MODERN MORAL PHILOSOPHY

In this magisterial study, one of our leading moral philosophers refutes the charge (originally made by Elizabeth Anscombe) that modern ethics is incoherent because it essentially depends on theological and religious assumptions that it cannot acknowledge. Stephen Darwall's panoramic picture starts with the seventeenth-century thinker Grotius and tells the story continuously down to the time of Kant, exploring what was in fact a completely new way of doing ethics based on secular ideas of human psychology and universal accountability. He shows that thinkers from Grotius to Kant are profoundly united by this modern approach, and that it helped them to create a theory of natural human rights that remains of great political relevance today. He further shows that this new way of thinking provides conceptual resources that are far from exhausted, and that moral philosophy in this idiom still has a vibrant future.

STEPHEN DARWALL teaches philosophy at Yale University. He is the author of *The British Moralists and the Internal 'Ought', 1640–1740* (Cambridge University Press, 1995), and of many other publications in moral philosophy and its history, including *The Second-Person Standpoint: Morality, Respect, and Accountability* (2006).

MODERN MORAL PHILOSOPHY

From Grotius to Kant

STEPHEN DARWALL
Yale University

Shaftesbury Road, Cambridge CB2 8EA, United Kingdom

One Liberty Plaza, 20th Floor, New York, NY 10006, USA

477 Williamstown Road, Port Melbourne, VIC 3207, Australia

314–321, 3rd Floor, Plot 3, Splendor Forum, Jasola District Centre, New Delhi – 110025, India

103 Penang Road, #05-06/07, Visioncrest Commercial, Singapore 238467

Cambridge University Press is part of Cambridge University Press & Assessment, a department of the University of Cambridge.

We share the University's mission to contribute to society through the pursuit of education, learning and research at the highest international levels of excellence.

www.cambridge.org
Information on this title: www.cambridge.org/9780521677790

DOI: 10.1017/9781139025065

© Stephen Darwall 2023

This publication is in copyright. Subject to statutory exception and to the provisions of relevant collective licensing agreements, no reproduction of any part may take place without the written permission of Cambridge University Press & Assessment.

First published 2023
First paperback edition 2025

A catalogue record for this publication is available from the British Library

ISBN 978-0-521-86047-5 Hardback
ISBN 978-0-521-67779-0 Paperback

Cambridge University Press & Assessment has no responsibility for the persistence or accuracy of URLs for external or third-party internet websites referred to in this publication and does not guarantee that any content on such websites is, or will remain, accurate or appropriate.

For Jerry, David, and Bill

CONTENTS

Preface xi
Acknowledgments xiv

Introduction 1
  Anscombe's Challenge 1
  Sidgwick's Contrast 4
  Modern Moral Philosophy's Shadow I 6
  Modern Metaethics 7
  Modern Moral Philosophy's Shadow II 8
  The Case of Kant 10
  (Relatively) Modest Aspirations 10

1 Grotius 15
  Classical Natural Law: Aquinas and Suárez 16
  Grotius on "*ius*," Morality, and Obligation 20
  Morality as a Distinctive Source of Reasons 25
  Freedom, Self-Rule, and the Right to Punish 31
  Publicly Articulable General Principles: A "Science" of Morality 34
  Sociability as the "Fountain of Right" 36

2 Hobbes and Pufendorf 39
  Hobbes 43
  Desire and the Good 44
  Obligation and the Right 48
  Grounding the Right in the Good? 52
  Irreducibly Deontic Laws of Nature? 54
  A Metaethics of Right? 59
  Pufendorf 61
  Moral Powers I 65
  A "Sociable" Attitude 70
  Equal Human Dignity 73
  Holding to Obligations in the Natural State 76

Moral Powers II   79
Moral Agency   82

3   Locke and Cumberland   87
   Locke: Natural Law, Motive, and Sanction   90
   Morality as Solution to the Human Natural Collective Action Problem   93
   Right and Good   95
   Law, Accountability, and Autonomy   98
   Cumberland   100
   Practical Propositions   102
   Obligation   103
   Empirical Grounds for the Law of Nature, Understood Egocentrically   104
   Practical Dictates of Reason, Agreement, and the Best End   105
   Obligation, Reconsidered   108

4   Spinoza, Cudworth, Shaftesbury, and Leibniz   111
   Spinoza   116
   Against Deontic Morality: Religious or Secular   116
   The Good: Knowledge, Power, and Perfection   119
   Revised Deontic Moral Concepts and Democratic Politics   122
   "Bear[ing] Calmly" and "Living Blessedly": Spinoza on Freedom, Happiness, and Power   125
   Cudworth   128
   Against Positivism   128
   Metaphysical Idealism?   130
   Ethical Idealism?   131
   Love   134
   Self-Determination   135
   Free Will and Obligation, Animal and Moral   137
   Shaftesbury   139
   An Ethics of Virtue   140
   Virtue and Moral Sense   142
   Virtue and Self-Reflective Moral Agency   145
   The "Obligation" to Virtue   146
   Authorship and Self-Determination   147
   Ancient or Modern?   151
   Leibniz   152
   Perfectionism: Identifying Goods (Personal and Impersonal) and Justice   154
   Freedom, Agency, and Necessity   157
   Right and Claim   158

5 Hutcheson and Butler   165
   Hutcheson   172
   Empiricist Naturalism and Moral Sense   173
   Moral Virtue Ethics: Constructing and Deriving Other Moral
   Notions and Standards   176
   Calm Desires, Reason, and Moral Sense   178
   Obligation   181
   Butler   183
   The Human Moral Psychological Economy   185
   Normative Practical Judgment: Wide and Narrow   188
   The Authority of Conscience   192
   The Right and the General Good   197
   Against Egoism   199

6 Hume and Smith   201
   Hume   203
   Against Practical Reason   206
   Against Moral Rationalism and for Moral Sentimentalism   207
   Justice, the Artificial Virtue   213
   Smith   222
   Sympathy: Attributing Mental States and Judging
   Their Propriety   224
   The Metaethics of Propriety   228
   Justice, Mutual Respect, and Accountability   231
   Dignity and Self-Command, the "Respectable" Virtue   234

7 The British Rationalists and Reid   237
   Fordyce   239
   Clarke   243
   Balguy   248
   Price   250
   Reid   258

8 Rousseau and Kant   269
   Rousseau   274
   Kant: *Groundwork I*   278
   Groundwork II: FUL   287
   Groundwork II: FH, FA, and FKE   299
   The Dignity of Persons and Autonomy of the Will   306
   Autonomy in *Groundwork III*   309
   The *Critique of Practical Reason*: Material vs. Formal
   Practical Principles   314
   The Fact of Reason   322

Necessitation and Respect   325
Kant on the Right and the Good   330
Freedom, Constraint, and Right in *The Metaphysics of Morals*   334
Kant's Racism and Sexism, and a Final Note of Humility   340

Works Cited   343
Index   363

PREFACE

This is the first of a projected two-volume work on the history of moral philosophy in the modern period, beginning with Grotius and extending through the end of the twentieth century, more or less. This first volume will end with Kant, and the next will begin with Fichte and Hegel. As the Introduction to follow makes clear, even at two completed volumes the work will be far from comprehensive. It will be framed by the challenge Elizabeth Anscombe famously issued in "Modern Moral Philosophy" that Western ethical philosophers' focus on deontic *morality* during this period has been substantially misplaced (Anscombe 1958).[1]

My attention will be devoted mainly to modern philosophers' attempts to respond to Anscombe's challenge (often *avant la lettre*), that is, to theorize, defend, and ground deontic morality. However, I will also be concerned with attempts to criticize or limit morality, for example, in Hegel, Marx, and Kierkegaard, as well as to undermine it completely, as in Nietzsche (and, arguably, Spinoza). As we shall see, these philosophers pay homage to the power and influence of the modern idea of morality as well, even as they seek to oppose or restrict it. And there will be discussions too of aspects of modern ethical thought that do not focus on deontic morality at all, for example, ethics of virtue and feminist critiques of orthodox moral theory in the late twentieth century.

I began to work on this project over twenty years ago.[2] Painfully aware of my ignorance of various periods and important figures, especially post-Kantian Continental thinkers, I undertook to fill in some of the gaps. Supported by a grant from the National Endowment for the Humanities in 1998–99, I began to study Fichte and Hegel and came upon Allen Wood's *Hegel's Ethical Thought*. There I found Wood's chapter on recognition and its section "Fichte's Theory of Recognition." I read this with something approaching ecstatic endorsement,

---

[1] I will thus be neglecting a number of figures who are less significant from this perspective, such as Descartes, Malebranche, Voltaire, Diderot, Montesquieu, and d'Holbach, among others.
[2] When Paul Guyer and Gary Hatfield invited me to contribute to a series of histories of modern philosophy they were editing for Cambridge University Press.

with a resounding "yes!" as Nietzsche might put it (Wood 1990: 77–93; Nietzsche 2007: 377). Encountering for the first time Fichte's idea that it takes a "summons" (*Aufforderung*) from another person to gain practical consciousness of our own freedom, and that this reciprocal awareness of summoned and summoner alike can ground fundamental principles of a theory of equal right, it felt as if the scales had fallen from my eyes (Fichte 2000: 35–83).

I came face-to-face with an idea that, as I allowed it to penetrate my thought fully over the weeks and months to come, seemed to me to provide the missing piece necessary to adequately ground morality, something I had been searching for perhaps my entire philosophical life. When I combined "Fichte's Point," as I came to call it, with Pufendorf and Grotius on sociability, Reid on the "social operations of the mind," Smith on the role of empathy ("sympathy") in judgments of justice, and, most importantly, Strawson on the role of the "participant" stance in moral responsibility, these insights appeared to me to point toward a fundamental reorientation of the foundations of morality and moral theory, providing a grounding for both in the "second-person standpoint."

I pretty much put my historical project on hold that year. The history of ethics could wait for a while; after all, the texts weren't going anywhere. I began to work on what became *The Second-Person Standpoint* almost immediately and for the last twenty years have pursued what I have taken to be the fruits of Fichte's insight (and the complementary insights of other historical figures) through many articles and books (Darwall 2006, 2013a, 2013b).

Some of those essays were explicitly historical – on Grotius, Pufendorf, Smith, Kant, and Nietzsche – as I found central elements of the second-personal framework in these writers, sometimes under attack, as in Nietzsche (Darwall 2013a, 2013b). Increasingly, I came to realize that even when modern philosophers did not make explicit use of Fichte's insight, it was implicit in their thought, nonetheless.

A good example is the distinction between law and counsel Suárez drew at the beginning of the early modern period, which influenced so much of the moral philosophy that followed.[3] Suárez notes a fundamental conceptual contrast between a normative area that is tied intrinsically to accountability and free moral agency (law) and one that is not (counsel). There can be beings who are agents having normative reasons but who lack the kind of freedom (moral agency) that Fichte relates distinctively to rights. (This, I came to see, was essentially the same as Cudworth's distinction between "animal free will" and "moral free will," which I discuss in Chapter 4.) Suárez's distinction was taken

---

[3] Suárez was not the first to draw this distinction, although his version was especially salient to modern moral philosophers who followed. Schneewind describes Grotius's invocation of it as following "the Scholastic tradition" (Schneewind 1998: 74). I am indebted to an anonymous referee to the Press for pressing this point.

up explicitly by Grotius, Hobbes, and Kant and implicitly by many others. It is in the background of almost all modern moral philosophy, as will begin to become clear in the Introduction.

If the texts stayed pretty much the same during the last twenty years, historical scholarship has not. The most prominent intervention has been Terence Irwin's magisterial *The Development of Ethics*, almost two volumes of which are devoted to the modern period (Irwin 2008, 2009). Many excellent smaller studies have appeared as well. Just within Fichte scholarship, both Michelle Kosch and Allen Wood have published superb works (Kosch 2018; Wood 2016). And Kosch has also brought out an unsurpassed treatment of Kierkegaard's ethics (Kosch 2006). These are only a few examples. The last twenty plus years have been a period of extraordinary flourishing in the history of modern philosophical ethics.[4]

I return to this project now with some trepidation, therefore, but also with real excitement. There really does seem to me to be an untold story of this period that emphasizes Anscombe's challenge and modern philosophers' attempts to deal with it. This volume, and the one to follow, are my attempt to tell that story.

There is, moreover, even greater reason now to consider whether such a story can be told, since Irwin's *Development of Ethics* expresses skepticism on this score. On Irwin's telling, the history of modern philosophical ethics is largely continuous with what he calls "Aristotelian Naturalism." In this respect, I will be writing against Irwin's account, echoing Anscombe and other historians who mark a significant contrast between modern ethical thought and the ancient and medieval philosophy that preceded it.[5]

Since I have "a horse in the race," readers will want to keep my philosophical biases in mind. I can only hope that my having something at stake as a philosopher makes for a more philosophically engaged (and engaging) historical account. My biases may make me sensitive to things others might not see, though perhaps I am just looking through "second-personal glasses" that distort my reading of texts and obscure important historical context. I hope my fellow historians of ethics, and you, dear reader, will keep me honest. Recalling the old Russian proverb that Reagan loved to quote to Gorbachev – "Trust, but verify" – I hope you will ignore the first and pursue the second.

---

[4] Another striking example is Hurka's study of British ethical thought from Sidgwick through Ewing (Hurka 2014).
[5] Here I have in mind Sidgwick, Schneewind, and Rawls, as I make clearer in the Introduction.

ACKNOWLEDGMENTS

I have been fortunate throughout my career in having mentors, colleagues, and students who have helped me both philosophically and as an historian. Two of the most prominent historians of ethics of the twentieth century were among my mentors. As a graduate student at the University of Pittsburgh, I was in the first seminar that J. B. Schneewind taught on Kant, along with Hobbes and Hume. At that point, Schneewind was mostly absorbed in his landmark work on Sidgwick, but one could already see in that seminar the seeds of what would emerge almost thirty years later as *The Invention of Autonomy*, one of the most important works on modern moral philosophy ever written (Schneewind 1977, 1998). Schneewind has been both a model and source of encouragement ever since.

The other great twentieth-century historian of modern ethics I was fortunate to learn from was William Frankena. Frankena published relatively little of his historical scholarship, but his knowledge of this period was vast and deep. I got to know him first in 1979–80 when he was a fellow at the National Humanities Center in North Carolina. I was then an assistant professor at the University of North Carolina at Chapel Hill, where I had also come under the tutelage of W. D. (David) Falk, from whom I got an almost spiritual sense of the importance of the early modern British moralists.[6] Falk was at the National Humanities Center that year as well, as were my former dissertation director Kurt Baier – with Falk, an important figure in the "good reasons" tradition in mid-twentieth century metaethics – and Annette Baier, who was in the process of becoming a leading figure on Hume. To say that this was an ideal environment in which to have nurtured an interest in the history of modern moral philosophy is understatement.[7]

---

[6] As I acknowledge in Darwall (1995: ix).
[7] I didn't actively pursue this interest right away, since I was still at work on *Impartial Reason* (1983). But it did not take long. In 1986–87, two years after I moved to Michigan, I spent a year in England doing research for *The British Moralists and the Internal 'Ought'* (1995). Much of this was in the British Library, where David Falk had first read the British moralists when he fled the Nazis. Falk did some of the first work on internalism in ethics. Indeed, he invented the term (Falk 1948). And he was a powerful proselytizer for it, both philosophically and in eighteenth-century British moral philosophy.

I spent the fall semester of 1982 as a visitor at the University of Michigan, talking often with Frankena. When I took a permanent position there in 1984, it was, in effect, to complete a new "Michigan Three," with Allan Gibbard and Peter Railton – the original three having been Frankena, Stevenson, and Brandt. (Ultimately, it became a "Michigan Five," with Elizabeth Anderson and David Velleman.) Gibbard jokes that his becoming a noncognitivist must have been determined by occupying Stevenson's old budget line. I'm not sure how it worked budgetarily, but Railton's ethical naturalism was certainly close to Brandt's, and my interests were uncannily akin to Frankena's. It was at Michigan that I first attempted to do serious history of ethics, in early modern British moral philosophy, certainly under Frankena's influence, and with the inspiration of Falk and Schneewind. It is with great gratitude that I dedicate this volume to Jerry, David, and Bill.

I should also express my deep gratitude to John Rawls. In addition to being the most important political philosopher of the twentieth century and having a deep appreciation of metaethical issues that he normally kept in the background, Rawls was a very careful reader of modern moral and political philosophy. His posthumously published *Lectures* on both subjects are both important works from which I here draw (Rawls 2000, 2007). It was mostly as a philosophical and human model that Rawls most influenced me, however. *A Theory of Justice* has shaped much of my own philosophy from the beginning, and I have always been very grateful for Rawls's interest in a young philosopher's work.

And then there is Yale. One of the attractions of the Yale Department, which I have certainly enjoyed since joining it, is that it provides the best mix of history of philosophy and philosophy proper of any department I know. All the historians have serious philosophical interests that inform their historical work, and almost all the non-historians are literate in and appreciative of philosophy's history. And that includes the graduate students. There is not a whiff of "Those who can, do philosophy, and those who cannot, do history of philosophy." It has been a pleasure and a privilege to be able to do this work in such a supportive atmosphere. I am especially grateful to my fellow historians of modern philosophy, Michael Della Rocca, Paul Franks, and Kenneth Winkler.

I owe a special debt to the students with whom I have done courses and worked on dissertations in the history of modern moral philosophy, both at Michigan and at Yale. Some of these seminars were taught with other faculty – Scott Shapiro, Matthew Smith, and Gideon Yaffe – from whom I have learned

---

On reflection now, it is clear to me that my pursuing the history of internalism in Darwall (1995) after having engaged with it as a metaethical position in Darwall (1983) is something like the pattern instantiated in the present historical project in relation to my own second-personal philosophizing (most obviously, in Darwall [2006]).

much. At Michigan, I was privileged to be able to sit in on courses with Edwin Curley, Louis Loeb, and Michelle Kosch. Also, I have discussed aspects of this book and been helped by countless scholars at these and other institutions, most prominently among those I remember: Kate Abramson, Julia Borcherding, Rachel Cohon, Remy Debes, Richard Dees, Aaron Garrett, Michael Gill, Charles Griswold, Paul Guyer, Thomas Hill Jr., T. H. Irwin, Christine Korsgaard, Matthew Leisinger, Sharon Lloyd, Tito Magri, Geoffrey Sayre-McCord, Tamar Schapiro, Kelley Schiffman, Susanne Sreedhar, Nicholas Sturgeon, and Allen Wood.

I am grateful more than I can express to those to whom I am closest. Julian has listened to me talk about figures in this volume since he was six and suggested as a title for my British moralists book *Philosophy in the Minds of Ten*. I always learn from our conversations. I have discussed philosophy and its history with Will for almost as long as we have conversed. No one holds my feet to the fire more (especially when it comes to Marx and Nietzsche, who will appear in the next volume). I owe the decision to include Spinoza to Will. Long conversations with Frank Marotta fed my soul towards the end of writing this volume, and Sidney Phillips helped keep me on an even keel throughout the writing. Finally, Laura has sustained me throughout, sometimes challenging but always supporting – invariably, just what I needed.

I owe many debts in connection with this book's publication, most especially to Paul Guyer and Gary Hatfield who first convinced me to write it over twenty years ago. Terence Moore was then my editor at Cambridge University Press. Both he and Hilary Gaskin since have provided very helpful advice, as did also an anonymous reader for the Press. For inestimable help in copyediting and other editorial assistance at late stages, I am very grateful to Molly Montgomery.

Finally, material from earlier publications is included here, and I am grateful to the publishers listed below:

"Grotius at the Creation of Modern Moral Philosophy," *Archiv für Geschichte der Philosophie* 94 (2012): 94–125. Reprinted with the permission of Walter de Gruyter.

"Pufendorf on Morality, Sociability, and Moral Powers," *The Journal of the History of Philosophy* 50 (2012): 213–38. Reprinted with the permission of *The Journal of the History of Philosophy*.

The British Moralists and the Internal 'Ought': 1640–1740. Reprinted with the permission of Cambridge University Press.

Introduction

Anscombe's Challenge

"Modern Moral Philosophy" is the title Elizabeth Anscombe gave to her famous broadside against the ethical philosophy she found around her in the middle of the twentieth century (Anscombe 1958).[1] Anscombe's chief complaint was that her contemporaries remained under the influence of a fundamentally mistaken turn that Western ethical thought had taken in the modern period, beginning roughly, I will suggest, with Hugo Grotius in the seventeenth century.[2]

Anscombe's most basic problem with modern ethical philosophy was that it is, as she put it, "*moral* philosophy." It concerns, even if not exclusively, what it calls *morality*: a set of putatively universal deontic or "juridical" norms of right and wrong that purport to *obligate* all normal human adults, indeed, all *moral agents,* as it terms beings who have the capacity to respond to obligation (5).[3] Anscombe called this a "law conception" of ethics (5), since it posits a moral law of right and wrong, what Grotius and his followers called "natural law."

All societies are structured by laws or social norms (*mores*) in some way, of course. But what modern ethical philosophers called and still call "morality" transcends socially constituted norms. Of any social or legal obligation, we can always ask whether it obligates us *morally*, that is, whether it would be morally wrong, and not just against social convention or illegal, or even our society's moral beliefs, to violate it. Moral right and wrong can never be settled by looking simply to a society's laws or *mores*. They concern *morality's* norms.

---

[1] Thomas Nagel also describes Anscombe's article as a "broadside" (Nagel 2022).
[2] Anscombe had other concerns also. Partly, her target was the "consequentialism" that characterized, she said, "every single English academic moral philosopher since Sidgwick" (1958: 10). By "consequentialism," she meant views according to which sufficiently extreme consequences might justify otherwise immoral acts. By this standard, even deontologists like W. D. Ross count as consequentialists. "Consequentialism" has come to have a narrower use, referring to theories of the right that are ultimately based on the goodness of consequences (either directly, of actions, or indirectly, of rules, practices, or motives that dictate them).
[3] Except when context requires it, I shall use these terms more or less synonymously, although strictly speaking, "deontic" terms express concepts that do not require actual socially constituted accountability structures to be instantiated, although "juridical" terms do.

This is not always apparent, since we use "morality" both as a count noun and as a non-count noun. In the count-noun sense there are as many moralities as there are societies with different *mores* (and perhaps different individual moral codes). Moralities, in this sense, are things we can count in the actual world. "Morality" in the sense that modern moral philosophers are concerned with, however, is not a countable aspect of actuality. It is an essentially normative deontic structure.[4] When modern moral philosophers use "morality" to refer to this normative structure, they are using it in a non-count sense that contrasts with the count-noun sense of "morality."

Moreover, what modern philosophers call "moral agents," those who are subject to morality, is determined not by membership in any actual society, but by having certain capacities of thought and will that philosophers dub "moral agency." These include the capacity to guide themselves by the moral law, which binds each simply as one moral agent among others. "Moral agent," or "Person," as Locke puts it, "is a Forensick Term" that "belongs only to intelligent Agents capable of a Law" (Locke 1975: 346).

Anscombe thought it obvious, however, that no practical law of any kind can exist without a lawgiver. So there can be a moral law only if it has a legislator whose jurisdiction transcends any posited earthly realm, even, indeed, that of the international law (*jus gentium*) that Grotius himself helped to originate in the early modern period.[5] Anscombe concluded that there can be such a thing as morality only if it is legislated by God.

The idea that morality binds only because it is divinely legislated has certainly been represented in modern moral philosophy, for example, in seventeenth-century natural lawyers like Pufendorf and Locke. But it has been a decidedly minority view. Most modern philosophers have been content to employ the essentially juridical concept of morality without any such grounding in divine legislation.[6] Grotius is an excellent example. And many deny that morality is even the kind of thing that *could* be legislated, even by God. It is not some actual thing that was made actual by creation or legislation. It is an essentially normative deontic structure.

---

[4] This also can also be confusing, since "normative" is often used, mostly outside of philosophy, to refer to actual social norms or to what is "normal" by their lights. For a helpful discussion, see Parfit's distinction between "rule-involving" and "reason-involving" conceptions of normativity (2011: I:144–148).
[5] Grotius's *De Jure Belli Ac Pacis* (*The Rights of War and Peace*) was published in 1625 (Grotius 2005).
[6] And even when philosophers like Pufendorf take this position, they often feel philosophical pressure to argue that the reasons that are distinctively tied to moral obligations are not *eudaimonistic* or egoistic. On this aspect of the modern view, see the next section. This is a crucial distinction between medieval theological voluntarists, like Ockham and Scotus, and modern ones. I am indebted to an anonymous reviewer for the Press for asking me to clarify this.

Anscombe thought that this left modern deontic concepts with no "discernible content except a certain compelling ['psychological'] force" (Anscombe 1958: 18). Deontic moral concepts certainly do not present as psychological concepts, however. How could they present as such and have the distinctive normative purport that has been thought to be morality's hallmark? We take morality to purport to be essentially normative, to provide us with *normative reasons* for acting.[7] Indeed, we take morality to purport to *obligate* us in an essentially normative way, to make violations not just unwise or imprudent but morally *wrong*: things we are accountable for not doing and for which we incur culpability and guilt when we do them without excuse. How could anything like that follow from psychological facts alone?

So powerful is this idea and so insidious is the moderns' error, Anscombe thought, that the concept of moral obligation is often invoked as a necessary ground even for divine law itself. In order for God's laws to obligate, it is said – for example, by the seventeenth-century Cambridge Platonist Ralph Cudworth – we must be obligated to follow God's legislation independently of his legislative act.[8] Any moral obligation to comply with God's commands cannot, Cudworth argued, itself be created by his commands. If Anscombe is right, however, the very idea of such a legislation-independent obligation is fundamentally confused. Philosophers who employ it end up deploying a contentless concept having only psychological force.

"Anscombe's Challenge," as we can call it, indicts much of the thought that ethical philosophers have produced in the West since the early seventeenth century. As we shall see, Anscombe is unquestionably right that a central feature of "modern moral philosophy" has been its fundamentally deontic or juridical character. Modern moral philosophers have indeed been concerned to articulate, understand, defend, and attempt to ground *morality* with its distinctively obligating normativity.

Even modern critics of the idea of morality – most prominently, Nietzsche, but also more qualified critics like Bernard Williams – have focused on the deontic features that Anscombe identifies. In seeking to overturn or at least rein in morality, they have implicitly accepted her point that deontic morality has been a, if not the, central focus of modern ethical thought (Nietzsche 2007; Williams 1985: 1–4, 174–196).

---

[7] Even those who deny that morality's imperatives are "categorical" and reason-giving for every person do not contest that they purport to be (see, e.g., Foot 1972).
[8] "It was never heard of, that any one founded all his Authority of Commanding others, and others' Obligation or Duty to Obey his Commands, in a Law of his own making, that men should be Required, Obliged, or Bound to Obey him" (Cudworth 1996: I.ii.3). For a discussion of Cudworth's claim, which, in effect, argues that it begs the question against the Anscombean view, see Schroeder 2005a.

To appreciate the distinctiveness of this conception of deontic morality, compare it to the view of ethics one finds in Plato and Aristotle. Notably, the term "morality" does not even appear in standard English translations of Plato's *Republic* or Aristotle's *Nicomachean Ethics*, though it sometimes does in commentaries on these texts.[9] For Plato and Aristotle, the central ethical concepts all concern species of the good: virtue, intrinsically good or noble (*kalon*) action, and the good or benefit (*eudaimonia*) of human beings. Much of what modern ethical philosophers consider under the heading of morality, Plato and Aristotle discuss under the virtue of justice or intrinsically good just action.

When Socrates is challenged by Glaucon and Adeimantus at the beginning of Plato's *Republic* to say why we should be just, his reply is not that justice is morally obligatory or that others' rights provide, in themselves, reasons to respect them. Rather, Plato has Socrates argue that justice is both instrumentally and intrinsically good for the just person.[10]

But consider how a modern like H. A. Prichard responded to arguments like this near the beginning of the twentieth century. Prichard maintains that such arguments "rest" "moral philosophy ... on a mistake" (Prichard 1912: 21–37). That complying with the moral law can benefit us, even intrinsically, is an important fact; but it is not one, Prichard argues, that can either explain why morality obligates us or establish any reason for being moral that might flow directly from its doing so. For these tasks, Socrates's argument provides a reason of the wrong kind.

Sidgwick's Contrast

The great nineteenth-century moral philosopher Henry Sidgwick made a similar point when he wrote that according to "the Greek schools" of ethics,

> Right action is commonly regarded as only a species of the Good. ... Their speculations can scarcely be understood by us unless with a certain effort we throw the quasi-jural notions of modern ethics aside, and ask (as they did) not "What is Duty and what is its ground?" but "Which of the objects that men think good is truly Good or the Highest Good?" (Sidgwick 1967: 105–106)[11]

---

[9] This can be confirmed by a search of electronically available translations, such as W. D. Ross's and Terence Irwin's translations of Aristotle's *Nicomachean Ethics*, or Benjamin Jowett's or Paul Shorey's translations of Plato's *Republic*. "Moral" appears in Aristotle, of course, for example, in his contrast between theoretical and moral virtue. But there it simply means virtues that are connected to character and the will.
[10] On this point and Prichard's response, discussed presently, see Brown 2007.
[11] John Rawls's *Lectures on the History of Moral Philosophy*, which aims to cover "Modern Moral Philosophy: 1600–1800," begins with an invocation and brief discussion of Sidgwick's contrast (Rawls 2000: 1–2). In my discussion of Sidgwick in the companion

As Anscombe would later, Sidgwick argued that modern moral philosophy differs from the ethical thought of the ancient Greeks in viewing the "quasi-jural" or deontic notion of moral duty or right as distinct from any "species of the Good."

Sidgwick drew a further, related contrast between ancient and modern ethics concerning what philosophers these days call "normativity" or the force of *normative reasons* or *oughts*:

> [I]n Greek moral philosophy generally, but one regulative and governing faculty is recognised under the name of Reason ...; in the modern ethical view, when it has worked itself clear, there are found to be two, — Universal Reason and Egoistic Reason, or Conscience and Self-love (1964: 198).[12]

Plato, Aristotle, and other ancient thinkers tend to be *eudaimonists*, holding that all normative reasons for action must derive from the agent's own good or happiness (*eudaimonia*) broadly conceived, even when it comes to virtue and justice.[13] In Socrates's exchange with Glaucon and Adeimantus, it is simply assumed by all parties that if Socrates cannot establish that it is intrinsically or extrinsically beneficial to the just person to be just, he will not have shown any reason for them to act justly rather than, say, simply to appear to be doing so.

According to Sidgwick, however, "the modern ethical view" allows for the position that Prichard clearly assumes, namely, that the fact that an action would unjustly wrong someone and therefore be morally wrong is or entails *in itself* sufficient reason not to do it. "Conscience," the mental power through which we make moral judgments, can be a "regulative and governing faculty" in its own right, an aspect of practical reason itself.[14] According to Sidgwick's moderns, deontic morality can provide an independent source of normative reasons and oughts that are additional to those provided by any species of the good. As we shall see, even modern *eudaimonists* or rational egoists who hold that all reasons for acting must come from (the agent's) good, like Locke, nonetheless often maintain that moral right and obligation are independent ethical ideas that cannot be reduced to any "species of the good."

---

volume to this one, I will discuss how Sidgwick himself uses deontic terms in a broader sense than the quasi-jural, accountability-entailing sense. In this, he is followed by Broad and Ross. Ewing notes the distinction between these in Ewing 2012a. For discussion, see Hurka, 2014. I am indebted to an anonymous reviewer for the Press for requesting clarification here.

[12] For an excellent discussion of this passage, see Frankena 1992. For a defense of a "reason-implying" conception of normativity, see Parfit 2011: I:144–148.

[13] The Stoics complicate this picture, though Irwin characterizes them as *eudaimonists* in Irwin 2003.

[14] For an excellent history of the idea of conscience, see Sorabji 2014.

There are two separate but related aspects to what we can call "Sidgwick's Contrast." First, many moderns claim that the deontic concept of moral right or obligation is irreducible to any species of the good. And second, an important strain of modern ethical philosophy, at least, holds that the right has a normative practical force that is additional to that of the good.

Modern Moral Philosophy's Shadow I

Obviously, I have chosen my title with Anscombe's essay in mind. I agree with Anscombe, Sidgwick, and others (most notably, John Rawls and J. B. Schneewind) that the "quasi-jural" or "law conception" of morality has been at the very heart of ethical philosophy in the West, roughly from Grotius on (Rawls 2000; Schneewind 1998). Of course, not all modern ethical philosophy can be categorized as *moral* philosophy in Anscombe's sense. Just to take one example, G. E. Moore famously argued in *Principia Ethica* (Moore 1993) that the concept of intrinsic good (though not that of a person's good) is the single fundamental ethical concept, an ineliminable kernel of any ethical concept.

About the concept of moral right, Moore there says that "to assert that a certain line of conduct is, at a given time, absolutely right or obligatory is obviously to assert that more good or less evil will exist in the world, if it be adopted than if anything else be done instead" (Moore 1993: 77). Clearly, there is nothing irreducibly juridical or deontic about the notions expressed by "right" and "obligatory" as Moore defines them in *Principia*. If what it means to say that an act is morally right or obligatory is just that it produces the most good, then the claim that it is morally right or obligatory to produce the most good is not a deontic normative claim. It is what Parfit calls a "concealed tautology" (Parfit 2011: II:276).

In using deontic moral terms like "right" and "obligatory" to express his views, however, Moore is arguing against and arguably trying to co-opt more orthodox deontologically minded moral philosophers of his time like Prichard. Thus, even though Moore's philosophical project is not itself moral philosophy in Anscombe's sense, his use of deontic moral terms is testimony to modern moral philosophy's powerful influence.

Even more obviously, if anyone counts as a modern ethical philosopher, Nietzsche surely does, though he is hardly a *moral* philosopher in Anscombe's sense. Even so, the idea of morality unquestionably looms large in Nietzsche's thought. *On the Genealogy of Morality* is devoted to understanding what Nietzsche argues to be the concept's questionable origins and to a critique of "the value of these [i.e., morality's] values" (Nietzsche 2007: 7).

Thus, even when ethical philosophers in the West from the seventeenth century on have not been doing moral philosophy, strictly so called, their thought has often been shaped by it. Either their terms bear the influence of modern moral philosophy, as with Moore; their projects are defined in opposition to it, as with Nietzsche; or their thought is formulated and received against modern moral philosophy's background and in its shadow.

Modern Metaethics

My aim in this book and the one to follow is to investigate central aspects of Western ethical philosophy from the publication of Hugo Grotius's *The Rights of War and Peace* in 1625 through the end of the twentieth century, using Anscombe's and Sidgwick's characterizations as reference points. Mostly I will be concerned with philosophers' attempts to understand, articulate, defend, and ground morality, as well as to grapple with the distinctive metaphysical and epistemological questions that arise in relation to it, *metaethical* questions, as we now call them. Are there moral truths, and if so, what makes them true? What is the relation between any metaphysical basis morality might require and that needed by the natural sciences that began to take a recognizably modern shape in the seventeenth century? Has modern moral philosophy the resources to respond adequately to Anscombe's Challenge and to Nietzsche's and his followers' critiques? On the epistemological side: can we acquire moral knowledge? And if so, how might that be related to moral motivation?

Although philosophers since the ancient Greeks have concerned themselves with fundamental metaphysical and epistemological questions about ethics, metaethics as a subfield of ethical philosophy did not exist before the modern era, arguably, not before the twentieth century.[15] It was only in the aftermath of Moore's *Principia Ethica* that philosophers began to distinguish and focus on so-called second-order issues about ethical language and concepts and their relation to questions in the philosophy of language and mind, metaphysics, and epistemology as a distinct area of inquiry, separable from "first-order" "normative ethics" (Mackie 1977).

Surely, one aspect of the modern period that stimulated metaethical thought was the decline of Aristotelian teleological metaphysics alongside the rise of modern science. If nature is not itself teleological, this forces the question of what place value can have "in a world of fact" (Köhler 1938). Another factor is that metaethical questions sometimes turn on technical issues in logic and the philosophies of language and mind, whose tools required the increasing specialization of the twentieth century to be developed sufficiently to pursue metaethics in a focused, fruitful way.

I speculate that a further important factor that led to metaethical reflection in the modern period, however, concerns Sidgwick's Contrast. So long as there is believed to be only a single fundamental ethical concept, the good, the question need not arise of what makes something an ethical or normative concept

---

[15] A search of JSTOR reveals "metaethics" first being used in its contemporary sense in Wisdom 1948.

in general, or of what the "sources of normativity" are (Korsgaard 1996a). No distinction between evaluative and normative concepts and questions seems possible. Once, however, there are thought to be two fundamental ethical notions, the good *and* the right, these more general and fundamental metaethical questions begin to seem unavoidable.[16]

Moreover, once it is believed, for example, by the early modern natural lawyer Francisco Suárez, that the deontic moral concept of right has a distinctive normative profile that differs from that of the good – that the morally right *obligates* whereas the good *recommends* – these philosophical questions can seem even more urgent. As we shall see, Suárez makes a fundamental distinction between *law* and *counsel*, the influence of which extends through Grotius, Hobbes, Kant, and the moral philosophy that follows them.[17] This focuses Prichard's question and also opens up philosophical space for thinkers like Nietzsche to argue that even if the good can be adequately grounded, the putatively obligatory normativity of morality (the right) cannot be.

In addition to these metaethical issues, modern moral philosophers have also grappled with substantive normative questions both at the level of normative moral theory and in thinking about specific cases. The familiar dispute between deontology and consequentialism is itself a creature of the modern period, requiring morality's hallmark deontic categories even to be formulated. It is worth bearing in mind that though it begins with a view about the good, consequentialism is itself a view about the good's relation to the *right*. Mill begins *Utilitarianism*, indeed, by saying that nothing is "more significant of the backward state" of ethical knowledge than the "little progress" that has been made in determining "the criterion of right and wrong" (Mill 2002: I:1). It is to this matter of deontic morality that utilitarianism and consequentialism more generally have historically been addressed.

Modern Moral Philosophy's Shadow II

Modern philosophy about morality will not, however, be my sole focus. I seek also to understand and situate aspects of modern ethical philosophy that are not moral philosophy in Anscombe's sense. Some of these concern traditional questions about the good – both, what kind of life is best for human beings,

---

[16] It was only toward the end of the twentieth century when Gibbard introduced the idea that there is a single *normative* concept, which can be expressed equivalently by "ought" or by "normative reason" (in Gibbard's terms, what "makes sense"), that metaethics came to be regarded as a species of the larger genus of metanormative theory, which concerns normativity more generally, including in, for example, normative epistemology (1990). As we shall see, Gibbard follows a strain of thought that arguably begins with Sidgwick's idea that ought is the fundamental ethical concept (Sidgwick 1967: 23–38).

[17] Suárez was not the first to draw this distinction. On this see Preface, n.3.

and, what is intrinsically choiceworthy – questions that have been a staple of ethical philosophizing since the ancient Greeks. But much such philosophy in the modern period, I shall be arguing, must nonetheless be understood in relation to modern moral philosophy, even when its aims are profoundly different. Sometimes this is because, as with Nietzsche and Williams, ethical conceptions are put forward in opposition to morality, as a replacement for or at least as a counterbalance to it. And sometimes, as with Moore, a philosopher's project may not itself concern deontic morality, but still be formulated in moral philosophy's distinctive deontic terms.

Different varieties of modern virtue ethics provide a particularly interesting example. Some virtue ethicists, like Francis Hutcheson in the seventeenth century and Rosalind Hursthouse in the late twentieth, put forward their theories in a moral philosophical idiom. Hutcheson is concerned with what he calls "moral goodness," which he distinguishes from "natural goodness." And Hursthouse draws on an account of moral virtue to ground a theory of what makes actions morally right or wrong (Hutcheson 2004; Hursthouse 1999). But modern virtue ethicists also often advance their virtue theories in opposition to deontic moral theories. Hume is a leading example. And a major aim of Anscombe's "Modern Moral Philosophy" in 1958, after all, was to wean her readers from that subject and return them to a virtue-centered Aristotelian approach.

As it happened, the 1960s and 1970s intervened, with movements for social and political equality that made issues of justice and rights inescapable, forming a backdrop for Rawls's monumental *A Theory of Justice*, which commanded the moral philosophical scene through the 1970s (Rawls 1971). This required deontic moral philosophy, since there can be no moral rights without moral duties.

It was only in the 1980s, in a very different sociopolitical climate, that the revival of virtue ethics for which Anscombe called began to take place, frequently formulated in non-deontic terms, as by writers like Alasdair MacIntyre and Annette Baier, and sometimes put forward in opposition to morality, as in Michael Slote's *From Morality to Virtue* (MacIntyre 1981; Baier 1985; Slote 1992).[18]

---

[18] Another precursor was Philippa Foot, whose landmark papers, "Moral Arguments" and "Moral Beliefs," appeared roughly contemporaneously with Anscombe's (1958 and 1959, respectively), and whose *Virtues and Vices* (Foot 1978), appeared just before the heyday of virtue of ethics in the 1980s. In effect, Foot worked out both the metaethics and normative ethics of the kind of neo-Aristotelian virtue ethics for which Anscombe called. And she expressed her skepticism of orthodox moral philosophy in "Morality as a System of Hypothetical Imperatives" (1972).

Baier's work was less concerned with the systematic development of virtue ethics than with defending a broadly Humean virtue approach against more orthodox normative moral theory (see, e.g., "Doing Without Moral Theory?" in Baier 1985).

The Case of Kant

Perhaps the most fascinating example of a philosopher whose thinking is shaped, and in some ways arguably distorted, by the modern moral philosophical frame, is Kant. On the face of it, Kant's ethics can seem a paradigm of moral philosophy in the modern idiom, a textbook example of deontological ethics and an archetypical theory of the "moral law." I shall argue, however, that on closer inspection the deontic categories of duty, obligation, and the moral law are, for Kant, only the shadow for finite rational beings of how a fully rational being would choose and act. Fully rational deliberation, according to Kant, always only involves questions of the good (albeit the intrinsically choiceworthy rather than agents' good – *das Gute* vs *das Wohl*) and not deontic moral questions.

This means that duty, obligation, and the moral law have no independent normative force for Kant. Kant's response to Anscombe's Challenge is that it is *reason* that commands us finite rational beings to do what it is best (what there is most reason) for us to do, hence what a fully rational being would do in our place. But two questions then arise. What can give reason this distinctively deontic power, if it is itself concerned exclusively with the good? And how can reason create any further reason to do something by commanding what it has already determined there is independently reason to do? Any such deontic aspect would seem to be normatively epiphenomenal. And if that is so, morality itself may end up being epiphenomenal on Kant's view also.

Despite this, Kant's emphasis on freedom and what he calls "autonomy" is unquestionably modern and unlike anything to be found among the ancient Greeks or in ethical philosophy of the medieval period that derives from them. Moreover, I shall argue that the emphasis on the distinctive freedom of a deliberating rational agent in modern philosophers like Cudworth, Locke, and Samuel Clarke even before Kant, as well as in Kant himself, derives from their taking it to be necessary for the very possibility of morality and moral obligation. And this surely is an essential feature of philosophers who follow in Kant's wake, most obviously, Fichte and Hegel, but also Kierkegaard and, arguably, even Nietzsche.

(Relatively) Modest Aspirations

I do not aspire to anything like a comprehensive treatment of modern ethics in this volume. Even were I capable of writing such a book, we already have in T. H. Irwin's magisterial, three-volume *The Development of Ethics* a more widely ranging and detailed treatment, even of just modern ethics, than perhaps anyone else can or will be able to provide (Irwin 2007, 2008, 2009). Irwin devotes almost all of his second and third volumes to the modern period, nearly nineteen hundred pages. I seek something significantly more modest.

There is a further difference between Irwin's treatment and what I aim for here. Irwin tends to downplay the significance of Anscombe's and Sidgwick's contrasts and argues that much of the modern period carries forward a tradition of ethical thought that is continuous with that of the ancient Greeks. What Irwin calls *Aristotelian naturalism* is a combination of views he finds first in Aristotle, but which he argues carries through the ancient Stoics, notably Cicero, Aquinas's classical theory of natural law, and, in Irwin's view, many modern figures from Grotius on, including Grotius himself.

Aristotelian naturalists, according to Irwin, hold a *teleological view of practical reason*; they maintain that rational action aims always and only at the good. They are also *eudaimonists*, holding that the final rational end is the agent's own good or *eudaimonia*. They thus deny that deontic standards of moral right or obligation can provide reasons for acting that are independent of the agent's good. As Irwin emphasizes, this does not mean that Aristotelian naturalists cannot recognize distinctively *moral* virtues or intrinsically good *moral* acts that differ from other nonmoral virtues or noble action. Like Cicero, they can recognize a category of *duty* (*officium*) or right action (*honestum*) and hold, moreover, that there is reason to conform to moral duty or right even when it is not advantageous in the sense of being instrumentally beneficial (*commodium* or *utile*), because it is *intrinsically* beneficial.

Nevertheless, for Aristotelian naturalists like Cicero and Aquinas, duty and right are not identified independently of the good; they rather concern a species of good, the *common good*. Also, any reason that agents have to comply with their moral duty depends on their own good or *eudaimonia*, albeit by virtue of compliance's being intrinsically, rather than just instrumentally, good for them. There is, as Cicero puts it, a *bonum honestum*, an intrinsic benefit in being moral and just, as indeed Socrates argues in *The Republic* and as Aristotle implies in the *Nicomachean Ethics* when he maintains that *eudaimonia* consists in virtuous (including just) activity (Irwin 2007: 620, 2008: 31–32).

Finally, Irwin calls this position Aristotelian *naturalism* since it maintains that an intrinsically beneficial, virtuous life is one that best realizes our rational human *nature*. This means that when Irwin classifies a modern moral theorist like Grotius as an Aristotelian naturalist, he is interpreting him as holding that morality's normative force derives from the fact that moral conduct realizes the agent's good by virtue of realizing his rational human nature. On an Aristotelian naturalist view, morality can have no normative force that is independent of the agent's good; nothing can. It can provide, in Suárez's terms, only counsel and not genuinely obligating law.

Irwin writes at the beginning of *The Development of Ethics* that were he to give his volumes an "ampler title" on the model of some seventeenth- or eighteenth-century works, he might have chosen *The Development of Ethics: being a selective historical study of moral philosophy in the Socratic tradition with special attention to Aristotelian naturalism* (2007: 1).

I agree that viewing the history of ethics, including that of the modern period, through the lens of Aristotelian naturalism provides an interesting and insightful interpretative prospect. But it is far from the only one. The history of modern ethics presented in this book will be guided by a very different viewpoint, one that, in my view, Irwin's *Development* insufficiently appreciates. The thread that will run throughout these volumes is that ethics in the modern period is best appreciated in relation to moral philosophy conceived in the deontic terms Anscombe identifies, through the lens of Sidgwick's claim that much modern ethical thought recognizes the morally right as having an independent normative force that is irreducible to that of the good.

I would like to say something in conclusion here, however inadequate, about race, sex, and gender as these enter into our history. No one can reasonably doubt that the larger culture that produced and supported philosophy and its publication during the modern period was, and remains, sexist and racist, patriarchal and white supremacist. It is not at all surprising, therefore, not just that so little published work was produced by women or people of color, but also that so many philosophers, including many here discussed, were themselves racist, sexist, or both. At least one philosopher who will be especially central to our story, Kant, himself produced a theory of races (Kant 2013b).

There is really no way to deal adequately with issues of race, sex, and gender, and other forms of epistemic and, indeed, philosophical oppression in a history such as this. I agree with Lucy Allais and Dilek Huseyinzadegan that, for example, Kant's racism is not a sufficient reason not to study his works (Allais 2016; Huseyinzadegan 2018). Kant's ideas have not simply had great importance for philosophy; his doctrine of the equal dignity of persons has also had special significance in movements to resist racist and sexual oppression.[19] Still,

---

[19] It is difficult to believe, for example, that it was simply a coincidence that in the years just following the civil rights movement, three important works of moral and political philosophy appeared in quick succession – Rawls's *A Theory of Justice*, Wolff's *In Defense of Anarchism*, and Nozick's *Anarchy, State, and Utopia* – all of which appealed to Kant's doctrine of equal dignity in their foundations (Rawls 1971; Wolff 1970; Nozick 1974). Hegel says, no doubt rightly, that philosophy's "owl of Minerva begins its flight only at the onset of dusk" only after progressive social and political changes have taken place. But even if Rawls's, Wolff's, and Nozick's Kantian philosophizing played no causal role in the civil rights movement, it seems pretty likely that Kant's notion of the equal dignity of persons played an important background role in helping to create the intellectual political culture that made the civil rights movement possible. That the idea had become undeniable in the 1960s was surely part of Kant's legacy.

Another important reason to study figures like Kant, including their most objectionable writings, is, as Allais argues, to help us better understand how someone like Kant could come to write what he did, so that we, who are no less subject to racist and sexist biases ourselves, might avoid similar errors of our own (Allais 2016). And the same arguably holds for other important figures we will be considering. As important as it is to pursue the genealogical and self-critical work Allais calls us to, however, this is not work we shall do here.

some of what Kant says certainly bears the imprint of his racial, sexual, class, and Eurocentric position, and, as Allais and Huseyinzadegan point out, studying his works in context provides an opportunity for us to think about how our own moral and philosophical thought and practice bear those marks as well (Allais 2016; Huseyinzadegan 2018). We shall have occasion to return to this theme at the end of this volume's final chapter, which is on Rousseau and Kant.

There will be many more men discussed in the following pages than women, as well as more white philosophers than philosophers of color.[20] Although women philosophers of the early modern period have begun to be more closely studied, many, like Mary Astell, Margaret Cavendish, Catharine Trotter Cockburn, Anne Conway, Mary Shepherd, and Princess Elisabeth of Bohemia, are more notable for their metaphysical and epistemological views than for their ethical philosophy (Atherton 1994).[21] It is only in the second half of twentieth century, beginning in the 1950s and 1960s, that women came to be widely recognized as important ethical philosophers. Anscombe's Challenge in "Modern Moral Philosophy" (in 1957) frames our study, albeit retrospectively. And the post–World War II period also features Foot, Beauvoir, and Murdoch, all of whom produced ethical philosophy of enduring value.[22] Their works and those of numerous later prominent women philosophers, like Hursthouse, (Annette) Baier, Wolf, and Korsgaard will be central to the closing chapters of the volume to follow.[23]

Finally, that volume will conclude with a chapter titled "Theorizing Oppression and Nonideal Theory," which will discuss a steadily growing movement by academic philosophers in the latter third of the twentieth century and early twenty-first attempting to come to terms with systematic sexual and racial oppression. This begins with philosophical responses to the civil rights movement and continues with discussions of affirmative action and other attempts

---

[20] The latter will begin to be discussed in the projected volume to follow the present one.

[21] Damaris Masham, who did have interesting views on love and friendship, will enter into our story because of the link she provides between Cudworth and Locke on free will. Some of her most interesting thoughts occur in her correspondence with Leibniz on metaphysical topics.

[22] See Benjamin Lipscomb's *The Women Are Up to Something* for a fascinating account of Anscombe, Foot, Murdoch, and Mary Midgley's philosophical lives, which began when they found themselves together as students at Oxford just before World War II (Lipscombe 2021).

[23] This may be an appropriate place to explain my pronoun use in this work. Following the well-argued proposal of Dembroff and Wodak, I shall use "they" for both singular and plural neutral pronouns (except within quotations) (Dembroff and Wodak 2018). Happily, this practice is becoming increasingly widespread. I shall not, however, pursue this practice inside quotations, except infrequently when context requires it. On reflection, it seems wisest to allow the philosophers I am quoting to speak for themselves. I am indebted here to counsel from Michael Della Rocca, Molly Montgomery, Laura Radwell, and Ken Winkler.

to address past racial and gender injustice and to eliminate it in the present (see, e.g., Boxill 1984, 2003). As formal and informal barriers to entry to academic philosophy began to be removed for women and philosophers of color, the topics that are considered to be moral philosophical topics of significance have changed accordingly.

The most notable development has been the pursuit of what has come to be called, following Charles Mills, "nonideal" moral and political theory, which attempts to theorize justice, not under ideal conditions, but in circumstances of historical and ongoing oppression, most especially the kind of white supremacy that has characterized the United States (Mills 1997, 2005). Although the terms "ideal" and "nonideal theory" come from Rawls, Mills has been the founding and central figure of nonideal theory, showing philosophers the need for moral- and political-philosophical accounts of urgent injustice that Rawls's ideal theory leaves out. Also important have been Elizabeth Anderson and Tommie Shelby (Anderson 2010, 2014; Shelby 2005, 2016). Nonideal moral and political theories have been pursued as well in fields like epistemology, as in Miranda Fricker's pathbreaking work on epistemic injustice (Fricker 2007).

All of this will be discussed at the end of the volume to follow the current one, which will take us from Fichte and Hegel through the end of a (long) twentieth century. The present volume, however, ends with Kant and begins with a moral philosopher who is justifiably regarded as the founding figure of modern moral philosophy, Hugo Grotius. To him we now turn.

1

Grotius

Courses in the history of modern philosophy generally focus on epistemology and metaphysics and begin with Descartes's engagement with skepticism in the *Meditations*. But where should a history of modern ethical thought begin? It has been widely believed, not least by early moderns themselves, that in the seventeenth century, ethical philosophy came to assume a self-consciously "modern" form, opposing itself to "ancient" Greek ideas and to medieval scholastic approaches that derived, at least in part, from Aristotle.

Many have thought that Hugo Grotius (1583–1645) helped initiate this modern form. In the mid-eighteenth century, Jean Barbeyrac's *Historical and Critical Account of the Science of Morality* praised Grotius as "the first who broke the ice" of "the *Scholastic Philosophy*; which [had] spread itself all over Europe" (Barbeyrac 1749: 66, 67). More recently, Knud Haakonssen has written that ethical philosophers of the time thought "that something decisively new happened with Grotius" (Haakonssen 1996: 15). To many thinkers of the early modern period, Grotius's *The Rights of War and Peace* (*RWP*), published in 1625, was not simply an original treatise on international law; it seemed to set a new agenda in ethical and political philosophy across the board.[1] A strong case can be made, indeed, that the very concepts to which "morality" and "science" in Barbeyrac's title referred were themselves substantially shaped by Grotius and his influence.[2]

So we begin our history of modern moral philosophy with Grotius, and in this chapter I shall attempt to say why.[3] This is a pressing question, since Irwin maintains that Barbeyrac "misunderstands Grotius in representing him as a pioneer" (Irwin 2008: 99). According to Irwin, Grotius follows the main lines of

---

[1] *De Jure Belli Ac Pacis* is also often translated as *On the Law of War and Peace*.
[2] For Barbeyrac, "morality" consists of a body of "rules" ("laws of morality") we are "obligat[ed]" to comply with just because we are "corporeal rational creature[s]" (Barbeyrac 1749: 2–3, 5). The modern project Barbeyrac terms the "science of morality" is the task of articulating and defending these "rules," including by providing some philosophical account of their distinctively *obligatory* character. This, I shall argue, is the problematic that Grotius bequeathed to early modern ethical philosophy, or at least, that many early moderns plausibly took to be his bequest.
[3] I draw heavily on Darwall (2012a).

an "Aristotelian naturalism," which also characterized classical Thomist natural law, with which Grotius's early modern natural law is frequently contrasted. If Irwin is right, however, there was nothing fundamentally original in Grotius.

What *was* importantly new in Grotius that helped produce a distinctively "modern" ethical philosophy? Schneewind has argued that Grotius's originality consisted in his "confrontation" with skepticism, which "was simply not an issue for the classical natural law theorists" who preceded him (Schneewind 1998: 71). If so, Grotius might stand to modern ethical philosophy in something like the relation Descartes stands to modern epistemology. But although *RWP* virtually begins with the skeptical challenge that justice is a mere "Chimera" since "Nature prompts all men ... to seek their own particular advantage," Irwin correctly notes that skeptical objections of this kind were well known to the ancients, as Grotius's putting it in the mouth of Carneades effectively acknowledges (Grotius 2005: I, 79, Irwin 2008: 94–96).[4] It is largely the same challenge that Glaucon and Adeimantus pose to Socrates in the *Republic*: Why should we be just when it is disadvantageous to be so? If, however, serious engagement with skepticism was not new with Grotius, what was?

In this chapter, I shall argue that what was novel in Grotius is a combination of three doctrines that will loom large throughout the modern period: (i) moral right (natural law) has a distinctively obligating normativity that cannot be reduced to normative reasons concerning the good that advise or "counsel" action rather than demand it; (ii) morality includes basic universal claim rights, what Grotius dubs "perfect rights" (thereby initiating the perfect/imperfect right and correlative perfect/imperfect duty distinctions); and (iii) morality would exist and obligate us "even if we were to suppose ... that there is no God" (Grotius 2005: I, xxiv).[5] By affirming that morality has obligating authority but not deriving it from God's command, Grotius made himself liable to Anscombe's Challenge.

Classical Natural Law: Aquinas and Suárez

For Grotius, morality is embodied in what he calls "natural law." But there is nothing exclusively modern in the idea of natural law itself. It goes back to the Stoics and was, in Aquinas's classical natural law theory, part of scholastic orthodoxy. What, if anything, was different about Grotius's conception?

---

[4] Because it is more generally available, I will be using the 2005 LibertyClassics edition (Grotius 2005), edited by Richard Tuck. It was translated by John Morrice (Grotius 2005: I: xxxv). In at least some places, which I will note below, Morrice appears to have worked from Barbeyrac's French translation, which is not entirely faithful to Grotius's Latin text. (Grotius 1724). When appropriate, I will supplement with Francis Kelsey's translation (Grotius 1925).

[5] This passage occurred in the Prolegomena to the first edition of *De Jure Belli*.

For Aquinas, laws of nature are *teleological* standards inherent in our rational nature that concern our common good (Aquinas 1997: Q91–93). This is familiar Aristotelian naturalist doctrine. But what makes these standards *laws*? There is, of course, a general sense in which "law" can refer to any standard or norm, but that is insufficient to distinguish Anscombe's juridical notion. Not just any standard involves *obligation* in the sense of something for which we are answerable, where issues of culpability, guilt, and innocence are automatically involved. If I believe the opposite of what is entailed by things I know, I violate a standard of reason (so a standard inherent in my rational nature), but, so far anyway, nothing juridical need be involved. No issue of culpability, guilt, or innocence necessarily arises. From the fact that someone manifests some mistake or fault of reasoning or errs in failing to respond to normative reasons, it does not follow that they are to blame or that this is *their fault* in that distinctive sense (Pink 2007). But this is precisely what is involved in the modern "law conception" of morality Anscombe identifies. So the fact that an ethical conception like Aquinas's is advanced in legal terms is not enough to make it a "law conception" in Anscombe's sense.

Even before Grotius, Francisco Suárez (1548–1617) criticized Aquinas's theory precisely on the grounds that it could not explain why we would have any *obligation* to follow natural law. Suárez agreed with Aquinas that, for example, telling falsehoods is intrinsically "repugnant" to rational nature, but he pointed out that this is insufficient to create any *obligation* to tell the truth (Suárez 1944: 181–183). To understand natural law as genuinely obligating law, Suárez believed, it is necessary to see its dictates as *authoritatively addressed demands* with which we are accountable for compliance. And this, he thought, requires seeing natural law as issuing from God's authoritative command.[6] In effect, Suárez held that Aquinas's view was not subject to Anscombe's Challenge because it was not even a theory of obligating law.

Suárez crystallized his idea in a fundamental distinction he made between law and "counsel," the influence of which would be felt throughout the early modern period. According to Suárez, law has a conceptual connection to obligating demands and accountability that normative reasons recommending an action as good (advisable) do not.

> [C]ounsel is excluded from law. ... The word promulgation implies an order for the purpose of creating an obligation and it is in this respect most of all that counsel differs from law [i.e., in not being "promulgated" and obligation creating] (Quoted in Schneewind 1990: I.74–75).[7]

---

[6] Here I draw on Darwall (2003).
[7] From *De Legibus*, first published in 1612. Jean Bodin made a related distinction between "command" and "counsel" in *The Six Books of the Republic*, published in 1577 (2004: 119). For discussion of Bodin's distinction and its role in early modern British thought, see Paul (2020).

It is difficult to overestimate the importance of Suárez's insight for the moral philosophy that followed him. The distinction between law (or command) and counsel is explicit in Grotius, Hobbes, and Kant. All these philosophers distinguish between normative reasons favoring or counseling an action, on the one hand, and the idea that the action is obligatory or demanded (commanded) through the moral law, on the other. And I shall be arguing that it is widely implicit elsewhere.

Several ideas are packed into Suárez's notion of obligating law. First, he says, "ordering pertains to the will," so obligating moral norms or laws must aim to *direct a will*; only thus can they have "binding force" (Suárez 1944: 66, 67). So, second, moral norms are God's will as *addressed to us*, hence to our rational wills second personally (Darwall 2006). But Suárez's idea is not that God seeks to determine our wills directly. If that were so, we could not fail to comply ("all these precepts would be executed"), since God is omnipotent (Suárez 1944: 55). Rather, God wills "to bind" his subjects by addressing legitimate demands *to* them through commands that they can then rationally choose to follow for what they can regard to be good reasons (55). Thus, third, the commands that create natural law must be addressed to human beings *as free and rational*. Laws of nature can exist "only in view of some rational creature; for law is imposed only upon a nature that is free, and has for its subject-matter free acts alone" (37). Finally, fourth, we are *accountable* for complying with moral obligations. If we do not "voluntarily observe the law," we are *culpable* ("legal culprits in the sight of God") (132).

In holding that the law of nature obligates because it is God's command, Suárez is implicitly accepting the premise of Anscombe's Challenge: any law such as morality purports to be can bind us only if it is divinely legislated. However, Suárez's theological voluntarism is not really essential to his conceptual distinction between law and counsel. Grotius, after all, invokes the distinction, as we shall see, but denies that moral obligation is grounded in divine command. The law, he says, would hold "even if we were to suppose ... that there is no God" (Grotius 2005: I, xxiv). This is what makes him subject to Anscombe's Challenge (as a modern moral philosopher).

The crucial conceptual distinction is between (deontic) concepts like law, authority, command, and obligation, which are conceptually tied to accountability and culpability, on the one hand, and the idea of normative reasons weighing in favor of or counseling action, which is not, on the other. Consistently with the conceptual connection between law and accountability, we might be accountable for complying with the moral law even if the latter did not depend on divine command. We might be accountable to one another, and ourselves, as representative persons or members of the moral community.[8]

---

[8] This is the view I argue for in Darwall (2006). Indeed, I argue there and in the next chapter on Pufendorf, that features internal to the logic of accountability make theological voluntarism inherently unstable as an account of the moral law.

Again, Grotius invokes Suárez's distinction between law and counsel, but denies his theological voluntarism.⁹ But if Suárez's objection has force against Aquinas, then why would it not also against Grotius? If Grotius rejects theological voluntarism as an explanation of the obligatory force of natural law, then what separates his view from Aquinas's? In the next section, I shall show how despite his rejection of theological voluntarism, Grotius's conception of natural law is nonetheless juridical in Anscombe's sense. And in the section following, I shall argue that, as against both Aquinas and Suárez central aspects of Grotius's view commit him to accepting Sidgwick's mark of the modern, that morality (natural law) provides a source of normative reasons that are additional to those provided by the agent's good, however broadly construed. Finally, we will consider Grotius's response to Anscombe's Challenge that morality requires a foundation in divine command. Grotius claims that our rational *and sociable* nature is sufficient to ground morality. This, he says, is the "fountain of right."

But why, first, would *Suárez* not count as a modern by Anscombe's standards? The reason is that although Suárez holds obligation to be essential to law, he does not think it is necessary for standards of moral right and wrong, nor for there to be normative reasons to comply with these standards. As odd as it may sound to modern ears, Suárez holds that an act's being morally wrong does not *in itself* entail any obligation not to do it.

Like Aquinas, Suárez is in this respect an Aristotelian naturalist (Irwin 2008: 38–41). Although Suárez holds that it takes God's command to create laws that place us under obligation, this *adds* obligation to what is already intrinsically right, and wrong not, to do.¹⁰ As Irwin puts it, Suárez believes that "if we

---

⁹ Tuck points out that in the Prolegomena to the first edition, Grotius says that the law of nature "necessarily derives from intrinsic principles of a human being" and that the law would hold "even if we were to suppose ... that there is no God, or that human affairs are of no concern to him" (Grotius 2005: I, xxiv; III, 1748–1749). Tuck notes that Grotius is less direct on this point in later editions. There Grotius says that "Natural Right [the Law of Nature] is the Rule and Dictate of Right Reason, shewing the Moral Deformity or Moral Necessity there is in any Act, according to its Suitableness or Unsuitableness to a reasonable Nature, and *consequently*, that such an Act is either forbid or commanded by GOD, the Author of Nature" (I, 150–151, emphasis added). This might encourage the Suárezian thought that genuinely obligating natural laws require an authoritative divine direction that is consequent upon any intrinsic reasonableness or unreasonableness and that the latter is impotent to provide this all by itself. However, Grotius then adds that actions that are thus suitable or unsuitable to a reasonable nature are "in themselves either Obligatory or Unlawful, and must, *consequently*, be understood to be either commanded or forbid by God himself" (I, 151–152, emphasis added). This means that the obligatory character of natural law depends not on divine legislation, but *vice versa*.

¹⁰ "This will of God, prohibition or prescription, is not the whole character of the goodness and badness that is present in the observance or transgression of natural law, but it assumes in the actions themselves some necessary rightness or wrongness, and joins to them a special obligation of divine law" (Suárez 1944: ii.6.11, quoted in Irwin 2008: 38n).

abstract divine commands from the natural law, what is left is morality (*honestas*), not just natural goodness" (31). God's commands do not make what is wrong wrong; they add an obligation to avoid the wrong, so that wrongful actions end up being, as it were, doubly wrong: wrong in and of themselves, but also because they disobey and so wrong God.

> Therefore it is necessary that it add some obligation of avoiding the evil that is evil from itself and by its own nature. Further, there is no contradiction if a thing that is right from itself has added to it an obligation to do it, or if a thing that is wrong from itself has added an obligation to avoid it (Suárez 1944: ii.6.12, Irwin 2008: 29b).

As Irwin emphasizes, Suárez follows Aquinas in holding (i) that standards of right and wrong are inherent in the nature of rational human beings; (ii) that moral rightness, so understood, is an intrinsically beneficial good, the "*bonum honestum*," which is distinct from the pleasant and the useful; and (iii) that this good provides the ultimate normative reasons agents have to do what is morally right for its own sake (Irwin 2008: 31, 2007: 606). As *eudaimonists*, Aquinas and Suárez both hold that *any* reasons agents have to do what is morally right must be rooted in their own good, where this is the intrinsic good of *bonum honestum*.

This ends up making Suárez pre-modern by Anscombe's *and* by Sidgwick's standards. Both Aquinas and Suárez have a way of marking out "moral" goods within the class of intrinsic goods, since only these goods and virtues distinctively concern the *common good* (Irwin 2007: 615–619, 2008: 66–67). But neither holds that moral right (*honestas*) is essentially juridical nor that it involves a non-*eudaimonist* source of normative reasons.

Since there is nothing essentially juridical about *honestas*, "morality" as Aquinas and Suárez conceive it is in this respect unlike morality in Anscombe's (allegedly) modern sense. And a similar point holds for Sidgwick's contrast. A mark of "ancient" ethics, for Sidgwick, again, is that "Virtue or Right action is commonly regarded as only a species of the Good" (Sidgwick 1967: 105–106). Since Suárez and Aquinas both hold that *honestas* provides no non-*eudaimonist* ground for action, but is instead a distinctive kind of intrinsic benefit (*honestum bonum*) whose normative weight can be fully captured within a *eudaimonist* framework, both count as pre-moderns by Sidgwick's standard also. Neither brings an intrinsic connection to obligation into their conception of "morality," and neither has any reason to think that morality requires a kind of reason for action that differs from *eudaimonist* considerations of the agent's own good.

Grotius on "*ius*," Morality, and Obligation

Grotius disagrees with Aquinas and Suárez on both counts. To begin to understand Grotius's position on these issues, however, we need to examine a three-way distinction he draws at the beginning of *RWP* between things correctly called *ius*.[11] First, Grotius says, "*ius*" can "signif[y] merely *that which is just*" or at least not unjust, where "that is unjust which is repugnant to the Nature of a Society of Reasonable Creatures" (Grotius 2005: I, 136). So far, this seems thoroughly within the classical natural law and Aristotelian naturalist framework; no essentially juridical notions need be involved.

Grotius then quotes Florentinus's remark that "*Nature has founded a kind of* Relation between us," and Seneca's saying that human beings "are born for Society, which cannot subsist but by a mutual Love and Defence of the Parts" (I, 136). He next distinguishes two different kinds of "relations" that are found in societies. Some are relations of "unequals," such as "Parents and Children, Masters and Servants, King and Subject," where one individual has authority over and the standing to govern another. Other relations are of "equal[s]," such as "Brothers, Citizens, Friends and Allies," where each party is conceived to be self-governing, at least so far as their relations to one another are concerned (I, 136). In the former instance, superiors have a "Right of Superiority"; in the latter, each has a "Right of Equality."[12] Grotius summarizes: "So that which is *just* takes place either among Equals, or amongst People whereof some are Governors and others governed, considered as such" (I, 137).

Grotius thus defines the human relations he is concerned with in terms of reciprocal recognition of relative *authority*. So understood, a relationship essentially includes the authority or standing those within it have to make claims on and demands of others to whom they are related by it; the relations are already conceived as inherently involving rights (*ius*) of this distinctive kind. Since relations of these sorts are essentially conceived in terms of *ius*, it follows straightway that anything that is contrary to the nature of people who are related *in these defined ways* will also be contrary to *ius* in a legal/juridical sense.

It is often noted that Grotius seeks to ground natural law in a form of "sociability" that is distinctive of human beings (I, 79–87). It is easy to mistake the force of his idea, however, since it can seem an attempt to derive moral obligations from some form of benevolent concern or affinity with others or some desire to be with or in agreement with them. But no such attempt can succeed in grounding juridical moral notions, especially since, as we shall see, Grotius himself distinguishes between what we owe to others and what we might properly be moved by love or by some sense of merit or desert to provide for them. Only in the former case, he holds, are genuine obligations (with associated rights) involved.

Moreover, we have seen that the distinctive *kind* of social relations Grotius has in mind are themselves already conceived in terms of relative authority, that is, in terms of the standing that the related parties have to make claims on

---

[11] Grotius's translators alternately translate "ius" as "law" or "right."
[12] Kelsey translates these as "rectorial law" and "equatorial law," respectively (Grotius 1925: 37).

and demands of one another.[13] This gives a distinctive color to Florentinus's remark that "Nature has founded a kind of Relation between us"; it suggests that this fundamental social relation must be conceived in terms of authority also. And that affects how Grotius's concept of "sociability" might most charitably be understood.

I shall argue that when Grotius says that "sociability" is "the Fountain of Right" (I, 85–86), the most promising philosophical option is to interpret him as holding that it is our *standing to make reasoned claims and demands of one another at all* that underlies the more specific rights and obligations that are contained in the law and right of nature. In other words, human beings share an equal authority over one other. Only such an interpretation of sociability can bring it into the conceptual space of law rather than "counsel."

To be clear, this interpretation goes well beyond what Grotius explicitly says. My point is that the idea of a standing to make claims on and demands of one another is implicit in aspects of his thought to which he is committed. And I maintain that it has a fundamental and distinctive importance for claims of moral obligation and rights that he, and after him so many philosophers of the modern period, wished to defend.

The second meaning of *ius* that Grotius mentions brings out the idea of authoritative standing even more clearly. Grotius says that this second sense is different from the first, "yet aris[es] from it." In the second sense, "*Right* is a *moral Quality* annexed to the Person, *enabling him to have, or do, something justly*" (I, 138). Here Grotius introduces his famous distinction, which will reverberate throughout the modern period, between perfect and imperfect rights (generating the modern distinction between perfect and imperfect duties or obligations).[14] A perfect right is a "*Faculty*" of the person, a normative "power" over oneself or, in special cases, over others, as when a relation of "superiority" like parent/child, master/servant, or king/subject obtains. Perfect rights are also implicated in property relations and contracts.

It is clear that Grotius identifies perfect rights with what we now call claim rights, which generate correlative obligations. Barbeyrac's French translation (from which Morrice's English translation draws) makes this explicit by adding

---

[13] It is worth noting in this connection that Pufendorf understands sociability (*socialitas*) in similar terms: "By a sociable attitude, we mean an attitude of each man towards every other person, by which each is understood to be bound to the other by … a mutual obligation" (1934: 208). Pufendorf of course differs from Grotius in seeking to derive natural law from divine command (including God's "fundamental" command to have a "sociable attitude") rather than from sociability. Even so, he and Grotius apparently agree in understanding sociability itself as involving relations of mutual right, obligation, and hence, authority, albeit understood formally.

[14] First, in Pufendorf (e.g., 1934: 90). On the significance of Grotius's distinction, see Schneewind (1998, esp. pp. 78–79, 133–134).

that perfect rights involve (in Morrice's English) "*The Faculty of demanding what is due*, and to this answers the *Obligation of rendering what is owing*" (I, 139).[15] It follows that there can be perfect rights only if natural law includes genuine obligations to respect them.

An imperfect right, on the other hand, is not a "*Faculty*" but an "*Aptitude*." Under this heading, Grotius includes considerations of "*Worth*" and "*Merit*" that can recommend actions as more or less worthy or meritorious, but that no one has standing to claim or demand (I, 141). "Prudent management in the gratuitous Distribution of Things" to which no individual or society has a valid claim may nonetheless recommend giving preference to "one of greater before one of less Merit, a Relation before a Stranger, a poor Man before one that is rich" (I, 88). However, Grotius insists that "Ancients" like Aristotle, and even "Moderns" who follow him are mistaken if they think this a matter of right, though they may take considerations of these kinds to be included within what they call "justice" (it is what Aristotle and his followers include under "distributive justice").[16] "Right, properly speaking, has a quite different Nature," namely, "doing for [others] what in Strictness they may demand" (I, 88–89).[17]

In its final sense, "*ius*" or "Right" "signifies the same Thing as *Law* when taken in its largest Extent, as being *a Rule of Moral Actions, obliging us*. ... I say *obliging*: for Counsels, and such other Precepts, which however honest and reasonable they be, lay us under no Obligation, come not under this Notion of *Law*, or *Right*" (I, 147–148).

Grotius here explicitly invokes Suárez's distinction between law and counsel. Even in "its largest Extent," *ius* is to be distinguished from counsel. It is of the nature of law and right to *obligate*; *ius* makes legitimate demands of us to which we are accountable for conforming. Normative reasons that simply weigh in favor of or "counsel" action lack this conceptual connection to the deontic; they do not obligate of themselves. This does not mean that there is not good reason to do what we are obligated to do. Far from it. It just means that being obligated to do something cannot itself be captured through the weight of reasons.

---

[15] In his notes, Barbeyrac defends this addition and argues that it should be read to apply not just to the case of contracts, as the Latin text might suggest, but to all perfect rights. Whether or not this is defensible as a translation, it seems clear that Barbeyrac is correct in thinking that if perfect rights are claim rights, then Grotius is committed to it.

[16] On the curious difference between this traditional notion and our contermporary notion of distributive justice, see Fleischacker (2004: 17–28).

[17] Kelsey translates this last passage from section 10 of the Prolegomena as "leaving to another that which belongs to him, or in fulfilling our obligations to him" (Grotius 1925: 13). Although it is clear from the text later that Grotius has Aristotle's distributive justice in mind, the language of "ancients" and "moderns" is Barbeyrac's. Kelsey has: "Long ago the view came to be held by many, that this discriminating allotment [distributive justice] is part of law" (1925: 13).

Grotius follows this with his definition of the "law" or "right" of nature:

> Natural Right *is the Rule and Dictate of Right Reason, shewing the Moral Deformity or Moral Necessity there is in any Act, according to its Suitableness to a reasonable Nature* (I, 150–151).

Barbeyrac notes that other editions interpolated "*and Sociable*" between "*reasonable*" and "*Nature*" and says there is some reason to believe that these were simply left out by a printer or transcriber (I, 151, note 2). As he points out, when Grotius distinguishes between *a priori* and *a posteriori* proofs of laws of nature, he brings in sociability explicitly. *A posteriori* proofs appeal to a *consentium gentium*, that is, to something being "generally believed to be" natural law "by all, or at least, the most civilized Nations" (I, 159). An *a priori* proof, by contrast, proceeds by "shewing the necessary Fitness or Unfitness of any Thing, with a reasonable and sociable Nature" (I, 159).

We shall return to how Grotius might hope to ground laws of nature in reasonable sociability in the final section. Since Grotius rejects Suárez's theological voluntarism, if he is to hold, like Suárez, that *ius* differs from counsel because of its distinctively obligating normativity, he needs some other way of accounting for this. Here, again, he faces Anscombe's Challenge.

Already, however, we can glimpse why Grotius might think that norms that can be justified in this way would have to be genuinely obligating. If, as we noted above, Grotius conceived of sociability as itself involving a *fundamental* standing to make claims and demands of one another, then being contrary to our reasonable *and sociable* character would mean being at odds with our standing to make *reasoned or reasonable claims and demands of each other*, not simply being contrary to standards of rational thought and action in general, even standards rooted in our rational nature however social that nature might be.[18] Only if it can be justified in some such way, indeed, would a "law of nature" be a genuine *ius*. Only if it can be grounded in an authority to issue demands would it be able to "lay us under" a genuine obligation in a way that a mere counsel cannot.

We can also now see that Grotius, unlike Suárez, is in no position to hold that obligation, though necessary for law, is inessential to moral right and wrong. Grotius ties his third definition of right – which he follows with his definition of natural right as "Suitableness to a reasonable Nature" – to *obligation*. Although he agrees with Aristotelian naturalists like Aquinas and Suárez that natural law and right are grounded in rational (and sociable) nature, he nonetheless holds that they entail obligation and that the latter does not come into existence through God imposing it on us through command. Moral right and wrong as Grotius

---

[18] For the difference between "sociability" in Grotius's sense and "social" in our ordinary sense and its philosophical significance, see Darwall (2014c).

understands them are already essentially juridical in Anscombe's (and Sidgwick's) sense. Something can be morally wrong only if we are under a legitimate demand not to do it. "Counsel," however reasonable, is an insufficient ground.

For Grotius, therefore, there is no notion of moral right and wrong that is independent of moral obligation. Considerations of common good, taken by themselves, are simply insufficient to show that anything is morally right or wrong in the sense with which Grotius is distinctively concerned. The most they can provide is counsel, not authoritative demand.

Morality as a Distinctive Source of Reasons

We turn now to Grotius's relation to Sidgwick's claim that modern ethical philosophers came to recognize morality (natural law) as a source of normative reasons for acting that is independent of the agent's good, therefore, *eudaimonist*. The point is somewhat delicate since, as Irwin has shown, a good bit of what Grotius says can be accommodated within an Aristotelian naturalist, *eudaimonist* framework according to which virtue – justice in particular – is intrinsically beneficial (part of the *bonum honestum*), whether or not it benefits agents instrumentally or promotes their partial interests, say, by making it likelier that others will act justly towards them in the future (Irwin 2003: 351–352).

A crucial passage occurs right at the outset of *RWP* when Grotius poses a fundamental skeptical challenge to his ideas, one that will be echoed later by Hobbes's "foole" (Hobbes 1994a: XV.§4), Hume's "sensible knave" (Hume 1975b: 256), and Kant's worry that morality might be a "chimerical idea without any truth" (Kant 1996a: 4:445). Who better to pose this challenge, Grotius says, than the ancient skeptic Carneades, who held that *"Laws ... were instituted by Men for the sake of Interest"* (Grotius 2005: I, 79).

> As to that which is called Natural Right, *it is a mere Chimera. Nature prompts all Men ... to seek their own particular Advantage: So that either there is no Justice at all, or if there is any it is extreme Folly, because it engages us to procure the Good of others, to our own Prejudice* (I, 79).[19]

---

[19] Cf. Hobbes:

> The fool hath said in his heart, there is no such thing as justice; and sometimes also with his tongue; seriously alleging that: "every man's conservation, and contentment, being committed to his own care, there could be no reason, why every man might not do what he thought conduced thereunto: and therefore also to make, or not make; keep, or not keep covenants, was not against reason, when it conduced to one's benefit" (Hobbes 1994a: XV.§4).

And Hume:

> [T]hough it is allowed, that, without a regard to property, no society could subsist; yet, according to the imperfect way in which human affairs are conducted, a

According to Carneades, there is only one source of reasons for acting, the agent's own interest or good; therefore, there can be no reason to follow any law that might conflict with that.

But what precisely is the challenge? If we were talking about law ordinarily so called – the laws of actual societies or even international law – egoism of this sort might pose no fundamental obstacle, since it seems no part of the concept of the law of any actual state or even of international law that such a law exists only if those subject to it have reason to respect it just because it applies to them. Laws of these kinds can exist even if the only motives for following them are self-interested desires to avoid sanctions.

This is not, however, the case with *natural* law, as that idea operated within both the classical theory deriving from Aquinas and the modern version I am claiming comes most clearly from Grotius. Something can be a natural law or right only if it entails normative reasons for agents to act. And if so, Carneades's challenge is that "natural right" so understood is a "mere Chimera." The only source of normative reasons is the agent's own interest.

Now it is important to see that although Aquinas and Suárez would certainly deny Carneades's claim that no law is such that there is necessarily reason to follow it, they nonetheless accept the *eudaimonist* assumption behind his claim, as Aristotelian naturalists do more generally. Aquinas and Suárez think there is necessarily reason to follow natural law because they believe that the agent's good necessarily coincides with it. In fact, for Aquinas, natural law and the agent's good turn out to provide the very same normative standard.

According to Aquinas, natural law is simply a formulation of "eternal law," God's ideal or archetype for all of nature – "the exemplar of divine wisdom … moving all things to their due end" – as it applies to rational human beings (Aquinas 1997: Q93.1). This is Thomas's synthesis of Aristotelian teleology with the idea of divine rule. Eternal law specifies the perfection or ideal state of every natural being, and so "rule[s] and measure[s]" them. Rational beings, however, are subject to eternal law in a special way since, having "a share of the eternal reason," they can act in the light of their awareness of eternal law, choosing to follow or flout it (Q91.3). What Aquinas calls "natural law" is simply the eternal law made accessible to and applicable by rational creatures in practice (Q91.2).

It follows that the content of natural law cannot differ from that of the eternal law for rational human beings *and* that, since what eternal law "requires"

> sensible knave, in particular incidents, may think, that an act of iniquity or infidelity will make a considerable addition to his fortune, without causing any considerable breach in the social union and confederacy. That *honesty is the best policy*, may be a good general rule; but is liable to many exceptions: And he, it may, perhaps, be thought, conducts himself with most wisdom, who observes the general rule, and takes advantage of all the exceptions (Hume 1975b: 256).

for any being is simply its good and perfection, natural law and the agent's own good are the very same normative standard. To follow natural law just is to pursue one's own good properly understood, and *vice versa*.[20]

It is also worth noting that on Aquinas's picture, since individual human beings realize their respective goods only within the overall teleological scheme specified by eternal law, any fundamental conflict between individuals' interests, properly understood, is ruled out – harmony is guaranteed by perfectionist-teleological metaphysics. The moderns who follow Grotius, however, assume that there can be genuine conflicts of interest; or at any rate, they believe that it cannot be assumed that there cannot be. Individuals will rationally believe that some rational conflicts are likely, even if that is only because no one can rationally believe that everyone else will believe that there won't be.

For most of Grotius's followers, the natural laws that comprise Barbeyrac's "morality" purport to provide a source of reasons that is distinct from and potentially in conflict with self-interest.[21] That is what makes Carneades's challenge genuine for them and explains why it compels the attention of thinkers as different as Hobbes, Hume, and Kant. For modern natural lawyers like Hobbes and Locke, moreover, it is central to their conception of the natural (moral) law that morality provides reasons for acting that trump considerations of self-interest in precisely those instances where the collective result of each individual's pursuing their own good, or their own conception of a good life for them would be worse for everyone.[22] As these Grotius-influenced moderns see it, the problem of social order is a *collective action problem* to which morality provides the solution.[23] Everyone does better if everyone follows the moral law than each would do were they to pursue their own good, or, at any rate, to pursue their own conception of their good.

From the perspective of his followers, then, the problem that Grotius appears to pose right at the outset of the modern period is how to show why individuals should respect such laws even when they would be better off individually (or, at least sensibly believe they would) by departing from them. In other words, since there cannot even *be* such a law unless it provides a source of reasons independent of self-interest, why suppose that such a law exists? The problem that Grotius thereby appears to set for the modern period is thus to show why collectively advantageous, putatively obligating laws are genuinely obligating

---

[20] At least, this equivalence holds with matters of common good.
[21] On this in relation to what Schneewind calls the "Grotian Problematic" (in Schneewind 1998: 119–129) see Darwall (1999a: 340–341).
[22] Although both of them believe that this is ultimately only because of sanctions (secular, for Hobbes, and divine, for Locke). See my discussions of Hobbes and Locke on this point in Darwall (1995: 36–44, 74–79).
[23] For the classic discussion of collective action problems, see Olson (1971).

and reason-giving rather than chimerical, as Carneades claims, even though following them is individually disadvantageous.

Even so, it is possible also to interpret Grotius, as Irwin does, as not himself posing this modern problematic, however central it might become to later writers (Irwin 2003: 351–352). It is certainly true, moreover, that Carneades's original challenge, as well as the way it was understood by the Aristotelian naturalist tradition before Grotius, does not require the modern Sidgwickean assumption that morality provides a source of reasons that is additional to the agent's own interest properly understood. Carneades himself challenged law and justice on roughly the same grounds that Glaucon and Adeimantus do in the *Republic* (359), namely, that they are no more than artificial conventions instituted for mutual *instrumental* advantage and that there is no intrinsic reason to follow them when it is contrary to one's (instrumental) interest to do so. And Grotius by and large just quotes Carneades's own challenge.[24]

Irwin notes that Aristotelian naturalists had a clear reply to Carneades's challenge that is fully consistent with *eudaimonism*. Moreover, some of what Grotius says certainly suggests that his own response to the skeptical challenge is simply that of Aristotelian (or as Irwin calls it elsewhere, "Stoic") naturalism, and hence that he accepts *eudaimonism* and so is not a modern by Sidgwick's lights (Irwin 2003). Grotius says that where Carneades goes wrong is in failing to appreciate that a "desire for society," or the "*Disposition the* Stoicks *termed* '*oikeiôsis*,'' [sociability]," is an essential aspect of human nature. The Stoics held that actions can be, as Irwin puts it, "morally right (*honestum*) because they are appropriate for human nature," given our natural sociability, and therefore that there is "a natural basis for justice, apart from the usefulness of justice in maintaining society" (2003: 352). And they held also that justice's being expressive of our nature and thus "natural" makes just action intrinsically *beneficial* to the just agent, whether it is useful, that is, instrumentally beneficial to them or not.

So understood, Grotius's reply to Carneadean skepticism is a response of the same general kind as Socrates's reply to Glaucon and Adeimantus in Plato's *Republic*. Plato and the Stoics might disagree about *why* justice is intrinsically beneficial to the just agent, and perhaps also about what justice is. But they agree that the fundamental reason to be just derives from the agent's own good. And so, Irwin argues, does Grotius.

However, this ancient reply to Carneadean skepticism will not do as a response to a skeptical challenge to the existence of natural law *as Grotius understands it*, and therefore as he must seek to defend it. The reason is, as Grotius himself explicitly points out, that "ancient" conceptions of right and law

---

[24] As it is reported in Lactantius's *Divine Institutes*: "*Nature prompts all Men ... to seek their own particular Advantage: So that either there is no Justice at all, or if there is any it is extreme Folly, because it engages us to procure the Good of others, to our own Prejudice*" (I, 79; see also Long 1986: 104).

lack any conceptual connection to *obligation* and *legitimate demands*. Grotius contrasts the Aristotelian conception of distributive justice that "ancients" and even some "moderns" include under the concept of right with right "properly speaking," since the latter includes doing for others "what in Strictness they may demand" (88–89). And he ties the broadest sense of right he is concerned with (the third sense of *ius* distinguished above) to *obligation* in the juridical Anscombean sense. Unlike "Counsels" and other "reasonable" "Precepts," law and right "lay us under … Obligation" (148).

The problem with the classical Stoic and Aristotelian naturalist reply is that it can provide no more than reasonable *counsel*, however weighty the reasons of the agent's good supporting the counsel might be. Therefore, even if it responds adequately to Carneades's challenge in the terms in which Carneades himself raised it, it is impotent to respond to a challenge to natural right and law, *as Grotius understands these*. However good it might be for us to comply with a standard or norm, that would not yet show that we lie under any *obligation* to comply with the standard or that that is something that can legitimately be *demanded* of us. The most the Aristotelian naturalist response can support is "reasonable counsel." It therefore cannot yet show that what we call natural law or right actually *is* a law or a right as Grotius understands these, since it would not yet have established its obligatory character.

Once we have the distinction between a mere "counsel," however well supported by reasons of extrinsic *or* of intrinsic value, on the one hand, and an obligating demand, on the other, we are committed to the idea that there must be a source of reasons for acting other than the agent's own good. The most the latter can provide is counsel, so if Grotius's natural law and right are to exist, there must be another source of reasons for following them. And if there is not, then the ideas of natural law and right are only chimerical and "there is no justice at all," just as Grotius has Carneades say.

It might be replied, however, that even if the arguments of the last two paragraphs show that *eudaimonist* reasons cannot establish natural law and right as genuinely obligating, they do not show that *eudaimonism* cannot provide an adequate account of the reasons for complying with the law. After all, that was Suárez's position. Why could it not have been Grotius's also?

Part of the problem is that, unlike Suárez, Grotius has no way of separating the grounds of natural law from the reasons for compliance. Suárez was an externalist in the sense that he held that what grounds something as obligating law, God's command, is distinct from what provides reasons for compliance. Only considerations of the agent's own good can supply the latter, even if some are related to God's commands, for example, through the good of obedience and the avoidance of sanctions.

Unlike Suárez however, Grotius has no independent way of grounding natural law. To the contrary, he appeals to human beings' rational and sociable nature both to reply to Carneades's challenge *and* as the "Fountain of Right"

(79–81, 86). In this respect, Grotius is an internalist. What grounds natural law and right as genuinely obligating must simultaneously supply normative reasons for compliance.

Although this ups the ante, it nonetheless gives Grotius a significantly more satisfying position philosophically. The externalist must hold that the fact that an action is legitimately demanded of an agent, and that they would be blameworthy for failing to comply were they to lack some further justification or excuse, does not *itself* entail any normative reason for them to comply. Any reasons for compliance must come from elsewhere – from the agent's own good for a *eudaimonist* like Suárez. But however broadly we construe the agent's welfare, as including, for example, the *bonum honestum* or obedience to God as intrinsic goods, it seems nonetheless to supply a "reason of the wrong kind" for their compliance with moral obligations and legitimate demands (Prichard 2002, Strawson 1968, Darwall 2006).

When we hold someone to account for doing something through what P. F. Strawson calls "reactive attitudes" like moral blame, we *thereby* imply that there were conclusive reasons for the agent not to have done what they did (Williams 1995, Gibbard 1990: 42). We presuppose that there are reasons for acting consisting in or entailed by the legitimate demands or obligations themselves, whether or not it will benefit the agent to comply. If, for example, we owe something to someone as a matter of *right*, it seems beside the point to ask whether discharging our obligation to them will benefit *us*.

We can agree with Irwin that nothing just said entails that Grotius himself saw that his conception of natural law requires a defense going beyond Aristotelian naturalism or that he rejects its *eudaimonism*. But there is no doubt that many of his followers saw this, as we can see from the way in which Grotius's Carneadean trope is repeated in Hobbes's reply to "the foole" (Hobbes 1994a: XV.§4), Hume's reply to the "sensible knave" (Hume 1975b: 256), and Kant's response to the charge that morality might be a "chimerical idea without any truth" (Kant 1996a: 4:445). These all assume that acting against morality might sometimes coincide with the agent's own interest in fact.[25] Consequently, they all assume that morality can exist only if *eudaimonism* is false, only if, that is, there can be reasons for agents to act that do not derive from their own good. Whether or not Grotius considered himself a modern in Sidgwick's sense, therefore, his account of moral right as entailing obligation and legitimate demand, and thus as being distinct from counsel, might reasonably have

---

[25] It is consistent with this that philosophers like Hobbes can hold that self-interested *eudaimonist* considerations still come in at another level. Hobbes is frequently seen as some kind of "rule" or "indirect" egoist. The point is that they do not deny the Carneadean claim that the wrong or unjust act may be beneficial. Obviously, for Kant, *eudaimonist* considerations don't enter at any level.

been seen by his followers as committing himself to the "modern" outlook as Sidgwick conceived it.

Freedom, Self-Rule, and the Right to Punish

An important theme of Richard Tuck's writings is that the moral/political conceptual framework we have inherited from the early moderns, one that bases political authority on the rights and dignity of individuals, begins with Grotius.[26] Part of Grotius's purpose in writing both *RWP* and the earlier *On the Law of Prize and Booty*[27] was to argue that organized groups of individuals, like the Dutch trading companies with which he and his family were involved, were like states in having a right to *punish* wrongs that did not violate their own rights but where the perpetrators might not otherwise be held responsible. Implicit throughout is a conception of individual persons as having the authority to rule themselves as well as the standing to hold one another responsible for respecting natural rights and law.

Consider, first, the following passage, which brings out Tuck's analogy between the personal and the political:

> But as there are several Ways of Living ... and every one may chuse which he pleases of all those Sorts; so a People may chuse what Form of Government they please: Neither is the Right which the Sovereign has over his Subjects to be measured ... but by the Extent of the Will of those who conferred it upon Him (Grotius 2005: I, 262).

Or the following, often cited by Tuck, from *On the Law of Prize and Booty*:

> God created man *autexousion*, "free and *sui iuris*," so that the actions of each individual and the use of his possessions were made subject not to another's will but to his own. Moreover, this view is sanctioned by the common consent of all nations. For what is that well-known concept, "natural liberty," other than the power of the individual to act in accordance with his own will? And liberty in regard to actions is equivalent to ownership in regard to property. Hence the saying: "every man is the governor and arbiter of affairs relative to his own property" (Grotius 1950: 18).

---

[26] "We take for granted that the language in which we still describe this autonomous, right-bearing individual is in fact a language to describe states or rulers. When Hart in his famous 1955 essay 'Are There Any Natural Rights?' said about promising that 'the promisee has a temporary authority or sovereignty in relation to some specific matter over another's will,' he was drawing on precisely this tradition which we find articulated for the first time in [Grotius's] *De Indis* [Grotius's favored title for *On the Law of Prize and Booty*]" (Tuck 2001: 84–85). See also Tuck (1981, 1993); and, especially, Tuck (2001: 1–9, 83–89).

[27] Grotius wrote *On the Law of Prize and Booty* between 1604 and 1606.

The "well-known concept" of "natural liberty," is a reference to Fernando Vázquez de Menchaca; but however well established the idea of self-rule was in some form or other, it seems clear that Grotius took the idea of a natural *right* to govern oneself significantly further. In Vázquez de Menchaca's hands, for example, "natural liberty" seems to refer alternately to a psychic faculty for free choice shared by rational agents, on the one hand, and to a Hohfeldian liberty, that is, to a range of permitted choices that violate no law or obligation, on the other.[28] With Grotius, however, the right to rule oneself evidently includes a Hohfeldian *claim* right and therefore entails a consequent obligation of others to allow one to do so.[29]

"Right properly and strictly so called," Grotius says, "consists in leaving others in quiet Possession of what is already their own [including the 'Power … over ourselves, which is term'd *Liberty*' (2005: I, 138)], or in doing for them what in Strictness they may demand" (I, 88–89). When we fail to abstain from what belongs to others (including, again, by interfering with their liberty), their right gives them standing to demand "Restitution" of what we have taken, insofar as this is possible, and "Reparation" of any "Damage done through our own Default" (I, 86). These reparative responses are all "due" to others not just in the sense that it is fitting that they have them or even that they deserve them, but also that these others have "the Faculty of demanding what is due," and that we consequently have "the Obligation of rendering what is owing" (I, 139). As Barbeyrac remarks in a footnote to the passage quoted at the beginning of the last paragraph, "When we Repair the Damage he has sustained in his Person, Goods, or Reputation, whether designedly or through Inadvertency, we restore what we had taken from him, and what was his own, *which he had a strict Right to demand*" (I, 88–89n).[30]

It follows that natural right, as Grotius understands it, includes obligation-entailing claim rights of individuals to demand that others conduct themselves toward them in various ways: "the Abstaining from that which is another's, the Restitution of what we have of another's, or of the Profit we have made by it, the Obligation of fulfilling Promises, [and] the Reparation

---

[28] For an excellent discussion of Vázquez de Menchaca on natural liberty, see Brett (1997: 165–204). Brett argues that Hobbes uses "natural liberty" to refer to these two things also (Brett 1997: 205–235). For Hohfeld's classification of rights, see Hohfeld (1923).

[29] Or, at least, it was taken to include such a claim right, as is shown by Barbeyrac's remarks quoted in the next paragraph.

[30] Similarly, when Grotius considers an argument on behalf of the Maccabees that "they acted by Vertue of the Right which their Nation had to demand Liberty, or the Power of governing themselves," which right we know from the first passage quoted above that Grotius must hold derives from individuals' right to choose, he implicitly accepts the premise that that right would include a right to "demand Liberty." (However, he also claims that the Maccabees had lost their right to liberty by earlier conquest (I, 359).)

of a Damage done through our own Default" (I, 86). And this shapes how the law of nature must itself be understood; it must include respect for these claim rights.[31]

Grotius's doctrine of natural right thus shapes his theory of natural law in the direction of a conception of morality as requiring protections of certain basic interests of individuals. But there is also a second way in which Grotius points toward what will become a signal modern idea: that the dignity of individuals is at the center of the moral law. In discussing Grotius's views on natural rights, Tuck aptly compares them to H. L. A. Hart's characterization of rights in his landmark paper, "Are There Any Natural Rights?" In Tuck's words, rights, for Grotius and Hart, "constitut[e] a kind of sovereignty for the individual over parts of his life" (Hart 1955, Tuck 2001: 9, see also 84–85).[32]

In addition, Grotius holds a view about the standing of individuals to punish violations of natural law that connects the law of nature to the dignity of individuals in yet a further way.

> Is the power to punish essentially a power that pertains to the state [*respublica*]? Not at all. On the contrary, just as every right of the magistrate comes to him from the state, so has the right come to the state from private individuals; and similarly, the power of the state is the result of collective agreement. ... Therefore, since no one is able to transfer a thing that he never possessed, it is evident that the right of chastisement was held by private persons before it was held by the state (Grotius 1950: 91).

---

[31] This is quite different from a conception of natural liberty as a Hohfeldian liberty (arguably, as in Vázquez de Menchaca and later in Hobbes), which simply entails permissions without any accompanying obligations. Hobbes's "right of nature," for example, of each "to use his own power, as he will himself, for the preservation of his own nature" (Hobbes 1994a: xiv, §4), entails no obligations of others to allow him to do so. It simply means that such an exercise of liberty by the agent themselves is "blameless." The term Hobbes uses in *The Elements of Law* is "blameless liberty.": "And that which is not against reason, men call RIGHT, or *jus*, or blameless liberty of using our own natural power and ability" (Hobbes 1994b: 79).

[32] An important additional aspect of Grotius's idea is best brought out by reference to another classic paper on rights, namely, Joel Feinberg's "The Nature and Value of Rights" (Feinberg 1980). This is the thought that claim rights involve the *authority* of the right holder *to claim or demand* certain treatment. This goes beyond it simply being the case that others should treat us in certain ways. It is the additional idea that right holders have the authority to demand that they be so treated and to demand restitution or reparation should they not be. As Feinberg puts it, "it is claiming that gives rights their special moral significance" (Feinberg 1980: 155). Without rights, although others might accept norms that require them to treat us in certain ways, we could not claim this is as our right. We would have, as Feinberg says, no place to "stand, ... look others in the eye" and make claims on one another (Feinberg 1980: 151). This gives us a dignity; as Feinberg stresses, it makes others accountable or answerable to us (Darwall 2006, 2013a). Better, our sharing these rights makes us *mutually* accountable.

As further evidence, Grotius adds an argument that will later be picked up by Locke in *The Second Treatise of Government* in support of his view that individuals in the state of nature have a right to punish that is additional to their right to seek reparation for violation of their own rights (Locke 1988: 272 (II.9)) – namely, that states normally claim the right to punish wrongs against not only their own citizens, but also against foreigners, "yet it derives no power over the latter from civil law, which is binding upon citizens only because they have given their own consent" (Grotius 1950: 91–92).[33]

According to Grotius, then, individuals have not only the authority to demand compliance with *their own* rights, and to demand restitution and reparation when these are violated, they also have the standing to demand that the moral law be complied with in respect of others' rights also. In effect, they have an authority of membership in an assumed moral community of mutually accountable equals.

This adds a distinctive element to the moral law. Since the law requires respect for each person's rights, it involves obligations that are, in the first instance at least, *to patients*, that is, those whom we affect by our actions. But patients are not the only ones who have the standing to demand compliance with these rights, and hence the law; all others do as well, since they have the standing to punish and not just to secure restitution or reparation on behalf of the victim. And since that is so, moral obligations involve, in the second instance, responsibilities *to* all persons and not just to patients. Here we have at least a strong suggestion, perhaps the first, of a conception of *moral community as mutual accountability*. Morality imposes genuine obligations that we are accountable for complying with, where this accountability involves being answerable to one another.

Publicly Articulable General Principles: A "Science" of Morality

It should now be evident that the central elements of the conception of natural law that in the mid-eighteenth century Barbeyrac referred to as "morality" were present already in Grotius (Barbeyrac 1749). Grotius holds that all individuals

---

[33] Grotius is not so explicit about individuals' right to punish in *RWP*. There he says that the "Person to whom the Right of Punishing belongs, is not determined by the Law of Nature" (II, 955). All "natural Reason" tells us for sure is that "a Malefactor may be punished, but not who ought to punish him" (II, 955). Though it "suggests ... it is fittest to be done by a Superior," it does not show that "to be absolutely necessary" (II, 955). Even if this seems weaker, there is no reason to think that Grotius has gone back on his earlier view. Indeed, in the passage where he proclaims sociability the "Fountain of Right," he adds that that this Right includes not just "Abstaining from that which is another's," "Restitution," "Reparation," and "the Obligation of fulfilling promises," as I mentioned before, but also "the Merit of Punishment among Men" (I, 86).

are subject to universal laws just by virtue of being rational sociable persons, irrespective of their local, national, or religious differences; that these laws impose genuine obligations; and, therefore, that agents are *responsible* for complying with them (and so subject to punishment if they do not). Moreover, these obligations include respecting natural *rights* that any rational moral agent has, including a right of autonomy or self-rule. The classic problem Grotius bequeathed to the modern period was how to establish that such universal genuinely *obligating* laws actually exist and are not merely chimerical, especially if their existence does not derive from divine command. Grotius initiated the form of modern moral philosophy that provoked Anscombe's Challenge.

I said at the beginning that Grotius was also an important source for what Barbeyrac called the "science of morality." This terminology is not Grotius's, nor is it familiar today, so we should ask what Barbeyrac intended by it. By a "science of morality," Barbeyrac means a publicly accessible *formulation* of basic "Principles and Rules of Morality" together, perhaps, with some account of their power to obligate (2).[34] He says that discovering moral "principles and rules" requires no "inquiry into the impenetrable Secrets of Nature,"[35] and that it is available to everyone, including "Persons, of the lowest Rank" (3).

It can be argued that a "science" of morality in this sense is precisely what Grotius was attempting himself to provide. It is worth quoting at length an excellent observation Tuck makes on this point in his introduction to *The Rights of War and Peace*:

> The Indian Ocean and the China Sea were an arena in which actors had to deal with one another without the overarching frameworks of common laws, customs, or religions; it was a proving ground for modern politics in general, as the states of Western Europe themselves came to terms with religious and cultural diversity. The principles that were to govern dealings of this kind had to be appropriately stripped down: there was no point in asserting to a king in Sumatra that Aristotelian moral philosophy was universally true (Grotius 2005: I, xviii).

Grotius's project was to formulate "minimalist" principles of obligation. The point was to specify principles that people can readily agree they should hold one another and themselves accountable for complying with regardless of national, cultural, and religious differences.

It is, indeed, because laws of nature (moral laws) purport to provide a basis for holding one another *answerable*, regardless of these more specific

---

[34] In his view, again, theological voluntarism provides the latter.
[35] "When we say, *That Man is subject to Law*; we mean nothing by *Man*, but a corporeal rational Creature: What the real Essence, or other Qualities of that Creature are, in this Case, is no Way consider'd" (1749: 4). Compare this to Locke's claim that "Person" is a "forensic term" (i.e., competent to be held accountable) that does not refer to a real essence (Locke 1975: 346).

differences, that they must be presumed to be publicly formulable and generally accessible without assuming any specific cultural or religious doctrine. Aristotle can intelligibly hold that someone of perfect virtue has a kind of practical wisdom that requires years of cultivation and experience and that may not even be possible for many people. Why think that everyone should be able to attain excellence of any kind or be capable of noble conduct?

Once, however, we have a conception of a standard that people can be held accountable for complying with, it seems that we must assume that anyone subject to it has what it takes to comply, that compliance requires no esoteric knowledge or special talents or wisdom that ordinary people cannot be presumed to have. The very idea of a standard of mutual accountability seems to require that it be capable of some public "minimalist" formulation, in something like the golden rule, which Hobbes says is "intelligible, even to the meanest capacity" (Hobbes 1994a: xv, 35), or the Categorical Imperative, or Grotius's injunction that we not deprive others of what is theirs. Of course, these formulations are not self-interpreting; they require judgment, and there can be reasonable disagreements about what they require. But the point remains that they require no special skill or controverted religious or cultural tradition that anyone subject to them cannot reasonably be supposed to share.

Seen in this light, Grotius's *a posteriori* arguments for putative laws of nature take on a new significance. A showing that a putative law, say, the obligation to keep promises, has "the Consent of all Nations" (Grotius 2005: I, 160–161), that it is part of a *consentium gentium*, is not just evidence that there are good reasons to keep promises. It is an argument that this is something we can reasonably demand of one another because we can reasonably expect (epistemically *and* morally) that others will reasonably accept it also.

So viewed, a "science" of morality is a distinctively modern project; it is an essential element of a mutually accountable social order having the same publicity requirements as the rule of law ordinarily so called.[36]

Sociability as the "Fountain of Right"

How are we to understand Grotius's claims that "Sociability" is "the Fountain of Right" (I, 85–86) and that what makes something in accord with or contrary to natural law is its "Fitness or Unfitness ... with a reasonable and sociable Nature" (I, 159)? The first statement of these ideas comes just after Carneades's challenge, to which Grotius replies by saying that human beings have a "Desire of Society" (I, 79). It is, however, important to understand just what Grotius takes our "sociable" nature to be, such that it might be able to ground natural law, as he understands it, that is, as a genuinely obligating law.

---

[36] For further elaboration of this point see Chapter 12 of Darwall (2006), especially the discussion of Bentham.

It seems clear, first, that sociability cannot be anything like benevolence, or the desire for the good of others or even of all, for at least two different reasons. First, even if such a desire were universal in the human species, it would be unable, by itself, to ground the idea that we are under any *obligation* to promote human welfare, that is, that we are responsible or accountable for doing so. In being benevolent, we see the flourishing of human beings as a good thing, but that is, by itself, insufficient to warrant the thought that we are *obligated* to bring this about, that it is something that can be legitimately *demanded* of us. Benevolence as such is focused on the good, not on the right, so it can only ground apparent counsel, not law.

Second, the very same form of collective action problem that arises with respect to individual good also arises with respect to the overall good. There are cases, notoriously those involving justice or fairness, where an agent could produce more overall good by violating a norm of justice as, for example, in Hume's famous example of restoring stolen property to a "seditious bigot."[37]

Neither can a desire to live among or in agreement with other human beings, or the Stoic idea that affiliation with other human beings is part of our common good, help to ground obligation and right. Like any consideration of good, the most such considerations can justify is some form of counsel, not obligating law.

Grotius is actually quite specific in defining the precise kind of "Desire of Society" that he has in mind.

> [A] certain Inclination to live with others of his own Kind, not in any Manner whatsoever, but peaceably, and in a Community regulated according to the best of His Understanding (I, 80–81).

To this he adds that mature human beings develop a "peculiar Instrument" that is necessary for such a "Community," namely, "the Use of Speech" (I, 85). And humans have also the related "Faculty of knowing and acting, according to some General Principles" (I, 85). Other animals live together, and many seem capable of acting out of something like affection or concern for at least some others of their kind. What is distinctive about human beings in this regard is their capacity for and disposition towards a particular kind of social order, namely, one mediated by the common acceptance of formulable, public "General Principles." Human beings thus have a capacity for and drive toward a distinctive *kind* of society, namely, "A Society of reasonable Creatures" (I, 136).

Recall the passages we considered earlier about the distinctive *relations* that define such a society, for example, Florentinus's remark that "*Nature has*

---

[37] "When a man of merit, of a beneficent disposition, restores a great fortune to a miser, or a seditious bigot, he has acted justly and laudably; but the public is a real sufferer" (Hume 1978: 497).

founded a kind of Relation between us" (I, 136). The examples that Grotius gives of social relations are all, again, relations of relative authority, involving standings to make claims and demands and to hold accountable, whether the relations are reciprocal (*"Right of Equality"*) or not (*"Right of Superiority"*) (I, 136–137). If we put these passages together with those quoted in the last paragraph concerning the "Social Faculty" (I, 87), what we get is a conception of sociability as the human capacity for and disposition toward a distinctive *kind* of social order, namely, the very kind of order that Grotius is himself trying to found in *RWP*. So understood, sociability is the fountain of an order involving all persons that is mediated by universal "General Principles" enshrining rights with which individual members take themselves to have standing to demand compliance.

This suggests that we might best understand Grotius as holding that the law and right of nature are grounded in the capacity of rational sociable persons to recognize their common competence and authority to make reasoned claims and demands against one another and to live with one another on terms that respect this common standing. Of course, this does not tell us much about how such a rationale might work in any detail. But it does point us toward a way of thinking about the modern conception of natural law (morality) that appreciates its legal/juridical aspect and, consequently, the distinguishing form the Carneadean challenge must take once there is a commitment, as Sidgwick says, to a source of normative reasons that is independent of self-interest.[38]

To sum up this chapter, Grotius put forward a moral conception according to which morality or natural law: (i) has a distinctively obligating normativity that cannot be reduced to normative reasons concerning the good that advise or "counsel" action rather than demanding it; (ii) includes basic universal claim rights, what Grotius dubs "perfect rights" (thereby initiating the perfect/imperfect right and perfect/imperfect duty distinctions); and (iii) would exist and obligate us "even if we were to suppose … that there is no God" (I, xxiv). This conjunction of claims played a significant role in shaping "modern moral philosophy." (i) and (iii) together lead to Anscombe's Challenge.

Moral philosophers who followed were unquestionably influenced by Grotius's approach to the subject. Although Grotius's answer to Anscombe's Challenge – that sociability is the "Fountain of Right" – was not explicitly taken up by many who directly followed him, we shall nonetheless see in the next chapter how a similar conception of sociability entered into Pufendorf's thought, although not as a fundamental ground. Whether or not modern moral philosophers have accepted Grotius's answer, many have clearly accepted the combination of Grotian views that make them subject to Anscombe's Challenge. It is a challenge we have been grappling with ever since Grotius.

---

[38] This idea has clear affinities with Scanlon's contractualist ideal of the moral community as one of mutual justification (Scanlon 1998; see also Darwall 2006).

2

Hobbes and Pufendorf

If it is widely believed that modern ethical thought began with Hugo Grotius, there is a virtual consensus that modern political thought began with Thomas Hobbes (1588–1679). The Hobbesian project of grounding political authority on the sparest assumptions consistent with the emerging modern sciences and without the "*Summum Bonum* … of the old moral philosophers" seemed to mark a new departure in political philosophy that was, if anything, even more recognizable and radical than the Grotian turn in ethical philosophy overall (Hobbes 1994a: XI.1).

In this chapter, we shall be concerned with Hobbes's similarly spare approach to ethics. Hobbes defines "moral philosophy" variously as "the science of the laws of nature," "the science of … good and evil," and "the science of virtue and vice" (XV.40). What makes moral philosophy a "science," in Hobbes's view, is its concern with "knowledge of consequences" (V.17), where "consequence" means conceptual or logical entailment rather than causal effect. "Ethics," Hobbes says, draws "[c]onsequences from the passions of men" (IX.table).

"Science" is the product of "reason," which is "nothing but *reckoning* … of the consequences of the general names agreed upon for the *marking* and *signifying* of our thoughts" (V.2). All thoughts originate in sense, whose cause is invariably some "external body, or object which presseth the organ proper to each sense" (I.2, 4). We use names to signify our experiences and "cogitate[e]" concerning their causes and effects (I.2; IV.3). The form of reasoning involved in Hobbesian science is not, however, inductive cogitation; it is drawing out deductive consequences of agreed "general names" signifying thoughts that originate in sense experience.

To this concept empiricism, Hobbes adds a materialist metaphysics. To have meaning and reference, names must refer either to some "*matter* or *body*," to "some accident or quality which we conceive to be in [bodies]," to "properties of our own bodies" such as sensings or imaginings ("fancies"), or to other names (IV.15–18). Where, however, can ethical thought and language fit into such a materialist, nominalist picture? It would seem that the most that a Hobbesian science could tell us is what *is* the case, not what *ought* to be or what we ought to do.

Hobbes makes it clear that he rejects the central concept of Aristotelian teleological metaphysics. "A final cause has no place but in such things that have sense and will" (Hobbes 1839: I.131), and here final causes are to be assimilated to efficient causes provided by desires and aversions (1994a: VI.2). It apparently follows that the language of Aristotelian naturalism can be no more than "insignificant words of the Schools" (IV.1).

If Hobbes was like Grotius in aiming to overthrow Scholastic orthodoxy, he was also like him in wanting to secure ethical and political thought on new foundations. Moreover, Hobbes shared the Grotian project of grounding a distinctively juridical ethical conception – a "science of the laws of nature" – a "modern moral philosophy" or "science of morality" (Barbeyrac 1749). Finally, Hobbes and Grotius were united in their concern to defend "minimalist" foundations for moral and political thought that could survive strong evaluative disagreements, whether international, as with Grotius, or intra-national, as with the religious differences of the English Civil War that Hobbes hoped to overcome.

But here the similarities end. Hobbes's empiricism and materialism impose philosophical constraints on his thought that go well beyond anything limiting Grotius. Grotius was a philosophical lawyer who began with agreed legal doctrines, a *consentium gentium*, and sought deeper rationales. Hobbes, by contrast, came to moral and political philosophy with prior commitments in metaphysics, epistemology, and the philosophies of language and mind. These constrained not just his method, but also his views about how ethical and political thought and their respective objects might be so much as possible.

This can make Hobbes's thought especially relevant to us today. Hobbes's materialism and empiricism force him to confront metaethical questions about the metaphysics of ethics, and related issues in the philosophies of language and mind, in something like the form they take in contemporary discussions. Moreover, Hobbes's own views bear an interpretation that is not unlike so-called anti-realist or expressivist positions in contemporary metaethics.

One obvious difference between Grotius and Hobbes concerns *sociability*. Both Hobbes and Grotius are "methodological individualists" in political philosophy in the sense that both seek to ground political authority in the perspective of independent individuals. But Hobbes's individualism runs deeper. Whereas Grotius arguably takes human sociability to entail a basic *interdependent* normative authority that can ground reciprocal claim rights (the "Fountain of Right"), Hobbes's fundamental commitments rule out any such mutual normative standing. Individual human beings no more instantiate natural normative relationships than do "mushrooms" "sprung out of the earth" (Hobbes 1983: 8.1). Obligations come into existence only as the result of individuals' voluntary acts "when a man hath ... abandoned or granted away his right" (1994a: XIV.7). "There [is] no obligation on any man which ariseth not from some act of his own" (XXI.10). Absent such undertakings, there is nothing in a state of nature to ground reciprocal obligations and claims.

The natural human condition, Hobbes says, is a basic right of liberty, not of claim.

> The RIGHT OF NATURE ... is the liberty each man hath to use his own power, as he will himself, for the preservation of ... his own life, and consequently of doing anything which, in his own judgment and reason, he shall conceive to be the aptest means thereunto (XIV.1).

Hobbes does say that "laws of nature" bind individuals even in the state of nature. But though he also says that these natural laws and the right of nature differ "as much as obligation and liberty," this juridical language substantially softens under analysis. First, in the state of nature when one cannot be assured that others will conform to natural laws, such as the first, to "*seek peace*," or the third, to "perform their covenants made," the laws of nature obligate only "*in foro interno*, that is to say, they bind to a desire they should take place" (XIV.4; XV.1, 36). And second, Hobbes says that the laws of nature are called "law, but improperly; for they are but the conclusions or theorems concerning what conduceth to the conservation and defence of themselves" (XV.41).

Taken literally, this last statement reduces laws of nature to empirical generalizations that lack any explicit ethical or normative force. Such generalizations are philosophically respectable by Hobbes's empiricist, materialist lights. But the cost seems to be that anything distinctively ethical or normative has been reduced away. Again the problem arises: If language and thought can only gain content by referring to material things and properties we are aware of through sense experience, how can there be meaningful ethical language and thought?

As a modern, indeed, Hobbes actually faces two distinct problems here. How can there be contentful claims and thoughts about the good? And how can there be such claims and thoughts about obligation and the right?

Samuel Pufendorf (1632–1694) will give us an especially apt comparative perspective in this chapter. Like Hobbes, Pufendorf is concerned with placing morality ("moral entities") in relation to an empirically graspable realm of "physical entities" (Pufendorf 1934: 5). But Hobbes and Pufendorf disagree radically about what brings juridical morality into play. Pufendorf is a theological voluntarist who holds that obligations all derive ultimately from "imposition" by God's authoritative command. For Hobbes, by contrast, it is only by voluntarily laying down natural liberties that individuals become obligated to one another.

There is actually an issue for Hobbes here that Pufendorf more actively confronts. How exactly is it possible to "lay down" a right and thereby create an obligation? As we shall see, Hobbes seems simply to assume the existence of what Pufendorf calls "moral powers" ("normative powers," in contemporary terms), the voluntary exercise of which can put us under obligation (Raz 1972), like the power to promise or contract. It turns out that Pufendorf has thought through what such powers must consist in and imply in ways that Hobbes apparently has not.

It is important to see that Hobbes and Pufendorf agree about the fundamental role of normative "moral powers" in underwriting moral obligations. For Hobbes, genuine obligations can arise only from exercising a power to undertake them voluntarily by laying down rights (liberties). And for Pufendorf, all moral obligations derive from God's "imposition" through exercising his moral power as a superior. As we shall see, both ultimately face the problem Cudworth raised for all such voluntarist views, namely, that the very existence of moral powers may presuppose moral obligations already in the background.

Pufendorf also provides an interesting counterpoint to Hobbes on sociability. Pufendorf agrees with Hobbes, against Grotius, that no natural basis for reciprocal claim rights can exist without the exercise of moral powers. According to Hobbes, we become obligated to one another by laying down rights through covenant in establishing the sovereign's authority. According to Pufendorf, all obligations ultimately derive from God's exercising his moral power of authoritative command. But despite agreeing on this, Hobbes and Pufendorf fundamentally disagree about the natural moral state human beings are in in relation to one another before any human beings have exercised *their* moral powers on each other.

According to Pufendorf, the fundamental law of nature derives from God's commanding us to "cultivate and preserve towards others a sociable attitude," where this involves viewing one another with mutual respect as having a dignity that grounds equal basic reciprocal obligations and rights (Pufendorf 1934: 208). In effect, Pufendorf's position is that our fundamental obligation to God is to view one another as *sociable in Grotius's sense*, that is, as sources of mutual obligations and claim rights, what Rawls will call toward the end of the twentieth century "self-originating source[s] of valid claims" (Rawls 1980: 546). According to Hobbes, however, human beings can have no obligations to or rights against one another without voluntarily laying down or transferring natural liberty rights. Pufendorf is a sharp critic of this Hobbesian position.

These interrelations between Grotius, Hobbes, and Pufendorf crystallize in their respective views of war and peace. Grotius's founding work is titled *The Rights of War and Peace*. And Hobbes's first law of nature is "to *endeavour peace*" so long as there is hope of "obtaining it," but otherwise to "seek and use all helps and advantages of war" (Hobbes 1994a: XIV.4). Pufendorf, for his part, defines peace as the state human beings are in when they bear one another a reciprocally respectful, sociable attitude:

> Peace is that state in which men dwell together in quiet and ... render their mutual dues, as of obligation ... (Pufendorf 1934).

However, Grotius, Hobbes, and Pufendorf exemplify three fundamentally different positions on this topic of common vital concern. Grotius holds that human beings naturally instantiate a basic normative sociable, hence peaceful, relation independently of any voluntary undertaking or the exercise of any moral power. Pufendorf agrees with Grotius that such a basis for mutually respectful peaceful relations exists independently of any voluntary *human* undertaking, but nonetheless agrees with Hobbes, and against Grotius, that it takes a voluntary action – God's exercise of his moral power of command – to ground this natural sociable state. Finally, Hobbes holds that the state of nature is not one of reciprocal obligation and right (so, is not a Pufendorfian state of peace) in any sense, thus disagreeing with both Grotius and Pufendorf. As Hobbes sees it, the only way peace can be achieved is through human covenants in which people lay down their (liberty) right to all things and authorize and agree to obey a sovereign who can provide the background institutional conditions necessary to make peace possible.

Hobbes

We turn now to Hobbes's attempts to work out an ethical philosophy whose tenets can be both "significant" and philosophically defensible.[1] Recall that Hobbes treats "ethics" and "moral philosophy" as *sciences*, therefore, as rational inquiries into the "consequences" of the "general names" with which they are concerned. Ethics seeks "consequences from the passions of men." And the part of moral philosophy that concerns obligations and claim rights, "the *Science* of JUST and UNJUST," seeks "Consequences from speech … *[i]n contracting*" (Hobbes 1994a: IX.table).[2]

We can put the two questions about the good and the right we raised above in Hobbes's scientific idiom. It would seem, first, that any consequences that might follow from "the passions of men" can only concern the nature and circumstances of human passions *in fact*. But claims about the good, for example, are not claims about what people actually desire; they are about what is *worthy* of desire, what is *desirable* or there is reason *to* desire. So if ethics concerns consequences of the passions, and these include only what follows from our passions in fact, how can genuinely ethical claims about the good be part of a philosophically respectable ethics, as Hobbes understands it?

Similarly, second, Hobbes holds that strictly juridical matters of obligation, claim right, and justice arise only through contract. Since the very idea of a promise or contract is to undertake some kind of obligation, Hobbes might

---

[1] "Significant" in Hobbes's sense of meaningful and securing reference to the material world.
[2] See Pettit 2009 for an account of Hobbes that stresses this aspect. Cf. the discussion of the role of language in Grotian sociability in Chapter 1.

seem to be on firmer ground in holding that the "science of just and unjust" consists of "consequences from speech in contracting." Even so, a dilemma looms: either whether a promise or contract has been executed is itself a normative matter or it is not. If it is, that will assure normative "consequences" from contracting, but then it will be hard to see how contracting can itself consist in the simple holding of material facts concerning speech and social convention. On the other horn, the more empirically and materialistically respectable we make contracting, the harder it will be to see how any genuinely obligating normativity can follow from it. And there will remain as well the further problem I alluded to briefly above concerning how to understand the normative power to contract within the normative materials that Hobbes's state of nature provides.

We shall investigate these matters in turn presently. When we get to Hobbes on the right, it will be important to bear in mind that although Hobbes's official view of obligation is that it can arise only through a voluntary laying down of right, as in contract, Hobbes also sometimes says that laws of nature obligate, and he defines natural laws in explicitly deontic terms. A law of nature, he says, "is a precept or general rule, found out by reason, by which a man is forbidden" to act in certain ways (as it happens, "to do that which is destructive of his life or taketh away the means of preserving the same") (XIV.3). "Forbidden" is a deontic term. So there will be two separate problems of right. How can any precept that can forbid action follow from the passions of men? And how can obligation, more strictly so called, follow as a consequence of "speech in contracting"?

Desire and the Good

We turn now to Hobbes on the good. The dominant view has been that Hobbes has a very simple way of answering the question of how claims about the good can be consequences of human passions, namely, by holding that these claims are about the desires of those who make them. A common view is that Hobbes is a value subjectivist (Gauthier 1969: 7; 1979: 548; Hampton 1986: 29; Kavka 1986: 47). When Hobbes writes that "*[g]ood* and *evil* are names that signify our appetites" (Hobbes 1994a: XV.40), and that whatever a person desires they "calleth good" (XV.7), he is frequently read as saying that "good" means something like "desired by me."

But although this makes good sense of Hobbes's claim that ethical propositions of the good concern consequences of human desires, it gives him the burden of explaining how facts about an agent's psychology can have normative practical force. Why does the fact that I actually desire something make it the case that there is a reason *for* me to desire and seek it? That I do desire something seems to be one thing; that it is desirable or good, something I *should* desire or seek, another. Reductionism seems to change the subject from ethics to psychology.

There is a further problem with subjectivism that must also infect a subjectivist interpretation of Hobbes. When two people, A and B, say of something, X, that it is good and that it is not good, respectively, they seem to disagree about some matter concerning which both cannot be correct. If subjectivism is true, however, what A really says is that she, A, desires X, and what B says is that he, B, does not. But if this is so, then there is no issue on which A and B differ. A will not be affirming what B denies, nor *vice versa*. Moreover, subjectivism is not simply problematic in its own right. It is especially dubious as an interpretation of Hobbes, since Hobbes says that disagreements about good and evil can be grave enough to lead to war (XV.40).

A major reason given for attributing a subjectivist view to Hobbes, again, is his saying that what we desire we call good, and that what we are averse to or "hate" we call evil (VI.7). But this no more supports subjectivism than would saying that whatever we believe we call true support subjectivism about truth. No one would claim that when we say that something is true, we are saying that we believe it. That would run over a distinction between *expressing* and *self-attributing* a belief, just as the subjectivist interpretation of Hobbes's text blurs the analogous distinction between expressing and self-attributing a desire.

It is more charitable, both philosophically and interpretatively, to read Hobbes as holding something closer to what is nowadays called expressivism or projectivism than it is to interpret him as a metaethical subjectivist (see, e.g., Blackburn 1984; Gibbard 1990).[3] When people say that something is good, they are not saying that they desire it; they are expressing their desire for it and, perhaps, projecting a property (goodness) onto the object of their desire in something like the way that Hobbes holds, following Galileo, that our color sense projects colors onto objects: "[T]he real and very object seems invested with the [color] fancy it begets in us" (Hobbes 1994a: I.4).

Hobbes explicitly analogizes the case of value to that of color. Though there is nothing more to color metaphysically, Hobbes says, than "motion caused by the action of external objects," these motions are nonetheless "to the sight" as "light and colour" (VI.9). Similarly, Hobbes holds that although desires are similarly motions in our bodies, these also have appearances, in this case as of an object's having the property of being good.

Chapter VI of *Leviathan*, "Of the … Passions, and the Speeches by Which They Are Expressed," contains a careful analysis of "the Interiour Beginnings of Voluntary Motion" in appetites and aversions. Desires always have some "fancied" object toward which they move us (VI.1, 2). The fancy (imagining of an object) that accompanies desire is "delight" or "pleasure" (VI.10).

> As in sense that which is really within us is … only motion caused by the action of external objects (but in appearance, to the sight, light and

---

[3] In the following paragraphs, I draw from Darwall 2000.

colour ...) so when the action is continued ... to the heart, the real effect there is nothing but motion or endeavour [desire or aversion] ... But to the appearance ... is that we either call DELIGHT, or TROUBLE OF MIND (VI.9).

This delight or pleasure, Hobbes says, is "the appearance, or sense, of good; and *molestation* or *displeasure*, the appearance, or sense, of evil" (VI.11). Just as color sensation projects apparently real, but non-existent, color properties onto objects, so too do desire and aversion project the ethical properties of goodness and evil onto their respective objects. When I see a banana, the material thing before me causes me to project the property of yellow onto the banana, as though it had this property intrinsically. Similarly, when the sight of a banana stimulates a desire in me to eat it, that causes me to see the banana as though it, or at least eating it, has the property of goodness intrinsically.

This interpretation explains how Hobbes can hold that disagreements about the good are capable of leading to "controversies, and at last war" (XV.40). According to a subjectivist account, people who utter apparently conflicting sentences about the good are not really expressing disagreement; to the contrary, they agree about their disagreeing attitudes. But on an expressivist or projectivist interpretation, this is not true. People uttering such sentences are expressing their conflicting desires, hence their disagreement. Such passionate disagreements can indeed lead to war.

But what about Hobbes's claim that "*[g]ood* and *evil* are names that signify our appetites and aversions" (XV.40)? Here again, Hobbes treats claims about good and evil as being on par with those involving color. With color, Hobbes says, "we bring into account the properties of our own bodies whereby we make such distinction" (IV.17). Similarly, all that can "enter into account" for the good metaphysically are material motions, in this case, desires and aversions (IV.15). Nevertheless, when we judge objects to be colored or good, we do not judge or see them *as* causing these material motions; we see them as though they have an intrinsic property that Hobbes believes they do not actually possess, in one case a phenomenal color property, in the other, an evaluative or normative property.[4]

---

[4] Hobbes also says that "good" and "evil" are "ever used with relation to the person that useth them," and that although there is no rule of good inherent in "the nature of objects themselves," a rule can be given by "the person of the man" (VI.7). Moreover, Hobbes frequently talks about good and evil in an explicitly relativized way. "The voluntary acts of every man," he says, invariably aim at "some *good to himself*" (XIV.8). And he defines benevolence as "desire of good to another" (VI.22). Don't all these remarks point in the direction of subjectivism rather than projectivism? Not necessarily. If speakers use "good" and "evil" to express their desires, then they use them "with relation to" themselves even if they do not assert some relation to themselves (as subjectivism requires). When Hobbes speaks of things being good *to* people, this can easily be interpreted as referring to what people *think*

Would not, however, knowledge of the projective character of ethical judgments undermine ethical thought and practice? Should not Hobbes have believed that in putting forward a projective theory of value judgment he was placing a significant obstacle in his readers' way in accepting the normative propositions he wished to convince them of in *Leviathan*?

Hobbes does not directly confront this question, but he might answer it by arguing that since evaluative thought is always an expression of desires, it is simply unavoidable for us so long as we have desires. "[L]ife itself is but motion, and can never be without desire" (VI.58). Once we are in the state of desire, we are *per force* deliberating and subject to deliberative ethical thought.[5]

All deliberation begins with desire (VI.49). And "[f]rom desire, ariseth the thought of some means we have seen produce the like of that which we aim at ... till we come to some beginning within our own power" (III.4). "[I]n deliberation," Hobbes adds, "the appetites and aversions are raised by the foresight of the good and evil consequences and sequels of the action whereof we deliberate" (VI.57). The relevant evaluative "foresight" must itself be provided by desires that are upstream in the deliberative process. Under the influence of the desires that begin deliberation, we are disposed to see some consequences of alternative actions as good and others as evil, and these thoughts then give rise to further (instrumental) desires leading ultimately to the "last appetite" (will or volition) and finally to action.

In effect, Hobbes is working with a distinction between theoretical and practical standpoints. Thought and discourse about good and evil encode an agent's view from the deliberative perspective their desires provide. Thus although Hobbes calls "moral philosophy ... the science of what is *good* and

---

good or what appears good to them. And we can understand Hobbes's claim that voluntary action invariably aims at some good to the agent as saying that voluntary action invariably aims at something the agent thinks good or that seems good to her. Since Hobbes holds that all voluntary motions result from desires and aversions, it will be true that all voluntary motion aims at something that seems good to the agent. As opposed to *"vital* motion," "animal" or "voluntary motion" invariably involves a "fancy" or "imagination," a "precedent thought of *whither, which way,* and *what*" (VI.1), which is "the appearance, or sense, of good" (VI.1,11).

[5] Even if we cannot stop it appearing to us as though some things are good and ought to be brought about, might we nonetheless become alienated from these appearances? Compare the case of color. A projectivist about color can hold that although, strictly speaking, all color judgments are false, our practical purposes are nonetheless better served by speaking and thinking as though they are not, normalizing our color judgments to the experiences of the normally sighted under normal conditions. We can easily imagine a philosophically sophisticated, projectivist interior decorator whose "first-order" thought and speech about color are regimented in this way. Such a philosophical position would apparently pose no obstacle to facility, even expertise, in color judgments for practical purposes as a decorator. Similarly, Hobbes might reply that the point and function of ethical terms and concepts is practical – even more so, indeed, than those of color.

evil" (XV.40), he must have held that it is a science we engage in from a practical point of view, as we discover how the consequences to be drawn from "the passions of men" bear on the ends that drive our deliberative thought.[6]

Since the good is the currency of desires, and deliberation is driven by desires, the good must be the currency of practical reason. Where, then, can Hobbes locate the right or judgments of right? Considerations of right can provide normative reasons for action only under "the guise of the good." This would not rule out considerations of right from being or entailing normative practical reasons. It would just mean that it is impossible for someone to take deontic considerations as reasons and act on them without a desire whose appearance and expression is that such action would be good.

Obligation and the Right

It is common to interpret Hobbes as holding that the normativity of the "laws of nature" ultimately derives from how conformance (or perhaps the disposition to conform) advances agents' self-preservation or good (Gauthier 1967, 1979; Hampton 1986; Kavka 1986, 1995; Darwall 1995). This interpretation is encouraged by Hobbes's saying that laws of nature are really "theorems concerning what conduceth to the conservation and defense of themselves" (Hobbes 1994a: XV.41). But while such good-based, instrumentalist approaches can plausibly claim to ground a kind of normativity for the laws of nature, it is ultimately one of the good. Such approaches cannot explain how Hobbes might account for any deontic sense in which someone might be "forbidden" to act against self-preservation.

We shall return to how Hobbes might reasonably hope to provide a more satisfyingly independent metaethics of right, one that is similar to his metaethics of good, presently. First, however, we should consider what Hobbes says about the distinctive deontic claims of right to which he is explicitly committed,

---

[6] This does not mean that Hobbes thought his readers' ethics would have been entirely unaffected by accepting his analogy between color and value. To the contrary, Hobbes must have thought they *would* be affected and for the good. Hobbes was a notorious critic of religious "superstition" and its intellectual expression in the metaphysics of the schools. When superstitious believers expressed their ethical convictions, he thought, they were simply giving voice to desires, albeit ones highly disciplined by religious ritual and practice. The faithful themselves, however, likely saw both their desires and their ethical convictions as responding to real objective values or "final causes." Hobbes of course thought that this was nothing but "insignificant speech" and that nothing stood behind their ethics but the desires of which their thought was an appearance and their discourse an expression. Even so, he might also have believed that their ethics were, at least partly, "ideological" in the sense that some of the desires their ethics expressed would not have existed but for their superstitious metaphysical beliefs. Convincing his readers of an expressivist metaethics of the good might help unmask and overturn their ideological ethics.

namely, the obligations that are created by voluntarily laying down or transferring rights.[7]

It is the right of nature that individuals are said to lay down in creating the sovereign's authority by contract. Although Hobbes holds that it is only by laying down this right that genuine obligations are created, the right of nature is itself a putative deontic moral fact. It is a *moral* liberty. This is brought out by Hobbes's *De Cive* formulation that it is not "reprehensible ... for a man to use all his endeavours to preserve and defend his body" (1983: I.7), and by his calling the right of nature a "blameless liberty" (1994b: 14.6). Even if the laws of nature are ultimately to be interpreted in non-deontic terms, the right of nature itself purports to be a truth about how it is *morally permissible* for agents to act.

Hobbes is clear, however, that when the right of nature is abandoned or laid down, this gives rise to genuine obligations. Hobbes defines obligation, indeed, as the upshot of such voluntary undertakings: "When a man hath in either manner abandoned or granted away his right, then he is said to be OBLIGED or BOUND not to hinder those" from benefiting from the right (1994a: XIV.7). The question we must now investigate is: How can Hobbes account for such voluntarily created obligations within his metaethical framework?

Hobbes gives different answers to this question in his earlier works, *De Cive* and *The Elements of Law*, and in *Leviathan*, respectively.[8] The key to his earlier answer has to do with conceptual connections Hobbes makes between obligation, liberty, and deliberation, and with the idea, which he abandons in *Leviathan*, that when people contract to do something, they thereby conclude deliberation about whether to do it. Hobbes's later answer in *Leviathan* is what scholars have devoted the greatest attention to, interpreting it either in instrumentalist terms (Gauthier 1969, 1979; Hampton 1986; Kavka 1986; Darwall 1995) or as grounded in a fundamental "reciprocity theorem" (Lloyd 2009).

A central move in Hobbes's earlier works is the idea that when deliberation has concluded in an intention not to perform some act, we are no longer free to take it, and "where Liberty ceaseth, there beginneth Obligation" (Hobbes 1983: II.10). We can begin to see how this is supposed to work with contracting by considering what Hobbes says in *De Cive* about "natural obligation," a species of obligation he does not recognize in his later works:

> [T]here are two Species of *natural obligation*, one when liberty is taken away by corporall impediments. ... The other when it is taken away by hope, or fear, according to which the weaker despairing of his own power to resist, cannot but yield to the stronger (1983: XV.7).

---

[7] For an excellent account, see Abizadeh 2018.
[8] The paragraphs to follow draw from Darwall 1995.

The first sense does not even purport to be deontic. It is roughly the sense in which we say we were "obliged" not to do something when circumstances prevented us from doing it, which Hart famously contrasted with obligation (Hart 1961: 6–8). The second sense, however, is one that Hobbes intends for deontic purposes, since he holds it to be the sense in virtue of which God has superior *authority* over us. What this authority consists in, according to Hobbes, is God's *irresistible* power over us, which we cannot but despair of opposing.

This gives Hobbes's *Leviathan* claim, also in *De Cive*, that no human being's power is irresistible, since "the weakest man [can] kill the strongest," normative relevance (Hobbes 1983: I.3). Because of this natural fact, no human being can be under natural obligation to any other. But this is not the case with our relation to God: "there is no kicking against the pricks" (XV.7). Although attempting to oppose human power is always an open deliberative option, it can never be one with respect to God, since God controls the very power with which we would try to resist. We therefore despair of opposing God's power, and this closes deliberation about whether to try to do so. And when our deliberation with respect to an alternative is removed by despair, we are no longer free to do that alternative. "He that deliberates is so farre forth free" (II.8). The "last act of deliberating" is that "whereby the liberty of non-performance is abolisht" (II.10). And "where Liberty ceaseth, there beginneth Obligation" (II.10).

Hobbes's problem, again, is to account for obligation, or at least obligation *judgments* (similarly to judgments of good), within a materialistic framework. We can at least see how this is supposed to work with the natural obligations owed to God, though we may wonder how anything genuinely normatively deontic has been accounted for. In his earlier works, Hobbes attempts to account for obligations that contracts create along similar lines. In *De Cive*, Hobbes holds that once a contract is executed, that closes the parties' deliberations about whether to perform as contracted, thereby limiting their liberty to do so.

> The *promises* which are therefore made for some *benefit* received (which are also Covenants) are tokens of the Will; that is, ... of the last act of deliberating, whereby the liberty of non-performance is abolisht, and by consequence are obligatory; for where Liberty ceaseth, there beginneth Obligation (II.11).

If an agent's liberty not to perform is to be restricted by concluding a deliberation, it cannot be by forming an intention to contract, but only by intending to perform the contracted action. But Hobbes identifies these normally distinguished intentions: "For by contracting for some future action, he wills it done" (III.3; see also II.14).[9]

---

[9] Hobbes distinguishes the deliberation-concluding, hence obligating, will in contract from a promise of future free gift, which fails to obligate. When one person promises to benefit

Hobbes underscores this point with an analogy between *injury*, the breaking of a contract, and *absurdity*, the maintaining of contradictory propositions in disputation. "For by contracting for some future action, he wills it done; by not doing it, he wills it not done, which is to will a thing done and not done at the same time, which is a contradiction" (III.3; see also 1994b: I.xvi.2).

De Cive's account of the obligation created by contract fits well within Hobbes's materialistic framework, even if it is implausible on other grounds. But *Leviathan*'s approach is quite different. Hobbes retains the thesis that concluding deliberation restricts liberty, but he explicitly rejects *De Cive*'s analysis of why that is. "Every *deliberation* is then said to *end*, when that whereof they deliberate, is either done, or thought impossible, because till then we retain the liberty of doing or omitting" (1994a: VI.52).[10] Of course, Hobbes is not committed to thinking in *De Cive* that it is literally impossible to violate contract. He treats the situation of a contracting party as that of an individual forming an intention to do something in the future. Obviously, such an individual may fail to follow through when the time comes. It follows that the only kind of contract that can possibly limit the liberty to perform must be one to perform immediately.

Gone also is any talk of natural obligation. Nor do we find Hobbes saying in *Leviathan* that contract ends deliberation, thereby limiting liberty and, for that reason, obligating performance. The contrast between non-obligating promises of free gift and obligating contract is described without any mention of their respective relations to deliberation and freedom.[11]

Importantly, *Leviathan* gives a non-reductive definition of obligation as the condition that results when a person has "abandoned or granted away his right" (XIV.7). Since Hobbes defines "contract" as a "mutual transferring of right," that people are obligated to keep their covenants will simply follow as a theorem of the "science of just and unjust" (XIV.11, IX.table).[12]

---

another in the future, receiving nothing now in return, not even a reciprocal promise, "a promiser of this kind must be understood to have time to deliberate, and power to change that affection as well as he to whom he made that promise, may alter his desert" (II.8). Since "he that deliberates is so farre forth free," he cannot be said to be obligated. But Hobbes thinks this is not true with contracts. Contracts obligate precisely because they conclude deliberation about performance.

[10] But see LeBuffe 2003.
[11] Hobbes does retain the analogy between injury and contradiction, but in more cautious terms. He no longer says that a violated contract involves an absurd willing and unwilling of the same action. Rather, the injury is "to undo that which, from the beginning, he had voluntarily done," which might plausibly be taken to mean that violating a contract is like trying to undo it (1994a: XIV.7).
[12] Hobbes reserves "covenant" for a contract to perform in the future in return for the other's earlier performance (XIV.11).

Grounding the Right in the Good?

But although this is assured as a conceptual truth, Hobbes seems to appreciate that more needs to be done to establish that covenanters are obligated in any genuinely normative sense. No substantive normative claim can follow from a definition. It is notable that in addition to this definition, Hobbes both introduces as a third law of nature "that men perform their covenants made" *and* then argues for this law across several of the most important paragraphs in *Leviathan* (XV.1–6). These include the famous challenge of the fool that seems, as we noted in Chapter 1, so clearly to echo Carneades's skeptical challenge, which Grotius discusses. The fool argues that whether or not breaking covenants "may be called injustice," such actions are not against reason when they are not against the agent's good (XV.4). And if they are not against reason, it would seem to follow that such actions are not violations of obligation in any genuinely normative sense.

To focus the issue, Hobbes considers cases in which there is no reasonable suspicion that the other covenanter will not perform their part as, for example, when they have "performed already" (XV.5). Commentators generally agree that Hobbes's reply to the fool emphasizes the potential costs to the agent of violating covenant, or of being someone who is disposed to do so, including being excluded from valuable agreements as an unreliable partner, which agreements Hobbes thinks offer the only exit from a violent state of nature. There is also consensus that Hobbes grants the fool's premise that, despite these costs, there can be cases in which violating covenant actually can pay. But Hobbes urges that even though unforeseeable circumstances might "turn" violation to the violator's "benefit, such events do not make it reasonably or wisely done" (XV.5). Being able to maintain one's reputation while violating covenant is something no one can "reckon upon" (XV.5).

One way to take Hobbes is as arguing that benefiting by violating contract can never "reasonably be expected" (XV.7).[13] To use contemporary jargon, it can never maximize *expected* utility, or maximize the utility we should reasonably expect given our evidence, to violate contract, and because this is so, doing so is always against reason. It is hard to believe, however, that this would always be true. But even if there are exceptions when we would most reasonably expect violation to be optimific, Hobbes might still argue that even in these cases, violation would nonetheless be imprudent.

The problem with doing what seems best by the light of available evidence is that poor evidence sheds poor light. Hobbes seems willing to grant the fool that if we could know that violating contract would be for our good, we should

---

[13] Hobbes actually uses this phrase in a slightly different context later in the paragraph – gaining sovereignty by rebellion – but to a similar purpose.

violate; it would be contrary to reason not to. The problem, he appears to be saying, is that we are never able to know this, and the stakes are so high that no matter how close to knowledge we may seem, we are never close enough to warrant taking a chance (Kavka 1986, 1995).

So far, this is an argument for the third law of nature, "that men perform their covenants made." But how does this relate to any *obligation* that contract might create? The right that covenanting parties in the state of nature are said to "lay down" is the right of nature: the agent's liberty "of doing any thing, which in his own judgment, and reason, he shall conceive to be the aptest means" to "the preservation of his own nature" and good (Hobbes 1994a: XIV.1). We have just seen that because of the central role covenant plays in extricating human beings from the state of nature and keeping them in civil society, the third law of nature dictates keeping covenant even when contracting parties believe, however reasonably, their interests would be better served by violating it.

It follows that the right of nature must be qualified for the case of contract. When contract is involved, right reasoning in the service of the agent's own good is not then the same as what the agent "in his own judgment, and reason ... shall conceive to be the aptest means thereunto." In this case, right reasoning recommends keeping contract regardless of what the agent believes, even reasonably, the relation to be between doing so and their own preservation and good. It follows, therefore, that when an agent contracts, it then becomes true that the full and unqualified right of nature no longer applies to the act they have contracted to perform. By covenanting a person does something that makes it no longer advisable for them to base their determination of whether to keep covenant on their own preservation and good.

Hobbes might thus argue that there is a sense in which in the case of covenant, the right of nature does not apply and is, therefore, "laid down." And because it is, the person ends up obligated in Hobbes's official sense (as a theorem of the science of just and unjust) with normative force being provided by the third law of nature, backed by Hobbes's reasoning in his reply to the fool.

While this line of reasoning goes some way to addressing the problem Hobbes faces, there are various reasons why it cannot be fully satisfying. The problem, recall, is how to account for the normativity of right in Hobbes's framework. The most significant difficulty with Hobbes's reply as we have so far interpreted it is that it remains grounded entirely in the agent's *good*. Even on the most sophisticated version, which argues that agents will do better if they *treat* covenants as binding, and as giving them overriding reasons for acting, even when the obligatory action goes against the agent's good, normativity is ultimately coming only from the good. It is being argued, in effect, that agents' goods are best promoted when they reason *as though* they were bound by independent normative constraints of right. But, as Prichard would later argue, this seems an argument of the wrong kind to show that deontic moral requirements of right are genuinely valid and binding on their own. It just shows that we each do better if we suppose that.

Irreducibly Deontic Laws of Nature?

But perhaps there is a way of interpreting Hobbes that avoids attributing to him an implausible, arguably impossible, attempt to account for the normativity of the right (or judgments of the right) solely in terms of that of the good (or judgments of the good). Sharon Lloyd argues that there is substantial textual evidence that Hobbes was committed to a fundamental ideal of reciprocity or reasonableness that is like the idea of "the reasonable" as it operates in the moral and political thought of John Rawls and T. M. Scanlon in the late twentieth century (Lloyd 2009; Rawls 1971, 1980; Scanlon 1998). What Lloyd calls Hobbes's "Reciprocity Theorem" is a formulation of the Golden Rule that Hobbes says summarizes the laws of nature: "*Do not that to another, which thou wouldst not have done to thyself*" (Hobbes 1994a: XV.35). An even better formulation for Lloyd's purposes is: "*Do not that to another, which thou thinkest unreasonable to be done by another to oneself*" (XXVI.13).

So interpreted, the laws of nature embody constraints on *reasonable* conduct, where "the reasonable" is conceived not in terms of advancing the agent's good, even indirectly – what Rawls calls "the rational" – but within the irreducible conceptual space of the right. Conduct is reasonable or morally permissible, on this view, when there is no reasonable objection to it. And conduct is unreasonable, or morally wrong, when there is such reasonable objection, when people could reasonably demand that one not do it – as Hobbes puts it in terms of "the law of the Gospel," "whatsoever you require that others should do to you, that do ye to them" (XIV.5).

An interpretation of laws of nature in terms of reasonable requirement or demand would explain why they are formulated in deontic terms as "precept[s] ... by which a man is forbidden to do that which is destructive of his life" (XIV.3). It also puts them on the "law" side of Suárez's law/counsel contrast. Hobbes himself draws the distinction between law and counsel somewhat differently, since he prefers to reserve "law," properly so called, for commands of the sovereign (or God) whom we are "formerly obliged" to obey (XXVI.2).[14]

---

[14] As Curley's glossary makes clear, by "formerly obliged," Hobbes means obliged by a former command. Cf. also: "They who less seriously consider the force of words, do sometimes confound law with counsel. ... We must fetch the distinction between counsel and law, from the difference between counsel and command. Now COUNSEL is a precept, in which the reason of my obeying it is taken from the thing itself which is advised; but COMMAND is a precept, in which the cause of my obedience depends on the will of the commander. For it is not properly said, thus I will and thus I command, except the will stand for a reason. Now when obedience is yielded to the laws, not for the thing itself, but

His official use of "law" ties it conceptually to "obligation" in his technical sense of the bond that derives from contracting. But that does not stop him from using deontic language in defining laws of nature. Nor does it stop him from holding that we are accountable for conforming to the laws of nature and that violations are *culpable*. Indeed, he says that the reason the laws of nature must be able to be summed into a readily usable formula like the Golden Rule is that otherwise we could not be justifiably blamed for violations.

> [T]o leave all men inexcusable, they [the laws of nature] have been contracted into one easy sum, intelligible, even to the meanest capacity; and that is, *Do not that to another, which thou wouldest not have done to thyself* (XV.35).

To this he adds:

> [H]e has no more to do in learning the laws of nature, but (when weighing the actions of other men with his own, they seem too heavy) to put them into the other part of the balance, and his own into their place, that his own passions, and self-love may add nothing to the weight; and then there is none of these laws of nature that will not appear unto him very reasonable (XV.35).

To work out whether demands of others are reasonable or not, we must consider whether we can accept others' making the very same demands of us in similar situations. Similarly, we should permit ourselves to do things to others only if we are prepared to permit others to do the very same thing to us in similar conditions.

This also provides a plausible reading of the right of nature, the "blameless liberty" of action in the state of nature. As noted above, Hobbes writes in *De Cive* that it is not "reprehensible ... for a man to use all his endeavours to preserve and defend his body" (1983: I.7). What the right of nature is saying, on this interpretation, is that there is no reasonable objection – no one can be justifiably blamed – for doing what they believe necessary to preserve themselves in the state of nature (Lloyd 2009: 18–19). If others could be relied on to treat each other in peaceful ways, then one would be bound to treat them peacefully also. But given the insecurities of the state of nature, no one can reasonably rely on this. And because they cannot, no one can reasonably demand that others forego doing what they think necessary to preserve themselves.

> by reason of the adviser's will, the law is not a counsel, but a command, and is defined thus: LAW is the command of that person (whether man or court) whose precept contains in it the reason of obedience: as the precepts of God in regard of men, of magistrates in respect of their subjects, and universally of all the powerful in respect of them who cannot resist, may be termed their laws" (Hobbes 1983: XIV.1; see also Hobbes 1994a: XXV).

So far, this is all evidence that Hobbes understands the laws of nature as independent norms of right that people are appropriately *held* to and that "oblige conscience" (Hobbes 1983: III.28). But what about evidence that seems to count against this reading and in favor of a more orthodox instrumentalist good-based interpretation: Hobbes's reply to the fool and his doctrine that the laws of nature do not bind *in foro externo* and are not genuine *laws* without the backing of the sovereign?[15]

The first thing to notice is that even if Hobbes's reply to the fool *is* that fools would do better were they to pursue their interests indirectly and reason by the third law of nature, thereby keeping contracts even when this is expectably against their interest, this would not commit Hobbes to thinking that the authority of natural laws derives from this fact. So far as the dialectic goes, this reply could simply be one that proceeds from premises that Hobbes accepts *arguendo* for dialectical purposes. On reflection, it is somewhat puzzling that interpreters have given so much weight to this passage as evidence for Hobbes's most fundamental normative justificatory views. So far as the text goes, the situation could be much the same as in Bishop Butler's famous "cool hour" passage, in which Butler assumes for the sake of argument something he actually denies, namely, that the authority of conscience depends on support from self-interest.[16] Moreover, there are ways of interpreting Hobbes's reply within the kind of interpretation we have just been considering.

Hobbes says that the fool "*declares* he thinks it reason to deceive those that help him"; and again: "he *declareth* that he thinks he may with reason do so" (1994a: XV.5, emphasis added). Why does Hobbes represent the fool as "declaring" these things?[17] If what were in question were simply how one might most sensibly promote one's interest, whether directly or indirectly, why would Hobbes be talking about the fool's *declarations*? Surely the fool would try to cover his tracks and be more or less successful in doing so. If, however, what is in question is a principle of right, of what one may legitimately *demand* of people and what one may not, of what people *may* and *may not* do, then this is indeed properly determined by what the fool is prepared to declare and endorse *publicly*. If they necessarily concern mutual accountability, principles of right are subject to a test of public endorsability by their very nature.[18]

---

[15] Lloyd argues against the orthodox interpretation of Hobbes's reply to fool in Lloyd 2009: 302–317.

[16] Butler argues that even if reasons for acting were ultimately grounded in self-interest, there would still be reason to be virtuous, since a virtuous life will give the virtuous agent the best life possible (Butler 2017: XI.20). For discussion, see Darwall 1995: 265n–266n, and Chapter 5 below.

[17] For a different explanation see Hoekstra 1997. See also Lloyd 2009: 310–312 for a criticism of Hoekstra that is closer to the view presented here.

[18] On this point, see Darwall 2006: 313–315.

Note next that what Hobbes then says is that a fool *who declares* the view that covenants *may* be breached or falsely entered into when that turns out to be useful can be accepted into society through covenant "only by the error of them that receive him" (XV.5). The orthodox interpretation is that someone who reasons egoistically rather than by the third law of nature will be received into society only by others' *mistaking his real intentions*. An alternative interpretation that is closer to the text, however, is that someone who puts forward what the fool "declares" *as a proposition of right* cannot be so received, except by way of a mistake *not* about the fool's intentions, but about the obligation to keep covenants and so about the right itself. So understood, the mistake that both the fool and his potential covenanters make is not a *strategic* error in advancing their respective interests; both make a mistake of right. A covenant, by its very nature, is something that transfers a right; but no such transfer is possible if both parties know that one of them has no intention of following through. Even "reasonable suspicion" of non-performance is enough, Hobbes says, to render a covenant "void" (XIV.18). In other words, the view that covenants *may* be broken or entered into falsely for reasons of self-interest is itself mistaken as a proposition of right. And anyone who attempts to covenant with someone who declares such a view must mistake the nature of covenants, since covenants are void on any "reasonable suspicion" of non-performance.

What then, about Hobbes's view that the laws of nature bind to external conduct but rarely in the state of nature and require the sovereign's sanctions to provide genuinely obligating law? Here again, it might seem that Hobbes is saying that the normative force of any duty or obligation to follow natural law must derive from reasons of self-interest coming from the sovereign's sanctions.

Although Hobbes clearly does say that it takes the sovereign's commands to create genuine law, even to make the "improperly called" laws of nature *laws* properly so-called, it is nonetheless of great importance to him that subjects see themselves as *obligated* to follow the sovereign's commands and not just as having reasons of self-interest for doing so (1983: II.10; 1994a: XIII.13, XXVI.*passim*). Sovereigns are established, as it were, either from below, by subjects covenanting with one another to authorize and follow a sovereign (1994a: XVII), or from above, by conquest. An obligation to follow the sovereign's commands follows directly from the covenant authorizing him. Even in conquest, Hobbes is clear that "it is not ... victory that giveth the right of dominion over the vanquished, but his own covenant," which the vanquished enter into when they submit to the conqueror and promise to obey as the price of survival (XX.11). Hobbes distinguishes between the condition of a slave who is kept in thrall by chains and threats of reprisals, on the one hand, and a "servant" who "upon promise not to run away, nor to do violence to his master, is trusted by him" (XX.10, 12), on the other. And he explicitly analogizes the case of servants to that of submitting subjects.

If masters and sovereigns genuinely trust covenanting servants and subjects, respectively, they must think that believing oneself to be obligated can make a difference in conduct that cannot fully be explained by motives of self-interest. And this is far from the only place in which Hobbes relies on this difference between motivation by self-interest and motivation by a sense of right. The most central, of course, is in the making of the covenant itself. Since a covenant involves a transfer of rights by its very nature, it is only possible if the covenanting parties see themselves as giving themselves and one another a reason to comply that is not reducible to self-interest. Or to put the point the other way around, individuals who recognize and know one another to recognize only reasons of self-interest cannot covenant.

There are many other places also where Hobbes recognizes the possibility of conscientious conduct. Some particularly important examples for his political philosophy are instances in which sovereigns' commands conflict with subjects' consciences or, contrariwise, when a proposed act of sedition would violate conscience. Thus, Hobbes says that "subjects will hardly be drawn into the field and fight with courage against their consciences" (2014: 130).[19]

We should also note that even if Hobbes's official view is that it takes the sovereign's command to make genuine law, Hobbes cannot possibly think that this is also necessary for obligation, since the sovereign can himself exist only if a covenant that establishes him and his authority obligates independently of his command. Moreover, there are reasons of *right* why, at least in Hobbes's view, it takes the sovereign's command to create genuine law. These reasons fit, briefly, under two main headings: publicity and assurance.

Genuine law requires genuine publicity – public practices and institutions – and those are unavailable in the state of nature by definition. Second, like any covenant, the covenant establishing the sovereign requires joint performance and is void under reasonable suspicion of non-performance. Covenanters will need assurance, therefore, not just that there will be reasons of right to comply, but that less conscientious individuals will have reasons to comply beyond their being obligated to.

The crucial point is not that the covenanters might have a strategic, self-interested reason for this assurance; *they have reasons for assurance that are grounded in the authority of right itself.* Perfectly conscientious beings who know one another to be so might not need the assurance provided by the sovereign's sanctions, but ordinary human beings, knowing one another to be guided both by conscience *and* by self-interest, do. Since reasonable suspicion of non-performance voids contract, even conscientious subjects have reasons of right for wanting there to be reasons of self-interest for compliance

---

[19] And that "though a man be discontent, yet if in his own opinion there be no just cause of stirring against, or resisting the government established, nor any pretence to justify his resistance, and to procure aid, he will never show it" (1994b: II.8).

also. But this does not mean that the reasons of right derive their authority from self-interest in any way. It just means that they would not bind to performance *in foro externo* unless sanction-creating reasons of self-interest were in play also.

Suppose, therefore, that we understand Hobbes to hold that the laws and right of nature are genuinely deontic propositions of right that cannot be reduced to propositions of good (despite Hobbes's saying that they are really "theorems" about what conduces to the good of self-preservation (1994a: XV.41)). A substantial metaethical problem remains, namely, that although Hobbes provides a metaethical account of claims about the good, he provides no independent account of claims of right. Moreover, it would seem to follow from his claims about deliberation and desires that the only way considerations of right can enter practical reasoning is by being translated into terms of the good.

A Metaethics of Right?

It is worth considering, therefore, whether Hobbes might nonetheless be able to provide such an independent metaethics of right that could satisfy the same empiricist, materialist constraints that help motivate his metaethics of good. I believe he could, by tying deontic moral claims to the expression, not of desires, but of the distinctive attitudes through which we hold ourselves and one another accountable, "reactive attitudes," as Strawson famously calls them, attitudes like guilt, moral blame, and what Strawson calls the "sense of obligation" (Strawson 1968: 86).

We have already seen how Hobbes holds both laws and the right of nature to a standard of justified blame. The right of nature is a "blameless liberty," and the laws of nature must be formulable in something like the Golden Rule in order to leave "men inexcusable" (Hobbes 1983: I.7; 1994a: XV.35).

In *The Elements of Law*, Hobbes contrasts human beings with other "living creatures" who "have no conception of right and wrong" (1994b: I.19.5). Such creatures, Hobbes says, experience "pleasure and pain" and so have desires and aversions. What they lack is any attitude of "censure of one another" (I.19.5). If Hobbes were to accept a projectivist metaethics of right according to which judgments of right and their conceptual correlates express reactive attitudes like indignation, blame, and censure, he could then explain why in lacking these attitudes, other creatures lack a "conception of right and wrong," though they are capable of desire, deliberation, and will. Such beings would lack a conscience.

We have seen that Hobbes regards the concepts of moral right and wrong as intrinsically related to moral responsibility, blame, and excuse. And Strawsonian reactive attitudes find their way into his moral psychology also. For example, Hobbes says that "indignation" is "[a]nger for great hurt done to another, when we conceive the same to be done injury" (1994a: VI:21).[20] Of course, if Hobbes were to think that indignation is a reaction to a prior *belief* about injury and wrong, he could not then say that these beliefs about right project the reactive attitude. But there is no philosophical reason for Hobbes to be a "judgmentalist" about reactive attitudes that would not apply also to being a judgmentalist about desire. Neither view, moreover, seems to fit with Hobbes's fundamental philosophical orientations.

The idea would not be that deontic claims of right express attitudes like blame and guilt directly. The normative claims that apparently directly express these attitudes are claims of blameworthiness and culpability. A metaethics of right that is analogous to, but nonetheless independent of, Hobbes's metaethics of good could then exploit a conceptual connection that seems to exist between wrongness and blameworthiness. It is an apparent conceptual truth that an act is morally wrong if, and only if, it is an act of a kind that it would be blameworthy to perform were the agent to do so without excuse (Mill 2002: V.14; Brandt 1979: 163–176; Gibbard 1990: 42; Skorupski 1999: 142; Darwall 2006). Hobbes could thus say that claims of right express attitudes of censure and blame indirectly via this conceptual connection.

How, then, would a projectivism about the right fit with a projectivism about the good? Hobbes believes that deliberation is but the succession of appetites and aversions and that the will is simply the last appetite before action. There is no doubt that such a stripped-down view of deliberation and the will fits less comfortably with a doctrine of the authority of right than a moral psychology and philosophy of action that connect these more tightly to autonomous agency. Only the latter, it would seem, can best fit with a moral and political philosophy that give authority and consent fundamental roles.

Nonetheless, there is nothing flatly inconsistent between Hobbesian deliberation and a projectivist metaethics of right. Just as a Kantian ethics and moral psychology can fit with a sufficiently formal Humean theory of motivation (e.g., by making Rawls's distinction between object-dependent and principle-dependent desires), so also might a projectivism about the right fit with a Hobbesian projectivism about the good (Rawls 2000). Thus we might regard one of the "subjects" that Hobbes discusses in the passage quoted above – the subject who forbears self-interested rebellion because they lack "just cause" – as having their reactive attitudes affect their desires in ways that make their judgments of good influenced by their judgments of right. Realizing that such rebellion would be blameworthy by imaginatively placing themselves in an impartial position and blaming rebellion from that perspective, they desire not

---

[20] See also Hobbes on "revengefulness": "desire, by doing hurt to another, to make him condemn some [act] of his own" (1994: VI.34). I am indebted here to Moya Mapps.

to rebel, which they express with the judgment that that would be bad to do (and good to forbear doing) because it would be wrong.

I know of no evidence that Hobbes considered a projectivist ethics of right along these lines. The point is that it is a metaethical position that can fit with his normative claims of right that resists reduction to claims about the good. And it would fit into his empiricist materialist framework no less well than does his projectivist metaethics of good.

In conclusion, I want to note one last problem that Hobbes's views face even if he can adequately underwrite the independent normative claims of right that are embodied in the laws and right of nature. When Hobbes defines obligation as the state resulting from the transfer or laying down of a right in contract, this definition rings true because of its association with our ordinary conceptions of how contractors can give one another rights. But is this a plausibility to which Hobbes is really entitled? Our ordinary notion of contract is like that of promise in being something that comes about through the exercise of normative or moral powers that the contracting parties (or promisor and promisee) reciprocally recognize each other as having and exercising. It is impossible to contract or to promise without the normative power to do so and without a partner who recognizes both themselves and one as having that power.

Even if, consequently, Hobbes can ground both the laws and the right of nature as genuine deontic facts, the question will remain whether these normative materials are sufficient to explain the existence of normative powers that individuals must possess in order to contract or lay down their rights. We turn next to examine the views of a philosopher, Samuel Pufendorf, who thought extensively about what such normative powers must consist in and presuppose and who criticized Hobbes partly on the grounds that the normative materials provided by a Hobbesian state of nature are insufficient to underwrite these powers.

Pufendorf

It is only relatively recently that scholars have begun to appreciate Samuel Pufendorf's importance to the history of ethics.[21] The signal element of Pufendorf's ethics for recent commentators is his idea that morality arises "by imposition," by God imposing his superior will on a world that, if not completely value free, nonetheless can contain no *moral* value of or on its own. But how, exactly, is imposition accomplished? According to Pufendorf, human beings do not simply defer to God in the way elephant seals do to a dominant male. Rather, imposition is realized through human *recognition* of God's authority

---

[21] Thanks largely to Schneewind 1987 and 1998, and Haakonssen 1996. See also Korsgaard 1996 and Irwin 2008. What follows draws heavily from Darwall 2012.

to direct and hold us answerable. This brings into play a whole battery of concepts – recognition, accountability, imputation, and authority – along with the capacities to operate with them in practical thought.

What is brilliantly original in Pufendorf, and less well noted by commentators, is his appreciation of these conceptual connections along with his awareness of their implications for moral psychology. Authority is a normative "moral power," as Pufendorf calls it, which agents can exercise only within a mutually recognized social, moral space that is constituted by their respective obligations to and rights against one another, and whose exercise directly affects those rights and obligations. As Pufendorf sees it, only "sociable" beings with the capacity for mutual recognition are capable of moral obligation.

Pufendorf was far from the first thinker to hold some version of a divine command theory of morality. But he may have been the first to try to work out what such a view must look like if it is to take seriously the conceptual links between authority, recognition, and accountability, as well as the psychology necessary for these to be realized in moral life. This may, however, introduce instability into Pufendorf's overall view. Whereas Pufendorf seeks to derive human moral powers, equal dignity, and sociability from God's superior moral power, the very idea of moral powers, including God's, may already presuppose a more basic moral power or dignity that is shared by any being who is capable of sociable relations. This is a view that, as we saw, is much closer to Grotius's.

If, as Sidgwick maintained, modern ethical philosophy is characterized by its focus on the "quasi-jural" concepts of morality and moral obligation, arguably no early modern thinker had a more juridical theory of these concepts, or more legalistic normative moral theories deploying them, than Pufendorf (Sidgwick 1967: 6). Pufendorf's works, *Elements of Universal Jurisprudence* (1660), *The Law of Nature and Nations* (1672), and *On the Duty of Man and Citizen According to Natural Law* (1673), were among the most significant moral and political texts of the seventeenth century (Pufendorf 1934, 1991, and 2009). If less philosophically powerful than Hobbes, Pufendorf stands as the most systematic expositor of the modern natural law tradition, more philosophically insightful than Grotius and Cumberland, and arguably no less so than Locke.

The most prominent aspect of Pufendorf's thought is his theological voluntarism. Like Suárez before him, Pufendorf holds that any genuine law must *obligate* and that it can do so only if it consists of legitimate demands from a superior authority.[22] It follows that there can be moral obligations, hence a natural law, only if we are subject to God's commands.

At the same time, Pufendorf was definitely a post-Grotian. He follows Grotius's distinction between *perfect* and *imperfect* human *rights*, which like Grotius, he makes central to his account of morality, and which he carries forward

---

[22] For Suárez, see Schneewind 1998: 58–66, Darwall 2003: 116-118, and Irwin 2008: 1–69.

with a correlative distinction between perfect and imperfect *obligations*.²³ Pufendorf's characterization of the former distinction broadly follows Grotius. Grotius says that a perfect right involves a "power of demanding" that to which one has the right (Grotius 2005: I, 139). Pufendorf also speaks of an "active qualit[y] ... by virtue of [which] something can be demanded of another" (Pufendorf 1934: 19) and adds to this a "power" "to compel" others not to violate the right, whether by "directing action against [them] before a judge, or, where there is no place for that, by force" (1934: 19; 2009: 92).

Imperfect rights, by contrast, involve for Grotius and Pufendorf only an "aptitude" rather than a "faculty" or "power." An imperfect right to beneficence, for example, consists in another person's having a moral reason, perhaps a weighty one, to benefit the rightholder, where beneficence is nothing that "can be extorted from him against his will" (Pufendorf 1934: 20) or that "in Strictness [one] may demand" (Grotius 2005: I, 89). Pufendorf and Grotius differ in their language somewhat, since Grotius reserves "obligation" for Pufendorf's "perfect obligations," which entail perfect rights. Where Pufendorf speaks of "imperfect obligations," Grotius seems happier saying that anything but rights "strictly so called" "lay us under no obligation" (Grotius 2005: I, 88, 148). But there is no real difference here. To bring their usages into alignment, we need only interpret Pufendorf's "imperfect obligation" to mean something that Grotius would say gives moral counsel but does not obligate.

A second Grotian element in Pufendorf's thought is his emphasis on human "sociality" or "sociability" (*socialitas*). The ways in which Pufendorf and Grotius employ the concept seem very different, however, at least at first sight. Whereas Grotius says that "Sociability ... is the Fountain of Right, properly so called" (I, 85–86), *socialitas* figures in Pufendorf's thought not as the foundation of natural law or right, but as the central constituent of the "fundamental law of nature['s]" *content*: "Every man, so far as in him lies, should cultivate and preserve toward others a sociable attitude" (Pufendorf 1934: 208; cf. 1991: 35). There are two differences here. One is that, according to Grotius, sociability grounds natural law, whereas for Pufendorf, natural law can only be grounded in God's superior (foundational) authority. Moreover, Pufendorf does not simply hold, as Suárez did, that God's authority is necessary only for moral

---

²³ Mautner 1999 understands Tuck as holding that Pufendorf denies natural perfect rights, since according to Tuck, Pufendorf maintains that perfect rights require a "network of social relations" through which they entail correlative obligations to right holders. (See Tuck 1981: 161). I shall argue presently that although Pufendorf does believe that perfect rights and obligations are social – indeed, they partly constitute the condition Pufendorf calls sociability (*socialitas*) – that does not mean they are not natural. It is worth remembering that Grotius himself held that perfect rights entail correlative obligations, since he held that a perfect right includes a "[f]aculty of demanding what is due," to which "answers the Obligation of rendering what is owing" (Grotius 2005: I, 139).

obligation, with our rational (and social) nature being sufficient to ground natural moral rightness and wrongness, as on the Thomist classical natural law view.[24] Pufendorf thinks that the whole moral realm, moral properties and moral "entities" of every kind, depends on the "imposition" of natural law through God's supremely authoritative will (1934: 5–8). Not even "good repute and turpitude can be conceived to exist before law, and without the imposition of a superior" (27).[25]

The second difference is that Pufendorf holds that perfect rights and obligations between human beings derive from a fundamental natural law, obedience to which is owed to God. In other words, it is only because God commands a "sociable attitude" between us and because this attitude itself involves an acknowledgment of perfect, "mutual" obligations that these reciprocal obligations and rights between human beings exist. Contrary to Grotius, therefore, Pufendorf believes that without God's authoritative will *neither* natural law in general *nor* rights and ("directed" or "bipolar") obligations *between* human beings could possibly exist.[26]

Despite these differences, there is an important similarity between Grotius's and Pufendorf's conceptions of sociability. Both understand *socialitas* as essentially involving relationships that are already conceived in terms of mutual recognition of individuals' respective authorities or normative "powers," that is, in terms of their capacities to have obligations to and rights against one another. "By a sociable attitude," Pufendorf says, "we mean an attitude ... by which each is understood to be bound to one another ... by a mutual obligation" (208). As we noted in Chapter 1, Grotius's notion of sociability can be interpreted similarly. Grotius quotes Seneca's saying that "*[n]ature has founded a kind of Relation between us*" (Grotius 2005: 136), which Grotius interprets in terms of mutual recognition of relative authority, involving either a "*Right of Equality*" or some justifiable "*Right of Superiority*" (136–137). Moreover, an essential aspect of Pufendorf's theory, as we shall see, is that mutual perfect obligations are tied to a view of the equal dignity of any being capable of sociability and, accordingly, to the idea that persons share a basic authority over themselves and their own lives. This also echoes Grotius.

Of even more fundamental importance is the role that authorities and "moral powers" play, according to Pufendorf, in constituting the whole of morality, both making it up and bringing it about. It is no exaggeration to say that Pufendorf's expressed view is that every obligation, whether owed to God or to other human beings, can exist only through the exercise of moral powers, either God's power to obligate human beings through his authoritative direction or

---

[24] A point that Irwin emphasizes in Irwin 2008.
[25] Likewise, "we call an action good morally, or in moral estimation, which agrees with law" (1934: 114).
[26] For a discussion of "bipolar obligation" see Thompson 2004 and Darwall 2013a.

our power to obligate ourselves to one another through agreements and "pacts." However, Pufendorf cannot, in the end, sustain this position. And seeing why this is so makes it possible to appreciate something profoundly significant in the very idea of a normative power to bind oneself or others as Pufendorf conceives of it and as it came to be conceived in a tradition of moral philosophical thought that derived from him and flourishes still.

Moral Powers I

The concept of "moral power" lies at the core of Pufendorf's moral theory.[27] God creates the law of nature, and so morality itself, by exercising a moral power, his authority over us. And Pufendorf holds that the fundamental natural law he thereby creates demands a sociability that itself includes recognizing various moral powers human beings have regarding one another, including the power to obligate ourselves through "pacts," from which, like Hobbes, Pufendorf believes that civil society and the authority of the state derives. If Hobbes and Grotius can be read, as they commonly are, as trying to base morality and natural law on rational self-interest (or perhaps reciprocity) and sociability, respectively, then Pufendorf is best interpreted as making it derive from moral powers. According to Pufendorf, all moral obligations, indeed, any "moral entity" or "mode" at all, exist only through the exercise of moral powers.

The idea of "normative" or moral power has become familiar in contemporary philosophy, first, through Hohfeld's famous distinctions between species of rights and correlative obligations – claims, liberties, privileges, and powers – and, more recently, by Joseph Raz's writings on "normative powers" (Hohfeld 1923; Raz 1972 and 2002a: 98–104). The basic idea can be gotten across with either of two examples that play an important role in Raz's work – promises and authoritative directives (or orders) (Raz 1977 and 2002b: 3–27).

When someone promises to do something, they voluntarily take on an obligation to a promisee by addressing the intended promisee in a distinctive way. As Pufendorf puts it, when I make a "perfect promise," "I not only intend in fact to be obligated, but also confer a right upon another to demand what I promise as quite simply owed to him" (Pufendorf 1991: 70). Promising presupposes the moral or normative power that is exercised in making a promise, namely, the power to bind oneself to another with the promise.[28] This is a power to change the moral relations obtaining between promiser and promisee – their respective rights against and (directed or bipolar) obligations to one another – by a voluntary address, a promise *to* the promisee. Similarly, when someone in authority orders another to do something, they thereby make the person who

---

[27] One source is Suárez. See Schneewind 1990: 70.
[28] For accounts of promising that stress this aspect see Raz 1977, Watson 2009, and Darwall 2013i.

is subject to their authority obligated to them to comply. As with the power to bind oneself by a promise, someone can obligate another through an order only if they have the relevant moral or normative power, in this case, the authority to issue the order and thereby bind someone subject to their authority.

As Pufendorf brings out with beautiful clarity, powers of the kind involved in pacts and authoritative demands are fully normative or "moral." By exercising the power, someone directly changes their moral relations to the person they address. These changes are what Pufendorf calls the power's "moral effects" (1934: 18). Exercising moral powers creates new rights and obligations, not just by creating some change in the natural or physical world that, when combined with existing moral obligations, has moral implications for the changed physical or natural circumstances, as, for example, when one incurs an obligation to make amends to someone by having said something hurtful. In such a case, one is already under an obligation to make amends to anyone one hurts, whether one has already hurt someone or not. A promise, by contrast, creates a new bipolar obligation to the promisee. We can of course say that a general obligation to keep promises or comply with authoritative orders already exists, but any such general obligation will itself depend on the normative powers to voluntarily create the more specific bipolar obligations of which promise and authority themselves respectively consist.

Pufendorf defines a moral power as "that by which a man is able to do something legally and *with a moral effect*" (18, emphasis added). "Moral effects" are simply the newly created rights and obligations together with the accountability and legitimate sanctions they entail.[29] They are part of a moral order or "space," as Pufendorf calls it, which he explicitly analogizes to natural or physical space (6–7). To grasp the precise character and significance of his idea, we should note its relation to a fundamental distinction Pufendorf makes between moral entities, on the one hand, and natural or physical entities, on the other.[30]

Physical things, their attributes, and modes occupy space and time and are related to one another through causal laws. The physical causal order, brought into existence by God's creative act, is "physically complete" (5–6). Moral entities and their various modes are "superadded," Pufendorf says, "by intelligent agency to physical things and modes" (5). Whereas "the original way of producing physical entities is creation, the way in which moral entities are produced" is through "*imposition*" (5). Pufendorf does hold that imposition occurs when God creates human beings with their distinctive nature, including the

---

[29] "*Power* is that by which a man is able to do something legally and with a moral effect. This effect is that an obligation is laid upon another to perform some task, or to admit as valid some of his actions, or not to hinder them, or that he shall be able to confer upon another a power of action or possession, which the other did not formerly possess" (1934: 18).

[30] Compare Kant's later distinction between a realm governed by causal laws of nature and a moral realm governed by laws of freedom.

capacity to understand his will for them, but it is only by God's *imposing* his will *on* human beings through making manifest his will *to* them through his creative act that moral entities and modes are produced. As we shall see, genuine imposition can occur only within a reciprocally recognitional social space.

Moral entities and aspects are not themselves part of the "physically complete" natural world God creates. Unlike any physical "active force" consisting in an "ability to produce any physical motion or change in any thing," the distinctive "active force" of moral entities "consist[s] only in this, that it is made clear to men along what line they *should* govern their liberty of action" (6, emphasis added).[31] Moral entities are inherently *directive*; their laws are inherently *normative* in a way that the causal laws of physical nature are not. And they entail accountability and legitimate sanctions: "[I]n a special way men are made capable of receiving some good or evil and of directing certain actions towards others with a particular effect" (6). The "particular effect" is not physical or natural, but "moral."

Moral entities' "efficacy" "flows from the fact that, as man's creator," God "has the right to set certain limits to the liberty of will" and, therefore, to impose *legitimate* sanctions should these be violated (6).[32] It is God's authority or moral power that enables him to obligate his creatures through his will. Since the rights and obligations that are created by God's commands are *perfect* rights and obligations, it follows on Pufendorf's view that the power to create such "moral effects" includes the authority or power to justifiably use sanctions and coercion to secure compliance with the obligations ("by the threat of some evil" (6)). This has important implications for Pufendorf's account of the will and moral motivation, as we shall consider below.

The only obligations that flow directly from God's commands are obligations human subjects owe *to him*. Thus far, therefore, the only moral power in play is God's. But God commands us to be *sociable* to one another and, as will be evident presently, Pufendorf thinks that sociability includes the mutual

---

[31] Compare Basil Kennett's translation: Moral entities' "force" consists in "in shewing men how they ought to govern their Freedom of Action" (Pufendorf 1710: 3).

[32] Compare Kennett: "[H]e [God] by his Right of Creation hath the Power of circumscribing, within proper Limits, that Liberty of Will with which he indulg'd Mankind, and when it grows refractory, of turning it which way soever he pleaseth, by the Force of some threatned Evil" (Pufendorf 1710: 3). (Compare the following passage from *De Officio*: "An obligation is introduced into a man's mind by a superior, by one who has not only the strength to inflict some injury on the recalcitrant, but also just cause to require us to curtail the liberty of our will at his discretion" (1991: 28)). Knud Haakonssen has impressed upon me that the Latin text mentions no "right of creation," but only that as creator, God is free to circumscribe his creatures' will. It is clear, however, that Pufendorf distinguishes between a superior's power to threaten natural evils and his "moral power" to create "moral effects," which includes inferiors' being held accountable and therefore subject to *deserved* sanctions.

recognition of an equal human dignity that grounds basic *human* moral powers, for example, to bind ourselves to one another through pacts of the sort that are necessary to legitimate civic association and the state.

Here again, Pufendorf distinguishes between human natural and moral powers along with the respective natural and moral effects of their exercise:

> In man the power to act is twofold. One is *natural* power to act, through which he is able by his natural strength to perform an action, or to neglect it. ... But *moral* power in man is that whereby he is able to perform a voluntary action legitimately and with a moral effect, that is to say, so that this action shall ... be able to produce moral effects in others (2009: 229).

A "moral effect," again, "is that an obligation is laid upon" someone (1934: 18). And since the obligation is a perfect one, it includes the standing to "deman[d]" and, within proper procedures, to "compel" compliance (1934: 19; 2009: 92). It follows that the exercise of moral powers, whether by God or derivatively by human beings, brings about obligations that make men "capable of receiving some good or evil" in a distinctively *legal* way, that is, as justly deserved benefits or sanctions (1934: 6). The obligations that are created by exercising a moral power entail a standing to hold those obligated to one *accountable*.

Pufendorf's theory is thus designed to capture the conceptual intuition about the right that we mentioned earlier in connection with Suárez and Hobbes, namely, that something can be genuinely obligatory only if those who are obligated can justifiably be held responsible or *accountable* for compliance. By addressing his will to human beings, God makes them "moral causes," that is, agents to whom actions and their effects can be *imputed* and for which they are thereby accountable.

The formal nature of a moral action, Pufendorf says, "consists of its 'imputativity'," "whereby the effect of a voluntary action can be imputed to an agent." Whether the effects be "good or evil," "he must be responsible for both" (68). Pufendorf's Latin makes clearer that he means "accountable." What can be imputed to us as a "moral cause" is what we must answer for or provide some account of ("*ratione rederre*") (1672: 61).[33] The "primary axiom in morals," Pufendorf says, is that "a man can be asked for a reckoning" for anything in his power.[34] Or, equivalently, "any action controllable according to a moral law, the accomplishment or avoidance of which is within the power of a man, may be imputed to him" (1934: 70).

---

[33] I am indebted here to Knud Haakonssen.
[34] Compare a parallel passage from *De Officio*: "The primary axiom in moral disciplines which look at the subject from the point of view of the human court is held to be: a man may be held accountable for those actions which it is in his power whether they are done or not" (Pufendorf 1991: 23).

Pufendorf holds, again, that all moral "entities" and "modes," all things properly considered "moral," depend upon God's having exercised his moral power to impose law. Pufendorf recognizes a sense of "natural goodness" that is independent of imposition ("the native power to produce an effect good and useful to mankind"), but this is insufficient "to constitute an action in the field of morals" (28). Any moral "entity," quality, or "mode" whatsoever, he thinks, exists only because of authoritatively imposed law. "That reason should be able to discover any morality in the actions of a man without reference to a law, is as impossible as for a man born blind to judge between colours" (28).

This is an illuminating analogy. Hobbes was but the first of a number of modern philosophers who would analogize the metaphysics of the ethical to that of color. In the eighteenth century, Hutcheson and Hume would draw a similar analogy between color sense and "moral sense" or sentiment.[35] For Pufendorf, however, the perspective from which we attribute moral qualities is neither that of desire nor of any sentiment or attitude like moral approbation or admiration, but rather the point of view of a will under authoritative direction, that is, of one will being addressed demands by another who has the authority or "moral power" to make demands of, and so to direct, them legitimately, *and* who has, by virtue of that, the standing to hold them accountable through legitimate sanctions.

The way Pufendorf connects moral obligation, accountability, and legitimate sanctions to his theory of the will and moral motivation will occupy us further below. So also will the question of how precisely "mutual" (bipolar) perfect human obligations and rights, including human moral powers, along with an equal basic human dignity underlying them, can all be grounded in God's moral power. Before we turn to these questions, however, we should briefly note a fundamental problem, which we shall consider in more detail below, that afflicts any attempt to construct the whole of morality from the exercise of moral powers. Pufendorf seems dimly aware of this problem, but I think he has no good solution to it.

Pufendorf makes a crucial distinction between imposing oneself on another('s will) by force and doing so legitimately, with authority. And he connects this to an equally fundamental, and reciprocal, distinction within the obligated agent's motivation and practical reasoning between being moved by fear of a threatened sanction ("sense of an impending evil"), on the one hand, and being moved by respect for the legitimacy of the sanction (seeing that the evil "falls upon him justly"), on the other (91). In the latter case, Pufendorf says, the obligated will must be able "to judge itself worthy of some censure, unless it conforms to a prescribed rule" (91). Moral agency, he holds, requires the capacity for conscientious *self*-judgment.

---

[35] Thus Hume: "Vice and virtue, therefore, may be compared to sounds, colours, heat, and cold, which, according to modern philosophy, are not qualities in objects, but perceptions in the mind" (Hume 1978: 486).

We have seen already that Pufendorf holds that someone can be put under obligation only through the exercise of a moral power.[36] And we know too that he thinks any human moral power must derive ultimately from God, specifically, from the obligation to follow the fundamental law of nature, which God legislates by exercising his moral power. But where does God's moral power come from? In imposing his will, God makes natural law. But Pufendorf also says that "we are obligated by a law, because we owed beforehand obedience to its author" (89). And this now seems to close a circle: God imposes obligations on us by exercising his moral power, which he apparently has only if we are already obligated to act as he directs "beforehand."[37]

This need pose no insoluble *metaphysical* problem, since Pufendorf can consistently hold that God's creative act *simultaneously* gives him moral power to direct us – by making it the case that we are indebted to him (through gratitude) for the great benefit of creation – and expresses his manifest will for (and to) us, and so exercises this moral power over us, thereby creating obligations to act as he directs.[38] Granted, this isn't quite "beforehand," but that doesn't seem required anyway. What matters is only that God have moral power at the time he exercises it. However, a normative or moral issue will remain. God's authority to obligate by imposing his will must be *normatively* independent of its exercise. That is, the moral fact that, as Pufendorf holds, God's gift indebts his creatures to him to follow his will cannot *itself* depend on God's will, since God's will can obligate only if that fact independently holds.

Still, Pufendorf can consistently maintain that no actual obligations (and in this sense no "moral entities") exist before God's creative, will-imposing act, and not just trivially, that is, because before that there exist no subjects to be obligated. Pufendorf can hold that it takes God's creative act to bring into existence any actual moral powers, including God's, and therefore any moral effects or obligations. Nevertheless, the problem remains that for that to be the case it must be independently true – true independently of God's will – that any such creative benefaction *would* make the created rational beneficiaries their creator's legitimate *subjects* (in a fully normative sense) and, consequently, that their creator would have moral power over them.

A "Sociable" Attitude

We turn now from the obligation to comply with laws of nature in general, which derives from God's moral power to obligate us through his superior will, to "mutual" (directed or bipolar) human obligations and the moral powers that human beings have to directly affect their moral relations and create new

---

[36] For this claim and its defense, see Mautner 1999: 175.
[37] Again, this is Cudworth's objection to all forms of metaethical voluntarism.
[38] Below I shall show that Pufendorf pursues this line.

bipolar obligations and rights. All obligations to follow the laws of nature are, in the first instance, owed to God. Even when God directs us to benefit and not harm other human beings, any obligations that are *thereby* created are owed only to God. No obligation *to others* to act in these ways directly follows. As far as laws of nature in general are concerned, the only being with grounds for complaint about non-compliance is God.

So far, therefore, we lack any account of human perfect rights. Like Grotius, however, Pufendorf holds that human beings have natural perfect rights (and, Pufendorf adds, perfect obligations) and that these entail the standing to demand compliance and even to compel it when directive judicial procedures run out. What brings human moral powers and rights into view is the law of nature's demand to take a sociable attitude to one another.

"It is," Pufendorf says,

> [A] fundamental law of nature, that "Every man, so far as in him lies, should cultivate a sociable attitude, which is peaceful and agreeable at all times to the nature and end of the human race" (208).

But how does this make us obligated *to one another*? Assume, for example, that we are required by the fundamental natural law to cultivate benevolence and act beneficently toward each other. This would not entail that others have any right to our beneficence or that we are obligated *to them* to act beneficently. Of course, Pufendorf does not believe that there is any perfect right to beneficence. But he does think we have perfect rights not to be harmed in various ways and that these imply correlative obligations *to others* not to harm them (128). Nonetheless, from the simple fact that God commands that we not harm one another, no reciprocal rights and obligations follow. If "mutual" human obligations and rights are to follow from the fundamental law of nature, therefore, a "sociable attitude" must be understood in some other way.

And Pufendorf does seem to understand sociability differently, indeed, in such a way that mutual obligations are already built into it. "By a sociable attitude," he says,

> We mean an attitude of each man towards every other man, by which each is understood to be bound to the other by kindness, peace, and love, and therefore by a mutual obligation (208).

Pufendorf evidently understands sociability as itself including the recognition of mutual obligations. Regarding others from the perspective of this attitude must be already to see them as having rights against one and, consequently, to regard oneself as obligated to them. It must be to see them as related to others by the same equal "relationship" of mutual accountability that Grotius holds sociability to include.

As Pufendorf understands inherently "social" attitudes of kindness, peace, and love, these already involve a kind of mutual recognition and respect. Indeed, Pufendorf explicitly defines peace, and its contrary war, in terms of mutual obligations whose reciprocal recognition the state of peace includes.

> [P]eace is that state in which men dwell together in quiet and without violent injuries, and render their mutual dues, as of obligation (9).

The part of sociability consisting in peacefulness, therefore, must already include recognition of reciprocal human rights and duties inherent in it.

Similarly, war is "the state of men who are naturally inflicting or repelling injuries [violations of rights] or are striving to extort by force what is due to them" (9). It follows that human beings cannot see themselves as at peace *or* at war without taking themselves to have reciprocal rights and obligations, indeed, perfect ones. To view other human beings sociably in Pufendorf's sense, whether in war or in peace, is to view them as having rights and obligations that justify directive and sometimes coercive action that would otherwise amount to brute force. This, if you like, is what it is *to view someone as a fellow human being as opposed to as a brute.*

We could put the same point by saying that, for Pufendorf, the natural state of human beings is an inherently social one, not just in the sense of involving affiliating attitudes and relations that lead human beings naturally to want to live together without conflict, but also as including social attitudes in which recognition of reciprocal human rights and obligations is already intrinsic.

Recall Pufendorf's fundamental distinction between the physical order, with its distinctive physical entities, powers, and (temporal and spatial) states, and the "super-added" "moral" order with its own entities, powers, and states created by "imposition." Concerning the latter, Pufendorf says, "every state presupposes in the man who is said to be in that state a certain respect and attitude toward others, since, indeed, every state is accompanied by a right or obligation which cannot be understood without an object for its force" (9). Because of God's imposition at the creation, human beings find themselves in a moral state in relation to him by virtue of his moral power. In addition, God's command that we cultivate sociability puts us also into a moral relation *to one another*, that is, into moral "states" that, Pufendorf says, "more expressly denote a relation toward other men," "since they signify distinctly the mode in which men mutually transact their business" (9).[39]

---

[39] Note that the idea is not that mutual recognition is the natural human state, but that it is inherent to the moral state that God commands his creatures to be in regarding one another. I am indebted to Knud Haakonssen for pressing me on this.

Equal Human Dignity

Human beings thus enjoy "an *equality of right*, which has its origin in the fact that an obligation to cultivate a social life is equally binding on all men, since it is an integral part of human nature as such" (333).[40] Because, Pufendorf writes, "[H]uman nature belongs equally to all men, and no one can live a social life with a person by whom he is not rated as a fellow man" it follows, as a precept of natural law, that "[e]very man should esteem and treat another man as his equal by nature, or as much a man as he is himself" (330).[41] This is a corollary of the fundamental natural law. A sociable attitude, as Pufendorf understands it, includes mutual respect for one another's equal dignity as human beings. It is a "precept of natural law," therefore, that everyone should "*permit others to enjoy the same right that he himself does*" (336).[42]

To regard others socially, consequently, is to see them as sharing a common basic standing with oneself that grounds or includes an ensemble of basic human rights to make demands of one another and hold each other to those demands. People "who, from a special feeling of their own superiority, would have every liberty reserved for themselves alone … and claim honor before all other men" are "plainly unsocial" (336). It is not too much to say that Pufendorf holds that complying with the fundamental law of nature requires viewing others as having a sociability that can be, as Grotius holds, "the Fountain of Right."

Sociability thus includes the recognition of all men as equally entitled to fundamental respect or, as Pufendorf usually puts it, "esteem." "Esteem of persons in communal life … outside of states consists in this, that [the other] is regarded as the kind of person with whom … it may be possible to have intercourse" (2009: 94). "Intercourse," like "sociable," is a normatively loaded term for Pufendorf. Just as taking a "sociable attitude" toward someone is already to view them as entitled to certain forms of treatment and to hold others to these, so likewise, to relate to someone as apt for "intercourse" is to recognize them as having this same fundamental dignity and thereby to respect (in Pufendorf's term, "esteem") them as an equal to whom one is accountable for complying with "mutual" obligation and correlative rights.

"Esteem" refers to a form of valuation Pufendorf uniquely applies to "persons" and their distinctive value: "the value of persons in common life" (1934: 1229). He contrasts esteem with the way "things" are valued. "In common life," Pufendorf says, persons are "valued by" esteem and things are valued by their

---

[40] "Suitable" may be a better translation of Pufendorf's "*comitetur*" than the Oldfathers' "integral." I am indebted to Knud Haakonssen here.
[41] Knud Haakonssen suggests that a better translation than "treat another man as his equal by nature" is "treat another man as if his equal by nature."
[42] Cf. Hobbes on "the law of the Gospel," "whatsoever you require that others should do to you, that do ye to them" (1994a: XIV.5).

"price," anticipating Kant's later distinction between dignity and price (Kant 1996a: 4: 435), but in a way that understands, perhaps more explicitly than Kant will, esteem or respect for human dignity to be a form of "sociability" or interpersonal *relating* (Darwall 2008). To esteem or respect others in this sense is to regard them as having the standing for "intercourse" as equals, along with whatever moral powers that standing involves (including the power to promise and enter into pacts).

In connecting rights and dignity in this way, Pufendorf begins a line of thought that will prove powerful and influential. Human beings carry with them "a most sensitive self-esteem" and are "rarely less and often more disturbed" by disrespect for their dignity "than if an injury were being offered [to their] person and property" (Pufendorf 1934: 330). When one's person or property is violated, the injury is generally twofold, indeed, since some insult is at least implicitly added, and so a second injury of disrespect, to the primary injury. The "most telling reply with which the rude insults of other men is met is, 'I am not a dog or a beast, but as much a man as you are'" (330).

Because of these connections between sociability, respect for equal dignity, and rights, arrogance "giv[es] occasion to a breach of peace" (335–336). Peace just *is* the condition in which people acknowledge one another's dignity and rights, so anyone who, in word or deed, presumes a superiority over others that cannot itself be justified from a fundamental standpoint of equality – like, for example, that of a political official that is properly grounded in an agreement or "pact" – undermines peace and threatens war. To be peaceful, one must treat others not as "inferiors," but as equal "men."[43]

Pufendorf contrasts his account of natural human equality with Hobbes's in two respects. Concerning Hobbes's idea that human powers are sufficiently equal to ground mutual "diffidence" or distrust, Pufendorf replies that a great

---

[43] Pufendorf holds that husbands have unequal rights over their wives because these are grounded in the "matrimonial pact" (Pufendorf 2009: 370–371).
Human obligations based on equal dignity are reciprocal or "mutual" in senses going beyond their involving mutual treatment. People can expect the compliance of others, in the non-epistemic sense of being entitled to expect compliance *of* them, only if they comply themselves. "[I]f a man wishes to avail himself of the assistance of other men ..., he must in turn lend his own talents to their accommodation" (1934: 335). The point is not one of prudence, that others will only cooperate if one reciprocates oneself. It concerns rather the *reciprocity of right*: Others will no longer be obligated *to one* to cooperate if one does not cooperate with them. "In this respect," Pufendorf says, "the obligation to exercise the duties of natural law toward others, although enjoined by the supreme will of God, agrees with an obligation arising from a convention [or 'mutual agreement']." Just as someone who makes an agreement but fails to do their share loses any claim to others' compliance and is rightly subject to their complaint and legal action, so someone who fails to discharge their obligations to others "cannot demand any longer those duties from the other, and the other has the further right to use force in making him render satisfaction" (1934: 333; see also 264).

"variety" of natural powers can actually exist in a "just harmony" precisely because of an equality of right that human beings can jointly recognize (Hobbes 1994a: XIII.4; Pufendorf 1934: 332). Second, Pufendorf rejects Hobbes's natural "right to all things" as not a "real right," since it entails no correlative "moral effect" (obligation) "in the rest of [humankind]," "those who have the same nature as I" (Pufendorf 1934: 391). "[I]t is absurd to try to designate as a right ... [something] which all other men have an equal right to prevent one from exercising" (391). For Hobbes, the "right of nature" is a "blameless liberty" that does not purport to give one a claim or right to demand anything from others (Hobbes 1983: I.14.6). By Pufendorf's lights, however, this effectively *defines* the state of nature as a state of war of all against all.

There are fundamental issues that confront Pufendorf's attempt to ground morality in moral powers. First, Pufendorf's basing human moral powers, equal dignity, and mutual obligations and rights on God's authoritative will faces the problem that taking a sociable *attitude* toward others is arguably not the kind of thing that can be done in obedience to anyone else's legitimate demands, not even God's. We regard others sociably if we regard *them* as having the standing to make claims on us because of our shared rational and social nature. There seems to be no way that this common human dignity could arise by God's commands, for example, as by a delegation of his authority. We will return to this problem in the next section.

More generally, as Pufendorf is himself dimly aware, it is possible for any being, God or human beings, to create obligations and rights through the exercise of their moral powers only if the parties who come thereby to have the new obligations and rights (i.e., through the power's exercise) are already related to one another morally in ways that entail mutual obligations. Whether the moral powers in question are human or divine, Pufendorf seems committed to thinking that the very existence of a moral power presupposes that both the person having it and those with respect to whom it may legitimately be exercised are already obligated to one another not to use violence or force, that is, to be "sociable" to one another.

This distinction between force and respectful sociable intercourse is reflected further in a distinction Pufendorf makes in his account of practical reasoning and moral motivation between the will's being moved by "compulsion," on the one hand, and by "obligation," on the other (Pufendorf 1934: 386). In the former, "the mind is forced to something by mere external violence," whereas "whatever we do from an obligation is understood to come from an intrinsic impulse of the mind" (386). Obligation thus requires the possibility of conscientious motivation that differs from fear of sanctions. At the same time, however, sanctions, most especially God's, play a virtually ineliminable role in Pufendorf's overall picture. For Pufendorf, the moral motive is a combination of "fear mingled with reverence" (1934: 95; 1991: 28).

Holding to Obligations in the Natural State

We should now consider two fundamentally different ways, defined reciprocally in terms of two different kinds of standing or authority, in which human beings are *responsible* for complying with moral obligations, according to Pufendorf. Obligations to comply with laws of nature in general are owed to God. Even when natural laws concern our actions toward other human beings, even indeed, when they concern the very actions to which others may have a perfect right, the fact that these acts are required by *natural law* entails only that God has the authority to demand that we perform them and to hold us responsible for doing so. At the same time, God commands us to cultivate a "sociable attitude," and since this attitude itself involves regarding one another (and ourselves) as having equal dignity and perfect rights, we can comply with this fundamental natural law only if we "esteem" each other as equals and hold ourselves responsible *to one another* for according each other our perfect rights.

Complying with our obligations to God consequently requires us to see ourselves as obligated to one another. And we can do that only by recognizing our shared authority to demand certain treatment and to hold each other responsible for this treatment. Human obligations to one another are "mutual" in the sense that they imply correlative rights *and* that rights to others' peaceable actions toward us are conditional on peaceable treatment of them. Nature does not "allow," Pufendorf says, that one can violate their obligations to another, "while the other remains bound [to him] to keep the peace with him" (1934: 264–265).[44]

So long as we give others no cause for complaint of our actions toward them, we retain the right that they act peacefully and sociably toward us. Threats to our person can therefore legitimate self-defense and uses of force that would otherwise count as violence (i.e., forceful violations of others' rights), and violations of our personal rights can warrant compensation and forceful attempts to secure it (1934: 264–265; 2009: 92).[45]

---

[44] If someone "undertakes against me such things as tend to my destruction, it would be a most impudent thing for him to demand of me that I should thereupon hold his person inviolate" (265).

[45] Someone's violent taking (i.e., without right) of that to which one has a perfect right constitutes injury or "damage" (*damnum*) to which one thereby acquires a right to compensation (1934: 314). Natural law "requires that men voluntarily perform and do for each other what they, for any reason, owe others, and freely offer to make good any damage which has been done to others" (825).

The authority to demand respect for perfect rights, recognized in common law, thus includes the standing to direct others forcefully in ways that would otherwise violently injure or "damage" them and so give them cause for similar forceful "complaint," as well as to demand compensation when others violate their rights.

Powers of these kinds are like those that victims are generally taken to have under the law of torts; both involve a distinctive form of accountability to the victim. Only the right

Although individuals may lose their right to demand respect for their perfect rights when they violate others', this does not mean that others are thereby relieved from the obligation of *natural law* to act peaceably toward them. Violation of a reciprocal or "mutual" obligation cancels individuals' reciprocal rights, but the natural law may still require actions to which these individuals are no longer entitled since "that wherein the other party fell short of justice, can be made up by the author of the obligation" (1934: 333). God creates natural law by imposing his authoritative will on human beings and simultaneously laying on sanctions for violators as well as benefits that can compensate victims.[46]

Since someone who actually violates your rights shows themselves willing to do so, Pufendorf holds that in addition to demanding compensation, victims may also demand that the wrongdoer "repent" and "give his word that he will not offend in the future" (825). But Pufendorf is clear that individuals have no standing to punish the wrong or "defect" itself nor to try to collect anything like punitive damages. "[W]hen reparation of damages has been offered," the victim's "loss" made good, and the wrongdoer has given the victim "guarantees … for the future," then the victim incurs an obligation to "freely pardon the other when he requests it" and "live with him thereafter on peaceful terms" (825, 1160). Further punitive measures make a victim "responsible for the breach of peace and the altercation that follows" (825).

    holder has the standing to decide whether or not to seek compensation for violations of their rights, only they can forgive the violator, only they can consent to what would otherwise constitute violation of their rights, and so on. But now note an important difference between the responsibilities and powers that are involved in reciprocal human obligations to and rights against one another, on the one hand, and those involved in the obligation to comply with natural law in general, which mirrors the familiar distinction between tort law and criminal law.

    Whereas tort law is concerned with compensation, criminal law is concerned with punishment. And whereas it is up to the victim whether to bring a tort action, whether to prosecute and punish violations of criminal law is not appropriately the victim's decision; it is up to the people and their representatives. Now, as we have seen, Pufendorf holds that human beings have natural perfect rights that legitimate actions defending them and seeking compensation for their violation. But he holds that no person in a state of nature has the authority to *punish* violations of natural right or law; only God has that authority or power. This is because genuine punishment can be done only with superior authority or "sovereignty," and the only natural sovereignty is God's. Human beings are natural equals, and human sovereignty can arise only through conventions and pacts (1934: 1161; 2009: 296).

[46] Individuals do have the standing to demand and defend their perfect rights, and to hold others accountable for violating them by seeking compensation, but only God has the standing to punish violations of natural law. These two standings, corresponding to those implicit, respectively, in tort and criminal law, are reflected in a distinction Pufendorf makes between two different "features" or "factors" of wrongful treatment of human beings, namely, between the "loss" that wrongs "directly or indirectly bring upon another" (the tortious injury or "damage") and the amount or degree of "the deviation … from the law" that the wrong itself involves (the criminal wrong and its culpability) (1160).

Unlike Grotius, Pufendorf takes the view that there is no natural human authority to punish. Outside the state, in the condition of "natural liberty," there is no such thing as human punishment. "In the proper sense of the word," human punishment "follows upon human sovereignty" and right, and the natural human condition is an equality of dignity ("esteem") and right in which no one has any standing or power in the state of nature to punish any other (1161). Forcible defenses of human rights, including "by means of war," are not "punishments in the proper sense of the term" (1161).[47]

We return now to the problem I noted briefly in the last section, namely, how human dignity, mutual human powers, and rights can be derived or grounded in God's authoritative command. We might think solutions to both problems can be found in the idea of *delegated* powers and authorities. Surely, God's authority might encompass the power to delegate his power to punish, so perhaps there is some way for states and magistrates to acquire their punitive powers in this way (2009: 212). Similarly, might we not regard individuals' authorities to demand certain treatment of themselves, seek compensation, defend themselves, and so on, as delegated powers? So considered, human beings would ultimately be acting on God's behalf when they make and defend claims. They would have certain "legal" powers so to act in defense of themselves, but such self-defense would be duly authorized ultimately by God – ultimately, they would be defending, as it were, God's right that his orders be complied with and that his creatures not be damaged against his expressed will.

There is no obvious problem in thinking of human beings as having certain derived legal powers and rights in this way. The problem is that what God demands of human beings, according to Pufendorf, is that they take a sociable *attitude* and that this attitude involves a form of *regard* for human beings, respect or "esteem," as having an equal basic dignity just because they are rational and sociable, that is, as being worthy of esteem just because they are beings "with whom ... it may be possible to have intercourse" (2009: 94). To have sociable respect or "esteem" for someone in this sense is not just to count them as fitting some legal category, as an official with delegated authority might recognize someone as qualifying for certain legal treatment. It is to view or regard them as having an intrinsic dignity or value in themselves and so being intrinsically worthy of respect or "esteem" for no further reason. Despite the fact that Pufendorf holds that the mutual obligations entailed within sociability themselves derive from God's command (the "fundamental law of nature"), it simply seems impossible to come to have a sociable attitude of esteem for someone

---

[47] However, civil magistrates do have the right to punish. Human sovereignty and unequal authority arise by convention or pact (949–966). But even assuming that human beings have the moral power to bind themselves to collectively constituted authority, it is not clear, as Grotius had argued before, how any such authority could thereby acquire a right to do a kind of thing, punish, that no individual had the authority to do in the first place.

for the reason that God commands it. One could, of course, desire to acquire the attitude for this reason, or undertake steps to try to inculcate it for this reason. But trying to see someone as intrinsically worthy of esteem or respect for this reason would be like trying to form an intrinsic desire for a saucer of mud for some external reason having nothing to do with any features of mud that one might be able to see as intrinsically desirable.

We can put the same point by saying that even if God's commands give us a reason of some kind for being in the mental state of thinking that human beings have dignity and equal perfect rights, they give us no reason whatsoever for thinking that the propositions we would thereby affirm would actually be true.[48] This would mean that a theory like Pufendorf's might have to be an "error theory" of human mutual rights and obligations. It might explain why we have reason, indeed are morally obligated, to *think* in terms of mutual human obligations and rights and their associated human moral powers, but would nonetheless hold that, unlike thoughts about God's authority and our obligations to him, these propositions are not actually true.

Moral Powers II

We turn now to whether it is possible to derive all of morality from God's authoritative will, that is, through his exercising his moral powers, and the way the issue of its possibility is reflected in Pufendorf's theory of moral agency and the will. I believe this is not possible, that Pufendorf is aware of this problem, and that this awareness shows itself in some deeply significant things he says about obligation and moral motivation (though these are in tension with other central aspects of his view). Whether or not Pufendorf's views fully hang together, analyzing them can help us see things of fundamental importance about the nature of moral obligation and moral or normative powers that will reverberate through modern moral philosophy.

Pufendorf's awareness of these issues comes in his discussion of certain differences between obligations created by law through an exercise of the moral power of sovereignty or authority, and obligations created by agreements, that is, exercises of the power to promise and create pacts. A central difference, he says, is that "[s]ince *agreements* depend in their origin upon our choice, *it is first determined what is to be done before we are obligated in action*" (1934: 89). With laws and authoritative commands, however, the order is reversed: "*[W]e are first obligated in action, and then what is to be done is determined*" (89). It is only when a promise or pact is consummated that the obligation we thereby undertake exists, but "we are obligated by a law, because we owed beforehand

---

[48] The reasons would be what Parfit calls "state-given" rather than "object-given" reasons (Parfit 2011). For further discussion of this problem, see Darwall 2006: for example, 15–17.

obedience to its author" (89). Laws thus presuppose that we are already obligated before their promulgation in ways that agreements do not. But if we can be obligated by God's commands only if we are obligated "beforehand" to obey him, then not all obligations can come through God's exercising his moral power of command. There must be at least one obligation existing already.

Now if this were as far as things had to go, the problem might be easily enough contained. Even if Pufendorf must admit that God's moral power or authority to command cannot itself derive from the exercise of that very authority, he might nonetheless hold that no actual obligations "in action" exist until God exercises this power. It must be true independently of God's exercising his authority, of course, that anyone *would* be obligated by his commands *were* God to issue any. Even so, any actual obligations to act or forbear action would await God's command.

But we can press the problem further. In virtue of what does God have his superior authority? If Pufendorf took God's authority simply to be a brute normative fact, he might deflect this question. He does not, however, and for good philosophical reasons that are reflected in his theories of moral motivation and the will. As we will examine in more detail presently, Pufendorf makes a crucial distinction between the practical reasoning of an agent under obligation and one who is moved by the desire to avoid harmful consequences or negative sanctions. The idea seems to be that, owing to the conceptual connections that Pufendorf insists on between obligation and accountability, someone can be under a moral obligation to do something only if they can hold themselves to the relevant demand through recognizing its legitimacy. "An obligation affects the will morally," he says; "it is forced of itself to weigh its own actions, and to judge itself worthy of some censure, unless it conforms to a prescribed rule" (91). Someone can be accountable only by *holding themselves* accountable. If, consequently, moral obligations are that for which we are appropriately held answerable by God, it follows that any such obligations must be things God can expect us to accept as legitimate demands and judge ourselves censurable for failing to obey.[49]

It would follow that God's authority, indeed any authority over us whatsoever, must be something we are able to accept just by virtue of our being in a position to be obligated to him. Either, therefore, this authority must be self-evident to any rational human being or it must be something any such being can appreciate good reasons for accepting. And Pufendorf holds that there are such reasons. Mere power is insufficient to "lay an obligation," though Pufendorf does hold that the ability to create negative consequences or sanctions is necessary. What is needed in addition to this, he says, is either that the putative

---

[49] Note also Pufendorf's remark that in order for law to exist it must be "communicated to the subject in such a way that he recognizes he must bend himself to it" (1934: 89).

authority "have done me some special service" or "that I should of my own accord consent to his direction" (101). Whatever force the former condition has in general, "this is all the more true if I am indebted to him for my very being" (101). God's authority is thus grounded in the greatest debt of gratitude that a person could possibly have.

Whatever we think about such an idea in its own terms, it creates an obvious problem for the position that all moral obligations derive from God's exercising his moral power over us. For now it seems, as we saw before, that God can have this moral power only if there already exists a freestanding obligation of gratitude.[50] Even so, however, Pufendorf might still hold that, in a way, all actual moral obligations depend on God's exercising his moral power, since God's benefaction and legal imposition might be conceived to be a single action accomplished in the creation that *simultaneously* creates his authority and exercises it.

In any case, there is also a different issue that Pufendorf faces in maintaining that all of morality derives from God's exercising his authority over us, which afflicts any attempt to understand moral powers as prior to obligation. The problem is that, properly understood – and as Pufendorf seems to understand it – the idea of a moral power presupposes that those who exercise it and those with and for whom it is exercised (for whom the "moral effects" of correlative obligations and rights are created) must already have a moral relationship that entails obligations to and rights against one another.

To see this, we can begin with the human power to obligate through pacts. By virtue of agreements or "conventions," individuals obligate themselves to one another to obey and give each other the right to expect their obedience. Thus is political sovereignty created by "consent." But note how sovereignty, consent, and agreement function in this line of thought. The natural human condition is an "equality of right" where it takes individuals' consent to justify directing and using force against them as a putative authority would (333). It is part of the very idea of a moral power of consent that consenting legitimates direction and force that *without consent would have been wrong*, indeed that *would have wronged the consenter had they not consented*. The same is true of the ideas of agreement, convention, or pact. It is part of the very idea that one can create an obligation, say, to give someone something as a part of an agreement, that it would be wrong for the other simply to take the thing from one if one had not agreed, and, indeed, that one would be wronged by such an unjustified taking.

The general point is that the exercise of a moral power can legitimate direction and the use of force if, and only if, it is assumed by the reciprocally recognizing parties to its exercise that the thereby legitimated coercive action would

---

[50] A further problem is that Pufendorf holds the obligation of gratitude to be imperfect (Schneewind 1998: 136).

have wronged its recipient were the directing agent to have lacked the relevant power or were somehow to have exercised it improperly. The very existence of moral powers to create new obligations and rights therefore apparently presupposes *already* existing moral relationships, with already existing mutual rights and obligations, between those who have the power and those with respect to whom it can legitimately be exercised. Finally, since this is a point about moral powers in general, moreover, the same would seem to apply to God's authority over his human subjects.

The arguments of the last three paragraphs have been entirely conceptual, drawing out consequences of the concepts of consent, agreement, and the exercise of moral powers in general. I am not saying that Pufendorf was himself aware of these entailments or even that he would have accepted them had they been pointed out to him. But if they hold, as I submit they do, then they pose a fundamental challenge to any attempt to derive all moral relations from the exercise of moral power, God's or any other beings.

There are places where Pufendorf seems implicitly to accept the general point.

> So that a man may not be able to complain that wrong has been done him when he is compelled to adapt himself to the free choice of a second person, it is necessary that the authority in question also be legitimate (2009: 206).

If this is implicit in the moral power of authority, it will obviously apply as much to God's as to any human authority. Although Pufendorf believes that God has an authority over human beings that may legitimate whatever directive treatment of them he pleases, it seems that he is committed by an aspect of the idea of moral power that he himself accepts to thinking that the created beings with respect to whom God exercises his moral power must have moral standing independently of his superior authority. (Of course, they would not have had that power unless he created them, but that is another matter.) Indeed, it seems to follow, oddly enough, that God could not have the superior authority that he distinctively has unless it were already the case that human beings had an authority they share with him, that is, a standing that makes unauthorized forceful treatment of them wrong, indeed, that would make it *wrong them*.

Moral Agency

I have been arguing that Pufendorf is committed to a fundamental distinction between authorized directive or forceful action, which is legitimated by moral powers and mutual obligations and rights and which therefore does no wrong or "damage" to its recipient, on the one hand, and illegitimate force, which does wrong and injury, on the other. In other words, the very framework of moral powers seems to presuppose that brute force and coercion – force that is not so legitimated – is both wrong and wrongs its recipients (violates their rights and the dignity that gives them standing to complain). If that is so, then whatever authorities or powers exist, it is guaranteed to be the case that anyone with whom one can have sociable "intercourse" in the sense of a reciprocally recognizing exercise of moral power must already be assumed to be able to be wronged by brute coercion and, therefore, that they likewise have the power to complain about unauthorized use of force against them. It apparently follows that the very idea of moral powers would commit Pufendorf to holding not only that God has moral powers that cannot be created by their exercise, but that *so also must anyone who can be affected "morally" by the exercise of moral powers* – that is, any agent who can acquire new obligations and rights through the exercise of moral powers in social intercourse.

In this last section, I want to bring out a way in which this distinction in the space of interpersonal relations is reflected in a distinction that Pufendorf makes in the internal space of moral phenomenology in his account of moral agency and conscience. Both distinctions, it is useful to see, amount to a contrast with Hobbes's philosophy, at least, as Pufendorf understands Hobbes.[51] Just as Pufendorf is concerned to argue against Hobbes that the state of nature involves a robust equality of right that cannot be reduced to equal natural power (or a right that is merely a "blameless liberty"), so also is he concerned to argue that conscience and the sense of obligation cannot be reduced to the fear of sanctions.

It is useful to begin with an insightful distinction Pufendorf makes between shame and conscience. This arises in connection with an objection he considers that "because the very blood seems to have a kind of natural sense of base deeds, since it brings blushes to our cheeks … as we … feel ashamed," our sense of the moral quality of actions must also therefore be able to be caused naturally just by considering the nature of the actions themselves, independently of any "law" or "imposition" (1934: 31). Pufendorf grants that we can feel shame in response to moral wrongs and defects of moral character among other things, but he denies that shame is especially attuned to the moral. "[S]hame arises not merely because of some base action, but also from anything, even though not morally base, which is thought to diminish our reputation," like "shortness of stature, lameness, baldness" and so on (31–32). Since shame doesn't distinguish between the moral and the non-moral, it can give us no distinctive sense of the former. So the fact that it arises naturally without imposition is no evidence that any distinctively moral emotion might be independent of imposition.

---

[51] Pufendorf's picture of Hobbes is something of a caricature. Hobbes also distinguishes, as we saw, between slaves who are moved only by fear of the "natural" consequences of disobedience and servants who, having promised to obey, are bound "in conscience" (1994a: xx.10).

Pufendorf contrasts shame with conscience. Conscience, he says, is a "judgment passed on moral actions by the understanding, in so far as it can take cognizance of laws, and so is responsible to the lawgiver for their execution and observance" (41). But though it involves the "understanding," Pufendorf conceives of conscience also in affective or emotional terms. Conscience's judgment when contemplating action already taken ("consequent conscience") involves the agent's "approving" or "condemning," "attended by peace of mind or agitation" (1934: 41; see also 2009: 266). Similarly, when it comes to conscience's role in deliberation ("antecedent conscience"), Pufendorf draws a contrast intrapersonally, as we have seen, between "compulsion" and action from obligation, in a way that echoes the interpersonal distinction between brute coercion and legitimate direction we noted above.

> This forms the main difference between obligation and compulsion, since in the latter the mind is forced to something by merely external violence contrary to its intrinsic inclination, while whatever we do from obligation is understood to come from an intrinsic impulse of the mind, and with the full approbation of its own judgment (1934: 386).

And again:

> An obligation differs in a special way from coercion ... the latter only shakes the will with an external force, and impels it to choose ... only by the sense of an impending evil (91).

An obligation, by contrast, "affects the will" not "by some natural weight," but "morally." It "fills [the agent or will's] very being with such a particular sense, that it is forced of itself to weigh its own actions, and to judge itself worthy of some censure, unless it conforms to a prescribed rule" (91).

Nothing could seem clearer than the contrast these passages draw between the will's autonomous motivation to comply with obligation and external, "violent," "coercive" avoidance of negative "natural" consequences to which someone displeased with the agent's conduct, even a displeased God, might have the power to subject the agent. Things are not so neat, however. When we view what is left out of the passage quoted toward the beginning of the last paragraph, we see that Pufendorf says that the "peace of mind and agitation" of consequent conscience come from an expectation "of the blessing or the wrath of the lawgiver, as well as the goodwill or anger of other men" (41), not just from the agent's own approval or censure, as reading without the elided passages might lead us to expect. Moreover, in the context from which the passage in the last paragraph comes, we find Pufendorf saying that "nothing can constrain the human mind, as it deliberates on the future to do or avoid anything, except reflections on the good and evil which will befall others and ourselves from what we do" (91). This suggests that, contrary to what we might have expected when Pufendorf says that action from obligation involves an "intrinsic impulse of the mind," the only thing that can move an agent is desire to have or to avoid (naturally) good and evil consequences. And if this is right, then what can the real difference be between the will's complying with obligation "of its own accord" and its doing so to avoid evil consequences?

It seems likely that Pufendorf's thought is in some tension here. On the one hand, the elements of his thought that I have been emphasizing push in the direction of a firm distinction between motivation by sanctions and conscientious motivation. On the other, Pufendorf apparently lacks a theory of the will that is fully adequate to capturing the distinction: "it belongs to the nature of the will always to seek what is inherently good, and to avoid what is inherently evil" (56). All motivation is apparently good regarding rather than right regarding. Pufendorf tries to maintain the distinction, however, but in a way that can be accommodated within his theory of the will. He says that while both avoidance of natural evils and obligation involve fear of an evil or "some object of terror," in the case of obligation a man is forced "to acknowledge of himself that the evil ... falls upon him justly" (91)[52]

Pufendorf consistently maintains that there must be actual sanctions in order for a person genuinely to be obligated. "An obligation is properly laid on the mind of man by a superior, that is, by one who has both the strength to threaten some evil against those who resist him, and just reasons why he can demand that the liberty of our will be limited at his pleasure" (1934: 95; cf. 1991: 28). The threat of actual sanctions is thus necessary for obligation. But Pufendorf emphasizes that his view differs from Hobbes's, at least as he understands Hobbes, since he holds that sanctions are not sufficient to obligate. It is also necessary that there be "just reasons" for the sanction, hence that it falls on one justly. The moral motive, again, is "fear mingled with reverence" (1934: 95).

It is a sign of the tension in Pufendorf's thought that it is not clear exactly how to understand the desire to avoid *justified* sanctions when, as Pufendorf seems to be supposing, it involves no desire to avoid what *would justify* sanctions. To hold that the threat of actual sanctions is necessary for obligation and moral motivation, Pufendorf must be thinking that the agent's own judgment that his action is worthy of censure and sanction can do no independent motivational work. It is as if conscience involves being "forced of itself to weigh its own actions," but also that judging that a specific action would make one "worthy of some censure" leaves one unaffected until one judges that some sanction (or censure) *other than one's own censure* would actually take place. But what motivational work is conscience then doing? It is as if the judgment that one is worthy of censure is utterly external and without affect; in other words, that it involves no implicit censure or blame *of oneself*.

---

[52] More precisely, the evil is "*non immerito*" (not unmerited). I am indebted here to Knud Haakonssen.

Motivationally, it is hard to see the difference between a desire to avoid justified sanctions *that involves no desire to avoid what would justify sanction* and the desire to avoid sanctions period. But Pufendorf is at pains to distinguish these. Of course, if someone were to lack a general desire to avoid sanctions and desired to avoid them *only* on the condition they were justified, then the desire to avoid justified sanctions would clearly be motivationally distinct from the desire to avoid sanctions generally. But Pufendorf of course thinks that we do have a general desire to avoid sanctions, whether they are justified or not. Someone who wants to avoid sanctions on the condition they are justified is most plausibly seen as wanting to avoid what would justify sanctions, whether or not the sanction will actually be applied.[53]

Pufendorf's attempt to account for morality as a realm of moral "entities" and properties that arise through God's exercising his moral power to impose obligations on human beings, including mutual obligations and rights they acquire through the demand to be sociable, thus ends up a fascinating, but unstable, balance of elements from Grotius and Hobbes. Like Grotius, Pufendorf emphasizes sociability, which he ties explicitly to the recognition of equal dignity and mutual rights, something that is only implicit in Grotius. But whereas sociability is foundational for Grotius, it is derivative for Pufendorf, and in a way that I have argued makes Pufendorf's view unstable. On the other hand, a connection between morality and the "natural" power to impose sanctions, which is so important for Hobbes in creating a robust realm of obligations *in foro externo*, is no less essential for Pufendorf. But here again, this introduces instability into Pufendorf's theory, since he is at pains to distinguish his moral psychology and view of the natural moral condition from Hobbes's.

In the end, however, what seems most interesting in Pufendorf is the centrality of moral powers and its connection to reciprocal recognition and accountability. But here again, we encounter a fundamental instability, since the idea of a "moral power" as Pufendorf understands it seems already to presuppose a fundamentally equal sociability, dignity, and right, even though Pufendorf seeks to derive these equal moral powers from God's superior moral power.

---

[53] Of course, the sanctions might be justified simply by the fact that they are legitimated by the authority of the agent or body who sets them, say, God or some civil authority. I am not suggesting that anything in Pufendorf's thought requires justification on a case-by-case basis.

3

Locke and Cumberland

All three of the philosophers we have considered so far – Grotius, Hobbes, and Pufendorf – are canonical representatives of the early modern natural law tradition. In this chapter, we consider the tradition's other two main figures: John Locke (1632–1704) and Richard Cumberland (1631–1718). Locke is justly famous, of course, though more for his political philosophy and the more familiar topics in epistemology and metaphysics treated in the *Essay Concerning Human Understanding* than for his ethics. Cumberland is much less well known. However, Cumberland's contemporaries saw him, along with Grotius and Pufendorf, as one of a "triumvirate of seventeenth-century founders of the 'modern' school of natural law" (Haakonssen 2001: 29). Moreover, Cumberland has special relevance to moral philosophy of the present day, since he was among the first to attempt to "locate" moral truths and facts in relation to, and perhaps reduce them to, those that are confirmable by the empirical sciences, a naturalist program that remains vital today.[1]

The early modern natural lawyers put the juridical idea of morality (natural law) at the center of ethical thought. But the word "morality" rarely appears in translations of Grotius and Pufendorf (nor, indeed, in Hobbes), though it features frequently in Barbeyrac's notes to his early eighteenth-century translations and, of course, in his *Historical and Critical Account of the Science of Morality*, which preceded his 1729 translation of Pufendorf's *De Jure Naturae et Gentium*.

By the time Locke published his *Essay* in 1690, however, the use of "morality" in our contemporary deontic sense to refer to universal deontic norms that obligate all "moral agents" was evidently sufficiently well established in Britain that Locke could refer to the golden rule, called by Hobbes the "sum" of the laws of nature (Hobbes 1994b: XV.35), as "that most unshaken Rule of Morality" (Locke 1975: 68).[2] Indeed, according to James Tyrell, the very project of

---

[1] See Jackson 1998 on the "location problem."
[2] Locke says in the *Essay* that "Person is a forensick term, appropriating actions and their merit; and so belongs only to intelligent Agents capable of a law" (1975: 346). About this, Edmund Law writes, "Now the word person, as is well observed by Mr. Locke ... is ... used in the strict forensic sense, denoting some such quality or modification in man as

the *Essay* had its roots in discussions Locke had in or before 1671 "about the principles of morality and revealed religion" (Woolhouse 2007: 98).[3] A central Lockean claim in the *Essay*, in fact, is that "*Morality* [*is*] *amongst the Sciences capable of Demonstration*" (Locke 1975: 549).

That "morality" had its modern deontic sense in England by this time is illustrated also by Cumberland. Cumberland's *De legibus naturae disquisitio philosophica* originally appeared in 1672, although it was not translated into English until 1727 as *A Treatise of the Laws of Nature*. Like Locke, Cumberland is concerned to argue that the "rules" or "principles of morality" are not innate, but that a "science of morality" can nonetheless be firmly established through philosophical reflection on materials that are given through observation and experience (Cumberland 2005: 264, 297, 489).

Although he is much less well known than Locke now, Cumberland actually has greater significance for the history of ethics, although not, of course, for the history of political thought. Important present-day positions in moral philosophy – for example, reductionist forms of ethical naturalism and empirical naturalist strains of utilitarianism – arguably find their first formulation in Cumberland.

Cumberland is a reductionist both in normative ethics and in metaethics. At the normative level, he argues that "all the Laws of Nature" or "true Rules of Morality" can be "reduc'd to that one, of Benevolence towards all Rationals," where benevolence is understood to aim at the "common Happiness of all rational Beings" (237, 413).[4] Metaethically, Cumberland's project is to show that "the Whole of *moral Philosophy*, and of the Laws of Nature, is ultimately resolv'd into *natural observations* known by the Experience of all Men, or into Conclusions of *Natural Philosophy*" (291). Unlike contemporary naturalists, however, and certainly unlike Hobbes, Cumberland hastens to add that he intends "natural philosophy" to be understood in "a large Sense" that includes empirical inquiry into "the Nature of Souls" no less than "natural Bodies" (291).

Both Cumberland and Locke conceive of morality in terms of natural law, following Grotius, Hobbes, and Pufendorf. But whereas the latter writers, I have been stressing, maintain essentially juridical elements in their conceptions of natural law, right, and obligation, Cumberland and, in some ways,

---

denominates him a moral agent, or an accountable creature; renders him the proper subject of laws, and a true object of rewards or punishments" (Law 1824: III, 179).

[3] Draft B of the *Essay* contains a Table of Contents that includes within Locke's projected critique of innate ideas: "The goodnesse of god never imprinted those Ideas of him that are to be found in mens minds. Noe god, noe idea of morality, which yet may be approved, moral rules & conscience about them prove them not innate" (Locke 1990: 87). See also note 8 regarding this use of "morality" in Locke's manuscripts on the law of nature, composed in the 1660s.

[4] "True Rules of Morality" is Maxwell's translation of "*veris Morum regulis*" (Cumberland 1683: 118–119).

Locke, attempt to account for and ground a juridical conception of morality in non-juridical terms, more specifically in good-based considerations that necessarily weigh with a rational agent from a practical or deliberative point of view.

Accounting for morality's normative force motivationally arguably operates at some level in Hobbes's thought also, but Cumberland's reductionism goes farther than anything in Hobbes. And Cumberland attempts to derive conclusions that are explicitly unHobbesian. He advertises that in his *Treatise*, "Mr. Hobbes's Philosophy, as well Moral as Civil, are consider'd and refuted" (236). More specifically, Cumberland aims to demonstrate that an empirically based ethical philosophy leads not toward a Hobbesian "Epicurean[ism]," but in the direction of what will later be called utilitarianism.[5]

What practical reason recommends to each agent, according to Cumberland, is not the agent's own interest considered independently of others, but rather the "happiness of all rational Beings." Hobbes never attempts to reduce moral or ethical thought or discourse to natural philosophy, holding that, like thought and talk about color, it *expresses* rather than describes users' mental, and ultimately bodily, states. Cumberland holds, by contrast, that "practical Propositions" and "Dictate[s] of Reason" can be formulated equivalently as oughts, as obligating laws, or as propositions of natural philosophy concerning what best conduces to the common happiness. "In my Opinion," he writes, "*these several Forms* of Speech, relating to the Law of Nature, mean the *same thing*" (482–483).

In this way, Cumberland anticipates yet another important strand of modern ethical thought. In eighteenth-century British moral philosophy, "obligation" comes frequently to operate as a synonym for a rational motive or normative reason for acting. Shaftesbury's *Inquiry Concerning Virtue or Merit* (1711) provides an excellent example. In Part I, Shaftesbury considers what virtue is and then asks, in Part II, "[W]hat obligation is there to virtue, or what reason to embrace it?" (Shaftesbury 2001: 192). Similarly, Hutcheson and Hume distinguish between "natural" and "moral obligations" (Hume 1978: 3.2.2.23), holding the first to consist, in Hutcheson's words, in "a Motive from Self-interest, sufficient to determine all those who duly consider it" (Hutcheson 2004: 177). Moreover, Hume and Hutcheson both understand moral obligation not as an irreducibly deontic or juridical concept, but in terms of moral sense or sentiment.

In this chapter, we shall consider "naturalizing" moves that Cumberland, and also Locke, make in these directions in attempting to understand morality and its normativity. Cumberland, especially, is an important influence on Hutcheson, and through him, on Hume. Both Cumberland and Locke hold

---

[5] 252–253, where Cumberland explains his dialectical reasons for not basing a defense of "natural *Religion* and *Morality*" on Platonism. These include that such a basis "*can never be prov'd* against the *Epicureans*, with whom is our chief Controversy."

that in being morally obligated to do something, the obligated agent must have normative reasons to do it (what I call "morality/reasons existence internalism").[6] And both hold that such normative reasons can exist only if the agent could, under appropriate conditions, be motivated so to act ("reasons/motives existence internalism").[7] That said, there are also significant elements in the thought of both that tie both to the juridical moral philosophizing of Grotius and, especially, Pufendorf.

Cumberland presents himself throughout as faithful to the theological voluntarist idea that morality and natural law cannot exist without a lawgiver, although, by the time he has finished, Cumberland's idea of the divine will seems almost indistinguishable from his notion of practical reason. And an important line of thought leading Locke to revise his views on freedom of the will in the second edition of the *Essay* runs right through a connection Locke assumes between moral obligation and justified punishment or accountability. In these ways, Cumberland and Locke are important transitional figures between more explicitly juridical theories of morality represented by Grotius, Pufendorf, and, to a lesser extent, Hobbes, and less legalistic moral philosophies to follow, including many that criticized the modern natural law tradition, like those of Shaftesbury, Leibniz, Hutcheson, and Hume.

Locke: Natural Law, Motive, and Sanction

We begin with Locke. Although Locke's *Essay* (published in 1690) was the main repository of his moral philosophy published during his lifetime, Locke's first theorizing about morality and natural law were contained in Latin manuscripts composed in the 1660s that are now referred to as *Essays on the Law of Nature* (Locke 2002).[8] The main lines of Locke's views in the *Essays* are not dissimilar to Pufendorf's *Elements of Universal Jurisprudence*, which Locke evidently acquired soon after its publication in 1660 (Locke 2002: 38). Like Pufendorf, Locke holds that morality and natural law depend upon divine command. And though Locke has nothing like Pufendorf's sophisticated, systematic theory of "moral powers," something akin to Pufendorf's distinction between moral and physical entities, along with the "imposed" and essentially "directive" character

---

[6] Although Locke, as we shall see, does not think that moral facts or thoughts – for example, that an action would be morally required – are intrinsically motivating themselves. In this respect, he is an externalist. For a discussion of different species of internalism and externalism in moral philosophy, see Darwall 1997.
[7] In Darwall 1995, I argue that both Cumberland and Locke can be placed within an empirical naturalist tradition of British internalism about morality.
[8] Note that the "modern" use of "morality" noted above appears also here, for example, "rules of morality" ("*morum regulas*") (Locke 2002: 166–167).

of the former, seems to lie behind Locke's *Essay* distinction between "ectypal" and "archetypal" concepts, his corresponding distinction between "real" and "nominal essences," and his associated claim that "*Morality* [is] *amongst the Sciences capable of Demonstration*" (because moral concepts are archetypal and thus concern nominal and not real essences, which can only be discovered empirically) (1975: 549).

Where Locke departs decisively from Pufendorf, and also from Grotius, is in the latter's doctrine that human moral agency essentially involves a social nature. By the time of the *Essay*, Locke is explicitly a rational egoistic hedonist, holding that normative reasons for acting can come only from considerations of the agent's own pleasure. Already in the *Essays*, Locke holds that the very raison d'être of morality derives from rationally irresolvable conflicts of self-interest to which the only solution is divine, sanction-backed legislation. Moreover, if it wasn't already clear in the *Essays*, it is in Locke's later writing, that since he holds the agent's pleasure to be the only source of normative reasons, he cannot accept the fundamental distinction Pufendorf draws between being moved by the *legitimacy* of sanctions and being moved by fear of sanctions pure and simple.

This is a deep difference between Locke and Pufendorf. I have been suggesting that much more is packed into sociable nature, as Pufendorf and Grotius understand it, than is normally appreciated. To play the role it does in their thought, sociability cannot just be an affiliative nature, like Stoic *oikeiôsis*, that gives human beings a genuinely common good. It must involve a reciprocally recognizable common standing or authority that can justify legitimate claims and demands. So Locke's disagreement with Pufendorf and Grotius concerns not simply human psychology, or even the nature of human good. It concerns whether moral agency essentially includes the capacity to recognize and be guided by normative reasons of a kind that differ from those of good conceptually, viz., legitimate claims and demands of *right* that presuppose the capacity for accountability and reciprocal recognition of authority.

Locke is clear, however, that morality and moral obligation are themselves to be understood not in terms of agents' goods, but in irreducibly juridical terms. Natural law contains "all the requisites of a law" (2002: 111). "It is the decree of a superior will"; "it lays down what is and what is not to be done"; and "it binds men, for it contains in itself all that is requisite to create an obligation" (111–113). Like Pufendorf, Locke holds that natural law comes into existence through divine imposition. Because God has superior authority over us and so the "right" to our obedience, we become obligated through his decreed will.[9]

---

[9] Somewhat like Pufendorf, but also in ways that anticipate his labor theory of property in the *Second Treatise*, Locke holds that God acquires this right through the creation (Locke 2002: 185).

Now so far, Locke could simply be taking Suárez's position, as did his British contemporary, Nathaniel Culverwell.[10] Suárez rejected Aquinas's view that a teleological order, Aquinas's "eternal law," with a robust common human good, is sufficient to constitute natural *law*. Thomist eternal law is sufficient, Suárez held, to provide natural law's content, but not yet to give it the *form* of law. For this, something explicitly juridical, God's authoritative command, is required. But though authoritative imposition is necessary for a law of any kind, it is not necessary, Suárez held, for what Irwin calls "natural rightness" (Irwin 2008: 28–61). The standards of conduct that give natural law's content are provided by the teleological order of nature, which also grounds natural law's reason-giving force. Independently of divine command, there would be reason enough to comply with natural law owing to the common goods it realizes that are essential to human agents' *telos*. God's imposition simply adds a further reason (of obedience).

This is not, however, Locke's position in the *Essays*. Locke declares at the outset that he assumes "there will be no one to deny the existence of God, provided he recognizes … that there is a thing that deserves to be called virtue or vice" (2002: 109). Locke assumes, that is, that people will recognize that there cannot be right or wrong, virtue or vice, without God's command. Like Pufendorf, Locke holds that all moral properties and "entities," obligations and "moral good or virtue," depend on a moral law that is authoritatively imposed by God (2009: 109). Moreover, Locke holds that the content of natural law is not provided by what is good for agents to do independently of authoritative demand.

> Utility is not the basis of the law or the ground of obligation, but the consequence of obedience to it. Surely, it is one thing for an action of itself to yield some profit, another for it to be useful because it is in accordance with the law, so that if the law were abolished it would have no utility whatever: for example, to stand by one's promise, though it were to one's own hindrance (2002: 215).

It is true, as Irwin frequently notes, that Suárez and Aristotelian naturalists more generally distinguish between what is useful or expedient (*utile*) and naturally right actions that are intrinsically good (the "right as good" or *bonum honestum*) (Irwin 2008: 31, 34). However, Locke can hardly be saying that natural law consists of standards that dictate acts that are inexpedient, but nonetheless beneficial to agents since they realize intrinsic common goods. If Locke thought that, he would not say that natural law can require one "to stand by one's promise, though it were to one's own hindrance."

Locke's view is that goods and evils that come to an agent from following or violating natural law derive not, or at least not always, from the acts themselves

---

[10] For a discussion of Culverwell, see Darwall 1995, esp. pp. 27–33.

considered independently of their being morally required or forbidden, but from consequences of their respecting or violating the law, that is, from their being obedient or disobedient.

> In fact we must distinguish between an action as such and obedient action, for an action itself can be inexpedient ... whereas an obedient action is useful in so far as it averts a penalty due to a crime ... And thus the rightness of an action does not depend on its utility; on the contrary, its utility is a consequence of its rightness (Locke 2002: 215).

This rejection of Suárezian natural rightness is literally the last word of Locke's *Essays*. And it makes clear the central role of divine sanctions in his view.

Locke holds that both God and "the immortality of souls ... must be necessarily presupposed if natural law is to exist" (173). Without God, there will be no law-maker and so no source for natural law. But why the immortality of souls? Just as, Locke says, "[T]here is no law without a law-maker," "law is to no purpose without punishment" (173). Natural law must presuppose immortality of the soul because (eternal) divine sanctions are necessary for law, and these require that human souls be immortal so that the requisite punishment can be meted out.

Morality as Solution to the Human Natural Collective Action Problem

Locke must be thinking that the reason divine supernatural sanctions are necessary for natural law is that without them human beings would lack adequate reason to comply with natural law. We know he thinks that adequate reasons cannot be independent of God's authoritative command. But if the soul's immortality is necessary for the kind of punishment that natural law requires, it must be because natural law requires sanctions of a kind that only God could mete out supernaturally, through eternal goods and evils.

Locke's egoistic hedonism is clearer in the *Essay*:

> If willing be but the being better pleased, as has been shewn, it is easie to know what 'tis determines the Will, what 'tis pleases best: every one knows 'tis Happiness, or that which makes any part of Happiness, or contributes to it; and that is it we call *Good* (1975: 249n).

Some form of egoism is already evident in the *Essays*, however, in Locke's holding that divine sanctions are necessary to establish natural law and give it a "purpose." A second reason Locke gives for thinking that the natural law cannot be grounded simply in agents' interests is the fact that human interests can conflict. If natural law were grounded simply in agents' interests, conflicts of interest would make it impossible for people jointly to obey natural law. But "it is impossible that the primary law of nature is such that its violation is unavoidable" (2002: 211).

Human goods conflict because of natural scarcity. Nature's goods "have been bestowed in a definite way and in a predetermined quantity; they have not been fortuitously produced nor are they increasing in proportion to what men need or covet. Clothes are not born with us, nor do men like tortoises, possess and carry about shelters" (211). And when one person takes away from the common stock of natural goods, "he takes away from another man's heap the amount he adds to his own" (211).

These themes are familiar from the *Second Treatise*, but already in the *Essays* Locke is concerned about the role of property in human good. It is the human need and desire to appropriate that makes for conflicts of interest that human beings cannot resolve without divine intervention in the form of supernatural-sanction-backed natural law. "The strongest protection of each man's private property," Locke writes in the *Essays*, "is the law of nature," which enables a man to "be master of his property ... and pursue his own advantage" without undermining others' capacity to pursue theirs (207).

Left to our own devices, we human beings face a classic collective action problem, something like an n-person prisoners' dilemma, which our created egoistic nature bequeaths to us. We humans see that this is so, moreover, and the very empirical evidence of divine design that persuades us that a supremely wise, benevolent, and powerful creator exists, can convince us also that God must command us to act on mutually advantageous laws to solve our collective action problem. Natural law or morality is the solution to the collective action problem that human beings face that would otherwise defeat them.

Since we know that God is perfectly wise, powerful, and benevolent, we have sufficient evidence that he wills us to conform to principles that it is in the interest of each that all follow. But since, as Locke supposes, only agents' own goods give them reasons for acting, however broadly their good may be conceived, it follows also that God's will would be vain if he did not provide further incentives, in the form of eternal sanctions, to comply with the law. And for these to exist, the soul must be immortal. In other words, from the evidence that supports the existence of an omnipotent, omniscient, and omnibenevolent creator, Locke believes we can draw the following further conclusions: the existence of natural law and eternal supernatural sanctions, and the immortality of the soul. All, he must be thinking, are necessary conditions for the very possibility of morality and reasonable social order, given the circumstances of human life as we find it.

The role of divine sanctions in giving human beings incentives without which they would lack good reason to comply with natural law is even clearer in later writings and the *Essay*.[11] Before we consider these, however, we should

---

[11] See, however, Sheridan 2007, which notes that there are places where Locke allows that the pleasure of doing our duty or love can motivate moral action, for example: "Happiness ... is annexed to loving others or our doing our duty" (Locke 1997: 319).

notice a deep tension already apparent in the *Essays* between Locke's egoism and his juridical view of moral obligation. We have seen that Locke is clear that there is a conceptual difference between natural law and (agents') good. Showing that something will benefit an agent, intrinsically or extrinsically, does not establish that it is legitimately demanded of them. No claim of right follows from these facts of good. For deontic claims to hold, authority and accountability relations must be in place that can legitimate demands and make the agent answerable for complying with them. Neither can the content of legitimate demands be given by the agent's good. Rather, natural laws consist of norms directing agents to perform acts, like keeping their promises or respecting the property of others, even to their own "hindrance." Everyone's conforming to such norms benefits everyone, however.

Right and Good

Natural law is thus juridical in concept and form. Like Suárez and Pufendorf, Locke holds that something does not count as law and cannot create genuine obligations unless it exists within a framework of authority and accountability. This is the conceptual or formal difference between the deontic concepts of law, right, and moral obligation, on the one hand, and the concept of good, whether extrinsic (*utile*) or intrinsic and common goods (*bonum honestum*), on the other. Further, Locke disagrees with Suárez, and agrees with Pufendorf, in thinking that natural law differs from the good also as a matter of content. There is no natural moral rightness that is a species of intrinsic (common) good. The right cannot be understood as a *bonum honestum*.

But this does not mean that human agents lack adequate reasons of self-interest for complying with natural laws created by God's commands. To the contrary, since God punishes disobedience, there is always adequate self-interested reason to comply. Still, though God's sanctions are what give agents reasons to comply with his legitimate demands, they are not what *obligate* them to do so.

> All obligation binds conscience and lays a bond on the mind itself, so that not fear of punishment, but a rational apprehension of what is right, puts us under an obligation, and conscience passes judgment on morals, and, if we are guilty of a crime, declares that we deserve punishment (185).

This means, as we shall see more clearly presently, that there is, for Locke, a gap between conscientious judgments of right, legitimate demand, obligation, and deserved punishment, on the one hand, and rational motivation on the other. Though it is guaranteed that there will always be sufficient reasons to comply with moral obligations, that is not because moral obligations entail or create reasons for acting themselves.

The coincidence between obligation and practical reasons is guaranteed *extrinsically* through divine sanctions. In this sense, Locke is a moral externalist. He is a judgment externalist, since he thinks that the judgment that something is morally obligatory is not inherently motivating. And he is, in one important sense, a (morality/reasons) existence externalist, since he thinks that something's being morally obligatory does not *in itself* give him any reason, much less overriding reason, to do it.[12]

We should compare Locke's view with Pufendorf's distinction between being moved by fear of sanctions and acting "from obligation" through an "intrinsic impulse of the mind" consisting in the agent's own "censure" of violating moral obligations and their sense that they would be subject to sanctions that would fall upon them "justly" (Pufendorf 1934: 91, 386). As we noted, Pufendorf also says things that suggest a view of motivation that is more like Locke's. But in the quoted passages, at least, Pufendorf clearly distinguishes himself from Locke in holding that genuine obligation is impossible unless moral agents have the capacity to be moved by moral obligations intrinsically through their own acceptance of authority that legitimates demands, and through their capacity to hold *themselves* responsible to authority through their own censure.

That this is not Locke's view is even clearer in his later works. Thus we find in a 1693 entry in his *Commonplace Book*:

> The pleasure that a man takes in any action or expects as a consequence of it is indeed a Good in it self able & proper to move the will. But the Moral Rectitude of it considered barely in it self is not good or evil nor in any way moves the will but as pleasure & pain accompanies the action it self or is looked on to be a consequence of it. W^{ch} is evident from the punishments & rewards wch god has annexed to moral rectitude or pravity as proper motives by ye will wch would be needless if moral rectitude were it self good and moral pravity evil (quoted in Colman 1983: 48–49).

In the *Essay*, Locke holds that "Good and Evil … are nothing but Pleasure and Pain" and, that since

> it would be utterly in vain, to suppose a Rule set to the free Actions of Man, without annexing to it some Enforcement of Good and Evil, to determine his Will, we must, where-ever we suppose a Law, suppose also some Reward or Punishment annexed to that Law (Locke 1975: 351).

Locke distinguishes three different kinds of laws – divine law, civil law, and the law of "Opinion or Reputation" by their respective "Enforcements, or Rewards and Punishments" (351).

---

[12] In another sense, he is a morality/reasons existence internalist, since morality can only exist through God's commands and sanctions, which guarantee that there is always sufficient self-interested reason for complying with morality.

In the *Essay*'s final chapter, Locke advances a three-fold division of knowledge: logic and semantics, theoretical knowledge or natural philosophy, and practical knowledge (1720).[13] Practical knowledge concerns "[t]hat which Man himself ought to do, as a rational and voluntary Agent, for the attainment of any End, especially Happiness." And Locke defines "Ethicks," as "the seeking out those Rules, and Measures of humane Actions, which lead to Happiness, and the Means to practise them" (1975: 720).

It is the connection to agents' pleasure or happiness, their only rational motive, that gives ethical thought its practical point for Locke. The writings of ethical writers like "Aristotle" or "Confucius," which attempt to pick out virtues and vices, "evaporat[e] only into words, disputes, and niceties." "Without showing a law that commands or forbids them," and that includes sanctions for disobedience, "moral goodness will be but an empty sound" (King 1830: 129–130). What makes the conceptions figuring in natural law and moral good and evil more than mere names is their *practical* force. It is because God's sanctions connect natural law to agents' *goods* that they become practical. Only in this way can human beings acquire motives to make the world fit archetypal moral notions and make them genuinely practical.

Locke contrasts the intrinsically practical knowledge at which ethics aims with knowledge of "[t]he Nature of Things, as they are in themselves, their Relations, and their manner of Operation" (1975: 720). Knowledge of our moral obligations does not require knowledge of real essences or substances, most importantly, of human beings themselves. "For as to Substances, when concerned in moral Discourses, their divers Nature are not so much enquir'd into as supposed, *v.g.* when we say that *Man is subject to Law*: We mean nothing by *Man* but a corporeal rational Creature: What the real Essence or other Qualities of that Creature are in this Case, is no way considered" (516). The basis for the law of nature thus involves nothing about the real essence of human beings.

This marks a real difference between Locke and Suárez – and a similarity between Locke and Pufendorf – that points in the direction of the difference between views called "constructivist" in contemporary discussion and "naturalist" views, whether Aristotelian naturalist in Irwin's sense, or in our contemporary sense of non-teleological ethical naturalism. There is an important way in which Locke "naturalizes" natural law, since he holds that the juridical, obligating character of natural law is, from a practical point of view, a fifth wheel. It has no intrinsic deliberative role, and without being connected to human motivation (through sanctions that are, albeit, supernatural), moral, irreducibly juridical concepts appear to be mere names lacking practical force, which are no part of "Ethicks," by Locke's criterion.

---

[13] Here, I follow Darwall 1995: 45–46.

Even so, once we have the concept of a person, that is, a rational corporeal creature subject to law (346, 516), know that rational creatures can act only on their own good, and know enough about the human situation to draw conclusions about God's will and sanctions, we know enough to draw conclusions about natural law. No further inquiry into the real essence of human beings is required.[14]

Law, Accountability, and Autonomy

Before turning to Cumberland, we should note one further feature of Locke's view that manifests a tension he copes with between holding that moral concepts are essentially deontic or juridical, and so irreducible to the good, on the one hand, and holding, on the other, that only the agent's good gives them normative reasons for acting and so is intrinsically "practical" and therefore "ethical." Since morality is tied to accountability through the nature of juridical concepts and, since, Locke came to believe, somewhat like Pufendorf, someone can intelligibly be held answerable for complying with law only if they have the agential capacities sufficient to determine themselves to comply with it, Locke required a theory of free will sufficient to explain how human agents could intelligibly be thought subject to natural law.

In the first edition of the *Essay*, Locke already declares his agreement with "those who cannot conceive, how any thing can be capable of a Law, that is not a free Agent" (76). By "capable of law," again, Locke means capable of being subject to law and obligated by it. But Locke's view of freedom there, that freedom consists in the absence of obstacles to agents' doing what they will, was largely Hobbesian (276). And he follows Hobbes also in holding that the question about whether the will itself can be free involves a category error (241, 247). In the first edition, Locke has no conception of a capacity for free determination of the will itself, that is, of autonomy or self-determination.

---

[14] There are places in the *Essays* where Locke's view can seem much like Suárez's, for example, when Locke uses Suárez's term *"debitum naturale,"* saying that there is a "natural obligation ... to fulfil the duty which it lies upon one to perform by reason of one's nature" (Locke 2002: 181). But Locke there adds: "or else submit to the penalty due to the perpetrated crime" (181). For Locke, sanctions for violating divinely imposed law are necessary to give natural law normative or practical force, whereas Suárez's idea of a natural duty consists of a standard agents already have sufficient *eudaimonistic* reason to comply with (*bonum honestum*) independently of God's commands and sanctions. What Locke obviously means by "duty which it lies upon one to perform by reasons of one's nature" is that the content of natural law derives from incontestable features of the human condition that require no inquiry into human essences: corporeal rational beings placed in circumstances of relative scarcity with some means for mutually advantageous collective action, but who are unable, without God's sanctioned law, rationally to undertake it.

But why would such a conception be necessary? Why after all, are only "free Agent[s]" "capable of a Law"? The answer has to do with conceptual connections Locke sees between the concepts of person, imputation, and accountability. "Person," Locke says, "is a Forensick Term appropriating Actions and their Merit; and so belongs only to intelligent Agents capable of a Law" (346). The identity of a person over time, "whereby it becomes ... accountable," presupposes an agent who consciously "owns and imputes to it *self* past Actions" on the same grounds "that it does the present" (346).

Still, why does such agency require anything beyond the human capacity to grasp natural law and that God punishes disobedience? If people were able to do whatever they think will be best for them in the long run, nothing more might be necessary, since once they are aware of divine sanctions, they would naturally prefer not to violate natural law. By the time of the second edition, however, Locke came to believe that this is not so and significantly revised his account of free agency.[15]

> *What is it that determines the Will in regard to our Actions?* And that upon second thoughts I am apt to imagine is not, as is generally supposed, the greater good in view: But some (and for the most part the most pressing) *uneasiness* a Man is at present under (250–251).

The problem is that even if people know that they will be punished for violating natural law, and even if they believe complying with the law is important for their greater long-term good, they will not comply with it if the threat of punishment does not make them sufficiently uneasy or if they do not desire to avoid the punishment first and foremost.[16]

If, consequently, human agents are to have the capacity to guide themselves by natural law, they will require some capacity to bring the strength of desire ("present uneasiness") into alignment with their assessments of long-term benefit. In the *Essay*'s second edition, Locke describes precisely such a power of self-determination.

> For the mind having in most cases, as evident in Experience, a power *to suspend* the execution and satisfaction of any of its desires, and so all, one after another, is at liberty to consider the objects of them; examine them on all sides, and weight them with others. In this lies the liberty Man has; and from the not using of it right comes all that variety of mistakes, errors, and faults which we run into, in the conduct of our lives, and our endeavours after happiness (263).

---

[15] Mostly, in Chapter 21, "Of Power." These are analyzed much more fully in Darwall 1995: 149–175, from which I here draw, and Yaffe 2000.

[16] One example Locke gives in the second edition is humorous when viewed against our contemporary background (say, after doing a Google search on "akrasia" and "smoking"): "Bread or Tobacco may be neglected, where they are shewn to be useful to health, because of an indifferency or disrelish to them" (1975: 280).

However strong our current desires, we have the power to step back from them and "examine" their objects "on all sides." "Thus, by a due consideration and examining any good proposed, it is in our power to raise our desires, in a due proportion to the value of that good, whereby in its turn, and place, it may come to work upon the *will*, and be pursued" (262). "[H]e that has a power to act, or not to act according as such determination directs," Locke concludes, "is a *free Agent*" (266).

Despite the fact that human beings always act on their strongest desire, then, they can nonetheless be held "answerable" and "justly incur punishment" when they violate natural law. "If the neglect or abuse of the Liberty he had, to examine what would really and truly make for his Happiness, misleads him, the miscarriages that follow on it, must be imputed to his own election" (271).

Locke's doctrine of self-determination, though prompted by the very same consideration of natural law's conceptual connection to accountability as Pufendorf's account of moral agency, nonetheless proceeds entirely within an egoistic hedonist framework. Contra Pufendorf, though we must be self-determining agents to be answerable and so "capable of a Law," this does not include any "intrinsic impulse of the mind" to recognize and hold ourselves accountable to legitimate authority. For Locke deontic moral thoughts are, in themselves, motivationally inert. That the capacity for free agency is made necessary by the moral law does not mean that morality must have any intrinsic practical "force" for the agent itself. God's sanctions bring a coincidence between natural law and our greatest long-run pleasure, and self-determining moral agency is a hedonistic capacity to bring the strengths of our current desires into alignment with that long-run pleasure. For Locke, any normative force the right has can come only from the good.

The connection Locke draws between autonomy or self-determination and being subject to the moral law is one whose power and influence reverberated throughout the history of modern moral thought. It is possible that Locke himself first encountered the idea in the philosophy of the Cambridge Platonist Ralph Cudworth, to be discussed in the next chapter.[17] We will find other versions of this notion in the thought of Shaftesbury, Butler, Rousseau, and Kant, as well as in forms of neo-Kantian moral philosophy of the late twentieth century.

Cumberland

We turn now to Cumberland. Cumberland is best known for being, as Ernest Albee put it, "the true founder of English utilitarianism" (Albee 1957: 1). Although historians of ethics duly note this, they tend to take less account of

---

[17] In Darwall 1995, I suggest that Locke may have had access to Cudworth's manuscripts on freedom of the will (see Darwall 1995: 172–175). However, see Broad 2006, which argues that this is unlikely, and that it is more likely that Locke learned Cudworth's ideas through

Cumberland's views concerning the nature of practical reason and its relation to morality.[18] It may be, however, that these foundational aspects of Cumberland's thought have even more historical significance.[19]

We have been stressing the Sidgwick/Anscombe thesis that much of modern moral philosophy departs from an Aristotelian naturalist framework by insisting on the juridical or deontic character of the right as a normative notion that cannot adequately be conceived as a "species of the Good" (Sidgwick 1967: 105–106). But there is a second way in which some modern thinkers diverged from Aristotelian naturalism, even about the good, namely, by rejecting the *eudaimonist* thesis that practical reason necessarily aims fundamentally at *eudaimonia* or the *agent's own* good.

Cumberland makes an important move here. Arguing against Hobbesian egoism, he maintains that others' goods are no less good than the agent's own and therefore are no less choiceworthy. He holds, first, that as a matter of rational will and action, it is no less *possible* for agents to aim directly at the good of others than it is for them to aim at their own. And second, he holds they have no less reason to do so. Thus begins a tradition according to which practical reason includes rational benevolence no less than self-regard that runs through Hutcheson and Sidgwick.

Cumberland also arguably stands at the beginning of another, empirical naturalist tradition in metaethics that seeks to "resolv[e]" "the Whole of *moral Philosophy* ... into *natural Observations* known by the Experience of all Men, or into Conclusions of true *Natural Philosophy*" (Cumberland 2005: 291).[20] Cumberland advances a naturalist account of the good: the "best Effect" accomplishable by human action is the "greatest Happiness of all rational Agents" (258, 487). And although he is formally a theological voluntarist, and recognizes that without its distinctive deontic features, morality will not take the form of a law, he ultimately seeks to reduce these naturalistically as well.

A Treatise of the Law of Nature, Cumberland says, is "a Confutation of the Elements of *Mr. Hobbes's* PHILOSOPHY" (287). Against Hobbes, Cumberland seeks to establish that there are "certain *Propositions of unchangeable Truth, which direct our voluntary Actions* ... *and impose an Obligation*

---

conversations with Damaris Cudworth Masham, in whose house Locke spent his last years (Broad 2006). Carter 2010 notes contrary evidence.

[18] See Albee 1957: 1–51, Sidgwick 1964: 173–175. See also Sharp 1912, Haakonssen 1996: 50–51 and 2001, and Crisp 2019: 33–48.

[19] I follow closely, and sometimes draw text from, Darwall 1995: 80–108.

[20] But note: "*Natural Philosophy*, in the large Sense I now use it, does not only comprehend all those *Appearances of natural Bodies*, which we know from Experiment, but also inquires into the Nature of our *Souls*, from Observations made upon their Actions and distinguishing Perfections, and at length leads Men, by the Chain of natural Causes, to the Knowledge of the *first Mover*, and acknowledges him to be the Cause of all necessary Effects" (2005: 291).

to external Actions, even without Civil Laws, and laying aside all Consideration of those Compacts, which constitute Civil Government" (289). We will consider his accounts of the *directive* and of the *obligatory* aspects of natural law in turn.

Practical Propositions

To "direct" human action, natural philosophy must establish what Cumberland calls "practical propositions." Cumberland accepts the traditional Aristotelian/Thomist account of action as invariably aiming at the good, though he seeks also to reinterpret it. As we've just noted, he holds that agents can aim at others' goods directly and not just as a species of their own. And Cumberland's version of the traditional account is empirical naturalist. An end is simply an "Effect" the idea of which, "preconceiv'd in the Mind, first moves a Rational Agent to intend the producing it" (506). *Practical propositions* therefore "pronounc[e] concerning the Consequences of human Action" (258).

For laws of nature to be practical propositions, then, they must concern "effects." But this can hardly be sufficient for them to be directive. Any empirically confirmable proposition concerning what will happen if one does something counts as practical by this standard. Laws of nature aim, however, to direct action more specifically, to say what one should do when doing one thing would have one effect and doing something else would have another. More is required for directing action than just pointing out the consequences of various alternatives before the agent. The practical question is *which* alternative to choose.

The law of nature directs us to benevolence or concern for the common good. Unlike other practical propositions, whose guidance depends entirely upon an *optional* end – for example, those that concern what will happen if one performs some geometrical construction – "the Effects of a care of the common Good ... nearly concern all" (263). We are not free not to have the end the law of nature directs us to; we have it necessarily.

It is not entirely clear exactly what Cumberland supposes this necessary end to be. Here is his statement of the "fountain" of all natural law:

> *The greatest Benevolence of every rational Agent towards all, forms the happiest State of every, and of all the Benevolent, as far as it is in their Power, and is necessarily requisite to the happiest State, which they can attain, and therefore the common Good is the supreme Law* (292).

It is natural to assume that "Effects of a care of the common Good" at least *include* the agent's own happiness. Given some other things Cumberland says, we might suppose that he is saying that the law of nature directs every agent to be benevolent because that is necessary to the agent's own happiness.

[A]n Action is ... necessary to a rational Agent, when it is certainly of the Causes necessarily requisite to that Happiness, which he naturally, and consequently necessarily, desires (554).

As we will see, however, Cumberland clearly thinks we can *at least* no less rationally aim at others' happiness as we can aim at our own. And his considered view seems to be that the happiness of all is a *better* end to aim at, indeed that it is the "best effect" or end.

Obligation

So far, then, we have the idea that the law of nature *directs* us to benevolent concern for all because the "Effects of a care of the common Good" inescapably concern any rational agent. We shall return to the further issue we have just broached – whether the inescapable end is to be understood egocentrically or impartially – presently. First, however, let us begin to understand the sense in which Cumberland thinks the law of nature *obligates*.

This is essentially the same issue as whether morality provides genuine *law*. "Laws," Cumberland holds, are "nothing but *practical Propositions, with Rewards and Punishments annex'd, promulg'd by competent Authority*" (253; see also 543). So far, this is basically the same view as Locke's and Pufendorf's. But there are important differences in Cumberland. First, it is important to Locke's view that morality's sanctions are supernatural. Our natural condition, Locke thinks, is like a prisoner's dilemma, which can be solved only by God's creating supernatural, eternal rewards and punishments that can offset natural *individual* advantages of *collectively* disadvantageous action. And second, it is crucial to Locke's view that these be genuine *sanctions*, that is, that the rewards and punishments be consequences, respectively, of *obedience* and disobedience of God's authoritative will.

Both are differences from what Cumberland holds. Although Cumberland accepts eternal sanctions in Locke's sense (600), they play no role in establishing natural law. The "*Rewards and Punishments*" with which he is mostly concerned are those that are "naturally connected" to the actions natural law directs. The natural connection between benevolence and "the happiest state of any and all the Benevolent" is sufficient to make the latter a *reward*. If this natural connection can be established and "reduc'd into the Form of [a] Practical Propositio[n]," then that is "all that is *essential to a Law*" (499).

Cumberland believes that human beings can solve their collective problems with motives they already have at hand in knowing the natural consequences of their motivated actions. The "*Rewards and Punishments*" through which God enacts practical propositions that constitute the law of nature are none other than those referred to in the law of nature itself. Thus, unlike both Locke and

Pufendorf, Cumberland holds that the fact that the law of nature proceeds from God plays no role in giving human agents motives to follow it. If the natural realm were to exist without God, human agents would have the same reasons to be mutually benevolent. Unlike Locke and Pufendorf, therefore, Cumberland does not hold that agents' motives for compliance with natural law depend upon its being *law*, formally so called. The thought that in contravening natural law one is *disobeying* God or violating his authoritative will has no motivational force.

Formally, again, Cumberland holds that law must be "*promulg'd by competent authority*" (253). But God's authority turns out not to be independent of a proper understanding of natural law itself. As Cumberland puts it,

> [I]t amounts to the same thing, when we *say*, "That the Obligation is an Act of the Legislator", or the First Cause; as if in this place we had *call'd* it, "An Act of the Law of Nature." For the Legislator obliges by the Law sufficiently promulg'd, and he sufficiently promulges it, when he *discovers* to our Minds, "That the prosecution of the Common Good is the Cause necessarily requisite to that Happiness, which every one necessarily desires" (555).

It turns out, therefore, that the existence of normative reason for following natural law's "direction" *and* the obligatory normative force that is distinctive of moral law are both reduced to the empirical naturalistic generalization that is the natural law's content. Thus are "moral Philosophy" and "the Laws of Nature ... ultimately resolv'd into *natural Observations* known by the Experience of all Men, or into Conclusions of true *Natural Philosophy*" (291).

Empirical Grounds for the Law of Nature, Understood Egocentrically

So far, we have said nothing about why Cumberland thinks the natural law holds as a matter of empirical fact. We have provisionally understood the law to assert that all rational human agents are likeliest to have the happiest lives within their power if they act with the greatest benevolence "to all rationals" – to fellow human beings and to God. But why does Cumberland think this is so? All his foundational theses would count for nothing against Hobbes unless he can establish this apparently unlikely empirical claim in the face of Hobbes's powerful arguments to the contrary.

Unlike Hobbes and Locke's Epicureanism, Cumberland holds a more Aristotelian theory of well-being as the enjoyable exercise of human faculties (523). As we shall better appreciate in the next section, Cumberland believes he can reasonably claim that acting with universal benevolence more satisfyingly exercises our powers than does acting with purely self-regarding motives (266). An extensive benevolence is also intrinsically satisfying because it maximally actualizes the joy of love and the tranquility of a mind without any conflict between what it wills for itself and what it wills for others. Benevolence is useful as well, moreover, since it makes agents less vulnerable to various maladies (both psychological and physiological) that afflict the self-absorbed. "*Hatred* and *Envy*, which fill the Mind of him who regards *his own Good only*, are necessarily accompanied with *Trouble* and *Sadness*, *Fear* and a *Solitary State*, which are evidently inconsistent with a *Happy Life*" (528). Finally, many of the most important human goods are *common* goods, through which human beings enjoy in common their joint exercise of natural powers.[21]

Part of Cumberland's disagreement with Hobbes thus concerns the nature of human good. Hobbes sees the state of nature as one of conflict owing to natural human desires for power, glory, and scarce resources. Cumberland, by contrast, holds that the peace that derives from mutual non-aggression and, even more, from mutual benevolence, is not only the best outcome agents can rationally hope for given the power behind others' interests. Rather, mutual benevolence and its fruits fulfill human beings' most important needs and desires.

We need not worry about the details of Cumberland's empirical arguments. Whether the law of nature provides every agent with adequate reasons, based in their own good, for being benevolent may matter less to his overall argument than it initially seems. We shall see why in the next section.

Practical Dictates of Reason, Agreement, and the Best End

We begin with Cumberland's account of the will. Cumberland holds the traditional view that all action aims at some good, but he modifies it in two important ways. First, as we have seen, he takes action to be fundamentally *instrumental*, and therefore, to be capable of being justified only by the goodness of natural *effects* it realizes. And second, he takes these justifying effects to include others' goods no less than the agent's, since they are no less good. It is possible, Cumberland argues, for human agents "to exercise Love, not only towards themselves, but also towards God, and Men, partaking of the same rational Nature with themselves" (312). "'[T]he Understanding is capable of judging, what promotes the Good of others, as well as what promotes our own;' nor is there any *Reason*, 'Why we cannot will those same things, which we have judg'd to be good'" (473).[22]

---

[21] We might say that this is an Aristotelian Naturalist strain of his thought in Irwin's sense.
[22] Sharp points out that "the principle ... that egoism and altruism have the same psychological root" "lies at the very foundation of [Cumberland's] system," since Cumberland believes that "the good as such, independently of its relationship to this or that possible possessor, tends to arouse the desire to realize it" (Sharp 1912: 380). As we will see in the next point, all desirable goods are goods *of* some being or other. This also would be Hutcheson's view, arguably under Cumberland's influence.

Cumberland's account of action and practical reason involves three significant moves. The first, again, is that rational will is *instrumental* and exclusively *consequence* directed. The agent's end is always some (believed) good effect, that is, some state of the world that is naturally producible by some action in the agent's power.

Cumberland's second move is to hold that the value of a consequential state is itself resolvable into the natural *goods* (well-being) of affected persons. This is a move that becomes characteristic of reductive naturalist utilitarianism, so long as it is supposed, as Cumberland does, that the good of person can be understood naturalistically.

It is a consequence of these first two claims that when an effect is aimed at *as good*, the will's object is invariably the good *of someone*. Thus, Cumberland agrees with Locke that it is impossible for anyone to desire or be motivated directly by the right or by *moral* good; all desires are for *natural goods*, that is, for the natural states that constitute well-being. Where Cumberland departs from Locke is in holding that people can directly desire the goods of others no less than their own.

This is Cumberland's third move: that the good of others is no less good, and so no less choiceworthy, than is the agent's own good. It follows, Cumberland argues, that since an agent has reason to will an end just insofar as it is a good effect, and since the good of others is no less good than the agent's own, the agent has the same reason to aim at the good of others that they do to aim at their own.

Because we can equally well act for others' sake as we can for our own, the moral question arises when people's goods conflict of whose good it is *morally right* to realize.

> There is no doubt, but that Man has a *natural Power*, or *Will*, which he himself may *determine* to act which way he pleases. But when we are inquiring into the *Right* of Acting, the *Question* is, "Which among those Actions which are in our *power*, are *lawful?*" ... Any one *can* either hang, or throw down a Precipice, either himself, or any other innocent person (359–360).

If the goodness of effects or ends is the only source of normative reasons, the fact that an act will be good for the agent cannot be a reason to act for his sake *as opposed to someone else's*, if an alternative would be no less good for someone else. Cumberland will conclude that the "best end" for practical reason to aim at must be the greatest good of all.

This line of thought lies behind remarks Cumberland makes about consistency and agreement. We noted earlier Cumberland's claim that someone who wills the same for themselves as they do for others has a kind of "inward *Peace*" (296). But Cumberland goes farther to say that the costs of willing different effects for ourselves than for others is not just psychic turmoil but a kind of deep unreasonableness.

It is *evident*, "That *no Action relating to others can be consistent* with those necessary and right *Actions conducing to our own Good*, unless the *Practical Dictates of Reason*, by which we are determin'd to *that Action*, ... enjoin us to *desire such things to them as to our-selves*" *(525).*

Cumberland objects on these grounds to the thinking underlying Hobbes's right of nature:

> The reason of *Hobbes's* making so gross a *Blunder* in this Argument was because he did not *observe*, "That there was the *same* Standard to *all*, by which the Reason of every one is to be tried, whether it be right or no" (381).

Of course, in one obvious sense, the right of nature *does* give all the same standard. The problem, from Cumberland's point of view, given his instrumentalist conception of rational action, is that any standard of practical reason can be derived only from the goodness of ends or effects. The requisite rational standards can only come from an "*End* necessary to all rational Beings" (381). Cumberland is clearly ruling out any agent-relative standard that gives each agent a different target effect or state, and so a different end. What is needed for there to be a common standard of practical reason is for there to be a *common end*.

"*Reason* will not suffer," Cumberland says, "that the greatest *Private* Good should be propos'd as the *ultimate End*" (529). Were that so, "*Actions* truly *Good* will be in *mutual opposition* to one another, which is impossible" (529). When people's goods conflict, moreover, "there is no Cause, why the Happiness of any one of these [say, the agent themselves] should be his ultimate End, rather than the Happiness of another should likewise be his ultimate End" (529). Cumberland therefore concludes that

> Reason dictates to neither, that he should propose to himself his own Happiness only, as his greatest End, but to every one, rather his own in conjunction with the Happiness of others; and this is that *Common Good*, which we contend is to be sought after (529).

This is a line of reasoning that is similar to Sidgwick's leading to his principle of Rational Benevolence, which comes from the thought that "the good of any one individual is of no more importance from ... the point of view of the Universe." And it is similar also to Moore's famous "refutation" of egoism in *Principia Ethica* (Sidgwick 1967: 381; Moore, 1993: 99–102). Of course, neither Sidgwick nor Moore are ethical naturalists, but otherwise Cumberland's idea is very similar.

For Cumberland, there is one fundamental ethical standard, the good, more precisely, the goodness of states of the world or "effects." Whether conduct is justified, dictated by practical reason, depends on the goodness of its effects, and others' goods are no less good than is the agent's own. It follows that reason must dictate to every agent that they pursue their own good "in conjunction with the Happiness of others." "Let *Hobbes* tell me," Cumberland writes, "what the addition of a *proper name* does, toward making the former Proposition [that each act only for their own self-preservation] a *more evident* Dictate of Reason," than that each should promote the happiness of all (Cumberland 2005: 532). What Cumberland is objecting to, of course, is not really Hobbes's use of proper names; that might be ruled out as inappropriately particularistic in a universal norm. It is, rather, Hobbes's use of the reflexive first-person pronoun. The ruling out of agent-relativity is a deep feature of a view of practical reason that takes the goodness (*simpliciter*) of an effect as what most fundamentally underlies there being reason to aim at it.

Cumberland concludes that the "common Good is the best and greatest End, which [rational beings] can propose to themselves" (269). There are, again, three steps that lead Cumberland to this conclusion. The first is that the best end is the best *effect*, the best state of affairs producible by any act in the agent's power. The second is the reductive naturalist move that the goodness of a state is constituted by the natural goods of individuals. Thus, once he has established the two theses, Cumberland thinks he has a very short argument (his third step) for the conclusion that practical reason dictates promoting the greatest aggregate good:

> "The Happiness of All is greater than the like Happiness of any smaller Number." But "that Happiness is greatest, which is greater than any other assignable." Nor is it a different Judgment, that by which we *affirm*, "The greatest Happiness of all Rational Beings is the greatest or chief End, which any Rational Agent can pursue" (537).

"The greatest overall happiness," is, if you like, the naturalistic content of "best end." Cumberland says that his "*Method*" is to show "[h]ow to reduce whatsoever the Moralists have said concerning the Means of obtaining the best End into *Theorems* concerning the *Power* of human Actions in producing the Effects propos'd" (259). Once "best end" is interpreted naturalistically as "greatest overall happiness," natural philosophy suffices to establish truths concerning what will best promote it. Importantly, Cumberland notes that the "happiness of all" provides a *common public standard* of action to which every moral agent has access. He explicitly contrasts this standard with Aristotelian practical wisdom, which only the virtuous can achieve (275).[23]

Obligation, Reconsidered

If any ideas are likely to prove resistant to Cumberland's program of naturalist reduction, they are the deontic ideas of authority, right, and obligation. How are we to understand the law of nature as genuinely obligating law?

---

[23] On this point, see Heydt 2014: 19.

Cumberland is formally a theological voluntarist, holding that anything with the form of law requires both competent promulgation and authoritative sanctions. These aspects of his view, however, appear ultimately to be removable formal scaffolding.

This is revealed in his view of the source of God's authority or right of rule. Cumberland says that he used, "as most others do, to deduce the Divine Dominion intirely from his being the Creator" (672). This, of course, is Locke's view, as it is in essentials, Pufendorf's also. But Cumberland tells us that he came to realize that "all Right is a Power granted or permitted by some Law ... But Law there is none prior to the *Natural* Law, of that *Dictate* of the Divine *Wisdom*, concerning the *Best End*, and the *Means* thereto *necessary*" (672). The ground for God's right that we obey the law of nature is simply *that it is the law of nature*, that it indicates the "*Best End*, and the *Means* thereto *necessary*." Indeed, Cumberland holds that we can judge the truth and bindingness of the law of nature for ourselves: "*God will determine the same End and Means* to be *best*, which the *Reason of any Man truly judges to be so*" (537). Once we have determined that the best end is the good of all, and that benevolence is the best means to our necessary end,

> there is no room to *doubt*, but that we shall *here also have God's concurrence*. For, since He himself is *Rational*, and it cannot be conceiv'd, how he can act *rationally, without* proposing an *End* to himself, nor can there be a *greater* End than the aforesaid *Aggregate of all Good Things*; we cannot but think, he judges this to be the best End that he can propose to himself (537–538).

Cumberland goes so far, indeed, as to say that we "believe the sacred Scriptures to be the Word of God, the Author of Nature, *because* they every where illustrated, confirm, and promote the Law of Nature" (281).

In the end, Cumberland's position has the effect of making not just God's authority epiphenomenal, but the very ideas of right, obligation, and authority epiphenomenal also. In his view, there simply is no genuine normative standard or "dictate of practical reason" that is independent of the good. "There is nothing that can superinduce a *Necessity* of doing or forbearing anything, upon a Human Mind deliberating upon a thing future, except Thoughts or *Propositions* promising Good or Evil, to ourselves or others, consequent upon what we are about to do" (554).

Ultimately, therefore, there are three reductionist programs represented in Cumberland. We have mentioned two before: reductive naturalism and the reduction of moral norms or laws of nature to Cumberland's one utilitarian formulation. But there is also a third, namely, Cumberland's project of cloaking his thought in the deontic terms of the right that are characteristic of modern moral philosophy while nonetheless maintaining that these terms can ultimately be explained away so that ultimately there is only one final normative standard: the good, which can be given the naturalistic interpretation he proposes. Later moral philosophers took up all three of these projects. In the next chapter, we turn to the thought of thinkers who, whether they were prepared to think deontic thoughts or not, nonetheless were all profoundly critical of the early modern natural law tradition we have been investigating to this point.

4

Spinoza, Cudworth, Shaftesbury, and Leibniz

All the philosophers we have considered to this point have been representatives of the early modern natural law tradition. The seventeenth-century natural lawyers conceived of morality in fundamentally deontic or juridical terms, and they attempted to explain morality's power to obligate in ways that might link satisfactorily with complementary theories of accountable moral agency and practical reason. Although there were non-voluntarist versions – Grotius's and, in some ways, Cumberland's – the most influential forms were voluntarist, mostly theological voluntarisms of the sort defended by Locke and Pufendorf.

In this chapter, we consider a group of philosophers who formed their views in opposition to voluntarist natural law. Although there are important differences between Baruch (Bento or Benedict) Spinoza (1632–1677), Ralph Cudworth (1617–1688), Anthony Ashley Cooper (the 3rd Earl of Shaftesbury (1671–1713)), and Gottfried Wilhelm Leibniz (1646–1714), all four were united by their opposition to voluntarism.[1] For voluntarists, even natural law is a kind of positive law since it is created by God's discretionary imposition. Against this, Cudworth complained that voluntarism makes morality "positive, arbitrary and factitious only" and unable to explain morality's "eternal and immutable" character (Cudworth 1996: I.i.1). Fundamental moral truths such as the wrongness of gratuitously harming an innocent do not simply happen to obtain; they hold independently of the contingencies of any possible world. Neither can morality depend on discretionary legislation, even God's. What makes such an act wrong is the kind of act it is; an act cannot be made wrong "by will," but only by "its own nature" (I.ii.3).

Cudworth also complained about the way natural law theories tend to focus on external conduct rather than on internal motive and character. He contrasts a *"dead Law of outward Works"* with the "inward *Soul* and *Principle of Divine*

---

[1] All but Spinoza were united also by their personal and intellectual connections to Ralph Cudworth's daughter, Damaris Cudworth Masham (1659–1708). As noted in the last chapter, it was likely because of Masham that Locke learned of Cudworth's views on autonomy and freedom of the will. Locke was also a close mentor of Shaftesbury and introduced him to Masham. Finally, Masham also had a philosophical correspondence with Leibniz. See Broad 2006 and Hutton 1993.

Life ... that enliveneth and quickeneth ... all our outward Performances" (1969: 123). Although Cudworth is anxious also to account for morality's power to obligate, and to provide an account of self-determining moral agency he argues to be necessary for moral accountability and obligation, he nonetheless understands morality as most fundamentally involving the virtuous human capacity to manifest and share God's *love* (the "*Principle of Divine Life*"). Indeed, Cudworth ties morality and love together. The moral law is ultimately a "law of love" (124). And the "moral free will" that Cudworth holds to be necessary for accountable moral agency essentially includes the capacity for love.

Recall Locke's view of self-determination as the capacity to step back from desires, form a judgment of what will bring the agent the greatest long-run pleasure, and then act on that considered judgment. Like Locke, Cudworth holds that free will involves self-conscious practical judgment.[2] But the Lockean form that judges "private utility" Cudworth calls "animal free will," and Cudworth holds that this is insufficient for accountable moral agency (~1670: 4980.171, 4982.89). "Moral free will" requires, "besides the spring of animal life," that we also have a "spring or principle of another superior intellectual life," namely, the "love or charity" that is the "life and soul of all morality" (~1670: 4982.20; 1678: I.iv.9).

In turning from natural law's focus on conduct to motive, character, and virtue, Cudworth provided an alternative to the law conception that resonated with Shaftesbury and Leibniz. Like Cudworth, Shaftesbury and Leibniz argue that theological voluntarism is powerless to explain God's own goodness or justice as deriving from God's commands (Shaftesbury 2001: I.iii.2.49; Leibniz 1988: 64–75). And Leibniz echoes Cudworth's complaint that voluntarism could not explain morality's "eternal truths" (Leibniz 1988: 71).

For Shaftesbury and Leibniz, Cudworth's most important move, though, was his change in focus from act to motive, and specifically, to love. Shaftesbury writes in his Preface to the *Sermons* of Cudworth's fellow Cambridge Platonist Benjamin Whichcote that "it is unaccountable that men who profess a religion where *love* is chiefly enjoined, where the heart is expressly called for, and outward action without that is disregarded ... should combine to degrade the principle of good nature, and refer all to reward" (Shaftesbury 1698).

Whereas Leibniz's anti-positivism was provoked by Pufendorf, Shaftesbury's was prompted by Locke. Shaftesbury objects against Locke that by arguing that human moral conduct is possible only through divine sanctions, Locke "struck at all fundamentals, threw all order and virtue out of the world" (1900: 403). Similarly, Leibniz complains against Pufendorf that a morally good person is

---

[2] Indeed, as I suggested in the last chapter, there is reason to think that Locke was influenced to adopt this view by his exposure to Cudworth's ideas, either directly by Cudworth's manuscripts on freedom of the will or by conversation with Damaris Cudworth Masham.

not one who simply performs certain "external acts." He does what is good and right, "not out of hope or fear" of sanctions, but from a core "inclination of his soul," "love for God or ... neighbor" (Leibniz 1988: 72, 73).

Even more than Cudworth, Shaftesbury puts forward an ethics of virtue in opposition to an ethics of law, one that provides a model for the later virtue ethics of Hutcheson and Hume. And Shaftesbury's thought inspired Hume's and Hutcheson's in yet a further way. Hume is famous for his doctrine that "moral distinctions [are] not derived from reason," but "from a moral sense" (Hume 1978: 455, 470). The phrase "moral sense" comes into Hume's thought most directly from Hutcheson, who made his theory of the moral sense the foundation of his moral philosophy. However, Hutcheson took the phrase "moral sense" from Shaftesbury (Shaftesbury 2001: II.46).

In Hutcheson and Hume's hands, the idea of a moral sense or sentiment is deployed in opposition to eighteenth-century forms of ethical rationalism, represented in the English context by contemporaries like Samuel Clarke, John Balguy, William Wollaston, and, later, Richard Price. But the debates between rationalism and sentimentalism that were a staple of eighteenth-century moral philosophy were much more sharply focused than anything we can find in the earlier philosophers investigated in this chapter. Cudworth, Shaftesbury, and Leibniz can fruitfully be seen as important bridge figures between early modern natural law and the eighteenth-century rationalists and sentimentalists. The latter's sharply drawn distinctions were much more muted in the earlier writers.

Cudworth was an important influence on Richard Price. But Price and the other British rationalists were more clearly rational intuitionists, and their ethical theorizing took a more deontological form. Where Cudworth identified moral reason with an essentially practical form of love, the eighteenth-century rationalists tended to see it as an intuitive perception or cognition of deontic moral truths or facts. Their sentimentalist opponents found Cudworth's virtue-centered approach much more to their liking than the deontological theories of the eighteenth-century British rationalists.

Similarly, when Shaftesbury talked of a "moral sense," he did not mean to distinguish it from reason, as his followers Hutcheson and Hume would. To the contrary, Shaftesbury's thought was much closer to that of Cambridge Platonists like Cudworth and Whichcote, who tended to blur lines between the rational and the affective. Like the Cambridge Platonists, Shaftesbury argues that moral goodness is ultimately grounded in creative and practical powers that are intrinsic to the mind. Here again, we find thinkers we investigate in this chapter functioning as bridge figures to later writers who develop one or another aspect of their thought in a more single-minded way.

For his part, Spinoza is also a bridge figure, but of an importantly different kind. In many ways, Spinoza stands apart from the main trends of moral philosophy in the seventeenth and eighteenth centuries. He does not so much bridge developments within early modern ethics as form a bridge from modern ethical thought back to premodern Aristotelian naturalist forms and forward to later ethical philosophers like Nietzsche. Not that Spinoza is an Aristotelian. Like Hobbes, Spinoza rejects final causes and a human *telos*. Also, freedom plays a central role in his thought that it did not for the ancients. Spinoza is a *eudaimonist*, however, indeed a perfectionist *eudaimonist,* like Aristotle. His is an ethics of virtue that ultimately identifies all of the following: knowledge, virtue, right, and well-being. Also like Aristotelian naturalists, Spinoza claims that virtue promotes the *common* good, thereby unifying personal and impartial good, and rejecting the modern division between them (Spinoza 1985a: 128).[3]

Spinoza is a unifier *par excellence*. He is, first and foremost, a systematic metaphysician who presents his views in *more geometrico*. And his metaphysics does not simply ground his ethics. Since, for Spinoza, all ethical concepts are ultimately metaphysical, every ethical claim he makes is really a metaphysical claim. Spinoza's "ethics" consists of metaphysical propositions expressed with ethical language. And his metaphysics is obviously unified also; it is a form of metaphysical monism. Spinoza believes that there is only one substance – Nature with its necessary laws – and that all other metaphysical categories – for example, properties and what we take to be the (Aristotelian) substances that instantiate them – are either attributes of Nature or modes of those attributes.

The most obvious contrast is with Descartes's dualism. For Spinoza, consciousness and extension are not properties of distinct substances, mind and matter, but attributes of one and the same substance (Nature). And individual thinking beings and extended bodies are modes of these different attributes, respectively. Natural necessities and causal relations obtain within attributes but not across them. Thus, causal relations are impossible between mental and bodily phenomena. Bodies and minds are modes of fundamentally distinct attributes of the same substance.

Spinoza titled his great metaphysical work *Ethics*, but this is something of a misnomer, since relatively little of it is focused on traditional ethical questions, not to mention issues of deontic morality. Spinoza recognizes, as we shall see, no concept of moral obligation or right that is distinct from that of the good. And his theorizing about the good life (alternatively, "virtue" or "perfection") is, again, reducible to propositions of metaphysics.

This is perhaps clearest in Spinoza's account of perfection. Typically, perfectionists like Aristotle or Aquinas advance their views in irreducibly teleological terms that set ideals of perfection for different natural (teleological) kinds. But Spinoza thinks this involves a fundamental metaphysical error, since "Nature

---

[3] For the role of the common good in Aristotelian naturalists, see Irwin 2007: 515–619; 2008: 66–67.

does nothing on account of an end" (1985: 544). Spinoza does think that every natural thing has a directed nature, what he calls a *conatus* or "striving." But this just means that everything has a nature that is expressible in natural laws of efficient causation, rather than involving anything like final causation in Aristotle's sense.

For Spinoza, there are (naturally necessary) truths about how every natural thing will tend to behave if it is not perturbed by external causes acting on it. What it is for something to be perfect in the sense in which Spinoza is concerned in his ethical writings, then, is simply for the process of its striving in this efficient causal sense to be unimpeded. This makes perfection, as Curley notes, "a nonevaluative, metaphysical" notion (Spinoza 1985b: 650). "By perfection," Spinoza says, "I understand only reality," hence nothing about how reality is not and ought to be (252).

Thus not only, as we shall see, does Spinoza not recognize any notion of right that is distinct from that of good, but so also are all ethical (or other normative) notions ultimately metaphysical for him. Far from facing the problem of how to account for distinct normativities of right and good, therefore, Spinoza sidesteps the whole problem. Nothing in his thought corresponds to normativity as ethical philosophers normally conceive it. There are no oughts, only is's.

Spinoza is especially skeptical of morality as it is conceived by modern moral philosophers. He rejects deontic moral notions, the psychological attitudes he takes to be connected to them (like indignation and blame), and the presuppositions of free will they require. Like theological voluntarists, he takes these all to be most at home when tied to a doctrine of eternal sanctions. But he rejects the personal God that doctrine requires. Moreover, differently from Pufendorf, he takes the requisite sanctions not to be tied to a sense of their justifiability that can motivate, but only to motivation through fear. Far from realizing moral virtue, conduct that is motivated in this way is, by definition, imperfect, unfree, and, strictly speaking, as we shall see, a matter of "passion" rather than our own "action" (493, 497).

Like Nietzsche, who acknowledges Spinoza's influence in this respect, Spinoza both decisively rejects the doctrine of free will necessary for deontic morality and diagnoses the latter as unhealthy, what Nietzsche will call an "illness" (Nietzsche 2007: 7). We will see resonances of this latter idea also in Shaftesbury and Hume. Arguably, Spinoza begins a kind of naturalistic critique of deontic morality that runs through Hume, Nietzsche, and into the twentieth century with Foot, Williams, and Annette Baier (Foot 2002; Williams 1985; Baier 1993). Although in many ways he is a bridge to premodern ethics, in others, he can seem the most modern thinker discussed in this book.

Perhaps Spinoza's greatest influence outside his metaphysics was his massive effect on eighteenth-century political philosophy. As Jonathan Israel has shown, Spinoza provided much of the inspiration for a democratic, egalitarian, libertarian movement of political thought that Israel calls the "Radical Enlightenment" (Israel 2001). The central work here is Spinoza's *Theological-Political Treatise*, which sets out Spinoza's democratic views. As we are interested in Spinoza's ethics, we will consider his democratic politics less for their own sake than for their grounding in Spinoza's ethical and metaphysical views.

Spinoza

What seemed most radical to Spinoza's contemporaries was his atheism. Spinoza rejected this characterization himself. Indeed, on Spinoza's definition – "a substance consisting of an infinity of attributes" – God is foundational for his metaphysics (Spinoza 1985b: 409). "God" is Spinoza's term for the one necessarily existing substance, which Spinoza also calls "Nature," and whose necessary essence determines everything, from the motion of the tiniest physical particle to the most brilliant cogitations and courageous actions of human beings (549).

Spinoza thus denied the orthodoxy of Christian Europe and of his own Jewish immigrant community in Amsterdam. That this made Spinoza an outsider is an understatement, as Spinoza was ultimately excluded even from his own community.[4] Spinoza thus became an outsider even to a group that were perennially excluded themselves. And the situation was more complicated still. The Portuguese Jews of Amsterdam had suffered through the Inquisition in Portugal, surviving largely as *conversos*, or converts to Christianity, at least publicly. Those, like Spinoza's family, who wished to continue to live as Jews, could do so only secretly until they were forced to emigrate from Portugal. This required them to manage two identities simultaneously – a public Christian persona and a private Jewish one. Yovel plausibly claims that this cultural experience carried seeds of the liberalism we find in Spinoza's thought (Yovel 1992). Liberal separation of church and state became a central tenet of the Radical Enlightenment and the political philosophy that followed in its wake, culminating, perhaps, in Rawls's *Political Liberalism* at the end of the twentieth century (Rawls 1993).

Against Deontic Morality: Religious or Secular

Despite these liberal aspects, there were elements of Spinoza's thought that cut against the main lines of the modern conception of morality that was so important for the Radical Enlightenment. There can be natural rights, after all, only if there are natural duties, and for most philosophers of the early modern period, duties are conceptually connected to accountability and, for many, to divine punishment. On the orthodox view, God punishes wrongdoers who (freely)

---

[4] For an excellent account of this and Spinoza's life more generally, see Nadler 2018.

violate his law. For theological voluntarists like Pufendorf and Locke, the very existence of morality depends on God's superior authority to hold human beings accountable. Spinoza denies that any such personal God can possibly exist, however. Where orthodoxy defines God as "omniscient, omnipotent, ... [and] infinite[ly] compassion[ate]" (Spinoza 1985a: 88), Spinoza claims that none of these properties can hold of a necessarily existing substance:

> [T]hese things [properties] are only certain modes of the thinking thing ... [and] can neither be nor be understood without that substance of which they are modes. That is why they cannot be attributed to him, who is a being existing of himself, without anything else (89).

Spinoza's "him" and "himself" retain the cover of his claim to theism, but his argument ensures that anyone convinced by it can no longer be an orthodox Christian or Jew.

Thought and extension, for Spinoza, are attributes that necessarily presuppose a substance, Nature, to which they apply. Individual thinking and extended things are nothing but modes of these attributes, as are all mental and bodily phenomena. It follows that any particular action or willing that orthodoxy supposes to be instantiated by God and human beings, respectively, cannot have the properties orthodoxy attributes to them, including the authority relations that voluntarists like Locke and Pufendorf hold to be necessary for the existence of deontic morality. Even non-voluntarists like Cudworth and Leibniz must therefore be mistaken in thinking that God could be a perfectly loving mind who wishes his creatures well and, therefore, that they act in ways that will promote their good.

A second blow against orthodox doctrine was what Spinoza's critics called his "fatalism." All natural events are necessarily determined by earlier ones in accordance with natural law, including human actions that modern moralists take to result from free will. Against this, Spinoza's correspondent, Henry Oldenburg, complained that it makes deontic morality's connection to accountability impossible to justify.

> You appear to postulate a fatalistic necessity in all things and actions. If this is conceded and affirmed, they say, the sinews of all laws, all virtue and religion are severed, and all rewards and punishments are pointless. ... [N]o one will thus be without excuse in the sight of God (quoted in Nadler 2006: 84).

There is yet a third respect in which Spinoza's *Ethics* threatened modern orthodoxy, both religious and secular versions. It is a central plank of modern thought that moral conduct expresses our nature as *free* moral *agents*. On Spinoza's metaphysics and moral psychology, however, the only motive that sanctions can create is fear, whether the sanctions are divine or secular. And any conduct that is motivated by fear, according to Spinoza, cannot be self-determined or even an instance of willed "*action*," properly speaking: something we really *do*. As we shall see, Spinoza holds it to be an instance of "*passion*" in which we are "acted upon" by things external to us. Action takes place only "when something happens, in us or outside us, of which we are the adequate cause" (Spinoza 1985b: 493).

On the mainstream view, when we avoid wrongdoing because it would be wrong, we exercise our capacity for autonomous moral agency. Spinoza turns this view on its head. He thinks we are most *unfree*, and do not strictly speaking even act at all, when we are motivated by accountability concerns, since these are realized in our psychic economy only through fear, a passion that puts us in "bondage" rather than enabling free action (505, 548). Unlike Pufendorf and Cudworth, Spinoza lacks anything like conscience in his moral psychology.

Other passions that Spinoza takes to be involved in deontic morality are even more toxic: blame, indignation, and – he holds – hate, anticipating Nietzsche. "Indignation is Hate toward someone who has done evil to another," and "[h]ate can never be good" (535, 571). Indignation, blame, hate, and the like are all negative emotions and can have no intrinsic value.

We feel these negative emotions, moreover, only through our own ignorance. When we fully understand someone's behavior – someone else's or our own – we cannot really be angry with them, since their behavior is simply the necessary result of the one necessarily existing substance; indeed, their behavior is the causal consequence of factors outside of them rather than their own actions. True knowledge yields "true love of one's fellow man, which ... disposes us so that we never hate him, or are angry with him, but are instead inclined to help him and bring him into a better condition" (1985a: 128).

"Remorse and Repentance," Spinoza says, "occur only by surprise" (114). It is impossible for us to grasp that something is good and not do it. If it turns out not to be good, its lack of goodness must take us "by surprise." Moreover, there is nothing good in these feelings themselves. "[O]n the contrary," they are "injurious [in themselves], and consequently evil ... and to be shunned and fled" (115). Here again, Spinoza sounds themes that will be developed by Nietzsche. Indeed, many elements of Spinoza's ethics – including his doctrine of *conatus* and power, his critique of deontic morality and freedom of the will, and his emphasis on value as positive and bad as lack or privation ("perfection" as "reality") – find later expression in Nietzsche. When Nietzsche first discovered Spinoza's writings, he wrote to a friend, "I have a forerunner. And what a forerunner" (quoted in Young 2010: 319).

There are, however, significant differences between Spinoza and Nietzsche. One of the most striking is what we might call the "flatness" of Spinoza's moral psychology in contrast with the depth of Nietzsche's. There is nothing in Spinoza like *ressentiment* or Nietzsche's "dark workshop" of the unconscious. And complex and turbulent emotions like hatred and jealousy, which Nietzsche reveals to be tortuously and torturously targeted in the human psyche, are significantly simplified and compressed in Spinoza's psychology. "Blame," for example, is *"the Sadness with which we are averse to [someone's] action"* (Spinoza 1985b: 510). "Hate" is "Sadness, accompanied also by the idea of an external cause" (511), and *"Jealousy ... is ... nothing but a vacillation of mind born of Love and Hatred together, accompanied by the idea of another who is envied"* (514). "Sadness," moreover, is simply Spinoza's term for the most general negative response to the transition from a more to a less perfect state *of oneself* (500). All things considered, one feels it likelier that Nietzsche does justice to the subtlety, complexity, and depths of the human psyche than that Spinoza does.

The Good: Knowledge, Power, and Perfection

We turn now to Spinoza on the good. In the end, something's being good and its being determined by the laws of its nature amount to the same thing for Spinoza. "[N]othing happens in nature which can be attributed to any defect in it" (492). Every occurrence is determined by Substance's necessary nature, and every natural thing's *conatus* determines it to remain in existence as the natural thing it is. When something is realized in this natural-law-determined sense, it is thereby "perfected," independently of any telos or end. This, however, can be impeded by other things and their contrary strivings; and when that occurs, there is necessarily imperfection or bad, which is simply the lack of perfection or good. There is no such thing as intrinsic badness, for Spinoza, just the lack of intrinsic goodness.

When bad occurs for some natural thing, that means that some other thing or things impede its perfection but thereby perfect themselves. "[G]ood and evil are nothing but relations" (1985a: 92).

> [G]ood and evil, say Peter's goodness and Judas's evil, have no definitions apart from the [particular] essence[s] of Judas and Peter, for these [essences] alone [a]re in Nature, and without them [the goodness of Peter and the evil of Judas] cannot be defined (93).[5]

When bad for one thing occurs, good must occur for others. And the good of the system of Nature as a whole is always necessarily continuously realized, since that just consists in everything's being determined by its necessary nature.

Spinoza realizes, like Hobbes, however, that even if "good and evil are not things ... which are in Nature," we speak and think as though they are. And he has, also like Hobbes, an error theory that explains why we do. Spinoza and Hobbes agree that the language of good and evil (bad), and thoughts we formulate with it, are expressions of practical states of mind. Hobbes holds, recall,

---

[5] See Curley's note at 1985a: 93n.

that whatever we desire, we call good (Hobbes 1994a: VI.7). Similarly, Spinoza says that "each one, from his own affect, judges, *or* evaluates, what is good and what is bad" (Spinoza 1985b: 516). And even more emphatically:

> [W]e neither strive for, nor will, neither want, nor desire anything because we judge it to be good; on the contrary, we judge something to be good because we strive for it, will it, want it, or desire it (500).

Hobbes's projectivist account of value judgment is more detailed (and explicitly modeled on his Galilean account of color) than Spinoza's is; but in essentials, they are the same. We speak and think with the concepts of good and evil when we have desires and aversions. These practical states of mind include seeing their objects as good and bad *themselves*.

Something that is distinctive in Spinoza, and absent from Hobbes, however, is an account of objective good that is projected by *will* rather than by desire. We will consider this distinction in more detail below when we examine Spinoza's views on the kind of freedom the will realizes in contrast with the bondage of desire and appetite, and will's relation to knowledge and ignorance. The relevant point here is that although for Hobbes, will is simply the "last appetite" before action, Spinoza distinguishes between appetites and desires, and the behavior they cause, on the one hand, and will and *action*, in his distinctive senses, on the other. And he makes a related distinction between *apparent good* and *objective good*.[6] Spinoza's distinction between will and desire is based on a distinction between practical states that are grounded in knowledge and understanding and those that are not. Spinoza defines "Will" as a thing's "striving" when it is "related only to the Mind" or "Intellect" and is based on "adequate" rather than "inadequate" or "confused" ideas of its object (498–500).

Guided only by the Intellect, the Will is informed by "clear and distinct ideas," whereas desires and appetites are based on "confused ideas" (499). Will and genuine action are informed by the Intellect and its clear view of Nature. Unlike Descartes, from whom the language of "clear and distinct" obviously derives, and who distinguishes between will and intellect, Spinoza holds that no such distinction exists (Della Rocca 2008: 23, 134). The Mind or Intellect has its own striving, and that is what Spinoza means by "Will." There is no real distinction between Will and Intellect for Spinoza.

This makes possible a companion account of real or objective good in contrast with the apparent good projected by desires and appetites. Objective good is what we see the objects of will as having when we have adequate ideas of their real (non-ethical) nature, and (merely) apparent good is what we see the objects of desire as having when we have confused ideas of their

---

[6] These are my terms, not Spinoza's.

nature.[7] This account is still projectivist; it denies that there are any value properties (that are not reducible to natural non-evaluative properties) in nature. And it remains relational: objective goodness is always in relation to individual beings. "[G]ood and evil" are thus "nothing but relations" (Spinoza 1985a: 92). Objective goodness is the property that the will projects onto its objects, where will is the practical attitude that is based on an adequate intellectual grasp of its objects' real (non-ethical) nature. Obviously, this latter grasp cannot involve projection itself.

But although objective good is relational, Spinoza holds that objective good is universal with respect to the beings who share a nature. We humans all individually will the completion or perfection of human nature *in ourselves*.

> I shall understand by good what we know certainly is a means by which we may approach nearer and nearer to the model of human nature that we set before ourselves. By evil, what we certainly know prevents us from becoming like that model (1985b).

By "model of human nature," Spinoza cannot mean some ideal at which we *ought* to aim in an irreducibly normative sense. There are, again, no oughts that are not reducible to is's. A "model of human nature" is simply a fact about what one's intellectual striving *would* lead to were it not impeded by the strivings of others, where that includes not just other human beings, but anything external to us whatsoever. Spinoza identifies human perfection, so understood, with "virtue" and "power," which he defines as perfection; "insofar as we attribute something to them ... that involves ... lack of power," "we call them imperfect" (545). As Nadler notes, "we can set up the following equation for Spinoza: virtue=knowledge=activity=freedom=power=perfection" (Nadler 2006: 256).

Here again are ideas from which Nietzsche will obviously draw. Everything, Spinoza thinks, has a *conatus* for power that Nietzsche will call the "will to power." For Spinoza, this only counts as "will," properly so called, when it is the conatus of Mind or Intellect, which necessarily realizes freedom and overcomes the bondage of appetites and non-intellectual affections. But this also is a doctrine with which Nietzsche will largely agree; it is only when we grasp the way nature actually works, and the genealogy of our own ideas and desires, Nietzsche holds, that we can throw off the superstitious, shackling, and unhealthy modern notion of morality and become genuinely free and autonomous. All of this – together with the idea that good is essentially positive and that bad is merely its lack – Nietzsche gets from Spinoza.

Even though objective good involves a "model of human nature," it remains an agent-relative, *eudaimonist* concept. Spinoza has no notion of agent-neutral

---

[7] Cf. the discussion of Hutcheson's distinction between calm desires and passions and his related accounts of the good in Chapter 5.

or of impartial good – what Hutcheson will term "public good," what Sidgwick will call "good from the point of view of the universe," or what Moore will dub, "intrinsic value" (Hutcheson 2004: 102; Sidgwick 1967: 381; Moore 1993). It is consistent with objective good in Spinoza's *eudaimonist* sense that our objective goods might be irremediably at odds. If human nature were essentially competitive, then it would simply be impossible for human virtue, power, and perfection to be realized jointly. If any were to realize the perfection and power toward which their *conatus* tends, it would be at the cost of others not realizing their objective goods.

Spinoza's solution to this problem is like that of Aristotelian naturalists. Human nature is essentially *non*-competitive, and much of what is good for human beings is good for us in *common*. Spinoza accepts Aristotle's characterization of human beings as social animals (Spinoza 1985b: 564). No one seems more excellent to us, Spinoza says, "than those that agree entirely with our nature." When "two individuals" work together, they "compose an individual twice as powerful as each one." Therefore, "to man, then, there is nothing more useful than man" (556).

> Man ... can wish for nothing more helpful to the preservation of his being than that all should so agree in all things that the Minds and Bodies of all would compose, as it were, one Mind and one Body; that all should strive together, as far as they can, to preserve their being; and that all, together, should seek for themselves the common advantage of all (556).

Given our common intellectual nature, each of us will realize our own virtue, perfection, good, and power only if we can do so together.

Revised Deontic Moral Concepts and Democratic Politics

Presently, we will consider how Spinoza's idea of the common good underlies his democratic political philosophy. First, however, we should see how Spinoza provides a revisionary account of deontic moral concepts, one that is not unlike similarly subversive accounts in Shaftesbury, Leibniz, Hutcheson, and Hume.

Again, as Israel emphasizes, Spinoza's democratic politics were especially important for the Radical Enlightenment, and, as we noted, deontic morality was an essential companion to Enlightenment ideas of natural rights. For Spinoza's views to be maximally helpful for the Radical Enlightenment, therefore, it was essential that Spinoza have non-deontic replacements that could do the conceptual work of natural duties and rights within his non-deontic ethical framework.

Because Spinoza is a thoroughgoing monist, he cannot accept that good and right are fundamentally distinct ethical notions, a distinction Sidgwick claimed as a mark of modern moral thought. For Spinoza, there can be only one ethical notion, the good, understood *eudaimonistically*. And even that must be identified with the metaphysical fact of a thing realizing its natural tendencies, unimpeded by others' natural strivings. What Spinoza calls "ethics" is ultimately a non-normative subject, part of metaphysics.

What is at issue here, however, is the connection between the good, as Spinoza theorizes it, and the concept of right or moral duty, both as it functions within moral and political philosophy and as Spinoza can understand it within his framework. Here is a helpful passage for seeing how Spinoza attempts to do this:

> [H]uman power is very limited and infinitely surpassed by the power of external causes. So we do not have an absolute power to adapt things outside us to our use. Nevertheless, we shall bear calmly those things which happen to us contrary to what the principle of our advantage demands, if we are conscious that we have done our duty, that the power we have could not have extended itself to the point where we could have avoided those things, and that we are a part of the whole of nature, whose order we follow (594).

Note, first, Spinoza's language of "demands" and "duty," and his saying that the demand in question comes from "our advantage," as is required if moral duty is ultimately to be understood *eudaimonistically*. Next note a distinction that Spinoza implies that is similar to a familiar distinction within moral philosophy between subjective and objective duty or rightness.

What is objectively right is whatever would realize our greatest good if our actions were not impeded. Since, however, we are only "a part of the whole of nature," others may frustrate our best efforts (as might also imperfect information and perhaps yet other things). So we should "bear calmly" when things don't proceed as planned. When we do our best, given the obstacles we could reckon on, Spinoza says, "we have done our duty." Of course, we will not necessarily have done what was objectively right in the sense of what would have brought about our greatest good absent these obstacles. So Spinoza must be here intending "duty" in a different, more subjective sense.

However this might be worked out in detail, several things emerge from this passage. Most obviously, Spinoza understands (objective) duty in terms of actions that are necessary to bring about the perfection of the agent's nature, where this is simply what the agent themselves would bring about if their efforts were not impeded by "external causes." This is "what the principle of our advantage demands" or, as he says elsewhere, "what reason prescribes to us" (555, 594). Moreover, such action is *naturally* (hence, for Spinoza, rationally) necessary – the only non-normative sense of "necessity" that Spinoza recognizes – in two distinct ways. It is, first, causally necessary in order to achieve the agent's perfection; it is a necessary means. And second, it is naturally necessary that a perfect agent *would* take the requisite action and that it would achieve the agent's perfection, were there no impediments to its doing so. That is a naturally necessary truth.

In this way, Spinoza achieves three conceptual reductions that reform the orthodox modern concept of moral duty or obligation. First, he reduces the idea of instrumental rationality to that of causally necessary means and naturally necessary action. Second, he reduces the idea of moral duty and obligation to that of an act's being instrumentally required to achieve the agent's good. And third, he reduces the (identical) notions of moral duty, virtue, perfection, and the agent's good to the aforementioned natural necessities. The right is reduced to the good and the good is reduced to the naturally necessary. There are no unreduced oughts, including the moral ought.

These identities are reflected in the following passage:

> For a perfect man is moved to help his fellow man only by necessity without any other cause. And therefore he finds himself all the more obliged to help ... [those who] have greater need ... (1985a: 117).

Significantly, this is a case of acting to benefit another in need. By definition, as we have seen, perfection concerns the realization of the agent's own good. This example thus illustrates Spinoza's view that since we are social, intellectual beings, our goods are common in ways they might otherwise not be. They are jointly realizable; so a perfect human realizes their own good in cases like this by responding to the greater needs of others. Moreover, the virtuous do what they do by natural "necessity." They simply do what they would do (if unimpeded) in accordance with the laws of their nature. They are thus "obliged." This can be seen as a version of Augustine's "Love and do what you want" (Augustine 1990: XIV.110). Spinoza's might read: "Understand (your nature) and do what you will."

This clearly reshapes the deontic concept of moral duty in a subversive way. It stipulates meanings for deontic vocabulary so that the concepts they express can fit within a *eudaimonistic* virtue ethics. We will see an identical move in two of Spinoza's rough contemporaries who are also critics of early modern natural law: Shaftesbury and Leibniz. Shaftesbury repurposes "obligation" to mean a reason provided for the agent's own good when he argues that agents have an "obligation to virtue" in the fact that they will live happier lives if they are virtuous (Shaftesbury 2001: II.i.2.173). Hutcheson and Hume, who follow Shaftesbury's moral sentimentalism, also follow him in this usage, which Hume dubs "interested obligation" (Hume 1975b: 278).

For his part, Leibniz understands moral obligation or "moral necessity" in a way that reduces the deontic concept to one involving (non-normative) natural necessity and *eudaimonist* virtue. Differently from Spinoza, and looking forward more to Hutcheson, Leibniz understands virtue in terms of benevolence or "charity." "Moral necessity," he says, "is equivalent to 'natural' for a good man" (Leibniz 1988: 171).[8] Unexpectedly, perhaps, we will find a similar usage in Kant.[9]

If we revise the concept of moral duty in the way we have outlined, we can see how Spinoza can ground his (suitably revised) democratic political philosophy in his *eudaimonist* ethical monism. The crucial element will be the conception of common good on display in the two passages last quoted. Individuals realize their own good in concert with others, and since Intellect is essential to the nature of each, the concert must be intellectual. Collective intellectual work in the political sphere is what democracy is: the people working out what to do in their common life by reasoning together. Thus Spinoza writes: "*A man who is guided by reason is more free in a state, where he lives according to common decision, than in solitude, where he obeys only himself*" (Spinoza 1985b: 587). We will see this same theme in Rousseau in Chapter 9.

It was Spinoza's *Theological-Political Treatise*, published anonymously in 1670, that set the democratic political agenda for the Radical Enlightenment (2016).[10] It is written in deontic, juridical terms without explicit instructions about how these are to be understood in Spinoza's revisionist lexicon. Spinoza's readers thus read its claims about natural right and its justification of the state in comparison with Hobbes's and likely interpreted their terms similarly. Two signal differences between their systems were Spinoza's championing of democracy and his claim that individuals need not give up their natural rights to establish the state, as against Hobbes's view that it takes a contract through which all lay down their natural rights to establish an absolute sovereign. What grounds both of Spinoza's positions is his monistic metaphysics along with his view of our intellectual collaborative nature.

"Bear[ing] Calmly" and "Living Blessedly": Spinoza on Freedom, Happiness, and Power

Spinoza tells us that "the Desire ... to live blessedly, *or* well, to act, etc. is the very essence of man" (1985b: 557–558). Spinoza's "etc." covers a lot. In addition to the items in Nadler's "identity – virtue=knowledge=activity=freedom=power= perfection, we could add happiness, and living and "bearing calmly" (Nadler 2006: 256). All are roughly identical for Spinoza. "[T]he foundation of virtue is this very striving to preserve one's own being, and ... happiness consists in man's being able to preserve his being" (Spinoza 1985b: 555–556). "Activity" is conduct that realizes our (intellectual) nature as we necessarily strive to do as

---

[8] Similarly, Leibniz defines justice as the "charity of the wise," thereby reducing justice to benevolence in a way that is like, but different from, Hutcheson (Leibniz 1988: 171). For Hutcheson, see the discussion in Chapter 5.
[9] See Chapter 8.
[10] See Jonathan Israel's introduction to Spinoza 2007 and Israel 2001.

the kind of beings we are. And this activity is, simultaneously, virtuous, perfecting, power exercising and power realizing, free, and that in which our happiness consists.

Spinoza's Hebrew name was "Baruch," or "blessed." Perhaps one of Spinoza's greatest achievements was to show how it is possible, both in theory and in practice, to "live blessedly" outside a religious context. In his own life, Spinoza faced extraordinary challenges. An excluded Jew who was officially separated from his own community in Amsterdam, he made his living as a lens grinder and died at the age of forty-four, probably from pulmonary tuberculosis brought on by the silica in glass dust (Nadler 2006: 407). By all accounts, however, Spinoza lived largely without complaint and unaffected by the negative passions and emotions that make it difficult to "bear" life "calmly." To put it in the reductive terms of our own age, Spinoza lived "positively," and didn't give in to "negative stuff."

If these contemporary terms seem overly simple or superficial, they are not far from Spinoza's own formulations. Somewhat like Hobbes, Spinoza has a taxonomy of the emotions that works with two valences, positive and negative "affect," with every passion or emotion, however complex, being composed of a combination of beliefs or imaginings and positive or negative affects toward the believed or imagined state. To take an example, Joy and Sadness, which are basic affects for Spinoza, are felt when "*the Mind passes to a greater perfection*" and when "*it passes to a lesser perfection*," respectively (1985b: 501). This is only one instance of how Spinoza's psychology flattens our internal life. Sadness in, say, the loss of a child hardly seems well captured by this formula. "Grief" does not appear in Spinoza's lexicon.

Similarly, "Hate" is simply "an inclination to avoid something which has caused some evil," which is only the privation of good, and "Hatred toward him who has done evil to another" is "Indignation" (1985a: 107; 1985b: 507). This significantly deflates both hatred and indignation, taking, as it were, the "fire" out of both.

Similarly with Love, which for Spinoza is simply a species of Joy "accompanied by the idea of an external cause" (1985b: 511). As Spinoza analyzes it, love is not really an attitude toward any being *for their sake*. Neither is it connected to deeply felt attitudes like joy, sadness, and grief on the beloved's behalf. Spinoza's love seems to lack the emotional depth of heartfelt human connection.

Throughout, it is important to bear in mind that Spinoza holds that negative emotions always involve the error of failing to understand the world as it really is. "Hate, then, the direct opposite of Love, arises from that error which comes from opinion" (1985a: 101). The way to "bear" things "calmly," therefore, is simply to *understand*, to perfect our intellectual nature, as we naturally strive to do. We are subject to passions or affects only when, not having exercised our intellectual powers, we have inadequate or confused ideas. Acting on such confusion is not really *action*, properly so called, nor does it result from will, again, properly so called. As such, "*[t]he Mind strives to imagine only those things that posit its power of acting*" (1985b: 525). Only good can come from our intellectual striving: perfection, action, virtue, happiness, and blessedness. And only bad from emotions and passions, including from love as we ordinarily understand it, namely, as involving emotional vulnerability to another.

Spinoza's view of the relation of reason, passion, and action is quite close to Hutcheson and Hume on the "calm" versus the "violent" passions, and Hume's famous claim that "reason is the slave of the passions" (Hutcheson 2002; Hume 1978: 415). Spinoza does hold that it is only through the Intellect that we are able to break the bondage of non-rational affects and realize free action, through our intellectual nature's being an "adequate cause" (Spinoza 1985b: 493). This may make it seem as if reason is the master, rather than the slave, of the passions, as Hume says. But there is no real difference with Hume. The doctrine that Hume opposes is the one we find in Plato and, among the moderns, in Butler and Kant, among many others, that reason is the faculty of normative judgment and that it can motivate, that there is such a thing as what Kant calls "practical reason."

Spinoza denies this doctrine also. What the Intellect grasps, according to Spinoza, is nothing normative; it grasps "laws of nature" rather than "laws of freedom," as Kant will put it (Kant 1996b: 5: 65). And although it is important to Spinoza that passions' strengths, indeed, that their very existence, depend on the absence of Intellect, he decidedly does not hold, as Plato and Kant do, that we can do what is good and right, regardless of the strengths of the passions. And he also denies the mainstream modern moral philosophical view, again, that anyone subject to morality can comply with it simply by exercising the capacity for free moral agency that makes them thus subject. On all these points, he agrees with Hutcheson and Hume (and, of course, with Nietzsche).

Spinoza's distinction between passion and will thus anticipates Hutcheson's and Hume's distinctions between the "calm" and "violent passions." Like Spinoza, Hume and Hutcheson draw the line based on whether a motivating state is informed by reason or intellect. Violent passions are those that are not, in the current terms, "reasons responsive," those that do not stem from reason or intellect. Hutcheson also holds a version of Spinoza's thesis that we are moved to bring about good when we maximize "calmness" through theoretical reason or intellect. The difference is that Spinoza's view is steadfastly *eudaimonist*, whereas Hutcheson holds the "modern" view that "calm desires" can either be for the agent's own good or for good impartially considered.

Cudworth

A particularly interesting comparison and contrast with Spinoza is the Cambridge Platonist Ralph Cudworth.[11] Like Spinoza, Cudworth is a rationalist and, moreover, one who, unlike the eighteenth-century British rationalists who draw from him, emphasizes non-deontic over deontic ethical aspects. But Cudworth is quite unlike Spinoza in holding that ethics cannot be reduced to (non-ethical) metaphysics and that reason is the faculty of irreducibly ethical cognition.

Cudworth was best known during his lifetime for his metaphysical thought and for his masterful command of classical philosophical and theological texts. Both were on display in his massive work, *The True Intellectual System of the Universe*, the only work he ever published, in 1678. But just as Locke's *Essay* was written with an eye to issues "about the principles of morality and revealed religion" (Woolhouse 2007: 98), so also had Cudworth's *System* a moral agenda. Cudworth tells us in the Preface that he originally projected three volumes, all to be concerned with divine government. The first was to focus on refuting arguments for atheism and "democritick fatalism," the second, to argue for an essentially good God, and the third to argue that there is "a *Liberty*, or *Sui-Potestas*, in *Rational Creatures*, as may render them *Accountable*," "that we are so far forth … *Masters* of our own *Actions*, as to be *Accountable* to *Justice* for them, or to make us *Guilty* and *Blame-worthy* for what we doe Amiss" (Cudworth 1678: Preface).

In the event, Cudworth published only the first volume. The projected second and third books of the *System* remained unpublished, although the posthumously published *Treatise Concerning Eternal and Immutable Morality* (1731) probably included material from the second. Cudworth left lengthy manuscripts, many on freedom of the will, which must represent attempts at the third.[12] Thus even in the *System* Cudworth is attempting to come to grips with metaphysical issues that are especially relevant to morality conceived as standards with which we are distinctively accountable for compliance.

Against Positivism

We shall return to Cudworth's writings on moral accountability and "moral free will" presently. They represent some of the most philosophically sophisticated reflections of the period on autonomy and the will. Moreover, they show

---

[11] For a more detailed version, see Darwall 1995: 109–148, from which I here draw. Also, the *Cambridge Platonism Sourcebook* is a treasure trove of Cudworth's writings and Cambridge Platonism more generally. Most important for our purposes, it has digital transcriptions of Cudworth's manuscripts with which we shall be concerned. www.cambridge-platonism.divinity.cam.ac.uk/about-the-cambridge-platonists/circle-network-constellation

[12] Cudworth ~1670. Only one of these (Mss. 4978) has ever been published: *A Treatise of Freewill*, which is included with Cudworth 1996. (It was originally published in 1838.) For a useful overall discussion of the provenance, history, and contents of the manuscripts, see Passmore 1951: 107–113.

that Cudworth was concerned, as Pufendorf and Locke had been in their own ways, with coming to terms with the conceptual demands placed on our ethical thought, and on our moral psychology, by morality's fundamentally deontic character. First, however, we should consider Cudworth's criticisms of voluntarist attempts to ground moral deontology.

This is a primary focus of the *Treatise*, which seeks to argue against any view of morality as "positive, arbitrary, and factitious only," whether this view takes a Hobbesian form or is advanced by "modern theologians" who seek to derive morality from the will of God (1996a: I.i.1,5). Against these views, Cudworth argues that if fundamental moral terms like "moral good and evil, just and unjust" are to have meaning, and if they are not "names for nothing else, but willed and commanded," then what they refer to "cannot possibly be arbitrary things, made by will without nature" (I.ii.1). Cudworth thinks he can exclude the second alternative, that moral terms include reference to will or command in their content. If, for example, "morally wrong" simply meant being contrary to the sovereign's or God's command, then "it is wrong to act contrary the sovereign's or God's command" would become a mere tautology without normative force. For moral propositions to be essentially normative, then, some further claim of the legitimacy of the sovereign's or God's commands must either be asserted or assumed. Moreover, Cudworth continues,

> it was never heard of, that anyone founded all his authority of commanding others, and others' obligation or duty to obey his commands, in a law of his own making, that men should be required, obliged, or bound to obey him. ... For if they were obliged before, then this law would be in vain and to no purpose. And if they were not before obliged, then they could not be obliged by any positive law, because they were not previously bound to obey such a person's commands (I.ii.3).

Any authority necessary for God's commands to obligate can therefore not itself be created by God's command.

As we noted in earlier chapters, this is a point that Locke and Pufendorf effectively grant, since they hold that God has authority by virtue of our complete dependency on him for all that is good in our lives. So although they think that all (other) facts about our moral obligations depend upon God's legislative will, they nonetheless must implicitly accept a background moral fact, namely, that God has an authority that makes his commands binding obligations for his creatures, an authority that is grounded in our dependency on him, not in his commands. They can still hold, as we also noted, that any actual obligations depend on God's positive legislative acts. But they are committed to the background moral fact necessary for God's legislation actually to bind nonetheless.

The thrust of Cudworth's anti-voluntarist arguments in the *Treatise* is to show that moral properties must depend on the nature of things that have them and that natures are "eternal and immutable." If stealing is wrong, it is because it has a nature that makes it wrong. Not even God can make stealing not be wrong by fiat, any more than he can make the angles of a triangle sum to something other than two right angles. To change an action's moral properties, therefore, it would have to be possible to change its nature without, *per impossible*, changing what it is.

Metaphysical Idealism?

Now this might seem to suggest a kind of Platonic realism that holds that moral properties and facts are completely mind independent. But although Cudworth's thought clearly owes much to Plato, it may owe more to a neo-Platonist like Plotinus.[13] Cudworth considers the question, "where these immutable entities do exist," and answers, "first that as they are considered formally, they do not properly exist in the individuals without us" (IV.iv.4). Natural philosophy has shown that no substantial forms exist in material bodies. But, he continues, "[n]either do they exist somewhere else apart for [*sic*] the individual sensibles, and without the mind" (IV.iv.4). "These intelligible ideas or essences of things ... exist, nowhere but in the mind it self."

Cudworth remarks that he actually agrees with Hobbesian nominalism that, quoting Hobbes, "'There is nothing in the world universal but names,'" if this be taken, Cudworth adds, to include all things "existing without the mind" (IV. iii.15). What Cudworth denies is that universal natures and essences, including "eternal and immutable morality," though mind dependent, are not real. Writing about relations like cause and effect and whole and part, he says that though these are "notions of the mind and modes of conceiving in us that only signify what things are relatively to intellect," this does not make them less real. To the contrary, mind or "intellect ... hath more of entity in it than matter or body" (IV.ii.5).

Cudworth's metaphysics are, therefore, some form of idealism, as we shall see is borne out also by what he says about moral properties and facts more specifically. As is often the case with idealisms, Cudworth's is driven largely by epistemological considerations. Knowledge of objects is impossible without universal notions. Since these cannot be extracted from experience, they must be prior to it. "Knowledge," he says, "is a comprehension of a thing proleptically, and as it were *a priori*" (III.iii.5). And this means that the categories that make knowledge possible must be present in the very activity of mind. He therefore holds all knowledge to be ultimately reflexive: "Knowledge and intellection doth ... comprehend its object within itself, and is the same with it." "The intellect and the thing known are really one and the same" (III.iii.4). It

---

[13] Passmore notes that Coleridge thought that Cudworth should be described as a Plotinist rather than a Platonist (Passmore 1951: 14).

follows that the "intelligible forms by which things are understood or known, are not stamps or impressions passively printed upon the soul from without, but ideas vitally protended or actively exerted from within itself" (IV.i.1).[14]

All universal natures and essences, including moral ones, therefore, are modifications of mind. They have reality only so long as mind, specifically, God's archetypal mind of which all created minds are ectypes, exists. Although he is no theological voluntarist, Cudworth actually agrees with Pufendorf and Locke, that morality could not exist without God. No universal natures could. "If … there be *Eternal Intelligibles* or *Ideas*, and *Eternal Truths*; … then must there be an *Eternal Mind Necessarily Existing*, since these *Truths* and *Intelligible Essences* cannot possibly be any where but in a *Mind*" (1678: 736).

Ethical Idealism?

Since Cudworth holds fundamental moral truths to be "eternal and immutable," it would seem that these too would have to have the same mind dependence. This is borne out in the *Treatise*'s anti-voluntarist arguments. Cudworth distinguishes between "natural" and "positive" goodness and justice in the process of arguing against the voluntarists that unless at least something is naturally just or good (e.g., complying with a sovereign's commands in general), then nothing can be positively just or good. Notice, however, *how* Cudworth makes the distinction.

> [T]here are some things which the intellectual nature obligeth to of itself (*per se*) and directly. … Other things there are which the same intellectual nature obligeth to by accident only, and hypothetically, upon condition of some voluntary action of our own or some other person's … (1996a: I.ii.4).

Since Cudworth's doctrine is that it is the eternal and immutable character of the act that makes it right or wrong, required or prohibited, we might expect him to say that the obligation derives directly from that. But Cudworth emphasizes that the obligation consists in a "relation to the intellectual nature" and also that in cases when someone is obligated by a positive command, that "it is not the mere will and pleasure him that commandeth that obligeth to do positive things commanded, but the intellectual nature of him that is commanded" (I.ii.4).[15]

---

[14] A. O. Lovejoy remarked that Cudworth's epistemology involved a "Copernican Revolution" not unlike the more familiar Kantian version: "Knowledge depends upon the 'conformity of objects to our mode of cognition' rather than upon the conformity of our mode of cognition to objects" (Lovejoy 1908). Universal natures exist formally by way of cognitive modes – thus does Cudworth's epistemology drive his metaphysics.

[15] Gill writes that "the intellectual nature that obliges to do what is naturally good does not seem to be *our* intellectual nature, but rather *the* intellectual nature, that is the nature of

Once we recall that Cudworth believes that all "intelligible essences" and "eternal truths" are "modifications of mind and intellect" (IV.v.8), these claims are no longer puzzling. Anything having universal reality must involve some relation to intellectual nature.

What is especially notable is that Cudworth holds that the "modifications of mind" in which moral natures and facts consist are essentially *practical, motivating* states of mind. This comes out in two remarkable passages. One occurs early in the *Treatise*, closely following the passages about obligation and intellectual nature we just noted:

> [I]f the rational or intellectual nature in itself were indetermined and unobliged to any thing, and so destitute of all morality, it were not possible that any things should be made morally good or evil, obligatory or unlawful (*debitum* or *illicitum*) or that any moral obligation should be begotten by any will or command whatsoever (I.ii.6).

Note the connection Cudworth draws here between being obligated to do something and being "determined" to do it. If it is not clear already in this passage that Cudworth has in mind a form of practical determination or *motivation* that is not necessarily in play with other intellectual essences, it becomes clear in a following remarkable passage in which Cudworth claims agreement with, of all philosophers, Hobbes. Here is what Cudworth says:

> [I]t is truly affirmed by the author of the *Leviathan*, "That there is no common rule of good and evil to be taken from the nature of the objects themselves," that is either considered absolutely in themselves, or relatively to external sense only, but according to some other interior analogy which things have to a certain inward determination in the soul itself (IV.iv.4).

So far, this just asserts Cudworth's agreement with Hobbesian nominalism so far as mind-independent aspects of "the world" are concerned. But Cudworth then goes on to distinguish the distinctively practical modifications of mind in which moral natures and facts consist:

> Not that the anticipations of morality spring merely from intellectual forms and notional ideas of the mind ... but from some other more inward and vital principle, in intellectual beings as such, whereby they have a *natural determination to do some things and to avoid others* (IV.iv.4, emphasis added).

---

reality as it exists eternally and immutably, independent of our particular minds" (Gill 277). It will become clear below, however, that Cudworth holds that we are capable of being obligated only because we ourselves can *share* (God's perfect) intellectual nature.

Cudworth concludes that if the soul "hath no innate active principle of its own, ... upon this hypothesis there could be no such thing as morality" (IV.iv.4).[16]

As we've seen, Cudworth holds that all universal essences exist by way of mind, ultimately God's archetypal mind. It follows that the existence of morality, like any universal essence or fact, depends upon the existence of God. But notice how Cudworth puts the point:

> [I]t is not possible that there should be any such thing as morality, unless there be a God, that is, an infinite eternal mind that is the first original and source of all things, whose nature is the first rule and exemplar of morality (IV.vi.13).

God's idea of a triangle must serve as the archetype of triangles, but even if this is a modification of God's mind, this does not mean that God's *nature* is "the first rule and exemplar" of triangularity.

The reason that God's nature is the rule and exemplar of morality is that God is, for Cudworth, an *ideal of moral agency*. Perfect mind is essentially practical; it is in its nature "determined to do some things and avoid others." Cudworth is

---

[16] In Darwall 1995 I argue that this distinguishes Cudworth's view from that of the eighteenth-century British rational intuitionists like Clark and Price. And I argue there that Cudworth's view amounts to a kind of *autonomist internalism*, according to which obligation consists in motivation that arises through the agent's exercise of their power for self-determination. Michael Gill criticizes my arguments for these claims and argues that Cudworth is best seen as an intuitionist for whom moral truths are akin to truths of geometry (Gill 2006: 275–277). Gill acknowledges that Cudworth holds morality to be mind dependent, but argues that morality "cannot be constituted by the motives of human agents" (275). That is of course true, but it does not mean that moral *obligation* cannot depend on human motives. In my view, Cudworth holds, like Kant, that the possibility of moral obligation only arises for imperfect rational beings who have in addition to what Kant calls "pure practical reason" other, not purely rational, sources of motivation. So any motivation that is part of intellectual nature that can be necessary for or part of moral obligation must be shared by human moral agents.

Gill claims that Cudworth's arguments against voluntarism "imply that morality consists of principles that are independent of anyone's motives," including God's. Although it seems clear that Cudworth is assuming the goodness of God's love as a background fact that is itself independent of any fact about what God necessarily (lovingly) desires, it does not follow from this that facts about moral conduct are also thus independent. Hutcheson, for example, holds that facts about the moral choiceworthiness of acts derive from the moral goodness of benevolence. What moral agents should do, he thinks, is whatever we would do if perfectly benevolent. Of course, Hutcheson holds the moral goodness of benevolence to be contingent, and Cudworth holds it to be necessary, but their views might otherwise be similar in this respect. So long as it is a necessary truth that God is loving, and a necessary truth also what a perfectly loving being would want for the circumstances of human life, moral truths will be "eternal and immutable." For a criticism of Gill's claim that for Cudworth the truths of morality are like those of geometry, see Leisinger 2019.

of course careful to distinguish his view from theological voluntarists. Morality does not depend upon God's arbitrary will. If God's will were utterly arbitrary, there would be no such thing as morality. According to the theological voluntarists, "there is no pattern or archetypal exemplar of morality in God" (~1670: 4979.87).[17] It is only because God's perfect mind does provide an exemplar of will and motivation – that is, because perfect mind is essentially practical – that eternal and immutable morality exists.

Love

However, what motivation *is* essential to perfect mind? Cudworth does not say in the *Treatise*, but the general shape of his answer is clear from his other writings. In the process of discussing Plato's Form of the Good in the *System*, Cudworth complains that "*Plato* sometimes talks too Metaphysically and Cloudily about it." "Nevertheless," he continues, "he plainly intimates … that this Nature of Good which is also the Nature of God, includes *Benignity* in it" (1678: 205). Then he writes,

> But the Holy Scripture without any Metaphysical Pomp and Obscurity, tells us plainly Both what is that Highest Perfection of Intellectual Beings, which is … *Better than Reason and Knowledge,* and which is also the Source, Life and Soul of all Morality, namely that it is *Love or Charity* (205).

From there Cudworth proceeds to quote at length the famous passage on love from Paul's First Epistle to the Corinthians, adding that without love, "I have no Inward Satisfaction, Peace or True Happiness" and an "destitute of all True Morality, Vertue, and Grace."

The fundamental ethical motive, essential to perfect mind, thus, is love.[18] Cudworth tells us little about love's precise character. He says love "dispenses it self Uninvidiously," with an equal regard of some sort, but he does not try to formulate any principle like Cumberland's "common good of all rationals." Since Cudworth says that "justice is an essential branch of this Divine Goodness," he must hold that love and justice cannot conflict. But it is impossible to be sure whether he holds that love is benevolence tempered by justice, or whether he thinks that justice can somehow be resolved into benevolence (I.iv.9).[19] It should not be surprising that Cudworth is unclear on this point since the fact that universal benevolence might conflict with other moral concerns such as

---

[17] This passage comes from Cudworth's manuscripts on freedom of the will.
[18] Indeed, at one point, Cudworth, like Cumberland, identifies God with love: "in a Rectified and Qualified sence, this may pass for true Theology; That *Love* is the *Supreme Deity* and *original* of all things: namely, if by it be meant, Eternal, Self-originated, Intellectual Love" (1678: 123, misnumbered 117).
[19] I am indebted to Roberts unpublished for this passage.

justice or honesty was not well appreciated until Butler's *Dissertation upon the Nature of Virtue* some fifty or so years later.

As mentioned earlier, Cudworth opposes an ethics of love to a "*dead Law of outward Works*" (123). God's love makes morality possible; without it there would be no distinction between moral good and evil. Because we can participate in God's (practical) intellectual nature, we can be moral agents. "Love is at once a Freedome from all Law, a State of purest Liberty, and yet a Law too, of the most constraining and indispensable Necessity" (1969: 124).

Unlike the natural lawyers, Cudworth's ethics do not start from the problem of obligation. Even so, as the passages quoted earlier from the *System* show, the legitimation of moral obligation is a primary purpose behind Cudworth's metaphysical speculations as well as his writings on freedom of the will. Although his ethics is at bottom an ethics of love, Cudworth also aims to argue that love grounds moral obligation. We are obligated, most fundamentally, to give expression to the source of morality we have within, thereby enlivening what would otherwise be the "dead carkasse" of outward acts. The agent's "intellectual nature" is what makes them obligated, and love is the practical form of the intellect.

This motivational source is, however, only one necessary condition of moral obligation. The other is what Cudworth calls "free will," the agent's capacity to determine conduct by freely forming their own practical *judgment*.

Self-Determination

This is the subject of Cudworth's surviving manuscripts, which are galvanized by the problem of accountability: conditions for the very possibility of moral "guilt" and "blame" (1678: Preface). If obligation is distinctive of morality, it is distinctive of obligation that we are accountable for acting as we are obligated. When we take up an attitude toward, make a judgment of, or act in response to persons as responsible for their acts, we *impute* their acts *to them*. We regard persons as the causes of their own acts, imputing to the person the determination of the act.

Although there is a weak sense in which someone might "blame" a defective alarm clock as the cause of their oversleeping, Cudworth notes that they do not "imput[e] to [the clock] its being the cause of its own moving well or ill" (1996: 155). By contrast, when "we blame a man for any wicked actions, … we blame him not only as doing otherwise than ought to have been done, but also than he might have done, …, so that he was himself the cause of the evil thereof" (155). Our blame takes a self-determining *person* as object. Commendation or blame not "only signif[ies] our approbation or dislike of the [acts] themselves … but doth also reflect upon the person as the cause of either to himself when it was possible he might not have been so" (~1670: 4980.31).

Cudworth holds that morality can genuinely obligate only agents who can determine themselves to act morally. He uses a variety of terms for the requisite power, *sui potestas*, as well as some of his own coinage: "autexousy" and "autexousious power".[20] Cudworth contrasts his account of self-determining imputable agency with Hobbes's account of the will as the "last appetite." The will, Cudworth says, "is no particular appetite." It involves "the soul comprehending its whole self." Volition is the agent's "last practical judgment," he says, using this phrase in his own technical sense of a more (or less) considered judgment made actively by the agent themselves in comprehension, more or less, of their various motives (4982.80).

Hobbes's account of will as "nothing but alternate passions where the victory at last falls to that passion whose necessary force is most prepondering" might aptly describe the behavior of "brutes." But they lack the self-awareness necessary for accountable agency. "[T]here is no ... thing in them [brutes] that takes notice of all, no reduplicate self-active principle that ... exerting itself more or less can oversway things one way or the other" (4980.7).[21]

In addition to Hobbes's theory, Cudworth rejects two other views he thinks do not adequately capture the role of "self-comprehensive" practical thinking and judgment in forming the will. One is the indifference view, which holds that agents simply plump for some option or other after the "last dictate of the understanding" (1996: 168). This alternative makes free choice blind and "mere irrationality" (169). A second view agrees with this criticism of the first, but holds that rational action is the result of a necessary process in which agents always do what they believe best. Cudworth rejects this account because it reduces moral agency to processes that occur *in* an agent rather than anything the agent themselves directs. A belief of "the understanding" is something the agent *has* or a state they are *in*. By contrast, a *considered* practical *judgment* is something the agent themselves *makes* (178–179). An agent's power of self-determination consists in its capacity to act, not just *from* itself, but also "on itself," to be "at once both agent and patient," as it directs its own practical all-things-considered deliberation and act on the basis of that (~1670: 4982.4).

As Locke would later, Cudworth makes an important distinction between merely *believing* that an action is the best thing to do and actively *judging* it to be so as the result of the agent's own deliberative thought.[22] Were the understanding directly to determine the will, then there would "nee[d] nothing else to be done in order to virtue [*sic*] but only the informing of a man's speculative

---

[20] "Autonomy" only had a political use before English translations of Kant's "*autonomie.*"
[21] As we shall see, Cudworth maintains there is a kind of free will whose scope covers actions motivated by desires for our overall happiness. But though he calls this "animal free will," he does not mean that (other) animals actually have it.
[22] As mentioned in the last chapter, it is arguably under Cudworth's influence that Locke makes this distinction.

understanding concerning the nature of good" (4982.10).[23] Like Locke in the revised *Essay*, Cudworth holds that we do not always do what we think best, but that we *do* always do what we ourselves *judge* best on the basis of our own (more or less) considered self-reflection. The will just is the "last practical judgment," which is the conclusion to this motivation-infused process (4982.80).

"[W]e are not," Cudworth writes, "merely passive to our own practical judgments and to the appearances of good, but contribute something of our own to them" (1996: 179). Human beings can do nothing to affect their fundamental sources of motivation. These are, as Cudworth puts it, motives of the "animal" and "divine life," respectively, that together constitute our "necessary nature" (4980.56). What we can do (in addition to acquiring virtuous habits (4980.57, 61)) is to undertake to get a more or less comprehensive grasp of our own practical situation in self-comprehensive deliberation.

An agent can thereby affect the "light" in which they view options, or even what options they have in view, as "these may be very different accordingly as we more or less intensely consider or deliberate which is a thing … in our own power" (1996: 179). Thus, "we ourselves finish or determine the last conclusive *visum* or phantasy of good, which is called the last or ruling practical judgment" (~1670: 4980.239). The requisite practical judgment can thus only be made by agents with free will. "[It] is made up partly from nature, some natural congruity or other, higher or lower, partly from we ourselves, the soul self-comprehensive or self-active" (4980.239).

Cudworth distinguishes between successful guidance by correct perceptions of value ("liberty" or "*sui potens*"), which God has, from "free will" or "*sui potestas*," the power we imperfect rational beings have to make and act on considered, self-reflective practical judgments to the best of our ability (4980.31, 44). In addition to these, there is also the voluntariness of exercising or failing to exercise this power. Sin or fault "is not to be imputed to free will as if it were actively exercised by freewill." Rather "it is nothing but a voluntary deficiency of a good power" (4982: 22).[24] What makes wrongdoing voluntary is that the agent "might have made a better judgment than now he did, had he more intensely considered, and more maturely deliberated" (1996: 179). The agent "is conscious also that it has a self-active autexousious power to excite and command a full consultation, deliberation, and search" (~1670: 4980.66).

Free Will and Obligation, Animal and Moral

The capacity for self-comprehensive choice is not, however, sufficient for moral accountability and, therefore, for moral obligation. Cudworth distinguishes

---

[23] On this, see Leisinger 2021.
[24] Roberts unpublished emphasizes this "asymmetrical" character of Cudworthian liberty.

between a kind of agency and free will, "animal free will," which though it involves self-reflective self-determination is not yet sufficient for "moral free will," and therefore, for moral agency and obligation.

According to Cudworth, human beings participate in two "stories of life" – "animal life" and "divine life." The former is composed of desires, feelings, and experiences arising from our bodily, "animal" nature; the latter, of the instincts of love and "honesty" that are essential to perfect mind. A being might have only animal ends and still have a kind of rationality, one Cudworth calls "inferior reason," that involves a "larger comprehension of [its] own utility" (4979.5). Cudworth stresses that this is different from particular animal passions and appetites, even when they are combined with instrumental rationality individually. Inferior reason's "larger comprehension of our own utility" is tethered neither to specific desires nor to any particular point in time (4980.6).[25]

A being restricted to animal desires and inferior reason can still have a kind of free will, which Cudworth calls "animal free will." And Cudworth holds that this is sufficient for a kind of "animal" obligation.

> [I]t is possible that the soul may be here defective in the exertions of this autexousious faculty ... in ... succumbing passively to the urging importunity of the present appetite ... and then it is conscious to itself that it is faulty and blameworthy, not as guilty of any moral evil properly called sin, [but] because it was wanting to itself within the sphere of the animal life as to private utility, and hereupon follows ... regret of mind, self-displeasure (4982.17).

Animal free will, including inferior reason, is necessary for animal obligation. And the proper exercise of this power is sufficient to discharge the obligation.

Animal free will and inferior reason are, however, insufficient for moral obligation. Cudworth pointedly notes (with an eye to Hobbes) that were agents only so far equipped, "there is no doubt but they might have societies, polities, and laws ... enforced with punishments and rewards to good purpose, in order to the advantage of private persons and the safety of the whole, which is the very constitution of the Leviathan" (4980.9). But this would not be an "obligation truly moral." Against Hobbes, Cudworth echoes Pufendorf: "Laws could no otherwise operate or seize upon them than by taking hold of their animal selfish passions ... and that will allow of no other moral obligation than this utterly destroys morality" (4980.9).[26]

In order to have moral obligations, an agent must have "moral free will," which involves the same power of self-comprehensive self-command, but combined with the distinctive motives of the divine life and, therefore, "superior

---

[25] "Utility" here is restricted to animals' desires only.
[26] Compare this with Shaftesbury's similar remark that by making morality depend on sanctions, Locke "threw ... virtue out of the world."

reason," alongside animal desires and inferior reason. "For the better explanation" of moral obligation, Cudworth writes, "it must first be supposed that besides the spring of animal life, there is in the soul, a spring or principle of another superior intellectual life" (4982.20). What Cudworth calls alternately "superior reason," "love," "the principle of honesty," and "conscience" exists in us not as God's overflowing love is in him. God is love essentially and necessarily. Though we participate in the divine life, we have "a principle of animal life in us besides" (4982.20). So, unlike God, we imperfect rational beings require a power of free will to enable us to self-reflectively guide our lives by this superior motive. We require moral free will. In this way, Cudworth combines an ethics of love with the characteristics of moral agency necessary for morality to obligate us.

Shaftesbury

Anthony Ashley Cooper, the 3rd Earl of Shaftesbury, was the grandson of the 1st Earl, the famous Whit politician. When Shaftesbury was three, his grandfather assumed his formal guardianship and turned over the direction of much of his education to the 1st Earl's medical attendant and sometime advisor and secretary, John Locke. Thus began a complex relationship.[27] Shaftesbury remained indebted to Locke, but his philosophical instincts ran directly opposite to Locke's.[28]

Shaftesbury was more attracted to the Cambridge Platonists' affective rationalism, represented by Cudworth. He especially reviled Locke's voluntarism, since it made morality external to the moral agent and reduced moral motivation to prods and pulls rather than anything expressive of the agent's own virtue or moral character. As Shaftesbury saw it, Locke's voluntarism was even more pernicious than Hobbes's, since the latter's "slavish" political views made his form of voluntarism less likely to get a foothold. "It was Locke," Shaftesbury wrote, "that struck the home blow ... [and] threw all order and virtue out of the world" (Shaftesbury 1900: 403).

Shaftesbury also opposed Locke's methods. Anglophone philosophy of the modern period was generally marked by a desire for analytical rigor and consonance with developing scientific understanding. Even Cudworth was a member of the Royal Society.[29] In his first *Enquiry* (1748), Hume famously distinguished between philosophy that seeks to edify and a more scientific sort that seeks "those original principles, by which, in every science, all human curiosity must be bounded" (Hume 1975a: 5). Shaftesbury's philosophy is more of the edifying

---

[27] For details, see Voitle (1984).
[28] In what follows, I draw from Darwall 1995: 176–206.
[29] Formally called The Royal Society of London for Improving Natural Knowledge.

sort. He frequently scorns the metaphysical and epistemological writings of contemporaries who, like Locke, are stimulated by advances in natural philosophy: "What specious exercise is found in those which are called 'Philosophical Speculations'? The formation of ideas, their compositions, comparisons, agreement and disagreement" (Shaftesbury 1900: 267). Such inquiries, he complains, make a person "neither better, nor happier, nor wiser" (269). "The most ingenious way of becoming foolish," Shaftesbury famously remarked, "is *by a System*" (2001: I.290). For Shaftesbury, philosophy is the edifying study of the good – an attempt to find, or more accurately, to *inspire in* the agent a fixed and steady aim necessary for them to project an enduring, integral self.[30]

It is ironic, therefore, that Shaftesbury is best remembered among anglophone philosophers for his idea of the "moral sense," which inspired Hutcheson's and Hume's empiricist moral sentimentalism. Sidgwick, for example, treats Shaftesbury as the first moralist to make the empirical study of mental phenomena the basis of ethics, thereby leading to Hutcheson and Hume's sentimentalism (Sidgwick 1964: 184–191).[31] But Shaftesbury's moral sense has greater affinities to the affective or practical rationalist themes we found in Cudworth. Cassirer wrote, indeed, that it was "principally Shaftesbury" who saved "the Cambridge School from the fate of a learned curiosity" and made it a "philosophic force in the centuries to come" (Cassirer 1953: 160; see also Cassirer 1951).

An Ethics of Virtue

Shaftesbury's ethics mark a radical departure from early modern natural law. Deontic notions are almost entirely absent from Shaftesbury's writings, and when they enter, Shaftesbury tends to recast them in subversive ways. For example, after having provided an account of "what virtue is and to whom the character belongs" in Book I of the *Inquiry*, Shaftesbury begins Book II by saying that "[i]t remains to inquire, *What Obligation* there is *to* Virtue" (Shaftesbury 2001: II.78). Any impression that Shaftesbury is attempting to account for deontic aspects of morality within an ethics of virtue is immediately dispelled, however, when he continues: "or *what Reason* to embrace it" (II.78). This

---

[30] Diderot wrote in his *Encyclopédie*, "There are very few errors in Locke and two few truths in milord Shaftesbury: the former is only a man of vast intellect, penetrating and exact, while the latter is a genius of the first order." Whereas "Locke has seen, Shaftesbury has created, constructed, and edified. To Locke we owe some great truths coldly perceived, methodically developed, and dryly presented; and to Shaftesbury, some brilliant schemes often poorly grounded, though full of sublime truths" (translated and quoted in Grean 1967: x–xi).

[31] Martineau said that Hutcheson worked out Shaftesbury's "fruitful hints and construct[ed] from them a systematical psychology" (Martineau 1901 v. 2, 514). And Albee wrote, "it is customary to regard Hutcheson's system as the logical development of Shaftesbury's" (Albee 1957: 58).

already is a move from a notion on the law or command side of Suárez's distinction, obligation, to a counsel notion. Moreover, Shaftesbury's *eudaimonism* leads him to interpret this question of practical reason in self-interested terms. The question of whether there is an obligation to virtue, in Shaftesbury's hands, becomes that of whether a virtuous life best realizes the virtuous agent's good. Hutcheson and Hume will follow Shaftesbury's revisionist lead. What Shaftesbury calls obligation will be what Hume calls "natural" or "interested" obligation (Hume 1975b: 268; 1978: 498).

So viewed, what makes something "obligating" has nothing to do with legitimate demand or accountability, not even with a reformed notion of natural law such as we find in Cumberland, nor even with Cudworth's idea of a "law of love." For Shaftesbury, morality primarily concerns good motives or "affections" rather than conduct. "[I]t is by affection merely that a Creature is esteem'd good or ill" (II.22). And when Shaftesbury talks about wrongful actions, he tends to have in mind actions that result from bad motives (II.32), turning a law-based ethical conception on its head.

Shaftesbury's ethics are steadfastly an ethics of virtue. What makes an affection a good one? Shaftesbury's answer derives from his theory of nature: a good affection is a *natural* one. Indeed, "natural" is often synonymous with "good" for Shaftesbury. Thus, the passage quoted in the last paragraph ends: "good or ill, *natural* or *unnatural*" (II.22). In the background is a teleological picture of nature in which subsystems function together to realize a well-functioning whole. All species and individual members have natural constitutions that are fitted, indeed designed, for specific functional roles in the "System *of all Things*" or "*Universal Nature*" (II.20, 105). Whether an individual or species is "really" good or ill depends on whether it enhances or detracts from the good functioning of the whole (II.20).

Though ultimately good and ill must be reckoned in relation to the whole system of nature, Shaftesbury generally writes as though whether an affection is good or bad primarily concerns how it relates to the flourishing of the species, which he generally calls the "publick Interest" (II.31). An animal whose violent instincts must be kept in check by "*fear of his Keeper*" is not good themselves, just as Hobbes and Locke's human agents, kept in check by fear of God, cannot be good on Shaftesbury's picture (II.26).[32]

---

[32] Shaftesbury sometimes writes as if natural affections have the public interest as object, but his considered view seems to be that natural affections are those functionally suited to promote the public interest, regardless of their object (Trianosky 1978). "A good Creature is such a one as by the natural Temper or Bent of his Affections is carry'd *primarily and immediately*, and not *secondarily and accidentally*, to Good, and against Ill" (Shaftesbury 2001: II.26). Good affections are those whose primary function is to realize species good. "When in general, all the Affections or Passions are suted to the publick Good, or good of the Species, ... then is the *natural Temper* intirely good" (II.27).

There can also be natural and unnatural *degrees* of affections like self-love and benevolence. Self-love tends to be "injurious to social Life" only when immoderate, so only an immoderate degree of self-love is unnatural (II.140). Similarly, "even as to *Kindness* and *Love* of the most natural sort, (such as that of any Creature for its Offspring) if it be immoderate and beyond a certain degree," it can be unnatural also (II.27).

Virtue and Moral Sense

Although having affections adapted to species' goods is sufficient for the "mere *Goodness*" of any sensible creature, Shaftesbury maintains that "that which is call'd Virtue or Merit" can be realized only by a self-reflective rational agent (II.28). Only an agent who is guided by reflective assessments of their own character and motive (through "moral sense") or moral conscience can direct their moral life in a way that is genuinely virtuous. Shaftesbury here embarks on a path that will prove influential, leading to Butler's idea of the authority of conscience and arguably even to Kant on moral worth. Interestingly, however, it is not a path that his main sentimentalist followers, Hutcheson and Hume, will follow. To the contrary, the idea that moral goodness must involve the agent's moral self-direction is more characteristic of writers who stress morality's deontic character and connection to accountability. Rationalists like Clarke and Price take this position, as does Butler. Shaftesbury's reasons for taking the position are different, as we shall see.

For rational beings "capable of forming general Notions of Things, not only the outward Beings which offer themselves to the Sense," but also actions and affections can be "fram[ed]" in thought as "*rational Objects*" and contemplated, along with their relation to the rest of nature (II.28, 36). When natural affections, "being brought into the Mind by Reflection, become Objects, ... there arises another kind of Affection towards those very Affections themselves, which have been already felt, and are now become the Subject of a new Liking or Dislike" (II.28). This "reflex approbation," as Butler puts it, or "natural *moral Sense*," as Shaftesbury does, is a second-order approval of natural affections (Butler 2017: Pr.26; Shaftesbury 2001: II.28, 46).

But what guarantees that moral agents will approve of *natural* affections, affections that tend toward the public interest, on reflection? The answer has to do with Shaftesbury's teleology of nature, his "aestheticism," and his view of the nature of beauty.

> The Mind, which is Spectator or Auditor of *other Minds*, cannot be without its *Eye* and *Ear*, so as to discern Proportion, distinguish Sound, and scan each Sentiment or Thought which comes before it. It can let nothing escape its Censure. It feels the Soft and the Harsh, the Agreeable and Disagreeable, in the Affections; and finds a *Foul* and *Fair*, a *Harmonious*

and a *Dissonant*, as really and truly here, as in any musical Numbers, or in the outward Forms or Representations of sensible Things. Nor can it withhold its *Admiration* and *Exstasy*, its *Aversion* and *Scorn*, any more in what relates to one than to the other of these subjects (Shaftesbury 2001: II.29).

Moral goodness, for Shaftesbury, is a species of beauty: a harmony, proportion, or beauty of the mind. Since beauty is naturally agreeable – something we contemplate with pleasure – we cannot but approve it.

Functional adaptation and order are part of what beauty is. "*Beauty* and *Truth* are plainly join'd with the Notion of *Utility* and *Convenience*, even in the Apprehension of every ingenious Artist" (III.181). Similarly, the "*inward Beauty of the* Body" is "the Harmony and just Measures of the rising Pulses, the circulating Humours, and the moving Airs or Spirits" (III.181). Thus, the adaptation of natural affections to their end, the public interest, is beautiful and agreeable also. Virtue is "moral beauty," as Hume will hold also (Shaftesbury II. 29; Hume 1978: 527).

Shaftesbury says that beauty and deformity are "immediately perceiv'd by a plain internal Sensation" (Shaftesbury 2001: II.285). Nevertheless, "moral sense" is, for him, plainly a *cultivated* taste, one that develops through free public critical discourse about the public good and "liberal Education" (II.293). "Taste or *Judgment* ... can hardly come ready form'd with us into the World;" "antecedent *Labour* and *Pains* of Criticism" are necessary (III.164,165). In free conversation we "polish one another, and rub off our Corners and rough Sides by a sort of *amicable Collision*" (I. 64). "There is no real Love of Virtue, without the knowledge of *Publick Good*. And where absolute Power is, there is no Publick" (I.107). The sense of moral beauty, even if immediate when properly cultivated, nonetheless develops through public liberal critical discourse informed by reflection on the public good.

But what makes the relevant perception a feeling? How do we "feel" moral beauty and respond to it in agreeable way? What makes virtue "amiable"? Shaftesbury holds that though there may be "no *real* Amiableness or Deformity in moral Acts, there is at least *an imaginary one* of full force. Tho perhaps the Thing itself shou'd not be allow'd in Nature, the Imagination or Fancy of it must be allow'd to be from Nature alone" (II.43). Natural affections' suitability to public good is itself part of nature, but their agreeableness is not. It is response dependent. Here we see seeds of the moral sentimentalism of Hutcheson and Hume.

But quite unlike the later empiricist sentimentalists, Shaftesbury does not hold that the agreeable and disagreeable responses of "moral sense" are contingent features of human nature. When Shaftesbury says that the imaginative reflective response to natural affections is "from Nature alone," he does not mean just that it has aspects of nature as object, or even that it is the product of natural causation. Those are true of Hutcheson's and Hume's versions of the moral sense or sentiment also. He means that it is a product of the same organizing rational principle or mind that is immanent in nature, in which we as contemplating rational minds sympathetically participate. Shaftesbury's theology, philosophy of nature, and notions of "noble *Enthusiasm*" (III.33), love, creative inspiration, and mind come together to create a version of the doctrine of moral sense that is far from the empiricist sentimentalism of Hutcheson and Hume and closer to Cambridge Platonists like Cudworth. Although moral sense clearly involves feeling for Shaftesbury, it is more accurate to think of him as a kind of rationalist moral sense theorist. Moral sense involves the creative, framing power of reason, not the passive reception of sensations.

The form and structure manifested by the natural affections, and by all natural beauty, evidence the design of a unifying creative mind. Shaftesbury's deity is not the God of orthodox religion.[33] The creative mind evident in nature is not a transcendent being but an organizing principle immanent in nature. A "Theist" believes that "every thing is govern'd, order'd, or regulated *for the best*, by a designing Principle or Mind, necessarily good and permanent" (II.11). Since atheism, and worse, "daemonism," conflict with the contemplation of natural affections as aspects of a benevolently designed natural order, these outlooks tend to undermine the reflective love or admiration on which virtue supervenes.[34] "[H]ow little dispos'd must a Person be, to love or admire any thing as *orderly* in the Universe, who thinks the Universe it-self is a Pattern of *Disorder*" (II.70). Therefore, "the Perfection and Height of Virtue must be owing to *the Belief of a* God" (II.77)).

It is important to Shaftesbury's view that the contemplation of beauty, including moral beauty, involves a kind of feeling that itself depends on rational reflection or "framing" (II.36). Although Shaftesbury is a sharp critic of the sectarian emotionalism generally called "enthusiasm" in early modern England, he vigorously defends what he calls "noble *Enthusiasm*" (III.33). The former is arational or irrational; the latter, the result of creative imaginative activity involved in rationally grasping order and design. This is the "Inspiration" he calls "*a real* feeling of the Divine Presence" (I.53). Inspiration by the divine is but a heightened version of our capacity to be moved by beauty and order more generally: "Is there a rational and admired enthusiasm that belongs to architecture, painting, music, and not to this [the order of the universe]?" (1900: 33).

When we admire and are inspired by beauty, Shaftesbury holds, the ultimate object of our attitude is the ordering mind beauty manifests. Though the

---

[33] See Grean 1967, chs. 4, 5, and 7, for a helpful discussion of Shaftesbury's religious and theological views.

[34] Shaftesbury's categories of atheism and daemonism correspond to Cudworth's "atheistical" fatalism and "divine fate immoral," respectively.

occasion for our agreeable experience will be the beautiful object we contemplate, what we really admire is the designing mind that formed the object.

> "The art then is the *Beauty*." "Right." "And *the Art* is that which beautifies." "The same." So that the Beautifying, not the Beautify'd, is the really *Beautiful* … "[T]he Beautiful … [is] in the… *forming Power*." … What is it you admire, but Mind, or the Effect of *Mind*? 'Tis *Mind* alone which forms (2002: II.404, 405).

Similarly, the contemplation of beauty involves creative, forming mental powers. "[N]either can Man by the same *Sense* or brutish Part, conceive or enjoy *Beauty*: But all the *Beauty* and *Good* he enjoys is in a nobler way, and by the help of what is noblest, his Mind and Reason" (II.425). When we contemplate beauty, we therefore have sympathetic union with the same creative intelligence that formed the beauty we contemplate. We are inspired and moved by the creative mind we thereby share.

Virtue and Self-Reflective Moral Agency

Recall Shaftesbury's thesis that although all affections that tend to the public good are natural or good, only agents who can self-reflectively approve their own good affections are genuinely virtuous. Why is this? One answer is implicit in what we have just noticed about the ultimate object of our contemplation of beauty being beautifying mind. Natural affections are beautiful, but if they are in no way regulated by the agent's own moral sense, the mind to which their beauty must be referred is not the agent's but the creative mind that is implicit in all natural order. If that were so, beauty would be in the agent's mind no differently than it would be in the workings of a healthy body. The agent's mind would only be the "beautified," not also "beautifying." The beauty displayed by their mind would be *in* them, but not really *theirs*. But if they have the capacity to shape their conduct and affections by their own moral sense, they become not just a place where beauty is displayed, but a creator of moral beauty themselves. The "first Order of Beauty," Shaftesbury says, has "a power of making other Forms," of "*forming Forms*" (II.405). Virtue, Shaftesbury may be thinking, is moral beauty of the "first order."

This rationale for emphasizing moral autonomy or authorship is rather different from the one we found in Cudworth and Locke, which is related to accountability. But although Shaftesbury focus is elsewhere, there is at least one place where he sounds Locke and Cudworth's theme.

> Neither can any Weakness or Imperfection in the Senses be the occasion of *Iniquity* or *Wrong*; if the Object of the Mind it-self be not at any time absurdly fram'd, nor any way improper, but sutable, just, and worthy of the Opinion and Affection apply'd to it. For if we will suppose a Man who,

> being sound and intire both in his Reason and Affection, has nevertheless so deprav'd a Constitution or Frame of Body, that the natural Objects are, thro' his Organs of Sense, as thro' ill Glasses, falsely convey'd and misrepresented; 'twill be soon observ'd, in such a Person's case, that since his Failure is not in his principal or leading Part; he cannot in himself be esteem'd *iniquitous*, or unjust (II.32-33).

In the background of this remark, as we shall appreciate better presently, is a view of self-critical self-determination that is very similar to those we found in Cudworth and Locke. Whatever direct influence there is of Cudworth and Locke here, the intellectual source Shaftesbury claims is Epictetus.[35] Rational agents have a "ruling," "leading," or "governing principle," a *hegemonikon*, that gives them critical leverage over their opinions and affections (1900: 112, 113, 130).

This is the point of Shaftesbury's contrast between an agent whose injuring behavior results from defective "Organs of Sense," and one whose actions reflect "absurdly fram'd" opinions and affections. In the former case, "since his Failure is not in his principal or leading Part; he cannot in himself be esteem'd *iniquitous*, or unjust" (2001: II.32-33). We cannot attribute the defect properly to *them* rather than, say, to their eyes.

The "Obligation" to Virtue

Having determined in Book I of the *Inquiry Concerning Virtue or Merit* what virtue is, Shaftesbury writes at the beginning of Book II: "It remains to inquire, *What Obligation* there is *to* Virtue; or *what Reason* to embrace it" (II.78). As we noted earlier, in posing the question in this way, Shaftesbury runs right over Suárez's distinction between law and obligation, on the one hand, and normative reasons for acting, or "counsel," on the other. Hobbes and Cumberland, who did much to naturalize natural law, still felt the need to work within it. And even Cudworth, who rejected natural law's focus on external conduct, was nonetheless concerned to show that we are accountable for conforming to a "law of love." By the time we reach Shaftesbury's *Inquiry* (1711), however, the natural law framework had been so revised from within, and recast from without, that it was possible for Shaftesbury to pose his question in superficially deontic terms without apparently feeling he had to provide any justification for doing so. After arguing in Book II that a virtuous life best realizes the virtuous agent's good, Shaftesbury concludes that there is indeed an "obligation to virtue," even, indeed, on the Cartesian supposition, that our life is but a dream, thereby using "obligation" for only the second time in the book.

---

[35] For references and further discussion of Shaftesbury's relation to Ralph Cudworth, Damaris Cudworth Masham, and Locke, see Darwall 1995: 191n.

Although Shaftesbury's account of virtue stresses other-regarding natural affections, he is nonetheless a *eudaimonist*. To argue that there is an obligation to virtue, in Shaftesbury's deflationary sense, it is necessary to show that the virtuous life promotes the virtuous agent's good: "[T]he *Judgment* we are to make of Interest, and *the Opinion we shou'd have of* Advantage *and* Good ... is what must necessarily determine us in our Conduct, and prove the leading Principle of our Lives" (2001: I.307). Hutcheson and Butler later criticize Shaftesbury for his rational egoism, but his *eudaimonism* was of the sort Irwin calls Aristotelian naturalism, which held that natural affections and virtue are *intrinsically* beneficial for the virtuous person. Hutcheson would later hold that others' goods are no less capable of motivating rational action than is the agent's. And Butler would hold that conscience, a close relative of Shaftesbury's moral sense, is a more authoritative source of reasons than *either* the agent's good or the good of others.

The human psyche is a system, and the harmony that moral sense disinterestedly approves of is no less essential to the agent's flourishing. Shaftesbury argues that a virtuous character is essential for psychic balance, both because it is the only balanced way of having diverse satisfactions and because it is also balance enhancing in itself. Love, in some ways a master virtue for Shaftesbury, is also the *"Master-Pleasure"*; "out of ... *Community or Participation* in the *Pleasures of others*, and *Belief of meriting well from others...* wou'd arise more than nineTenths of whatever is enjoy'd in Life" (II.104, 109). We want not only esteem from others, but "*merited Esteem*," Shaftesbury says, sounding a theme that will loom large also in Adam Smith's moral philosophy (II.112).

Noting that his argument is cast almost entirely in terms of the internal, psychological benefits of virtues, Shaftesbury concludes by remarking that it survives even Cartesian skepticism:

> Nor is it of any concern to our Argument, how these exterior Objects stand; whether they are Realitys or mere Illusions; whether we wake or dream. ... In this Dream of Life, therefore, our Demonstrations have the same force; our *Balance* and *OEconomy* hold good, and our Obligation to Virtue is in every respect the same. (II.173)

Authorship and Self-Determination

When we earlier considered Shaftesbury's reasons for holding that genuine virtue requires self-direction through moral sense, I mentioned that he relies on a Lockean/Cudworthian account of self-determination that he attributes to Epictetus. Both in *Advice to an Author* and in his Stoic-inspired notebooks, Shaftesbury elaborates on this process at some length (2001: I.154–364; 1900). Though the former is formally addressed to literary authors, Shaftesbury remarks elsewhere that this is "Pretence"; his real aim is "to correct *Manners,* and regulate *Lives*" (2001: III.187). He argues that through the self-reflective process he calls "soliloquy" (also "self-converse"), agents can genuinely author their own conduct and lives.

Cudworth and Locke hold the power of self-critical self-determination to be necessary for moral agency because they think we could not otherwise be accountable for acting morally. Shaftesbury also argues that exercising this power is necessary to be morally good, but his reasons have less to do with accountability than with the nature of aesthetic creation and authorship, as well as with the integrity of the self. Even so, Shaftesbury describes a form of self-determination that involves agents taking something like a juridical or deontic attitude toward themselves, that is, as a robust form of self-*government*.

Shaftesburean soliloquy is a distinctive form of self-therapy that involves not just a reflective grasp of motivations and vivid imagination of their objects, or even bringing these impressions together to make all-things-considered judgments. In addition, Shaftesbury describes a form of self-analytic reality therapy in which an agent seeks an objective picture of the sources of their desires and the desires' place in the natural order. He agrees with Locke that there is no direct correlation between the press of present desire and the real contribution its object would make to the agent's good. Locke's strategy is imaginative examination of the real nature of desires' objects. This may work so long as the lack of congruence is the result of misapprehension or distorted salience. But the existence and strength of desire may bear no simple relation to the agent's conception of its object. The desire may have a different motivational source.

One kind of case that concerns Shaftesbury involves motivated ignorance, where a relatively superficial desire is partly explained by another, deeper desire that motivates the first, explained also by an ignorance of that motivation. Getting an adequate conception of the superficial desire's object may leave the motivational force of the secretly motivating desire unaffected. To gain leverage on this, an agent must somehow bring the relation to the deeper desire to consciousness.

The very capacity of rational agents to be aware of their own desires may require that deeper motivating desires be "sly" and "insinuating" (I.173). If an agent would be less likely to act on a desire were they to be aware of having it, then the desire may motivate a more surreptitious pursuit of its object, motivating superficial desires the satisfaction of which will also tend to satisfy the deeper desire and mask its operation at the same time.

"One would think," Shaftesbury writes, "there was nothing easier for us, than to know our own Minds, and understand ... what we plainly drove at, and what we propos'd to our-selves, as our *End*, in every Occurrence of our Lives" (I.171). But this is not so. Ignorance of some of our desires is motivated by those desires. "[T]he chief Interest of *Ambition, Avarice, Corruption,* and every sly insinuating *Vice*, is to prevent this Interview" of ourselves and the consequent discovery of the vices (I.173). Vicious desires are likely to express themselves "tacitly and murmuringly," "by a whisper and indirect insinuation, imperfectly, indistinctly, and confusedly" (1900: 166). Vanity, for instance, may motivate a desire for political office out of proportion to the attraction this would otherwise have and in such a way that the desire's real motivational source remains hidden.

A different kind of case is the sort of false enthusiasm or emotional contagion that Shaftesbury sarcastically calls the "inspiring Disease" (2001: I.45). Here one catches a feeling or passion neither by responding to its object, nor by a desire to emulate, but by "insensible Transpiration" (I.45). Here again, a desire's strength will be relatively independent of one's conception of its object and may be relatively immune to having a more accurate conception.

Cases of these kinds require a form of self-analysis through which agents bring their desires and their mutual relations to light and realistically examine them. So long as an agent views things only from the perspectives of their desires and emotions, the agent is in the grip of those desires and emotions. Avowing a desire is already a step away from being possessed by it. One now occupies a different standpoint (not *from* the desires, but *on* the desire). The desiring view of things can be seen for what it is, a view of things one has by virtue of having the desire.

Shaftesbury also calls soliloquy "self-converse" (I.166), because it involves both giving desires voice and addressing oneself and them from a more realistic perspective. Listening to one's own unconstrained soliloquizing can enable one to identify desires that would otherwise have remained hidden. Moreover, privacy disarms the desire to please, enabling one to be more honest with oneself. "There is nothing in the management of the *visa*," Shaftesbury writes, "than to have a sort of custom of putting them into words, making them speak out and explain themselves as it were *viva-voce*, and not tacitly and murmuringly" (1900: 166).[36] As "our own Subjects of Practice" we can "divide our-selves into *two Partys*" and make our thoughts and feelings the objects of our own awareness and consideration (2001: I.169).

The agent can then interrogate the source of their desires:

> Thus I contend with Fancy and Opinion; and search the Mint and Foundery of *Imagination*. For here the Appetites and Desires are fabricated. Hence they derive their Privilege and Currency. If I can stop the Mischief here, and prevent false coinage; I am safe (I.320).

Desires aim to take over the agent's practical perspective and, in effect, to impersonate the agent. Shaftesbury's "advice to authors," therefore, is that they directly address their desires in a way that disarms their motivational

---

[36] Cf. Cudworth on determining the last "*visum*" or practical judgment before acting.

leverage. "*Idea!* wait a-while till I have examin'd thee, whence thou art, and to whom thou retain'st. Art thou of *Ambition*'s Train? Or dost thou promise only *Pleasure*" (I.320). When a desire's strength depends partly on ignorance of its source, appreciating its etiology can help an agent affect its strength in the direction of their overall good.

After this scrutinizing of desires and their causes, the agent must still "recollect" themselves and place present desires in the framework of their most important concerns over time. "Thus at last a Mind, by knowing *it-self,* and its own proper Powers and Virtues, becomes *free,* and independent. It sees its Hindrances and Obstructions, and finds they are wholly from *it-self,* and from *Opinions wrong-conceived.* The more it conquers in this respect ... the more it is its own *Master*" (III.204).

Although Shaftesbury shares Locke's rational egoism, he rejects his hedonism. To the contrary, the more reflective half of Shaftesbury's divided self is a *better* or nobler self who represents an ideal of character (given by their own moral sense) to which they are committed and on which the goodness of their life is staked.

> And thus as long as I find Men either *angry* or *revengeful, proud* or *asham'd,* I am safe: For they conceive *an Honourable* and *Dishonourable,* a *Foul* and *Fair,* as well as I (II.421).

Shaftesburean self-converse involves responsibility to a personification of an ideal of character to which the agent is committed. The agent views themselves from the perspective of someone who realizes, or respectably pursues, their character ideal and, identifying with their better self, judges what course they should take, taking account of the higher values on which their self-esteem is staked. Consciousness of being a scoundrel makes life miserable, but that is because one thinks villainy base, not vice versa. "[W]e can never really blush for anything beside what we think truly *Shameful*, and what we shou'd still blush for, were we ever so secure as to our Interest" (II.419).

More clearly than Locke, and even more than Cudworth, Shaftesbury conceives of self-critical self-determination in juridical terms as *self-government*. This is really the only place where deontic notions play an important role in his thought. "How do I govern myself?" "This," he writes in his notebooks, "is a matter, and the only matter" (1900: 102). For Shaftesbury, soliloquy involves recognizing and subjecting ourselves to the authoritative prescriptions of our better selves, our "ruling principle." In dividing ourselves into two, we give one perspective authority as "our Counsellor and Governor" (2001: I. 169). "As cruel a Court as *the Inquisition* appears; there must, it seems, be full as formidable a one, erected in our-selves" (I.186). There must be a "superior part which disciplines, instructs, and manages," one with "authority and command" (1900: 169).

Shaftesbury connects the capacity for self-government to the ability to unify and give integrity to a life and to agency over time. Through self-governing soliloquy, we "gain ... *a Will*" (2001: I.187). Only in this way can an agent "be sure of his own Meaning and Design; and as to all his Desires, Opinions, and Inclinations, be warranted *one and the same* Person to day as yesterday, and to morrow and to day" (I.187). Identifying soliloquy with philosophy itself, Shaftesbury writes, "[T]is the known Province of Philosophy to teach us *our-selves*, keep us the *self-same* Persons, and so regulate our governing Fancys, Passions, and Humours, as to make us comprehensible to our selves" (I.283).

Ancient or Modern?

Shaftesbury does not fit easily into Sidgwick's categories. On the one hand, his fundamental philosophical commitments conform to Irwin's Aristotelian naturalist model: (i) *eudaimonism* about practical reason, (ii) the claim that virtue is an intrinsic good (for the virtuous agent), and (iii) the thesis that this good realizes the agent's nature. Furthermore, Shaftesbury steadfastly rejects law-based ethical conceptions, especially in prominent voluntarist formulations, and defends an ethics of virtue. On the other hand, there are elements of Shaftesbury's thought that lend themselves to development in more distinctively modern ways by philosophers who follow him. The clearest example is Shaftesbury's "moral sense," which Hutcheson and Hume will work out in an empiricist framework that is consonant with the emerging empirical sciences. In Hutcheson's hands, a Shaftesburean ethics of virtue takes a distinctively modern form with moral goodness being determined entirely by disinterested approval from an impartial perspective completely independently of the agent's flourishing. And Shaftesbury's focus on other-regarding virtues of natural benevolence and love will help inspire Hutcheson's repudiation of ancient *eudaimonism*; Hutcheson will argue that benevolence is no less an ultimate source of motivation than self-love.[37]

Finally, Shaftesbury's focus on authorship and autonomy and his doctrine that genuine virtue must involve the moral agent's determining themselves by their own moral judgment will also loom large in the modern period, for example, in Butler's doctrine of the authority of conscience and Kant's idea that genuine moral worth must be self-reflectively moral. It is notable in this connection that the one place where deontic notions figure prominently in Shaftesbury's thought is in his view of autonomy as self-government through which an agent holds themselves to be obligated by the judgments of their better self. Here again we see ideas that will be taken in a more explicitly modern direction by Butler and Kant. In these ways Shaftesbury is, like Cudworth, a bridge figure.

---

[37] Another influence on Hutcheson is Cumberland. On this, see Chapter 4.

Leibniz

Leibniz is a bridge figure also. Like Shaftesbury, Leibniz sounds classical (Aristotelian) naturalist themes, though with a more systematic metaphysical underpinning. Both are philosophical optimists, holding that reality is a harmonious whole. But Leibniz's theology is more orthodox and philosophically elaborated than Shaftesbury's. Leibniz's God is a transcendent being who creates "the best of all possible worlds" (Leibniz 1985: 228). And Leibniz's theodicy is rooted in explicit doctrines concerning the natures of being and perfection, the principle of sufficient reason, the identity of indiscernibles, and the analyticity of all truth. Leibniz is concerned less with edification, and more with working out a comprehensive rationalist metaphysics that can fit with modern science.[38]

Leibniz was also a harmonizer by philosophical temperament. He sought to bridge differences between Protestants and Catholics, and although he was definitely sensitive to conceptual differences between the good and the right, he attempted to demonstrate fundamental coincidences between them even so.

Schneewind writes that Leibniz's conception of morality is "centered on love," with "law and obligation hav[ing] a vanishingly small part to play" (Schneewind 1998: 246). This is correct in the main, but deontic ideas nonetheless enter into Leibniz's thought in surprising and interesting ways, as we shall see.

Like Cudworth and Shaftesbury, Leibniz is a sharp critic of all forms of voluntarism, both secular and theological. But whereas Cudworth and Shaftesbury focus their criticisms on Hobbes and Locke, respectively, Leibniz's main opponent is Pufendorf. Also, like Cudworth, Leibniz holds that God's loving nature is a perfectly virtuous exemplar we are to emulate. More, Leibniz's official view is that moral obligation or "moral necessity" derives from this. "Moral" in "moral necessity," he says, means "that which is equivalent to 'natural' for a good man" (Leibniz 1988: 171). In other words, what a perfectly virtuous being *would* do is what we imperfect beings morally *should* do. To say that something is obligatory on this definition is not to say anything intrinsically deontic or juridical. It is rather to say that it is what a perfectly virtuous exemplar would do as a matter of natural necessity. Like Shaftesbury's, this appears to be a revisionary view of obligation.[39]

Leibniz seeks also to understand justice in terms of the universal benevolence of the ideally virtuous, apparently reducing justice to benevolence, and so the right to the good. Justice is, he says, "the charity of the wise" (171). Because "the good man is benevolent toward all," "the highest rule of right is that *everything is directed to the greatest general good* or common felicity" (quoted in

---

[38] It should be remembered not only that Leibniz helped invent the calculus, but also that he thought his dynamic teleological doctrines of monads provided a necessary foundation for the emerging natural philosophy (science).

[39] In Chapter 8 I shall argue that, remarkably, Kant also holds a version of this same doctrine.

Johns 2013: 83). At one point, indeed, Leibniz formulates this in terms that will be taken up by Hutcheson and later utilitarians as the greatest happiness principle: "to act in accordance with supreme reason is to act in such a manner that the greatest quantity of good available is obtained for the greatest multitude possible and that as much felicity is diffused as the reason of things can bear" (Hruschka 1991: 166).[40]

But this apparent reduction of the right to the good is deceiving. Some of Leibniz's earliest writings concern jurisprudence and the "science of right" (Johns 2013).[41] And various arguments and observations Leibniz makes concerning his theory of justice as rationally regulated benevolence also suggest that he takes conceptual connections between the right and legitimate *demands* to underlie and affect the interpretation of his theory. As an example, Leibniz holds that justice (conceptually) concerns acting in ways to which no one has a legitimate *complaint*. "Everyone will perhaps agree, perhaps, to this nominal definition, that justice is a constant will to act in such a way that no one has a reason to complain of us" (Leibniz 1988: 53).[42] Leibniz parlays this conceptual claim into a fundamental principle of equity or reciprocity that it is always unjust not to provide others what one would ask or demand from them. Any case for anything approaching utilitarianism on *this* basis is less on the grounds of equal love than on the grounds of equal respect for all persons as having a common authority to make claims and demands of one another.

Another aspect of Leibniz's importance for the moral philosophy that will follow him is his significance for Kant. Much of Kant's critical or transcendental turn in moral philosophy, similar to that in the *Critique of Pure Reason*, came from his rejection of Wolffian rationalism, which was close to Leibniz's. Kant was especially critical of Leibniz's compatibilist view of freedom, which he disdainfully called "the freedom of a turnspit" (Kant 1996b: 5:97). Despite this, the details of Kant's account of moral obligation will mirror Leibniz's idea of moral necessity. For Kant, as for Leibniz, obligation derives from laws of the nature of a perfect agent (in Kant's terms, a "holy will"). The major difference concerns their respective views of what such laws consist in. For Leibniz, they are perfectionist standards that at once unify the agent's good, justice, and the good of all. For Kant, they are "laws of freedom." This is the signature Kantian doctrine of "autonomy": "the property of the will by which it is a law to itself (independently of any property of the objects of volition)" (Kant 1996a: 440). This difference notwithstanding, however, Kant's moral philosophy, often

---

[40] According to Hruschka 1991, Hutcheson gives his own translation of this passage of Leibniz's as stating his own view in Hutcheson 2004: 125.
[41] *New Method for Learning and Teaching Jurisprudence* was written in 1667. Johns 2013 contains a translation and analysis of this work from which I shall quote below.
[42] From *Meditation on the Common Concept of Justice*, written in 1702–1703.

taken to be a paradigm of deontological ethics, turns out to retain Leibnizian elements that require significant alteration in this common view.

As we noted above, we must complicate the kind of characterization of Leibniz's ethics that Schneewind gives. To be sure, the most prominent elements of Leibniz's thought are a good-based ethics of virtue with justice and obligation being ultimately either reduced to or identified with God's perfectly virtuous universal benevolence. However, as I have indicated, there are also irreducibly deontic elements that resist such an analysis that significantly complicate the picture.

Perfectionism: Identifying Goods (Personal and Impersonal) and Justice

Let us begin, though, with the better-known elements of Leibniz's thought. Most fundamentally, Leibniz's ethics are, like Shaftesbury's, an ethics of virtue. Against the natural lawyers' focus on conduct or "external acts," Leibniz objects that moral goodness concerns the agent's motives (Leibniz 1988: 73). Moreover, Leibniz treats justice primarily as a virtue, holding even that the justice of actions depends on motivation.

> [H]e who acts well, not out of hope or fear, but by an inclination of his soul, is so far from not behaving justly that, on the contrary, he acts more justly than all others, imitating, in a certain way, as a man, divine justice (72).

Against voluntarists like Pufendorf, Leibniz argues that their theory makes it impossible to say that God himself is good and just, since goodness and justice could not possibly themselves derive simply from God's commands. It is rather, Leibniz argues, God's benevolent goodness that underwrites his authority and therefore the legitimacy of his commands. Of course, neither Pufendorf nor Locke denies that God's *goodness* is independent of his command. Their position is that without his actual commands there is no deontic morality, nothing that genuinely *obligates* moral agents.

Leibniz might argue, however, that they effectively credit God's goodness as the source of his authority of command in arguing, as at least Pufendorf seems to, that God's authority derives from something like a debt of gratitude. If it is ultimately because of God's goodness to us that we owe him obedience, then his authority is ultimately rooted in his benevolence.

Not only goodness, however, but justice itself is "an essential attribute of God" (71). So the standard of justice cannot derive from God's "free will." When God acts or wills justly, there must be reasons – reasons of justice – that weigh with him and make his resulting will and actions just. Leibniz concludes that for us to act justly, we should act on these reasons also and thereby "imitate divine justice" (72). Indeed, it appears to follow that we would have these reasons even if God did not exist, though there are complications here that we must consider below.

When he comes to discuss obligation, Leibniz takes over Grotius and Pufendorf's term "moral necessity," but gives it a subversive redefinition that seems to rob it of any distinctively deontic normativity (Grotius 2005: I, 150–151; Pufendorf 1934: 20). Whereas moral necessity for Grotius and Pufendorf is tied to accountability for compliance with legitimate demands, Leibniz identifies moral necessity with a necessity of the virtuous person's *nature*. "Right is a kind of moral possibility, and obligation is a moral necessity. By moral I mean that which is equivalent to 'natural' for a good man" (Leibniz 1988: 171). Leibniz uses "right" and "morally possible," as we shall see presently, to mean actions that do no wrong (are morally permissible) and that wrong no one (do not violate anyone's rights). And clearly he intends moral necessity to entail wrongness, that is, being morally impermissible, or wrong not to do. Indeed, Leibniz works out a deontic logic, which he calls "modes of right," in his *Elements of Natural Right* (1669–1671), which makes these entailments explicit (Johns 2013: 48–56).

What I want to focus on now, however, is the way Leibniz reduces moral possibility (also "moral power" in his earlier text on the "science of right") and moral necessity to what is composable with, and what is necessary to, God's wise and benevolent nature, respectively. Plainly there is nothing essentially deontic or juridical in the ideas of perfect wisdom and perfect benevolence. "A good man," Leibniz says, "is one who loves everybody, in so far as reason permits" (Leibniz 1988: 171). Leibniz follows this with his famous definition of justice as "the charity of the wise man" (1988: 171). If there is any doubt about Leibniz's meaning, it is cleared up in the following passage: "moral necessity ... is always followed by its effect in the wise. This kind of necessity is happy and desirable" (1985: 395). Moral necessity is natural necessity, that is, nomological necessity, of the wise person's nature. It is what such a person invariably does or would do. And what they would do is what we imperfect beings should do, what we are, Leibniz says, obligated to do.

Similarly, "right," for Leibniz, has the meaning of "not wrong." And something is not wrong, hence right, if it is not contrary to the wise person's nature, if it is something the wise person *might* do, consistently with their nature. If an action is something a wise person might do, if it is composable with their nature, then it is something imperfect beings *may* do. Like Shaftesbury's implicit definition of obligation in terms of normative reasons, these are revisionary definitions of obligation and right, respectively. There is nothing essentially deontic or juridical in them, nothing that puts them on the law or demand, as opposed to on the counsel, side of the Suárezian ledger.

Moreover, like Aquinas's classical natural law view, Leibniz's position requires a metaphysical guarantee of harmonies and coincidences, both within morality and between morality and self-interest. Within morality, Leibniz's perfectionism leads him ultimately to identify all of the following: justice, enlightened benevolence, wisdom, virtue, and happiness. (We're beginning to get into Spinoza territory here. What we would need to get all the way there would be to be identify all of these with reality itself.)

First, again, justice is "the charity of the wise," so whatever an enlightened love of all leads to is just. Subject to some caveats we shall note presently, this guarantees a connection between justice and overall good. Indeed, even in his early jurisprudential writings, Leibniz identifies justice and injustice with "what is useful or harmful to the public," respectively (Johns 2013: 153).

But neither are wisdom and benevolence really distinct, for Leibniz. Every being's good is its perfection, and though the good life is pleasurable, that is not because pleasure is intrinsically good. Rather, "[p]leasure is a knowledge or feeling of perfection, not only in ourselves, but also in others" (Leibniz 1988: 83). This assures that knowledge of (the prospect of) good (perfection) in *anyone* will lead to a desire for it for its own sake. Indeed, it apparently follows that this knowledge itself constitutes either pleasure in or a desire for the good of others, depending on whether the latter is actual or envisioned as a possibility in prospect. Since wisdom includes knowledge of perfection, virtue or justice can also be described as "the habit of acting according to wisdom" (83).

Leibniz's identification of moral goodness and justice with universal benevolence led him to assert a version of the greatest happiness principle, for perhaps the first time in the history of ethical thought: "To act in accordance with supreme reason is to act in such a manner that the greatest quantity of good available is obtained for the greatest multitude possible and that as much felicity is diffused as the reason of things can bear."[43] The utilitarians would reject Leibniz's perfectionism, but formally draw the same maximizing consequences from equal concern for the good of all.

Despite Leibniz's stress on benevolence, however, he is ultimately a *eudaimonist* for whom genuine normative reasons must be grounded in the agent's own good. But his perfectionism and views about the relation between knowledge of perfection and pleasure and desire assure that there cannot be any deep conflict between the agent's goodness and the good of all. This is confirmed in a criticism Leibniz makes of Grotius's response to Carneades's challenge that justice is foolish since it is "folly to care for another at loss to oneself" (quoted in Johns 2013: 28). Grotius, recall, argues that justice is grounded in sociability and not in the agent's own good, however broadly construed. To this Leibniz replies that acting against one's own good is indeed foolish, and that the proper

---

[43] This comes from a review Leibniz published anonymously, "Observationes de Principio Juris," published in 1700 in *Monathlicher Auszug/Aus Allerhand Neu-herausgegebenen/ Nützlichen und Artigen Büchern* (Hanover: 1700), p. 378. It is quoted (and translated) in Hruschka 1991: 166. Hruschka argues that this is the first formulation of the greatest happiness principle.

response to the Carneadean challenge is the Ciceronian one that justice realizes an essential *intrinsic* benefit (what Cicero calls *bonum honestum*) even when it is disadvantageous (not instrumentally beneficial or *utile*).[44] Knowledge that an action will bring about others' good is pleasurable in itself.

Despite these coincidences between justice, overall good, and the agent's good, Leibniz nonetheless argues that not everyone is sufficiently wise to appreciate them. "If God did not exist" and did not reward and punish virtue and vice, respectively, Leibniz writes, even "wise men would have no more cause to be benevolent than such as would be required for their own welfare."[45] But no problem arises for the wise, since they appreciate the connections between justice, public good, and the agent's good that Leibniz draws. Eternal sanctions are necessary, however, for the rest of us who truly believe *eudaimonism* (that our own good is the only source of normative practical reasons) but fail to appreciate Leibnizian perfectionist connections. God thereby "ensures that every good act will be beneficial, and every bad one harmful, to the agent. So that not even a man who endures torture and death for the public good can be regarded as an idiot" (Hostler 1975: 59). God assures a harmony between even the *apparent* eternal interests of all members of the "Universal Republic of Spirits" or "Kingdom of Grace," guaranteeing for each a coincidence between virtue and good (17).

Freedom, Agency, and Necessity

If only because they were to constitute such an important point of departure for Kant, it is important to say something about Leibniz's views on free agency and necessity and how these interact with his ethical claims. Leibniz famously distinguishes between metaphysical necessity and moral necessity. Something is metaphysically necessary if it is something that must take place "because the opposite implies a contradiction" (Johns 2013: 129). A moral necessity, by contrast, is one "whereby a wise being chooses the best, and every mind follows the strongest inclination."[46]

God creates the best of all possible worlds and does so by moral necessity. God, like any agent, does what seems best to him, and God, in his wisdom, sees, and is thereby moved to create, the best world. But there were other possible worlds in the sense that their existence would in themselves imply no contradiction. A contradiction only arises when we add in their having to have been created by God.

---

[44] See Johns 2013: 28. For a discussion of Cicero on this point, see Irwin 2007: 600.
[45] Translated and quoted in Hostler 1975: 59.
[46] These passages come from Leibniz's correspondence with Clarke. They are quoted in Johns 2013: 56. Leibniz accuses Clarke of failing to make this distinction.

If this is the best of all possible worlds, the question might arise, what reason can we have to do one thing rather than another? It is a central aspect of Leibniz's metaphysics, however, that all substances act teleologically with some form of perception and appetite. There is a sense, therefore, in which all substances act for reasons coming from their apprehension, often confused, unconscious, and subrational, of the good. All activity, whether God's, our imperfect rational activity, or the activity of subrational substances aims at the good. The best of all possible worlds is thus composed of substances that aim at their respective goods. It is therefore essential to the world as we find it that rational substances face the question of what is the greatest good they can achieve for themselves.

Leibniz is a compatibilist. All substances aim at the good, and their choices are necessitated by their nature through their perception, however confused, of their goods. But Leibniz holds that this necessitation in no way impedes freedom. Liberty or freedom, for Leibniz, is a *power* of action. And action is, in its nature, aimed at the good. So genuinely free action is action where this aim succeeds, where we are determined by perceptions and appetites that successfully lead us to genuine good. In this way, moral necessity is thoroughly compatible with genuine freedom or liberty.

Leibniz denies not just the liberty of indifference, that also that there exists or need be anything like a faculty of will that can choose arbitrarily. Locke and Cudworth deny these, but they hold that in addition to beliefs and desires, genuinely free agents also have a self-reflective capacity to direct their attention – as Locke puts it, "exerting that dominion [the mind] takes itself to have over any part of a man" (Locke 1975: II.21.15). According to Leibniz, all beings act for the good; rational beings differ from subrational ones only in being determined by less confused and more accurate perceptions of it.

Right and Claim

To this point, I have been emphasizing the non-deontic character of Leibniz's ethics, both his *eudaimonism* and his apparent reduction of justice to universal benevolence. But this is only part of the story, albeit its dominant theme. There are also irreducibly deontic elements in Leibniz's thought. These are most notable in his early writings on jurisprudence, both in his "science of right" (*New Method of Learning and Teaching Jurisprudence*) and in his *Elements of Natural Right*. Just to give a sense of the deontic theme, consider the following passage from the *Elements*:

> The just is not accurately enough defined as the public useful, since it may be permitted to prefer the ruin of many to my own ruin. ... The just is the balanced relationship between the love of myself and the love of neighbor (quoted in Johns 2013: 32).

From the perspective of universal benevolence, the ruin of many is clearly worse than an individual's ruin, as Leibniz himself here acknowledges. Nevertheless, it is not unjust, Leibniz is saying, for an agent to act to protect themselves even at greater universal cost. Justice is the "balanced relationship" between self-love and the love of others. And Leibniz seems to be ruling out the possibility that this balance is to be determined in terms of universal *good*, that is, in terms of what maximizes benefit overall.

If this is indeed Leibniz's view, it follows that he cannot consistently hold that the deontic ideas of right, obligation, and the like – those on the law side of the Suárezian divide – can be reduced to those of good – those on the normative reasons or counsel side. We get some more indication of how Leibniz must be thinking in his "science of right."

We can begin with his definition of right and obligation. As Christopher Johns points out, Leibniz writes in later notes, "Right and obligation are not to be treated separately. They constitute one relation composed from both."[47] This suggests something like the kind of correlativity claim associated with Hohfeld and Michael Thompson (Hohfeld 1923; Thompson 2004). Obligations that are owed *to* someone entail the latter's claim right to the obligation's being fulfilled. There is really just a single deontic/juridical relation viewed from two different "poles," as Thompson puts it (Thompson 2004: 335).

When, however, we look at Leibniz's initial definitions of right and obligation in this early work from the perspective of his later definitions, this suggestion may seem dispelled. "*The morality*," Leibniz writes, "that is, the justice or injustice of the act," "springs from" a "moral quality" of the person (Johns 2013: 154). This quality is "twofold, namely, the *power* to act and the *necessity* to act; therefore, moral power is called *right*, and moral necessity is called *obligation*" (154). Recall now from Leibniz's deontic logic that "right" must have the force of "all right" or not wrong, as opposed to right in the sense of obligatory. After all, Leibniz is here distinguishing right from obligation.

But when we take this together with Leibniz's later accounts of justice and moral necessity as "the charity of the wise," we apparently get accounts that lack distinctively deontic/juridical entailments. Being right, or not unjust, simply means being compossible with God's wise benevolence, something that deliberation from the perspective of equal concern for all would not rule out. Similarly, being obligatory or morally necessary means being an act that these (good-based) grounds of action converge on.

Indeed, even if we read "right" as expressing an irreducibly deontic relation, being not unjust is only a Hohfeldian liberty right (that one does no wrong or does no one a wrong), not a claim right that would entail a correlative obligation. This, recall, was the difference between Hobbes's right of nature and

---

[47] From "Notae in Tabulam Jurisprudentiae" (1696). Quoted in Johns 2013: 9.

the natural rights that Pufendorf recognizes (and consequently, the source of Pufendorf's objections to Hobbes). A liberty right consists just in the absence of obligation to act otherwise; it entails no obligations to others like the correlatives of claim rights.

Two sections later, however, Leibniz writes:

> The causes of right in one person are a kind of loss of right in another; that is, the second person has an obligation to the first. Conversely, acquiring an obligation from another is the cause of recuperation of right (156).

This is, of course, precisely the correlativity point about directed (bipolar) obligations and claim rights. Moreover, Leibniz sketches out on this basis a jurisprudence that bears a remarkable resemblance to Kant's *Doctrine of Right*. Each person has a fundamental right of freedom, which includes a right to the body. Everyone's right of freedom imposes correlative obligations on others and is constrained by their similar rights. Moreover, this "right in persons is called right to coercion," justifying the use of force in its defense (154).

Obviously, this line of thought requires an irreducibly deontic/juridical framework. There is simply no way to get the relevant entailments to go through on Leibniz's official good-based definitions of justice, right, and obligation. Moreover, Leibniz derives from his fundamental moral qualities three deontic "precepts" of decreasing stringency: (i) "strict right": do no harm, (ii) "equity": give everyone their due, and (iii) "piety": live honorably and respect authority.

We find similarly irreducibly deontic thoughts in Leibniz's *Elements of Natural Right* where Leibniz elaborates the precept of equity in terms of reciprocal claims or demands: "The *equitable* is to grant to the other as much as one would *demand* from another" (32). Since it is formulated in terms of demands, this is a deontic formulation of the Golden Rule. The root idea is that it is a fundamental violation of justice as reciprocity to deny others not what one might hope or be pleased by from them, but what one would claim or demand from them.

We find corollary ideas in Leibniz's *Meditation on the Common Concept of Justice*.

> Everyone will agree, perhaps, to this nominal definition, that justice is a constant will to act in such a way that no one has a reason to complain of us (Leibniz 1988: 53).

There is an obvious affinity between this formulation and that concerning reciprocal demands from the *Elements*. Whatever can justify complaint can justify a demand, and *vice versa*.

In an especially interesting series of steps, beginning with the obligation of strict right – to do no harm – Leibniz then justifies increasingly expansive duties in terms of the Golden Rule, expressed, as above, in terms of reciprocal claims and demands. The first concerns helping someone avoid an evil when one can do so at little cost.

> Let him ask himself what he would say and hope for if he should find himself actually on the point of falling into an evil, which another could make him avoid by a turn of his hand (54).

Leibniz assumes his readers will easily agree that refusing such help would justify complaint, which one can check by applying the Golden Rule formulated in terms of demand or complaint to oneself.

Next Leibniz considers a case where someone cannot prevent evil, but can relieve it at little cost. Suppose one is drowning and another will not throw one a rope, as they could easily do. Would not one, would not anyone, complain? And next, a case where another is in a position to help one acquire a good.

> A great good is going to come to you; an impediment appears; I can remove that impediment without pain: would you not believe yourself to have a right to ask it of me, and to remind me that I would ask it of you, if I were in a similar position? (55)

Leibniz's final step is to pose a case in which he asks, "[H]ow will you refuse the only remaining request, that is to secure a great good for me, when you can do it without inconveniencing yourself in any way?" and can only give as a reason for refusal "a simple 'I don't want to'." (55). In all these cases, others would have "reasons of complaint."

Leibniz concludes with a "principle of equity," which holds "that one should grant [to others] whatever one would wish in a similar situation, without claiming to be privileged ... or to be able to allege one's will as a reason" (56). It is clear from the context, that by "wish," Leibniz means something that is naturally addressed to its object, like a request, claim, or demand, that is, not an idle wish, or even an ardent desire that one would not impose on others. The basic idea is that equity is rooted in the idea that any claims we make on others must be grounded in a common basic authority to make claims of one another. So understood, equity is a fundamentally deontic or juridical idea, squarely on the law or command side of the Suárezian idea. Indeed, it seems closely related to Grotius's claim that sociability is the "fountain of right."

How should we relate the deontic themes we have just been discussing to Leibniz's identification of justice with the charity of the wise? And to his related support for something like the principle of utility or the "greatest happiness"? If Leibniz aims to *reduce* justice to universal good as a metaethical thesis, holding that the good is the only fundamental notion of which justice can be understood as a "species," to use Sidgwick's terms, then these deontological claims apparently conflict with that. On the other hand, if Leibniz is making the substantive normative claim that promoting overall good is the fundamental just-making feature, there may be no deep conflict.

This is brought out in Leibniz's response to an objection that a judge could never justly sentence a criminal because they would not want to be sentenced were they in the criminal's shoes.

> The reply is easy: the judge must put himself not only in the place of the criminal, but also in that of others who are interested that the crime be punished. And the balance of good (in which the lesser evil is included) must determine it (1988: 46).

As Irwin points out, reasoning of this kind would seem to be able to justify the kinds of trade-offs for which utilitarianism is famous (or infamous) (Irwin 2008: 319). Indeed, it appears to be an argument of the very same kind that R. M. Hare will advance in the late twentieth century for act utilitarianism as an ideal morality (Hare 1982). The important thing to realize, however, is that if an argument like this one of Leibniz's ends up supporting utilitarianism, it does so on very different grounds than that this is what is recommended from the standpoint of universal *benevolence*. It derives it from a principle of universal *respect* for individuals' authority or standing to make claims and demands. Indeed, Leibniz says, "there is in justice a certain respect for the good of others" (Leibniz 1969: 136).

It is important to be clear that the ethical position that, following Bentham and Mill, we call utilitarianism is a *normative* ethical position, and, more particularly, that it is a normative thesis about the *right*. It is the view that the determinant of whether an action is morally right or not is its relation (direct or indirect) to promoting universal good or happiness. It is not simply a claim about the good.

Historically, there have been three different ways of supporting this normative deontic view. One has been to anchor it in universal benevolence or care, as Hutcheson does. A second is to argue that from an impartial or impersonal point of view, everyone's good or happiness matters equally. Sidgwick explicitly does this with respect to good, and early chapters of Mill's *Utilitarianism* might be read as implicitly doing it with respect to happiness. And a third is to derive utilitarianism from universal respect. As I see it, economic forms of utilitarianism that give equal weight to preferences ("consumer sovereignty") implicitly invoke universal respect in this way.

Respect and benevolence or care are different attitudes (Darwall 2006: 126–130). Benevolence and care involve desires for someone's good or happiness, however that might come about. (Recognition) respect, on the other hand, is concerned fundamentally with how we conduct ourselves toward someone. Whereas benevolence is targeted on the good, respect is focused on the right – on doing right by, or justice to, its object.

Leibniz's ideas seem to hover between these. On the one hand, he lays out an ethics of virtue with his leading virtues being forms of love and benevolence. On the other, he discusses fundamental relations of right, and some of his arguments for universal beneficence (if not benevolence) are rooted in a principle of equity or equal respect. Finally, there are places, as we noted above, where Leibniz seems to pull away from the kind of impartial weighing of interests that universal beneficence requires. If I am "permitted to prefer the ruin of many to my own ruin" (quoted in Johns 2013), then anyone is. So perhaps justice and morality does not demand universal beneficence.

Thinking along these lines might lead us to favor as a theory of right not act utilitarianism but a form of rule utilitarianism. We start with the idea that everyone has the same claim-making authority but want to know what demands we can justifiably make of one another. We then restate this question as "Given that we all have the same claim-making authority, what demand-warranting principles or rules should there be?" Since our equal authority warrants weighing everyone's preferences equally, we then reinterpret this as "What demand-warranting principles or rules are there such that their acceptance would maximize preference-satisfaction?" It seems clear, as rule utilitarians of all stripes have historically argued, that such rules would not require universal beneficence.

In thinking about Leibniz's view in relation to the good and the right, it is worth noting some criticisms Barbeyrac makes of Leibniz and of Leibniz's critique of Pufendorf, together with some comments about these by Schneewind and Irwin. These center around Barbeyrac's complaint that, unlike Pufendorf, Leibniz fails to appreciate the fundamentally deontic character of morality and that moral obligations purport to give us reasons that cannot be reduced to our own good. Barbeyrac's most important criticism, according to Schneewind, is that whereas Leibniz holds "that all reasons for action, and hence all motives, arise from considerations of just one kind," "moral law brings into our deliberations reasons for action that are different in kind" from considerations of our own good (Schneewind 1998: 256). To this we might add that deontic considerations of moral obligation differ also from those of universal or impersonal good, even if the moral law requires universal beneficence.

Irwin defends Leibniz, and implicitly, Aristotelian naturalism, against this critique (Irwin 2008: 327–330). He notes that Barbeyrac oversimplifies Leibniz's *eudaimonism*. As can be seen in Leibniz's comments on Grotius's response to Carneades's challenge, Leibniz (and Aristotelian naturalists generally) can distinguish between the agent's *advantage* or narrow or instrumental interests and the *intrinsic* benefit that is realized by benevolent actions for the common good (the *bonum honestum*). Secondly, Barbeyrac's critique that Leibniz fails to appreciate morality's deontic character, which Pufendorf's account explains better, rests, Irwin argues, on the implausible voluntarist view that obligation must be voluntarily imposed.

Both of these defenses can be resisted. As we noted in connection with Grotius's response to the Carneadean challenge, the *bonum honestum* provides a reason of a fundamentally different kind from (deontic) morality as Grotius understands it, and hence, a reason of the wrong kind to support or be entailed by it. This is essentially Barbeyrac's "deeper criticism," as Schneewind presents it. And second, Irwin is assuming that the criterion for being on the law, command, or obligation side of the Suárezian divide is *imposition* by superior authority. It is certainly true that Suárez and Pufendorf, as theological voluntarists, would agree with this second point. But there is a more fundamental conceptual connection between these deontic notions and accountability. The voluntarists accept this connection, but hold that one can be accountable only for what has been imposed by superior authority. However, this can be denied, as it was, indeed, by Grotius and has been by later philosophers like Butler, the British rationalists, and many philosophers today.

One of the things that is so interesting about Leibniz is that he actually insists on this connection, as his "nominal definition" of justice in terms of justified complaint and his formulation of the principle of equity make clear. At the same time, however, the dominant elements of his thought are a perfectionist theory of virtue and the good that recall classical naturalist themes.

5

Hutcheson and Butler

Francis Hutcheson (1694–1746) and Bishop Joseph Butler (1692–1752) were true contemporaries whose lives overlapped for fifty years, and whose best-known works appeared within a year of one another. Although they also had similar intellectual temperaments and styles, their philosophical approaches differed in important ways that reverberated through the moral philosophy that followed.

Hutcheson's *An Inquiry into the Original of Our Ideas of Beauty and Virtue* was first published in 1725 (2004), and Butler's *Sermons* appeared in 1726 (2017). Both were sharply analytical thinkers, and both shared a keen insight into aspects of human psychology centrally involved in moral life, what we now call moral psychology. Moreover, both laid great stress on a feature of moral psychology they held to be implicated in moral judgment. Hutcheson called this, following Shaftesbury, "moral sense," and Butler referred to it alternately as the "principle of reflection" or "conscience."

For both Hutcheson and Butler, as for Shaftesbury, moral judgment involves the human capacity to reflect upon and respond affectively to motives, characters, and actions in a way that abstracts (more or less) from self-interest and other forms of partiality as well as from the effects of mood and passion. However, the role of disinterested, dispassionate moral reflection for these two philosophers is profoundly different. According to Hutcheson, it is an *observer's* moral sense that enables a person to make moral evaluations of motivation and actions, but these evaluations are not self-reflexive – the agent is not evaluating their own, or even others', moral sense. For Butler, on the other hand, conscience is a moral faculty by which agents crucially make judgments of *themselves*, judgments they employ to shape their own actions. Conscience is action-guiding for Butler in a way that moral sense is not for Hutcheson.

Butler agrees, moreover, with the Shaftesburean doctrine that genuine virtue requires self-reflective moral agency. Indeed, Butler holds that conscience is a necessary condition for moral agency itself. For Hutcheson, by contrast, moral sense is inessential in virtuous conduct, at best, and, at worst, it can undermine virtue by giving an otherwise virtuous agent motive to indulge complacently in reflecting on their own virtue. It can give them, in Bernard Williams's words, "one thought too many" (Williams 1981a: 18).

Considering Hutcheson and Butler's respective relations to Leibniz can bring out a related difference. Like Leibniz, Hutcheson takes the most virtuous (morally best) motive to be a universal form of benevolence or love. Though morally best, Hutchesonian love is not itself moralized. It is a desire for what Hutcheson calls the "natural good" (well-being or benefit) of all beings. This entails the point we just noted. Unlike Shaftesbury and Butler, and perhaps like Leibniz, virtue for Hutcheson does not itself require moral judgment or moral sense.[1] Indeed, since Hutcheson holds that all desires (other than arational appetites and passions) have someone's welfare or natural good as their object, Hutcheson holds that it is actually impossible for moral sense to motivate action directly. Butler, again, holds that virtue consists in conscientious self-guidance.

A second difference springs from this. The object of universal benevolence is, Hutcheson and Leibniz believe, the greatest happiness of all. In fact, as we noted in the last chapter, Hutcheson may have taken the formulation of the greatest happiness principle in his *Inquiry* directly from Leibniz.[2] Butler, however, argues against Hutcheson that virtue cannot be reduced to benevolence. Partly he has in mind the Shaftesburean (and later Kantian) doctrine we have just mentioned: genuine virtue involves moral autonomy, that is, the agent's directing themselves by their own moral judgment. But Butler also rejects the proto-utilitarian thesis that morality always requires, or even recommends, the action that would bring the greatest happiness overall. There are other morally relevant considerations, like justice and honesty, that, Butler argues, cannot be reduced to promoting the general welfare.

Hutcheson is perhaps most significant for his influence on Hume. Several familiar Humean doctrines – for example, that morality is derived from sentiment rather than reason, that reason is incapable of motivating, and Hume's account of obligation – come directly from Hutcheson. Hume is drawn to Hutcheson because Hutcheson provides a promising way of accounting for key features of ethics and ethical judgment within a fundamentally empiricist framework that is consonant with the emerging experimental sciences. At the same time, there are important differences between Hutcheson and Hume that make Hutcheson a particularly interesting figure from the perspective of the history of modern moral philosophy.

As may have been evident in what we have just noted about Hutcheson's ethics of virtue as universal love, explicitly *deontic* morality is not at the center of his theorizing. When, indeed, he embraces the greatest happiness principle, it

---

[1] I say, "perhaps like Leibniz," since we noted some passages where Leibniz seems to hold that virtue involves *respect* for others' goods, and respect (recognition of others' moral standing) is moralized in its nature.

[2] See Chapter 5, footnote 39.

is not as an account of moral obligation or right, but more precisely of the morally *choiceworthy* (of what moral sense recommends concerning "election") (Hutcheson 2004: 125). In his *Illustrations on the Moral Sense*, Hutcheson goes so far, indeed, as to term "ought" an "unlucky Word in Morals" (2002: 156).

These Hutchesonian ideas have clear resonances in Hume. Like Hutcheson's moral sense, what Hume calls moral sentiment is a disinterested response to motive and character. As Hume memorably puts it: "[T]he external performance has no merit" (Hume 1978: 477). And like Hutcheson's, Hume's ethics are decidedly virtue theoretic. The only place that genuinely deontic notions enter for Hume, like the ancients, is the virtue of justice, which Hume holds to be an "artificial" rather than a natural virtue. Quite unlike Hume, however, Hutcheson holds that there is a bright line between *moral* goodness and other estimable or praiseworthy natural abilities and talents. This, indeed, is a direct consequence of Hutcheson's doctrine of the moral sense, which Hume also rejects, though both are moral sentimentalists.

The *Inquiry*'s signature thesis is that the ideas of moral goodness and moral evil cannot be reduced to those of natural goods and evils. Hutcheson accepts Locke's concept empiricism according to which simple, no-further-analyzable ideas can be received only through some sense. It follows that if, as Hutcheson believes, moral goodness and evil are to be understood in terms of the distinctive responses of "approbation" and "condemnation," respectively, and if "Approbation and Condemnation are probably simple ideas, which cannot be farther explained" (Hutcheson 2004: 217), then there must be a dedicated sense, the moral sense, through which we have these ideas. Hutcheson therefore recognizes a fundamental distinction between moral approval and disapproval ("condemnation"), on the one hand, and other, non-moral forms of esteem and disesteem, however disinterested and dispassionate these may be. Hume will reject both doctrines. He will reject Hutcheson's theory of moral sense in favor of his thesis that moral sentiment is produced by the same general psychological mechanisms (sympathy and the association ideas) that are in play in non-moral esteem and disesteem. And whereas Hutcheson claims that "involuntary Disadvantage[s]" and "Fortune" cannot "exclude any Mortal from the most heroick Virtue," Hume will hold that the difference between "moral virtues" and "natural abilities" is merely "verbal" and not worry much about the relation of virtue to luck (Hutcheson 2004: 134; Hume 1975a: 279).

Unlike ancient versions, Hutcheson's virtue ethics is a theory of distinctively *moral* virtue, not in Aristotle's sense of concerning passions and actions rather than intellect, but as eliciting responses that are constitutive of a distinctive kind of non-Aristotelian value: *moral* goodness. As Hutcheson understands them, virtues realize moral goodness by eliciting, or being such as to elicit, the irreducibly moral idea he calls "approbation," which non-morally estimable traits and characters do not elicit. Canvassing cardinal Aristotelian virtues such as temperance and courage, Hutcheson says that these are genuine virtues only to the extent that they are "dispositions universally necessary to promote publick Good, and denote Affections toward rational Agents" (Hutcheson 2004: 102).

In this way, then, Hutcheson counts as a modern moral philosopher. His theories of moral goodness and the morally choiceworthy are intended to have narrower scope than the kinds of goodness that are in play in ancient ethics. They implicate responses, approbation and condemnation, that Hutcheson takes to be distinctive of morality. When Hutcheson puts forward a version of the greatest happiness principle, it is "[i]n comparing the moral Qualitys of Actions" (with moral sense) "in order to regulate our Election among various Actions propos'd" (125).

Despite this modern moral focus, deontic language and notions of obligation and right enter into Hutcheson's thinking only as derivative of moral goodness. Hutcheson derives both his principle of moral choiceworthiness and his theses about justice and rights from his fundamental theory of moral good.

There is another way in which Hutcheson rejects the Aristotelian naturalism that is typical of ancient ethics; Hutcheson denies any form of *eudaimonism*. He holds that considerations of other people's welfare or "natural good" are no less rationally choiceworthy than those concerning the agent's own. Though he believes that reason *by itself* cannot motivate an agent to pursue others' good or, for that matter, the agent's own, he nonetheless thinks that calm rational reflection can produce *both* self-regarding and other-regarding desires. As we shall see, Hutcheson believes there are "two grand determinations" of our nature: "one toward our own greatest happiness, the other toward the greatest general good" (1755: 50). In this he follows Cumberland. Although Sidgwick cites Butler as the source of his own "dualism of practical reason," it is more accurate to say that Sidgwick's predecessors are Cumberland and Hutcheson (Sidgwick 1967: x–xi).

This brings us to Butler. The Butlerian dualism to which Sidgwick pointed was not between egoism (or self-love) and universal benevolence, but between self-love and conscience. Butler was famous for the doctrine that conscience has a unique "authority," but he also says that conscience and self-love are "the chief or superior principles in the nature of man: because an action may be suitable to this nature, though all other principles be violated; but becomes unsuitable, if either of those are" (Butler 2017: III.9). Being *natural* or *suitable to our nature* are normative properties for Butler. Butler's claim, in a more contemporary idiom, is, roughly, that being contrary to the agent's good and being ruled out by conscience, that is, being morally wrong in the agent's own view, are both sufficient reasons not to do something.

Despite this passage's appearances, however, Butler's position is not that self-love and conscience are equals in what Butler calls "authority." Butler is careful to use "authority" only in connection with conscience and never with self-love.

> It is by this faculty [conscience], natural to man, that he is a moral agent, that he is a law to himself: by this faculty, I say, not to be merely considered as a principle in his heart, which is to have some influence as well as others; but considered as a faculty in kind and in nature supreme over all others, and which bears its own authority of being so (II.8).

Like Shaftesbury and Hutcheson, Butler sees our psychology as a kind of system. Though he uses a variety of metaphors to describe it – that of an economy, for example – his favored way of putting his idea is that the human psyche has a *constitution*, where this is to be understood in the same juridical terms that apply to a political body or state. It is only by treating conscience as authoritative, Butler argues, by *respecting* its authority, that we are able to constitute ourselves as moral agents.

Butler's doctrine of the authority of conscience puts his ethics into a fundamentally different normative space than Hutcheson's. It puts moral autonomy – the agent's capacity to be a "law to himself" – at the heart, not just of Butler's view of moral virtue, but of what it is to be a moral agent. And it understands the autonomy that grounds moral agency in essentially deontic or juridical terms.

Conscience, both for Butler and in our contemporary sense, is not a capacity to make just any assessments of ourselves. It is a faculty with which we make a distinctive kind of deontic judgment through which we hold ourselves accountable (Darwall 2014b; Sorabji 2014). "[T]here is no man," Butler writes, "but would choose, after having had the pleasure or advantage of a vicious action, to be free of the guilt of it, to be in the state of an innocent man" (Butler 2017: VII.16). "[V]ice," he concludes, cannot be the happiness, but must upon the whole be the misery, of such a creature as man …, an accountable agent" (VII.16). If, consequently, an action cannot be suitable to our nature if it is contrary to either self-love or conscience, it is not because these have equal authority. Butler believes that the vicious implicitly acknowledge the superior authority of their own consciences (over self-love) through feeling guilt.

It is important to appreciate how Butler's non-*eudaimonist* identification of autonomy with the authority of conscience differs from the way autonomy features in the thought of Cudworth, Locke, and Shaftesbury. Although Locke and Cudworth are led to accounts of autonomy because they think it necessary for moral agency, and though Cudworth distinguishes between the autonomy ("moral free will") that is necessary for moral agency and an "animal free will" that is sufficient for a self-reflective rational agency that falls short of full accountability, neither Cudworth nor Locke questions a fundamentally *eudaimonist* framework. Most obviously, Locke's egoistic hedonism forces him to the view both that human agents have adequate reason to avoid moral wrong only by virtue of divine sanctions and that autonomy consists in the capacity to step back from the press of current desires and think about the long-term consequences of wrongdoing *for the agent* so that they can bring their current desires into line with their judgments about the latter. But even Cudworth, for whom Lockean autonomy would amount only to animal free will, understands moral free will not in terms of responsiveness to non-*eudaimonistic* considerations of right but to higher goods. Even when deontic morality is in play, it is not, for Cudworth, as a source of reasons that are irreducible to the agent's good. And the same is true of Shaftesbury.

Butler's doctrine of the authority of conscience marks an important departure from this view. Indeed, Butler criticizes Shaftesbury on precisely these grounds: "The not taking into consideration this authority, which is implied in the idea of reflex approbation or disapprobation, seems a material deficiency or omission in Lord Shaftesbury's *Inquiry concerning Virtue*" (Pr.26). Though Shaftesbury has shown "beyond all contradiction, that virtue is naturally the interest or happiness, and vice the misery, of such a creature as man," he has not shown that moral sense or conscience has authority *itself*, an authority, indeed, that can override considerations of the agent's good, whether it is conceived in terms of higher goods or not (Pr.26).

Recall Sidgwick's claim that modern moral philosophy differs from ancient ethics in recognizing two ultimate sources of normative reasons:

> [I]n Greek moral philosophy generally, but one regulative and governing faculty is recognised under the name of Reason ...; in the modern ethical view, when it has worked itself clear, there are found to be two,— Universal Reason and Egoistic Reason, or Conscience and Self-love (Sidgwick 1964: 198).

In these terms, we might say that it is with Butler's view of the authority of conscience that "the modern ethical view ... work[s] itself clear."

Butler is not the first philosopher to hold that agents are capable of acting rationally for ends other than their own good. Both Cumberland and Hutcheson hold that an agent can aim rationally at others' goods no less than at their own. However, in holding that both their own good (considered from a first-person perspective) and universal good (considered third personally) are the two "grand determinations" of a rational human agent, Hutcheson also maintains that there is no deliberative perspective that agents can occupy that can enable them to decide between these should they conflict. It falls to God to ensure that the correct results from these two perspectives always coincide. Butler rejects this view. He denies that virtue can be reduced to benevolence, holds that morality can require us to act in ways that are neither recommended by the agent's or by others' goods, *and* holds that accountable moral agents must be able to treat these requirements as authoritative reasons.

Butler's view differs also from Cumberland's. Unlike Hutcheson, Cumberland maintains that agents can ask whether they should pursue their own or universal good, in the case that these conflict. Indeed, that they can do this plays a significant role in his argument for the rationality of universal benevolence and the greatest good of all being the "best end." But although this is so, Cumberland holds a fundamentally teleological conception of practical reason, according to which all normative reasons for action are reducible to goods. Butler denies this. He rejects Hutcheson and Cumberland's view that virtue can be reduced to benevolence, as noted above, and holds that conduct can be ruled out by conscience on grounds other than the good. Conscience may disapprove of injustice, for example, even if it produces an "overbalance of happiness" (Butler 2017: D.8).

Significantly, Butler reserves the deontic/juridical term "authority" for conscience. In so doing, however, he slides over a distinction between a different sense of "authority" that is also not well marked among contemporary philosophers these days. Sometimes in present-day philosophical discussion, "authority" can express a broadly normative notion. When philosophers discuss, for example, "first-person authority" in epistemology and the philosophy of mind, they are not concerned with anything distinctively deontic or juridical. They are simply considering whether, say, the fact that someone believes they are in pain provides normative reason to believe they are that is not created by the beliefs of other observers. Similarly, philosophers querying the "authority of desire" are asking whether the fact that an agent desires something creates any normative reason for them to bring it about. In neither case is anything essentially deontic in question.

Used more narrowly, however, "authority," has an essentially deontic/juridical use that is conceptually connected to obligation and accountability in ways that put it on the law or demand side of Suárez's distinction between law and counsel. Clearly, this is the use that is in play when we consider issues of political legitimacy or of one person's authority over another. But it is also the sense that is distinctively concerned with deontic morality and moral obligation. To be sure, there are also uses of "obligation" in early modern writers like Shaftesbury, Leibniz, and, as we shall see, Hutcheson and Hume, that are non-deontic. But these are reformative and subversive. The sense in which conscience in "the modern ethical view" is held to be authoritative is not just that it responds to especially weighty normative reasons, but also that these can *obligate* in the sense that we are accountable for complying with them.

As we shall see, Butler tends to include both of these claims when he says that conscience has supreme authority. Conscience is the faculty necessary for accountable moral agency, through which we recognize morality's distinctive capacity to obligate. But Butler holds as well that conscience, which he also calls the "principle of reflection," is necessary for genuinely rational agency in general. In this latter case, conscience is a broader capacity not just to recognize deontic obligatory norms, but also to make and guide ourselves by judgments of normative reasons more generally. It will be important to keep these claims separate and to try to understand the relation between them in his thought. Generally, I will use "conscience" to refer to the former and "principle of reflection" to refer to the latter.

Butler identifies practical normative judgment in deontic terms. In doing so, he turns *eudaimonism* on its head. Whereas *eudaimonism* grounds all normative practical reasons in the agent's good, Butler's view can appear to ground them all in the right, as if there would be no normative reason to pursue self-interest unless there were an obligation to do so. A sympathetic reading distinguishes, however, between narrower and broader notions of conscience in Butler's thought. So understood, Butler's "broader" claim of the authority of the "principle of reflection" is that rational autonomy involves agents' guiding themselves by their own judgments of normative reasons, and that doing so requires distinguishing whether an action will benefit the agent and whether there is therefore reason for them to perform it as *different questions*. "Everything is what it is and not another thing" (Pr.39).

A central question of metaethics as it has been pursued in the twentieth and twenty-first centuries has concerned the nature or "sources of normativity," where this latter is understood in terms of the grounds of normative reasons understood most generally (e.g., Korsgaard 1996a). On a *eudaimonist* or Aristotelian naturalist view, there is only one fundamental normative concept: the good. So long as the good is held to be the only source of normative reasons, there can seem no important conceptual distinction between the good and normative reasons. Once, however, a second normative concept, the right, is distinguished, the separate, more fundamental concept of normative reason or ought comes more clearly into view. In addition to issues concerning the nature and grounds of the good and the right, there is the more fundamental question of the nature of normative reasons and oughts, hence of normativity itself. Arguably, Butler's doctrine of the authority of conscience put modern moral philosophy on a track to distinguish and ultimately focus on this latter question.

Hutcheson

We noted in the last chapter that it has become customary to view Shaftesbury's thought retrospectively, through the lens of the moral sentimentalism his writings inspired in Hutcheson and Hume. Shaftesbury's thought was unquestionably salient for Hutcheson. To the title of *Inquiry*'s first edition (originally published in 1725) Hutcheson appended: "In which the principles of the late Earl of Shaftesbury are Explain'd and Defended, against the Author of *The Fable of the Bees*" (Hutcheson 2004: 199).[3] What was primarily at issue between Shaftesbury and Mandeville was whether all human motivation is ultimately egoistic or whether there is such a thing as disinterested benevolence.

But although Hutcheson clearly sided with Shaftesbury on the question of psychological egoism, there are many ways in which his thought departed from Shaftesbury's and in which he understood himself to be doing so. Whereas Shaftesbury's moral sense must be understood within a broadly rationalist epistemology that owes much to the Cambridge Platonists, Hutcheson's epistemology is more thoroughly Lockean. That moral concepts and judgments require a special sense follows from what Hutcheson argues is the simplicity or irreducibility of fundamental moral ideas together with the Lockean premise that simple ideas can only be received through senses. Unlike Shaftesbury, Hutcheson was thoroughly in the empirical naturalist tradition of Hobbes, Cumberland, and Locke.

Hutcheson follows Shaftesbury's virtue ethics, but, as we noted, denies Shaftesbury's claim that genuine virtue must involve self-reflective guidance through moral sense.[4] And Hutcheson also denies Shaftesbury's claim that the "obligation to virtue" is *eudaimonistic*, derived from the agent's own good. Hutcheson agrees with Shaftesbury's attempt to reform the use of "obligation" away from expressing a distinctively deontic/juridical notion and toward the more general idea of normative reasons and oughts. But he denies that the normative reasons that ground virtue must ultimately be *eudaimonistic*. He praised Shaftesbury's project of demonstrating the congruence of virtue and interest as "the principal Business of the moral Philosopher" (179), and asserted throughout his writings that self-interest constitutes *an* obligation to virtue. But he also insisted against Shaftesbury that the virtuous person has normative reason to act virtuously quite independently of any good to self, intrinsic or extrinsic, just in the fact that the action would benefit others or, more accurately, in the fact that it would benefit *someone*. And Hutcheson introduced a second reformative use of "obligation" – what Hume would later call "moral obligation" – that is tied directly to the approval of moral sense (Hume 1978: 498).

Empiricist Naturalism and Moral Sense

It is illuminating to view Hutcheson's *Inquiry* as an extended argument that morality can be understood, in all its complexity, within the framework of empiricist naturalism. Broadly accepting Lockean doctrines about the powers of

---

[3] Bernard Mandeville's *Fable of the Bees* was published in 1714 (Mandeville 1988). Hereafter, I will omit the original dates of publication of Hutcheson's, Butler's, and Hume's writings.

[4] In what follows, I draw from Darwall 1995: 207–243.

reason and the empirical sources of ideas and knowledge, Hutcheson attempts to show, against Hobbes and Locke, that morality has its own natural place. Most significant, he argues, is a fundamental distinction between moral and natural good that can be located naturalistically. *Natural good* is benefit or welfare, which Hutcheson follows Locke in identifying with pleasure.[5] *Moral good*, by contrast, is realized only in the motives of a moral agent and is recognized when contemplating those motives disinterestedly. Moral good is irreducible to natural good, but that does not make it any less a natural feature or aspect of nature. Whether a motive is morally good is determined entirely by facts of nature and is just as open to empirical investigation as natural good is.

As we will see presently, Hutcheson holds that moral good and evil are definable, respectively, in terms of the simple ideas of "approbation" and "condemnation." Roughly, moral goods are motives whose contemplation elicits approbation, and moral evils are motives that elicit condemnation. Hutcheson holds that all other moral qualities – the morally choiceworthy, rights (along with the distinction between perfect and imperfect rights), and moral obligation – are definable in terms of moral good and evil, hence approbation and condemnation. Placing moral value properly in nature therefore provides a naturalistic foundation for all of morality.

Later editions of the *Inquiry* begin with the following definition:

> The word MORAL GOODNESS, in this Treatise, denotes our Idea of some Quality apprehended in Actions, which procures Approbation, attended with Desire of the Agent's Happiness. MORAL EVIL, denotes our Idea of a contrary Quality, which excites Condemnation or Dislike (Hutcheson 2004: 85, 217).

To this, Hutcheson adds: "Approbation and Condemnation are probably simple Ideas, which cannot be farther explained" (217). Any impression of a hedge with "probably" is removed by Hutcheson's definition of moral sense:

> A Determination of our Minds to receive the simple Ideas of Approbation or Condemnation, from Actions observ'd, antecedent to any Opinions of Advantage or Loss to redound to ourselves from them (100, 221).

Since Hutcheson defines a sense, in general, as "a Determination of the Mind, to receive any Idea from the Presence of an Object, which occurs to us, independent on our Will" (90), the simple, irreducible character of approbation and condemnation entails Hutcheson's hypothesis of the moral sense.

When Hutcheson says that moral goodness is a quality of actions "that procures Approbation," he evidently means that it is the apprehension or

---

[5] "The Pleasure in our sensible Perceptions of any kind, gives us our first Idea of natural Good, or Happiness" (2004: 86).

contemplation of the quality that does so, not the quality directly itself. Moral goodness elicits approbation by way of its contemplation. And Hutcheson's view is that the qualities of actions that do elicit approbation are all and always *motives* of action, most directly, at least. Moral qualities, for Hutcheson, are always of actions *as motivated*. As he sometimes puts it, the simple moral ideas of approbation and condemnation arise only from contemplating "Affections of rational Agents" (90).

Moral good contrasts with natural good in two ways. Natural good is simply whatever causes pleasure, mediately or immediately, but moral good is that the contemplation of which causes approbation. What is morally good is the contemplated quality itself. Hutcheson does hold that approbation is a kind of pleasure. So, to whatever extent moral good tends to cause pleasant contemplation of itself, this will make moral good (mediately) naturally good for the person contemplating it. But this does not make moral goodness a species of natural goodness. A quality might be no less morally good even if its existence did not occasion its own pleasurable contemplation, if, say, it tended to distract attention from itself.

The second thing that distinguishes moral good from natural good in general is that Hutcheson takes approbation to be a specific *kind* of pleasure – a simple idea, in Hutcheson's empiricist theory of concepts – just as he takes condemnation to be a distinctive kind of pain. This point will prove especially important in a disagreement Hutcheson has with Hume over whether the most plausible form of moral sentimentalism is a moral sense theory, or whether, as Hume believes, approbation can be explained as resulting from more general psychological mechanisms: sympathy and the association of ideas and impressions.

Finally, it is worth noting that Hutcheson says not that moral goodness is the property of causing approbation and love, but that it is *that quality* (motive), if any, that causes these (when contemplated). He appends to his definitions of moral good and evil: "We must be contented with these imperfect Descriptions, until we discover ... what general Foundation there is in Nature for this Difference of Actions, as morally Good or Evil" (85). Empirical inquiry is necessary to see whether some natural quality actually fits this description.

This suggests that Hutcheson intends his definition as a reference fixer, pointing to a place in the natural causal order and identifying moral good with whatever happens to occupy it. His hypothesis is that every quality that fills the bill is some form of benevolence. If this hypothesis proves to be correct, then moral good turns out to be identical with benevolence.

However, there are other places where Hutcheson seems to identify moral goodness with something like the disposition to cause approbation (on reflection).[6] He sometimes treats beauty as depending on an "internal sense"

---

[6] I am indebted here to Nicholas Sturgeon.

in this way.⁷ And he gives his readers every reason to think he regards beauty and moral goodness as having the same ontological status. In the *Illustrations*, moreover, he says that the ideas received by both moral and internal senses are, like those of "*Colours, Sounds, Tastes, Smells, Pleasure, Pain,*" "only *Perceptions* in our own Minds, and not Images of any like *external Quality*" (2002: 177).⁸

However we read Hutcheson on this issue, it is clear that he holds moral good to be a feature of the natural order and that he thinks that every quality the contemplation of which causes approbation is some form of benevolence.⁹ Section I of the *Inquiry* is devoted to showing that we all do experience distinctive pleasurable and painful states of mind when we contemplate certain motives disinterestedly, that is, that we have a moral sense. And Section II argues that every motive whose contemplation causes approbation either is a form of benevolence (desire for someone's natural good) or is approved because of its relation to benevolence. Hutcheson argues also that our approval of benevolence increases depending upon the extent of the benevolence we are contemplating, with the greatest approbation being of universal benevolence.¹⁰ In every case, Hutcheson's method of argument is the same: appeal to introspection guided by judiciously selected cases.

Moral Virtue Ethics: Constructing and Deriving Other Moral Notions and Standards

Moral good and evil are constructed in a straightforward way from the simple ideas of approbation and condemnation, as qualities (motives) of action that, when contemplated, give rise to approbation and condemnation, respectively. So understood, moral good and evil are features that are assessed from an observer's rather than an agent's perspective. We apprehend these qualities not in deliberating about what to do, hence looking for reasons (motives) to guide action. Rather we encounter them as features of motivated actions, once an

---

[7] "[W]ere there no Mind with a *Sense of Beauty* to contemplate Objects, I see not how they could be call'd *Beautiful*" (2004: 27).

[8] Hutcheson contrasts these with the ideas of "*Extension, Motion, Rest.*" He also consider the possibility that God could have constituted us with a moral sense that approved of "Barbarity, Cruelty, and Fraud," rather than benevolence, and implies, but does not say, that this would make these traits morally good (2004: 197).

[9] For discussion of the issue of whether Hutcheson deserves to be called a "moral realist," see Norton 1982, Winkler 1985, and Kail 2001. See also Frankena 1955.

[10] "*Benevolence* is a Word fit enough in general, to denote the internal Spring of Virtue. ... But to understand this more distinctly, 'tis highly necessary to observe, that under this Name are included very different Dispositions of the Soul. Sometimes it denotes a calm, extensive Affection, or Good-will toward all Beings capable of Happiness or Misery. ... [This] sort is above all amiable and excellent" (2004: 237).

agent has already settled the practical question for themselves of how to act or has acted on some reason or motive.

Moral good and evil are identical with vice and virtue, for Hutcheson, but it is important to see that Hutcheson's is a narrower, distinctively moral, conception of virtue and vice than that of ancient ethicists like Aristotle. Hutcheson's is a *moral* virtue ethics. What makes something a virtue, for Hutcheson, is not that it is a human excellence through which we flourish, or that contemplating it gives rise to esteem of a broader kind, but that it gives rise to a distinctively moral kind of approbation. And vices are features that elicit not contempt, shame, or disgust, but rather *condemnation*. Although deontic ideas are not, as we shall see, at the center of Hutcheson's thought, condemnation suggests the deontic/juridical nexus of accountability, culpability, and guilt. This grounds a profound disparity between Hutcheson and Hume, who will deny that any real difference between moral virtue and non-moral forms of human excellence exists.

Approbation and condemnation arise, again, from an observer's, rather than from an agent's, perspective. Knowing which motives are morally good does not directly answer an agent's question of what, or of what there is most moral reason, *to* do. However, it is clear that Hutcheson thinks it can provide an answer *indirectly* if we assume, as he evidently does, that we should approach the deliberative question from the perspective provided by the motive that is morally best.

Moral sense can "regulate our Election among various Actions propos'd" (2004: 125) indirectly by, first, determining that universal benevolence is the morally best motive and then working out which act is most highly recommended from the perspective of that motive. Since the object of universal benevolence is the greatest natural good or happiness of all, Hutcheson concludes that "that Action is best, which procures the greatest Happiness for the greatest Numbers; and that worst, which, in like Manner, occasions Misery" (125). In this way, the most morally choiceworthy act is derived from the morally best motive.

Hutcheson's formula is a proto-utilitarian account of the morally choiceworthy that is arguably closer to Bentham and Mill than to Cumberland's "common good of all rationals." But it is important to see that Hutcheson gets to the greatest happiness principle in a profoundly different way, from within an ethics of virtue, than do the later utilitarian writers. For Hutcheson, it is the moral goodness of universal benevolence, the fact that benevolence elicits the simple moral idea of approbation, that grounds everything.

It is significant that Hutcheson uses the term "best" (most morally choiceworthy) rather than morally "*right*," as later utilitarians will. Like Shaftesbury before him, and Hume after, Hutcheson is a virtue ethicist who is, at best, ambivalent about deontic moral conceptions. Although his "condemnation" has a definite deontic resonance, he subversively redefines moral obligation in aretaic terms.

Hutcheson is most explicit about his project of constructing all moral notions out of the two simple, distinctively moral ideas in the *Inquiry*'s Section VII: "*A Deduction of some Complex moral Ideas, viz. of Obligation, and Right, Perfect, Imperfect*, and *External, Alienable*, and *Unalienable, from this moral Sense*" (177). Just as Hutcheson's virtue ethics of universal benevolence lead to a proto-utilitarian theory of moral choiceworthiness, so also does he derive a proto-utilitarian theory of rights, perhaps the first in the history of ethics, on the same basis.

"The true Original of moral Ideas," Hutcheson reiterates, is "[t]his moral Sense of Excellence in every Appearance, or Evidence of Benevolence" (177). And "[f]rom this Sense too we derive our Ideas of RIGHTS" (183).

> Whenever it appears to us, that a Faculty of doing, demanding, or possessing any thing, universally allow'd in certain Circumstances, would in the Whole tend to the general Good, we say, that any Person in such Circumstances, has a Right to do, possess, or demand that Thing. And according as this Tendency to the publick Good is greater or less, the Right is greater or less (183).

Hutcheson then accounts for distinctions among rights within this proto-utilitarian framework. Rights are "perfect" (coercively enforceable) if what they protect is so important to the public good that their universal violation "would make human Life intolerable" and if "allow[ing] a violent Defence, or Prosecution of such Rights," even outside of civil government, would have better consequences than "the Violation of them with Impunity" (183). Imperfect rights, by contrast, are those that are not appropriately coercively enforced, where "a violent Prosecution of such Rights, would generally occasion greater Evil than the Violation of them" (184). Similarly, the distinction between alienable and inalienable rights depends on whether "a Power ... to transfer such *Rights* may serve some valuable Purpose" (186).[11]

Calm Desires, Reason, and Moral Sense

In the next section, we will consider Hutcheson's view of obligation, specifically of what Hume will call later "moral obligation" (Hume 1978: 498). First, however, we should look more carefully at Hutcheson's rejection of *eudaimonism* and his view of practical reason, from which Hume will also borrow.

In *An Essay Concerning the Passions and the Affections*, Hutcheson lays out a systematic theory of action and practical reason. His main object is to argue that disinterested desires for the good of others are no less possible, and indeed, no less

---

[11] For more detail, see Darwall 2022.

rational in the only philosophically respectable sense, than self-regarding desires. As Hutcheson sees it, the main obstacle to "conceiving *disinterested Desires*" has been that philosophers, like Locke, have misconceived desires as "*uneasy Sensation[s] in the absence of good*," rather than as simple ideas that can only be identified by their functional role in motivating action (Hutcheson 2002: 28). "*Desire* is as distinct from any *Sensation*, as the *Will* is from the *Understanding* or Senses. This everyone must acknowledge, who speaks of *desiring to remove Uneasiness or Pain*" (28–29). Once the clear distinction between desire and (unpleasant) sensation is made, Hutcheson thinks, it should appear obvious that disinterested desires are no less possible (or, indeed, "rational") than interested ones.

Although Hutcheson argues famously in his *Illustrations on the Moral Sense*, from which Hume will borrow liberally, that reason is motivationally inert in itself, he nonetheless thinks that action and motivation can be more or less based on *rational apprehension*. Indeed, he makes a fundamental distinction between "desires" or "affections," on the one hand, and "passions" and "appetites" that operate not through rational apprehension of their objects but through sensation, on the other. "*Desire*" and "*pure Affection* … arise necessarily from a rational Apprehension of Good or Evil," whereas "there are in our Nature violent *confused Sensations*, connected with *bodily Motions*," which are "denominated *Passions*" (51).

The goods or evils the rational apprehension of which gives rise to desires and affections are *natural* goods and evils (pleasure or welfare and pain or illfare). As Hutcheson argues in *Illustrations*, desire does not result from rational apprehension alone; some motivational susceptibility or "*Instinct*" is required (51). But it is important to see that the requisite instinct embeds a conception of rationality. It is a disposition to desire natural goods (as it will turn out, *both* for self and for others) *when these are rationally apprehended* – as Hutcheson says, "calmly." In this way calm desires and affections are, unlike passions and appetites, "rational Desire[s]" (52). On this basis, he defines "[t]he *Will*, or *Appetitus Rationalis*" as "the disposition of Soul to pursue what is presented as good, and to shun Evil" (214).

The *Essay* lays out some twenty "*Natural Laws of pure Affection*" (13) that describe our tendency to desire good, "as it appears to our *Reason* or *Reflection*," without the attendant sensual confusion and violence of the passions (31). Taken together, these imply that rational reflection on our own good leads us to desire our own greatest good or pleasure, and that rational reflection on natural goods, conceived disinterestedly, leads us to desire the greatest happiness of the greatest number. "The *Strength* either of the *private* or *publick* Desire of any Event, is proportioned to the imagined *Quantity of Good*" (37).

Hutcheson is not claiming that we all tend to desire the greatest good of all or even our own greatest good. Rather, he is claiming that it is a law of our psychological nature that we tend to desire in proportion to quantity of good *when we contemplate the latter calmly and rationally*.

> When the Soul is calm and attentive to the Constitution and Powers of other Beings, their natural Actions and Capacities of Happiness and Misery, and when the selfish Appetites and Compassions and Desires are asleep, ... there is a calm impulse of the Soul to desire the greatest Happiness and Perfection of the largest System within the Compass of its Knowledge (1755: 10).

Similarly, in the intrapersonal case, "there is found in the human Mind, when it recollects itself, a calm determination toward personal happiness of the highest kind it has any notice of" (50).

Hutcheson's laws of calm desire thus embed an ideal of rational deliberation. They are empirical generalizations, but about an ideal human agent whose deliberations are free of the perturbing influence of passion and appetite, and who is perfectly informed about, and attentively considering, all natural goods in prospect. When human beings instantiate this ideal, they raise the "two grand determinations" of our nature: "one toward our own greatest happiness, the other toward the greatest general good" (50).

Since all desires must have natural goods as objects, it is easy to see why Hutcheson was committed to holding that moral sense cannot motivate directly. Hutcheson did hold that the motive we mostly highly approve through moral sense, calm "extensive" (universal) benevolence, is one that rational deliberation on natural goods will give us. But he believed that not only was an apprehension of the moral goodness or virtue of benevolence not itself necessary for moral virtue – it could actually interfere with it. The only way he had of understanding Shaftesbury's (and later, Butler's) doctrine that self-reflective approval is necessary for genuine virtue was that such self-approbation offers the agent a natural good: the "secret Sense of Pleasure" of contemplating his own virtue (2004: 87).

Hutcheson rightly believed he had sketched in the *Essay* a substantial alternative to Shaftesbury. Shaftesbury included benevolent motivation in human nature but thought it could form no basis for a reflective endorsement of the good life. Shaftesbury's "obligation to virtue" remained steadfastly *eudaimonist*, only the agent's interest on the whole can provide, he thought, a framework necessary to order pursuits in a rational way. The *Essay*'s central thesis, by contrast, is that "calm extensive benevolence" gives rationally reflective human agents a second organizing motive. Just as agents can order the goods they can realize for themselves within their good on the whole, so can they likewise order goods they can realize impersonally. Particular benevolence stands to calm extensive benevolence as agents' desires for specific personal goods stands to calm self-love or the desire for their own greatest good.

Ultimately, there are three reasons why Hutcheson was committed to the view, denied by Butler, that moral sense cannot directly motivate the actions of which it approves. First, moral sense receives sensations, and Hutcheson explicitly distinguishes these from desires, which can exclusively motivate. Second, all calm desires are for natural goods, for oneself or others, and never for moral good itself. And third, Hutchesonian moral sense approves of motives and not acts considered independently of these and so cannot possibly motivate action.

Obligation

This brings us to Hutcheson's view of obligation. Here again, Hutcheson departs from Shaftesbury. Hutcheson rejected both Shaftesbury's view that agential self-direction through moral sense is necessary for genuine virtue and that the (only) "obligation to virtue" is provided by motives of self-interest. Hutcheson agreed with Shaftesbury that virtue ultimately *coincides* with self-interest. Otherwise, the two "grand determinations" of practical reasoning, universal benevolence and self-love, would conflict with no possible deliberative perspective to resolve them. But Hutcheson rejected Shaftesbury's *eudaimonism* and so his view that normative reasons to be virtuous are all grounded in the agent's own good. Universal benevolence is no less a source of normative reasons than is self-love.

Shaftesbury's reduction of the obligation to virtue to "*what Reason* [there is] to embrace it" (Shaftesbury 2001: II.78), and then, to *eudaimonist* reasons of the agent's good, was, as we have noted, a subversive redefinition that reduces away any Suárezian deontic/juridical content. Hutcheson shared Shaftesbury's desire to center his ethics on virtue rather than on deontic morality, and so shared also Shaftesbury's rationale for reforming definition of deontic notions. "[O]*ught*," Hutcheson said, is an "unlucky Word in Morals" (Hutcheson 2002: 156).

Hutcheson might naturally have followed Shaftesbury's reduction of obligation to normative reasons. From there he could have departed and said that the obligation to virtue was not (simply) self-interest, but also the very considerations of others' (or impersonal) natural good, anyone's weal and woe, to which the morally best motive, universal benevolence, responds. He did not, however, take that route.

Like Shaftesbury, Hutcheson accepts a species of obligation that Hume will later call "natural obligation" or, more helpfully, "interested obligation" (Hume 1978: 498; 1985b: 278):

> A Motive from Self-Interest, sufficient to determine all those who duly consider it, and pursue their own Advantage wisely, to a certain Course of Actions (Hutcheson 2004: 177).

But to this he adds a second species, what Hume will call "moral obligation," which involves moral sense. There are subtle differences between his account in the *Inquiry* and his later *Illustrations* account. The latter is cleaner and gives his mature contrast between the obligation of self-interest and that of moral sense:

> When we say one is obliged to an Action we either mean, 1. *That the Action is necessary to obtain Happiness to the Agent, or to avoid Misery*: Or, 2. *That every Spectator, or he himself upon Reflection, must approve his Action, and disapprove his omitting it, if he considers fully all its Circumstances* (2002: 146).

In defining moral obligation in relation to moral sense in this way, it might be thought that Hutcheson had no real disagreement with Shaftesbury. Although Shaftesbury did not call the approval of moral sense obligation, this might be thought more of a semantic than a substantive disagreement.

There were, however, two substantial disagreements. First, as we have noted, Hutcheson holds that moral sense cannot directly motivate, since all motives are for natural goods. Second, later editions of the *Inquiry* make clear that what Hutcheson has in mind by moral sense is not just any second-order "Liking or Dislike," as Shaftesbury put it (Shaftesbury 2001: II.28), but a disposition to have distinctive moral responses of approbation and condemnation, the "simple ideas" that define moral sense and from which, Hutcheson believes, all other (complex) moral notions can be deduced (Hutcheson 2004: 100, 217, 221).

Once Hutcheson had accepted Shaftesbury's reduction of one species of obligation to normative reasons of self-interest, it might seem natural to understand a moral species of obligation as consisting in the consideration of disinterested natural good to which the morally best motive, benevolence, responds. In tying moral obligation to the approbation and condemnation of moral sense, however, Hutcheson ties it to sensations or perceptions that he believes are incapable of motivation. We might reasonably ask Hutcheson, then, what is the genus of which his different senses of "obligation" are both species? What can unify them?[12]

---

[12] Hutcheson faces a similar unification problem in his account of practical reasoning. Like Sidgwick's dualism of practical reason, Hutcheson holds that practical reasoning can be grounded *either* in calm self-love (the agent's overall interest) or calm extensive (universal) benevolence (the greatest good of all). By the time he wrote *A System of Moral Philosophy* he no longer found it satisfactory to think that rational deliberation could be bifurcated in this way.

> But here arises a new perplexity in this complex structure where these two principles seem to draw different ways. Must the generous determination, and all its particular affections, yield to the selfish one. … Or must the selfish yield to the generous? Or can we suppose that in this complex system there are two ultimate principles which may often oppose each other, without any umpire to reconcile their differences (1975: 50–51).

The *Essay* doctrine was that there can be no *practical* umpire between calm benevolence and calm self-love. Through moral sense we *approve* of benevolence and not self-love (except when we consider ourselves disinterestedly), but this approbation is, in itself, deliberatively inert. It can give considerations of general happiness no greater weight as *practical reasons*. But if no human deliberative adjudication is possible, neither is any

Butler

We turn now to Butler. In light of his influence on modern moral philosophy, it is remarkable how little of Butler's life was actually devoted to writing on the subject. When Hume listed Butler as one of "some late philosophers

needed. Since God has designed a pre-established harmony between self-love and benevolence, the consistency of rational human agency is preserved.

In the *System*, however, Hutcheson writes that this "must appear a complex confused fabric, without any order or regular consistent design" (74). Moreover, he adds that its solution requires "a distinct consideration of [the] moral faculty. By means of it, all is capable of harmony" (74). But how can this be, given that moral sense is practically inert?

The *System* bears the clear imprint of Butler's influence. Given his moral psychology, and his reduction of virtue to benevolence, Hutcheson can hardly take Butler's authority of conscience into his system in Butler's own terms. It is fascinating, however, to see how Butler's idea can be recast in Hutchesonian idiom.

At his most Butlerian, Hutcheson writes that the "moral sense from its very nature appears to be designed for regulating and controlling all our powers" (61). But note Hutcheson's twist:

> This moral faculty plainly shews that we are also capable of calm settled universal benevolence, and that this is destined, as the supreme determination of the generous kind, to govern and control our particular generous as well as selfish affections; as the heart must entirely approve its doing thus in its calmest reflections (74).

Butler of course holds that it is conscience that ultimately governs. Hutcheson, however, holds, against Butler, both that the will can aim only at natural goods (rather than directly at moral good *or* at the right), and that moral sense approves of universal benevolence overriding all other desires for natural goods, including calm self-love.

But this really gives us no more than we had before the *System*. Although moral sense approves of benevolence over self-love, nothing whatsoever follows from this about the relative weight of the agent's good and the good of all as normative reasons for acting. Thus Hutcheson faces a dilemma in the *System*. On the one hand, his theory of practical reasoning and the will, carried forward from the *Essay*, restricts rational motivation to calm self-love and benevolence and seems to provide no place for genuinely *practical* judgment between these should they conflict. On the other, he wants to hold some version of Butler's position that the moral faculty provides the agent with just such a perspective.

His solution is grounded in a doctrine of superior and inferior pleasures that closely resembles Mill's more familiar later version together with the observation that apparently self-sacrificing benevolent actions provide higher pleasures than those that seem less self-sacrificing. These higher pleasures always erase the conflict between benevolence and self-love and always make the sacrifice only apparent and never real.

The doctrine of higher and lower pleasures is already in the *Essay*. Like Mill, Hutcheson takes the testimony of experienced judges to determine superiority and inferiority of pleasures. "It is obvious that 'those alone are capable of judging, who have experienced all the several *kinds of Pleasure*, and have their *Senses* acute and fully exercised in them all'" (2002: 89). Moreover, Hutcheson also there says that the pleasures of virtue are superior to all others. "[A]ll virtuous Men have given *Virtue* this testimony, that its Pleasures are superior to any other, nay to all others jointly" (89). That this is the testimony of the virtuous themselves should not be dismissed as self-serving bias. To the contrary, since they alone in England, who have begun to put the science of man on a new footing," he was judging Butler on the strength of several sermons preached at the Roll Chapel in London and published as part of a collection in 1726 (Hume 1978: xvi; Butler 2017). Although others of Butler's *Sermons* have had continuing interest – for example, those on resentment and self-deceit – Butler's central ethical ideas are mainly laid out in only five sermons (and a preface), three on human nature and the superior authority of conscience, and two on "the love of our neighbor." Besides his "Dissertation of the Nature of Virtue," Butler's only other philosophical work was his massive *Analogy of Religion* (1736), with which the "Dissertation" was published, which argued that revealed religion is fully consistent with then current experimental science. Mostly, Butler was an Anglican clergyman, then bishop, who devoted himself to church affairs.

Butler's ethics have had a profound and continuing influence on the subject. His impact on Hume, Hutcheson, and Adam Smith was substantial. And the *Sermons* were reprinted more during the nineteenth century than any other British ethical work (Schneewind 1977: 7). Sidgwick's *Methods of Ethics* is full of references to Butler. Also, as I mentioned earlier, the terms Sidgwick uses to refer to the two "regulative and governing facult[ies]" that he claims modern moral philosophy comes to recognize are Butler's: "conscience" and "self-love" (Sidgwick 1964: 198). Even if Cumberland and Hutcheson stand more clearly behind Sidgwick's "dualism of practical reason," it was Butler's "authority of ... conscience" that more evidently marked modern moral philosophy's expression of the independent normativity of the right (Sidgwick 1967: x–xi; Butler 2017: Pr.14). Cumberland and Hutcheson's views were dualisms of the good.[13]

---

will have had their "*Senses* acute and fully exercised" in their benevolence, their testimony is dispositive evidence.

Hutcheson makes clear that the superior pleasures of benevolence consist not just in the joyful sense that others are benefited, but also in the awareness that one has benefited them oneself and also, he seems to add, that this is morally good.

> These joys are different from the sympathetick, which may arise from that happiness of others to which our affections and actions contributed nothing. ... When we find our own whole soul kind and benign, we must have a joyful approbation: and a further and higher joy arises from exercising these affections in wise and beneficent offices (1975: 1331).

Even if, therefore, moral sense cannot regulate *deliberation* and so directly govern in the way required by Butler's authority of conscience, it is nonetheless integral to a harmony of practical reason that God affords us. Whereas Butler makes moral autonomy the center of moral virtue and unity something the agent can themselves achieve in their own practical reasoning, albeit with God-given materials, both Hutchesonian virtue and unified practical reasoning depend more directly on God's grace.

[13] As, actually, was Sidgwick's.

Analytical moral philosophy of more recent times is also greatly indebted to Butler. Butler was a master of subtle, important distinctions. His marvelous remark, "[e]verything is what it is, and not another thing" (Butler 2017: Pr.39), provided the epigraph for G. E. Moore's agenda-setting work of twentieth-century analytical ethics, *Principia Ethica*.[14] And Butler's distinction between "*mere power* and *authority*" (II.14) anticipated Sidgwick's contrast between non-normative judgments and normative or "ethical judgments," as well as Moore's juxtaposition of naturalistic properties with the irreducible property of goodness (Sidgwick 1967: 23–38; Moore, 1993: 53–88). Finally, W. D. Ross's famous "deontological" objections to Moore's "ideal utilitarianism" – that considerations other than the goodness of consequences "make right acts right" – bear a clear relation to Butler's objections, in his *Dissertation*, to Hutcheson's claim that "virtue is resolvable into benevolence" (Ross 2003). There Butler argues, anticipating Ross, that we "condemn falsehood, unprovoked violence, [and] injustice" and "approve of benevolence to some preferably to others, abstracted from all consideration, which conduct is likeliest to produce an overbalance of happiness or misery" (Butler 2017: D.8).

The Human Moral Psychological Economy

What is most notable in Butler is his sophisticated and systematic moral psychology, along with his penetrating analysis of different motivational sources within the human psychic "economy" or "constitution," and his powerful, suggestive ideas of how these fit together within moral agents – or, better, how moral agents fit them together themselves in autonomously determining their own moral conduct.

Following Shaftesbury, Butler distinguishes between "private" and "public" "passions and affections" based on their function and tendency to promote individual and overall good, respectively, whether or not they have these as intentional objects. Thus, hunger is a private passion, since it leads people even without "any conviction from reason of the desirableness of life" to preserve themselves and their own good (I.7). Butler does not intend these categories to be mutually exclusive. A passion can be both public and private, as are, for example, "desires of esteem from others" (I.7).

"Everything is what it is, and not another thing" (Pr.39). And what distinguishes different passions is that they are *for* one thing rather than for another. Butler insists that desires invariably have specific intentional objects. It is essential to his famous argument against psychological egoistic hedonism that "all particular appetites and passions are towards *external things themselves*, distinct from the *pleasure arising from them*" (XI.6).

---

[14] Saul Kripke invokes it also in Kripke 1981: 94.

> There could be no enjoyment or delight for one thing more than another, from eating food more than from swallowing a stone, if there were not an affection or appetite to one thing more than another (XI.6).

A person's good or "happiness," Butler holds, "consists only in the enjoyment of those objects, which are by nature suited to our several particular appetites, passions, and affections" (XI.9).

Self-love, it follows, is a second-order desire for the satisfaction of one's first-order desires. Benevolence is likewise second-order; it is the desire for the satisfaction of others' first-order desires. We will consider some implications of these claims that Butler makes use of in arguing against psychological egoism below. Here, however, we should note that benevolence and self-love are alike in standing "above" particular public and private desires, respectively, if not yet in an order of justification, in the sense that an agent must be able to view first-order desires with reflective distance even to have these second-order sources of motivation. They are desires of which only mutually aware, self-reflective beings are capable.

Butler uses the language of normative hierarchy, "superiority" and "inferiority," to express the claim that there is normative reason to act on one desire rather than another. In this way, Butler calls self-love a "superior principle" to specific private desires. Moreover, as we have already noted, Butler classes self-love with conscience as being "the chief or superior principles in the nature of man: because an action may be suitable to this nature, though all other principles be violated; but becomes unsuitable, if either of those are" (III.9).

This might suggest a Sidgwickian "dualism of practical reason," like Hutcheson's, with conscience playing the dual to self-love that universal (calm extensive) benevolence plays in Hutcheson's view. For Hutcheson, recall, self-love and universal benevolence are independent, final, incommensurable sources of normative practical reasons. Butler's statement might suggest, as Sidgwick took it, that this is what Butler held about self-love and conscience (Sidgwick 1967: xi).

There is, however, a fundamental difference between self-love and conscience that is central to Butler's claim that only conscience has what he calls "authority." As Butler understands self-love, namely, as a second-order desire for the satisfaction of one's first-order desires, it has no normative content. But that is what precisely is not true of the "principle of reflection" or conscience. As Butler conceives it, the principle of reflection uniquely has *authority*, because it uniquely makes normative *judgments*.

> But there is a superior principle of reflection or conscience in every man, which distinguishes between the internal principles of his heart, as well as his external actions: which passes judgment upon himself and them (Butler 2017: II.8).

The terms of judgment that Butler then mentions are distinctively moral and deontic. Conscience "pronounces determinately some actions to be just, right, good; others to be in themselves evil, wrong, unjust" (II.8). This suggests that Butler takes the judgments of conscience always to be judgments of deontic morality.

However, Butler clearly thinks we make normative practical judgments that are not distinctively moral in the deontic sense. Someone's "strongest desire" might be for some "present gratification" even at the cost of "certain ruin." In such a situation, Butler says, self-love is "*superior*" to the former desire, however strong the former might be (II.10). In such a case, "without particular consideration of conscience, we may have a clear conception of the *superior nature* of one inward principle to another" (II.11). Acting on the stronger desire is "unnatural," Butler asserts, using "unnatural" in the same normative sense as "inferior" to express the claim that the desire for present gratification, even if stronger than self-love, gives rise to less weighty normative reasons for action than does self-love.

Butler clearly intends his claim that self-love is a superior principle to the stronger desire for lesser gratification, or that acting on the latter desire is *unnatural* or contrary to our nature, as a normative judgment. It is, again, a judgment we might express in a contemporary idiom by saying that there is, or that the agent has, weightier normative reason to do what is for their greater good in the long run rather than to act for lesser but closer goods. But the only faculty of normative practical judgment in Butler's moral psychology is the principle of reflection or conscience, conceived in the broad sense. It is a signal difference between Hutcheson's and Butler's pictures that Butler takes the capacity for self-regulating normative judgment via the principle of reflection to be an essential feature of autonomous agency. Whereas Hutcheson holds that there is no deliberative perspective from which agents can decide between self-love and benevolence, Butler conceives the principle of reflection to be unlike Hutchesonian moral sense in being a faculty of *practical* normative judgment by which agents determine themselves in their own deliberations. It is, he says, what makes autonomous agency possible.

In the case in question, however, the kind of normative judgment that is called for, between self-love and the desire for a lesser, closer pleasure, is not one of deontic morality. That is why Butler says that we can judge the normative superiority of self-love "without particular consideration of conscience" (II.11). Since what is at issue is not a deontic moral question, no issue of conscience in this narrower sense is involved. But there is a broader sense in which the "principle of reflection," which phrase I shall use to express this sense, is the seat of normative practical judgment in Butler's moral psychology.[15] In this

---

[15] Henceforth, I will reserve "conscience" for the faculty through which we make judgments of deontic morality, as well as judgments, for example, of moral goodness that derive from deontic morality.

wider sense, we make judgments of superiority/inferiority and naturalness/unnaturalness through our principle of reflection.

Thus Butler says in the Preface to the *Sermons* that his aim is to show that virtue accords with our nature, using "nature" in the same wider normative sense we have just been using. And he notes there what he describes as an "inward feeling" or "inward conviction" of the "ancient moralists," "which they chose to express in this manner, that ... [virtue] consists in following nature" (Pr.13). To this Butler adds, that such "inward perceptions ... deman[d] in all cases to govern such a creature as man" (Pr.16). This makes it clear that Butler's view is that the "inward" judgments of naturalness and superiority – in our terms, judgments of normative practical reasons – employ the principle of reflection: "you cannot form a notion of this faculty ... without taking in judgment, direction, superintendency" (II.14). Autonomous agents can be a law to themselves only because they have the capacity to make, and act on, their own normative practical judgments.

Normative Practical Judgment: Wide and Narrow

The theme of autonomy and making one's own judgments is evident throughout the *Sermons* from the outset. The Preface begins with these words:

> Though it is scarce possible to avoid judging, in some way or other, of almost everything which offers itself to one's thoughts; yet it is certain, that many persons, from different causes, never exercise their judgment, upon what comes before them, in the way of determining whether it be conclusive, and holds (Pr.1).

"Arguments are often wanted for some accidental purpose," Butler continues, "but proof as such is what they never want for themselves, for their own satisfaction of mind, or conduct in life" (Pr.1; see also Pr.2–7).

Although judgment of some kind is at least implicit in virtually all thought, Butler decries the self-indulgent rationalization, self-deception (IV, VI, X), inattentive thought, and complacent reluctance to make careful judgments that he finds around him. "People habituate themselves to let things pass through their mind ... rather than to think of them." "Review and attention, and even forming a judgment, becomes fatigue, and to lay anything before them that requires it, is putting them quite out of their way" (Pr.4).

The theme here is of people failing to make use of their faculty of judgment, both generally and in "conduct in life" (Pr.1). The latter faculty is the "principle of reflection." To make the best sense of Butler's idea, again, we need to distinguish between a narrower reflective faculty that makes deontic moral judgments, "conscience," and a broader faculty of normative practical judgment in general, for which we are reserving "the principle of reflection." When Butler argues, for example, in Sermon II, that we have reason to live a morally virtuous life (in his terms, that such a life accords with our nature), we should regard this argument as addressed to our principle of reflection and not to our conscience in the narrow deontically moral sense.

It is a tautology that it is wrong to do what is wrong, which we can only judge with narrow conscience. Butler obviously thinks he is making an argument in Sermon II and not just pointing to a tautology. He must think that in arguing that, in our terms, there is sufficient reason not to do wrong, he is not just arguing that wrongdoing violates moral obligation or goes against the balance of *moral* reasons. He is aiming to support the further claim that wrongdoing is against what one has reason to do all things considered, or against the balance of normative practical reasons *sans phrase*.

It is also clear that when Butler argues, throughout the *Sermons*, that virtue accords with our nature, or that vice and morally wrong conduct are unnatural, he is not simply asserting what Irwin calls the Aristotelian naturalist claim that virtue, because it realizes human nature, realizes *eudaimonia* or human good or well-being. Aristotelian naturalism is *eudaimonist*, so were we to interpret Butler's claims in this way, he would be grounding normative reasons to be virtuous or to act rightly in the agent's good. But that would commit Butler to the view that self-love is the only ultimate source of normative reasons. Even if Butler were to hold, as Sidgwick sometimes interprets him, that self-love and conscience are independent sources of normative reasons that are on a par, he would have to reject this *eudaimonist* view.

Butler explicitly considers Shaftesbury's view that the "obligation to virtue" consists in reasons for acting grounded in the agent's interest. Like Hutcheson, Butler grants that Shaftesbury "has shewn beyond all contradiction, that virtue is naturally the interest or happiness, and vice the misery, of such a creature as man" (Pr.26). But Butler explicitly denies Shaftesbury's *eudaimonism*. "[W]hatever their opinion be concerning the happiness of virtue," he writes, people are still "under the strictest moral obligations" to avoid wrongdoing and vice (Pr.27).[16]

It is an important fact that the object of self-love, for Butler – the satisfaction of the agent's first-order desires, their "happiness" – is itself non-normative. Of course, Butler believes that all agents have reason to further their happiness. But that this is so is a further normative claim or judgment that is not entailed

---

[16] Butler's famous "cool hour" passage might be thought to be some evidence against this: "Let it be allowed, though virtue or moral rectitude does indeed consist in affection to and pursue of what is right and good, as such; yet, that when we sit down in a cool hour, we can neither justify to ourselves this or any other pursuit, till we are convinced that it will be for our happiness, or at least not contrary to it" (XI.20). It is clear enough, however, that Butler's "Let it be allowed" signals a dialectical supposition rather than any assertion of *eudaimonism*. I discuss this more carefully at Darwall 1995: 265n–266n.

by the natures of happiness and self-love themselves. The judgment that something will promote the agent's happiness is "one thing," we might say, echoing Butler's famous phrase, and the judgment that there is therefore reason to do it is "another." The second is a normative judgment, while the first is not.

Though self-love responds to normative practical reasons, it does not itself make or involve normative judgments. The only sources of normative judgment are the principle of reflection and conscience. As we are using Butler's terms, as we noted above, conscience is the faculty we employ when we judge actions in moral deontic terms. And the principle of reflection is the faculty through which we judge the existence of normative practical reasons and oughts in general.

Consider in this light the evidence Butler cites that human beings actually have a principle of reflection or conscience. Butler asks us to imagine "a man" who has helped "an innocent person in great distress" but who also "in the fury of anger" does "great mischief to a person who had given no just cause of offence" (I.8).

> Let the man ... coolly reflect upon them afterwards, without regard to their consequences to himself: to assert that any common man would be affected in the same way towards these different actions, that he would make no distinction between them, but approve or disapprove of them equally, is too glaring a falsity to need being confuted (I.8).

Several things about this example are worthy of comment. First, although we are told that the man acts in anger in the second case, we are not told what the motive of action actually is in either case. The object of reflective judgment is an act in a circumstance (we can consider the agent's anger as part of the circumstances). In this way, both wide and narrow Butlerian reflective judgment (the principle of reflection and conscience) differ from *both* Hutcheson's moral sense and Hume's moral sentiment. The direct object of the latter is always, at least in the first instance, an agent's motive, whereas the object of Butlerian reflective judgment is standardly an action in a circumstance.[17]

A related, second point is that the standard case of conscience or the principle of reflection is that of an agent reflecting on *their own* actions and situations, whether from the deliberative perspective or post hoc, considering what they did given the circumstances of choice that faced them. Again, this is no part of the Hutcheson/Hume view of moral sense/moral sentiment. Of course, Hutcheson and Hume believe that, in principle, observers can judge the moral goodness and badness of their own motives no less than they can those of others (supposing that they are capable of disinterestedly bracketing

---

[17] Direct, because Hutcheson holds that moral sense can indirectly (and derivatively) approve of acts as choiceworthy.

their own interests). And, also of course, Butler holds that reflective judgments they make of themselves commit agents to making similar judgments of others in the same situation. Butler's point is not that in the agent's distinguishing their judgments of their action toward the innocent in distress in the first case from their judgment of angry injury of someone against whom they had no just claim, the agent would be likely to make a different judgment *of themselves* than they would of someone else in the very same situation. To the contrary, Butler is clearly assuming that such judgments would have to be identical on pain of inconsistency.

Rather, Butler's point is that an agent's reflective judgment of themselves plays a fundamentally different role in their moral psychological economy than their judgments of others' actions possibly can because, first, it occurs within the agent's *own* "economy," and, second, because it purports to play an authoritative, directive role within that economy. In judging that they really should not have angrily injured someone who had done nothing to deserve their ill usage, they do not merely note a fact about themselves. They come to a normative judgment that can play a role in holding themselves to the norm whose acceptance the normative judgment expresses.

Third, and this is shared with Hutchesonian moral sense, the deliverances of conscience purport to be *disinterested* and *dispassionate*. Taking it for granted that, in the heat of anger, the "man" may well have construed his situation as one in which his victim "had it coming," Butler asks him to "coolly reflect" on what he has done when anger's heat has subsided. Moreover, he is to reflect back on his actions "without regard to their consequences for himself." This does not mean that consequences for, as it were, "the agent," are to be abstracted. What he is to ignore is that the agent was he himself. Thus even though it is important, as we noted in the last point, that judgments of the principle of reflection or conscience are reflective, that is, that agents make these judgments about *themselves*, it is also important that agents make these judgments about themselves *as agents facing specific kinds of alternatives in a specific kind of situation*. This commits agents to making identical judgments of others in the very same kind of circumstance facing the very same kinds of alternatives.

Notice now that these conditions are no less relevant to practical normative judgment than they are to deontic moral judgments. Thus consider Butler's example of someone who does not defer a lesser gratification at the cost of losing a much greater one later. (In Butler's actual example, the cost is "certain ruin" (II.10).) Even if, as we may suppose, no deontic question of right or wrong is at issue, we can well imagine Butler saying that it would be "too glaring a falsity to need being confuted" (I.8) to assert that someone could decide they had equally good reason to act prudently and to act imprudently for no creditable purpose after they had considered both options coolly and disinterestedly. Both deontic moral judgments *and* normative practical judgments in general purport, equally, to be dispassionate, disinterested, and to be based on an informed and adequate grasp of their objects.

It is no argument against this that, as Butler is clearly assuming, there are practical normative reasons for agents to act for *their own* interests and to pursue other forms of self-partiality. This means that agents will correctly take the fact that an action is in their interest as a normative reason to do it. But though this fact is "interested" (i.e., self-interested, a fact about *their* interests), the fact that this (self-interested) fact is a normative reason for them is *not* self-interested. It is not essentially about *their* interests. The fact that an action is in my interest is a reason for me to take it if, and only if, the fact that an act is in *the agent's* interest is a reason for that agent to take it. To assess these facts, I have to abstract from their relation to *my* interests as such.

The Authority of Conscience

In the Preface and Sermon I, Butler argues that our moral psychological economy contains various specific public and private desires, self-love, benevolence, and the principle of reflection. In Sermon II he turns to arguing that there are normative differences of superiority and inferiority between these, and that it is uniquely true of conscience or the principle of reflection that it has *authority*: that it alone is "in nature supreme" over all other principles, that it "ought to preside over and govern all the rest" (II.1).[18]

It is Sermon II where Butler attempts to demonstrate the existence of distinctive "moral obligations" (II.1) as against Shaftesbury's view that the obligation to virtue consists (*eudaimonistically*) only in self-interest (Pr.26). Butler is also implicitly arguing against Hutcheson's view that moral obligation can be grounded in a third-personal, observer's mental state that can get no direct purchase in deliberation. His aim is to show that moral obligations are grounded in conscience's supreme *deliberative* authority.

There are three distinguishable strains of argument in Sermon II for conscience's deliberative authority and thus for the claim that we should govern deliberation by its deliverances. One is a teleological/functional argument that appeals to conscience's manifestly superintendent function. A second places the first in a theological framework, arguing that it is manifestly God's purpose that we function in this way. There is clear textual support for both of these arguments, but both face apparently insuperable objections to which Butler himself seems committed. A third argument seems both more promising

---

[18] Note that though we are using "principle of reflection" and "conscience" to refer, respectively, to faculties of all-things-considered practical judgment and deontic moral judgment, Butler does not himself distinguish these. His claim here applies most obviously to overall practical judgment.

philosophically, and truer to Butler's claim that it is by virtue of conscience that human beings "are a law to themselves" and that they are "moral agent[s]" (II.4, 8, 9). Because this argument proceeds from necessary conditions for the very possibility of moral agency, we can call it Butler's "transcendental argument." It holds that the validity of moral obligation, and normative reasons to act as obligated, are necessary conditions of the possibility of moral agency.[19]

Let us consider Butler's teleological/functional argument first. Butler first discusses conscience's functional role in Sermon I. It is evident, he argues, that conscience restrains us from doing harm and leads us to do good to others. In this way, its function is the same as any "public" principle. But conscience, by its nature, is less vulnerable to the effects of mood and passion, so it can move us when natural affections are challenged. Thus, Butler points out, parents who may find their love and affections for their children taxed by "labour and difficulties" can be "carrie[d]" to care for them by their conscientious sense that doing so is their "proper business" as parents (I.8).

In Sermon I, though, Butler is content to argue that conscience is simply *a* principle in our nature, that it has some independent role in our moral psychological economy. In Sermon II, Butler argues not just that conscience is designed to lead us to do good when it "happen[s] to be stronger than other principles," but that we are so designed that "the *whole* character be formed upon thought and reflection; that *every* action be directed by some determinate rule, some rule other than the strength and prevalency of any principle or passion" (II.3). So Butler now asks, "What sign is there in our nature ... that this was intended by its Author?" (II.3). What evidence does our nature provide that it has a design in which conscience's function is to superintend?

The most obvious consideration, Butler thinks, is that conscience uniquely represents itself as superintendent. Butler also offers a second, coordinate consideration. Benevolence, self-love, and other public and private affections are all "in a degree equally natural," and are all equally part of our natural design. However, "we have no method of seeing the particular degrees in which one or the other is placed in us by nature" (II.8). So we cannot successfully govern ourselves by any of these more specific principles *or* by a judgment of their naturalness, understood teleologically. When they conflict, we have no way of telling, by looking to their place in our design, which we should follow. None of these can be a "law to us" (II.8).

Conscience is God's solution to this design problem. Butler continues:

> But there is a superior principle of reflection or conscience in every man, which distinguishes between the internal principles of his heart, as well as his external actions: which passes judgment upon himself and them;

---

[19] What follows draws on Darwall 1995: 262–283.

pronounces determinately some actions to be in themselves just, right, good; others to be in themselves evil, wrong, unjust (II.8).

By giving us intuitive judgments of which principles we should follow and which actions we should perform, God has given us a way of regulating ourselves that does not require detailed knowledge of the precise place of specific principles in our design.

Assume, then, that Butler has shown that, in the terms of his famous metaphor, we function properly when we virtuously follow conscience much as a watch functions properly when it accurately gives the time (Pr.14). Add that this is God's evident intention. The problem is that these premises can hardly be dispositive by themselves, without additional normative premises, for beings that have a principle of reflection.

Butler himself makes the relevant point in the Preface just after the watch analogy. Machines, like watches, are "inanimate and passive: but we are agents. Our constitution is put in our own power. We are charged with it: and therefore are accountable for any disorder or violation of it" (Pr.14). The principle of reflection makes possible our moral agency, our existence as accountable moral beings. Of course, Butler is supposing here that it makes us accountable for "any disorder or violation" in our functioning. But that can be true only if it is independently true that we should function properly and/or align ourselves with God's intentions, *and* that we can judge our alignment through our principle of reflection. Otherwise, we can hardly intelligibly be held accountable for our proper functioning.

Of course, there is a notion of correct or proper functioning on which, if we are designed to be governed by conscience, it simply follows that we function properly only if we are so governed. But it is hard to see how any normative practical reasons can follow from this. Any normative reason we could have to realize proper functioning so understood must be judged independently of any such function-relative norm. And Butler is committed to the view that we can make normative judgments only by employing our principle of reflection itself.

Also of course, Butler holds that what determines our proper functioning is not just any design, but that of an omniscient, omnibenevolent designer. That there is normative reason to realize our proper functioning seems much more plausible in light of that fact. But here again, any plausibility this normative hypothesis has, Butler has to think, is something we can judge only by employing our principle of reflection. Ultimately, therefore, it is hard to see how any argument from design – wise and benevolent, or otherwise – can work without already assuming that we should govern ourselves by our principle of reflection. The reason this is so, again, is Butler's claim that we are accountable for following conscience. This engages the Pufendorfian point that we can be held so accountable only if we can judge our accountability through conscience itself.

Let us turn now to the transcendental strain in Butler's thinking. The metaphor that Butler uses most frequently for our moral psychology is that of a *constitution*. He clearly has in mind "constitution" not just in the generic sense of what something is made of, but in the juridical/political sense of a constitutional order. Viewed in this light, the thesis of conscience's authority has a distinctive juridical/deontic cast. It ties Butler's claim to his themes of self-government, being a "law to [one]self," and to his contrast between "*mere power* and *authority*" (II.8, 14) in a special way. A constitutional order determines the identity and form of government of a political state. It establishes the possibility of the rule of *law* and what will count as the state's judgment on matters of law and governance.

A constitutional order requires something from which authority flows, and for Butler, the seat of authority is the principle of reflection or conscience. It is what makes possible a person's making their own normative judgments and guiding themselves by them, thereby being a "law to" themselves. Following our distinction between narrow conscience, which makes deontic moral judgment, and a broader principle of reflection, which makes judgments of normative practical reasons in general, we may distinguish similarly between Butlerian claims about necessary conditions for the possibility of autonomous rational agency in general and for moral agency in particular.

Taking autonomous rational agency first, this just is an agent's guiding themselves by their own normative practical-reason judgments, which is only possible if they have the capacity to make such (putatively dispassionate, disinterested, reflective) judgments through a principle of reflection. Such an agent can hardly put in question whether they should follow their principle of reflection as their ultimate court of appeal without putting in question their very capacity for reasoned action. They can of course doubt their judgment on particular matters in the sense that they can doubt that they are judging correctly. But they can hardly ask, in general, what reason they have to do what they themselves judge they have reason to do without fundamentally undermining the rational self-trust necessary for reasoned agency. In this sense, following the direction of their principle of reflection is just what reasoned agency is.

Once, however, we have the distinction between the broader principle of reflection and narrow conscience, it would seem to be possible for a rational agent to sensibly ask whether, and if so, why, they should follow their (narrow) *conscience*. Butler claims that *moral* agency is impossible without conscience, and this seems importantly correct. His point is not just that autonomous moral agency is impossible without it, but that anything worth calling moral agency at all is impossible without it. This is the claim he shares with Shaftesbury against Hutcheson. Although there is undeniably something good about ingenuous benevolence, a benevolent being who was not even capable of morally assessing their own conduct or guiding themselves by that assessment would not really be morally virtuous or even a moral agent yet.

Essential to the capacity for moral agency, Butler holds, is accountability. Unlike a "passive" mechanism like a watch, moral agents are accountable for their own operations (Pr.14). Accountability for complying with deontic moral norms, however, requires not just the ability to accord with the norms, but to *follow* them in the sense of *holding* oneself to them. And this requires the capacity to make and be moved by deontic normative judgments.

There is a minimal sense of rational agency, namely responsiveness to normative reasons, that does not require reflective normative judgment. And it is of course true that rational agents, indeed moral agents, may better accord with normative reasons, or even moral obligations, if they respond correctly to the facts that are reasons (or their moral obligations), irrespective of their own normative reasons (or obligation) (see, e.g., Arpaly 2004). But as Pufendorf pointed out, someone can intelligibly be held accountable for discharging their obligations only if they can hold themselves to them, and this requires, in Butler's terminology, conscience.

But what is the relation between conscience and the principle of reflection? Might not a moral agent judge themselves obligated to do something through conscience, but still ask, using their principle of reflection, whether they have sufficient normative reason to discharge their obligation? Although this is plainly a more coherent question than whether they have reason to do what (they judge) they have reason to do, there may nonetheless be features of accountable moral agency that effectively close it in the way Butler clearly thinks it closed.

Recall Butler's remark that "vice cannot be the happiness, but must upon the whole be the misery, of such a creature as man ..., an accountable agent" (Butler 2017: VII.16). The reason this is so, to the extent that it is, is due to the fact that conscience is not merely the faculty of judgment in the sense of judging whether something is the case. It is also the faculty through which we judge ourselves and our actions in a deontic sense. And not just in the sense of estimating our positive and negative features, but in coming to what P. F. Strawson calls "reactive attitudes" that express *verdicts* toward our actions, like guilt and blame. I think it is fair to say that Butler would recognize his own doctrine of the authority of conscience in the following passage from Samuel Clarke's 1705 Boyle Lectures.

> For the Judgment and Conscience of a Man's own Mind ... that his Actions should be conformed to such or such a Rule or Law; is the truest or formallest Obligation. ... For whoever acts contrary to this sense and conscience of his own mind is necessarily self-condemned (Selby-Bigge: 1964: I.165).

The reason that acknowledged, unexcused wrongdoing can make moral agents miserable is that they hold themselves accountable through the attitude of self-blame or guilt, that is, by having a guilty conscience.

Narrow conscience is thus a faculty through which we make not just any normative assessments of ourselves. It is one whose currency are distinctive (reactive) attitudes through which we hold ourselves accountable (Darwall 2006 and 2014b). But this means that the deliverances of (narrow) conscience have implications for normative reasons, hence judgments of the (broad) principle of reflection.

It is arguably a presumption of blame as a holding-accountable attitude that there cannot be sufficient reason to perform culpable wrongs. It is a kind of self-contradiction to blame someone but simultaneously to acknowledge that they had sufficient reason to do what one is blaming them for (Darwall 2006: 98; Williams 1995: 40–44; Gibbard 1990: 299–300; Shafer-Landau 2003: 181–183; Skorupski 1999: 42–43). But if that is so, then blame cannot be warranted, an act cannot be culpable, unless there is, by virtue of its culpability, sufficient reason not to perform it.

Even if such a line of thought can establish normative practical reasons to act morally, or, in Butler's terms, that vice is unnatural, it would not yet establish that there actually is such a thing as morality and its distinctive obligating normativity. It would not yet, that is, fully respond to the Carneadean challenge that morality might be chimerical. It would just mean that *if* there is such a thing as moral right and wrong, then there is never sufficient reason to do what is wrong.

But where can skepticism about the right get a foothold that would not apply equally to the good? Once we have the general concept of normativity that seems implicit in both the good *and* the right, then any skepticism about normativity in general will apply equally to both. Butler's distinction between self-love and the principle of reflection opens up the space to distinguish the general notion of normative reasons. The dialectic should then naturally turn to examining the way in which normativity enters into the concepts of good and right. An attractive view is Sidgwick's, that the concept of the good involves that of (reason-supported) justified desire. If the concept of right is tied to accountability, as Butler seems to be supposing, then a complementary thought to Sidgwick's is that the right is therefore also tied to normative reasons, in this case, reasons for the distinctive attitudes through which we hold one another accountable, reactive attitudes such as guilt and blame (Gibbard 1990: 42). As Mill puts the point, "We do not call anything wrong, unless we mean to imply that a person ought to be punished for doing it … [for example], by the reproaches of his own conscience" (Mill 2002: 5.14). Unless a skeptic can give some argument for doubting the existence of normative reasons for the attitudes of conscience that would not also apply to other attitudes, such as desire, then it would seem that conscience and therefore morality's authority is vindicated (Darwall 2016).

The Right and the General Good

Conscience, as Butler understands it, is unlike Hutcheson's moral sense in having an essentially practical role. The capacity to govern deliberation by conscientious normative judgment makes human beings "moral agents" and a "law to themselves" (Butler 2017: II.4, 8). For Hutcheson, moral sense always has motives and motivated actions in view, seen from an observer's perspective (which an agent might of course adopt themselves). Butler's conscience, on the other hand, is essentially *agential*. Not only motives, but also "external actions" themselves are objects of conscientious judgment (II.8). It is essential to moral agency, as Butler conceives it, that moral agents are capable of deciding not to do something on the grounds that, as they judge through conscience, it would be wrong.

So far, we have two contrasts between Hutcheson and Butler that go together. For Hutcheson, moral sense always has a motive as object, whereas for Butler, we can also approve of actions (in circumstances) directly. And second, the perspective of moral sense for Hutcheson is that of an observer, whereas Butlerian conscience is agential. Yet a third contrast flows from these two. Hutcheson holds that all approved motives are desires for states of affairs in which natural goods are realized. Butler, however, holds that among the "external actions" that conscience approves are deeds considered not just for their naturally good or evil consequences, but also on the basis of other right- and wrong-making features of the acts themselves.

Thus, Butler rejects Hutcheson's view that "virtue is resolvable into benevolence" (Butler 2017: D.8), not just on the grounds that genuine virtue must involve moral self-government through conscience, but also because conscience approves and disapproves of conduct on other, non-consequentialist grounds.

> The fact then appears to be, that we are constituted so as to condemn falsehood, unprovoked violence, injustice, and to approve of benevolence to some preferably to others, abstracted from all consideration, which conduct is likeliest to produce an overbalance of happiness or misery (D.8).[20]

Butler makes, moreover, a point that will loom large in defense of indirect utilitarian theories of right to follow, such as rule-utilitarianism, namely, that there is no reason to think that it would maximize the general happiness for human beings to be governed by a desire to maximize it. It may be that God is universally benevolent and "that He foresaw that this [non-utilitarian] constitute of our nature would produce more happiness, than forming us with a temper of mere general benevolence" (D.8). From this, Butler draws the same conclusion as later indirect or rule-utilitarians: what we are obligated to do is not to promote overall net happiness but to follow dictates, the general internalization of which has these good effects.

---

[20] The similarity between this list and Ross's examples of nonconsequentialist *prima facie* duties is uncanny (Ross 2003).

Against Egoism

In addition to his claims about the authority of conscience and his critique of Hutcheson's proto-utilitarian focus on benevolence, Butler is best known for his "refutation" of psychological egoism. This is somewhat ironic since many of the considerations Butler draws on are common to Shaftesbury and Hutcheson also. However, Butler's arguments are crisp and convincing and have proven the most memorable.

Butler notes that it is tautologous, in one sense, that people always do what they desire, but that this is impotent to show anything about the *objects* of their desires. It is the latter, however, that is really in dispute between those who hold that all human motivation is egoistic and those who deny this. Then Butler points out that whenever something makes someone happy or gives them pleasure, this invariably involves the person's having some positive attitude to some particular thing that makes them happy or that gives them pleasure. "There could be no enjoyment or delight from one thing more than another, from eating food more than from swallowing a stone, if there were not an affection or appetite to one thing more than another" (XI.6). If I get pleasure from eating pad Thai but not from swallowing stones or iPads, that must be because I like the former experience and do not like the latter. It simply cannot be the case that the only thing I like or desire is pleasure, conceived generically, since I could not get pleasure from eating pad Thai unless I liked features of the experience that are intrinsic to it.

Like Hutcheson and Shaftesbury, Butler was concerned not just to show that we have desires that are independent of self-love or a desire for our own good or happiness. He also wanted to establish that we can desire things beyond our own experiences, including the good of others and moral action. However, neither of the arguments mentioned so far can establish that. It is consistent with them that all desires are for experiences of various kinds or, more generally, for states of oneself. But Butler believed that psychological egoism can only seem to be plausible when we think, mistakenly, as he has shown, that it is supported by some such confusion as the arguments we have already mentioned unmask. And once we see that what is at issue is an empirical question, the evidence will be overwhelming that people are capable of taking pleasure in, or being made happy by, things other than their own experiences, for example, by the happiness of others. Whether benevolence exists "is ... to be judged of and determined in the same way other facts or matters of natural history are." By that standard, "that there is some degree of benevolence amongst men, may be as strongly and plainly proved in all these ways, as it could possibly be proved, supposing there was this affection in our nature" (I.6n).

If the object of self-love can be accomplished only when we satisfy our desires for specific objects, among which may be the good of others, we already have the result that a person's interest may not be advanced to the degree that they concern themselves with it. It will be realized only insofar as they realize the *objects* of their various desires. Moreover, Butler argues, a person may have too great a concern for their own good for their own good. Like the person at a party who constantly asks, "Are we having fun yet?" they may be too focused on being happy to enjoy things that would make them happy. "*Disengagement* is absolutely necessary to enjoyment; and a person may have so steady and fixed an eye upon his own interest, whatever he places it in, as may hinder him from *attending* to gratifications within his reach, which others have their minds free and open to" (XI.9). Butler refers to this as a kind of paradox (Sidgwick called Butler's point the "paradox of egoistic hedonism" (Sidgwick 1967: 136)). But it is fundamentally the same kind of point Butler makes against universal benevolence. Just as universal benevolence, universally realized, is unlikely actually to bring about the greatest overall happiness that is its object, so also is self-love, realized in an individual agent, unlikely to bring about its object.[21]

Despite the relative brevity of his philosophical writings, Butler ended up making several significant contributions to the history of modern moral philosophy. In normative moral theory, Butler articulated what would become standard objections to consequentialism, but he also made points, those noted in the last paragraph, that would point the way to "indirect" consequentialist theories. By his sharp conceptual distinctions, for example, between power and authority, and his insistence on the independent normative authority of right and conscience, Butler's thought served to "work clear," in Sidgwick's terms, the modern idea of the independence of right and good in a way that could clarify the distinctively metaethical question of the sources of normativity in general, as well as that of moral right in particular. Finally, Butler's subtle and careful treatment of human moral psychology and of the role of conscience within it took important steps in the direction of articulating a conception of accountable moral agency necessary for a modern moral philosophy.

---

[21] This is what Parfit calls being "indirectly self-defeating" in Parfit 1986.

6

Hume and Smith

Like Butler and Hutcheson, David Hume (1711–1776) and Adam Smith (1723–1790) were contemporaries. More, they were interlocutors, compatriots, and friends, who, along with Hutcheson, helped shape the remarkable period of intellectual activity in eighteenth-century Scotland known as the Scottish Enlightenment. Hume and Smith inherited Hutcheson's sentimentalist approach: a form of moral empiricism that is opposed to ethical rationalism and that continues to find resonance today. Hume's version has had the greatest influence; he is, of course, one of the greatest philosophers of all time. Though the main lines of Hume's critique of rationalism come straight from Hutcheson, Hume pushed them farther and more memorably. It was Hume, moreover, who placed moral philosophy most compellingly within an empiricist naturalist framework.

We also owe to Hume a formulation of perhaps the most fundamental problem of metaethics, what Michael Smith calls the "moral problem" (Smith 1994). Moral judgments, Hume says, "go beyond the calm and indolent judgments of the understanding" in seeming to be intrinsically motivating (Hume 1978: 457). When someone's expressed moral or ethical judgments leave them utterly unmoved, we doubt their judgments' sincerity. But Hume famously held that only desires can motivate. According to the "Humean theory of motivation," belief and reason are motivationally inert (Smith 1994). Nonetheless, ethical judgments also seem belief-like in being subject to genuine disagreement concerning their correctness or truth. The metaethical challenge is how to reconcile these three things.

Hume raises a related issue in his famous "is"/"ought" passage, which questions how reasoning from non-normative premises formulated with "is"s can arrive at conclusions expressed with "ought"'s. This "*ought*, or *ought not*," Hume writes, "expresses some new relation or affirmation" (Hume 1978: 469). This leads to the question: What is the "source" of "ought"'s "normativity?" as Christine Korsgaard puts it (Korsgaard 1996a). Following Hume, it is often thought that normative judgments necessarily play a role in guiding the attitudes they normatively assess in a way that non-normative judgments do not.

For his part, Adam Smith is, of course, best known for his writings on economics. But Smith's *Theory of Moral Sentiments* is arguably one of the greatest works on moral psychology ever written, whose moral philosophical significance may only now be becoming clear (Fleischacker 1991, 2013; Griswold 1999; Darwall 2004, 2006). Smith shows the ubiquity of imaginative perspective-taking in our mental moral lives, both in attributing mental states to others (getting "inside their heads") and in everyday normative judgments of the fittingness, or "propriety" as Smith calls it, of attitudes to the objects they have in view.

For example, we often grasp that another person is angry and what they are angry at by imaginatively placing ourselves in their perspective and imagining what is in view from that standpoint and how to respond to it. Determining what their state of mind is is not itself a matter of ethical or normative judgment. But we do also often judge whether someone's response to some object of thought is a justified or "proper" one. According to Smith, this is something we do by an imaginative projection into the other's "shoes" – though the projection is regulated impartially (with Smith's "impartial spectator"), so that we enter into their shoes not *as* them, or even as ourselves, but as *someone* in their situation. If we share their response after such an impartially regulated projection – in Smith's terms, "sympathize" or have "fellow-feeling" with it – we judge their response *proper* or justified in the sense of being fitting to its object.

Smith makes an important connection between fellow-feeling and mutual respect and accountability. Our capacity to take on others' perspectives and regulate our conduct toward them from an informed and impartial second-personal point of view figures centrally both in Smith's account of justice and in his connection between the human capacity for unforced agreement (in particular, free economic exchange) and mutual respect.

This turns out to be central to solving what has been called the "Adam Smith Problem": How can Smith both praise the free market's "invisible hand" for turning *self-interestedly* motivated conduct into public benefits, and also be as concerned as he is with *moral* sentiments? How could the same mind have produced both *The Wealth of Nations* and *The Theory of Moral Sentiments*?

The answer is that Smith thinks that these are inextricably connected. In the very section of *The Wealth of Nations* in which Smith attributes the division of labor on which national wealth depends to the human capacity for "truck, barter, and exchange," he remarks that this capacity makes possible a relation of mutual respect (Grotius and Pufendorf's "sociability") between human beings that other species cannot have (Smith 1976: 25).

As we will see, Smith echoes Pufendorf's connection between sociability, mutual respect, equal dignity, and mutual accountability. "A moral being is an accountable being," Smith writes (1982: 111). When another person injures us, Smith says, what "chiefly enrages us … is the little account he seems to make of us, the unreasonable preference which he gives to himself over us" (96). We are outraged by the violation of our dignity and what Kant will call the other's "self-conceit" (Kant 1996b: 5: 73–77).[1] As with Kant, this focus on individual dignity gives Smith a principled way of opposing the imposition of costs on some for the greater benefit of others. Here, Smith writes, our concern is rightly not for overall utility, but for the "very individual who [would be] injured" (Smith 1982: 90).

Hume is more equivocal on these matters. Like Smith, and unlike Hutcheson, he stresses the contrast between justice and public utility in individual instances, but argues that the moral foundation of justice is ultimately utility nonetheless. Hume lacks Pufendorf's or Smith's focus on equal dignity or mutual respect and any related emphasis on autonomy and accountability. Indeed, he also rejects Hutcheson's sharp separation of moral evaluation from other forms of esteem. What leads Hume to these positions is his "experimental" approach, which he pursues from the perspective of an "anatomist" concerned to discover the mind's "most secret Springs and Principles" (Hume 1932: I.32–33; 1978: xi, 620).[2] Frequently, when Hume uses "moral philosophy," it is to refer to empirical moral psychology, analogously to "natural philosophy"'s early modern reference to the emerging natural sciences.

At the same time, Hume is also a moral philosopher in our contemporary, normative sense. But even here, his approach is decidedly tied to an observer's third-person perspective rather than the first-person standpoint of a deliberating agent or the second-person point of view of mutually accountable moral agents.[3]

Hume

Hume's empiricist naturalism is on display from outset of *A Treatise of Human Nature*, the first two volumes of which Hume published in 1739 at the age of twenty-eight. Its subtitle announces the *Treatise* as "an attempt to introduce the experimental method of reasoning into moral subjects" (Hume 1978: xi). Hume's ambition, it is often said, was to be the "Newton of the moral sciences" (Passmore 1968: 131).[4] Although Hutcheson also broadly shared this approach, Hume's Newtonianism led him to deny two central tenets of Hutcheson's

---

[1] On this element of Smith, see Debes 2012.
[2] Although Hume's contrast between the approach of the painter and the anatomist is familiar from the *Treatise*, this characterization comes from a letter to Hutcheson. On this, see Immerwahr 1991; see also Abramson 2007.
[3] For an argument that Hume can provide a first-personal account of moral agency, see Abramson 2002.
[4] See, however, McIntyre 1994 for an argument that Samuel Clarke was actually an earlier contender for this title.

moral sentimentalism. These were, first, Hutcheson's hypothesis of a dedicated moral sense, what Hume termed an "original instinct," and second, Hutcheson's claim that the object of moral sense, *moral* goodness or virtue, is fundamentally distinct from other estimable qualities to which we respond in non-moral ways. Hume argued on Newtonian grounds that a simpler explanation of approbation and disapprobation is provided by all-purpose mechanisms of sympathy and the association of ideas that are in play throughout our psychology. No independent moral "sense" is required. Further, Hume argued that any distinction between "moral virtues" and estimable "natural abilities" is purely verbal (Hume 1978: 606).

Hume's ethics are, like Hutcheson's, an ethics of virtue, but Hume denied the tenet that made Hutcheson's a modern *moral* virtue ethics in contrast to Aristotle's. Like Shaftesbury, Hutcheson rejected the juridical model of the modern natural lawyers. But he nonetheless insisted against ancient ethical theorists that *moral* good and evil differ fundamentally from other things the ancients and their followers called virtues and vices, like temperance and gluttony. Only the former were objects of the distinctively *moral* approval and disapproval that he called "approbation" and condemnation, respectively. Moreover, Hutcheson held that all moral goodness consists in forms of benevolent concern for human (non-moral) good. And he argued that because universal benevolence is the morally best motive, and because universal benevolence aims at the "greatest happiness of the greatest number," this goal provides the standard of moral choiceworthiness. These ideas led him to embrace one of Sidgwick's marks of "modern moral philosophy," namely, that universal benevolence is no less a source of normative reasons than is egoistic concern for the agent's own good. And this led naturally, in Sidgwick and later writers, to utilitarian and consequentialist theories of moral conduct more generally.

According to Hutcheson, moral good and evil are qualities the contemplation of which gives rise to irreducible moral feelings or "ideas" of approbation and condemnation, respectively. Hume denied that any such distinctive feelings requiring an "original instinct" or "sense" exist, however. Sympathy and the association of ideas can explain our human contemplative responses quite generally, and what Hutcheson *called* moral goodness is only one of a wide variety of things that evoke favorable disinterested contemplative response. Any distinction between "moral virtues" and "natural abilities" like wit, Hume said, is only "verbal." Finally, Hume also denied that benevolence enjoys anything like the priority even among moral virtues that Hutcheson claimed. Hume agreed with Butler that virtues like justice and fidelity can conflict with benevolence and sometimes trump it.

Hume's appreciation of the differences between benevolence and justice, and of the latter's special connection to problems of collective action that can be solved only through mutually advantageous practices and institutions in which participants do their fair share, marked an important contribution to the history of ethical thought. Hume showed that just practices are vulnerable not just to free-riding "sensible knave[s]" who wish to advance their self-interest, but also to unjust benevolence, as when someone seeks to advance the public good rather than repay a loan to a "seditious bigot" (1975a: 282–283; 1978: 497).

It is essential to Hume's view that justice is established by conventions or rules that are not simply beneficial overall but mutually advantageous in the sense that their benefits extend to pretty much everyone who is bound by them.[5] Even so, Hume's account of what he calls the "moral obligation" of justice is in terms of public utility, which sympathy and the association of ideas turn into observers' approbation. This means that for Hume it is the beneficial consequences of justice overall, though not in every specific case, that grounds its moral value. This gives Hume an especially interesting relation to utilitarianism.

Hume is not a utilitarian in the sense of Bentham and Mill. To begin with, Hume is a virtue theorist and uninterested in articulating what Mill will call a "criterion of right and wrong" (Mill 2002: I.1). This he shares with Hutcheson. However, Hutcheson, unlike Hume, does put forward a standard of moral *choiceworthiness*, and that standard is, moreover, a utilitarian one: Moral sense, Hutcheson says, "regulate[s] our Election" by preferring acts to the degree that they "procur[e] the greatest Happiness for the greatest Numbers" (Hutcheson 2004: 125). Even so, Hutcheson does not accept a consequentialist, much less a utilitarian, theory of virtue. The moral goodness of benevolence is intrinsic and fundamental, irrespective of its consequences, as is evident to moral sense.

Broadly speaking, however, Hume *is* a consequentialist in these respects. It is our sympathy with the good effects of virtuous traits and the practice of justice that leads us to approve of them. This was not lost on Bentham. Bentham wrote that when he read the *Treatise*, he "felt as if the scales had fallen from [his] eyes"; he "learned to see that *utility* was the test and measure of all virtue" (Bentham 1838: 268n).[6]

As we noted in the last chapter, Butler's objections to Hutcheson's claim that "virtue is resolvable into benevolence," that justice, fidelity, and truth telling are moral obligation-making independently of their consequences, would become stock counterexamples to utilitarianism for later critics. There was, though, a further issue regarding whether moral goodness can be reduced to benevolence that concerned Butler's doctrine of the authority of conscience. Here Butler held, as against Hutcheson, that genuine moral virtue involves

---

[5] Hume restricts, however, just practices to those having a roughly equal antecedent standing. I will discuss a passage in which this becomes starkly clear below (Hume 1985: 190). For a discussion of Hume's racism, see Garrett 2004.

[6] For more discussion, see Darwall 1994.

moral *autonomy*: self-guidance by the moral agent's own conscientious moral judgments. And Butler held, again, that ordinary moral agents' judgments are not utilitarian.

This illustrates what would become a deep difference between utilitarians and their opponents. Like Butler, deontological critics of utilitarianism generally give a central role to moral autonomy. They frequently see self-direction as essential both to a morally good life – as in Kant's doctrine that genuine moral worth involves conduct resulting from agents' own conception of their moral duty – and as a source of non-utilitarian duties and rights – for example, rights to lead one's own life and to be treated, as Kant says, never simply as means but always as an end – and the correlative moral duties these rights entail.

It is significant, in this connection, that Hume gives so little weight to moral autonomy. Indeed, when Hutcheson, impressed by Butler's defense of the authority of conscience, attempted to give it some role in his later works (e.g., in *System of Moral Philosophy* (Hutcheson 1755)), albeit still holding that moral sense or conscience is motivationally inert, Hume criticized him.[7] Hume wrote to Hutcheson: "You seem here to embrace Dr. Butler's Opinion" that conscience "has an Authority distinct from its Force and Durableness, and that because we think it *ought* to prevail" (Hume 1932: I.47). Against this, Hume urged that conscience or moral sense is simply like any "Instinct or Principle" in "approv[ing] of itself upon reflection" (I.47). If anything, then, Hume downplays moral autonomy even more than Hutcheson.

Against Practical Reason

Hume mounts his major metaethical arguments, first, against rationalism, and second, for moral sentimentalism, at the beginning of Book III of the *Treatise*. However, a central premise in these arguments, that neither actions nor passions can be "contrary to truth or reason" (1978: 415), is argued for in II.ii.3 ("Of the Influencing Motives of the Will"). "Nothing is more usual in philosophy," Hume says, than "talk of the combat of passion and reason," including by philosophers, like Butler, who say that every motive is to be brought into "conformity with that superior principle" (413). Against this, Hume announces that he will argue for two claims: (a) "reason alone cannot be a motive to any action of the will," and (b) reason "can never oppose passion in the direction of the will" (413).

The first is what Michael Smith calls the "Humean theory of motivation," though Hume generally prefers to say that *reason* rather than belief is impotent to motivate. (On Hume's theory of reason, these come to the same thing.)

---

[7] Hutcheson's *System* was published posthumously in 1755. Hume read an earlier copy that circulated among friends. For discussion, see Darwall 1995: 237–242.

Hume recognizes two kinds of reasoning: demonstrative reasoning concerning the "relations of our ideas" and probabilistic reasoning about "causes and effects" (413–414). Reasoning of either kind can directly affect only our beliefs. It is only when beliefs are combined with desires that action is motivated. And when this happens, it is passion or desire that provides the motivational impetus.

It appears to follow immediately that in one sense reason and belief "can never oppose passion": They cannot counter passion's motivational impetus. But Hume also argues that reason cannot oppose passions and actions in a different way; passions and actions can neither be "contrary or conformable to reason" since they cannot *themselves* be reasonable nor unreasonable.

This follows rather directly from Hume's conception of reason, which he tells us in Book III is "the discovery of truth and falsehood" (485). It is a consequence that only what can be true or false can be reasonable or unreasonable. Passions and actions have no "representative quality"; unlike ideas, including those with the "vivacity" to be beliefs, passions do not purport to be "copies" of "objects which they represent" (97, 415). A belief is "contradictory to truth and reason" if it is in "disagreement" "with those objects which [it] represent[s]" (415). Actions and passions cannot be unreasonable in this way.

Hume allows that we sometimes *call* passions and actions "unreasonable" when they are accompanied by or based on false beliefs, but it is really only the beliefs that are unreasonable "strictly and philosophically" (415–416). "'Tis not contrary to reason," he concludes, "for me to chuse my total ruin, to prevent the least uneasiness of an *Indian* or person wholly unknown to me. 'Tis as little contrary to reason to prefer even my own acknowledg'd lesser good to my greater, and have a more ardent affection for the former than the latter" (416).

Against Moral Rationalism and for Moral Sentimentalism

Having made these arguments about reason and the will in Book II, Hume begins Book III by arguing on their basis that "*Moral Distinctions*" are "*not deriv'd from Reason*" (455). Although he gives a battery of other considerations, the central arguments against metaethical rationalism depend on these two. If it is impossible for passions and actions to be in accord with or contrary to reason, then a passion or action can hardly be against morality *because* it is against reason. If reason just is "the discovery of truth and falshood" (458), then reason cannot dictate passions and actions. Therefore, morality cannot dictate an action or passion on the grounds that reason does.

Obviously, this Humean argument depends entirely on Hume's definition of reason, which even many modern-day Humeans would reject as overly narrow, since they often want to hold that there is such a thing as instrumental irrationality: failing to take necessary means to ends. Hume himself held that even such irrationality is not against reason, "strictly and philosophically" (415). At best, it typically involves irrational belief. Kant will later argue that reason imposes formal constraints on practical reasoning: "hypothetical imperatives" of instrumental rationality, but also "categorical imperatives" that are grounded in the conditions of free rational agency. For this dispute between Hume and his critics to be more than definitional, it must be set in the context of a whole network of substantive philosophical issues concerning the nature of practical reason, deliberation, and the will.

By far Hume's most influential argument against metaethical rationalism depends on his claim that ethical judgments "go beyond the calm and indolent judgments of the understanding" (457) together with the Humean theory of motivation advanced in Book II. The direct argument from his definition of reason attempts to show that morality cannot be derived from reason *metaphysically*, that moral dictates are neither grounded nor consist in dictates of reason. Reason can only dictate belief and not action. The *motivational argument* attempts to show that neither can moral distinctions derive from reason *epistemically*. Moral knowledge and judgment go "beyond" anything with which reason or belief provides us, since moral judgments can move us directly.

For this argument to establish its conclusion, it must hold not just that there is some connection between moral judgment and motivation, but that the latter is intrinsic to the former. Otherwise, moral judgments might be made by reason with motivation being provided by some passion that is connected to it, perhaps even necessarily. Kant himself actually agrees that motivation always requires desire; he just holds that some desires derive from reason ("pure practical reason").[8]

Ethical rationalists like Samuel Clarke held that through reason we can perceive relations of "fitness" between actions and circumstances (e.g., that gratitude is a fitting response to benevolence). Hume argued that this rationalist position faced the challenge of proving "*a priori*, that these relations, if they really existed and were perceiv'd, wou'd be universally forcible and obligatory," by which he meant motivating (466). Not all rationalists have accepted this internalist challenge – prominently, Ross does not – but the eighteenth-century rationalists usually did, as we shall later see.

It is not clear, indeed, exactly what connection between ethical judgment and motivation Hume himself accepts (Brown 1988). His challenge to the rationalists that they must show an *a priori* connection to motivation is rooted in the fact that they hold morality to be "eternal and immutable," in Cudworth's phrase. Since Hume does not hold this view, he need not face this challenge. Hume holds that it is contingent psychological human processes of sympathy

---

[8] "Desire is the faculty to be, by means of one's representations, the cause of the objects of these representations" (Kant 1996c: 6:211; see also Kant 1996b: 5:9).

and the association of ideas that make ethical judgments motivating. Whether this motivation is intrinsic to ethical judgment depends on exactly what Hume takes such judgments to be, and this is, at best, a complicated matter. Whatever the details of Hume's own view, there is no question that, as Michael Smith's formulation of "the moral problem" makes clear, the claim that motivation is intrinsic to moral judgment has had a powerful influence in contemporary metaethics, leading many philosophers to forms of anti-realism, whether expressivist or error-theoretic (e.g., Stevenson 1937; Mackie 1977).

Again, Hume holds that reasoning can only establish analytic propositions about "relations of our ideas" or "matters of fact" through probabilistic causal reasoning (Hume 1978: 413, 468). No substantive ethical proposition is analytic, so that means reasoning can establish ethical propositions only if they are "matters of fact." And here, Hume invites us to consider how ethical judgment actually works. Of course, it must begin with "matters of fact" concerning the object we are judging. But that does not mean the judgment with which we conclude itself concerns a matter of fact.

> Take any action allow'd to be vicious; Wilful murder, for instance. Examine it in all lights, and see if you can find that matter of fact, or real existence, which you call *vice*. In which-ever way you take it, you find only certain passions, motives, volitions, and thoughts. There is no other matter of fact in the case. The vice entirely escapes you, as long as you consider the object. You never can find it, till you turn your reflexion into your own breast, and find a sentiment of disapprobation, which arises in you, towards this action (468).

When we make ethical judgments, it is *on the basis of* what we take to be "matters of fact" concerning the thing we are judging. Our concluding judgment cannot then be just another such fact; it is a further judgment that "go[e]s beyond" the facts.

So far, this should be uncontroversial. Indeed, the irreducibility of normative ethical judgments to non-normative "matters of fact" on whose basis ethical judgments are made is something on which ethical rationalists themselves generally insist. A conceptual distinction between the normative and the non-normative is implicit in Butler's distinction between power and authority and, later, in Richard Price's claim that "right" and "wrong" express "simple ideas" (Price 1974: 41). It is even clearer, of course, in Sidgwick on the irreducibility of "ought" and Moore on the "naturalistic fallacy" (Sidgwick 1967: 25; Moore 1993).

When, therefore, Hume famously proclaims a conceptual gap between claims expressed with "is" and those expressed with "ought," this is common ground with his rationalist opponents. Where Hume departs in a way that he believes rationalists cannot follow is in holding that moral judgments "go beyond the calm and indolent judgments of the understanding" because the former have, and the latter lack, motivational impetus. It is because ethical judgments express or somehow otherwise involve *sentiment* that there is no rational path to them from beliefs about matters of fact.

Hume's sentimentalism has been a source of inspiration to recent philosophers who have developed a variety of anti-rationalist metaethical views, from naturalist versions of subjectivism and constructivism, to forms of expressivism and error theory (e.g., Brandt 1979; Railton, 1986; Dreier 1990; Street 2008; Stevenson 1937; Blackburn 1984; Gibbard 1990; Mackie 1977). The differences between these later views depend on subtle distinctions – for example, between expressing and attributing sentiments – that Hume himself does not make or, at least, consistently observe. It is probably ahistorical folly to attempt to determine exactly what metaethical position Hume held in any fine-grained way.

For instance, right after the passage quoted above, Hume writes, "So that when you pronounce any action or character to be vicious, you mean nothing, but that from the constitution of your nature you have a feeling or sentiment of blame from the contemplation of it" (Hume 1978: 469). Taken literally, this is a version of subjectivism: ethical judgments self-attribute sentiments (Dreier 1990). However, Hume also says that "[w]e do not infer a character to be virtuous, because it pleases: But in feeling that it pleases after such a particular manner, we in effect feel that it is virtuous" (1978: 471). This runs against subjectivism. It suggests something closer to the projectivist or expressivist account of value judgment that we found in Hobbes. Similarly, in the second *Enquiry*, Hume contrasts reason-based judgments of the understanding and ethical judgments in the following terms:

> The former conveys the knowledge of truth and falsehood: the latter gives the sentiment of beauty and deformity, vice and virtue. The one discovers objects as they really stand in nature, without addition or diminution: the other has a productive faculty, and gilding or staining all natural objects with the colours, borrowed from internal sentiment, raises in a manner a new creation (1975a: 294).

This also suggests a projectivist or expressivist view (Blackburn 1984: 210–212).

However its details are developed, Hume clearly espouses some version of metaethical sentimentalism in opposition to any form of rationalist realism. As we noted earlier, this was common ground with Hutcheson, even if Hutcheson tended more single-mindedly to metaethical subjectivist naturalism than Hume with his expressivist leanings. Hume titles the main sentimentalist section of the *Treatise* (III.i.2) in explicitly Hutchesonian terms: "Moral Distinctions Deriv'd From a Moral Sense." However, just after delimiting moral sentiment as of the "*peculiar* kind which makes us praise or condemn," suggesting Hutcheson's doctrine of the moral sense and its "simple," irreducibly moral "ideas" of approbation and condemnation, Hume makes a turn to explicitly reject Hutcheson's view (1978: 472).

"*From what principles*," he then asks, does moral sentiment derive (473)? What is the underlying psychological mechanism? Hume's Newtonianism leads him to seek the simplest explanation. Hutcheson thought he had a sufficiently simple explanation since he thought the object of approbation is always some form of benevolence; a dedicated sense that approves of it is simple enough. But, like Butler, Hume rejected Hutcheson's normative theory of moral goodness, if only because justice can conflict with benevolence no less than it can with self-interest. There are many different kinds of things we approve, and "'tis absurd to imagine, that in every particular instance, these sentiments are produced by an *original* quality and *primary* constitution" (473). Any hypothesis of a dedicated "moral sense" must thus be suspect on Newtonian grounds.

Moreover, Hume rejected Hutcheson's bright line between moral goodness and estimable "natural abilities" such as wit. He thought he had a simpler explanation that could encompass all our approvals and disapprovals without distinguishing between moral and non-moral approbation. The materials of this explanation were quite general phenomena of "sympathy" (in Hume's special sense) and the association of ideas that are involved throughout our mental lives.

What Hume calls "sympathy" is a psychological process through which an idea of a feeling or passion is "converted into an impression, and acquires such a degree of force and vivacity, as to become the very passion itself" (317). Sympathy, for Hume, is much like what psychologists these days call "emotional contagion" in which we catch feelings from others, but not by taking their perspective or considering the object that others' feelings have in view. "The human countenance, says Horace, borrows smiles or tears from the human countenance" (1975a: 220). This example just *is* emotional contagion: "catching" others' feelings in their presence. The mechanism of sympathy at work in Hume's account of the moral sentiment is, however, somewhat different, since it can be employed in solitary thought from the armchair.

Hume's mechanism, again, transforms an *idea* of a feeling into the feeling "itself." For example, if I have the idea of someone feeling pleasure, sympathy then transmutes that idea into a pleasant feeling (impression) in me. The sentiments implicated in ethical judgment are felt impressions, and it is Humean sympathy that brings these feelings into our mental economy in making ethical judgments. The rest of the work is done by the association of ideas, a general mechanism that takes us from idea to idea, when these are related by "*resemblance, contiguity*, and *causation*" (1978: 60). Putting these two mechanisms together provides a significantly simpler explanation of our moral sentiments, Hume argues, than any that can be provided by the hypothesis of a moral sense.

Hume's explanatory theory also ends up valorizing a broadly consequentialist, almost utilitarian, normative theory of virtue and vice. As the chapter titles of the second *Enquiry* make clear, Hume believes that all virtues are qualities that are either "immediately agreeable" or "useful" to ourselves or to others (1975a: 233, 250, 261). To see how his psychology of moral sentiment works, consider benevolence. When we contemplate the motive or trait of benevolence, our thoughts are carried by an association of ideas to the normal and usual consequences of benevolence, that is, the pleasurable states of mind of those who benefit from actions motivated by it or by directly pleasurably engaging with the benevolent person. Sympathy then transforms ideas of these pleasurable states into pleasant feelings in us, which we associate back with the benevolent motives or traits we are contemplating. We express these pleasant contemplative feelings when we judge the motive or trait of benevolence itself to be good or virtuous.

There are some important wrinkles in Hume's view. First, Hume holds that our judgments involve less the actual consequences of some motive or trait on particular occasions than their *normal* consequences. "Virtue in rags is still virtue" (1978: 584). Second and more importantly, because we tend to sympathize more with people who are psychologically closer to us, we have to "correc[t] our sentiments, or at least ... our language" by fixing on some "*steady* and *general* points of view" and thinking and speaking as though we occupied them (581–582). "[N]otwithstanding [the] variation of our sympathy, we give the same moral approbation to the same moral qualities in *China* as in *England*" (581).

We "correct" the sentiments that sympathy and the association of ideas themselves provide by "plac[ing] ourselves" in a common "*general*" point of view. And we correct our language by "apply[ing] the terms expressive of our liking or dislike ... as if we remain'd in one point of view. Experience soon teaches us this method of correcting our sentiments, or at least, of correcting our language" (582).

In the *Treatise,* Hume's perhaps idiosyncratic view of how we do this is by fastening on the perspective of someone in "that narrow circle, in which [the agent who is the object of our judgment] moves" (602). In the *Enquiry,* he offers a more social-constructionist proposal. There he speaks of "render[ing] our sentiments more public and social" (1975a: 229). "The intercourse of sentiments, therefore, in society and conversation, makes us form some general unalterable standard, by which we may approve or disapprove of characters and manners" (229).

In public moral discourse, sympathy helps supply a general standard that can solve the problem that "variation ... of sympathy" in private moral judgment itself causes. Moral discussion expresses sentiments, and interlocutors sympathetically reverberate with one another's feelings. We can think of moral discussion of morals, then, as a kind of tuning of a large social orchestra, where what brings the various instruments into tune is their reverberation with one another.

Justice, the Artificial Virtue

Hume's ethics are, like Hutcheson's, an ethics of virtue. Both are opposed to the modern natural lawyers' focus on conduct and obligation. And both carry forward Shaftesbury's subversive reconceptualizing of obligation in non-deontic terms. When Shaftesbury asked, "*What Obligation* there is *to* Virtue" (Shaftesbury 2001: II.78), he was inquiring what normative reason we have to be virtuous (and assuming that any such reasons would have to be self-interested). To this, Hutcheson added the non-*eudaimonist* premise that any person's good can ground normative reasons, not just the agent's. This, again, was his "modern turn." And he added a sense of "obligation" consisting in the deliverances of moral sense. Hume follows Hutcheson, holding that, in addition to the "*natural* obligation" of self-interest, moral sentiment provides a "*moral* obligation" (Hume 1978: 497, 498). This becomes clearest in Hume's discussion of justice, to which we now turn.

In one way, Hume goes farther in the direction of a virtue ethics than Hutcheson does. Though Hutcheson downplays questions of morally right and wrong conduct, and though virtue or moral goodness is for him, in the first instance, anyway, a matter of *motive* and not of conduct, Hutcheson does recognize and theorize a kind of morally good *conduct*, namely, the morally choiceworthy, considered independently of its motive. As we saw, this is where he formulates his version of the greatest happiness principle. Hume does not follow him in this. At the beginning of *Treatise* III.2, on justice, Hume writes, "[W]hen we praise any actions, we regard only the motives that produced them, and consider the actions as signs or indications of certain principles in the mind and temper. The external performance has no merit" (477).

Hume's analysis of justice in terms of mutually advantageous rule-governed cooperative practices is path breaking and brilliant. However, it is important to bear in mind, as the passage just quoted makes clear, that his primary focus is on the *virtue* of justice, and this, for Hume, must consist in some kind of motive. Nevertheless, justice differs fundamentally from other motives, like benevolence, in that its object *is* a kind of conduct considered independently of its consequences, rather than some result, like someone's natural good, whether the agent's, like self-interest, or someone else's, like benevolence.

Hume distinguishes between virtues he calls "natural" and those he calls "artificial." The distinction is roughly this: artificial virtues require a background of conventional rule-governed practices in order to be realized; the natural virtues do not. In holding that there are both natural and artificial virtues, Hume places himself between Hobbes and Hutcheson. As against Hobbes, and with Hutcheson, Hume holds that there can be virtue or moral goodness in a state of nature. Benevolence is to be approved of whether or not there exists law or custom. But as against Hutcheson, and with Hobbes, Hume holds that there are moral traits that do require human artifice, and that do not reduce to benevolence in any of its forms – namely, justice. This latter claim is an echo of Butler, with a distinctly Hobbesian twist.

Since virtues for Hume, as for Hutcheson, consist in virtuous motives, Hume argues for the artificiality of the virtue of justice by arguing that no reliable motive to justice "proceeds immediately from original principles," like benevolence or self-love, "without the intervention of thought or reflexion" (484). Neither self-love nor "regard to publick interest" leads us to be just directly.

As far as the former is concerned, "'tis certain that self-love, when it acts at its liberty, instead of engaging us to honest actions, is the source of all injustice and violence" (480). Regarding the latter, Hume gives several reasons why regard for the public interest cannot be the motive to just acts. One is that, like self-interest, the public interest can conflict with justice in particular cases. Thus a loan "to a seditious bigot" might be secret and its being repaid be contrary to the public interest, however much justice requires its repayment (497). Second, we have but limited generosity, and "experience sufficiently proves that men, in the ordinary conduct of life, look not so far as the public interest, when they pay their creditors, perform their promises, and abstain from theft, and robbery, and injustice of every kind" (481).

The virtue of justice thus cannot be identical either with self-love or with benevolence, since neither reliably motivates just action, even, indeed, when rules of justice have been conventionally established. But what about the moral sentiment? Hume thinks that does occur naturally. And he certainly thinks we approve of justice – otherwise we could not judge justice a virtue. Even so, Hume holds that there is a conceptual bar to the moral sentiment being, as he puts it, the "first motive" to just acts. The reason, again, is that the "external performance" of a just act can have no "merit" in itself, since it derives any merit it has from its motive (477). Therefore, "[t]o suppose, that the mere regard to the virtue of the action, may be the first motive, which produc'd the action, and render'd it virtuous, is to reason in a circle" (478).

Like Hutcheson, Hume holds that since the moral sentiment approves of motives, it is impotent to motivate any act itself, any choice of a thing to do, considered independently of motivation. Hutcheson didn't think, however, that justice posed any special problem in this regard, since he thought that justice and the public interest never conflict, so the virtuous motive of benevolence is sufficient to motivate just acts. No separate virtuous motive of justice is required. Hume, however, denied this.

A sense in which the virtue of justice, unlike benevolence, is artificial, according to Hume, is that we only require such a virtue because of contingent features of human life that make necessary the conventional establishment of rule-governed practices of property, promise, and contract. If human generosity were unlimited, or human goods superabundant, we might have no need for such practices and there would be no virtue of justice. By contrast, natural virtues like benevolence are not conditional on the instituting of human practices to deal with such human limitations.

What Rawls would call, after Hume's account, the "circumstances of justice" – limited generosity and moderate scarcity – create the need and the opportunity for individuals to establish mutually advantageous rule-governed practices of property, promise, and contract (Rawls 1971: 126–129). To see how Hume thinks this works, consider the case of property.

Without an institution of property, because of moderate scarcity and limited generosity, our access to many goods will be relatively unstable. We will not, absent some special remedy, be able to rely on strangers not to take the benefits of our own industry. But, though neither self-love nor benevolence can be relied upon to motivate others to leave us in possession of our goods, "nature provides a remedy in the judgment and understanding, for what is irregular and incommodious in the affections" (Hume 1978: 489). We can come to see *together* that it is mutually advantageous to jointly accept and follow some set of rules concerning the legitimate acquisition and transfer of property, rules that forbid appropriating without consent what others have legitimately acquired.

Thus "members of [a] society" gain a "general sense of common interest" in everyone's abiding by a rule that, say, requires people to restrain from taking the possessions of friends and strangers alike, even when it is in their own interest to do so (490). Each "observe[s] that it will be for his own interest to leave another in the possession of his goods, *provided* he will act in the same manner with regard to me" (490). This sense of common interest does not however remain, as it were, in members' individual private consciousnesses. It is rather made "public and social" by, Hume says, "all the members of the society express[ing it] to one another" (1975a: 229; 1978: 490). "When this common sense of interest is mutually express'd, and is known to both," Hume writes, "it produces a suitable resolution and behaviour. And this may properly enough be called a convention or agreement betwixt us" (490).

Although we often use the term "convention" to refer to customs or rules, what Hume means by it is more like a convergence or convening of society members' minds, the creation of a kind of "common mind" (Pettit 1993) that somehow establishes rules. The latter, like those that structure property, are both the object and the upshot of the convention. There are some puzzles, however, about exactly how they are. It is clear that Hume thinks that the convention *produces* a "suitable resolution" of members "to regulate their conduct by certain rules," for example, those of property (Hume 1978: 490). And it is also clear that Hume thinks, as against Hobbes, that they do not, indeed, that they cannot, do this by anything like a mutual contract or promise. Hobbes faced the problem, recall, of explaining how the normative power to enter into any contract to establish the sovereign can be explained from the meager normative materials he provides. For Hume, any normative power of promise or contract would itself depend on social rules that it would take a convention to establish. So the convention cannot be a mutual promise or contract itself.

It seems closest to Hume's meaning to take the convention to consist simply in the mutually expressed "general sense of common interest" in everyone's regulating their conduct by the rules. In his famous example, "[t]wo men who pull the oars of a boat, do it by an agreement or convention, tho' they have never given promises to each other" (490). If you and I each simply want to get across a lake, not caring whether the other does, but realize that we each can only if we row together, then our "general sense of common interest" will be sufficient to motivate us to do what we need to do to get across. No joint resolution is required.

If we take our cue from the rowing example, then Hume would be saying, at least initially, that a mutually expressed "general sense of the common interest" in everyone regulating their conduct by rules of justice, such as those structuring an institution of property, can be sufficient to produce a "suitable resolution" of members "to regulate their conduct" by these rules. So although self-love is often a source of "injustice and violence" (480), reflection on the mutual benefits of restraining ourselves from taking the property of others can be a sufficient motive to make us do so. "There is no passion," Hume writes, that can control "the interested affection, but the very affection itself, by an alteration of its direction" (492).

However, there are special features of the rowing example that are not generalizable to all attempts to produce a sufficiently widespread resolution to comply with rules of justice. Rowers are easily able to surveil their partners and withhold their contribution when their partners do. And they enjoy the benefits of their partners' rowing just in case their partners enjoy their reciprocal benefits, indeed, simultaneously. None of this is true with all attempts to establish rules of justice. Finally, and perhaps most importantly for Hume's account of the virtue of justice, a well-established rule-governed practice of property will exist only if a sufficient number of members of society develop a new motive. A rule-governed practice of justice requires that a sufficient number take what Hart called an "internal point of view" on the rules and *accept* them as obligating norms (Hart 1961: 55–57). Nothing like this is involved in the rowing example, although of course, the rowers might have a *natural* sense of justice or reciprocity requiring them to do their fair share in a cooperative enterprise. But this is something Hume explicitly denies. Justice, he thinks, is an artificial virtue.

This means that Hume cannot really escape a version of the problem that beset Hobbes's attempt to derive obligations of justice from a covenant to establish the sovereign without sufficient normative materials to explain the normative power to make and be obligated by such a covenant in the first place. Hume rejects the Hobbesian project of grounding justice in contract or promise, since whatever is required to explain the obligating power of promises would have to be able to ground justice itself already. Hume holds, of course, that promises gain their power to obligate only because a social convention to regulate conduct by a rule of promise-keeping exists. But if the convention just consists in a "general sense of common interest," even when this is mutually expressed, it will only give members *self-interested* reasons to comply and then only when this is necessary to produce others' compliance. A convention, understood in these *interested* terms, is impotent to establish rules that people can genuinely respect or violate and to create the *acceptance* of such rules upon which a rule-governed practice depends.

Hobbes and Hume both see clearly that there are strong self-interested reasons to want justice practices in place (whether these require an absolute sovereign, as Hobbes believes, or not). This insight is not, of course, new to the modern period. When Glaucon challenges Socrates to justify justice in Plato's *Republic*, he states what he takes to be the common view that people are benefited by others' just conduct; he just wants Socrates to tell him why people should act justly themselves in cases where it is not necessary to procure others' justice (as it would not be if one had the ring of Gyges). He wants to know what non-instrumental motive people have to be just. I mentioned this at the outset of this book because the only such non-instrumental motives Socrates considers are intrinsic benefits of self-interest, not any motive of right that, Sidgwick claims, the moderns begin to recognize when they "work" their "idea[s] clear" (Sidgwick 1964: 198).

Hume calls self-interest the "*natural* obligation" to justice (in the *Enquiry*: "interested *obligation*") (Hume 1978: 498; 1975a: 278). He does think that the natural obligation of self-interest is initially sufficient to get justice practices started. "To the imposition, then, and observance of these rules, both in general, and in every particular instance, they are at first mov'd only by a regard to interest; and this motive, on the first formation of society, is sufficiently strong and forcible" (1978: 499). But only initially. When society becomes sufficiently "numerous," and the effects of injustice are sufficiently dispersed and diffuse, self-interest turns from being an ally to an enemy of justice. When that happens, any natural obligation to justice is insufficient. There must then also be a *moral obligation* to be just if rule-governed practices of justice are to flourish or even survive (499).

The basic problem, of course, is that of the "free rider," of which Hume's "sensible knave" provides a textbook example (1975a: 282). "[H]onesty" or justice is often "*the best policy*," but while good as a "general rule," it is nonetheless "liable to many exceptions." Someone "conducts himself with the most wisdom," says the knave, "who observes the general rule, and takes advantage of all the exceptions" (1975a: 282–283). To use Rawls's famous contrast between a "summary" and a "practice" conception of rules, the knave treats rules of justice as summary "rules of thumb" that have no binding force except as guides to their own interest (Rawls 1955). Rules of justice cannot, however, be so conceived and survive. It is only when conceived as *practice* rules that can be *respected* or *violated* that rules can structure practices of justice like property, promise, and contract.

Hume suggests at various points that the non-self-interested motive that practices of justice require is a distinctively moral one. He says that their "very equity and merit" is the only "universal motive for observing the laws of equity" (Hume 1978: 483). Also, "we have no motive leading us to the performance of promises, distinct from a sense of duty" (518). But now a problem emerges.

Like Hutcheson, Hume understands moral obligation in terms of the moral sentiment. To say we are morally obligated to something is just to say that moral sentiment or sense approves of it. But also like Hutcheson, Hume holds that moral sentiment only directly approves of *motives* and never acts considered independently of them. Indeed, Hume goes farther in this than Hutcheson, since Hutcheson defends a *derived* sense in which moral sense can approve of acts as choiceworthy – that is, as options considered from a deliberative perspective. Unlike Hutcheson, Hume gives no account of such deliberative judgments.

This commits Hume to the view that the moral sentiment is impotent to motivate action from the deliberative point of view. Approbation is something we feel from an *observer's* (third-personal) standpoint when we consider motive and character and the motivated actions that flow from these. Therefore, despite the fact that Hume seems to be saying that just acts can be – indeed that they often are – motivated by a sense of moral obligation and duty, such a statement is actually inconsistent with his considered view of the moral sentiment.

For Hume, the virtue of justice, like any virtue, must be expressed in a motive. But what is the motive of justice? On what motive does a just person act? If we rule out a sense of moral duty or obligation on the grounds just mentioned, then what motives are left? We have seen that both self-interest and benevolence are also ruled out. The "natural obligation" of self-interest may be sufficient to help constitute a convention to establish rules of justice initially, but when society becomes "numerous" it will not reliably motivate compliance. Benevolence is ruled out, first, because its limitation is one of the "circumstances of justice" that make just practices necessary, and, second, because, as in the case of a loan to a "seditious bigot," benevolence conflicts with justice.

We can see our way to a possible solution if we note a further puzzle in Hume's text. Hume writes that only *after* the "convention, concerning abstinence from the possessions of others, is enter'd into ... there immediately arise the ideas of justice and injustice; as also those of *property, right,* and *obligation*" (490). This suggests that *all* of these ideas are "artificial" in Hume's sense that they have no application outside the artifice of convention.[9] Moreover, "obligation" in *this* sense would, like "property," be defined *within* the rules of justice. We have already noted two senses in which Hume uses "obligation" that are defined independently of rules of justice. Although Hume thinks that there is a natural obligation and a moral obligation to be just, these species of obligation are not themselves artificial in the way Hume thinks justice is. Neither depends upon conventionally established rule-governed practices of justice.

The kinds of rules Hume is concerned with are directive in their nature. A rule of property, for example, directs agents to abstain from others' possessions.[10] It requires that people so abstain; if they do not, they *violate* the rule. We might say, meaning nothing more, that it obligates them to abstain. We can call this third Humean sense *rule obligation*. Recall Hart's distinction between the "internal" and "external" aspects of rules (Hart 1961: 55–57). From an external third-personal point of view, we can say, at a given social stage, that rules of justice have been established when a sufficient number of people respect and regulate their conduct by the rules and forbear violating them. Here we speak, as it were, not from the "internal" perspective of members who so regulate themselves, but from an "external" observer's standpoint. From this perspective, any talk of obligation and justice is *de facto* and non-normative. When, however, we speak from the perspective of those respecting and regulating their conduct by the rules, we take up an "internal" standpoint, and when we use "obligation" from this perspective, it now has a *de jure* normative sense.

Above I mentioned that a fundamental problem faces any philosopher, like Hobbes or Hume, who wants to move from a self-interested justification for individuals to desire the existence of a social order in which they are bound by normative bonds of the *right*, obligations, that differ from normative reasons grounded in their own *good* (or, for that matter, in the good of others). It will be impossible to establish any such order *on those grounds*, since it provides a reason of the wrong kind to support claims of right and obligation in their own terms. (We also noted that Pufendorf faces a version of this problem, albeit a different version, when he attempts to ground mutual accountability and the dignity of persons in divine command.)

Any such attempt must ultimately "rest" its "moral philosophy on a mistake," in Prichard's memorable phrase (Prichard 1912). Rules of justice are only established when sufficient numbers *accept* the rules and treat them as obligating norms, that is, as giving them adequate reason to be just simply because

---

[9] As we saw in Chapter 3, Hobbes says similarly that the ideas of justice and obligation apply only after the covenant, though, like Hume, he needs these ideas elsewhere, for example, to ground the covenant itself.
[10] Hereinafter, I follow Darwall 1995: 297–318.

they are so obligated, quite independently of whether the just conduct is for their good, or, for that matter, whether it promotes the public good.

In many places, Hume describes the motive of justice in something approaching these terms. Just people "lay themselves under the restraint of such rules"; they observe them "strict[ly]," and treat them as "sacred and inviolable" (Hume 1978: 499, 533–534). One way of solving the problem his views about moral sentiment, virtuous motive, and the lack of merit of "external performance[s]" create would be for him to hold that the virtue of justice consists in the distinctive form of motivation involved in *accepting* rules of justice as binding norms. So understood, just acts, considered independently of their motivation, would still lack moral goodness or "merit" in themselves. They would nonetheless be obligatory in the sense of instantiating rule obligation. And when just actions are motivated by the just person's acceptance of the rules as binding norms, we can *then* say that such actions are morally good or have merit.

All virtues, for Hume, recall, must either be useful or beneficial, either to the agent or to others. And Hume specifically says that "sympathy *with public interest is the source of the* moral approbation, *which attends*" the virtue of justice (499–500). As with all the virtues, the idea is that when we contemplate the just person's motivating sense of justice, we are carried by an association of ideas to thoughts of its usual consequences, generally, pleasures constituting the "public interest," and sympathy then turns thoughts of these pleasures into a suitably "general" or disinterested pleasing sentiment in the observer, which constitutes their moral approbation.

To summarize this way of interpreting Hume's theory of justice, then: there is, first, the *natural obligation* to justice, which is the self-interested motive members of society have to bring about conventions establishing rules of justice. There is the *rule obligation* that is internal to the established rules. And there is the moral obligation to justice consisting in approbation of the just person's characteristic motivation, a sense of justice consisting in *acceptance* of the rules, by sympathy with this motive's usual publicly beneficial effects.

To be sure, for Hume to hold this view of the motive of justice, he would have to revise the theory of motivation he takes from Hutcheson, according to which all actions seek to promote goods. "The will," Hume says, "exerts itself, when either the good or the absence of the evil can be attain'd by any action of the mind or body" (439; see also 399).[11] But no other major changes in view would seem to be required.

To complete this discussion of Hume on justice, we should note a remark that Hume makes about the extent of justice in the *Enquiry* that illustrates justice's artificial character from Hume's perspective and that will mark an important contrast with Smith.

---

[11] We noted in Chapter 2 that a similar point holds for Hobbes and Pufendorf.

> Were there a species of creatures intermingled with men, which, though rational, were possessed of such inferior strength, both of body and mind, that they were incapable of all resistance, and could never, upon the highest provocation, make us feel the effects of their resentment; the necessary consequence, I think, is that we should be bound, by the laws of humanity to give gentle usage to these creatures, but should not, properly speaking, lie under any restraint of justice with regard to them, nor could they possess any right or property (1975a: 190).

The reason Hume thinks we would owe no obligations of justice to any creatures, however rational, who "could never ... make us feel the effects of their resentment," is that no convention for mutual restraint could possibly be advantageous to us. Failing to give them "gentle usage" would still be every bit as vicious as it would otherwise be. But such creatures could have no right to this and failing to give it to them would not be a violation of a just claim they could justifiably resent.

This brings out an important aspect of Hume's artificiality claim that will mark a significant contrast with Smith. For Hume, resentment functions to create costs for the resented that have to be figured in to determine whether accepting rules that give victims specific convention-based authorities and right would be mutually advantageous or not. If others' power is sufficiently inferior, then restraining our treatment of them by such rules will not be advantageous to us, and we will consequently owe them no obligations of justice. For Smith, by contrast, whether we owe someone an obligation of justice depends on whether their resentment would be *justified*, or, in Smith's term, "proper." To be sure, the "effects" of resentment that Hume most likely has in mind include sympathetic ones. And his point might partly be that we would be unable to have effective moral discourse with such creatures, since such discourse is carried by a sympathy-infused intercourse of sentiments, and sympathy varies with psychic distance. But here again, a deep difference with Smith emerges.

Humean sympathy operates from an observer's third-person perspective, whereas, for Smith, we judge whether a sentiment like resentment is proper by putting ourselves in the shoes of the person we are judging. For Hume, moral judgments are akin to aesthetic assessment; they concern what he often calls "moral beauty" (e.g., 1978: 465). For Smith, the locus of moral judgment is interpersonal and, sometimes, as with justice, second personal. We judge propriety by placing ourselves in one another's perspective; and we assess justice by considering whether holding-accountable emotions (what Strawson called "reactive attitudes") like resentment would be justified from that point of view (Strawson 1968; Darwall 2006). It is thus not surprising that Smith, like Butler and Kant, and unlike Hutcheson and Hume, places great weight on the moral autonomy we must grant others if we are to insist on their answerability for their own choices.

Smith

In the last chapter, we noted that an important difference between Butler and Hutcheson, and we can now add Hume, is Butler's emphasis on the "authority of conscience." As we saw, Butler takes the faculty of "conscience" or the "principle of reflection" to be a necessary condition of moral agency, and he takes virtue to consist in the excellent exercise of this faculty. In the latter, Butler follows Shaftesbury, who distinguishes between "natural" (estimable) motives of which conscience or "reflex approbation" approves, and genuine "virtue or merit," which consists in a moral agent's directing themselves by their own reflective moral judgments (Butler 2017: Pr.26; Shaftesbury 2001: II.28).

For Hutcheson and Hume, virtue or merit consists not in any motivation provided by moral sense or sentiment but in motives of which it approves. Indeed, since Hutcheson and Hume both hold that the object of approbation is always in the first instance motives and never acts considered from a deliberative perspective independently of motives, it is impossible for moral sentiment to provide what Hume calls the "first motive" to any virtuous conduct (Hume 1978: 478). Strictly speaking, approbation cannot motivate from a (first-person) deliberative standpoint at all; it is an observer's third-person response to contemplated motive and motivated action.

In this dispute, Adam Smith is decidedly with Butler (and Shaftesbury) against Hutcheson and Hume. So last chapter's debate between Hutcheson and Butler is carried forward in this chapter between Hume and Smith, with Smith taking Butler's part. Smith holds both that the capacity for moral autonomy or "self-command" – to direct our lives by our own moral judgments – is essential for moral agency and that its excellent exercise constitutes "perfec[t] virt[ue]" (Smith 1982: 237, 241, 266).[12]

Hutcheson and Hume hold, again, that moral judgments fundamentally concern motives and motivated actions, viewed from an observer's third-personal perspective. For Hutcheson, moral sense is a disinterested response to motives considered in themselves, quite independently of their effect and of their response to the agent's deliberative context. For Hume, we form moral judgments by sympathy with the target motive's usual effects. For Smith, by contrast, basic moral judgments, indeed basic *normative* judgments, concern what Smith calls a mental state's "*propriety*," which is what contemporary philosophers call its "fit" or "fittingness" to its objects, *viewed from the agent's perspective* (D'Arms and Jacobson 2000a and 2000b; Chappell 2012).

Attitudes and emotions, including intentions and choices, all have *intentional objects*, which they standardly represent or "construe" in evaluative or normative terms (Roberts 2003). Desires, for example, represent their objects as

---

[12] "Self-command is not only itself a great virtue, but from it all the other virtues seem to derive their principal lustre" (1982: 241).

desirable, as something there is reason to desire. Resentment construes its object as resentable in the sense of involving injury or unjust treatment to the resenter. Intentions represent an intended action as something *to be* done. And so on.

Something is said to be a fitting object of desire, then, just in case it *is* desirable; it is a fitting object of resentment just in case it is resentable (warrants resentment); or it is a fitting object of intention just in case it is an act that is to be done. In general, an object X is a fitting object of attitude A just in case X is "A-able" or "A-worthy" (on the model of "desirable" or "blameworthy"), that is, worthy of being A-ed *in virtue of features of it* (i.e., of X together with what Smith calls the "situation" in which X is presented in deliberation to the agent). These are features that would correctly be taken by the agent as normative reasons *to* have attitude A and on the basis of which the agent could form the attitude. Attitudes are mental states that agents have *for reasons* (Anscombe 1957). And they are fitting to their objects just in case the object in the presented situation has features that give the agent "reasons of the right kind" to form the relevant attitude (Hieronymi 2005, 2013). When this is true, then X is "A-able" or "A-worthy," and so it is fitting to have A toward X.

Parfit gets at roughly the same idea when he distinguishes between "object-based" and "state-based" reasons for having an attitude. Reasons are of the "wrong," state-based kind when they are given, not by features of the attitude's object in the presented "situation," but, for example, by pragmatic reasons why it would be a good thing for the agent to have that attitude (to be in that "state") (Parfit 2011). Suppose someone offers you a prize to form a desire for something that is utterly undesirable, like a saucer of mud. Any reason that might give you to have that desire could not, by hypothesis, bear on the mud's desirability; neither is it a consideration on the basis of which you could form a desire for the mud from a deliberative point of view (though you could so form a desire to have that desire). An attitude, A, then, is fitting to its object, just in case the object is "A-able" or "A-worthy," that is, an object that warrants having attitude A toward it in virtue of object-based reasons, which are A-able-making features, where these are reasons *to* have A toward X and on the basis of which the agent could form the attitude.

Now for Smith, again, basic normative judgments concern what he calls "*propriety.*" But this turns out to be same thing as fittingness, as we will see presently. For now, however, note that if it is, this means that Smith brings the agent's point of view into moral judgments in a way that Hutcheson and Hume do not. The question of whether benevolence is proper in the sense of fitting to its object in the situation as it is presented to a deliberating agent is simply a different matter than whether it is the object of moral sense, in Hutcheson's sense, or whether it would tend to have pleasurable consequences that Humean sympathy would transmute into contemplative pleasure from a third-person standpoint (Hume's "moral sentiment").

Sympathy: Attributing Mental States and Judging Their Propriety

Hume, recall, uses "sympathy" to refer to a process that takes an observer from an idea of an attitude or feeling to a version of the feeling itself. Like emotional contagion, it involves catching others' feelings, but does not require being in others' presence. Humean sympathy can work from the armchair. Emotional contagion and Humean sympathy share a fundamental feature, however, that contrasts with what Smith calls sympathy, namely, that they need not be directed to the same object.

Take emotional contagion first. I may "catch" another's anger by seeing their angry face without putting myself in their shoes to attempt to grasp what they are angry at. It might even make me angry at them. From the point of view of emotional contagion, the object does not matter; we catch the other's feeling but supply an object ourselves. Similarly, when in the armchair I come to have a version of others' pleasure through Humean sympathy by first having the idea of their pleasure, there is nothing in the process that takes me imaginatively into their perspective so that our pleasures will have the same object.

For Smith, however, "[s]ympathy ... does not arise so much from the view of [a] passion," as with Hume, "as from that of the situation which excites it" (Smith 1982: 12). We sympathize by putting ourselves in others' "situations" in their shoes, that is, by viewing the objects of their mental states as they are presented to others from their view of their situation.

Now, we are concerned mostly with the role that sympathy plays, according to Smith, in judgments of mental states' propriety, that is, as fitting or "suitable to their objects." "To approve of the passions of another ... as suitable to their objects," Smith writes, "is the same thing as to observe that we entirely sympathize with them" (16). And again, the point we should continue to consider is that Smith holds that we sympathize with others in the sense he has in mind by placing ourselves in their perspectives and viewing the objects of their mental states from that standpoint.

First, however, we should note that Smith holds that imaginative projection into others' points of view is also central even just to *attributing* mental states to them and to grasping what their situation is like *for them*, regardless of their mental states' normative status. Here Smith anticipates the notion of "simulation" as it figures in contemporary philosophy of mind (Goldman 1992; Gordon 1992). "As we have no immediate experience of what other men feel," Smith writes, "we can form no idea of the manner in which they are affected, but by conceiving what we ourselves should feel in the like situation" (Smith 1982: 9). This we do by "plac[ing] ourselves" in others' "situation[s]" imaginatively (9).[13]

---

[13] There is empirical evidence for Smith's simulationist account. For example, Amos Tversky presented subjects with the following story:

When the function of imaginative projection is *epistemic*, as it is in mental state attribution or in trying to grasp what someone's experience is like, as when "our brother is upon the rack" and we want to know "what he suffers," then the imaginative exercise is to imaginatively take on as many features of the person into whose shoes we are projecting as possible, to "become in some measure the same person with him" (9). Here the knowledge we gain is not normative. It is of how things actually are with the person we are trying to know.

But Smith holds that we also make normative judgments of propriety by imaginative projection. And here the exercise must be somewhat different, since there has to be critical distance between what mental state someone actually is in and whether that state is proper in the sense of fitting or "suitable to its object." It cannot be the case that determining *what* someone is feeling also establishes that their feeling or attitude is proper.

Note also that what Smith calls "sympathy" is not the imaginative projection itself, but a sharing of feeling as a result of it. "Sympathy" "denote[s] our fellow-feeling with any passion whatever," and that can be determined only after we know what passion another person actually has, Smith thinks, by imaginative projection (10).

The question of whether a mental state is proper is not particularistic in the way that the question about what some person's mental state actually is is. We imaginatively become the "very person" to determine the latter, but we cannot do that and attain the critical distance necessary to judge the latter. Rather, the question of whether a mental state is proper or suitable to its object is the question of what would be a suitable or proper response for *someone* facing the deliberative "situation" that the particular person confronts.

"To approve of another man's opinions is to adopt those opinions, and to adopt them is to approve of them" (17). The "objects" to which beliefs or opinions are proper or suitable are the believed propositions together with the epistemic "situation" confronting those who hold them, that is, what they take as

> Mr. Crane and Mr. Tees were scheduled to leave the airport on different flights, at the same time. They traveled from town in the same limousine, were caught in a traffic jam, and arrived at the airport 30 minutes after the scheduled departure time of their flights. Mr. Crane is told that his flight left on time. Mr. Tees is told that his was delayed, and just left five minutes ago. Who is more upset? (Kahneman and Tversky 1982).
>
> If you are like 96 percent of Tversky's subjects, you will say more or less instantly that Mr. Tees is more upset than Mr. Crane. How did you decide? Alvin Goldman argues that it is unlikely that we all possess common-sense theories that overlap on a generalization that we apply to the instant case or that we all think consciously about how we ourselves have felt in the past and infer by analogy (Goldman 1992). It seems far likelier that you simply unconsciously projected into Tees's and Crane's respective situations and imaginatively simulated feelings "in their shoes."

evidence or reasons *to* hold their opinions. We determine the propriety of others' opinions by imaginatively confronting their epistemic situation and deliberating about what seems true (hence, what to believe) from that point of view. This is not the same thing, again, as determining what they actually do think. When we are considering whether someone's beliefs are proper, we assume that we already know what they think and consider the further normative question of what *to* think (or what there is reason for them to think) in light of the epistemic situation confronting them. This is not a particularistic question; it is the question of what *one* should think given the evidence. And because it is, then, unless there are relevant differences between the other's epistemic situation and our own, there is no difference between judging the other's opinions proper and adopting them ourselves (unless, of course, we are epistemically weak-willed).

And what holds for opinions holds also for other mental states, at least for those one can adopt *for reasons*, like emotions and attitudes, including intention and choice. To judge that a mental state is suitable to its object and situation, as these present themselves to the agent in deliberation, just is, according to Smith, to attempt to sympathize with, that is, to "adopt" the attitude oneself imaginatively feels when one projects into the agent's deliberative situation. Suppose, for example, that someone is angry with another person for having stepped on their foot. To work out whether their anger is proper, one puts oneself imaginatively in the position of someone who has had their foot stepped on, along with any other relevant features of their situation. To sympathize or have "fellow-feeling" with their anger is to share it from that perspective. If one does, one judges their anger proper.

Suppose one judges their anger improper, that it is out of proportion to what has provoked it. There is a sense in which one might nonetheless still sympathize with this particular individual being thus angry. One might attempt imaginatively to become "the same person" (9), that is, that very individual with their own foibles, personal history, and so on, in order to appreciate what it is like *for that particular person* to have their feet stepped on. You might still think their response is not suitable to its object, though you can see how this individual person *would* have it. There are reasons that *explain* the person's response without, however, justifying it.

The general lesson is that it is always necessary to factor the agent's circumstances, in the broadest sense, into two parts. What Smith generally means by the agent's "situation" is the set of situational features to which the agent responds – the situation that the agent faces or confronts. The question of propriety is whether a mental state is suitable or proper to the situation confronting the agent and to which the state is a response. From this perspective, the agent drops out of the picture as the particular agent they are. They confront a situation that, in principle, anyway, anyone might face.

In deliberating about what to feel or do in that situation, they do not face a question that is essentially about them as the particular individual they are. In addition to this first set of features, however, there will be further *particularizing* features that together comprise the second set and that explain why they, *as particular individuals*, respond as they do to the situation characterized by the first set.

Suppose, for example, that I have an irrational fear of flying, that my fear is improper because it is not suitable to the danger to which it responds. My fear may have many different causes, and if someone wants to comprehend my fear and what it is like, and not assess its propriety, they will have to imaginatively take on my particular idiosyncrasies from this second set that, because they are no part of the situation I am confronting (but rather characterize me as I actually confront it), are irrelevant to my fear's propriety. "When I condole with you for the loss of your only son," Smith writes, "I consider what I should suffer if I was really you, and I not only change circumstances with you, but I change persons and characters" (317). Condolence seeks not normative assessment of others' responses to misfortune, but to compassionate their responses as they actually are.

Normative assessment of states of mind as proper or improper is different, however. Here it is a mistake to take on features from the second set that are not present in the first. The issue is how *to* respond to a presented situation (features in the first set), what response would be proper or suitable to it, not what explains an actual response or what that response is like. This is where Smith's idea of the "impartial spectator" enters. Because the question of propriety is always about how *an agent* should response to a presented situation, what matters is not how the other actually responds, or even how one would actually respond oneself. To grasp these (perhaps potential) *actualities*, we must imagine ourselves in the other's situation not *as them*, as we do in condolence, *or*, in the latter case, *as ourselves*. Knowing that I have an irrational fear of flying, for example, I can't imagine being in an airplane passenger's position *as myself* without importing my irrational fear. But that is obviously irrelevant to what level of fear is proper.

Smith's phrase "impartial spectator" can misleadingly suggest an observer's third-personal view. But when he says we should "consider what will be the sentiments of the cool and impartial spectator" (38), he is not recommending our considering the kind of third-personal response involved in Hutchesonian or Humean moral sense or sentiment. Neither of those involves sympathy in Smith's distinctive sense, that is, sharing the agent's response *to* the presented "situation" *from their point of view*. Rather, we think as "cool and impartial spectators" when we imagine ourselves into the other's situation *as someone*, rather than as any particular person, whether ourselves or the person themselves.

So the difference between the imaginative exercise involved in understanding the other's mental state and assessing its propriety is between taking on all of the features of the both sets, on the one hand, and taking on only the features of the first in order to imagine what to feel or do as someone facing the agent's deliberative situation and, Smith therefore thinks, what they *should* feel or do. There is no reason, of course, to suppose that anyone can flawlessly pursue the latter imaginative exercise by themselves or that people's attempts will automatically converge. So Smithian moral epistemology will inevitably involve taking other people's sympathetic propriety judgments into account. This is a further aspect of the "impartial spectator" idea. Attempting to put myself in someone's situation as someone, I will inevitably be influenced by factors in *my* second set that are irrelevant to what a proper response to a situation comprised by the first set would be. Each of us attempts to make such judgments impartially (as someone), but we are all subject to errors we can hope to correct only by reasoning *together* in ways that reveal previously unacknowledged partialities.

We should note also that we can ask more fine-grained normative questions by bringing in features from the second set. For example, even though the features to which an improper (irrational) fear respond – the seeming danger – do not warrant that fear or acting as if the dangers were real, we can still ask what someone should do *given their irrational fear*. Even though it is thinking about a particular person's situation that generates it, this question is still not particularistic in the way questions about what a particular mental state is or is like for the person having it are. In the latter case we attempt imaginatively to take on all features from both sets, as noted above, while in the first we take only those features from the second set that are part of the (more fine-grained) deliberative situation the particular agent faces, not further features from the second set that might explain how *they* would in fact respond to it.

The Metaethics of Propriety

At the outset of Part VII of *TMS*, "Of Systems of Moral Philosophy," Smith distinguishes two questions that a systematic treatment of moral philosophy must answer. One is a fundamental normative question: "[W]herein does virtue consist?" The second is "[B]y what power or faculty in the mind is it, that this character, whatever it be, is recommended to us" (265). As Smith understands it, this second question is not the purely epistemic issue of how we know virtue and what it consists in. Rather, he is concerned with what "recommends" virtue, with the power or faculty through which we recognize virtue's *normativity*, such that we ought or have normative reason to be virtuous so understood.

Smith canvasses four answers to this metaethical question. The first is the one implicit in Shaftesbury's argument for the "obligation to virtue": that virtue is "recommended to us by self-love" (266).[14] The second is offered by rationalists, like Clarke, Balguy, and Price, that virtue is recommended "by reason, which points out to us the difference between one character and another, in the same manner as it does that between truth and falsehood" (266). The third is Hutcheson's hypothesized "moral sense." And the fourth is "some other principle in human nature, such as a modification of sympathy" (266). Smith includes Hume in this fourth category with himself, but explicitly distinguishes between their views.

Smith regards Hutcheson as having decisively refuted both egoistic and rationalist responses (315–321). He allows that reason has a role to play in determining "general maxims of morality," but only "from experience and induction" (319). In terms of Mill's contrast in *Utilitarianism* between the "intuitive" and "inductive" schools of ethical philosophy, Smith counts as an inductivist. Reason cannot give us our "first perceptions of right and wrong," Smith writes; these are "founded… [upon] immediate sense and feeling," as Hutcheson had shown (320–321).

Smith agrees with Hume, against Hutcheson, that the theory of the moral sense is to be rejected in favor of the idea that we judge moral qualities through sympathy. But he disagrees sharply with Hume about *how* sympathy enters into moral judgment and, relatedly, what the object of moral judgment most fundamentally is, that is, the answer to the *first* question: "Wherein does virtue consist?" For Hume and Hutcheson, the moral sentiment assesses motives, considered either in themselves (Hutcheson) or in relation to their usual effects (Hume). For Smith, by contrast, moral judgments, and normative judgments more generally, most fundamentally concern the *relation* between agents' mental states and the "situations," faced from the agent's perspective, to which the mental states respond. The fundamental normative property for Smith is fittingness or propriety.

So Smith's own answer to the first question is propriety, and he thinks there are really only two alternatives to propriety: benevolence and prudence (267). I mentioned above that Smith sides with Butler against Hutcheson and Hume on the role of moral self-direction or autonomy in moral virtue. For Smith, this follows from the fact that virtue is propriety. If that is so, then virtue consists not "in any one species of affections," whether considered in themselves or through their usual effects, "but in the proper government and direction of all our affections … according to the objects they pursue, and the degree of 'vehemence' with which they pursue them" (286). Smith evidently thinks that "proper government and direction" of the affections and maintaining proper affections amount to the same thing.

---

[14] See the discussion of this point in Shaftesbury in Chapter 4.

We will return to the centrality of "self-government" to Smith's ethics, in contrast, again, to Hutcheson and Hume below. To conclude this section, however, we should return to metaethics. Smith clearly considers himself a sentimentalist, but of a different kind than Hutcheson and Hume. Like Hume, he rejects a Hutchesonian moral sense, but the way sympathy enters into his metaethics is profoundly different than the way it enters Hume's. Humean sympathy works from a third-person perspective on an evaluated agent, whereas sympathy of the kind that Smith believes is at work in judgments of propriety can arise only after an imaginative projection into the agent's point of view.

For Hume, sympathy's role in moral judgment is identical to its role in aesthetic judgments of beauty; indeed, Hume frequently refers to virtue as moral beauty. Both involve contemplation from an observer's third-personal point of view. Smith explicitly rejects this Humean view. As it happens, Smith accepts Hume's theory of *aesthetic* judgment. Hume is right, he thinks, that our judgments of beauty, for example, of a "convenient and well-contrived building" are ultimately grounded in utility, which lead through *Humean* sympathy to pleasure in a contemplating observer. Smith notes that Hume takes the same aesthetic view of virtue.

> The same ingenious and agreeable author who first explained why utility pleases, has been so struck with this view of things, as to resolve our whole approbation of virtue into a perception of this species of beauty which results from the appearance of utility (188).

However, Smith rejects Hume's aestheticizing of moral judgment and virtue. "The sentiment of approbation always involves in it a sense of propriety quite distinct from the perception of utility" (188). Whether a given motive or intention is proper is a matter of whether it responds fittingly to the deliberative situation that an agent confronts. And this is something we can judge not by remaining in an observer's third-person position, but by projecting into the agent's perspective and judging the situation as it confronted them.

Smith makes another argument against identifying moral judgments with aesthetic judgments. Since the latter do not implicate an essentially interpersonal point of view, a person might "grow up" "without any communication with society" and still be as disposed to note aesthetic features, including of their own actions and affections. They might view their "own temper and character with that sort of satisfaction with which we consider a well-contrived machine ... or with that sort of distaste of dissatisfaction with which we regard a very awkward and clumsy contrivance" (192). But these responses would differ fundamentally from moral praise or blame. "He would not exult from the notion of deserving reward in the one case, nor tremble from the suspicion of meriting punishment in the other" (193). These latter sentiments "suppose the idea of some other being" who can hold the person accountable (193).

Smith's answer to his second, "normativity" question is thus, like Hume's, a version of the fourth, "sympathy" approach, but a very different version than Hume's. As with Hume, there are various more finely delimited metaethical views that might be consistent with Smith's approach. One can imagine a naturalist empiricist view on which propriety consists in the convergence of fellow-feeling with a given attitude when imaginative projection meets some naturalistically specifiable impartiality conditions. Or there might be an expressivist version according to which propriety judgments express sympathy with a given attitude, perhaps under conditions meeting impartiality standards that one accepts. Or there might be a projectivist, error-theoretical view that takes a similar shape. All seem consistent with what Smith actually says; as with Hume, it is ahistorical folly to attempt to place Smith determinately into one or the other of these.

Justice, Mutual Respect, and Accountability

Smith may be somewhat overstating his contrast between judgments of propriety and aesthetic judgments. It is certainly true that the former differs from the latter in involving a projection into the agent's point of view in a way that aesthetic judgments do not. Smith's considered view is that it is only moral judgments of merit and demerit, especially as these implicate judgments of *justice*, that involve the distinctive responses that P. F. Strawson will call "reactive attitudes" (two centuries later) and that are held from an essentially "participant," that is, "interpersonal" or second-personal, perspective of mutually accountable equals (Strawson 1968; Darwall 2006).

Justice, for Smith, is a kind of demerit, where merit and demerit are distinguished among moral qualities by their respective relations to patients' warranted reactive feelings, specifically, to proper gratitude and resentment, and, consequently, to reward and punishment (Smith 1982: 67–108). "The sentiment which most immediately and directly prompts us to reward, is gratitude; that which most immediately and directly prompts us to punish, is resentment" (68).[15]

It is a necessary condition of merit and demerit that these attach to proper and improper actions and states of mind, respectively. But that is insufficient, since, for example, not all impropriety warrants resentment. Injustice consists in improper conduct (motivated by improper motives) to which the proper response is a reactive feeling like resentment and motives to challenge, resist, or punish the conduct forcefully.[16]

---

[15] Strawson cites gratitude and resentment as paradigmatic "reactive attitudes" that are felt from a second-personal perspective of implicit relating *to* someone (Strawson 1968).

[16] What follows draws from Darwall 1999b. Smith holds, of course, that these feelings can also be held *improperly* and, moreover, that "we ought always to punish with reluctance, and more from a sense of the propriety of punishing, than from any savage disposition to revenge." (1982: 172; see also 160–161).

This already sheds light on one important way in which Smith's treatment of justice differs from the tradition of Hutcheson and Hume. For Hutcheson, the primary moral fact from which all others derive is that universal benevolence is the morally best motive, this being established by moral esteem from an observer's point of view. Since universal benevolence aims at everyone's happiness equally, Hutcheson draws the conclusion that "that action is best, which procures the greatest happiness for the greatest numbers" (Hutcheson 2004: 125). A similar line of reasoning leads to Hutcheson's theory of rights. Someone has a right "to do, possess, or demand" something just in case "a faculty of doing, demanding, or possessing [it], universally allow'd in certain circumstances, would in the whole tend to the general good" (183). Hume's theory of justice differs from Hutcheson's in (at least) the respect that he holds that rules of justice cannot be established unless they are, and are seen to be, in *everyone's* interest, and not just for the general good. Nonetheless, Hume's account of the "moral obligation" to justice is roughly the same as Hutcheson's since it depends on justice's tendency to advance the "public interest."[17]

On Smith's view, however, we judge injustice, not from an observer's perspective, but by projecting ourselves impartially into the agent's *and*, crucially, into the *patient's* point of view. In particular, something is unjust only if it is proper to feel resentment toward it: "the violation of justice ... is the proper object of resentment" (Smith 1982: 79). And we can judge whether resentment is proper only by imagining what it would be like to be in the shoes of the parties who are affected and considering (impartially) what to feel – what any one of us would or should feel – in their situation. Since injustice is a vice, it is also essential that its motives be improper. But this it shares with every other vice. What is distinctive about injustice is that it is properly resented and resisted, and this is something we can assess only from the perspective of individual patients.

Earlier we noted in connection with Hume's theory of justice his remark that we would owe no obligations of justice to a "species of [rational] creatures" of such inferior strength that "they were incapable of all resistance, and could never, upon the highest provocation, makes us feel the effects of their resentment" (Hume 1975a: 190). For Hume, justice is an artificial virtue established, if at all, by a mutually advantageous convention. In such an instance, however, no such mutually advantageous convention would exist. Smith's view is importantly different in these respects. Justice is not conventional, for Smith. To determine whether such creatures might be unjustly treated by our "provocations," we look not to their relative power, but to whether putting ourselves (impartially) in their place would lead us to experience resentment

---

[17] "Sympathy with public interest is the source of the moral approbation which attends that virtue [justice]" (Hume 1978: 499–500; see also 498).

from that point of view. Whether the provokers were able to "feel the effects of [our] resentment" would obviously be irrelevant to whether *to* feel it (from the weaker species' point of view), and therefore whether their resentment would be proper, hence, whether the provocation would be unjust.

Although like all vicious action injustice proceeds from "motives which are naturally disapproved of," injustice is distinguished by causing "injury," "positive hurt to some particular persons" that is "the proper object of resentment, and of punishment, which is the natural consequence of resentment" (Smith 1982: 79). It is no surprise, therefore, to find Smith concluding that it is wrong for someone to injure another in order to benefit themselves "though the benefit to the one should be much greater than the hurt or injury to the other" (138). From an agent-neutral observer's standpoint, in which benefits and harms are accounted as off-setting gains or losses, such an action might seem justified. Nonetheless, Smith believes, we cannot justify it when we view things from the perspective of the injured parties themselves, if we enter impartially into their standpoint.

Smith thus endorses the "remarkable distinction between justice and all the other social virtues" that we first noted with Grotius (80). "[W]e feel ourselves to be under a stricter obligation to act according to justice, than agreeably to friendship, charity, or generosity" (80). Justice consists in "rules" we must strictly observe, the latter in recommended "precepts" we are not strictly obligated to follow (80). In his chapter on the "systems of moral philosophy," Smith distinguishes between what he calls "ethics" (roughly the "other social virtues") and natural jurisprudence or justice. Although the ancients have excellent accounts of the former, he thinks, it is only with the moderns that we begin to get adequate accounts of justice. "Grotius," he says, "seems to have been the first who attempted to give the world any thing like a system of those principles" (341–342).

Smith links this individual-relative metaethics of moral judgment (and patient-relative metaethics of justice) to a doctrine of the dignity of individuals and their mutual accountability. Because we judge that anyone would properly resent various kinds of injury and violation, we see these as forms of injustice that are appropriately resisted and reacted to with force. This gives us a way of grounding rules of justice that impose "strict," enforceable obligations and define rights of individuals that we are mutually accountable for respecting. "A moral being," Smith says, "is an accountable being," who "must give an account of its actions to some other, and that consequently must regulate them according to the good-liking of this other" (111n.3). Although Smith says that we are "principally accountable to God," he quickly adds that each "must necessarily conceive himself as accountable to his fellow-creatures, before he can form any idea of the Deity …" (111n.3).[18]

---

[18] Smith did not retain this passage in the sixth edition of *TMS*. I am indebted here to Charles Griswold and Vivienne Brown.

There is an element of Smith's thought here that echoes the theme of the equal dignity of persons that we saw in Pufendorf and will see perhaps most forcefully in Kant. We resent attempted injuries, not just to our possessions or bodies, but also to our *persons*. What most "enrages us against the man who injures or insults us, is the little account which he seems to make of *us*" – "that absurd self-love, by which he seems to imagine, that other people *may* be sacrificed at any time, to his conveniency" (96, emphases added). In other words, we resent disrespect of our dignity, our status as someone who *may not* (not to say, cannot) be treated in certain ways. What our resentment is "chiefly intent upon, is not so much to make our enemy feel pain in his turn, as ... to make him sensible, that the person whom he injured did not deserve to be treated in that manner" (95–96).[19] Punishment aims to make the other "sensible" of our dignity, to feel respect for us.

Smith's view of the equal dignity of individuals provides some of the moral underpinning for his praise of free markets in *The Wealth of Nations*. Market exchanges occur between independent equals who pursue their respective interests, not by "servile and fawning attention to obtain" each other's goodwill, but through mutually advantageous, respectful free exchange (1976: 26). Of course, Smith's main topic is the relation between markets and the creation of wealth, but even here the theme of equal dignity is in the background: "Masters of all sorts ... make better [though humiliating] bargains with their servants" during tough times when their servants are "more humble and dependent" (101, 412).[20]

Dignity and Self-Command, the "Respectable" Virtue

Earlier we noted that Smith follows Butler's (and Shaftesbury's) doctrine that virtue involves not simply estimable motives, but "self-government" or "self-command": agents governing themselves by their own consciences. Again, this is a significant contrast with Hutcheson and Hume.

This difference with Hume arises, indeed, within a distinction that Smith makes between what he calls the "amiable" and "respectable" virtues, which distinction he actually takes from Hume! In the *Treatise*, Hume distinguishes between "amiable" and "awful" virtues; contemplation of the former produces "love," whereas the latter inspires "esteem." "We could wish to meet with the one character in a friend; the other character we wou'd be ambitious of in ourselves" (1978: 607).

---

[19] In the introduction to their edition of *The Theory of Moral Sentiments*, Raphael and Macfie point out that Smith could, in his "Letter to the Editors of the *Edinburgh Review*" of July, 1775, "describe, from his own reading, ... Rousseau's *Discourse on Inequality*" (1982: 10).

[20] See Fleischacker 2005 for an account of Smith's concerns about justice for the poor.

Self-government is Smith's paradigm of a respectable virtue: "of that command of the passions which subjects all the movements of our nature to what our own dignity ... and the propriety of our own conduct require" (Smith 1982: 23). This connection between dignity, respect, and self-command shows up most powerfully in some remarks Smith makes about slavery. Smith regarded it as a symptom of the failure of all earlier social ideals that they depended on subservience and slavery. The classical republicans' focus on collective liberty and the virtues of civic participation was fine as far as it went, but it was necessarily confined to a narrow elite. And ancient ideals were decisively marred by their reliance on slavery (Smith 1976: 377–378; see Muller 1995). Smith's criticism of the chattel slavery of his own time is especially moving.

> There is not a negro from the coast of Africa who does not, in this respect, possess a degree of magnanimity which the soul of his sordid master is too often scarce capable of conceiving. Fortune never exerted more cruelty over her empire over mankind, than when she subjected those [African] nations of heroes to the refuse of the jails of Europe (1982: 206).

Magnanimity, for Smith, is a form of self-command, the ability to bear up with dignity in the face of violent emotions, to regulate grief, for example, by what an "impartial spectator" in the situation could sympathize with. As an aspect of self-command, magnanimity is a "respectable" rather than an "amiable" virtue. This is significant, since it is the link to self-command that evidently underlies slavery's special horror for Smith. The subjection of such dignified, self-commanding "heroes" to men so unable or unwilling to control their own arrogance and self-conceit that they appear powerless even to conceive the virtue of self-command is especially appalling to him.

Here we see, again, the Rousseauean theme in Smith that leads toward Kant. From our own egocentric standpoints, there is a tendency to judge value and importance by their importance *to us*, from our own points of view. To insist on this self-preference, however, is to manifest the "arrogance of ... self-love" (83). When, however, we view ourselves and our situation from a perspective anyone could take on us, we see that we are "but one of the multitude, in no respect better than any other in it" (137). Only from this impartial standpoint can a person assess the propriety of their own motives and achieve self-command, thereby "humbl[ing] the arrogance of his self-love" (83). From this perspective, blind self-preference seems "shamefu[l]" (137). Smith and Kant both stress that we are humbled also when we recognize this authority through the eyes of others, as when we appreciate their self-command. That is why self-command is an "awful" or "respectable," rather than amiable, virtue for Smith. In Kant's terms, the other's "example holds before me a law that strikes down my self-conceit" (Kant 1996b: 5:77).

There is an irony in the fact that Smith's emphasis on self-command occurs in the context of a distinction between the respectable and the amiable virtues that he takes from Hume. Whereas Smith links his paradigmatic respectable virtue, self-command, to themes of equal dignity and mutual accountability that are marks of a distinctively modern conception of morality, Hume introduces the category of virtues that are "awful" rather than "amiable" as part of an argument that "natural abilities" like wit that occasion esteem rather than love have no less merit, and that the modern distinction between "moral virtues" and "natural abilities" is merely a verbal one (Hume 1978: 606).

7

The British Rationalists and Reid

Hume's claim that "moral distinctions derive" from sentiment rather than reason, echoed in different ways by Hutcheson and Smith, was advanced in opposition to a group of philosophers writing in the early eighteenth century now known as the "British rationalists," which included Samuel Clarke (1675–1729), John Balguy (1686–1748), and William Wollaston (1659–1724). Richard Price's *Review of the Principles of Morals* (1758) was a later entrant in this debate on the rationalist side as, in some ways, was Thomas Reid's *Essays on the Active Powers of the Human Mind* (originally published in 1788), though Reid, like Butler, was hesitant to characterize himself as a rationalist. (Price lived from 1723 to 1791 and Reid from 1710 to 1796.) In this chapter, we shall focus on the central elements of eighteenth-century British rationalism, beginning with Clarke and Balguy, but concentrating mostly on the more philosophically developed and interesting versions in Price and Reid.

The philosophical, metaethical claims that divided rationalists and sentimentalists were primarily epistemological and metaphysical. Concerning epistemology: How and through what faculties do we judge, and perhaps know the truth of, moral and ethical propositions? And metaphysically: In what do moral and ethical properties consist (if they exist)? Are there moral and ethical facts, and, if so, how do they relate to facts of other kinds? The most obvious disagreement was epistemological: whether the faculty of moral judgment and knowledge is some version of the understanding, intellect, or reason, or whether it consists in sentimental or affective sensibility of some other kind. But these epistemological differences were often grounded in metaphysical disagreements.

The rationalists followed Cudworth in arguing that morality is "eternal and immutable" and that it could not, therefore, be response-dependent in the ways moral sentimentalism affirms (Clarke 1978a, 1978b: 596; Price 1974: 50). Moral obligations hold at the most fundamental level not just for moral agents, constituted as they are in, say, the human species, but for any possible moral agent. For Hume, however, "[v]ice and virtue ... may be compared to sounds [and] colours," which "according to modern philosophers," are secondary qualities that depend essentially on contingent human sensibilities like our sense of color (Hume 1978: 468). Because they thought morality to be "eternal and immutable," the rationalists held that moral propositions could not be judged by any such sensibility or sense that a possible moral agent might lack.

There was a related issue concerning the capacities that are necessary for moral agency and action. For Hutcheson and Hume, what Hume called the "first motive" to virtuous conduct is always some motive, like benevolence, that, as the rationalists saw it, a moral agent might conceivably lack. Rationalists like Balguy, for their part, tended to hold that moral virtue must involve motivation provided by a faculty that is necessary to be subject to morality at all as they saw it, the faculty of reason. "[S]upposing us void of *natural Compassion*, as well as *Benevolence*; might we not possibly be induced to attempt the Relief of a Person in Distress, merely from the *Reason* of the Thing, and the *Rectitude* of the Action?" (Balguy 1976: I. 12). Balguy decidedly answered "yes," as did Clarke and Price. Moral virtue, for them, involves the proper exercise of the faculty (reason) that is an essential feature of moral agency.

Partly what was at issue was the dispute that, as we have seen, divided Shaftesbury, Butler, and Smith, on the one side, and Hume and Hutcheson on the other – namely, whether virtue necessarily involves self-direction through an agent's own moral judgment or conscience. The rationalists followed Butler in this, holding that virtue is *conscientious* conduct and that conscience operates through the agent's own reason. Butler's doctrine does not strictly require rationalism, as the example of Smith, and perhaps Butler himself, proves. Some version of rationalism is difficult to avoid, however, if some form of reason is thought to be necessary and sufficient for moral agency.

Here it is significant that the British rationalists were all attempting to theorize a deontic conception of morality alongside a matching conception of moral agency, in a way that Hume and Hutcheson were not. Theirs was definitely a "law conception," which, like Suárez and his natural law followers, they took to be essentially related to accountability. Moral agents are, Clarke says, "Accountable Beings" whose wills can and morally must (it is "(morally speaking) necessary" that they) "be determined in every Action by the *Reason of the thing*, and the *Right of the Case*" (Clarke 1978b: 613). Price echoes this theme in a Butlerian idiom: "Every being endowed with reason, and conscious of right and wrong, is, as such, necessarily a *law* to himself" (Price 1974: 119). Because they have reason and conscience, moral agents are "accountable, guilty, and punishable" for wrongful conduct (119).

As we shall see, there is arguably a deep connection between the British rationalists' focus on deontic morality and their rationalism.[1] But this is not a necessary connection. Nothing rules out a sentimentalist metaethics of deontic morality in principle. Owing to the conceptual connection between deontic

---

[1] Here I follow Schiffman 2015.

moral concepts like obligation and accountability, there will indeed be dialectical pressure to hold, with Pufendorf, that an agent can be a subject of obligation, and hence a moral agent, only if they have whatever faculties are necessary to hold themselves accountable (in Butler's terms, to be a "law to themselves," or in Locke's, to be "capable of a law"). But these might involve sentiment, as Smith arguably held. I suggested earlier that we might develop a metaethics of judgments of right that ties them to reactive attitudes, considering Hobbes's claim that the "sense of right and wrong" that distinguishes human beings from other species consists in our susceptibility to (reactive) attitudes through which we "censure" one another.

As we shall see, a central plank of British rationalism in its most developed form, especially in Price, is the thesis that the deontic idea of moral obligation is a fundamental moral concept that resists definition in non-deontic-moral terms. They were not, however, the first to notice this or make this claim. Arguably, the first was David Fordyce (1711–1751), who was not a rationalist at all, but arguably a kind of sentimentalist.[2] It is remarkable, indeed, to see how closely Fordyce cleaves to the views we have already noted as characteristic of the British rationalists without embracing their rationalism. Before we begin to consider the rationalists' views in more detail, it might be useful to frame them with a short discussion of Fordyce.

Fordyce

What is most interesting about Fordyce from our perspective is that he insists on the indefinability of moral obligation, a thesis that looms large in the case for British ethical rationalism in its most developed form in Price. Unlike Price, however, Fordyce denies that the faculty of moral judgment is reason. Fordyce's view of reason seems thoroughly within an empiricist framework deriving from Locke by way of Hutcheson. Fordyce holds, like Locke and Hutcheson, that all ideas come from sense experience, and that different simple ideas come from different "senses" (Fordyce 2003: 34). That, recall, was what lay behind Hutcheson's doctrine of the moral sense, which, he held, receives the simple ideas of approbation and condemnation through which we attribute moral good and evil.

Fordyce agrees with Hutcheson's general epistemology, but the simple idea on which Fordyce focuses is not that through which an observer judges the *moral goodness of motive*s and motivated action, but the distinctively deontic idea of a *morally required act*. It is, "the Idea of *Moral Obligation*," he says, that we must "trace" "to our inmost Sense and Experience" (22). Fordyce uses Hutcheson's term, "moral sense." But he is referring to the conscientious sense

---

[2] William Frankena used to make this claim to me in conversation.

an agent has that they ought or must perform some *act*, not an observer's sense of the moral goodness of a motive (what Strawson calls the "sense of obligation" (Strawson 1968: 86)).

Although it is set within a Hutchesonian empiricist epistemology, Fordyce's view of the moral sense is actually much closer to Butler's conscience. Like Butler, Fordyce emphasizes conscience's "authority": "[T]here is another directing or controlling Principle, which we call Conscience, or the Moral Sense, which by a native kind of Authority, judges of Affections and Actions, pronouncing some *just* and *good*, and others *unjust* and *ill*" (19). Fordyce's including affections (motives) here might seem to diminish any difference from Hutcheson, but his examples make clear that, as with Butler, conscience has a major *agential* role in directing us to perform morally obligatory *acts*. The instances he gives of the sense of moral obligation have as their objects acts rather than motives. "Let us suppose, for instance, a Parent, a Friend, a Benefactor, reduced to a Condition of the utmost Indigence and Distress, and that it is in our Power to give them immediate Relief. To what Conduct are we *obliged?*" (24). Or "Again, let a Friend, a Neighbour, or even a Stranger, have lodged a *Deposit* in our Hands, and after some time reclaim it, no sooner do these Ideas of the Confidence reposed in us, and of Property not *transferred*, but *deposited*, occur, than we immediately and unavoidably feel, and recognize the Obligation to restore it" (24).

And the undefinable or simple idea that Fordyce insists on is the deontic idea of moral obligation. "[W]hen we use these Terms, *Obligation*, *Duty*, *Ought*, and the like, they stand for a simple Idea, an original uncompounded Feeling or Perception of the human Mind, as much as any Idea whatsoever, and can no more be defined than any other simple Idea" (28). This, of course is the idea that Shaftesbury, Hume, and Hutcheson subversively redefine in non-deontic terms of self-interest (Hume's "natural" or "interested obligation") or esteem and disesteem of motivation (Hume's "moral obligation").

Nonetheless, Fordyce insists, against what will be the main tendency of ethical rationalism, that the source of this fundamental deontic moral idea is not reason, but sentiment or sense. Like Hume and Hutcheson, he restricts reason to demonstrative and probabilistic reasoning, including of the aptness of means to accomplishing ends. And like both, he denies reason's capacity to motivate on its own: "*Reason* may perceive a *Fitness*, or *Aptitude* to a certain *End*, but without some *Sense* or *Affection* we cannot propose, or indeed have any Idea of an *End*, and without an *End* we cannot conceive any *Inducement* to Action" (35). "We might ... perceive all the possible Reasons, Relations, and Differences of Things, and yet be totally indifferent to this or that Conduct," he says, likely with Clarke in his sights (35).

In a passage that recalls Hume's challenge that one can establish through reason every "matter of fact in the case," and nonetheless find that "[t]he vice entirely escapes you" until sentiment is engaged (Hume 1978: 468), Fordyce writes:

> We employ *Reason*, and worthily employ it in examining the Condition, Relations, and other Circumstances of the Agent ... or, in other words, the *State of the Case* (Fordyce 2003: 27).

But this judgment of reason does not yet give us the idea of moral obligation. To make the further judgment that an agent is morally obligated to act in the circumstances that reason has determined to be the case, we require moral sense. Reason can tell us that property has been deposited with and not transferred to us, but it takes moral sense to conclude that we are morally obligated to return it.

Fordyce explicitly considers Samuel Clarke's rationalist view, which we shall examine below, that reason can judge relations and "*Finesses*" that constitute obligations in themselves (Fordyce 2003: 33). To Clarke's claim that it is self-evident to reason that gratitude is a fitting, obligatory response to benevolence, Fordyce acknowledges that through reason we can "compar[e]" "the Nature or Character of a *Benefactor*, and of a *Beneficiary*" and "the Relation between" them through reason (34). But he asks,

> Are any of these Ideas that which we understand by the *Moral Duty* or *Obligation*, the Idea of *Gratitude* due to the *Benefactor* from the *Beneficiary*? This is evidently a distinct Perception, obvious to some *Sense*, *Organ*, or *Power* of Perception, but not the Result of *Reasoning* (34).

Even as he insists on the irreducibility of moral obligation that is a hallmark of British rationalism, therefore, Fordyce remains steadfastly empiricist. "The Nature, the Reasons, and the Relations of things would never have suggested to us this simple Idea of *Moral Obligation* without a proper Sense susceptible of it" (40).

Fordyce's decidedly deontic focus does, however, run against the main lines of empiricist sentimentalism in Hutcheson and Hume, as does his focus on the authority of conscience. Connected to these is a doctrine he shares with Butler about the connection between moral goodness and conscientiousness, the agent's self-regulation through conscientious deontic moral judgment. The doctrine is a staple of British rationalism and opposes Hume's and Hutcheson's skepticism about the moral goodness, and even, indeed, the very possibility, of conscientious motivation. Fordyce defines "*morally good Action*" as action "to fulfil a *Moral Obligation* knowingly and willingly." "And a morally bad Action," or an immoral Action, is action "to violate a *Moral Obligation* knowingly and willingly" (25).

It is crucial to Fordyce, as it was to Butler, that Conscience makes us a "Law to Ourselves" (40). Both take conscience to be essential to moral agency, to be the very capacity that makes us subject to morality, and both hold that moral goodness or virtue consists in the excellent exercise of conscience. It is only because conscience or the moral sense "is interwoven with the very Frame and

Constitution of our Nature" that "*We* are in the strictest Sense a Law to Ourselves" (40).

It is a notable feature of the use of "obligation" in the moral philosophy of the seventeenth and eighteenth centuries that it sometimes refers to a motivational state and sometimes expresses a deontic normative relation. We see this in Fordyce (as we had in early British writers), and we will see it too in the British rationalists Clarke and Balguy and, remarkably, also in Kant. Price will make a special point of marking this ambiguity so that he can focus on the deontic normative relation.

At one point, Fordyce defines what he calls a "State of Moral Obligation" as "That State in which we feel ourselves moved … and prompted to a correspondent Conduct" by our sense (through conscience) that we "ought" to act (24). Conscience speaks to us "with a Voice irresistibly audible and commanding …, with an Authority which no person can silence without being self-condemned" (24). A state "in which we feel ourselves moved" is a motivational state. But what conscience tells us, of course, is that we ought to act, not just that we feel moved to, and this is a normative relation between us and the relevant act. Conscience's content or object is not a motivational state, but the normative relation or state of which it makes us aware: that we ought or are obligated to act.

Fordyce then describes "the State of Moral Obligation" in the following terms:

> that State in which a Creature, endued with such *Senses, Powers*, and *Affections* as *Man*, would condemn himself, and think he deserved the Condemnation of all others, should he refuse to fulfill it (25).

The "it" to be fulfilled is the obligation of which Conscience gives us the sense. Fordyce's way of describing the State of Moral Obligation here is thus notably not as the mental state of being moved. It is rather things being such that the agent *would* be in the mental state of condemning themselves were they not to have fulfilled the obligation of which their conscience gives them the sense. To be sure, this is still a motivational claim, only a counterfactual one. If, however, Fordyce had said not that the agent "would condemn himself," but that he should, that would make the relevant state normative rather than motivational or psychological.

In any case, Fordyce clearly sees obligation as something one can either succeed or fail at fulfilling, where success and failure are tied to accountability. This makes obligation something normative (or at least, believed to be normative) in a distinctive deontic sense. Falling short of an obligation is, moreover, failure to meet not just any normative standard, but one that elicits self-condemnation. Moral obligations are, in their nature, the sort of thing for which we hold ourselves accountable in our own conscience.

Clarke

We find this same ambiguity in Samuel Clarke, who is generally taken to be the originator of British Ethical Rationalism, though Price draws inspiration from Cudworth as much as from Clarke. Clarke's rationalism was doctrinally cleaner than Cudworth's, since Cudworth identifies "superior reason" with love. It was Clarke's rationalism, laid out in his Boyle Lectures of 1704 and 1705, to which Hutcheson, Hume, and, as we have just seen, Fordyce opposed their moral sentimentalism (Clarke 1978a, 1978b; Hutcheson 2002: 155–160).[3] And later British rationalists all recognized Clarke as their predecessor.

Clarke was most famous for the doctrine that there are eternal relations of "fitness" and "unfitness" between moral agents, deliberative circumstances, and actions that are self-evident to reason. There is a "Fitness or Suitableness of certain Circumstances to certain Persons, and an Unsuitableness of others, founded in the nature of Things and the Qualifications of Persons, antecedent to all positive appointment whatsoever," Clarke writes, in opposition to voluntarism of all forms (Clarke 1978b: 608). "'Tis undeniably more *Fit* ... that all Men should endeavour to promote the *universal good and welfare of all*" (609). This "Branch" of the "Rule of Righteousness" Clarke calls that of "Love" (619). But it is not the only one. The fundamental rule of right has another branch, "Equity," which Clarke formulates as reciprocity or the Golden Rule: "so to deal always with another, as he would reasonably expect that *Others* should in like Circumstances deal with him" (619). This also is self-evidently "*Fit*" (609). Unlike Butler, Clarke does not consider the possibility that Equity and Love might conflict.

Fitness, as Clarke understands it, is plainly a normative relation. He tends to use "reasonable," "fit" or "fitting," and "right" as rough synonyms. Thus, "'tis without dispute *Fit* and reasonable in itself" that we should "*preserve the Life* of an innocent" person who is in our power, or "deliver him from imminent danger" (609). Being "fit," for Clarke, is much the same as being *proper* for Smith. Recall that Smith takes propriety to be a relation that holds between some "case" or "situation" (what Clarke tends to call a "circumstance") that an agent confronts and some act or response they might have in the light of it.

---

[3] William Wollaston (1659–1724) is also a target of Hutcheson and Hume, but what is distinctive about his *The Religion of Nature Delimited* (originally published in 1728) is an attempt to reduce normative judgments and properties of moral good and right to the property of truth (Wollaston 1978). Wollaston argued that morally wrong actions express falsehoods, for example, in Wollaston's best case, that lying "says" that something false is true. Sentimentalists and rationalists were agreed that it is reason that judges truth and falsehood, but they generally denied that moral judgments and properties can be thus reduced. That was a centerpiece of Hume's argument that "moral distinctions" cannot "derive" from reason, after all (Hume 1978: 455, 470). Later rationalists like Price agreed (Price 1974: 125–126).

Similarly, an act is fitting for Clarke when it is a fitting response to the "circumstance" in which it is taken. Fittingness and propriety are normative relations for both Clarke and Smith. Clarke uses "fitting" in a way that is substantially the same as the way the term functions in metaethical debates in the twentieth and twenty-first centuries (Broad 1962; Ewing 2012a, 2012b; D'Arms and Jacobson 2002a, 2002b; Howard 2019). What is distinctive in Clarke is the claim that normative fittingness is something that can be self-evident to reason.

Clarke famously analogizes morality to mathematics: "that from the different relations of different Persons one to another, there necessarily arises a fitness or unfitness of certain manners of Behaviour of some persons towards others, is as manifest, as that the Properties which flow from the Essences of different mathematical Figures, have different congruities or incongruities between themselves" (Clarke 1978b: 608). But here an issue arises in understanding Clarke's view.

Clarke takes it to be undeniable by reason "[t]hat there are *Differences* of things; and *different Relations, Respects* or *Proportions*, of some things toward others" (608). These "Differences" and "Relations" derive from "the nature of Things"; they are *"natural relations"* (608, 615). In one sense even sentimentalists like Hume can agree that the analogy with mathematics carries through. That mathematical objects are what they are and have whatever properties they do in virtue of their natures is available to reason; for Hume, this concerns "relations between ideas" that are discoverable by reason.

Similarly, facts about "Circumstances" (Smith's "situations" and "cases") are what Hume calls "matters of fact" that probabilistic causal reasoning can reveal. As we recently saw, Fordyce also agrees with this: "We employ *Reason*, and worthily employ it in examining the Condition, Relations, and other Circumstances of the Agent ... or, in other words, the *State of the Case*" (Fordyce 2003: 27). Since in terms of Hume's "is"/"ought" distinction, these are all "is"'s, sentimentalists like Hume, Hutcheson, and Fordyce can happily agree that reason can determine them.

What they disagree about and what is consequently at issue is whether reason can determine the kind of normative claims we express with "ought." And here it is important to appreciate that Clarke himself distinguishes between natural "Differences" and "Relations" that constitute the "Circumstances" of action, on the one hand, and the normative judgment of an action, that it is "fit" or "reasonable," on the other. "Fitness or Suitableness" is, he says, "founded in the *nature of Things*" (Clarke 1978b: 608). The normative relation is grounded or "founded" in natural relations that make up circumstances. It is not itself constituted by them.

> These eternal and necessary differences of Things, make it *fit and reasonable* for Creatures so to act; they cause it to be their *Duty*, or lay an *Obligation* upon them so to do (596).

Clarke importantly distinguishes, therefore, between relations that themselves constitute the circumstances about which a normative judgment is made and normative judgments of fitness and reasonableness of action in those circumstances that are grounded in these. From the natural relations and differences that constitute the former, "there necessarily arises … a fitness or unfitness" they do not themselves constitute (608).

This is all common ground with the sentimentalists. All can agree with a basic "supervenience" claim that came to be a staple of metaethical debates in the twentieth century from G. E. Moore on: Things can differ in their normative properties only if they differ in the properties that constitute their natures (Moore 1993). As it came to be expressed, evaluative or normative properties are grounded in or supervene on properties constituting the nature of what is said to have the evaluative or normative property. Just as this would be shared by cognitivists like Moore and non-cognitivists like Hare in the twentieth century, so also was it common to Clarke, Fordyce, and Hume in the eighteenth.

What was at issue was what faculties we make the normative judgments with, the judgments Clarke expressed with terms like "fit" and "reasonable." Clarke held the view that these also were judgments of reason. And here, Clarke faced Fordyce's criticism. Fordyce agreed with Clarke that reason can determine, for example, the relations in which a benefactor stands to a beneficiary, but he denied that these necessarily give us "that which we understand by the *Moral Duty* or *Obligation*, the Idea of *Gratitude* due to the *Benefactor* from the *Beneficiary*." He held that "this is evidently a distinct Perception, obvious to some *Sense, Organ*, or *Power* of Perception, but not the Result of *Reasoning*" (Fordyce 2003: 33, 34). "The Nature, the Reasons, and the Relations of things," Fordyce argued, "would never have suggested to us this simple Idea of *Moral Obligation* without a proper Sense susceptible of it" (40).

Thus, Clarke distinguished between reason-made judgments of circumstances and the nature of things, on the one hand, and normative judgments that are based on them, on the other, just as the sentimentalists did. But he asserted against them that the latter are made by reason also. Clarke could not respond directly to the sentimentalist critique, since its first focused form in Hutcheson's *Illustrations Upon the Moral Sense* appeared only a year before Clarke died in 1729. To do so, however, he might have availed himself of the theme, central to later rationalists like Balguy and Price, that we mentioned earlier – namely, that normative judgments concerning "eternal and immutable" morality could not be made through a contingent human sensibility that possible moral agents might lack. The judgment, for example, that it is wrong to cause gratuitous harm, or that we should help "deliver" others "from imminent danger," evidently purports to concern any possible moral agent, and not just human beings (Clarke 1978a: 194). How could some contingent sensibility akin to the human color sense be sufficient to judge that?

This brings us to the tendency in eighteenth-century moral philosophy we remarked on earlier to use "obligation" to refer both to a normative relation and to a motivational state. Clarke also exemplifies this ambiguous usage. Generally, as in the passage quoted above, he understands "obligation" in the former way, as expressing, synonymously with "duty," a normative relation of fitness and unfitness that is grounded in "the eternal and necessary differences of Things" (596). The nature of the circumstances, he says, "lay an *Obligation*" on the agent (596).

There is, however, a notable exception.

> For the Judgment and Conscience of Man's own Mind, concerning the Reasonableness and Fitness of the thing, that his Actions should be conformed to such and such a Rule or Law; is the truest and formallest *Obligation* ... For whoever acts contrary to this sense and conscience of his own mind, is necessarily self-condemned (614).

Here is the same ambiguity we saw in Fordyce. And in both philosophers it is tied, significantly, to a Butlerian view of the authority of conscience along with a focus on deontic morality tied to accountability.

Clarke acknowledges that "the ambiguous use of ['obligation'] as a *Term of Art*, has caused some perplexity and confusion" (614). But he holds that there is an underlying unity in the ambiguity. "The original *Obligation* ... is the eternal *Reason* of Things," at least when this concerns reasons of *right* (614). When it does, judgments of fitness and reasonableness are expressible with deontic terms like "right," "duty," and "obligation." Clarke follows Butler (and Pufendorf) in holding that "the force" of moral obligations is "particularly discovered and applied to every Man" through each person's conscience with which they can hold themselves accountable by self-condemnation (614). It follows that obligation as a normative relation can be in force only if it is possible for agents who are subject to it to instantiate the relevant motivational state in themselves through conscience. Clarke's two uses of "obligation" thus go together in a way that the ambiguous, subversive uses by Shaftesbury, Hutcheson, and Hume do not.

Clarke holds that there are two fundamentally different aspects or "branches" of deontic morality or the "Rule of Righteousness" as regards our "*Fellow-Creatures*," which he calls "*Equity*" and "*Love*," respectively:

> *That in particular we so deal with every Man, as in like Circumstances we could reasonably expect he should deal with Us*; and *that in general we endeavour, by a universal Benevolence, to promote the welfare and happiness of all Men* (619).

He does not say, as Butler does, that what is morally right can sometimes conflict with the greatest overall good that universal benevolence would recommend. But unlike Hutcheson, universal benevolence does not function for Clarke as a source of moral direction that is independent of conscience and the rule of right. As with Butler, the latter is fundamental. Moral agency consists in conscientiously holding oneself accountable for compliance with the rule of right, and this requires both equitably asking no more of others than we would have them ask of us and promoting human good (though they may come to the same thing).

As we saw in the last chapter, a major prong of Hume's critique of rationalism is that the rationalists cannot explain the connection between moral judgment and motivation. One version Hume gives seems especially targeted on Clarke:

> In order, therefore, to prove, that the measures of right and wrong are eternal laws, *obligatory* on every rational mind, 'tis not sufficient to shew the relations upon which they are founded: We must also point out the connexion betwixt the relation and the will; and must prove that this connexion is so necessary, that in every well-disposed mind, it must take place and have its influence (Hume 1978: 465).

One might think that rationalists could have avoided Hume's critique by simply denying the motivational internalism that underlies it, as some twentieth-century intuitionist externalists, like Ross, did. Importantly, however, Clarke does not take this tack, and neither do Balguy and Price, who follow his lead.

There are, moreover, good philosophical reasons for them not to do so, owing to the connections between deontic morality, conscience, and accountable moral agency that, as we have just noted, they were all concerned to draw. If deontic morality is necessarily connected to (any possible) moral agent's capacity to hold themselves accountable through their own conscience, then moral agents must be able to be moved by deontic moral judgments of themselves.

Clarke is the first of the British rationalists to defend a motivational internalism by invoking a parallel between the way a rational mind is necessarily moved to believe what it judges to be true and the way the will is necessarily moved to what a rational agent judges to be fitting and right.

> '[T]is as *natural* and (morally speaking) *necessary*, that the *Will* should be determined in every Action by the *Reason of the thing*, and the *Right of the Case*; as 'tis *natural* and (absolutely speaking) *necessary*, that the *Understanding* should submit to a *demonstrated Truth* (Clarke 1978b: 613).

But note the distinction Clark makes between the theoretical and practical cases. Whereas believing a demonstrated truth is "absolutely" necessary, doing what one judges right is "morally" necessary.

> [A]ssent to a plain speculative *Truth*, is not in a Man's Power to withhold; but to *Act* according to the Plain *Right and Reason* of things, this he may, by the natural Liberty of his Will, forbear (613).

Balguy and Price will argue that the connection is tighter still.

Balguy

Like Cudworth and Leibniz, Clarke argued against all forms of voluntarism that they made moral right and wrong "positive" and "arbitrary" (Cudworth 1996: I.i.1; Clarke 1978b: 608). Sentimentalists also were opposed to the voluntarist's moral positivism. Balguy, however, argued against sentimentalism that it also made morality "positive". About Hutcheson's version, he wrote, "Virtue appears in it to be of an arbitrary and positive Nature; as entirely depending upon *Instincts*, that might originally have been otherwise" (Balguy 1976: 8–9).

Balguy argued that this was true in several ways. It is the case, first, that, for Hutcheson, the property of moral goodness or virtue is a contingent, response-dependent property, like color. Second, the response on which virtue depends, the moral sense, is not itself intrinsic to moral agency, according to Hutcheson. Possible moral agents might lack it. Hutcheson did not concede this point; he *proclaimed* it. Indeed, Hutcheson thought that virtuous moral conduct does not involve the agent's moral sense at all; it consists entirely in benevolence. Third, Balguy argued that benevolence is not intrinsic to or necessary for moral agency either. Had we "been formed destitute of *Natural Affection*" and "void of *natural Compassions*, as well as *Benevolence*," we would still be agents who are fully capable of moral virtue (12).

Like Butler and Clarke, Balguy holds that virtue is realized by exercising the faculty that makes us moral agents and subject to moral obligation. And Balguy follows Clarke in holding that the requisite faculty is reason. On Hutcheson's view, by contrast, non-rational beings can be virtuous no less than we can be. "[I]f Virtue be only kind *Instincts*, or *Affections*," then how can we "deny the Virtue of Brutes," Balguy asks (14). He holds that virtue consists entirely in agents' determining themselves by their own rational judgment. Nothing can "be Virtue, but what consists in a Rational Determination of the Mind" (41). "I cannot have any other Idea of *Moral Merit*, than *conforming*, or endeavouring to conform *our Actions to the Reasons of Things*" (60).

Reason-determined action is not only necessary for moral goodness, it is also sufficient. Therefore, as against Hutcheson, benevolence is not only insufficient, it is also not necessary. Even were we "void of *natural Compassion*, as well as *Benevolence*; might we not possibly be induced to attempt the Relief of a Person in Distress, merely from the *Reason* of the Thing, and the *Rectitude* of the Action?" (12). "Might not some such Maxim as that of doing as we would be done unto, offer it self to our Minds, and prevail with us to stretch out a helping hand upon such an occasion[?]" (12–13). Not only can reason effectively direct us to what is right, it also enables us to hold ourselves accountable if we do not follow its direction: It "would prompt us to undertake it, and condemn us if we omitted it" (13).

For Clarke and Balguy, rational agency and moral agency are coterminous. Unlike Butler, who seems implicitly to recognize a distinction between wider judgments of practical reason (the "principle of reflection") and narrower, fundamentally deontic judgments of conscience, Balguy speaks indifferently of conforming to "the *Reason* of the Thing" and to "the *Rectitude* of the Action." "The *End* of Rational Actions, and Rational Agents, consider'd as such," he says, "is *Reason* or *Moral Good*" (48).

This is most evident in the analogy Balguy takes over from Clarke between the way the rational will aims at doing what is right and reasonable, on the one hand, and the way theoretical reason aims at truth, on the other: "The same necessity which compels men to *assent* to what is *true*, forces them to approve what is *right* and fit" (45). By approval, it is important to see, Balguy does not mean the kind of observer's esteem for the motive of a completed or intended action that Hutcheson and Hume use "approbation" to express. He means a motivating state an *agent* is in when they view an act they consider from a deliberative perspective. "What is the *Reason exciting* a Person to the *Choice* of a Virtuous Action?" he asks, using Hutcheson's terminology for what contemporary philosophers call a "motivating reason" (Hutcheson 2002: 138). Balguy's answer: the agent's "very *Approbation* of it is itself a *sufficient* ['exciting'] *Reason*, wherever it is not over-ruled by another more powerful" (Balguy 1976: 45). When an agent judges an act they are considering to be "*right* and fit," they are then necessarily already in a state moving them to do it. Balguy allows that they might akratically fail to do it, but only through a more powerful motive. They require no additional desire to be motivated beyond what their judgment of practical reason itself provides.

Balguy goes farther in pursuing the analogy with belief and truth than Clarke. Clarke held that while it is "absolutely speaking" necessary that belief be determined by demonstrated truth, it is only "morally speaking" necessary that a rational agent do what they judge reasonable and fit. For Clarke the analogy breaks down owing to the "natural liberty of [the] will," which does not hold with assent or belief; neither can be voluntarily adopted (Clarke 1978b: 613). Balguy, however, does not make this distinction.

> [W]hy then do we approve? ... I answer in one word, *Necessity*. The same Necessity which compels Men to *assent* to what is *true*, forces them approve what is *right* and fit (Balguy 1976: 45).

Motivation is connected as necessarily to judging an act to be right and fit as belief is to seeing a demonstration that something must be true.

Like Clarke, Balguy calls the motivational state involved in judging the reasonableness of an act a kind of obligation.

> *Internal Obligation is a State of the Mind into which it is brought by the Perception of a plain reason for acting, or forbearing to act, arising from the Nature, Circumstances, or Relations of Persons or Things* (31).

As with Clarke, three things must be distinguished: (a) the circumstances and relations that make an act reasonable or fit (the facts that are "plain reason[s] for acting," like that an act would avoid harm), (b) the act's being reasonable or fit (owing to the facts in (a)), and (c) the mental (motivational) state of taking an act to be reasonable or fit (believing (b) in the light of (a)). (b) is a normative relation between an act and the non-normative facts in (a), and (c) is the non-normative state of accepting (b), which is a normative proposition or fact. Like Clarke, Balguy calls (c) a kind of obligation, but (c) consists in taking oneself to be under an obligation in the normative deontic sense (12).[4]

Price

Richard Price makes this very point in the course of arguing that the concept of obligation is indefinable. Quoting Balguy's definition of "internal obligation," Price notes that it conflates "the *effect* of obligation perceived" with "obligation itself" (Price 1974: 114). Noting the general tendency to use "obligation" to refer to a distinctive motivational state, including by Clarke, Price argues that this usage fails to distinguish sufficiently between "motive" and "obligation" (114, 118). As Price also puts it, it conflates "an act and object of the mind," "a perception and the truth perceived" (117).[5]

Price argues that "fit," "reasonable," "right," "morally good," "obligatory," and "ought" all express the same fundamental indefinable normative idea when applied to acts (41, 104–130). "*Fitness* and *unfitness* ... when applied to actions, ... generally signify the same with *right* and *wrong*" (104). Similarly, "*[m]orally good* and *evil*, *reasonable* and *unreasonable*" applied to acts "evidently mea[n] the same" as "*right* and *wrong, fit* and *unfit*" (104). Crucially, for Price, "*right*" and "wrong," are indefinable "simple ideas" in Locke's sense. "Our ideas of *right* and *wrong* are simple ideas, and must therefore be ascribed to some power of *immediate* perception in the human mind" (41). So also, therefore, are the ideas referred to by the synonymous terms "reasonable" and "unreasonable," "fit" and "unfit," and so on. They all express the same fundamental indefinable normative ideas.

Like Balguy and Clarke, Price does not mark Suárez's distinction between law and counsel, between being obligatory and being recommended by normative reasons for acting. The critical element of Suárez's contrast, again, is that obligations are necessarily connected to accountability; issues of culpability necessarily arise with obligations in a way they do not with choosing

---

[4] "[B]y the help of Reason and Reflection, [we can] discover ourselves to be under Obligations, and that we ought to return good Offices, or Thanks, according to our Abilities" (12).
[5] Price does note, however, that "in common language, the term *obligation* often stands for the sense and judgment of the mind concerning what is fit or unfit to be done" (117). Dafydd Daniels emphasizes this point in Daniels 2020.

less choiceworthy options. Price does hold that an intrinsic connection exists between obligation and accountability. "Would a person who either believes there is no God, or that he does not concern himself with human affairs, feel no *moral obligations*, and therefore not be at all accountable?" he asks, implying that accountability is entailed by obligation (106–107). But Price does not mark any contrast between the narrower deontic normative accountability-entailing relation expressed by "obligation" and the more general normative notion expressed by "normative reason" and "fit" and "unfit" when these are used in more general normative senses.

Also like Balguy, Price's foil in much of his moral philosophy is Hutcheson. Hutcheson too stressed that all moral thought involves simple fundamental moral ideas, but for Hutcheson, these were approbation and condemnation, ideas that we have from an observer's perspective when we contemplate motives and the intended or completed actions they motivate. For Price, however, the fundamental moral ideas of fitness and unfitness, right and wrong, are ideas we have in connection with alternatives for choice: acts, considered mostly independently of motive, as we might consider them from an agential perspective in deliberating about what to do. It is only when we form an intention or act that actual motivation is revealed in our reasons for so intending or acting. Here again, we see a contrast between deontic morality's focus on accountability and moral agency, on the one hand, and Hume and Hutcheson's virtue-ethical focus on motive and character, on the other.[6]

The difference with Hutcheson that Price is most concerned to stress, however, concerns the *source* of our fundamental moral ideas. Where Hutcheson is led by Lockean empiricism to infer the existence of a moral sense, Price defends the ethical rationalist thesis that fundamental moral ideas come from reason. Here he differs as well from Fordyce, who also holds that the idea of moral obligation is indefinable, but who argued against Clarke that the source of this idea is not reason but sense. Against Hutcheson (and Fordyce), Price declares:

> What is the power within us that perceives the distinctions of *right* and *wrong*?
> My answer is. The UNDERSTANDING (17).

Price complains that moral sense theories like Hutcheson's make moral judgments matters of taste and treat morality as response-dependent in the same way color is. So conceived, morality becomes "the effect of a *positive constitution* of our minds," resulting from "an *implanted* and *arbitrary* principle by which a *relish* is given us for certain moral objects and forms and aversion to others" (14). Moral sense theorists often opposed their ideas to early modern

---

[6] This is reflected in Gary Watson's distinction between "responsibility as accountability" and "responsibility as attributability" (Watson 1996).

forms of voluntarism that modeled morality on positive law. But Balguy and especially Price argued that the moral sense theory ultimately made morality depend no less on arbitrary posits, in this case contingent aspects of the human psyche rather than voluntary dictates of the will. Price argued, following Cudworth, that morality is "eternal and immutable": objective rather than subjective, inherently rational rather than arbitrary, necessary rather than contingent, and universally binding on any possible moral agent (52, 85, 89).

Against the sentimentalists' empiricist theory of ideas, Price contended that it could give no account, not just of moral ideas, but of a whole host of concepts that are of fundamental importance for thought in general, whether theoretical or practical. Drawing on Plato's *Theaetetus* and, especially, Cudworth's *True Intellectual System of the Universe*, Price argued that the concepts of universality, necessity, substance, power, causation, and the like, necessary for active thought at all, could not possibly derive from phenomenal sensations alone. Sense is essentially particularistic and passive – it receives particular images. (This, of course, is Berkeley's reason for rejecting "abstract ideas.") Sense "lies prostrate under its object," Price says, using a phrase of Cudworth's (19).[7] This is a familiar theme among rationalists (think of Descartes's piece of wax in the *Meditations*) (Descartes 2017). And the empiricists themselves acknowledged, sometimes happily, that many such thought-structuring ideas cannot derive from sense. Sometimes they outright rejected the rationalists' concepts (Berkeley on "abstract ideas") or attempted alternatively to provide "skeptical" ways of explaining them (like Hume on causation and, arguably, moral properties such as virtue).

In arguing so clearly that "the power ... that *understands* ... and that compares all the objects of thought, and *judges* of them, is a spring of new ideas" like universality and necessity, as well as the fundamental moral ideas involving these, Price's thought looks forward to Kant (18). "Sensation is only a mode of feeling in the mind; but knowledge implies an active and vital energy of the mind" (20). Thought and knowledge require something like the spontaneity of reason, no less in the practical than in the theoretical sphere. When we make moral judgments, taking, for example, someone to be under a moral obligation, we think with concepts that cannot come from sense, since they essentially involve the ideas of universality and necessity that cannot possibly derive from it.

Price and the intuitionists, however, give rational "intuition" or "immediate perception" of the understanding a fundamental role in their moral epistemology that it does not have in Kant's. "Some truths there must be, which can appear only by their own light, and which are incapable of proof; otherwise

---

[7] "Sense, that suffers from external objects, lies as it were prostrate under them" (Cudworth 1996: 54).

nothing could be proved, or known; in the same manner as ... if there were no simple or undefinable ideas, there could be no complex ideas" (98). Intuition is the source both of fundamental moral ideas and of our knowledge of the truth of propositions we are able to formulate with them. "It is on this power of intuition, essential, in some degree or other, to all rational minds, that the whole possibility of reasoning is founded" (98).

Price thus agrees with the sentimentalists that knowledge is grounded in immediate perception and expanded from that foundational basis by reasoning. And they agree also that all simple ideas must be given in "immediate perception."[8] But they disagree about what the requisite faculty of perception is. For empiricists, it is given entirely by sense experience, whereas for rational intuitionists like Price it is a form of intellectual perception that, like Cartesian "clear and distinct perception," is possible only with the rational mind or understanding.

Sense experience, Price argues, is irremediably imagistic, particularistic, and subjective, whereas knowledge requires, quite generally, formulation in universal concepts and objectivity. And fundamental moral knowledge, moreover, is necessary rather than contingent. "[M]orality is a branch of necessary truth" (85). Eternal and immutable morality is constituted by deontic standards that obligate any possible "moral agent." They are laws for moral agents as such.

Price stresses, again, that unlike sense experience, intuition or perception by the understanding is active rather than passive. It involves "an active and vital energy of the mind" (20). This contrast carries through also to Price's account of self-determining agency which plays a central role in his account of deontic morality.

As with Butler, it is important to Price that virtue or moral goodness consists not in any form of motivation to which a moral agent might be (passively) subject or simply have. It involves the agent determining *themselves* by their own judgment of how they morally should act, as Butler would put it, through their own conscience. "[A]n agent cannot justly be denominated *virtuous*," Price writes, "except he acts from a consciousness of rectitude" (184). "It is the actual conformity of the wills of moral agents to what they see or believe to be the fitnesses of things, that is the object of our praise and esteem" (184).

"Moral capacit[y]," the power or competence required to be subject to deontic moral standards of "rectitude" and to hold oneself accountable for compliance to them, requires "the power of *acting* and *determining*" (181). True agency, Price holds, cannot be understood through any form of causation or determination that one passively undergoes. Rather agency is something agents actively exercise and themselves determine, so that they cause their own actions. "As far as it is true of a being that he acts, so far he must *himself* be the

---

[8] "Given" in the sense of the "myth of the given" (Sellars 1956).

cause of the action" (181). Price calls this power "moral capacity" since he holds it to be essential to the accountability that deontic standards of "rectitude" necessarily involve.

> [I]t is hard to say what virtue and vice, commendation and blame, mean, if they do not suppose *agency*, free choice, and an absolute dominion over our resolutions.—It has always been the *general*, and it is evidently the *natural* sense of [humankind], that they cannot be accountable for what they have no power to avoid (182).

Here is another aspect of the contrast between Price's focus on deontic morality and the version of virtue ethics we find in Hutcheson and Hume. The latter feel no dialectical pressure in the direction of a theory and ideal of autonomous moral agency that Price so evidently does.

Price does not draw incompatibilist conclusions from his doctrine of "liberty" as agent causation. His focus is squarely on ethics rather than metaphysics.

> If ... advocates of the doctrine of necessity should find, that what they mean by necessity is not inconsistent with the ideas of *agency* and *self-determination*, there will be little room for farther disputes (183).

Price is happy to allow that doctrines of universal causation might be true as a metaphysical matter. All that matters is that the idea of self-determination be in good working order for the purposes of deontic morality.

Price holds that agents determine themselves by making their own judgments of what is fitting and right, and by acting on those.

> The intellectual nature is its own law. It has, within itself, a spring and guide of action which it cannot suppress or reject. Rectitude is itself an end, an ultimate end, an end superior to all other ends (187).

We determine ourselves by guiding ourselves by the law of our intellectual nature, which makes us active beings.

In a pointed contrast with Hutcheson, Price distinguishes between "*instinctive*" and "*rational*" benevolence. Whereas Hutcheson holds that virtue is benevolence pure and simple, with guidance by the moral sense being not only unnecessary, but not actually directly possible, Price claims that any such "*instinctive benevolence* is no principle of virtue" (191). "*Rational benevolence*" is virtuous, Price allows, but that is because "[r]*ational benevolence* entirely coincides with rectitude, and the actions proceeding from it, with the actions proceeding from a regard to rectitude" (191). Virtue always consists in the agent's doing what they think fitting and right because they themselves think so. That is obviously consistent with beneficence, and it can be consistent also with benevolence, so long as the agent's governing motivation is a "regard to rectitude."

Again, Price does not distinguish between rectitude in a narrower, distinctively deontic sense and a broader notion of fittingness or support by normative practical reasons. This gives him a very tight circle of concepts when it comes to the question of why be moral. We have seen that Butler can be interpreted in a way that makes this question at least superficially open by distinguishing between narrowly moral deontic judgments of right, made through conscience, on the one hand, and broader normative judgments of reason (what Butler calls "superiority" and "inferiority") that are made with the "principle of reflection." But Price makes no such distinction. He says that intellectual nature or rational agency aims at doing what is "fitting" and "right" indifferently.

This turns the question of "why be moral (do what is morally obligatory or right)?" into the question of "why do what is fitting (do what there is good reason to do)?" If that question asks for anything like justification, it is self-answering. But what explains why the agent's answering the normative question motivates them? This puts us back in the territory of Hume's challenge: How can we "prove *a priori* that these relations, if they really existed and were perceived, would be universally forcible and obligatory" (Hume 1978: 466)? What is the "connexion betwixt the relation and the will" (465)?

Price, like Clarke and Balguy, takes up this internalist challenge, refusing to take refuge in an externalist intuitionism as some later intuitionists, like Ross, do. "It seems extremely evident," Price says, "that excitement belongs to the very ideas of moral right and wrong" (Price 1974: 186). By this, Price clearly does not mean that an act's being unfitting or wrong is the same thing as the agent's being motivated not to do it, or even that the latter is entailed by the former. That would run over the distinction he is so concerned to make against Clarke and Balguy between the normative claim that an act is fitting, right, or obligatory, and the psychological proposition that someone perceives or accepts that and is moved by it. It would blur the distinction between normative and motivating reasons. Price clarifies his meaning, saying that "excitement" "is essentially inseparable from the apprehension of" the "ideas of moral right and wrong" (186). "When we are conscious that an act is *fit* to be done, or that it *ought* to be done," he continues, "it is not conceivable that we can remain *uninfluenced*, or want a *motive* to action" (186).

But Price thinks the explanation of this is so straightforward almost to be trivial. "Why a *reasonable* being … has a disposition to follow reason…; why he chuses to do what he knows he *should* do…, are questions which need not, and deserve not to be answered" (187). This follows directly from Price's account of rational agency, agent causation, and self-determination. Something does not so much count as the action of a self-determining rational agent unless it is chosen under the guise of the reasonable, fitting, and right. It is important, again, that these latter amount to the same concept for Price. He works with no distinction between law and counsel; if it so much as counsels, "reason *commands*" (188).

Although it may seem to, this need not rule out the possibility of *akrasia*, action contrary to the agent's considered beliefs about what they have most reason to do. Price could hold that there is a difference between the latter and what seems to the agent most fitting in the moment because of framing effects and the pressure of nonrational motivation. Price does not, however, make this move.

Price thus assembles in its most mature form among the British rationalists an account of deontic morality that puts together mutually supporting elements that appear also in Clarke and Balguy, as well as Cudworth and Butler.

1. Morality comprises a set of deontic norms, laws of "rectitude" that
2. universally bind all (any possible) moral agents,
3. making them accountable for compliance.
4. Moral agency involves the capacity for self-determination, which is
5. the capacity to do, and hold oneself accountable for doing, what one thinks right.
6. Morally good (virtuous) action consists in the excellent exercise of this capacity (action from "consciousness of rectitude").

This is not a potpourri of views. All six are at least mutually supporting and perhaps even mutually entailing. If there is a fundamental organizing idea, it is the notion that deontic norms of right involve accountability in their nature. As writers as diverse as Butler and Pufendorf illustrate, once we have that idea, the capacities necessary for accountable agency follow in its train, and good moral agency as their excellent exercise follows accordingly.

This package of views does not entail metaethical rationalism, even less rational intuitionism, as the example of Fordyce proves. But if, like Price, Clarke, and Balguy, one treats rational agency as coterminous with moral agency, and makes no distinction between what there is normative reason (what it is fitting) to do, and what is morally demanded, required, or obligatory, then some form of rationalism seems virtually unavoidable. If rational agency is sufficient to make one subject to moral obligation, then practical reason must be sufficient also for accountability. And if that is so, then reason itself must equip an agent with all that is necessary for right and wrong to be evident to them and for them to hold themselves to these standards.[9]

The central importance for Price of conscientious conduct shows itself also in a distinction he makes between "abstract" and "practical" forms of virtue. *Abstract virtue* is the same as fittingness and right. It is what "it is right *such* an agent, in *such* circumstances, should do," "considered independently of the *sense* [belief] of the agent" (177). *Practical virtue*, by contrast, is what an agent should do, given their beliefs. Since there are two ways this might be taken, it is important to see how Price understands it. By "practical virtue," Price does *not* mean what an agent should do, conditional on *what* they believe, that is, if their

---

[9] See here Schiffman 2015.

beliefs were to be true. Practical virtue rather means what an agent should do conditional on *their believing* as they do.

This goes farther than simply saying that moral goodness or virtue consists in the agent's following their conscience. It says, in addition, that the content of the agent's conscience also affects what they should *do*. Price no doubt thinks, like Butler, that most people's consciences are reliable much of the time. But he acknowledges that we can be mistaken. So he says that "[o]ur rule is to follow our consciences steadily and faithfully, after we have taken care to inform them in the best manner we can" (179). He counsels caution, however. "[W]here we doubt," we are "to take the *safest* side, and not venture to *do* any thing concerning which we have doubts, when we know there can be nothing amiss in *omitting* it" (179).

But what determines abstract virtue or moral right? Price formulates this as the question "[W]hat are the chief *heads* of virtue[?]" (meaning abstract virtue or right) (131). Here Price is an intuitionist also, but in a yet further normative-theoretic sense that became popular in the nineteenth and twentieth centuries. Like early twentieth-century intuitionists, such as Ross and Prichard, Price held that there are a multiplicity of principles of right (what Ross called "prima facie duties") that are self-evident to rational intuition and that can neither be derived from nor explained by more fundamental principles (Ross 2003). Price was what Sidgwick called a "dogmatic intuitionist," what Mill called an "intuitive" moralist, and what Rawls called simply an "intuitionist" (Sidgwick 1967: 102; Mill 2002: 2; Rawls 1971, 3).

Price's intuitionism in this pluralist sense closely follows Butler's critique of Hutcheson's doctrine that virtue can be "resolved into" benevolence, laid out in Butler's *Dissertation*, which Price quotes virtually in its entirety (Price 1974: 131–132). For his part, Price argues that the "heads" of virtue include duties to God, duties of self-regard, of beneficence, of gratitude, of veracity (under which he, implausibly, considers promissory obligations), and duties of justice (131–164). Although he evidently holds these "heads" or "principles" to be irreducibly *normatively* plural, he nonetheless says that "they all run up to one general idea, and should be considered as only different modifications and views of one original, all-governing law" (165). What he evidently means by this is not that there is a single principle from whose content the content of all the rest can be derived (in the way he thinks that the duty to keep promises can be derived from the duty to tell the truth), but just that they all "are alike our indispensable duty." "It is the same authority enjoins, the same truth and right that oblige, the same eternal reason that commands in them all" (165). All are equally part of the same *body* of law of "rectitude"; all derive from "intellectual nature" or reason.

Price recognizes that these different "principles" or "heads" can conflict. When they do, it can be difficult determinately to weigh their conflicting claims. "[S]o variously may different obligations combine or oppose each other in particular cases, and so imperfect are our discerning faculties, that it cannot but happen, that we should be frequently in the dark ..." (167). As with Ross, who will hold that it is only *prima facie* duties that are self-evident, and that how to balance them in particular cases may not be, so Price says that it is "[t]he principles themselves" that "are self-evident," even if "obscurity attend[s] several cases wherein a competition arises between the several principles of morality" (168).

Reid

We prefaced our examination of the canonical British ethical rationalists – Clarke, Balguy, and Price – with a short discussion of Fordyce. Fordyce accepts all the elements of the deontic moral conception that find their most mature formulation in Price, but he denies metaethical rationalism. He agrees that morality comprises a set of norms of right that obligate all moral agents, making them accountable for compliance, with moral agency including the capacities for self-determination and holding oneself accountable through conscience. And he accepts that virtuous or morally good action consists in the excellent exercise of this capacity; it is conscientious conduct. But whereas the rationalists identify conscience with reason, Fordyce claims it requires a "Moral Sense" (Fordyce 2003: 12).

What drives Fordyce to this conclusion is his Lockean theory of ideas. Like Hutcheson, he accepts that moral concepts involve a fundamental simple idea that can be received only through a distinct, moral sense. But Fordyce departs from Hutcheson on what the fundamental moral idea is. For Hutcheson, it is moral goodness of motives, the essential kernel of which is approbation, an observer's response upon contemplating the motive of benevolence. Against this, Fordyce agrees with the rationalists that the fundamental concept of morality is the deontic idea of moral duty or obligation (28).

As we have recently seen, Price makes this point a central part of his argument that the source of our moral ideas is reason or "The Understanding" rather than sense (Price 1974: 17, 41). No sense, as the empiricists understand them, could possibly give rise to the idea of moral duty with its entailments of necessity, universality, and objectivity.

To end this chapter, we turn to an important philosopher, Thomas Reid, who agreed with the rationalists on almost all these points, but who is nonetheless not a canonical ethical rationalist. Like Fordyce, Reid is prepared to call the "original power of the mind" through which we "have the notions of right and wrong" and also "perceive certain things to be right, and others to be wrong," "*moral sense*" (Reid 1969: 231). And Reid is skeptical about canonical rationalist formulations like "*acting contrary to the relations of things, ... to the fitness of things*" (472). Clarke and Balguy's "phrases have not the authority of common use" and so are no part of moral commonsense (472).

Like Butler, from whom he draws many of his arguments and terminology, Reid carefully avoids taking a definite side in the debate between rationalists and sentimentalists. In the *Dissertation*, Butler says that it matters little whether conscience is called "moral reason" or "moral sense" (Butler 2017: D.1) and then uses phrases that seem purposely designed to blur the lines: "sentiment of the understanding" and "perception of the heart" (D.1). Reid is similarly cagey, wishing not to enter into "subtile disputes among modern philosophers" about whether the moral "power of the mind" that is the source of moral ideas and perceptions "ought to be called *reason*, or be not rather some internal sense or taste" (Reid 1969: 71, 231). Reid also follows Butler in saying that the moral faculty is "cool," "dispassionate," and authoritative. It operates "in a manner so like to judgment or reason, that even those who do not allow it to be called by that name, endeavour to account for its having always had that name" (71).

Reid actually agrees with Price that no moral sense, as empiricists like Hume and Hutcheson understand it, could possibly be a source of moral ideas and knowledge. Reid's critique of the empiricist theory of ideas and sense experience is a centerpiece of his epistemology quite generally. As Reid sees it, the central problem with early modern empiricism is that it takes the objects of sense experience to be "sensations in our own minds" (458) rather than ordinary objects and their properties. Empiricists end up restricting the scope of justified empirical judgments to mental phenomena: sensations and feelings. This makes empirical judgment irremediably subjective.

Reid thinks, by contrast, that we use our senses to make justified objective empirical judgments directly about ordinary objects and their properties. Moreover, as we shall see presently, he advances a careful analysis of justified intuitive moral knowledge through moral sense. Thus, although Reid is happy to use Hutcheson's term "moral sense," he rejects Hutcheson's empiricist understanding of that term. "I find no fault with the name *moral sense*," Reid says (398). But he adds that "[m]odern philosophers have conceived of the external senses as having no other office but to give us certain sensations, or simple conceptions, which we could not have without them" (398–399). "[T]his notion has been applied to the moral sense. But it seems to me a mistaken notion in both" (399).

Reid's *Essays on the Active Powers of the Mind* (1788) virtually begins with the signature rationalist (and Butlerian) claim that "[e]very thing virtuous and praiseworthy must lie in the right use of our power; every thing vicious and blameable in the abuse of it" (1). The relevant "active power" is the "capacity of self-government," which Reid identifies with the capacity to govern oneself by a "conception of a law" and "its obligation" (2). Virtue is conscientious conduct, an agent's determining and holding themselves to the moral law. It is the excellent exercise of the capacity that makes them moral agents, subject to deontic morality, and accountable for compliance with it. "Two things are implied in the notion of a moral and accountable being; understanding and active power" (315). A moral agent "must understand the law to which he is bound, and his obligation to obey it" (315). And a moral agent must have the "power to do what he is accountable for" (316).

Reid defines "active power" as "an attribute in a being by which he can do certain things if he wills" (38). And he similarly defines "will" as a "power to determine, in things which he conceives to depend upon his determination" (57). With these, he advances a subtle theory of agency as agent causation that is significantly more sophisticated than Price's. Reid distinguishes the (active) power of will from the exercise of that power: "the act of determining" or "*volition*" (57). And he distinguishes the latter from all "motives" or "incitements" to the will, which other philosophers mistakenly identify as "modifications" of the will (58). The exercise of will is always (as Cudworth and Locke both emphasized) a self-conscious self-determining activity, rather than anything that happens in or to the agent.[10] Reid carefully botanizes the wide variety of motives and "incitements" to which human beings are subject, distinguishing between "mechanical" instincts and habits, "animal" appetites and passions, and "rational" motives of prudence and moral duty. Throughout, he is clear that it is always *the agent* that wills, and so causes, their own actions. Motives "influence" but do not cause actions. Only agents can do that.

An especially important part of Reid's action theory for his ethics is a mental state he calls "a fixed purpose or resolution with regard to our future conduct" (83). This is the kind of prospective intention on which philosophers only really came to focus in the wake of Michael Bratman's work on intention in the late twentieth century (Bratman 1987). It is close, however, to what Kant considers under the heading of adopting or "setting" an end (e.g., Kant 1996c 6:239). We form a fixed purpose or resolution when we form a firm intention to do something in the future. Resolutions thus involve the will for Reid in a way that motives like desire can never, however strong they might be.

Since Reid takes virtue necessarily to involve the will, it can never be constituted by motivating states, like desires, to which an agent is passively subject. Virtuous agency thus involves self-determination, and virtuous agents adopt fixed purposes and resolutions. The virtue of justice, Reid writes, is "nothing but a fixed purpose, or determination, to act according to the rules of justice" (Reid 1969: 85). So indeed, Reid says, are all virtues; "[t]hey are all fixed purposes of acting according to a certain rule" (85). (By "rule" here Reid means a rule of right.)

---

[10] Reid quotes approvingly Locke's definition of will as "an act of the mind, knowingly exerting that dominion it takes itself to have over any part of the man, by employing it in, or withholding it from any particular action" (58).

"By this," Reid says, "the virtues may be easily distinguished ... from natural affections that bear the same name" (85). Hutcheson, by contrast, identifies benevolence with a desire for the good of others (or for one's own good, impartially considered). Reid holds that, so understood, benevolence cannot be a virtue. According to Reid, "[t]he virtue of benevolence is a fixed purpose or resolution to do good when we have opportunity, from a conviction that it is right, and is our duty" (86).

The boundaries of virtue and right are coterminous with those of voluntary moral agency. "Hard would it be indeed to think, that a man should be born under a degree of reprobation, because he has the misfortune of a bad natural temper" (86). Reid analyzes active power into three "voluntary" "operations of mind" (76–89). Two of these, attention and deliberation, are familiar from Cudworth on the "autexousious power" and from Locke's account of "free agency" in the second edition of the *Essay*. Moral agents can voluntarily direct their attention to consider alternative choices before them in deliberating about what to do (though "[w]e ought not to deliberate in cases that are perfectly clear" (80)). To these, Reid adds the voluntary forming of fixed purposes or resolutions (83).

Together these constitute our job as moral agents and all we can be held accountable for:

> If any man could be found who, in the whole course of his life, had given due attention to the things that concern him, had deliberated duly and impartially about his conduct, had formed his resolutions, and executed them according to his best judgment and capacity, surely such a man might hold up his face before God and man, and plead innocence (92).

Like Butler, Reid treats both what Butler calls "reasonable self-love" and conscience as rational principles of action. "To act with a view of some distant interest, or to act from a sense of duty, seems to be proper to man as a reasonable being" (83). Both a regard to "what is good for us upon the whole" and the concern to do "what appears to us to be our duty" are "rational principles" (202–203). Both are "leading and governing principle[s]," in Butler's sense (202).

This raises a number of issues, however, as it did with Butler. The "rational principle of a regard to our good upon the whole" "is so similar to the moral principle, or conscience, and so interwoven with it," Reid says, "that both are commonly comprehended under the name of *reason*" (210). We are "self-condemned" when we go against our duty and when we pursue a nearer lesser good over a greater one in the further future (209). A regard to our own greatest good, like conscience, Reid writes, "gives us the conception of a *right* and a *wrong* in human conduct," but he quickly adds, "at least of a *wise* and a *foolish*" (210).

That is the problem. Reid's considered view is that the idea of right or moral obligation is a different notion from that of the agent's good. It is a distinctively deontic "relation of its own kind ... perhaps too simple to admit of logical definition" (229; see also 223). The idea of right contains a conceptual connection to accountable agency that the concept of the agent's own good does not have. To constitute the normative relation of obligation, an action must be "voluntary" and "within the sphere of [the agent's] natural power," and the agent must have the "understanding and will" enabling them to know their obligations and to hold themselves to them (229). Nothing like this is true of the concept of the agent's greatest a good or a rational concern for it.

Prudence and conscience are, therefore, "distinct principles" (210). It is conscience or the "*moral faculty*" that is the "original power of the mind" through which we "have the notions of right and wrong" and also "perceive certain things to be right, and others to be wrong" (231). Like Butler, Reid reserves "authority" for conscience rather than self-regard (254). It would seem to follow, as it does for Butler, therefore, that the only way acting against rational self-regard can make us self-condemned in the deontic accountability sense is if imprudence also violates conscience. Only conscience or the moral faculty provides us with the deontic conceptual materials to blame or condemn ourselves. These are, Reid emphasizes, "acts of judgment" that involve the "exercise [of the] moral faculty" (464). Moreover, Reid says, the idea of right that is essential to conscience's judgment cannot be "resolved into that" of our "interest, or what is most for our happiness" (223).

"Prudence is a virtue," like "benevolence," "fortitude," justice, and others. But the "essence and formal nature" of every virtue, including prudence, "must lie in something that is common to all these, and to every other virtue" (399). And this, Reid clearly says, "can be nothing else but the rectitude of such conduct ..., which is discerned by a good man" through the exercise of the moral faculty (399).[11]

A deeper point is that although the "regard to duty" and the "regard to our good on the whole" are both "motives" or "rational principles of action," Reid speaks only of conscience or the "moral faculty" as a "power," one involving both the power to understand the right and the active power to determine ourselves to act in light of it.[12] Butler does not make this distinction, as he has a less sophisticated theory of action than Reid does.

We noted in our discussion of Butler that it is possibly profitable to read him through the perspective of a distinction between a broader "principle of

---

[11] Cf., however, "We ought to prefer a greater good, though more distant, to a less. ... A regard to our own good, though we had no conscience, dictates this principle; and we cannot help disapproving the man that acts contrary to it" (362). This is like the passage in Butler's sermons where he says that, in a similar case, "we may have a clear conception of the *superior nature* of one inward principle to another" (self-love over a particular present appetite) "without particular consideration of conscience" (Butler 2017: II.11). See p. 179 above for discussion of this same issue in Butler.

[12] "Of Regard to our Good on the Whole," is the title of Essay III, Chapter II.

reflection" that makes normative judgments of practical reason in general, and conscience, which makes narrower judgments of deontic morality. It is more difficult to read such a distinction into Reid, however. The reason is that Reid explicitly says that the deliberative question is "whether the action under … deliberation ought to be done, or ought not," and for Reid, like the British rationalists, the only ought is the narrow deontic moral ought of right and obligation. "[T]he notion or conception of duty," Reid says, can be defined "only by synonymous words or phrases, … as when we say that it is what we ought to do" (223).

There seems to be no place in Reid's thought for the more general practical normative notion of what a person should do in the sense of what there is most normative reason for them to do. Had Reid theorized with this more general notion, he might have made a distinction between the moral active power and a more general active power of practical reason that could have had the power of rational prudence as a species.

Although Reid recognizes the difference between self-regard and conscience (regard to duty) as rational motives or "principles of action," he holds that Divine providence guarantees that there can be no genuine conflict between them. Any "opposition between the two governing principles … is merely imaginary" (256). So long as "the world is under a wise and benevolent administration, it is impossible, that any man should … be a loser by doing his duty" (256–257).

Reid's normative moral theory is laid out in his lectures on practical ethics (Reid 2007). He holds with Price that moral knowledge and reasoning must "rest upon one or more first principles of morals, whose truth is immediately perceived without reasoning" (1969: 235). And like many of the British rationalists, he makes the golden rule a "first principl[e] in morals": "that we ought not to do to another, what we should think wrong to be done to us in like circumstances" (234).

Of particular interest in Reid's metaethics is an argument he makes against empiricist sentimentalism, represented most clearly by Hume, that crystallizes, arguably for the first time, a contrast between cognitivism and non-cognitivism that will loom large in metaethical debates of the twentieth century. Reid crisply states the issue in terms that refer explicitly to the sentiment that figures centrally in the moral sentimentalism of Hutcheson and Hume.

> [F]or half a century, it has been a serious dispute among philosophers, what this approbation and disapprobation is, whether there be a real judgment included in it, which, like all other judgments, must be true or false; or, whether it includes no more but some agreeable or uneasy feeling, in the person who approves or disapproves (457).

For Hutcheson, approbation is the simple idea that moral sense receives and through which moral goodness is defined. And although Hume rejects moral sense as part of our *primary* constitution," approbation figures prominently in his sympathy-based sentimentalism (Hume 1978: 473).

When we discussed Hume, we noted that he formulates his view in different ways, some of which suggest a subjectivist form of cognitivism, some of which suggest a non-cognitivist or expressivist reading. Hume himself doesn't seem to notice the differences, so it seems anachronistic to attribute one or the other of the views clearly to him. But Reid, perhaps for the first time, shows precisely what the difference and issue is between these alternatives.

The key question, Reid says, is whether a given sentiment, like approbation, necessarily involves judgment. As Reid understands it, a judgment necessarily has an *object*, which is always some "proposition" that is capable of being true or false. "In judgment, we can distinguish the object about which we judge, from the act of the mind in judging of that object" (Reid 1969: 460). And "[e]very judgment must necessarily be true or false" (460). Feelings, by contrast, are distinguished by their felt phenomenal features, which may be either "agreeable" or "uneasy" (457).

Reid allows that in "many operations of the mind," feeling and judgment are "inseparably conjoined under one name." The crucial question is whether the sentiment expressed by what a moral sentimentalist calls moral "judgments" (as even sentimentalists are disposed to call them) necessarily involves a judgment in the sense that Reid distinguishes, namely, an attitude toward a proposition that is held to be true. Were Hume to confront the issue framed in this way, it would force him to make a choice. Since he holds that "reason is the discovery of truth and falsehood," then it will follow from the claim that moral "judgments" are made through sentiment rather than reason that they are not really judgments in Reid's sense. It would mean that Hume's holding that moral judgments express, rather than self-attribute, feelings would commit him to metaethical non-cognitivism, the view that moral judgments cannot be true or false.

In these terms, Hutcheson, however, would seem clearly to count as a cognitivist, since he holds that moral goodness is the property of (motivated) actions that "procures" approbation, in the sense that disinterestedly contemplating the action causes it. That is a proposition that can be straightforwardly true or false. The point is that, unlike Hutcheson, Hume seems tempted by non-cognitivism when he says such things as "morality is more properly felt than judged of" and that "we do not infer a character to be virtuous, because it pleases," but rather our "judgment" of virtue is itself an expression of our pleasure (Hume 1978: 470, 471).

Reid also offers two further arguments against understanding moral judgments in a subjectivist way. "Suppose ... my friend says, Such *a man did well and worthily; man's conduct is highly approvable*," and then "in relation to the same case ... says, *The man's conduct gave me a very agreeable feeling*." That these two statements mean different things is shown, first, by the fact that the friend's first statement is plainly not about themselves, whereas the second one is. A second "reason these two speeches cannot mean the same thing," Reid writes, is that one can deny the first, but not the second, "without an affront" (Reid 1969: 464–465). It is presumptuous and potentially insulting to deny that a person feels what they say they feel, though it is not to express disagreement with their moral opinions. These arguments work against only analytical or definition forms of subjectivism, and only crude ones at that. More sophisticated versions, like Hutcheson's can avoid them.

To conclude this chapter, we should note some particularly interesting and philosophically important aspects of Reid's claims about justice, especially in the context of his critique of Hume's claim that justice is an artificial virtue. These recall somewhat similar points in Smith and, in some ways, also look backward to Grotius and Pufendorf on sociability, and forward to later developments in Fichte and Hegel, as well as in recent moral philosophy.[13]

Hume's claim that justice is artificial, recall, is that justice requires a rule-structured *practice* that is established by a mutually advantageous "convention" (Hume 1978: 490). Reid concedes that a "conception of the virtue of justice" is impossible until people "have lived some time in society." But he denies that this shows that justice is conventional, since reason itself depends on development and maturation within a social context (Reid 1969: 405). The sense of justice arises simultaneously, he claims, with the capacity for moral judgment in general (406). Moreover, this sense already involves the apprehension of "an obligation to justice, abstracting from the consideration of its utility" (406).

As evidence of these claims, Reid cites the fact that the concepts of *favor* and *injury* come with normal human (social) development, independently of Humean conventions, and that these concepts presuppose those of justice and injustice. The very idea of a favor is of an intentional benefit that goes beyond anything its beneficiary has the standing to expect or demand as their just due. And the notion of an injury is of a harm that violates a norm of justice.[14] It is one thing to see ourselves as benefited or harmed by others, even intentionally, and another to regard another's act as a favor or injury. The latter only makes sense in relation to warranted expectations that Reid collects under the concept of justice. What justice requires and allows, as he puts it, "fills up the middle between these two" (410).

Reid explicitly connects these notions, moreover, to reactive attitudes in the same way Smith does: "A favour naturally produces gratitude. An injury done to ourselves produces resentment; and even when done to another, it produces indignation" (410). Before we have the concepts of favor and injury, we can, of

---

[13] For example, in Darwall 2006, 2013b, 2013c. In what follows I draw from Darwall 2006: 192–200.

[14] Obviously, what Reid means by "injury" is nothing physical or medical, but something that is appropriately resented, as in, "Sir, you do me an injury."

course, be pleased when we are benefited, especially when it is intentional, and displeased when we are harmed. But to have the concept of a favor or injury, we must have some notion of what we can justifiably *expect* or demand from others. Favor and injury thus presuppose a standing to have expectations and make demands of one another and hold each other accountable. "He perceives that injury is done to himself, and that he has a right to redress. … Even the injurious person is conscious of his doing injury; he dreads a just retaliation; and if it be in the power of the injured person, he expects it as due and deserved" (416–417).

Among the most interesting of Reid's criticisms are those he makes of Hume on the obligation to keep promises. Hume's account of promising is notoriously byzantine,[15] and it would take us too far afield to attempt to master all its intricacies. Suffice it to say that although Hume sensibly understands promising to involve the voluntary undertaking of an obligation ("the *willing* of that *obligation*, which arises from the promise"), his moral psychology and virtue ethics require that the obligation be understood via the moral sentiment's role in an individual's psychic economy (Hume 1978: 516–517). Against this, Reid points out that the ideas of promise and its resulting obligation are essentially social, they are *to others*, and, therefore, involve what he calls "social operations of the human mind." Social operations contrast with "solitary" ones in that the former, unlike the latter, "cannot exist without being expressed by words or signs" *to* another person (Reid 1969: 438).

Neither, Reid argues, can the obligation to keep promises depend on the usefulness of a conventional social practice of promising, as Hume supposes is true of the moral obligation to justice generally. Reid anticipates the recent psychology of moral development in arguing that children are capable of understanding, and naturally accept, the basic fairness and reciprocity involved in keeping faith long before they have any conception of its social utility (444).[16]

Reid stresses throughout the necessity of a pre-conventional form of reciprocally recognized mutual obligation and accountability that individuals must already implicitly recognize in order for them to come to have genuine conventional obligations at all. For this point, it does not much matter whether we reserve the words "promise" and "contract" for undertakings that require specific conventional contexts. If we do, then the point will remain that we could not come to have the conventionally established obligations of promise and contract unless we were capable of the pre-conventional second-personal obligations that make conventional obligations generally possible in the first place.

---

[15] Or, as Hume might have put it, "Romish," since he says that promising is "one of the most mysterious and incomprehensible operations that can possibly be imagin'd, and may even be compar'd to *transubstantiation*, or *holy orders*, where a certain form of words, along with a certain intention, changes entirely the nature of an external object, and even of a human creature" (Hume 1978: 524).

[16] See, for example, Engelmann and Tomasello 2019.

Suppose we reserve "promise" for a conventionally defined obligation that is undertaken with tokens of "promise" and its synonyms, and we reserve "contract" for those that require as context the law of contract. So defined, promise and contract will be essentially conventional, and whatever distinctive obligations they carry will depend in some way on their respective conventional contexts. They will depend, as Hume puts it, on a certain *"form of words"* and therefore on the employment of *"symbols* or *signs* instituted" by "the conventions of men" (522). But if Reid is right, these will themselves depend on the possibility of voluntarily undertaking reciprocal obligations that are *not* conventional. It must be possible for individuals to create binding conventions by a kind of agreement that is itself neither conventional (in the usual sense) nor simply a coordination of self-interested conditional intentions, as in Hume's boat-rowing example or in an iterated prisoner's dilemma.

Reid faults Hume for failing to grasp promising's essentially "social," reciprocally recognizing character. Commanding, testifying, requesting, bargaining, and promising are all, Reid argues, irreducibly "social": "They cannot exist without being expressed by words or signs, and known to the other party" (438). It is impossible, moreover, "to resolve" social operations "into any modification or composition of the solitary" (438). It is consequently impossible to understand promising in terms of such "solitary" Humean mental acts as "*willing* [an] obligation" (understanding "obligation" as Hume does) or as the expression of "a *resolution* to perform the promised act" (Hume 1978: 516–518).

Additionally, even if the distinctive forms that contract and promise take in established practices depend on "human invention," these nonetheless presuppose a second-personal sociality that makes conventional practices possible in the first place. Reid makes a similar claim about language. No doubt much of language is conventional also, but without a background of natural, non-conventional dispositions to respond reciprocally, conventional linguistic discourse would be impossible: "[T]his intercourse, in its beginning at least, must be carried on by natural signs, whose meaning is understood by both parties, previous to all compact or agreement" (Reid 1969: 439). "The power which [a human being] has of holding social intercourse with his kind, by asking and refusing, threatening and supplicating, commanding and obeying, testifying and promising," cannot be human invention, but must rather be a distinctive "part of our constitution, like the powers of seeing and hearing" (439).

Contemporary epistemological discussion has drawn from related Reidian claims about *testimony* (Coady 1992; Burge 1993; Moran 2005). Reid argues that our practices of reason-giving cannot get off the ground unless we are disposed to give others authority in theoretical reasoning. We must treat their testimony as providing reasons for belief in addition to any that others themselves offer in support of what they say. As Pettit and Smith argue, when we conduct serious "conversation of an intellectual kind," we must impute to one another the authority to give us reasons to believe things (Pettit and Smith 1996: 430–431).

Reid notes that "as soon as they are capable of understanding declarations," children "are led by their constitution to rely upon them." And "[t]hey are no less led by constitution to veracity and candour, on their own part" (Reid 1969: 444). Were children not naturally disposed to trust what they are told and to avow candidly their own beliefs, it is difficult to see how they could possibly be inducted into practices of theoretical reason-giving or even learn a language.

Reid argues that the analogous points must hold also with practical trustworthiness. Fidelity must be the natural default in the practical realm no less than in the theoretical. Children naturally trust others' assurances about their future actions no less than what they say about other matters (444). It would be impossible, moreover, for us to make agreements, promises, and contracts, unless we already took ourselves to be accountable to one another and accorded each other the authority to undertake these distinctive obligations. Violations of agreements or promises do not simply give the lie to declarations of future actions, of course. They are distinct forms of injustice with their own characteristic remedies. If I agree or promise to do something, then I am obligated to make that happen in a way I am not normally obligated to make what I assert true. I am obligated only to assert what is true, or what I believe to be true.

Again, it doesn't matter if we reserve "promise" and "contract" for distinctive conventionally defined methods of voluntarily undertaken reciprocal recognized obligations. Reid's point is that such conventional obligations will be possible only if we can presuppose an authority to make claims of one another and undertake voluntary obligations at all that does not itself depend upon antecedent conventions. We can hear in Reid's words echoes of Smith on exchange:

> One boy has a top, another a scourge; says the first to the other, if you will lend me your scourge as long as I can keep up my top with it, you shall next have the top as long as you can keep it up. Agreed, says the other. This is a contract perfectly understood by both parties, though they never heard of the definition given by Ulpian or by Titius. And each of them knows, that he is injured if the other breaks the bargain, and that he does wrong if he breaks it himself (437).

Like Smith, Reid thus brings mutual accountability, and reactive attitudes as their medium, directly into his account of justice. And, even more than Smith, he stresses the idea of a distinctive "social" authority that justice presupposes, most obviously in the case of mutually undertaken obligations through promise and contract. This gives what Grotius and Pufendorf called "sociability" an essential role in an adequate philosophical theory of justice. And it suggests the possibility that deontic morality itself, with its conceptual connection to accountability, cannot be adequately accounted for except in some such terms.[17]

---

[17] As I argue in Darwall 2006, 2013b, 2013c.

8

Rousseau and Kant

No philosopher is more strongly associated with deontological ethics or is a more canonical modern moral philosopher than Immanuel Kant (1724–1804).[1] In this chapter, we focus on Kant, though we begin, after a brief introduction of Kant and his historico-philosophical significance, with some discussion of Rousseau. Jean Jacques Rousseau (1712–1778) is best known as a political philosopher, but there are elements of his thought that have great importance for moral philosophy and its history and, especially, for Kant. Kant credits Rousseau as the source of his signature claim of the equal dignity of rational persons. And Rousseau's conception of political society as an "association" that "defend[s] and protect[s] the person and goods of each associate with the full common force," but where each "nevertheless obey[s] only himself," has obvious resonances with Kant's "kingdom of ends" in which all are governed by self-legislated law (Rousseau 2003: 49–50; Kant 1996a: 4:433). At the same time, Rousseau offers important points of contrast to Kant. Whereas Rousseau's emphasis is essentially social and political, Kant will attempt to argue for morality as a common law binding all agents that is grounded in practical reason alone. Rousseau, by contrast, points toward an alternative grounding in sociability that is reminiscent more of Grotius, Pufendorf, Smith, and Reid. We will consider this in more detail presently. First, however, let's set the stage for Kant.

Bernard Williams calls Kant "the philosopher who has given the purest, deepest, and most thorough representation of morality" (Williams 1985: 174). Williams's famous critique of the "morality system," whose "special significance in modern Western culture" he decries, largely targets Kant (1985: 6). The aspects on which Williams focuses are mainly the deontic features emphasized also by the British rationalists, namely, that morality comprises a set of deontic norms that universally bind all (and any possible) moral agents; that moral agency involves the rational capacity for free self-determination by these norms; and that moral virtue consists in the excellent exercise of this capacity in conscientious conduct.

---

[1] "If any philosopher is regarded as central to deontological moral theories, it is surely Immanuel Kant" (Alexander and Moore 2016).

As we saw, what underlay the British rationalists' account of free rational agency was their acceptance of the Suárezian conceptual connection between deontic morality and accountability. Moral agents can intelligibly be held accountable for compliance with deontic moral norms only if they have the capacity to hold themselves accountable in their own practical reasoning. The rationalists identified this capacity with reason and held it to include conscience, in Butler's narrower, distinctively moral sense.[2]

Notoriously, the rationalists provided no account of how reason includes conscience, but they made no apologies for this, since they thought any attempt to provide such an account would risk reducing ethics to psychology. This brings us to Kant.

Kant is a profoundly systematic thinker, so it is possible fully to grasp his moral thought only if we appreciate it within the context of his "Copernican revolution" and "critical philosophy" more generally. It is here that we find the deepest motivations for his Copernican turn in practical and moral philosophy, as against more "dogmatic" forms of rationalism represented by the British rationalists and, for Kant himself, by Leibniz and Christian Wolff (1679–1754). Kant held that just as theoretical philosophy, including natural philosophy and metaphysics of nature, is impossible without a prior "critique of pure [theoretical] reason," so also does moral philosophy require a critique of practical reason.

This is what prior rationalist moral philosophers failed to provide, according to Kant. Even when, like Cudworth and Price, they appreciated the incapacity of empiricist and sentimentalist accounts to explain fundamental concepts, like universality and necessity, and saw, as well, that theoretical and practical reason must be "active" faculties unlike any "passive" reception of sense impressions, they provided no systematic account or "critique" of reason's powers in which a proper theoretical or practical philosophy might adequately be situated.

From Kant's perspective, this was a failure in both theoretical and practical philosophy. Rationalist theoretical philosophers, like Leibniz and Wolff, failed to see that the powers of theoretical reason are limited by possible experience and the transcendental conditions of its possibility. Rationalist attempts to extend theoretical knowledge beyond these bounds and maintain, for example, a doctrine of universal causation, can always be countered by equally good arguments for the contrary position. Uncritical theoretical rationalisms unavoidably encounter "paralogisms" and "antinomies" of "pure reason" (Kant 1998).

Kant thought that this problem was compounded in practical or moral philosophy. Theoretical cognition is, by its nature, *of objects*. Although "[g]eneral logic abstracts ... from any relation of [cognition] to the object, and considers

---

[2] See the distinction made in Chapter 6 between Butlerian conscience in a narrow sense tied to deontic morality and the "principle of reflection" as a broader capacity of practical reason.

only ... the form of thinking in general," the "transcendental logic" from which the "categories" of empirical cognition are drawn necessarily concerns "rules of the pure thinking *of an object*" (1998: A55/B79–80, 102, emphasis added). Moreover, any object of human cognition must be experienced as "given" in space and time.

But whereas Kant famously holds that pure theoretical thought involving only "the form of thinking," without some content or putative object, is "empty," he maintains that the fundamental concepts of practical thought "have as their basis the *form of a pure will* as given within reason and therefore within the thinking faculty itself," irrespective of the will or practical thought's objects (1998: A51/B75; 1996b: 5:66). Kant calls the fundamental concepts of practical thought "categories of freedom." And he defines the "positive concept of freedom" that is realized in pure practical reason, which he calls "*autonomy*," as "the property of the will by which it is a law to itself (independently of any property of the objects of volition)" (1996a: 4:440, 446; 1996b: 5:65).

It follows that what Kant calls "practical law" and (under human conditions, as we shall see) "moral law," must be able to be grounded in a "formal principle" of the "pure will," or, as he also calls it, "pure practical reason" (1996b: 5:21–28). "If a rational being is to think of his maxims as practical universal laws, he can think of them only as principles that contain the determining ground of the will not by their matter," but through their form (5:27).

In the *Critique of Practical Reason*, Kant's argument is carried by a distinction between "material" and "formal" principles, where material principles are grounded empirically in inclination and formal principles are not. Kant's rationalist opponents agree that nothing that is empirically given can ground fundamental practical or moral norms. Rationalist principles would count as formal by Kant's definition in the second *Critique*. It seems clear in the *Groundwork*, however, that Kant intends his fundamental argument to cut more deeply. The difference between autonomy and heteronomy, which ultimately coincides with Kant's distinction between formal and material principles as well as that between categorical and hypothetical imperatives, is between principles of action that can be grounded entirely in the *form* of the will and those that cannot, that is, whether any content or object is provided by inclination *or* by "representations of reason" (1996a: 4:441). It is worth quoting what he says there at length.

> If the will seeks the law that is to determine it *anywhere else* than in the fitness of its maxims for its own giving of universal law—consequently if, in going beyond itself, it seeks this law in a property of any of its objects—*heteronomy* always results. The will in that case does not give itself the law; instead the object, by means of its relation to the will, gives the law to it. This relation, whether it rests upon inclination or upon representations of reason, lets only hypothetical imperatives become possible (4: 441).

This is only the briefest presentation of Kant's argument, which we will need to analyze at greater length. I present it briefly now to give some indication of how Kant's ethical rationalism differs from that of the British rationalists. By Kant's lights, all prior rationalists are "dogmatic," in the sense he outlines in the *Critique of Pure Reason* of attempting to "ge[t] on solely with pure cognition from (philosophical) concepts according to principles, which reason has been using for a long time without first inquiring in what way and by what right it has obtained them" (1998: Bxxxv). Prior rationalists proceeded *uncritically*. Had they pursued a proper critique of practical reason, Kant thinks, they would have seen that moral laws can be grounded only in the *form* of the will or autonomy, again, "the property of the will by which it is a law to itself (independently of any property of the objects of volition)" (1996a: 4:440).

Autonomy in this defined sense is only one of the things Kant means by "freedom." It is this autonomy he has in mind when he refers to practical laws as "laws of freedom," in contrast to the "laws of nature" that structure the objects of theoretical cognition, and when he calls the fundamental concepts of practical thought "categories of freedom" (1996a: 4:387; 1996b: 5:65). But this is far from the only sense of "freedom" featuring prominently in his thought. Another is "freedom of choice" (*Willkür*) – the "faculty to *do or refrain from doing as one pleases*" – which contrasts with pure practical reason or autonomy (*Wille*) and is exercised when agents determine themselves by self-given law (1996c: 6:213).

A third is an essentially *inter*personal sense, that in which one person can restrict or violate another person's freedom. This is the sense primarily in play in *The Doctrine of Right*, for example, in the Universal Principle of Right: "Any action is *right* if it can coexist with everyone's freedom in accordance with a universal law" (6:230). The freedom to which all persons are entitled is "external" freedom or "freedom in the *external* use of choice" (6:214). Freedom of choice is internal to the agent, whereas external freedom concerns our capacity actually to bring about what we choose, or would choose, to accomplish in the world; it concerns matters external to the agent.

In the Preface to the *Critique of Practical Reason*, Kant says that "the concept of freedom ... constitutes the *keystone* of the whole structure of a system of pure reason, even of speculative reason" (1996b: 5:3–4). "Freedom" here is akin to autonomy, the will's capacity to be a law to itself and, equivalently, Kant maintains, to be bound and to bind itself by the moral law. His argument in the second *Critique* is that we cannot avoid concluding that we are free in this sense because we are inescapably aware of being bound by the moral law ("the fact of freedom"), and that we could be so bound only if we are free: "freedom is real, for this idea reveals itself through the moral law" (5:4). Freedom in this sense is the linchpin of Kant's whole critical philosophy.

Our focus is Kant's moral philosophy, understood broadly to include his philosophy of right. So, in addition to appreciating autonomy's fundamental role in Kant's critical practical philosophy, we shall need to understand how this sense of "freedom" relates to the other senses – "freedom of choice" and "external freedom" – in Kant's systematic moral theories, including his theories of virtue and right in the *Metaphysics of Morals*.[3]

We should bear in mind throughout that the connection between deontic morality and accountability is an important source of the accounts of free moral agency in philosophers like Clarke, Price, and Reid. Only self-determining moral agents can, they thought, be intelligibly held accountable. This turns out to be much less clear with Kant. I shall be arguing that although some of Kant's arguments borrow plausibility from this idea, it does not, indeed it cannot, play any fundamental role in his thought. The reason is that for Kant, the distinctively deontic aspects of morality – in his terms, morality itself strictly so called – turn out not to be intrinsic to practical reason at all. They are normatively epiphenomenal features of the finite human perspective that can play a deliberative role only from that point of view and not from the standpoint of practical reason itself. In contemporary parlance, these deontic aspects neither create nor respond to any additional normative reasons. Even so, I shall argue, Kant's argument for freedom in the second *Critique* trades on accountability-related features of deontic morality. Ultimately, Kant's philosophical case for autonomy must rest on overall systematic considerations of transcendental idealism and the critical philosophy more generally.

That deontic moral concepts have no place in pure practical reason itself is Kant's view throughout his moral philosophical writings, although it becomes clearest in *The Critique of Practical Reason*: "Pure reason is practical of itself alone and gives (*to the human being*) a universal law which we call the *moral law*" (1996b: 5:31, emphasis added). There what Kant called in the *Groundwork* the Categorical Imperative and termed the "supreme principle of morality," he calls the "Fundamental Law of Pure Practical Reason" (1996a: 4:440; 1996b: 5:30). "The moral law is, in other words, for the will of a perfect being a law of *holiness*, but for the will of every finite rational being a law of *duty*, of moral necessitation and of the determination of his actions through *respect* for this law" (1996b: 5:82).

Morality and, in particular, moral obligation, is unique to finite beings who must restrain their inclinations through self-presented oughts and imperatives that are internal to the (phenomenal) feeling of respect, thereby "necessitating" their compliance not normatively, but by a natural law of *psychology*. Kant understands obligation to be what he calls "necessitation," by which he means a psychological process, mediated by the feeling of respect, through which finite agents overcome inclinations to diverge from practical law – as they see it, moral law – by representing reason's directives as imperatival *commands*. "For

---

[3] Guyer 2006 is especially good on this point.

human beings and all created rational beings moral necessity is necessitation, that is, obligation" (5:81).

It is only from a finite, self-restraining perspective – through the phenomenal feeling of respect – that the deontic moral concepts of ought, obligation, demands, and duty get purchase. They have no deliberative role from the perspective of practical reason itself. This makes moral obligation ultimately a psychological rather than a normative relation in a way that is not unlike what Price objected to in Balguy, Clarke, and sentimentalists like Hutcheson and Hume. We shall return to this aspect of Kant's view later.

Rousseau

It will provide useful context for our investigation of Kant's moral philosophy if we begin with a brief discussion of Rousseau. Central elements of Kant's view seem clearly to come from Rousseau, although Rousseau's theories rely on a grounding of morality that differs profoundly from Kant's in pure practical reason (from a first-person agential perspective). What is fundamental for Rousseau is something more like "sociability" as it operates in the thought of Grotius and Pufendorf. This grounding involves an essentially interpersonal, or second-personal, perspective.

Where Kant and Rousseau agree is on the equal dignity of persons and on a kind of freedom or autonomy that persons can realize when they comply with laws each legislates from a common (first-person plural) point of view. Kant credits Rousseau as having "set [him] straight" about the former. What gives human life the greatest value is not, as Kant had previously thought, admirable pursuits, like the search for "knowledge," that create a hierarchy of value depending on how excellently people pursue them, but something all human beings have in common. From Rousseau, Kant learned not to value the admirable as "constitut[ing] the honor of humanity," but rather to "honor men" themselves, each and every one, as having intrinsic value – Kant's "dignity" – on which basis it is possible to "establish the rights of humanity" (Kant 1904: 20:44). Rousseau thus revealed for Kant the equal dignity of persons, which stands in contrast to what Nietzsche will call the "rank-defining" values recognized in hierarchical orders by honor respect, esteem, and contempt (Nietzsche 2007: 11; Darwall 2013c).

In *Of the Social Contract*, Rousseau says that the fundamental problem of political philosophy is to "find a form of association that will defend and protect the person and goods of each associate with the full common force, and by means of which, each, uniting with all, nevertheless obey only himself and remain as free as before" (Rousseau 2003: 49–50). Rousseau goes on to say that "the social contract provides the solution" to this problem (50). Central to Roussseau's solution is his idea of the "*general will*": "[e]ach of us puts his person *and his full power in common under the supreme direction of the general will"* (50). In contrast with the "will of all" – the aggregate of "private interest[s]" – the general will is essentially public, general, and common in two distinct senses (60). Both the will's form and its content or object are general.

The will is formed from a shared, first-person plural perspective – it is what *we* will – and its object is never something particular, but always something universal or general (67). Only if these two conditions are met can what is willed be validated as *law*. Since the perspective of the general will is one that anyone who is subject to it can share (as a member of the association whose will it is), those who are required to comply with it end up "obey[ing] [themselves]" and are not simply subjected to external force.

Kant's treatment of the moral law and its relation to the kingdom of ends has the same structure, as we shall see. This is a second thing Kant gets from Rousseau. The perspective from which moral agents must be able to will the principles (maxims) of their wills, Kant says, is one in which they "abstract from … all the content of their private ends," therefore arriving at "common laws" in a "kingdom of ends" (Kant 1996a: 4:433). This means that moral persons are subject to laws that can issue from a "general will" in both of Rousseau's senses – from a shared general perspective and concerning matters of general principle rather than issues involving any individuals in particular.

Kant also gets from Rousseau the idea that in governing themselves by laws that can be grounded in this way, persons realize a kind of freedom or autonomy that differs from natural liberty or independence. In a state of nature, outside of a social contract, all persons equally share a "natural independence," which "common freedom is a consequence of man's nature" (Rousseau 2003: 42, 63). "[A]s soon as he has reached the age of reason, he is the sole judge of the means proper to preserve himself, he becomes his own master" (42). Every rational agent, consequently, has a claim right to autonomy to make their own decisions. But the kind of autonomy to which one can claim a right differs fundamentally from the kind that is realized by the social contract, what Rousseau calls "moral freedom." It is this moral freedom that is conceptually related to yet a third kind of freedom that Kant calls "autonomy."[4]

We can see the relations between these three different things that "autonomy" can mean by considering what Rousseau says about mastery and slavery. *The Social Contract* begins with this famous passage:

> Man is born free, and everywhere he is in chains. One believes himself the others' master, and yet is more a slave than he. How did this change come about? I do not know. What can make it legitimate? I believe I can solve this question (41).

---

[4] For the relations between these, see Darwall 2013g.

The freedom with which we are born is natural liberty or independence, the "common freedom" consisting in the claim right to be our "own master[s]" (42). Any attempt to usurp this freedom is therefore illegitimate. The only way this freedom can legitimately be constrained is by an individual's consent (through their private will) *or* by the general will (as it involves the individual's will as an equal member). Those who attempt to master others in slavery violate this "common freedom" without either legitimate consent or authorization from the general will.[5]

But what does Rousseau mean by saying that anyone who believes themselves an "others' master ... is more a slave than they" (41)? Even masters have the same right to autonomy, that is, natural independence or "common freedom," as those they seek to enslave. Rousseau does not appear here to be saying that they thereby forfeit that right. In what sense, then, do masters make themselves "more a slave"? The obvious answer is that they fail to obey themselves in the sense that those who govern themselves by the general will do. They therefore fail to realize autonomy as something that can be *achieved*. This is the same general sense of "autonomy" that philosophers have in mind when they talk about someone succeeding in governing themselves by their own values or moral principles. In Kant's terms, it consists in a moral agent's succeeding in following self-legislated law.

For Kant, this will bring yet a third kind of autonomy into play that Rousseau does not discuss: "autonomy of the will," that is, "the property of the will by which it is a law to itself (independently of any property of the objects of volition)" (Kant 1996a: 4:440). It is no understatement to say that autonomy in this sense is the linchpin of Kant's whole moral philosophy. The very possibility of morality, he thinks, depends upon autonomy of the will, which Kant ties to pure practical reason. The will instantiates autonomy if, and only if, it is practical reason. There is, therefore, practical reason only if the will has autonomy.

In the *Groundwork*, Kant attempts to show that autonomy in this sense is an inescapable presupposition of practical reasoning from the agent's (first-person) standpoint. As we shall see, however, it is doubtful that any such argument can succeed, as Kant himself seems to have appreciated when he wrote the *Critique of Practical Reason*.[6] Rousseau has no systematic moral philosophy, so he does not himself take a stand on this issue. He is, however, an acute observer and theorist of moral psychology. There are in his writings both an insightful appreciation of the complexity of our social nature and an implicit distinction between what Kant, following him, calls "unsociable sociability" and sociable sociability. It is a distinction that points to the possibility of a grounding of

---

[5] To justify this claim, Rousseau gives a classic argument against the possibility of individuals consenting to their own slavery on the grounds that any such attempt would be nullified by the fact that persons cannot renounce or alienate their own "quality as man" (45).

[6] See the discussion of the *Critique of Practical Reason* below.

morality (and, indeed, of autonomy of the *sociable* will) that is like the one we found in Grotius (Kant 2009: 13).

The central Rousseauean theme here is the distinction between what Rousseau calls *amour propre*, on the one hand, and sociability of the kind that makes morality and egalitarian politics possible, on the other. Rousseau introduces *amour propre* in *The Second Discourse on the Origin of Inequality*, published in 1754, eight years before *The Social Contract* (Rousseau 2019). There Rousseau notes the difference between two kinds of self-love: *amour de soi* and *amour propre*.[7] *Amour de soi* is the drive for self-preservation and other goods for the self that we have in common with the rest of the animal kingdom independently of society. *Amour propre*, on the other hand, is essentially social. It is only in societies that human beings begin to look at each other and take an interest in how they are looked at or regarded. This interest in others' (and one's own) esteem is what Rousseau means by "*amour propre*" (218). "Vanity," as it is sometimes translated, shows itself in a whole host of competitive and invidious syndromes that Rousseau contrasts with sociability among equals, as in morality and the social contract. To form a general will, members of a society must relate to one another as members and see one another as having a standing to participate independently of how they regard one another in terms of esteem or contempt.

In a famous passage from *Idea for a Universal History with a Cosmopolitan Aim*, Kant takes special note of the distinction between what he calls the "*unsociable sociability*" created by amour propre and the sociable sociability necessary for egalitarian society (Kant 2009: 13–14). Human beings naturally have a "propensity to enter into society, … combined with a thoroughgoing resistance that constantly threatens to break up this society." The "unsociable" aspect involves *amour propre*, including "spiteful competitive vanity" (14). Kant's point in the passage, however, is not to decry the threat that unsociable sociability poses to sociable sociability. It is rather to analyze the former's historical role in moving humanity from "an arcadian pastoral life of perfect concord, contentment and mutual love" that, however desirable in itself, would ultimately leave humanity impotent to achieve history's "cosmopolitan aim." Without competitive, rivalrous instincts, though human beings would be "as good natured as the sheep they ten[d]," human life would have no "greater worth than that of their domesticated beasts …, [and] humanity would eternally slumber undeveloped" (14).

All these themes are in Rousseau. In the second *Discourse*, Rousseau says that it is *amour propre* that allows "all our faculties [to be] developed," and "reason [to] become active" (Rousseau 2019: 170). Rousseau also notes that mutual love or "pity" characterizes humanity's natural pre-social state as it does those of

---

[7] For an excellent analysis, see Neuhouser 2008.

other animals (152). And Rousseau draws a contrast, as does Kant, between pity-motivated, loving conduct, on the one hand, and action that realizes what Rousseau calls "moral freedom" and Kant calls "moral worth," on the other (Kant 1996a: 4:398). Finally, Rousseau maintains, as Kant will also, that moral freedom consists in guiding oneself by a law that one wills for oneself from a shared perspective as an equal person, which requires equal respect for all.

The crucial difference between Rousseau and Kant resides in the transcendental ambitions of Kant's critical philosophy. Kant bids to ground morality in inescapable presuppositions of pure practical reason. Rousseau has no such ambitions; his aim is to solve the basic problem of political philosophy. His solution – grounding political legitimacy and obligation in a shared human capacity for sociable "moral freedom" – points the way toward a similar grounding for morality of the kind we encountered first in Grotius.

Kant: *Groundwork I*

Now to Kant. We begin with Kant's signature work, *The Groundwork of the Metaphysics of Morals*, published in 1785. Deontic morality's conceptual features are implicated in Kant's thought right from the outset. After distinguishing between the "laws of nature" and "laws of freedom" and their respective "sciences" – "physics" and "ethics" – Kant turns to a brief statement of the need for "a pure moral philosophy, completely cleansed of everything that may be only empirical" (4:388–389).

> For, that there must be such a philosophy is clear of itself from the common idea of duty and of moral laws. Everyone must grant that a law, if it is to hold morally, that is, as a ground of an obligation, must carry with it absolute necessity (4: 389).

"[T]he command 'thou shalt not lie'," he adds, "does not hold only for human beings, as if other rational beings did not have to heed it" (4:389).[8] This example may seem to presuppose Kant's notorious absolutism about lying, but all Kant's readers need grant is that in a case where it is agreed that it would be wrong for human beings to lie, it would be wrong also for any rational agent to, absent some distinguishing feature that would affect the wrongness of lying were that feature present in the human case.

All Kant needs for his illustration is that moral laws purport to hold in general for any being who has the capacity to be bound by them – for any rational agent (assuming for the moment that rational agency is necessary and sufficient for moral agency) – and that what moral laws dictate, they prescribe for any rational being who happens to be in the relevant situation. It will then

---

[8] Though, again, any such duty or command can apply only to finite rational agents.

follow "from the common idea of duty" that deontic moral truths, if they hold at all, necessarily hold universally for any possible rational agent (4:389).[9] And that will show that the foundations of morality must be *a priori*. (At this point, Kant is evidently assuming, like the rationalists, that rational agency is both necessary and sufficient for moral agency, though he will later revise that position, distinguishing between practical and moral laws, with moral laws holding only for finite rational agents like human beings and practical laws holding for all possible rational beings.)

The *Groundwork*'s project, Kant tells us, "is ... nothing more than the search for and establishment of the *supreme principle of morality*" (4:392). This, of course, is the Categorical Imperative (CI), which Kant formulates in different but, he argues, equivalent ways. Kant ends the *Preface* with an outline of the *Groundwork*'s method, which brings out the centrality of deontic morality to the book's structure.

Sections I and II are to proceed analytically by drawing out the consequences of what Kant hopes will seem like uncontroversial truisms about morality (4:392). At this point, Kant will simply be "explicating the generally received concept of morality" (4:445). By analyzing the concepts of morality – moral duty and moral goodness – and relying only on what is truistic concerning them, Kant believes he can show that the CI in its various formulations follows. Most importantly, by the end of Section II, Kant takes himself to have shown that if these truistic assumptions hold, then "[a]utonomy of the will," the will's being a law to itself "independently of any property of the objects of volition," follows as a consequence, and *vice versa* (4:440).

Kant is careful to point out, however, that no such analytical argument can establish that *any* of these assumptions and, hence, their consequences, actually holds. It is consistent with the soundness of his analytical arguments in Sections I and II that all of the ideas that he has argued stand together also all fall together and that deontic moral concepts turn out to be "chimerical idea[s] without any truth" (4:445). This is the functional equivalent in Kant's moral works of the challenges to morality posed by Grotius's Carneades, Hobbes's "foole," and Hume's "sensible knave," although it is not put in explicitly egoistic terms.[10] No analytical argument can establish morality's fundamental normative claims or its necessary presuppositions. That, Kant says, "requires a possible *synthetic use of pure practical reason*," and the only way of showing that is possible is by "a *critique* of [the practical] rational faculty itself" – a critique of practical reason, which Kant attempts in a first version in Section III of the *Groundwork* and pursues more systematically in the second *Critique* (4:445; 5:3–163).

---

[9] Kant's position seems to be that The Fundamental Law of Pure Practical Reason and the Categorical Imperative (the moral law) have the very same contents and so call for the same acts, but their prescriptions create duties or obligations only for finite rational agents.

[10] Discussed in Chapters 1, 2, and 6, respectively.

We can put Kant's point and plan in terms of what Allison calls the "reciprocity thesis," namely, that morality and the CI hold if and only if autonomy of the will does (Allison 1990: 201–213). This is what Kant's arguments in *Groundwork I* and *II* are supposed to establish. But these analytical arguments are insufficient to show that any of the key deontic moral ideas is not "chimerical." Establishing that requires a critique of practical reason. The critical strategy Kant pursues in *Groundwork III* differs substantially from his argument in the second *Critique*. In *Groundwork III*, Kant attempts to show that autonomy is an inescapable presupposition of deliberative practical rationality quite generally. From there, he can deduce the equivalent moral concepts and platitudes as consequences. In presupposing autonomy, deliberating agents are committed to morality. In the second *Critique*, however, Kant pursues something like the reverse strategy. He argues that awareness of being bound by the moral law is, if not a presupposition of any rational action (we will see why he cannot think that), nonetheless an undeniable feature of human practical consciousness. "Consciousness of [the] fundamental law" is, Kant says, "a fact of reason." Implicit in that consciousness is the realization that we can determine ourselves by the moral law, that our will has the property of autonomy (1996b: 5:30–31).

Kant's view that deontic moral concepts can have no place from the perspective of pure practical reason vastly complicates this second argument, since its plausibility trades, I shall argue, on accountability-related features of deontic morality. It is hard to see, therefore, how someone who accepts Kant's view of the normative epiphenomenality of deontic morality should be convinced that the fact that we must assume we are free when we are aware of being morally bound from the human perspective can show that we really are free, that autonomy of the will really holds. If Kant's argument in *Groundwork III* works, and autonomy really is an inescapable presupposition of practical reason, this would solve his problem. But Kant probably ended up thinking it does not, and, as we shall see, he was ultimately right to think it doesn't.

We turn now to a more careful laying out of Kant's analytical arguments, first in *Groundwork I*. Section I begins with Kant's famous claims about the unique goodness "without limitation" of a "good will" and his related claims about the moral worth of actions that express goodness of will – as he argues, actions that do not simply accord with duty but that are also done "from duty." These conclude with a short argument for morality's "supreme principle," CI, in its "universal law" formulation (FUL): "*I ought never to act except in such a way that I could also will that my maxim should become a universal law*" (1996a: 4:402).[11]

---

[11] I take the following abbreviations from Wood 1999: FUL (Formula of Universal Law), FLN (Formula of the Law of Nature), FH (Formula of Humanity as End-in-Itself), FA (Formula of Autonomy), FKE (Formula of the Kingdom of Ends).

It is worth analyzing Kant's claims and arguments in some detail in order to bring out both the ways in which Kant relies on familiar features of deontic morality to carry his arguments *and* how his understanding of moral obligation as a psychological process ("necessitation") – one through which finite human agents represent to themselves morality's distinctive deontic aspects (oughts, imperatives, and commands) that are normatively epiphenomenal from the perspective of pure practical reason – is essential to comprehending otherwise puzzling aspects of his claims in *Groundwork I*.

We should first get clear about the *kind* of evaluative claim Kant is making when he says that only a good will is "good without limitation" (4:393). Several things make it obvious that the evaluations with which Kant is concerned in *Groundwork I* are internal to (deontic) morality, that Kant is saying that the only thing that is *morally* good without limitation is a good will.

First, Kant tells us that his arguments in the first two sections aim to "explicat[e] the generally received concept of morality" (4:445). Second, it is evident that Kant intends his claims about the unique "moral worth" of actions done "from duty" to be understood as claims about actions that manifest good will, and he puts this also by saying that only such actions are "morally good" (4:390, 397–398). Third, Kant defines moral duty in terms of good will: "the concept of duty ... contains that of a good will though under certain subjective limitations" (4:397). This definition can seem puzzling, since if a good will is a will that acts from duty, how can duty itself be understood in terms of the good will without circularity? The key to unlocking this puzzle, as we shall see, is Kant's doctrine of necessitation, according to which duty is the presentational aspect under which a finite rational agent must represent the practical law in order to determine themselves by it.

Understood as a claim within morality about moral goodness, Kant's claim that the good will is uniquely "good without limitation" is truistic. If morality essentially concerns self-determined compliance with moral laws, then moral goodness can only be excellent moral self-governance, and the moral value of anything else must be reckoned in relation to that. Considered in themselves, there is nothing morally good about the talents of mind, temperament, and gifts of fortune with which Kant contrasts good will, however valuable, even intrinsically, these might be in other ways (4:393).

Kant's claim that the moral worth of actions depends on their being done from duty, and not just in accord with it, appears to follow fairly directly from the unique moral goodness of the good will. We have seen before in Butler and the British rationalists the claim that genuine moral virtue consists uniquely in self-consciously moral self-direction, and all these philosophers agree that that is realized by moral agents exercising the capacity that makes them subject to (deontic) morality in the first place.

Now ethical philosophers of pretty much any stripe can agree with Kant's claim that the prudent shopkeeper of his first example, who charges the same price to everyone, passing up opportunities to take advantage even of "inexperienced customer[s]," but only because honesty is the most expedient policy, does not display virtuous or morally worthy conduct (4:397). One does not have to accept a "modern" conception of deontic morality to agree with that.

It becomes clearest that Kant is relying on a shared deontic moral common sense in his third example, in which one person helps another not out of self-interest but from benevolence or sympathy (4:398). Kant actually describes the example in terms that suggest that the person's motive is ultimately self-serving, since he depicts the agent as "tak[ing] delight in the satisfaction of others so far as it is their own work" (4:398). His example would be cleaner if the person were motivated simply by care or benevolent concern focused entirely on another person and their welfare, being concerned to help them only if it is good for them. We do better to think about such a case.

Why, we might then ask, is Hutcheson not right that benevolent motivation is morally good irrespective of whether the agent is moved by duty? Kant says that the good will is (morally) good in itself, not in virtue either of "what it effects" or even "its fitness to attain some proposed end, but only because of its volition," because of its "maxim" or the "principle" that the agent actually acts on (4:394, 397–398). But Hutcheson agrees with that. The disposition to aid people simply because it will benefit them, he thinks, is morally good in itself, regardless of what benevolent action actually accomplishes. This, again, is a key difference between him and Hume. What can Kant say to a Hutchesonian reader of his (revised) third example?

It is instructive to compare Kant's praise of the good will at the beginning of *Groundwork I* to the famous passage about charity or love from Paul's *First Letter to the Corinthians*. About the good will, Kant says that "like a jewel, it would shine by itself," even if "by a special disfavor of fortune" it had no power to bring about good effects (4:394). Paul says something similar about love: "though I bestow all my goods to feed the poor, ... and have not charity [love], it profiteth me nothing" (1 Corinthians 13:3). Kant, Hutcheson, and Paul can all agree that the goodness with which they are all concerned is intrinsic to the agent's motivation or will.

Their disagreement concerns a fundamental difference in ethical conceptions. In the background of Kant's claims is obviously a deontic moral conception, which he evidently assumes his readers will share when they fully think things through. From the perspective of deontic morality, the problem with benevolent concern or love is that what it moves us to do can conflict with what we are morally obligated to do. This is a point on which Butler and the British rationalists insist. It is most obviously true when love is focused on the good of individuals or specific groups, but it is also true of Hutcheson's most favored moral motive, universal or "calm extensive benevolence," which aims at the greatest overall or "public good." Morality may sometimes require agents to forego promoting that also, if, for example, doing so is incompatible with justice. Indeed, even if act utilitarianism is correct, the concept of moral right is clearly different from that of optimally beneficent conduct.

The modern deontic conception of morality holds, moreover, that moral agents are accountable for complying with moral obligations and, therefore, that they should *hold themselves* to doing what is right and avoiding wrongdoing. Even if, consequently, moral agents' best attempts to hold themselves to deontic moral standards and do what is right were to lead them astray in a particular case – indeed, even if it were likelier to do so than their being motivated by benevolence – that would be irrelevant to their moral goodness. According to deontic morality, the question of an agent's goodness entirely concerns how excellently they exercise the capacity that makes them subject to morality and capable of being morally obligated in the first place.[12]

To see the point from a different perspective, recall Balguy's query that were we "void of *natural Compassion*, as well as *Benevolence*; might we not possibly be induced to attempt the Relief of a Person in Distress, merely from the *Reason* of the Thing, and the *Rectitude* of the Action?" (Balguy 1976: 12). If conscience or rational agency is sufficient to make one an accountable moral agent, there could be moral agents completely lacking benevolence. If, consequently, benevolence were itself a source of moral worth, there would be possible moral agents who completely lack the capacity for a form of moral goodness. From the perspective of deontic morality that is an absurd consequence.

It should be clear by this point that Kant's claims in the first half of *Groundwork I* borrow plausibility from an assumed deontic conception of morality. What I want now to show is that implicit also in this beginning part of the *Groundwork* is Kant's view of obligation as "necessitation," which ultimately makes deontic moral concepts and standards normatively epiphenomenal from the perspective of pure practical reason. Obviously, the British rationalists shared no part of this view of morality.

The point arises in two things Kant says in *Groundwork I* about the concept of duty. I have already mentioned the first, namely, Kant's remark that the idea of duty "contains that of a good will though under certain subjective limitations and hindrances" (Kant 1996a: 4:397). This already seems puzzling, since if a good will is moved by the thought that an act is a duty, it would seem that the idea of duty would have to be defined independently of the will. A similarly puzzling passage is what Kant calls "the third proposition," which occurs after his claims about the good will and the moral worth of actions from duty, and which he says follows from them: "*duty is the necessity of an action from respect for law*" (4:400). This also is puzzling. We might have thought that being a duty

---

[12] Irwin seems implicitly to be making this point in Irwin 2009: 26–27.

was a distinctive normative status – being required or called for by law – being, that is, necessary in a normative sense. What could Kant mean by the necessity of an action from *respect* for law? Respect and motivation by respect are psychological phenomena. What can they have to do with an action's being necessary in any normative sense?

The answer is that they do not, on Kant's view. We shall have to await a full discussion of the role of respect in Kant's moral psychology in the second *Critique* to see how this is supposed to work in detail. But we can already see that what Kant is implicitly referring to is what he calls "necessitation," a process that takes place in finite rational agents (in the "phenomenal world," as he calls in in the first *Critique* (Kant 1998: A273)). Through it, from the feeling of respect, they restrain inclinations contrary to practical reason's dictates and determine themselves to accord with those dictates by representing them as deontic laws. Those laws obligate them through what Kant calls a "command (of reason)" (4:413). Respect is a feeling that is the phenomenal cause (event cause in the phenomenal world) of the morally worthy actions that on the noumenal level moral agents cause themselves through pure practical reason. Respect works by representing practical reason's dictates in distinctively deontic imperatival terms.

The point here is that Kant takes deontic moral ideas, like duty, to be concepts whose function is to mediate this process. As he puts it in the *Metaphysics of Morals*, "[t]he very *concept of duty* is already the concept of a *necessitation* (constraint) of free choice through the law" (1996c: 6:379).[13] Similarly, in *Groundwork II*:

> The representation of an objective principle, insofar as it is necessitating for a will, is called a command (of reason), and the formula of the command is called an **imperative**.
>
> All imperatives are expressed by an *ought* and indicate by this the relation of an objective law of reason to a will that by its subjective constitution is not necessarily determined by it (a necessitation). They say that to do or to omit something would be good, but they say it to a will that does not always do something just because it is represented to it that it would be good to do that thing (1996a: 4:413).

The deontic notions of ought, obligation, duty, demands (commands), and imperatives are all defined, for Kant, in relation to "necessitation," thus always only in relation to finite, imperfect rational agents. Whereas perfect rational

---

[13] "Such a constraint, therefore, does not apply to rational beings as such (there could also be *holy* ones) but rather to *human beings,* rational *natural* beings, who are unholy enough that pleasure can induce them to break the moral law, even though they recognize its authority; and even when they do obey the law, they do it *reluctantly* (in the face of opposition from their inclinations), and it is in this that such *constraint* properly consists" (6:379).

agents deliberate in terms of the (practically) good – what would be choiceworthy or good to do – the practical thought of finite rational agents must be mediated by deontic moral notions. The latter have no place in pure practical rational thought.

For this reason, deontic moral notions end up being normatively epiphenomenal. The deontic claim that I *ought* or must (am under an imperative) to do something is the same normative claim as that it would be good or best that I do it ("they say that to do or to omit something would be good"), but *as addressed to* someone who does not automatically act for those reasons because they can have inclinations to do otherwise. The obligation gives me no further normative reason to act; all normative reasons are already figured into what makes the act good or best to do, and no additional reasons flow from duty or the ought. We shall return to this matter both in our discussion of Kant on imperatives and the CI and in seeking to understand Kant's view of the role of the feeling of respect.

Having seen now how Kant's claim about the good will and morally worthy (morally good) action in *Groundwork I* are most plausible within an assumed deontic moral framework, and also how what Kant says about the concept of duty has to be understood in terms of his view that deontic moral claims are ultimately normatively epiphenomenal, let us turn to the argument Kant there gives for the universal law formulation of the CI (FUL). The argument, which takes place in a breathtakingly swift two sentences, can be convincing only on the same deontic moral assumptions we needed to see how Kant's claim about the good will could be defended against Hutchesonian or Pauline objections.

Here is Kant's argument:

> But what kind of law can that be, the representation of which must determine the will, even without regard for the effect expected from it, in order for the will to be called good absolutely and without limitation? Since I have deprived the will of every impulse that could arise for it from obeying some law, nothing is left but the conformity of actions as such with universal law, which alone is to serve the will as its principle, that is, *I ought never to act except in such a way that I could also will that my maxim should become a universal law* (4:402).

We begin with the idea of a good will and then ask what must characterize any law by which such a will could be governed. Assume, then, that a good will is (morally) good in virtue of its principle or maxim. Again, someone who thinks that love or benevolence is intrinsically morally good can agree with that. To get the further Kantian claim that moral goodness consists in acting from duty, we must make the further deontic moral assumption that moral agents are accountably subject to morality by virtue of rational capacities that require nothing like love or benevolence, and that moral evaluation concerns how they exercise those capacities.

But is even that sufficient to yield FUL? Is the idea that the good will acts from and not only in accord with duty sufficient to show that duty requires acting only on principles (maxims) that one could will to be a universal law? That depends on how we understand duty and what it means to be moved by it. Begin with Kant's idea of practical law or an "objective law of reason" (4:413). If a law of reason says, "that to do or to omit something would be good," or even that it would be the best or most choiceworthy act, it is hard to see how treating it as a practical law in that sense and being governed by it would commit one to FUL. To see the problem, imagine someone who holds rational egoism as a theory of what it is most rationally choiceworthy to do, and who acts in their own interest only because they think that that is what practical law prescribes. Holding that will commit them to egoism as a universal law, and to thinking that everyone should follow it. But would it commit them to *willing*, or to being able rationally to will, that everyone follow it?[14]

To be clear, we are to imagine not just someone who desires most fundamentally that their interests be promoted and who happens (idly perhaps) to believe that promoting their interests themselves is rational. We need to consider someone who is disposed to promote their interests *only when and because* that is what it is best or most choiceworthy for them, or for anyone in their position, to do, that is, because it is dictated by a practical law in Kant's sense. We should imagine someone, then, who is reluctant to promote their own interests, so that doing so runs against their temperament, and who must restrain their self-denying inclinations to make themselves promote their own interests on principle. Someone can evidently fit this profile without willing or being prepared to will that others act on this principle also. They would have to believe, again, that others should act on this principle. But that would not itself give them any reason to will that others do so. Indeed, to the extent that agents' interests conflict, the principle they would be treating as practical law might dictate willing that others not follow it, or at least not willing that they do so.

If the concept of duty is identified with practical law, or even with the moral law as Kant officially understands that (practical law from a finite human perspective), it seems entirely possible to act from duty in this sense without being committed to FUL. But notice now how much more plausible Kant's argument for FUL is when we bring in the accountability-related aspects of duty as a deontic moral concept. If moral duty is the idea, not just of what agents have most reason to do, or of what it would be best or most choiceworthy for them to do, but of what they are *accountable* for doing through exercising the moral powers that make them thus accountable, then there is an obvious movement of ideas in the direction of FUL. What we are accountable for is only what can justifiably be *demanded* of us. And whatever else a demand involves, it is an

---

[14] On this point, see Aune 1979: 29–30 and Allison 1991.

expression of will. As Strawson points out, the states of mind through which we hold one another and ourselves accountable – blame and self-condemnation or guilt – implicitly make demands (Strawson 1968: 85). If moral duty and obligation are conceptually tied to accountability, then moral wrong is conceptually tied to justified demands and blameworthiness (lacking excuse) (Darwall 2006, 2013a, 2013b).

Imagine now that someone holds and is governed by the belief not just that it is always best for them (as for anyone) to do what is in their interest, but that acting in their own interest is a moral duty for which they and others are to be held accountable. Willing that they act in their own interest on *these* grounds will effectively be to will that the rational agent they happen to be do so. It will be part of holding themselves accountable for their conduct as one moral agent among others. They cannot consistently will on these grounds that they promote their own interest, therefore, unless they are simultaneously prepared to will that others do so as well. So understood, FUL seems something like a moral axiom or principle that is presupposed by the very idea of deontic morality.

It is no surprise, therefore, that principles of reciprocity or the golden rule that are close cousins of FUL are ubiquitous among deontic moral philosophers, including even Hobbes, but more obviously, British rationalists like Clarke, Balguy, and Price. When Balguy argues against Hutcheson that through the rational moral faculty we "might … be induced to attempt the Relief of a Person in Distress, merely from the *Reason* of the Thing, and the *Rectitude* of the Action," he adds: "Might not some such Maxim as that of doing as we would be done unto, offer it self to our Minds, and prevail with us to stretch out a helping hand upon such an occasion" (Balguy 1976: 12–13). Not only does reason effectively direct us to what is right, he thinks. It also enables us to hold ourselves accountable if we do not follow its direction: It "would prompt us to undertake it, and condemn us if we omitted it" (13).

If this is right, some principle of reciprocity like FUL is itself internal to the rational moral capacity that makes moral agents subject to deontic morality. The very idea of deontic morality presupposes that moral agents have what is necessary and sufficient to be subject to morality in the rational capacity to hold themselves and others accountable for compliance with deontic moral norms. This notion underlies both the most plausible version of Kant's claims that moral goodness of will and worth of actions involve the motive of duty *and* his argument for FUL on their basis.

Groundwork II: FUL

Section II of the *Groundwork* continues Kant's analysis of the "generally received concept of morality" (Kant 1996a: 4:445). Its main function is to elaborate and defend the different formulations Kant gives of the CI, which Kant argues are all equivalent to each other and to autonomy of the will. Section II thus establishes the "reciprocity thesis": The will is subject to the moral law, in each of its formulations, if, and only if, the will is autonomous. It is, Kant says, a "[t]ransition" to the synthetic "critique of pure practical reason" – which is necessary to establish that morality is "not a chimerical idea without any truth" – in *Groundwork III* (4:445).

The first formulation of the CI is FUL: "[A]*ct only in accordance with that maxim through which you can at the same time will that it become a universal law*" (4:421). As Guyer points out, Kant's argument for FUL in Section II reprises his argument in Section I, but this time he argues "from the analysis of the concept of a rational being" rather than "from the common-sense notions of good will and duty" (Guyer 2006: 184). In Section II, the argument goes through a connection between rational agency and action on practical norms or laws, Kant's distinction between hypothetical and categorical imperatives, and an analysis of the concept of a categorical imperative. Kant attempts in Section II "to derive [moral laws] from the universal concept of a rational being as such" (Kant 1996a: 4:412). I will claim, however, that Kant's argument can plausibly establish its conclusion only if we read into it the same accountability-related aspects of deontic moral concepts that we saw were necessary to shore up the parallel argument in Section I.

We can begin with a famous passage:

> Everything in nature works in accordance with laws. Only a rational being has the capacity to act *in accordance with the representation* of laws, that is, in accordance with principles, or has a *will*. Since *reason* is required for the derivation of actions from laws, the will is nothing other than practical reason (4:412).

There is an implied contrast here between two kinds of laws: "laws of nature," in accordance with which everything in nature works, and "laws of freedom," *normative* action-guiding principles on which rational agents act. The intuitive point can be put in terms of a distinction between explanatory and normative reasons and a distinctive kind of explanation of action in terms of *agents' reasons*.

If I pick up a rock from the ground to examine it and then drop it to return it to its previous place, there will be explanations of both my and the rock's behavior. My behavior might be explained in many ways, and some of these take the same form that reasons for the rock's behavior do – efficient causal explanations proceeding from prior states of the world. But there is a distinctive kind of explanation of my conduct that is unavailable in the case of the rock, namely, in terms of the reasons *on* or *for* which I acted – *my reasons* for having dropped the rock. Maybe I thought it would be better, for some reason or other, for the rock to be returned to the earth rather than remaining with me. Or maybe I did it simply because I wanted to, not in the sense that my mental state of wanting caused my action (though perhaps that was also true), but in the sense that I took my desire to be a reason for me *to* drop the rock. Whatever it was, my reason for acting will have been something I took to be a (normative) reason *to* drop the rock. Nothing was or could have been the rock's reason in this sense for falling. Only rational agents have *their* reasons (agents' reasons) for what they do, where those are considerations they themselves take to be normative reasons *for* them *to* act as they do (Darwall 1983: 30–31).

An agent's reasons in this sense are near enough to what Kant calls the "subjective principle" or "maxim" of an agent's will (Kant 1996a: 4:401n). The crucial point is the connection Kant draws between acting "in accordance with principles" and acting "in accordance with the representation of laws," where "laws" are not natural explanatory laws but the normative practical "laws of freedom" with which Kant contrasts explanatory laws. Maxims or principles in this sense are not themselves states of an agent's psychology, motivating "springs of action" in the early modern sense; they are rather considerations that can be formulated and acted upon, though of course an agent's doing so itself involves their psychology and motivational states.

Kant's thought is that to act on a principle in this sense is to act on something one represents as a universal norm that holds, at the most fundamental level, for any rational agent: a "practical law." In letting go of the rock for the reason that I do, I am committed to thinking that any rational agent would have a similar reason in similar circumstances. If my reason is that I simply want to let go of the rock, then I must grant that any rational agent would similarly have such a reason to do what they want. Or if I thought that the reason was that a disturbed part of nature should be returned to its undisturbed state, then I should think that all rational agents have reason to act according to this same principle. Whenever rational agents act, Kant is saying, they are committed to accepting some universal practical law by their action.

Having made this point, Kant turns to a brief discussion of *necessitation* in anticipation of distinguishing between hypothetical and categorical imperatives and, ultimately, giving his parallel derivation of FUL from the very idea of a categorical imperative and the "concept of a rational being as such" (4:412). If a being is perfectly rational in the sense that "reason infallibly determines the will," Kant says, then its actions "that are cognized as objectively necessary," that is, as fulfilling practical law, "are also subjectively necessary," in the sense that the action happens by what Kant calls an "inner necessity" of the agent's perfect rational nature (1996a: 4:412; 1996c: 6:222).[15] Perfectly rational beings invariably do (by a kind of nomological or natural necessity) whatever "reason independently of inclination cognizes as practically necessary, that is as good"

---

[15] "[A] practical law ... represents an action as necessary but takes no account of whether this action already inheres by an *inner* necessity in the acting subject (as in a holy being)" (1996c: 6:222).

(1996a: 4:412). This is an important point: The normative concept of pure practical reason is that of *good* or, as Kant also puts it, "practical good" (4:413). An "objective law of reason say[s] that to do or omit something would be good" (4:413).

When, however, actions that are "objectively necessary are subjectively contingent" – that is, when agents have potentially conflicting non-rational sources of motivation, what Kant calls "inclinations" – then "the determination of such a will in conformity with objective laws is *necessitation*" (4:405, 413). Finite rational agents do not accord with objective practical law through an "inner necessity" of their rational nature; they must somehow "restrain" inclinations that might lead them astray (1996c: 6:222, 6:481). Kant holds that they can do this only by representing practically necessary (i.e., *good*) conduct as *commanded* by reason and therefore what they ought or must do. And we do that, he claims, through the deontic, juridical lens provided by the feeling of respect (about which, more later).

> The representation of an objective principle, insofar as it is necessitating for a will, is called a command (of reason), and the formula of the command is called an **imperative** (1996a: 4:413).

"All imperatives are expressed by an *ought*," Kant says. They "indicate by this the relation of an objective law of reason to a will that by its subjective constitution is not necessarily determined by it (a necessitation)" (4:413).[16]

Perfect and imperfect rational wills both stand under objective or practical laws, but only imperfect ones are subject to oughts, imperatives, duties, and obligations, that is, to what Kant calls morality. Kant's reason for holding this is that the deontic moral concepts only have place and function within necessitation. "A perfectly good will would, therefore, equally stand under objective laws (of the good), but it could not on this account be represented as *necessitated* to actions in conformity with the law" (4:414). Necessitation can only take place in finite rational agents. "Hence no imperatives hold for the *divine* will and in general for a *holy* will: the 'ought' is out of place here, because volition is of itself necessary in accord with the law" (4:414).

The imperatival forms that moral laws take are "categorical imperatives." These represent actions as objectively necessary (and therefore, rationally commanded) in and of themselves, "without reference to another end" (4:414).

---

[16] This does not mean that the will of a perfectly rational agent *is* determined by a necessitation. To the contrary, as we shall soon see, necessitation can only take place in imperfect, finite agents. Kant's point is that the only way a finite agent can purposely act from practical reason is through a necessitation, but that they do not invariably do so; sometimes they give in to conflicting inclinations. Thus, imperatives "say that to do or to omit something would be good, but they say it to a will that does not always do something just because it is represented to it that it would be good to do that thing" (4:413).

"[H]ypothetical" imperatives, by contrast, represent actions as "good merely as a means to something else" (4:414).

To be imperatives at all, even hypothetical imperatives must go beyond claims about what it would be good to do, whether categorically or relative to some further assumed end. They must be expressible by oughts in the imperatival mood. But there are puzzles about how exactly this is supposed to work within Kant's picture of practical reason, puzzles that are reflected in recent debates about the nature of instrumental rationality. This famous passage is central to these debates: "Whoever wills the end also wills (insofar as reason has decisive influence on his actions) the indispensably necessary means to it that are within his power" (4:417). On this basis, Thomas Hill formulates what he calls "The Hypothetical Imperative," which stands in relation to specific hypothetical imperatives as the CI stands to specific categorical imperatives: "If a person wills an end and certain means are necessary to achieve that end and are within his power, then he ought to will those means" (Hill 1973: 429).

This might be taken as an axiom of instrumental rationality. But if it is, how is the "ought" claim to be understood? Recent discussions of this issue distinguish between "wide scope" and "narrow scope" readings. Read with wide scope, the ought does not occur within the conditional, but governs it. It says that agents ought to make it the case that: if they will an end and believe a means indispensably necessary, then they will the means. This they can do equally by taking the means or by renouncing the end, and the wide scope norm does not distinguish between these. On a narrow scope reading, "ought" occurs within the conditional, making it a genuine conditional "ought" that can be discharged by *modus ponens* if the conditions of the agent's having the relevant end (and belief) are met.

Considered as an axiom of instrumental reasoning, a wide scope reading would seem to have obvious advantages. Contemporary philosophers who defend this reading, like Michael Bratman, point out that a narrow scope reading has the unwelcome consequence that an agent can "bootstrap" themselves into having a reason for promoting any arbitrary end, whatever reasons there might be not to adopt it, just by adopting it (Bratman 1981). The right way to think of a norm of instrumental rationality, these philosophers argue, is as a norm of practical coherence. So understood, the norm says nothing whatsoever about what agents have normative reason to do, although it does dictate the transfer of the support of normative reasons from end to means (Darwall 1983: 14–16, 44–49). Similarly, it transfers lack of support from means back to ends.

It is very difficult to see how a narrow scope reading can plausibly be construed as a truistic axiom of practical reasoning. But how should we interpret Kant's dictum? Hill interprets it with wide scope, which makes it more plausible as a structuring principle of practical reason. Lending even more plausibility to this reading, Kant says that his claim is an analytic proposition (Kant 1996a: 4:417). How could that possibly be true if it is read with narrow scope? It would mean that philosophers, like Bratman, who deny the narrow scope reading are trapped in contradiction or conceptual incoherence themselves.

Despite this, there are strong reasons for thinking that a narrow scope reading is actually truer to Kant's text (Schroeder 2005b). For one thing, Kant makes a distinction between different kinds of hypothetical imperatives: "problematic" imperatives that concern possible ends and "assertoric" imperatives concerning ends an agent actually has that would be unmotivated on a wide scope reading. As interesting as these issues are in their own right, however, I propose mostly to ignore them. We should note, though, one puzzling thing Kant says about assertoric hypothetical imperatives in comparison with categorical imperatives that invokes Suárez's distinction between counsel and command or law, a distinction that has loomed so large in our reading of modern moral philosophy to this point.

Kant includes "imperatives of prudence" among assertoric hypothetical imperatives, since he thinks that human finite rational beings have their own happiness as an end "by a natural necessity" (Kant 1996a: 4:415, 4:417). Now on a narrow scope reading, hypothetical imperatives are genuine conditional oughts, no different in their logical form from statements like, "If you have made a promise to do something, you should do it," except that the condition concerns an agent's *optional* ends. But there is an important sense in which Kant holds that human agents having their own happiness as end is not optional, since they have it by "natural necessity." From the human perspective, therefore, it is hard to see what the analytical difference is between an ought that is conditional on an unavoidably satisfied condition and an unconditional ought.

However, Kant holds that although it is determinately the case that human beings have their own happiness as an end, this end is itself too indeterminate and vague to give definite rational guidance. In other words, there may be no actions that are "indispensably necessary" for this end or, more plausibly, even if some action or policy were to be indispensably necessary, no human agent would ever be able to know it. A human agent "is not capable of any principle by which to determine with complete certainty what would make him truly happy, because for this omniscience would be required" (4:418).

Kant says on this basis that "imperatives of prudence cannot, to speak precisely, command at all, that is, present actions objectively as practically *necessary*; that they are to be taken as counsels (*consilia*) rather than as commands (*praecepta*) of reason" (4:418). This obviously invokes the Suárezian vocabulary, but to make a very different contrast than the one Suárez made and that influenced early modern philosophers like Grotius and Hobbes. Even if some means is known to be indispensably necessary for an unavoidable end, that would show nothing about whether taking it was called for by obligating law in Suárez's sense of something one is accountable for complying with, where non-compliance is culpable lacking excuse. This is yet another instance where Kant does not so much account for deontic moral normativity as attempt to reinterpret it within his own theory.

We turn now to Kant's derivation of the first formulation of the CI (FUL) from "the concept of a rational being as such," which parallels *Groundwork I*'s argument for FUL based on the concepts of a good will and morally worthy action.

> [W]hen I think of a *categorical* imperative I know at once what it contains. For, since the imperative contains, beyond the law, only the necessity that the maxim be in conformity with this law ... nothing is left with which the maxim of action is to conform but the universality of a law as such; and this conformity alone is what the imperative properly represents as necessary.
>
> There is, therefore, only a single categorical imperative and it is this: *act only in accordance with that maxim through which you can at the same time will that it become a universal law* (4:420–421).

We know by an analysis of the concept of a rational agent that rational agents act on "*representation*[*s*] of laws," where these are practical laws that apply universally to all rational agents (4:412). The ideas of rational agent and (universal) practical law are matched concepts; each requires the other. There can be practical laws only if they can be represented as such and acted on by rational beings, considered as such. But that can be so, Kant here argues, only if FUL holds, only if rational agents are, as such, required to act only on maxims that they can will to become universal law.

This argument has the same logical structure as the one we examined before in *Groundwork I*, and it faces the same logical gap. It seems entirely possible for an agent both to treat a principle as a universal law applying equally to any rational agent *and* to be motivated to act on the principle entirely on those grounds without that committing them in any way to willing or being rationally able to will that every rational agent do so as well. Here again, they will be committed to thinking that any agent should act on the principle, but that is a different matter, which we can show with the same example we employed before. An agent might have a self-denying temperament and inclinations, hold a rational egoist theory of practical law, and (albeit reluctantly) guide their conduct by their (putative) representation of practical law, without that committing them to willing or being rationally able to will that all agents act on the same principle. It would, again, commit them to thinking that others should act on the egoist principle as well, but not to willing that they do so.

With the argument in *Groundwork I* we saw that this gap can be closed when the idea of moral duty is interpreted in the distinctively obligating terms that entail accountability. If a moral agent determines themselves to comply with moral obligation as part of holding themselves accountable for compliance then that does commit them to being able to will that others do so as well. But nothing in the bare concept of a rational agent commits us to anything like that. We will return to these issues in connection with the *Critique of Practical Reason*, where Kant argues that principles like that of rational egoism are material rather than formal, and that genuine practical laws must be formal. The point here is that nothing like this can fall out of any analysis of the "concept of a rational being as such" (4:412).

FUL is followed directly by FLN: "[*A*]*ct as if the maxim of your action were to become by your will a* **universal law of nature**" (4:421). Following Rawls and others, we can treat FUL and FLN together as involving the same CI procedure, as Rawls calls it (Rawls 2000).[17] Roughly, we test whether everyone's acting on the agent's maxim as if by a law of nature is something the agent could rationally will, consistently with their acting on the maxim themselves.

Since the CI invariably tests agents' maxims or subjective principles of acting, it cannot be applied until an agent's maxim exists or is at least assumed to exist. To apply it in practical reasoning, therefore, an agent must be tentatively decided to do something for some reason, or at least actively considering whether to act for that reason. The CI is then applied to whatever the agent's reason for acting would then be. Whether the agent will – or is actively deciding to – do something for a particular reason is a matter of psychological fact. If I am considering doing something for one set of reasons, and cannot rationally will a world (natural realm) in which as a matter of natural law everyone acts similarly for the same set of reasons, but there exists a second set of reasons, which are not my reasons for wanting to perform the relevant action, but which I could rationally will everyone to act on, that does not help. What matters is my actual maxim or reasons. Applying FUL in deliberation obviously requires self-awareness – if not, in many cases, brutal honesty with oneself. What CI dictates depends on the agent's actual maxim, and dishonest agents are only fooling themselves if they think they can game the system and, like tax lawyers, cook up more fine-grained universalizable maxims.

What Rawls calls the "Four-Step CI-Procedure" then goes roughly as follows: (a) formulate the agent's maxim (say, "Whenever in circumstances C, do A"), (b) formulate a universalized version of the maxim as a candidate for practical law (say, "Everyone should, when in circumstances C, do A"), (c) formulate a possible world in which it is a psychological law that everyone when in C does A (on the maxim) and always has, and (d) conjoin that world with the actual world to determine what a (c) world that is otherwise as close to the actual world would be like. We then apply FUL by determining whether the (d) world is something the agent could rationally will, consistent with acting on their tentative actual maxim as given in (a).

---

[17] Unless context clearly signals otherwise, I will use FUL to refer indeterminately to FUL and FLN.

Kant illustrates FUL with four examples, the same four he will use in illustrating the Formula of Humanity (FH). We need not consider all four. It will do to restrict ourselves to the two most commonly discussed. These will be sufficient to illustrate a basic distinction Kant holds FUL to reveal between cases where a possible world modeled on the agent's maxim (a (d) world) cannot "even be *thought* without contradiction," on the one hand, and, on the other, cases where such a world is a rationally thinkable possibility, but nonetheless not one that can be rationally *willed* (4:424). This distinction tracks and explains a related Kantian distinction in normative moral theory between "strict" or "narrow" duties and "wide" or "meritorious" duties, respectively. Roughly, strict duties narrowly dictate specific actions, whereas wide duties require more general ends, giving agents some discretion in how they promote them. Like most commentators, I will assume that this distinction is roughly the same as the one Kant marks out by speaking of "perfect" and "imperfect" duties," as he does more frequently.[18] Kant holds that strict duties are violated by actions the universalization of whose maxims cannot rationally be conceived – that involve a contradiction in thought – and that wide duties are violated by actions on maxims whose universalization can be rationally thought but not rationally willed.

Kant's first two examples are meant to illustrate two kinds of perfect duties, the first, toward oneself (against suicide) and the second, toward others (against insincere promises), both of which are characterized by the fact that, as Kant argues, a world in which agents acts on their conflicting maxims cannot even be rationally thought. And his second two are intended to exemplify imperfect duties – one toward oneself (to develop one's talents) and the other toward others (to come to their aid) – both of which are characterized by the fact that though their relevant (d) worlds can be thought, they cannot be willed rationally.

Consider first the second of Kant's four examples, which is supposed to illustrate a strict duty to others. An agent intends to borrow money with no intention of repaying the loan and plans to disguise this fact to the lender. To keep it simple, suppose the person does this just because they believe it to be in their interest to do so, abstracting from any features of urgent need that might complicate things. Their maxim is something like, "Whenever I am in circumstances in which it is in my interest to make an insincere promise, I will do so." Without going through all four steps of Rawls's CI procedure, let's consider the possibility of a world in which everyone acts on this maxim, whenever it applies to their situation and always has. The imagined world is otherwise like the actual world. Kant argues that such a possible world is not rationally conceivable, since if everyone were to act on the maxim, it would make the promise

---

[18] See, for example, Johnson 2016.

and the end one might have in it impossible, as all potential lenders "would laugh at all such expressions as vain pretenses" (4:422).

We should grant that credit would quickly dry up in a world of insincere promises and that this is certainly relevant to the moral impermissibility of self-serving insincere promises. But Kant's claim that such a world is not even thinkable is probably too strong, as reflection on our actual world might quickly show. Credit would no doubt be reduced, but that would not mean that people could not still sometimes find themselves facing a willing lender foolish enough to think they could sniff out insincerity. We need not worry about that problem though, since there are larger ones.

What seems to be doing the work in Kant's example, is the idea of a practice, in this case promising, that has certain background conditions, where departures prohibited by the practice tend to undermine the conditions on which the practice itself depends.[19] In such a case, one cannot imagine everyone making the practice-prohibited departures, because this removes the condition necessary for the practice, and hence for the practice-prohibited departures, to exist in the first place. But what moral force does this have? If the practice is, like promising, one that is valuable or mutually advantageous (or which an agent is otherwise committed to willing), then the fact that everyone's acting on a maxim will undermine the practice seems to count in favor of its being wrong for one to do so. But what if the practice has no particular value? Or better, what if the practice is thoroughly evil?

John Rawls describes a hypothetical practice he calls "telishment," which is like punishment except that innocent people are capriciously selected for sanctions, say, as part of a reign of terror (Rawls 1955). Suppose that this practice depends on official underlings who are called upon to administer telishment. The regime tells them that if they refuse to go along with the practice and telish innocents, other officials can be found who will. The regime has a name for disobeying a command to telish: *nullishing*. To forestall a fussy objection, suppose that it is intrinsic to the idea of nullishing that it can occur only when there is a going practice of telishment. Only an official who has been commanded to telish can nullish. Suppose finally that if a critical mass of officials were to nullish when commanded to telish, this would undermine the practice of telishment.

Now since one can nullish only if one has been commanded to telish, if nullishing tends to undermine the practice of telishing, it also tends to undermine the possibility of nullishing. In this respect nullishing is like promisebreaking. (There are still differences, of course. *If* someone were commanded to telish under the circumstances brought about by universal nullishing, they could still nullish, although one could not break a promise in circumstances

---

[19] Here I follow my discussion in Darwall 1998: 160–161.

brought about by universal false promising, since the promise could not have been made. In both cases, however, universal action on the maxim removes the opportunity to act on the maxim.) But imagine a public-spirited official who has been commanded to telish and who is considering nullishing in order to help destroy the practice of telishment. If we cannot rationally conceive a world in which everyone makes self-serving, false promises, so also would we be unable rationally to conceive a world in which everyone nullishes in such a situation. But how can this show that it is morally unacceptable to nullish, especially if one's purpose is to undermine the practice of telishing and, even more, if the practice is thoroughly evil?

Clearly something has gone wrong here. What has gone wrong, I think, is that Kant has been misled by certain features of his example and generalized too quickly. He would have done better to rely exclusively on the test of whether it is possible to *will* a world in which everyone acts on one's maxim. This gives us the "morally expected" answer in both the promising and telishing/nullishing cases. As Kant himself says about a self-serving false promise, if everyone were to act on the maxim that gives rise to it, "it would make the promise and the end one might have in it itself impossible" (Kant 1996a: 4:422). That matters because in making such a promise oneself, one wills this purpose (that others trust one so that one can benefit from their trust), but in willing everyone act on the maxim, one wills in contradiction with this purpose. This is not so in the nullishing case. The official who is determined to nullish in order to help end telishing does not will anything that is in conflict with what they will in willing that all act on their maxim. Quite the contrary.

Or just consider a person who, for whatever reason, is opposed to the practice of promising and who makes false promises not to advantage themselves, but as a step in bringing down the practice. Suppose they favor everyone's living more spontaneously without having to rely on formal guarantees. It is hard to see how the fact that everyone's acting on their maxim would tend to make it impossible to promise falsely should speak to them as a reason for them not to do so. "That is exactly why I intend to do it," they might reasonably say.

In sum, it is hard to see how Kant's contradiction-in-thought test creates anything but mischief for his view. It seems better to rely on the contradiction-in-will test, which would pretty readily rule out self-serving insincere promises in the kind of cases Kant has in mind, since they would tend to make it much less likely that the agent would be in a position to make the kind of promise they are tentatively considering.

Let us move to the fourth example where Kant explicitly applies the test. Here we are to consider a person who is in a position to help another, but decides not to do so, let us suppose, simply because it is not in their interest to do so. We can imagine them to be a rational egoist who will do anything, including aiding others, if – and only if – it advances their own interests. Their universalized maxim is: "Everyone should help others only if, and to the extent, that it advances their self-interest." Kant agrees that we can easily imagine an associated (d) world that is like our world except that everyone acts on this maxim as though it is a law of nature. The question is whether an agent can rationally will this world. Kant argues that they cannot, because any such attempt to will the requisite (d) world while willing also what one wills in acting that one act on the maxim oneself, would "conflict with itself" (4:423). The agent would be willing that their own interests be promoted (in acting on the maxim oneself), but also willing that they not be promoted, assuming that the (d) world would not be in their interests, since it would rob themselves "of all hope of [others'] assistance" (4:423).

This certainly seems a more promising line of moral analysis than the contradiction-in-thought test, and it seems to be getting at something genuinely morally significant. But there still appear to be obvious problems. Suppose someone is in a sufficiently powerful position such that in order to get the assistance they need they do not have to rely (much anyway) on other people being prepared to override their self-interested actions. When they need others' help, suppose, they can purchase it. Of course, they may want things from others that cannot be purchased, but Kant clearly does not intend his analysis to depend on anything like that. Suppose, then, that when a sufficiently powerful agent considers the (d) world associated with everyone's (including *their*) invariably self-serving action and compares it with a world in which everyone constrains their pursuit of self-interest when they can help others at little cost to themselves, they vastly prefer the former. What rational incoherence would there then be in their will?

If FUL would not rule out purely self-interested refusal to aid others, or perhaps even self-interested harming, that is problematic. It seems obvious that the basic idea that Kant is trying to get at with the Categorical Imperative should rule out conduct whose universalization is rationally acceptable only owing to knowledge of relatively advantageous circumstances. That the formulation does not already suggests that an improved formulation should rule out such self-serving construals.

There is a further issue. FUL seems addressed to the question of whether it is morally permissible for someone to perform some action on some specific maxim or principle. Take the second example, again. Even the contradiction-in-will test, it seems, can only show that it is wrong to make insincere promises if one does so in order to advantage oneself. The conflict in the will comes from willing that one promote one's own interests by insincerely promising, as willing that everyone do so is to will a (d) world that is against one's interest, since promissory credit will be too tight to be able to promise self-advantageously oneself. Suppose even that the problem we were just considering, that the agent might be prepared to accept the (d) world on balance because they have a highly advantageous bargaining position, can be solved. The further problem is that even if it can be shown that it would be morally impermissible to make insincere promises self-servingly, that would not show that making insincere promises would be wrong if done from other motives. Imagine, again, someone who is opposed to the practice of promising quite generally, and who promises insincerely to try to hasten the practice's demise. Here what the person wills in insincerely promising themselves is not in conflict with what they would will in willing its universalization in the associated (d) world. The two would be entirely in sync.

Groundwork II: FH, FA, and FKE

We might put the problem we just noted by saying that although FUL plausibly provides a principle of moral *consistency*, concerning what moral agents can permissibly do consistently with acting on their intended maxim, it seems powerless to generate claims about the wrongness of acts considered independently of motive. Or, at least, FUL can generate such results only if the argument can rely on some facts about ends to which agents are rationally committed independently of the universalization test. There needs to be some content in the agent's will to generate a conflict with a willed (d) world. In Kant's fourth example, the content comes from the agent's actual maxim, but if we don't have that, there seems to be nothing left to generate conflict, unless we can assume some content or end to which a rational agent is necessarily committed independently of FUL.

Kant seems to have something like this problem in mind when he considers rational action from the point of view of its *end*. Kant takes the capacity of "setting ... ends" to be intrinsic to "humanity" (1996c: 6:387). "[S]ubjective" ends "that a rational being proposes at his discretion as *effects* of his actions (material ends) are all only relative" and "can therefore furnish ... no practical laws" (1996a: 4:428). This problem would be solved, Kant says, if "there were something the *existence of which in itself* has an absolute worth, something which as *an end in itself* could be a ground of determinate laws" (4:428). He then famously declares:

> Now I say that the human being and in general every rational being *exists* as an end in itself, *not merely as a means* to be used by this or that will at its discretion (4:428).

Kant follows this with the Formula of Humanity (FH):

> *So act that you use humanity, whether in your own person or in the person of any other, always at the same time as an end, never merely as a means* (4:429).

It is difficult to overstate the philosophical, indeed historical, significance of this idea (or, more properly, *set* of ideas). Kant distinguishes between an end in the sense of a possible "effect" or state of the world that one might desire and therefore aim to bring about, on the one hand, and, on the other, a very different way of acting for someone or something's *sake*, namely, not to promote or bring it about, but as a distinctive way of *valuing* it – as a form of *respect*. Respect is like desire in that it can provide content to the will, but it does so in a fundamentally different way, by *regulating* one's conduct toward its object rather than motivating one to produce or acquire the object.

Kant's radical claim then is that irrespective of their specific talents and accomplishments all rational human beings have a common dignity as "persons" that "marks them out as an end it itself" (4:428). Kant credits Rousseau for this landmark idea:

> I am an investigator by inclination. I feel a great thirst for knowledge and an impatient eagerness to advance [it]. … There was a time when I thought that all this could constitute the honor of humanity, and I despised the mob, which knows nothing about it. Rousseau set me straight. This dazzling excellence vanishes; I learn to honor men, and would consider myself much less useful than common laborers if I did not believe that this consideration could give all the others a value, to establish the rights of humanity (Kant 1904: 20:44).

One can hardly think of a positive normative thesis has been more central to mainstream modern moral and political thought as it developed after Kant than the claim that all rational human persons have a common dignity that grounds equal basic human rights. We saw anticipations of this thought in Pufendorf and Adam Smith, but Kant's formulation and defense of it has certainly proven the most influential.

What is perhaps most remarkable is Kant's ambition of establishing this powerful normative thesis as part of a theory of practical reason inescapable from commitments of any rational agent in deliberation. Korsgaard and Wood have argued on Kant's behalf that agents can rationally value the ends they set themselves only if they value themselves (Korsgaard 1996a: 122; Wood 1999: 129–130). I have criticized these arguments elsewhere (Darwall 2006: 229–235; see also Cohon 2000 and Bukoski 2018). I agree, as a matter of normative moral theory, that the most plausible justification for respecting someone's will and choices, whether someone else's or, indeed, one's own, is respect for them and their dignity as equal moral persons, as being, in Rawls's terms, "self-originating source[s] of valid claims" (Rawls 1980: 546; Darwall 2013b: 93–114). What I question is how to ground this basic normative thesis in a theory of practical reason without assuming the philosophical baggage of Kant's transcendental idealism.[20] This issue will return when we consider Kant's defense of autonomy of the will, since the defense is ultimately the linchpin in Kant's

---

[20] In Darwall 2006, I argue that the most philosophically plausible grounding of the dignity of persons is within the second-person standpoint.

case that the whole package of mutually involving deontic moral ideas are not chimerical. I shall argue, again, that Kant's attempts to situate morality within pure practical reason cannot succeed, that crucial moves in his arguments borrow plausibility from deontic moral claims that can play no justifying role in his official framework, and that these are better grounded in a way that retains their distinctive normativity.

No matter how FH is justified or grounded, however, there are questions about how it is to be understood, applied, and related to the other formulations of the CI, especially if we seek interpretations on which these are all equivalent. If what it is to be a rational agent is to be able to act on a conception of law, that is, for reasons – importantly, *one's own* reasons – then to treat a rational agent as an end in the sense that Kant has in mind must involve respecting them as an independent will. As with FUL, we get a more determinate idea of what Kant thinks this requires in his discussion of his same four examples. Especially illuminating, again, are the second and fourth.

The second example, of a self-serving insincere promise, seems tailor made for Kant's characterization of "mak[ing] use of another human being *merely as a means*" (Kant 1996a: 4:429). Kant helpfully adds: "For, he whom I want to use for my purposes by such a promise cannot possibly agree to my way of behaving toward him and so himself contain the end of this action" (4:430). This naturally suggests that FH requires something like actual or at least hypothetical consent (Korsgaard 1996b: e.g., 110–114). Consent is a kind of authority – the power to permit or prohibit. Regulating conduct by it implicitly recognizes a kind of authority persons have just by having certain rational capacities. It treats their rational humanity as an end in itself, not as something to be promoted, but as something to be respected in the recognition sense (Darwall 1977, 2006, 2013d).

About the second example, Kant adds:

> This conflict with the principle of other human beings is seen more distinctly if examples of assaults on the freedom and property of others are brought forward. For then it is obvious that he who transgresses the rights of human beings intends to make use of the person of others merely as means, without taking into consideration that, as rational beings, they are always to be valued at the same time as end (Kant 1996a: 4:430).

This is an important linking text between the *Groundwork* and the *Doctrine of Right*. Although Kant's derivation of the Universal Principle of Right (UPR) in the latter is carried out primarily in terms that are internal to the theory of right, it is important to bear in mind that the UPR must also be anchored in Kant's moral philosophy. Rights require correlative duties, and what underlies these duties is FH and the equal dignity of persons.[21]

---

[21] Guyer emphasizes the centrality of freedom to this linking of FH to the Universal Principle of Right. To comply with FH, he argues, we must "act only on maxims that could be

Kant's analysis of his fourth example proceeds along somewhat different lines. Even if we must have others' actual or hypothetical consent to make use of them and their rational powers, we do not always need their consent to decline to advance their ends and projects. The duty to come to others' aid is a "wide," imperfect, or "meritorious duty" (4:424, 4:430). Barring emergencies, we do no wrong in privileging our own ends and projects over others'. The duty to aid requires, rather, that we make the happiness of others our end in some more general way. Others' happiness is "an end that is also a duty" (1996c: 6:382). In this sense, Kant says, the ends of others "must as far as possible be also *my* ends, if that representation is to have its *full* effect in me" (1996a: 4:430).

In what sense, however, must those with whom we interact be able to "contain the end" of our actions? Suppose, for example, that someone is convicted of an egregious tax fraud in accordance with due process in, we can add, a perfectly just republic. In what sense must the convicted person be able to "contain the end" of the sentencing judge's action? Must the sentenced be able to share the end of their own detention and, perhaps, reform?

It helps here to bring in what Kant counts as "the third practical principle of the will, as supreme condition of its harmony with universal practical reason" – what Wood calls the Formula of Autonomy (FA): "the idea of the will of every rational being as a will giving universal law" – and to read FH in light of it. (4:431; Wood 1999). Ultimately, we will want to have a way of understanding all the formulations of the CI as equivalent at the most fundamental level.

We give ourselves universal law, and so treat rational nature in ourselves as an end in itself, when we comply with FUL (as so far interpreted), namely, by acting only on principles whose universalization we ourselves can will. Similarly, it might be argued, we treat rational nature in others as an end in itself when we restrict our acts toward them to those on principles whose universalization *they* can will also. Even if someone convicted of tax fraud may not share the end of their own punishment, they are far likelier to be able to will the universalized form of the judge's maxim. They are unlikely to be anarchists. So long as they are not, they will be capable of sharing the judge's end in this lawgiving sense.

This may give us a way of linking FUL and FH through FA. We give ourselves the law, and treat ourselves as beings who do, Kant must think, when we regulate our practical reasoning by not acting on maxims that we cannot will as universal law (thus complying with FUL). So far, however, this only requires treating others as beings who can give themselves the law by regulating *their* conduct by FUL as well.

This would involve seeing ourselves and others as "lawgiver[s]" in the sense that Kant distinguishes in *The Metaphysics of Morals*, of being "author[s]" "of

accepted by everyone else as preserving their capacity for free choice as well" (Guyer 2006: 194–195).

the obligation in accordance with the law, but not always the author of the law" (1996c: 6:227). We "author" obligations when we impose the law on ourselves by regulating our own conduct by FUL through necessitation and respect. So far, this requires no particular treatment of others, except insofar as that is required by FUL already. We do not need the idea that rational persons are ends in themselves, and so must be treated as such, to fully regard them as lawgivers in this "author of obligation" sense. For FA to require FH and not just FUL, FA must require that rational moral agents be able to give themselves the law in some further sense.

We noted above that to the extent that FUL only prohibits acting on agents' actual maxims, it seems powerless to prohibit or require the performance of certain acts, or even, indeed, the adoption of certain ends, considered independently of the agent's actual maxims. To solve this problem a revision of FUL would have to permit action when a given maxim or principle *applies* (and not just when it is actually acted on) based on whether its associated (d) world can rationally be willed. It would thus have to seek to rule out or rule in action through conflicts between willing the associated (d) world and something the agent can be assumed to will as a rational (moral) person independently of FUL. It could not rely on conflicts with the agent's actual maxims.

This, again, seems exactly what the idea of rational nature as an end in itself is supposed to provide. And this suggests a further sense in which rational beings must be assumed to be "will[s] giving universal laws" that is additional to the sense of authoring obligation through the self-application of FUL (1996a: 4:431). The content of a law that can require more than moral consistency and prohibit or require certain actions or ends independently of agents' actual motives must somehow be grounded in "objective ends" that are provided, Kant holds, by rational beings as ends in themselves (4:427–428). And this means that rational beings must be able not just to author the *obligation* of the law whatever its content, but that rational nature as an end in itself must somehow ground the content of moral law.

Practical laws are, by definition, normative for rational beings. And moral laws are, by definition, requirements and prohibitions for human rational beings. But what is the content of practical and moral law? Whatever it is, it must be the same or common for all human rational agents. I can give myself the moral law in a "content-affecting" sense, therefore, only if any and every human moral agent can give themselves that same law. One and the same moral law must have its source in any and every rational agent's will. I alone can give myself my *obligation* to comply with the law (through "necessitation"), but I cannot by myself be the source of obligating law's content. That can have its source in my will only if its source is rational nature generally. And that can be true only if the candidate (d) world can be rationally willed also by those with whom I interact. And this gives us something like FH: *Act toward others only on, and according to, principles that they can will to be universal laws also.*

Failure to appreciate this more robust sense in which moral law must have its source in rational will is, Kant thinks, the explanation of why "all previous efforts that have ever been made to discover the principle of morality ... had to fail" (4:432). "[I]t never occurred" to earlier philosophers that a moral agent "is subject *only to laws given by himself but still universal* and that he is bound only to act in conformity with his own will" (4:432). It is hard not to hear in these remarks an echo of Rousseau's famous formulation of his aim in *The Social Contract*:

> To find a form of association that will defend and protect the person and goods of each associate with the full common force, and by means of which each, uniting with all, nevertheless obey only himself and remain free as before (Rousseau 2003: 49–50).

It is not surprising, therefore, that Kant proceeds directly to his idea of a "realm" or "kingdom" of ends.

> For, all rational beings stand under the *law* that each of them is to treat himself and all others *never merely as means* but always *at the same time as ends in themselves*. But from this there arises a systematic union of rational beings through common objective laws, that is, a kingdom, which can be called a kingdom of ends (Kant 1996a: 4:433).

The moral law is essentially a law for rational human agents *in common*. Consequently, the only way it can issue from the will of any particular agent is if it likewise issues from the will of every agent. And this can be so only if it can be grounded not in what some particular agent wills from their own perspective, but in what any and all agents rationally will from a perspective they can share and occupy in common.

Recall now the problem we faced with Kant's treatment of the fourth example of FUL, where we considered the possibility of an advantageously situated agent who was prepared to accept others' acting only in their own interest if the agent could thereby get the benefit of acting in their own interest themselves. Clearly, the fact that they themselves are thus advantageously situated has no bearing on whether what they propose to do or accept can be sanctioned by practical or moral law. If, consequently, their being prepared to will the relevant (d) world is conditional on this contingent circumstance, which is arbitrary with respect to the bindingness of practical law, then they can hardly take this to show that they are acting in accord with practical law.

To solve this problem within the CI procedure what we would need to know is not what (d) world the agent can rationally will from their own, perhaps idiosyncratic, perspective, but what they, and indeed any agent, could rationally will from a standpoint they can share in common as rational moral agents. Kant gives the following clue.

> Now since laws determine ends in terms of their universal validity, if we abstract from the personal differences of rational beings as well as from all the content of their private ends we shall be able to think of a whole of all ends in systematic connection ... that is, a kingdom of ends, which is possible in accordance with the above principles (4:433).

As Rawls points out, this suggests a "limit" on information that should be available in any perspective from which the question of whether a (d) world associated with some candidate principle can be rationally willed should be considered. Rawls's own device from *A Theory of Justice* of a veil of ignorance seems a necessary feature of any adequate CI procedure (Rawls 1971, 2000: 139).[22] It should ask not just what (d) worlds the agent, or even the particular persons they are interacting with, can rationally will, but what (d) worlds *a* person can rationally will from behind a veil of ignorance with respect to "personal differences," from the perspective, that is, of a rational human person as such.

A veil of ignorance will solve the idiosyncrasy problem, but, if anything, it exacerbates the difficulty of getting moral laws with content that require specific acts (and ends) in specific circumstances. We still need something to give content to rational willing from behind the veil. We need, in another words, something to play an equivalent role to that played by "primary goods" (and what Rawls later called "highest" and "higher order interests") in *A Theory of Justice* and his later writings (Rawls 1971, 1980). In discussing this aspect of Kant's views in *Lectures on the History of Moral Philosophy*, Rawls suggests that we import into the CI procedure some similar theory of "true human needs" (Rawls 2000: 232–234). If this seems overly contingent for Kant's purposes, we might rather employ an account of interests or needs for rational agents considered as such, which for the case in which rational agents are human, would approximate "true human needs."[23]

We might then model the perspective of rational willing relevant to common laws in a kingdom of ends quite closely on Rawls's hypothetical choice in his

---

[22] Rawls himself argues that such limits on information are already implicit in FUL and cites Kant's remark in the Typic in the second *Critique*: "[A]sk yourself whether, if the action you propose were to take place by a law of the nature of which you were yourself a part, you could indeed regard it as possible through your will. Everyone does, in fact, appraise actions as morally good or evil by this rule. Thus one says: if *everyone* permitted himself to deceive when he believed it to be to his advantage ... or looked with complete indifference on the need of others, and if you belonged to such an order of things, would you be in it with the assent of your will?" (1996b: 5:69). About this passage, Rawls writes that he "find[s] it hard to read" it "without feeling that such an idea [limits on information] is implicit" (Rawls 2000: 176).

[23] Though on some conceptions of human needs, these could differ from needs of rational persons who happen be human.

original position (1980). The veil of ignorance would "abstract from the personal differences of rational beings as well as from all the content of their private ends" (Kant 1996a: 4:433) and some theory of "primary goods" for rational persons considered as such could provide grounds for rationally willing (d) worlds from that perspective.

Guyer rightly emphasizes the role of freedom in connecting Kant's moral and political philosophy; in particular, the connection between FH and UPR: "Any action is *right* if it can coexist with everyone's freedom in accordance with a universal law" (1996c: 6:230). Thus, Guyer interprets FH as, "act only on maxims that could be accepted by everyone else as preserving their capacity for free choice as well" (Guyer 2006: 194). There is no doubt that Kant thinks that freedom in this sense is an interest, arguably the highest-order interest, of rational agents, considered as such. So interpreted, FH would be very close to a Formula of the Kingdom of Ends (FKE) interpreted along the Rawlsian lines I have just been suggesting: *"Act only on (or in accord with) principles that anyone could, from a perspective reflecting only their knowledge and interests as rational agents, will all rational agents to act on (for the case of being human)."* We might then regard FKE as the best formulation of the "very same law" that FUL, FH, and FA attempt to formulate, with increasing success, as they move in the direction of FKE. Where Rawls speaks of a "Kantian Interpretation" of his theory of justice as fairness, we might speak of a "Rawlsian Interpretation" of the CI.

The Dignity of Persons and Autonomy of the Will

"[M]orality," Kant says, "is the condition under which alone a rational being can be an end in itself, since only through this is it possible to be a lawgiving member in the kingdom of ends" (Kant 1996a: 4:435). "Hence morality, and humanity insofar as it is capable of morality, is that which alone has dignity" (4:435). Famously, Kant distinguishes between a kind of value that can be "priced" in something like the market sense of exchange for equivalents, which shows itself through strength of preference or desire, and a different sort of value, dignity, to which the evaluative response is a fundamentally different kind of attitude: *respect*. "[R]*espect* alone provides a becoming expression" for the attitude that responds to what has dignity (4:436). Dignity is an "incomparable worth" "raised above all price" (4:436, 4:434).

Kant's deep philosophical point concerns a distinction between different kinds of value that is manifested in different evaluative responses: desire and respect. This difference is reflected also in the different ways these evaluating states of mind respectively relate to action, to the different kinds of *ends* associated with each. The objects of desire are possible states of affairs that actions can promote or bring about as "effects" (even when the effect is the trivial one of an action's having been performed). Respect shows itself not in motivating action for the sake of some end in the "effect" sense – a possible state of the world – but rather through self-regulating deontic moral action, as when one acts "for the sake of duty" or the moral "law alone," or "from the idea of the *dignity* of a rational being" (Kant 1996b: 5:85, 5:81; 1996a: 4:434).

There is actually some unclarity concerning what Kant thinks the precise relations are between respect, moral law, morally good action and good will, the capacity for morally good (deontically self-regulating) conduct, and respect for persons exactly are. And a complicating factor is that there are also different kinds of respect *and* that Kant himself distinguishes between a kind of respect that shows itself in action (*"observantia"* or "respect in the practical sense") and the feeling of respect (*"reverentia"*) (1996c: 6:449, 6:402).

One important distinction between kinds of respect is that between "recognition respect" and "appraisal respect" (Darwall 1977). To see the difference, notice that we can think both that there is a sense in which all persons are entitled to respect and a sense in which how much respect a person deserves or has earned depends on how they conduct themselves. The former, recognition respect, consists in how we *treat* someone or something. We respect persons in the recognition sense when we constrain our conduct toward them, recognizing that it would be wrong (and wrong them) not to do so. We thereby regard and treat them as beings we are required to treat always as ends in themselves (in the relevant sense) and never as means only. Respect of the latter kind, appraisal respect, shows itself not directly in deliberate action or treatment, but in an appraising attitude (moral esteem) that responds to how the objects of our respect conduct themselves, their actions and character.

Kant's own distinction between *observantia* and *reverentia* does not map cleanly onto the difference between recognition and appraisal respect. *Observantia*, "respect in the practical sense," seems to be a form of recognition respect. But *reverentia*, or the "feeling" of respect, can arise both when we contemplate morally good actions and agents, and also when we impose the moral law on ourselves (*within* morally good action from the agent's point of view). These matters will prove crucial to understanding respect's role in Kant's theory of morally good action and the process of "necessitation" in the second *Critique*.

On the most common interpretation, Kant holds that persons, that is, beings with the capacity for moral action, have dignity as ends in themselves and can never (rightfully) be treated as mere means. But in the *Groundwork*, Kant also says that "a morally good disposition," "virtue," and the "cast of mind" "that practices" self-regulation by the moral law have dignity (1996a: 4:435–436).[24]

---

[24] For some of the complications here, see Dean 2006, Sensen 2011, and Darwall 2013e.

If we distinguish two distinct, but related, forms of dignity that can be objects, respectively, of recognition respect for persons (as ends in themselves) and of appraisal respect (moral esteem) for action and agents motivated by the former, then we can sort Kant's use of "dignity" out along these lines. Just as "respect" is ambiguous as between recognition and appraisal senses, so also might we distinguish between associated senses of "dignity."

Recall Kant's remark that Rousseau taught him that only by "honor[ing] men" in general could he adequately appreciate a kind of human value that could "establish the rights of humanity" (1904: 20:44). The idea that human rights are grounded in human dignity has proven an historically powerful idea. The beginning articles of Germany's *Grundgesetz* assert it with notable clarity:

> (Article 1) Human dignity shall be inviolable. To respect and protect it shall be the duty of all state authority.
>
> (Article 2) The German people therefore acknowledge inviolable and inalienable human rights as the basis of every community, of peace and of justice in the world (Tschentscher 2012).

Respect for rights is not, like moral esteem, something that can be earned. It can rather be demanded or claimed. This is the sense of "respect" and "dignity" that Kant must have mind in the following passage.

> But a human being regarded as a *person*, that is, as the subject of a morally practical reason, is exalted above any price ... he possesses a *dignity* (absolute inner worth) by which he exacts *respect* for himself from all other rational beings in the world. He can measure himself with every other being of this kind and value himself on a footing of equality with them.
>
> Humanity in his person is the object of the respect which he can demand from every other human being, but which he must also not forfeit (Kant 1996c: 6:434–435).

The only kind of respect we can "exact" or "demand" is recognition respect, in this case for our dignity as persons and for the rights this dignity grounds. Any connection between dignity and *rights*, therefore, will have to concern respect and dignity in the recognition rather than in the appraisal or esteem sense.

We have, then, a host of fundamental deontic moral claims that Kant regards as entailing one another: the unique moral goodness of the good will and self-governing moral conduct, the various formulations of CI (FUL, FH, FA, and FKE), and the claim that moral agents have a dignity that is "beyond price." Linking these ideas is Kant's thesis that "the dignity of humanity consists just in this capacity to give universal law, though with the condition of also being itself subject to this very lawgiving" (1996a: 4:440).

Kant then introduces his definition of *autonomy of the will*: "the property of the will by which it is a law to itself (independently of any property of the objects of volition)," which will play the central role in Kant's critique of practical reason, first, in *Groundwork III*, and later in Kant's second *Critique*. So defined, autonomy is, Kant claims, within the circle of mutually entailing fundamental moral claims just listed. If it can be validated, it assures the possibility of categorical imperatives grounded in the "capacity to give universal law, though with the condition of also being itself subject to this very lawgiving" (4:440). There can be a moral law only if those subject to it are assured the capacity to govern themselves by it, without having to assume any desire for any object or "effect," like benevolence. This is assured if, and only if, the will is autonomous in Kant's sense.

We noted above that connections like these can plausibly be drawn if we take adequate note of deontic morality's conceptual tie to accountability. It seems to go with the very idea of a moral law one is accountable for complying with that an agent can intelligibly be subject to it if, and only if, they have the capacity to hold themselves accountable for compliance in their own practical reasoning. This, again, was a central point of Pufendorf's. I have been arguing that even though Kant's arguments in *Groundwork I* and *II* borrow plausibility from morality's accountability-involving character, his view of the epiphenomenal nature of deontic concepts and claims from the perspective of pure practical reason does not permit him to take advantage of these conceptual connections.

Kant seeks to situate autonomy within a critique of practical reason in *Groundwork III* as an inescapable presupposition of pure practical reason, irrespective of deontic moral ideas. At the end of Section II, Kant says that until they can be validated by a critique of practical reason, it cannot be ruled out that all of the central (deontic moral) ideas and claims in play in Sections I and II, autonomy of the will included, are "chimerical idea[s] without any truth" (4:445). However, even if Kant's critical validation of autonomy in *Groundwork III* succeeds, I shall argue, his view of necessitation and the epiphenomenal character of the deontic may end up showing that even if autonomy of the will is not chimerical, there is a sense in which deontic moral concepts and claims are, for pure practical reason at least.

Autonomy in *Groundwork III*

Kant begins his argument with a "negative" definition of freedom as agent causation through the agent's own practical reasoning, "independently of alien causes *determining* it" (4:446). Kant will add to this a "positive concept of freedom," but first we should have before us the principle that will do the major work in Kant's argument: "[E]very being that cannot act otherwise than *under the idea of freedom* is just because of that really free in a practical respect" (4:448). We need not concern ourselves with the relation between freedom "in a practical respect" and "transcendental freedom" (1996a: 4:448, 1996b: 5:3). However central that question is to metaphysics, it would seem that if Kant can show that freedom is an inescapable deliberative presupposition of rational agency, that would be sufficient to establish its *bona fides* for moral philosophy, at least, insofar as it attempts to ground normative convictions from a practical point of view.

In one sense, it should be uncontroversial that a deliberating agent must presuppose that they can choose to act on the basis of their deliberation, for what they take be reasons for acting. We need not assume we are infallible, that everything we take to be reasons really are or that they have the weight we take them to have. Nor need we assume that we are not subject to biases of different kinds, though the fact that we are should make us epistemically humble and cautious and lead us, when necessary, to check our reasoning both intra- and interpersonally. We just have to assume we are not hopeless and proceed on the assumption that there are normative reasons for and against alternative actions, and that we can attempt (and are attempting) to determine what they are with an eye toward acting on our determination.

Suppose you believe, however, that your deliberative thoughts are being controlled by an evil demon, and that the demon will cause you to do the opposite of whatever you conclude you should do. Can you now deliberate? Simply having that belief about what will happen does not prevent you from turning your mind to the practical question of what *to do* and trying to answer it for yourself (Korsgaard 1996c). In your deliberation, you might simply try to ignore the belief. Can you deliberate with the belief in mind? Thinking does not so much as count as deliberation unless it is aimed at making up your mind between what you take to be practical alternatives of what you take to be normative reasons. The only way you can take account of the belief, consequently, is if you can see its *practical* relevance – as affecting what you have normative reason to do. That practical issue is simply a different question from the theoretical one we are supposing you have already made up your mind on, namely, your belief concerning how your reasoning and conduct will be determined in fact by the demon. To think about the practical question you will have to ignore, at some level of reflection anyway, the theoretical question of how your practical thinking is in fact proceeding. You will reason practically *as if* you were doing so "independently of alien causes."

That's not quite the same thing as assuming that your practical thinking actually is independent of causes that are "alien" in the sense of affecting it in untoward ways. But it may be close enough for Kant's purposes. It is the assumption of what Kant terms the "positive concept of freedom" that really matters for his argument, however, since Kant will be arguing that that is the concept of autonomy of the will. He will be claiming that since we cannot deliberate except under the assumption of autonomy, we are entitled to conclude all of the deontic moral claims that he claims follow from it. Having established in Section II that "a free will" in this positive sense "and a will under moral laws are one in the same," Kant can conclude the latter from the former inescapable assumption (Kant 1996a: 4:447).

We should grant that positive freedom of some form is a necessary deliberative assumption. There might be nothing "alien" causing one's practical thinking to go awry even as it misfires persistently; it might be a completely random process. We should grant, therefore, that deliberation requires the assumption that it is not, that one's practical thought can somehow be guided by normative reasons and whatever norms or practical laws these involve. Just as ordinary theoretical thought about the world must proceed, Kant argues, under the guise of "laws of nature," so also must practical deliberative thought be under the guise of "laws of freedom" or practical laws (4:387). (Kant tends not to use the currently familiar vocabulary of normative reasons, preferring to speak of actions that are dictated by practical law as being "good" to do. Imperatives drawn from practical law, he says, "say that to do or to omit something would be good" (4:413). However, we can translate between these two vocabularies if we simply understand normative reasons as facts that tend to make an action good to do in Kant's sense.)

Now so far, it is important to see that the relevant presuppositions of negative and positive freedom are in no way unique to or distinctive about practical reasoning.[25] Whether we deliberate about what to believe *or* what to do, we must assume that we can think freely of alien causes and in accordance with reasons and rational norms. And Kant says as much: "[O]ne cannot possibly think of a reason that would consciously receive direction from any other quarter with respect to its judgments, since the subject would then attribute the determination of his judgment not to his reason but to an impulse" (4:448).

However, Kant identifies the requisite positive practical freedom with autonomy of the will. "[W]hat, then, can freedom of the will be other than autonomy, that is, the will's property of being a law to itself? ['independently of any property of the objects of volition']" (4:447, 4:440). But why should we suppose that? Based on what we have said so far, the only sense in which Kant has vindicated a presupposition of positive freedom is one that is common to both practical and to theoretical reason. As we saw earlier, however, autonomy of the will has no structural analogue in theoretical reason in Kant's thought. General logic concerns the pure forms of theoretical thought, but it cannot generate contentful theoretical thought without bringing in pure concepts of the understanding (the categories) that have to do with the *objects* of thought and their possible properties. For Kant, the idea that theoretical reason or the understanding could be a law to itself independently of any properties of its possible objects is a non-starter. Pure theoretical thought involving only "the

---

[25] What follows draws from Darwall 2006: 224–229.

form of thinking," without some content or putative object, is, he says, "empty" (1998: A54/B78, A51/B75; 1996b: 5:66).

Perhaps, however, there is something about the practical standpoint in particular that requires a deliberating agent to presuppose autonomy. Consider, then, how deliberation ordinarily proceeds from the practical perspective. The primitive deliberative phenomenon is the act of taking some fact about the world as a reason to do something, a consideration that tends to make some action a good thing to do. Wondering how to spend a free evening, I scan the newspaper to find an attractive possibility, say, going to a film. What I take as reasons for wanting to go, and for going, are aspects of the possible state of seeing the film, on the basis of which I might want to see it. It would be enjoyable, say, or, if I cannot articulate any such reason, there is the fact that, as it might seem to me, seeing the film would be good, a possible state or outcome that there is some reason to bring about.[26] My reasons for going will derive from properties of the object of my desire (and so my volition); whether I go will depend on good-making features, as these seem from my perspective, of the possible state of the world that would be the outcome of my action. Nothing yet seems to require the thought that what I take to be normative reasons for acting must be grounded somehow in the pure form of the will.

But do we yet have genuine agency and a will? For Kant, rational action involves not just beliefs and desires, but also some norm or principle the agent accepts and implicitly makes their own in acting on it (1996a: 4: 412). To involve my will in an intelligent pursuit of an outcome I desire, I must deliberate on the basis of some rational norm, one I take to apply validly to any possible rational agent. And I must presuppose that I am bound by such norms as a condition of the intelligibility of my own deliberation. But does this require us to presuppose autonomy? For this assumption to amount to autonomy, I would have to be required by the logic of my deliberative situation to presuppose that (at least some) reason-involving norms are valid independently of any properties of the objects that the norms counsel me to bring about. What in the deliberative context forces us to assume this?

Consider what norm I might accept in deciding to go to the film because I expect the state of seeing it to be good (for whatever good-making reasons my consideration of the state presents me with)? The state of my enjoyably viewing the film will seem to me to be an intrinsically good thing, a state that, in Moore's words, "ought to exist for its own sake" (Moore, 1993: 34). A natural answer to the question of what norm I might accept is Moore's answer. I might

---

[26] Of course, these might include facts about myself, my expected mood, how I would expect to enjoy the film, and so on, that I take as reasons for going, and for wanting to go. But these are still facts about the objects of my desire most properly understood, not the fact that I have the desire itself.

accept the act-consequentialist norm of always doing whatever promotes good or desirable states or outcomes, and I might think, in accepting that, that any rational agent should do likewise.

Nothing in the deliberative context, I should make clear, forces the acceptance of this norm. The point is that nothing seems to preclude it and that accepting it would seem quite natural from an ordinary practical standpoint. Just as belief aims at accurate representation of the world as it actually is, so from the practical standpoint of an agent with desires might action seem to aim at bringing about intrinsically desirable states or outcomes, as these seem from the perspective of the agent's desires. Compare Kant: "[T]heoretical cognition [is] that through which I cognize **what exists,** and practical cognition as that through which I represent **what ought to exist**" (Kant 1998: A633/B661).

But do we even have an agent yet? Obviously, a being who deliberates about what to do simply from the perspective of their current desires and beliefs, and who is incapable of stepping back and critically revising these, is not an agent in any sense we should be interested in here. A deliberating agent must, as Korsgaard says, both be, and be able to see themselves as, "something over and above" their desires who "chooses which desire to act on" (Korsgaard 1996a: 100). But it is quite possible for an agent to do that without assuming autonomy of the will, although they will have to assume autonomy in the familiar sense of being able to act on critically revised desires and so to make their actions "their own." As we have been thinking of it, the ordinary agent's desires are identified with their current evaluations of the possible states of the world that are their objects. They can certainly step back from these and reevaluate, getting a better conception of the features of these states on which they take their value to supervene and, hence, of desired states' value (desirability).

Just as a theoretical reasoner can bring experience and reflection to bear on the dispositions to belief involved in their current experiences – for example, overriding or defeating any tendency to believe that an apparently bent stick in water before them really is bent – so also can a practical reasoner analogously critically revise their desires. Plainly, this picture of deliberation is still much too naïve. But my point in setting it out is not to defend it, but to suggest that nothing in the presuppositions to which a deliberating agent is committed seems to rule it out. It follows that Kant's argument for autonomy in *Groundwork III* fails. Naïve practical reasoning is surely intelligible, even if it is mistaken.[27] If it is to be ruled out, and autonomy of the will ruled in, it would have

---

[27] I have only recently been able to study Tamar Schapiro's *Feeling Like It* in which she gives a compelling systematic account of inclinations in Kant's sense as incompatible with this picture, which, as she points out, is that of the "standard" Humean desire/belief *and* more rationalist Scanlonian "practical thinking" accounts of motivation. Schapiro's account fits perfectly with Kant's and is intended to show how autonomy is implicated in "the moment

to be on systematic metaphysical, metaethical grounds provided by the critical philosophy and transcendental idealism more generally.

In setting out this flatfooted alternative to autonomy-grounded normative reasons and practical laws, I have helped myself to various notions – like that of an intrinsically desirable outcome – that are obviously problematic from Kant's point of view. My point has been that nothing in inescapable assumptions to which rational deliberation is committed seems to rule such notions out. It will become clearer in our consideration of the *Critique of Practical Reason* that Kant takes the sources of motives and normative reasons to include only ("material") "inclinations," on the one hand, and purely "formal" practical reason, on the other. We shall want to know what grounds this picture, which rules out the very possibility of motivating states of mind, like benevolence and love, for example, that apparently respond to sources of value that neither do nor could derive from autonomy of the will.

The *Critique of Practical Reason:* Material vs. Formal Practical Principles

However satisfied Kant was with his vindication of autonomy, and of morality on its basis, when he published the *Groundwork* in 1785, he had evidently grown dissatisfied by the time he published the *Critique of Practical Reason* (*Kritik der praktischen Vernunft* (*KpV*)) in 1788. Rather than arguing that we can establish the validity of morality through an independent argument for autonomy as an inescapable presupposition of practical reason, Kant here argues that although "freedom is indeed the *ratio essendi* of the moral law, the moral law is the *ratio cognoscendi* of freedom" (Kant 1996b: 5:4n). Through our awareness of moral obligation, of being subject to moral imperatives and oughts, we see that we must be capable of regulating our conduct by these. Here, I shall suggest, Kant implicitly relies on the same accountability-related considerations that underlie the British rationalists' arguments for freedom. If this is so, however, it will raise a fundamental problem for Kant, since he believed that deontic morality has no normative significance for pure practical reason. That this is his considered view is made evident again in the second *Critique*. Here he lays out the psychological details of necessitation (obligating self-constraint) in his account of the moral psychology of respect. This will mean, ultimately, that no argument for autonomy as an essential aspect of pure practical reason can be mounted based on what Kant calls the "fact of reason" – the human awareness

of drama" when an agent steps back from the perspective of inclination and deliberates rationally. Though Schapiro's account is doubtlessly closer to the human ("finite") case, it is still not clear how it must presuppose autonomy in Kant's sense, viz., that the form of the will alone is sufficient to provide normative grounds for action (Schapiro 2021).

of being morally obligated – since, on his view, it is not really a fact of pure practical reason at all (5:31).

Section I of Chapter I ("On the Principles of Pure Practical Reason") of *KpV* begins with definitions on the basis of which Kant proves three "theorems," ultimately deriving the *Critique*'s version of the CI (the *Groundwork*'s "supreme principle of morality"), which Kant here calls the "Fundamental Law of Pure Practical Reason" (1996a: 440, 1996b: 5:30). Unlike the *Groundwork*, whose first two sections proceed by analyzing the "generally received concept of morality" (1996a: 4:445), the arguments of *KpV* are meant not to rely on (deontic) moral premises at all. *KpV*'s arguments are to be based on necessary features of practical reason alone.

Kant begins by defining "[p]ractical *principles*" as "propositions that contain a general determination of the will, having under it several practical rules" (1996b: 5:19). Practical principles are "subjective, or *maxims*, when the condition is regarded by the subject as holding only for his will" (5:19). And they are "objective, or practical *laws*, when the condition is cognized as objective, that is as holding for the will of every rational being" (5:19).

Already, we face some complexities of interpretation. In our discussion of the *Groundwork*, we were understanding maxims ("subjective principles") in terms of agents' actual reasons for acting. Maxims, so interpreted, are necessarily connected to psychological states of an agent in a particular deliberative context, although it is a distinctive mental state the content of which can be *formulated*, from the agent's point of view, as a (putative) normative principle of action (in our contemporary parlance, in terms of putative normative reasons or practical oughts that provide the agent's reason for acting). If we were to carry that usage through here, the relevant "holding" would be psychological and not normative. A practical principle would hold, in this sense, if, and only if, it actually motivates the agent. It is doubtful, however, that this is how Kant regards subjective principles' "holding" in *KpV*, since he speaks of the agent regarding subjective principles as "holding" (only for their own wills). The relevant "holding" here must be normative, though "regard" obviously refers to a psychological state.

But who then is "the subject" whose "regard" determines whether a candidate principle is subjective or objective? Presumably, the subject to whom the normative principle is supposed to apply. This is not, however, some particular actual agent, as in the case of an actually motivated action. It is anyone to whom the principle applies as formulated. But then why would whether *the agent* regards the principle as holding (normatively) for their own will matter rather than whether a given practical principle validly holds normatively only for their will?

Similarly, Kant defines principles as "objective" practical principles or "practical *laws*, when the condition is cognized as objective, that is, as holding for the will of every rational being" (5:19). "Cognized," unlike "regarded," is factive, so it entails that the principle universally holds normatively, but even so, why is not this latter sufficient? Why does the principle also have to be *cognized* as universally normatively valid?

Nonetheless, Kant's practice is to speak of practical principles not just as normative formulae, but as essentially tied to agents in particular deliberative contexts. This is clear in his reasoning for Theorem I: "All practical principles that presuppose an *object* (matter) of the faculty of desire as the determining ground of the will are, without exception, empirical and can furnish no practical laws" (5:21). The "matter" of a desire is its object ("an object whose reality is desired"). Kant then says that "when the desire for this object precedes the practical rule and is the condition of its becoming a principle, then I say ... that this principle is in that case always empirical" (5:21). This last definition makes being "empirical" (later, Kant says "material") a matter of how the principle functions in a particular deliberative "case." When an agent begins with a desire for some object and then, simply out of that desire, adopts some practical rule or principle, then the resulting principle is empirical.

In such a particular "case," desire or inclination is doing all the motivational work and principles are, in Humean fashion, slaves to it. The "determining ground of choice" in that case is then the "representation of an object" from the perspective of the preceding desire "by which the faculty of desire is determined to realize the object" (5:21). "[I]n such a case the determining ground of choice must always be empirical," and as the principle is "based only" on this empirical condition, it cannot be regarded (or cognized) as a practical law, since no such empirical condition can be assumed to hold (either normatively or psychologically) for all rational beings (5:21–22).

It follows from this reasoning that if an agent adopts a practical principle or rule motivated only by their desires for specific (empirical) objects, in order to realize their desires' objects as their action's effects, then they cannot be cognizing the principle as a practical law. Suppose the principle is something like, "Do whatever will maximize the satisfaction of your desires," in universalized form: "Agents should maximize the satisfaction of their desires." If the only thing leading one to adopt such a principle for one's own conduct is desire, that can hardly justify acceptance of the principle as one on which all rational agents should act.

As important as that is, however, it would not rule out adopting the very same principle, with very same content, on other grounds, even, indeed, because the agent took the universalized version of it to be a practical law. A principle might be empirical or material in the sense that satisfying empirical desires is part of what the principle recommends, without its being true that in some particular deliberative "case" the agent in question adopts and acts on it only because they are motivated to do so by their empirical desires. Versions of *eudaimonism* or rational egoism have been advanced as theories of practical reason since the ancients. If anything, it has been the default view. Imagine someone who accepts rational egoism and who, like Butler, identifies agents' good or happiness with desire-satisfaction. Arguably, Kant accepts some such theory of happiness himself.

Imagine someone now who adopts the principle of maximizing their own desire satisfaction not because they are motivated to do so by their own desires, but because they accept that that is what any rational agent should do. Again, their acceptance of the latter is also not motivated by their own desires. Suppose they independently come to accept desire-satisfaction egoism as a theory of practical reason. If they do, then though their adopted principle (maxim) will have the very same content as "empirical" or "material" principles in Kant's sense, their principle will not count as "empirical" or "material" in the sense that Kant seems to be relying on. The agent's desires for specific objects will indeed "preced[e] the practical rule," but the desires will not be "the condition of its becoming a principle" in sense of the agent's adopting of the principle's being "based only" on such a "subjective condition of receptivity to a pleasure or displeasure" (5:21).

If "empirical" (or "material") principles are defined as those that are based only on empirical subjective conditions in this particular-agent-guiding sense, then Theorem I follows fairly readily. But so understood, both this definition and Theorem I concern not principles as individuated by their content but considered as particular *agents'* principles. What Theorem I then says is that if what motivates an agent's adopting and following a principle of whatever content is their empirical desires (what Kant generally calls "inclinations"), then the principle cannot be functioning as a practical law in the agent's reasoning. The agent cannot be treating the principle as an objective principle that applies to all rational agents.

So far, however, this says nothing about the content of empirical desires. It is consistent with the definition of empirical principles that the principle "Maximize desire-satisfaction" is not itself an empirical desire.

Ultimately, Kant wants to derive the Fundamental Law of Pure Practical Reason, *KpV*'s equivalent of the CI: "So act that the maxim of your will could always holds at the same time as a principle in a giving of universal law" (5:30). Theorem III is a key linking premise: "If a rational being is to think of his maxims as practical universal laws, he can think of them only as principles that contain the determining ground of the will not by their matter but only by their form" (5:27). If Kant can show that practical laws have to be grounded in the form of the will rather than anything that could independently give it content, then it would seem that that would establish autonomy of the will ("the property of the will by which it is a law to itself (independently of any property of the objects of volition)") (1996a: 4:440). And all the formulations of the CI would then follow from that by virtue of the analytical arguments of *Groundwork II*.

Unlike the *Groundwork*, however, *KpV*'s arguments are meant to be free of any premises about (deontic) morality. Kant's proofs of Theorems I through III, and of the Fundamental Law of Pure Practical Reason following from them, are, like those of *Groundwork I* and *II*, analytical, but they attempt to analyze the concepts of rational agency and norms of practical reason (practical laws). Even if Kant can show that the Fundamental Law follows from these concepts, however, that will not dispatch the worry he raises about the possibly "chimerical" character of morality. It *would* show that autonomy (and therefore, deontic moral concepts) are not only mutually entailing, but that they also entail, are entailed by, the concepts of rational agency and practical law. But it would follow from that entailment that deontic moral concepts are not chimerical only if it could be shown that the concepts of rational agency and practical law are not chimerical themselves. Such a claim could not be analytic; it would have to be synthetic *a priori*. And the only way to establish such a synthetic *a priori* truth, Kant thinks, is through a critique of practical reason (of the kind that Kant unsuccessfully attempted in *Groundwork III*). In *KpV*, Kant tries to establish the claim through his "fact of reason" argument, which we shall consider in the next section.

The question we face now is how Kant can get from Theorem I, considered in the particular-agent-guiding sense in which it is most plausible, to Theorem III, considered in the sense necessary to establish autonomy. Theorem III says, again, that "[i]f a rational being is to think of his maxims as practical laws, he can think of them only as principles that contain the determining ground of the will not by their matter but only by their form" (1996b: 5:27). For Theorem III to entail that the will is a "law to itself" independently of any possible contents ("objects of volition") (1996a: 4:440), it must be read in a way that rules out interpretations consistent with the particular-agent-guiding sense of Theorem I.

The issue is how to interpret Theorem III's requirement that to think of maxims as practical laws, the agent must see them as "contain[ing] the determining ground of the will not by their matter" (1996b: 5:27). What seems to follow from Theorem I as we have been interpreting it is that insofar as an agent is moved to adopt and act on a maxim *solely because* of their empirical desires, then they cannot be viewing their principle as a practical law. The "matter" is the "determining ground" of their will here, as their will is being formed entirely under the motivational influence of their empirical desires. As we saw, however, if it is interpreted in this way, Theorem I is consistent with the matter of an agent's desires being the "determining ground" of their will in a different sense that does not rule out their viewing the principle of their will as a practical law. To take the most obvious case, again, they might hold it to be a practical law that agents should maximize the satisfaction of their desires. They might not adopt this maxim simply owing to the motivational pressures of their desires.

How should Theorem III be interpreted if it is to follow from Theorem I? (Theorem II, that all material practical principles "come under the general principle of self-love," does no independent work in proving Theorem III (5:22).) The sense in which an agent must think of their maxims as "containing the determining ground of the will not by their matter" would have to be the same particular-agent-guiding sense. Interpreted thus far, indeed, Theorem III just *is* Theorem I. Theorem I states that agents must not regard their own adoption of and action on principles as being entirely motivationally driven by their (empirical) desires if they are to regard them as practical laws. But Theorem III adds a further positive requirement. To view principles as practical laws an agent must regard them as "containing the determining ground of the will ... only by their form" (5:27).

This, then, is the question we must therefore confront: how to interpret the phrase "only by their form" in order to make it true both that (i) Theorem III follows from the most plausible version of Theorem I and that (ii) Theorem III entails autonomy of the will, that the will can be a "law to itself" independently of any fact about its possible contents ("any property of the objects of volition")? And there seems to be no way to do this. Suppose we interpret "only by their form" in such a way that the agent we considered – the one who believes that adopting the principle of maximizing their desire satisfaction is dictated by a rational norm of action (practical law) – satisfies the "only by their form" condition. Theorem III will then follow from Theorem I all right, but it will not entail autonomy of the will. It will not follow from Theorem III that any, much less every, practical law is grounded only in the *form of the will*, independently of any properties of the will's possible content.

Or take a different kind of case, where an agent regards certain possible states of the world as intrinsically good or desirable in G. E. Moore's sense (Moore 1993). Imagine, for example, that benevolence or love involves regarding the realization of the good or happiness of the beloved as good in itself. Suppose then that a loving agent adopts the principle of acting to bring about the beloved person's good whenever that is possible. Their maxim need not be "empirical" or "material" in Theorem I's most plausible sense. Even if, indeed, they regard their appreciation of the intrinsic value of their beloved's welfare as being connected to their love or benevolence *epistemically* (which we can grant for these purposes involves an empirical desire), it does not follow that they would have to see their principle of action as itself grounded in their desire. To the contrary, they would see their desire as itself a response to their beloved's value and the intrinsic desirability of their well-being. They would regard the beloved's well-being as providing a(n agent-neutral) normative reason for them, but also, in principle, for anyone, to promote it (Darwall 2002: 69–72). In that sense, they would see their principle as a practical law. If, again, this were to count as their adopting the principle "only by [its] form," it would obviously not involve their seeing their principle as deriving simply from the pure form of the will.

There is also the case we considered in our discussion of *Groundwork I* and *II* that revealed a gap in Kant's arguments for the CI, both from the goodness of the good will and from the idea of rational action. An agent might adopt the principle of prudence, of doing whatever is good for them (whether that consists in desire-satisfaction or not), not out of their desire for their own good but because they think it is normative for rational agents (or rational human agents) as such. Again, that adoption would be grounded only in the principle's form in the sense that follows plausibly from Theorem I, but the principle would not necessarily be grounded in the pure *form of the will.*

Alternatively, we might try to interpret Theorem I in some different way that does entail an interpretation of Theorem III required for it to entail autonomy of the will. The problem will now be the reverse, namely, that the requisite definitions will no longer yield a Theorem I that is plausible and uncontroversial. The various possibilities we have just been considering will no longer be consistent with Theorem I so interpreted. But that will be because these alternatives to the idea that normative reasons and rational norms of action can be grounded only in the pure form of the will have been ruled out by definition in the first place.

At this point, we might step back from the letter of *KpV* and reflect on what we could think of as the spirit of Kant's critical philosophy in relation to it. The general thrust of Kant's Copernican Revolution is to seek the grounds of theoretical and practical cognition, not as "dogmatic" philosophers (like the British rationalists) supposed in what is somehow "given" to us, but in structures a mind must itself impose in order for there to be such a thing as theoretical or practical cognition at all. So viewed, autonomy is what would have to play the relevant structuring role on the practical side. As against the intuitionists, Kant does not grant the validity of practical norms independently of practical reason's exercise. Practical reason is not a faculty of intellectual perception of independent normative truths. Rather normative practical truths are made true by facts about the exercise of practical reason.

Constructivist or "procedural realist" interpretations of Kant, like those of Rawls and Korsgaard, emphasize this aspect of Kant's thought (Korsgaard 1996a, 1996b; Rawls 2000). What Rawls calls the CI procedure can be interpreted as a "procedure of construction" that is not simply an epistemic device for discovering deontic moral truth but a procedure the correct application of which *explains* deontic moral truth. Understood at this level, however, the CI procedure might be seen as a *normative* deontic moral theory rather than a metaethical theory that might compete with realist and irrealist theories (or be a version of either). It could be seen as operating at the same level as contractualism, as, for example, Derek Parfit understands what he calls the "Kantian Contractualist Formula" (Scanlon 1998; Parfit 2011).

Korsgaard's constructivist, "procedural realist" interpretation of Kant aims to cut more deeply to the metaphysical, metaethical level. It is of the nature of practical normative truth that it must be able to be grounded in an agent's deliberative context, from the practical point of view. Kant "start[s] from the fact that when we make a choice, we must regard its object as good" (Korsgaard 1996a: 122). We cannot, however, just take the goodness of the objects of our desires for granted. "Being human we must endorse our impulses before we can act on them" (122). We must ask whether what we take to be good really is, and what makes it good. "Rejecting one form of realism," Korsgaard continues, Kant "decided that the goodness was not in the objects themselves" (122). We would not find them good, after all, unless we desired them. "Kant saw that we take things to be important because they are important to us – and he concluded that we must therefore take ourselves to be important" (122).

This is the Kantian argument for FH that I mentioned in passing above (see also Wood 1999: 129–130). As I said there, although we can agree, as a matter of normative moral theory, that the most plausible justification for taking someone's will and choices, either one's own or someone else's, as reason giving is respect for them and their dignity as equal moral persons, there are insuperable objections to the argument at the level of the metaphysics of value (Darwall 2006: 229–235, 2013b: 93–114). The idea that the value of persons grounds a constructive procedure might be most plausible *within* deontic moral theory, in something like the way the Rawlsian interpretation of CI discussed above treats it.

Similarly, Korsgaard discusses an "appeal to autonomy" as a source of moral normativity according to "Kant and Kantian constructivists" like Rawls: "Kantians believe that the source of the normativity of moral claims must be found in the agent's own will" (Korsgaard 1996a: 19). This recalls the *Groundwork*'s FA: "the idea of the will of very rational being as a *will giving universal law*" (Kant 1996a: 4:432). As we discussed before, however, FA functions *within* deontic moral theory as a way of linking FUL to FH and FKE. It results from unpacking the "generally received concept of morality" (4:445). Nothing that underlies the attractiveness of FA and of autonomy as the source of moral normativity in that context, however, can support autonomy in a critique of practical reason of the kind Kant thinks necessary to establish that deontic morality is not chimerical.

Perhaps we do better, however, to regard Kant not as giving specific arguments for a constructivist metaethics but as putting forward a systematic metaethical alternative to forms of realism. Whether it should be accepted would ultimately require assessing the overall theoretical costs and benefits as judged in comparison with other metaethical theories. And to be sure, there is something undeniably attractive about the thought of being able to derive substantive normative practical conclusions from procedural constraints of practical reason. There can be widespread agreement that some rational requirements – for example, those of instrumental rationality and similar constraints of rational coherence that John Broome has studied – are built into the very possibility of rational agency (Broome 2013). But it can reasonably be doubted whether all normative reasons for acting or considerations that can make an action good (even indeed for any rational agent) must be able to be derived from procedural rationality and its requirements (Scanlon 2014: 90–11; Parfit 2011). To take perhaps the most powerful counterexample, benevolence and love seem to present us with access to the agent-neutral value of their objects as reason-giving in themselves, and it is difficult to see how any such value could be grounded in the form of the will or requirements of rational agency.

We are left, then, with the problem that we do not yet have any grounding for autonomy, as Kant seems to believe we need. *KpV*'s analytical arguments fail to establish autonomy and the Fundamental Law of Pure Practical Reason. Even if these analytical arguments were successful, however, that would simply widen the circle of reciprocal concepts. The (moral) analytical arguments of *Groundwork I* and *II* established the reciprocity thesis – that morality and autonomy imply one another. But that still left open the question of whether either concept was more than "chimerical." Similarly, were *KpV*'s (rational) analytical arguments to succeed, they would establish a wider reciprocity thesis – that morality, autonomy, and practical reason imply one another. But strictly speaking, it would be compatible with this wider reciprocity thesis that none of these concepts are instantiated, that all are chimerical.

The Fact of Reason

Groundwork III sought to fill this gap by arguing that autonomy is an inescapable presupposition of practical reason. If that strategy had succeeded, it would have shown, together with the reciprocity thesis, that any agent is rationally committed in their deliberations to morality, the CI, and the dignity of persons as well. And that would arguably be all the vindication that deontic morality would need or could possibly hope for.[28]

---

[28] But would it not then be true that if Kant could establish a wider reciprocity thesis between rational agency, practical law, autonomy, and morality, that a strategy similar to that of *Groundwork III*, but beginning from the premise that deliberation must assume some concepts of rational agency and practical law, could then work? The problem would be exactly how to understand "rational agency" and "practical law" in such a presuppositional argument. As we noted when we considered Kant's argument in *Groundwork III*, even if a deliberating agent has to assume *some* concept of rational agency and practical law in order to deliberate intelligibly at all, it seems not to be true that they need to assume concepts that are plausibly equivalent to autonomy and those of deontic morality. Even if, for example, they must presuppose rational requirements of procedural rationality, these will be insufficient in themselves to generate contentful normative practical reasons (practical-good-making, or choiceworthy, considerations). And even if a deliberating agent must assume

In *KpV*, Kant abandons this strategy, arguing that although "freedom is indeed the *ratio essendi* of the moral law, the moral law is the *ratio cognoscendi* of freedom" (1996b: 5:4n). What does the work is Kant's discussion of two vivid examples, the second of which exemplifies the way in which consciousness of the moral law is the *ratio cognoscendi* of freedom, what Kant calls "a fact of reason" (5:30–31). Based on this discussion, Kant asserts: "Consciousness of this fundamental law may be called a fact of reason because one cannot reason it out from antecedent data of reason, for example, from consciousness of freedom (since this is not antecedently given to us)" (5:31).

In the first example, Kant imagines "someone [who] asserts of his lustful inclination that, when the desired object and the opportunity are present, it is quite irresistible to him" (5:30). About this case, Kant dryly observes:

> [A]sk him whether, if a gallows were erected in front of the house where he finds this opportunity and he would be hanged on it immediately after gratifying his lust, he would not then control his inclination. One need not conjecture very long what he would reply (5:30).

This example illustrates a kind of freedom, but one that is entirely compatible with actions always being motivated by inclinations whose objects are invariably some "effect" beyond the will's exercising itself in a law-guided way. It just shows that if an agent were placed in a situation in which they were more strongly inclined toward something other than the object of their lust, they would be moved by that stronger inclination.

The first case serves as a foil to set up Kant's discussion of the second:

> But ask him whether, if his prince demanded, on the pain of the same immediate execution, that he give false testimony against an honorable man whom the prince would like to destroy under a plausible pretext, he would consider it possible to overcome his love of life, however great it may be (5:30).

By contrast with the first case, Kant hazards no speculation about what the person *would* do in the second instance, nor does he speculate about what the person themselves thinks they would do. He confidently declares that the person "must admit without hesitation that it would be possible for him" not to falsely testify about the "honorable man" (5:30). Kant then concludes: "He judges, therefore, that he can do something because he is aware that he ought to do it and cognizes freedom within him, which, without the moral law, would have remained unknown to him" (5:30).

that contentful normative practical reasons exist (and therefore that there are valid practical laws), that will not show that all or even any such reasons must be able to grounded in the form of the will or be accessible by the exercise of practical rationality (understood in some formal or procedural way) alone.

Several aspects of the second example in contrast with the first bear comment. The most obvious aspect of it, first, is Kant's contrast between what might be plausibly thought to be the strongest possible inclination and what the agent must assume to be a source of motivation other than inclination, a source that is capable of motivating contrary to even the strongest inclination.

Second, the kind of freedom the agent must unhesitatingly admit is not just that they are capable of performing an act of some given kind, considered independently of motive, for example, that they are capable of performing the physical actions that constitute forbearing false testimony against an honorable person. The agent must admit that they can successfully be moved not to do this *because they know it would be wrong.* The deep point is that in having this bit of deontic moral knowledge, agents also thereby implicitly know that they can comply with their moral obligation simply by exercising the capacity that makes them subject to the moral law.

To bring out the distinctive importance of this point, suppose that the person in the second example is threatened not with their own death, but with serious injury to someone they care for. And stipulate that the presence of this threat, like the death threat, does not change the wrongness of the false testimony. Love and benevolent concern are different from (mere) inclinations in that they involve seeing their objects and their well-being as having an agent-neutral value that is independent of any inclination or desire-like mental state through which the value is felt or appreciated (Darwall 2002: 69–72). But here again, Kant's diagnosis applies. In judging that it would be wrong to testify falsely against an innocent person, even at the cost of injury to a loved one, one seems committed to judging that one *can* not do so, indeed, that one can just because one knows it is wrong. Or suppose the threat is to destroy something else one thinks to have significant intrinsic value, say a library of precious books. The same reasoning seems to apply.

Most importantly, third, an essential aspect of Kant's thought experiment is that it involves consciousness of the *moral* law. "He judges, therefore, that he can do something because he is aware that he ought to do it" (Kant 1996b: 5:30). "[W]ithout the moral law," "freedom ... would have remained unknown to him" (5:30). Recall that for Kant, "ought," imperatives, and obligation are the mark of deontic morality, which are all distinctive of finite imperfect rational agential thought and which have no place in the reasoning of perfectly rational agents.

As we noted in our discussion of the British rationalists, there is a plausible line of thought explaining the fact of reason that has to do with deontic morality's conceptual connection to accountability. Since one can intelligibly hold accountable only agents who have the capacity to hold themselves accountable in their own practical thought, it seems a conceptually necessary truth that an agent's actions can be morally wrong, a violation of their moral obligation, if, and only if, they have the capacity to know that and be appropriately moved by this knowledge. It must be the case, in other words, that exercise of the very capacities that make them subject to the moral law and obligated by it suffices to enable them to comply. I submit that the plausibility of Kant's claims about the second example and, therefore, of the fact of reason, itself depends on deontic morality's accountability-involving character.

Again, Kant calls the capacity of rational agents to act on a law that is grounded only in the form of the will, independently of any facts about the "objects of volition," "autonomy" (1996a: 4:440). Autonomy thus involves the capacity to act for reasons and norms that are not based in the goodness of any states the will might bring about as effects, but in formal features of will. This is where the versions of Kant's second example we considered, in which agents take themselves to be morally obligated to forgo the promotion of agent-neutral goods, are especially apt. It might well be that many normative reasons for acting concern such agent-neutral goods, which we are nonetheless required by deontic morality, on occasion, to forgo. Especially in such cases, we see that in taking ourselves to be so obligated, we must "admit without hesitation" that we can do so just because we ought (in the deontic moral sense). The moral law might indeed be the only substantive norm of practical reason that is grounded in the form of the will, with autonomy being guaranteed by deontic morality's conceptual connection to accountability.

Necessitation and Respect

I have been emphasizing that, for Kant, deontic moral concepts play no role in pure practical reasoning; they function only in the "necessitating" practical thought of finite rational agents through which the imperfect agents "restrain" themselves to do what they already have, independently, good reason to do. Considerations of moral right and wrong themselves provide no further normative reasons. Kant develops an empirical account of how necessitation works through the feeling of respect in Chapter III of *KpV*, "On the incentives of pure practical reason," to which we now turn (1996b: 5:71).

An action can have "moral worth" only if "*the moral law determine[s] the will immediately*" (5:71). But how does this happen empirically? How is "immediately" free action on a law of pure practical reason possible in the empirical ("phenomenal") world? For Kant, all phenomenal events must have phenomenal causes. This is guaranteed transcendentally, since anything empirical, any possible object of experience, must be conceived through the category of causation in space and time. This is no less true of actions than it is of anything else that can be experienced in time. It follows for Kant that however much a moral action must be a product of free practical reason, its empirical manifestation must nonetheless be empirically caused.

Kant's candidate for this cause is the feeling of *respect*. When we freely choose to do something because morality requires it, we are moved, as a matter of empirical psychology, by the feeling of respect. Kant calls this an *a priori* feeling, since its existence can be established on *a priori* grounds (5:79). That there must be some such feeling follows from the fact that if moral actions, determined "immediately" by a law of pure practical reason, are to manifest themselves empirically, they must have empirical causes, and this, Kant thinks, must be a feeling of some kind.

Kant calls an "incentive" "the subjective determining ground of the will of a being whose reason does not by its nature necessarily conform with the objective law" (5:72). Only finite beings with an empirical nature are subject to incentives; a "divine will" is not (5:72). But although incentives operate through empirical (felt) causes by definition, the "determining ground" of the agent's will, the *reason for which* the agent acts, is not the empirical feeling itself. "[R]espect for the law is not the incentive to morality; instead it [respect] is morality itself subjectively considered as an incentive" (5:76). Moral action done "from duty," *for the reason that* the moral law requires it, expresses itself in the empirical world as action done from respect (5:81). It is through respect that the moral law manifests itself empirically and so can give rise "immediately" to moral action.

It is helpful to begin with the following remarkable passage:

> [B]efore a humble common man in whom I perceive uprightness of character in a higher degree than I am aware of in myself *my spirit bows*, whether I want it or whether I do not and hold my head ever so high, that he may not overlook my superior position. Why is this? His example holds before me a law that strikes down my self-conceit when I compare it with my conduct, and I see observance of that law and hence its *practicability* proved before me in fact (5:77).

"Humble," "eminent," and "superior position" all signal that Kant is here contrasting moral respect with the form that respect takes in recognizing *social status*. The passage comes directly after Kant's quotation of a saying of Fontenelle's: "*I bow before an eminent man, but my spirit does not bow*" (5:76). Bowing is an essentially social form of respect. It is a form of deference that supports or honors, and thereby helps constitute, a (high) social status. It is a species of *recognition respect*, *honor respect*, as I have elsewhere called it, that is the very medium through which hierarchies of honor and status are socially constructed (Darwall 1977, 2013d). To be "eminent" or to have "superior position" just is to be recognized as such through others' (publicly) treating one as having that status, for example, by bowing.

Fontenelle says that though he bows before an eminent man, his "spirit does not bow." This makes an important point. Eminent status need not be jeopardized by insincere expressions of honor. So long as his bow is *performatively received* as sincere by the *characters* in the the social drama in which he takes part, whether or not it is sincere or is even believed to be, that is enough to make it a genuine case of honor respect and to confirm or further enhance the eminent social status of the actual individual to whom the bow is made (Darwall 2013d). Of course, if an honoring gesture wears its insincerity on its sleeve, that can undermine a bow's social significance. All of the socially significant "action" goes on in public.

Kant tells us, first, that unlike Fontenelle who bows before an eminent man but whose "spirit does not bow," *his* spirit *does* bow before a "humble common man." And Kant adds that his spirit bows, "whether I want it or whether I do not and *hold my head ever so high, that he may not overlook my superior position*" (1996b: 5:77, emphasis added). The part I have italicized exemplifies performative contempt within the social drama in which Kant partakes (Darwall 2018). Holding one's head high so that a social inferior "may not overlook" one's superior position "puts" an "inferior" individual "in their place."

It seems most natural to take the kind of moral respect Kant here describes to be appraisal respect or moral esteem rather than recognition respect (Darwall 1977). Any reaction to someone's "uprightness of character" is from an observer's standpoint in appraising that person's (motivated) conduct or character; it is not from a deliberative perspective in deciding how to treat someone as a way of recognizing them.

The feeling of respect that manifests itself unbidden when we contemplate good will or "uprightness of character" is moral appraisal respect (1996b: 5:77). To play the role it is slated for in Kant's moral psychology, however, respect must be felt, and be able to motivate action, *from the deliberative standpoint*. It must be for the moral law, and for the dignity of persons as mandated by it, as making claims on our conduct. Only then is respect for "morality itself subjectively considered as an incentive" (5:76). It must be the form of respect that is realized in an upright person themselves when *they* deliberate about what to do.

What is front and center in Kant's example, however, is appraisal respect for an ordinary person of low status. Disarmed by their humility in the face of Kant's public pride, Kant involuntarily feels moral esteem for their character. It is important that this unbidden respect is for *uprightness*, not for anything especially ethically distinguished. It is for someone who conscientiously follows the very same deontic standards that obligate us all as one person among others, for an ordinary moral agent who simply does their job as a moral agent. The man's example, Kant says, "holds before me a law that strikes down my self-conceit when I compare it with my conduct, and I see observance of that law and hence its *practicability* proved before me in fact" (5:77).

Kant describes the experience of respect as a kind of humiliation. We do not simply find ourselves with unbidden moral esteem for a humble upright person, we also feel the force of a normative standard, the moral law, that "strikes down" or "humiliates" "self-conceit" in us. In feeling unbidden moral appraisal respect for them, one is brought face to face with a standard of conduct (the moral law) that applies equally to one as well. Their "example holds before me a law that strikes down my self-conceit" (5:77). And this, Kant must be thinking, leads unavoidably from moral appraisal respect for the upright person to moral *recognition* respect of the law itself, to emulating the moral recognition respect that the upright person themselves feels in being moved to comply with the moral law "immediately" or "by morality itself subjectively considered as an incentive" (5:76).

But what is self-conceit? And what is the "humiliation" it receives that Kant thinks is part of felt respect for the moral law? Kant distinguishes two forms of "self-regard": "self-love" and "self-conceit" (5:73). Self-love is a "predominant *benevolence* toward oneself," roughly caring more for oneself and more about one's well-being than about others'. Self-conceit, by contrast, consists in "*satisfaction with oneself*" or "esteem for oneself" that is independent of and unconstrained by the moral law.

Self-love need only by "restrict[ed]" "to the condition of agreement with" the moral law (5:73). Unlike self-conceit, self-love does not purport to provide any standard for esteem or satisfaction with ourselves at all, much less one that is unconstrained by the moral law. Concern for oneself or desire for one's own well-being, however strong, need not pronounce on estimability.

By self-conceit, however, Kant means forms of self-satisfaction or self-esteem on grounds that purport to be independent of and unconstrained by the moral law. At its most extreme, this can include forms of ego-obsession and involvement that entail seeing oneself as inherently better than or superior to others. But it also encompasses any standard of esteem that is independent of and unconstrained by the common moral standard of the moral law.

Internalized conceptions of social, racial, and gender privilege are paradigm examples. In our passage, Kant's gentleman is able to maintain his high social standing while feeling unbidden moral esteem for a "humble common man." So long as his continuing to enact his social superiority ("holding his head so high") is *just* an act, there may not yet be any self-conceit to be struck down. But suppose his "character" does not simply so act in the social drama, but that he, the individual playing this role, indulges in feeling *justified* in so acting. Now we have self-conceit. He, the actual human individual, is feeling self-satisfied esteem for himself as an honorable person to whom people should defer independently of the moral law.

It is this latter, self-esteem's form in self-conceit, that cannot coexist simultaneously with his moral esteem for the common humble upright person. Esteem for uprightness just *is* esteem for being governed "immediately" by the moral law, a normative standard that is common to all persons, irrespective of their rank, status, or personae, *any such considerations to the contrary notwithstanding*. From the perspective of moral appraisal respect for uprightness, we see that "all claims to esteem for oneself that precede accord with the moral law are null and quite unwarranted" (5:73). From this standpoint, any standard for esteem deriving from social status hierarchies are unmasked as mere pretension. And even standards of genuine human excellence are seen to be limited and regulated by the moral law.

Thus is self-conceit struck down or humiliated. Like humiliations of more familiar kinds, a "superior" person feeling moral esteem for a "lower" upright person cannot escape a felt lowering that implicitly recognizes that any standard that might rationalize their superiority is bogus (self-conceit's "illusion" (5:76)), since they cannot possibly be more estimable than an upright person who is governed by a law that binds both in common as persons (5:77). And this humiliation has a painful edge that Kant holds to be essential to respect (5:73).

In feeling respect for a common upright person's good will, one esteems them for their exercise of a capacity that is shared between respecter and respected. The upright person provides an "example" of "immediately" acting on the moral law ("from duty"), "and hence its *practicability* [is] proved before me in fact" (5:71, 5:77, 5:81). "Practicability" here cannot just mean that everyone can act in accordance with the moral law, that it never demands anything it is impossible to do. We hardly need the example of an upright person to prove that it is possible to keep our promises, tell the truth, and act in *conformity* with the moral law (as Kant says, "legally," in our external conduct (5:151)). What the common upright person shows by example is that, just like the respected, the respecter, *whoever they may be*, can also act "*immediately*" on the law, embodying its "*spirit*" and not just its "*letter*" (5:72). It demonstrates the possibility of acting not just in accord with duty, but from duty in a way that gives action "genuine moral worth" (1996a: 4:398).

This brings us to respect's relation to *necessitation* and, through it, to the deontic moral representations – duty, oughts, and imperatives – that mediate respect for the moral law. Kant lays this out in the following passage.

> The consciousness of a *free* submission of the will to the law, yet as combined with an unavoidable constraint put on all inclinations though

> only by one's own reason, is respect for the law. … An action that is objectively practical in accordance with this law, with the exclusion of every determining ground of inclination, is called *duty*, which, because of that exclusion, contains in its concept practical *necessitation*, that is, determination to actions however *reluctantly* they may be done (1996b: 5:80).

From the beginning of the *Groundwork*, Kant observes a distinction between practical law, which applies to all rational beings, perfect and imperfect alike, and the moral law and its associated duties, obligations, oughts, and imperatives, that apply only to finite, imperfect rational agents who, in addition to having practical reason, are subject also to inclinations. The latter must restrain potentially conflicting inclinations through their reason, and the process through which they do it is necessitation, mediated by the feeling of respect, which itself involves *deontic representations* of what one must do – what, Kant says, reason *commands* one to do. "The representation of an objective principle, insofar as it is necessitating for a will, is called a command (of reason), and the formula of the command is called an **imperative**" (1996a: 4:413). "[D]uty is," Kant says, "*the necessity of an action from respect for law*" (4:400).

> The moral law is, in other words, for the will of a perfect being a law of *holiness*, but for the will of every finite rational being a law of *duty*, of moral necessitation and of the determination of his actions through *respect* for this law (1996b: 5:83).

This means, again, that deontic notions of duty, wrong, requirement, prohibition, and so on, are no part of pure practical reason *per se*. They enter from the perspective of finite rational agents in whom pure reason can be practical only through necessitating representations of the practical law as something they must constrain themselves to comply with through respect for reason's commands.

Kant on the Right and the Good

Recall Sidgwick's claim that whereas the ancients thought of virtue and choiceworthy conduct as different species of the good, the modern period has been marked by philosophers who recognize duty as an independent ethical concept and who believe that moral agents have a "regulative or governing faculty," "conscience," that responds to it (Sidgwick 1964: 198). These moderns think, that is, that conscience is a part of practical reason in the sense that deontic morality is an independent source of normative reasons.

It follows from our analysis in the last section, however, that if conscience operates via moral necessitation, it cannot be part of pure practical reason, as Kant understands it, and therefore that Kant actually rejects this "modern" view. Perfectly rational beings have neither duties nor conscience, since the "moral necessitation" that is essential to these concepts is foreign to their nature. Deontic moral concepts like duty arise only from the perspective of an imperfect rational being who must conceive of practical laws as authoritative commands addressed to them and which they must hold themselves accountable for complying with in their conscience. Moral duty is impotent, for Kant, to provide any normative reason for acting itself. All normative reasons are registered already in the practical law, which is not itself deontic. If reason could create further reasons by commanding what there is most reason to do, it would be capable of indefinitely magnifying even small difference in the relative weight of reasons by infinite reiteration.[29]

What Kant calls "the wonderful capacity within us which we call conscience" arises only from the perspective of a finite rational agent requiring necessitation (1996b: 5:98). In *The Metaphysics of Morals*, Kant describes the process through which human beings can hold themselves accountable in their own conscience. "A human being who accuses himself in conscience must think of a dual personality in himself, a doubled self" (1996c: 6:438n). We erect "an ideal person (the authorized judge of conscience)" within ourselves who occupies the perspective of pure practical reason (6:439). This personification of reason "*impose[s] all obligation*," and "must be, or be thought as, a person in relation to whom all duties whatsoever are to be regarded as also his commands" (6:439). We thus see ourselves as subject to the authoritative commands of practical reason and hold ourselves accountable for complying with them.

The right in Sidgwick's deontic sense is thus not a concept of pure practical reason; it enters neither into practical laws nor into the practical reasoning of a perfectly rational being. "The only objects of a practical reason are therefore those of the *good* and the *evil*," Kant says, where these are respectively understood as the "necessary object[s] of the faculty of desire ... [and] aversion ... in accordance with a principle of reason," respectively (1996b: 5:58).

Rawls is famous for the claim that "the priority of right" over the good "is a central feature of Kant's ethics," as it is of Rawls's own conception of justice as fairness (Rawls 1971: 31). In support, Rawls cites a section of *KpV* (Rawls 2000: 230–232).[30] The best passage for Rawls's purposes is the following:

> [T]he concept of good and evil must not be determined before the moral law (for which, as it would seem, this concept would have to be made the basis) but only ... after it and by means of it (Kant 1996b: 5:63).

---

[29] Thus suppose that there is slightly more reason to do A than B. Reason might then command doing A, creating even more reason to do A. But because there is now more reason, reason might command doing A because of this greater reason, creating yet more reason to do A. And so on.

[30] Rawls refers to 5:62–65.

Kant certainly does hold that the concepts of good (*das Gute*) and evil (*das Böse*) must be distinguished from those of well-being (*das Wohl*) and ill-being (*das Übel*), respectively, and that the "objects of a practical reason" cannot be derived from these latter empirical concepts (5:58–60). Since Sidgwick and Rawls understand the good as well-being (*das Wohl*), it follows that Kant does hold that "the objects of a practical reason" cannot be derived from the good as Sidgwick and Rawls understand it.

When, however, Kant says that "the concept of good and evil must not be determined before the moral law," he means nothing beyond the *KpV*'s signature thesis that the object of pure practical reason must be conceived formally through freedom, and, therefore, in accordance with the Fundamental Law of Pure Practical Reason (5:63). For Kant, this is a claim about the practical *good*, not about deontic morality and right as he understands it. He does not mean that the concept of good (*das Gute*) must be determined subsequent to the moral law, conceived in the distinctively deontic terms through which it is given to imperfect rational beings. It remains true for Kant that "[t]he only objects" of pure practical reason are "those of the *good* and the *evil*" (5:58).[31] "Imperatives," for Kant, "say that to do or to omit something would be good, but they say it to a will that does not always do something just because it is represented to it that it would be good to do that thing" (1996a: 4:413).

The question before any rational agent is what it would be good or best to do in the sense of what there is most reason to do. When Kant says that "the concept of good is ... derived from an antecedent practical law," what he means is that the concept of good that is the object of pure practical reason is simply that of "practical good" or the choiceworthy: what it would be best *to do*, not well-being or what would be good *to happen* (either from the agent's point of view or from the "point of view of the universe" (agent-neutral value)) (Kant 1996b: 5:58, 5:114; Sidgwick 1967: 381). "*Good* or *evil* always signifies a reference to the *will* insofar as it is determined by the *law of reason*" (1996b: 5:60).

If "right" is taken in its distinctive deontic sense, therefore, Kant does not hold that the right is prior to the good as he, Kant, understands the good (*das Gute*). The question of pure practical reason is what is good or best to do. That must be determined independently of any issue of moral duty or obligation. The latter are simply the form that reason's deliverances of what it is good or best to do take from the perspective of a will that can have motives to act otherwise.

Rawls used the slogan "the right is prior to the good" to contrast his and Kant's view with teleological or consequentialist theories in which "the good

---

[31] Cf. "A perfectly good will would, therefore, equally stand under objective laws (of the good), but it could not on this account be represented as *necessitated* to actions in conformity with law since of itself, by its subjective constitution, it can be determined only through the representation of the good" (Kant 1996a: 4:414). For an insightful analysis of this passage and its significance, see Kosch, 2006: 47–50.

is defined independently of the right" and the right is determined by the good, usually as what maximizes it, either directly or indirectly (Rawls 1971: 25). Consequentialists frequently identify the good with well-being (*das Wohl*), and *always* with what is good *to happen* (with valuable states of affairs). Rawls is right to insist that Kant rejects any such view. Kant's point in the second *Critique* is that what it is good to do can only be determined by the free use of practical reason, hence not (simply anyway) by what would promote well-being or would be good to happen. This is identical with the *Groundwork*'s thesis of "autonomy of the will" (1996a: 4:440).

Nevertheless, if we understand the good (*das Gute*), as Kant does himself, to fundamentally concern "the *will* insofar as it is determined by the *law of reason*," then Kant does not hold that the right, conceived deontically, can provide a source of reasons that do not derive from the good (1996b: 5:60). Neither is it the case that considerations of moral duty can figure as good-making features of action, as providing reasons that bear on what it is good or best to do. The common thought that we might have had sufficient reason to do something if it had not been wrong or violated an obligation cannot get a foothold. Being moral obligatory or a duty is simply the shadow that good or reason-supported actions cast for imperfect rational agents.

We are left, finally, with the question of Kant's success in vindicating "the concept of freedom," which "constitutes the *keystone* of the whole structure of a system of pure reason" (5:3–4). Departing from *Groundwork III*'s strategy of arguing that autonomy is an inescapable presupposition of practical reason, Kant argues in *KpV* that we can be assured of our freedom through our awareness of being bound by the moral law (the "fact of reason") (5:30–31). I have argued, however, that the plausibility of Kant's analysis of his key example of the "fact of reason" relies on the same conceptual connection between deontic morality and accountability that underlay the British rationalists' arguments for free moral agency. It turns out, however, that Kant rejects Butler's and the British rationalists' view that conscience is a form of practical *reason*. So he cannot accept that when conscientious agents act from duty – having as *their reason* that their action is morally required and taking it that that (deontic moral) fact is itself conclusive normative reason for them so to act – that they are right. On Kant's considered view, deontic moral facts are no part of pure practical reason and can provide no normative reasons for acting at all. It follows that even if ordinary moral agents necessarily take the fact that they are morally obligated to act as guaranteeing that they have (as accountable agents) the capacity to comply for that very reason, Kant himself is committed, as a theorist, to thinking that they are acting on a kind of illusion. Any normative reason to act is figured already into what would have made their action a good thing to do independently of its being their moral duty.

I should emphasize, however, that in stressing Kant's treatment of the moral deontic as normatively epiphenomenal, I am not questioning his commitment to the claim that the *content* of the moral law – the CI in its various formulations – is grounded in pure practical reason. Indeed, that is part of my point. All the normative work, for Kant, is done by practical law: what practical reason establishes as good or best for agents to do. That an action is a moral requirement or duty normatively adds nothing. Neither am I questioning that what practical reason dictates, for Kant, is respect and support for the *freedom* of rational agents. Above we noted with approval Guyer's interpretation of FH as "act only on maxims that could be accepted by everyone else as preserving their capacity for free choice as well" (Guyer 2006: 194). It is undeniably Kant's view that this formulation of the CI, like FUL and FA, is a dictate of pure practical reason. I have, to be sure, disputed Kant's *arguments* for these claims in the *Groundwork* and in *KpV*. But that is unquestionably his view. I have suggested that the most promising defense of it lies in systematic considerations of the critical philosophy overall and what Rawls calls Kant's "moral constructivism" (Rawls 2000: 237). Even here, however, constructivism may prove to be a more promising account of the metaethics of morality than of practical reason more generally.

Freedom, Constraint, and Right in *The Metaphysics of Morals*

Necessitation is the process through which finite agents constrain their inclinations in order to comply with the law of their own will or practical reason, thereby realizing the freedom Kant calls "autonomy." This is, we might say, the "internal" account of the relation between freedom and constraint for Kant. Autonomy is realized in finite agents by "an internal but intellectual constraint," which we impose on ourselves through the feeling of respect (Kant 1996b: 5:32). When inclinations tempt us away from what it would be best to do, they require "a resistance of practical reason" (5:32).

Kant also has an "external" account of the relation between freedom and constraint, one that parallels his internal account of moral, "internal lawgiving," and opens up an entirely new philosophical area, which Kant pursues in the *Doctrine of Right* (included in his *Metaphysics of Morals* (originally published in 1797)).[32] Just as morality, for Kant, is fundamentally concerned with internal lawgiving, constraint, and freedom (autonomy), so, in parallel, is his philosophy of right, which examines "the external … relation of one person to another," concerned with "external lawgiving," constraint, and freedom (1996c: 6:229–230).

Hegel famously remarked in his *Elements of the Philosophy of Right*, published almost twenty-five years later in 1821, that "the right of subjective freedom is the

---

[32] We should note that Johann Gottlieb Fichte's *Foundations of Natural Right*, which observes a similar distinction between ethics and theory of right, was published just before, in 1796–1797 (Fichte 2000).

pivotal and focal point in the difference between antiquity and the modern age" (Hegel 1991: 151). Kant's *Doctrine of Right* is in this sense a thoroughly modern text, providing, along with Fichte's *Foundations of Natural Right* (1796–1797), the model for Hegel's philosophy of right and establishing freedom as a, if not *the*, central concept of political and legal philosophy ever since.

The Metaphysics of Morals begins with a discussion of "preliminary concepts," organized around the relation of different forms of freedom to "internal" and "external lawgiving" (Kant 1996c: 6:221–228). "Moral laws" involve "internal lawgiving" through necessitation (6:221–222). The moral deontic notions of "duty," the morally "permitted," and "obligation" are all defined in relation to self-constraint (6:222). "[O]bligation involves not merely practical necessity (such as a law in general asserts) but also *necessitation*," that is, the psychological process we have been analyzing (6:223). "Deed[s]" are actions only "insofar as [they] come under obligatory laws" and can be "imputed" to the "person" who is obligated to perform them (6:223). Moral laws thus admit only of "internal lawgiving" (6:220–221).

By contrast, Kant uses "external law" to refer to "[o]bligatory laws for which there can be an external lawgiving," where that can operate through external constraints in a way the "internal lawgiving" of the moral law cannot (6:220, 6:224). "All duties," Kant says, "involve a concept of *constraint* through a law" (6:394). "Ethical duties" can involve only internal lawgiving and constraint (through necessitation), and "duties of right involve a constraint for which external lawgiving is also possible" (6:394).

Ethical duties and duties of right mark out the two parts of *The Metaphysics of Morals*: *Doctrine of Right* and *Doctrine of Virtue*, respectively. It is important to keep in mind, however, that even though duties of right cannot be ethical duties in Kant's technical sense, he clearly thinks we are morally obligated not to do what duties of right proscribe.[33] The point of Kant's terminology is that what ethical duties require is not (external) actions but the adoption and maintenance of ends. They are "ends that are also duties," duties of "wide obligation," as he also puts it, such that we have some discretion (*Spielraum*) in determining which specific actions to perform in their pursuit (6:385). Duties of right are "of narrow obligation," requiring specific actions that are capable of being exacted by external constraint and legislation.

The *Doctrine of Virtue* systematically explores the two "ends that are also duties": "*one's own perfection*" and "*the happiness of others*" (6:385). The former, Kant considers to be duties to oneself under various headings: "as an *Animal Being*," "as a *Moral Being*," and so on. And the latter are all "duties to others," including the "*Duty of Love*" and "the *Duty of Respect*" (6:492–493).[34]

---

[33] On this point, see Guyer 2006: 240.
[34] I discuss the duty of respect in relation to Kant's views on respect in Darwall 2013e.

What makes them all ethical duties, again, is that it is impossible for them to be exacted by external constraint. Though "I can indeed be constrained by others to perform *actions* …, I can never be constrained by others *to have an end*: only I myself can *make* something my end" (6:381). I do so through free self-constraining necessitation; external constraint is of no avail.

Duties of right, by contrast, do admit of external constraint. Indeed, Kant holds, they can be rightfully coerced, and the *Doctrine of Right* lays out how this can be. What is especially interesting from the point of view of the themes we have been discussing is that Kant holds that what makes ethical duties and duties of right both duties is that both essentially involve *constraint*. "All duties," again, "involve a concept of *constraint* through law" (6:394). Indeed, though the Gregor translation usually reserves "necessitation" for the self-constraint involved in inner lawgiving, it sometimes uses "necessitation" to refer to *external* constraint.

> The very *concept of duty* is already the concept of a *necessitation* (constraint) of free choice through the law. This constraint may be an *external constraint* or a *self-constraint* (6:379).

Kant uses both *Zwang* ("force") and *Nöthigung* ("compulsion" or "constraint") to refer to self-constraint *and* to external constraint. The crucial point is that even when it is backed by reason, a constraint is itself the application of *force* rather than reason. Rousseau is famous (or infamous) for claiming in *The Social Contract* that citizens who go against the general will must be "forced to be free" (Rousseau 2003: 53). It seems no exaggeration to use this same language to describe Kant's position concerning both internal and external legislation.

We have seen how Kant thinks self-constraint works through the (painful) feeling of respect in response to what we represent to ourselves as reason's commands (from, as it were, a second-person standpoint of accountability for compliance), thereby forcing ourselves to realize autonomy (following the law of our own will). Even if this necessarily involves the appearance of further normative reason beyond those practical-good-making considerations that back reason's command (more on this presently), Kant's position is that any such appearance is illusory and therefore that we are only able to get ourselves to do what there is independently good reason to do through self-applied force (*Zwang*).

A major aim of the *Doctrine of Right* is to carry the idea of freedom-preserving constraint through law that is part of the concept of duty in general, and to demonstrate how practical reason also dictates external constraint to preserve external freedom. Kant defines a "doctrine of right" as "[t]he sum of those laws for which an external lawgiving is possible" (6:229). His method, therefore, is not, as Ripstein has stressed, to "apply general moral principles to the factual circumstances that make political society necessary" (Ripstein 2009: 1).

Rather Kant works from within what he takes to be the different conceptual space of the right.

> The concept of right, insofar as it is related to an obligation corresponding to it (i.e., the moral concept of right), has to do ... only with the external and indeed practical relation of one person to another (Kant 1996c: 6:230).

"All that is in question," Kant says, "is the *form* in the relation of choice on the part of both, insofar as choice is regarded as *free*, and whether the action of one can be united with the freedom of the other in accordance with a universal law" (6:230).

On this basis, Kant lays out the "Universal Principle of Right": "Any action is *right* if it can coexist with everyone's freedom in accordance with a universal law" (6:230). This idea drives Kant's argument. Actions that are rightful by the Universal Principle are thereby within a sphere of protected external freedom. If, consequently, someone "hinders" such an action, thereby doing something that cannot itself be rightful (because it cannot coexist with everyone's freedom in accordance with universal law), they not only do wrong, they *wrong the hindered agent*, thereby violating their right (6:230–231). More specifically, they violate what Kant calls the "one innate right": "[*f*]*reedom* (independence from being constrained by another's choice), insofar as it can coexist with the freedom of every other in accordance with a universal law" (6:237). It is "the only original right belonging to every man by virtue of his humanity" (6:237).

The crucial point for our purposes is that Kant takes the right to freedom to justify *external constraint*. When someone hinders another's external freedom, the hindered person is justified in compelling the hinderer to desist, thereby "hindering ... [the] hindrance" (6:231). That this is rightful and no wronging of the hinderer follows analytically, Kant thinks, from the Universal Principle of Right. "Hence there is connected with right by the principle of contradiction an authorization to coerce someone who infringes upon it" (6:231). "Right and authorization to use coercion," Kant says, "therefore mean one and the same thing" (6:232).[35]

For Kant, consequently, external restraint preserves external freedom in a way that is entirely analogous to the way internal self-constraint realizes freedom in the form of autonomy. Through the latter we force ourselves to comply with the moral law, while through the former we force others to keep their

---

[35] In 6:232–233, Kant lays out an analogy between a "construction" of the concept of right that exhibits the rightfulness of a "fully reciprocal and equal coercion" and analogous geometrical constructions. For a masterly discussion of this and the *Doctrine of Right* overall, see Ripstein 2009.

actions within the sphere of rightful external freedom under universal law. There is, however, a further, deeper way in which Kant's account of the role of constraint in duty – both in our duties of right to others and in our duties (period) under the moral law – substitutes force for any recognition of duties as entailing distinctive deontic reasons for acting.[36]

To see how this is so, notice how Kant's understanding of a right as a justification for coercion compares to the different notion (which we found, for example, in Grotius) of claim rights as a justification for claiming or demanding certain treatment. Grotius and Kant agree that interfering with another person's freedom in a way that violates the Universal Principle of Right *wrongs* them (6:230–231). What this means for Grotius is that it violates their claim right; it is something they have the authority to demand we not do. But Kant's innate right to freedom is not really a claim right, though he does use the language of *wronging*, which might be thought to entail, as a conceptual matter, the violation of a claim right (Kant 1999c: 6:256; Hohfeld 1923; Thompson 2004; Darwall 2013a). Rather, Kant's view seems to be that when one's freedom is hindered, one does no wrong (and, in Kant's lexicon, does not wrong the hinderer) if, in response, one hinders the hinderer by coercively restraining them.

This is a deep conceptual difference. When one makes a justified demand of another person, one presumes an authority to direct their conduct through a distinctive kind of reason for acting (what we might call an authority-based or, as I might put it, a "second-personal reason") that is grounded in one's authoritative demand. And this demand is grounded in one's assumed authority or claim right (Feinberg 1980; Darwall 2013a). The claim right against others not to be hindered by them is conceptually equivalent to their obligations *to one* not to hinder one (Hohfeld 1923). And just as accountability is conceptually implicated in moral obligations (period), so also is accountability *to the obligee* conceptually implicated in moral obligations owed *to them* and, correlatively, in the obligee's entailed claim rights (Darwall 2013a).

The contrast between this picture and Kant's is stark. It is the difference between an essentially interpersonal realm of joint reasoning – in which agents justify themselves to one another through reasons that depend upon their common authority to demand such justification – and a *multi*-personal realm in which agents have the authority to exert interpersonal force. On the first, the "realm of rights" is one in which agents are presumed to be able to recognize and act on essentially interpersonal deontic reasons. On the second, no such reasons are acknowledged, and force is substituted for authoritative direction through mutually acknowledged reasons of right.

---

[36] See Darwall 2013a for the distinction between "relational," "directed," or "bipolar obligations" owed *to* someone and moral obligations "period" (or "pure and simple").

This point can be brought out by considering Joseph Raz's theory of authority as involving the capacity to create "preemptive" and "exclusionary" reasons (Raz 1986). When someone with the authority to direct someone's contact issues a legitimate directive, Raz argues, they thereby create a new "preemptive" reason for that person to act as directed and exclude from their legitimate deliberative consideration any reasons there might otherwise have been for them to act differently (Raz 1986: 42). If this influential idea is correct, it follows that if someone holding a claim right has the authority to demand compliance with the right, then the right holder has the authority to create a reason for others to respect the right that would not have existed but for the right's and the authority's existence.[37]

Demanding respect for a claim right, on this picture, necessarily implicates a distinctively interpersonal form of reason-giving. On Kant's picture, by contrast, the innate right not to have one's freedom hindered creates no reason against hindering that one could authoritatively give to potential and actual hinderers in interpersonal practical reasoning. The authority that goes with the right is the authorization to coerce, to hinder others' hinderings. The right holder has the authority to say, "Stop!" as a way of causing or forcing the hinderer to desist, but not with the illocutionary force of a justified demand that creates preemptive or exclusionary reasons.

Consider now the case of *internal* self-constraint and legislation. External hinderings hinder rightful external freedom. Is there anything comparable to this in the internal case? Both internal and external constraints are hinderings of threats to freedom. External constraints hinder threats to external freedom, and internal self-constraint hinders threats to autonomy. But are both hinderings of hindrance? At one point, Kant calls inclinations that threaten compliance with the moral law "hindering impulses" (Kant 1996c: 6:405). So the hindered agent's hindering of these impulses is indeed a hindering of hindrances.

Recall that according to Kant's moral psychology, self-constraint always operates through the feeling of respect, which brings deontic notions and propositions into view. Perfect rational beings have no need of deontic morality's notions and stand only under practical law, not under moral law, strictly so called. Their deliberations proceed entirely in terms of what it would be good or best to do, what, as we might say, there is most reason for them to do. Finite imperfect rational beings, however, stand under moral imperatives that are

---

[37] Most usually, of course, the claim right is thought to entail a reason for compliance, whether or not that is actually demanded by the right holder. If you have a claim right that I not hinder your freedom, then you do not have to demand that I not do so in order for me to have a reason not to hinder you deriving from your right. In such cases, the authority to demand can be understood as an authority to "second" or "insist on" a justified demand that is assumed to already be "in force" by virtue of the right, which entails a reason for compliance that would not have existed but for the right.

"expressed by an *ought*" (1996a: 4:413). But this gives them no new reasons for acting. Imperatives "say that to do or to omit something would be good, but they say it to a will that does not always do something just because it is represented to it that it would be good to do that thing" (4:413). In other words, they express no new or different normative proposition – they express the same normative propositions the person would accept if perfectly rational – but they do so in a distinctively peremptory way.

Kant's view is that from the perspective of (the self-restraining feeling of) respect, imperatives have the apparent content of reason's commands. If Raz's influential picture is correct, however, authoritative directives like commands create preemptive and exclusionary reasons for acting. The reason-commanded agent would not only have good and sufficient reason to do something. They would also have a further preemptive reason to do it, one that would exclude any reasons to the contrary and with which they would be accountable for compliance (Darwall 2013f). On Kant's view, however, self-regulation through respect does not give the agent a further preemptive reason for complying with reason's demand. As Kant sees it, "the view from respect" is illusory; it is the misleading appearance of a non-rational goad that finite rational agents need to overcome their inclinations against doing what they have sufficient reason to do already. It is, like the interpersonal case, an application of force rather than reason, albeit one that, also like the interpersonal case, has reason's backing.

Kant's Racism and Sexism, and a Final Note of Humility

It is appropriate at this point in this chapter, and in the book overall, to say something about Kant's views on race, sex, and colonial position; how these affected his moral philosophy; and what we can learn from that about the history of modern moral philosophy more generally and about our own moral theorizing today. As I mentioned in the Preface, no one can doubt that the culture that produced and supported modern moral philosophy and its history was, and remains, sexist and racist, patriarchal and white supremacist. Testimony to this is the virtual absence from these pages of women and thinkers of color.

In recent years, however, scholars have become significantly more interested in the sociopolitical context of modern philosophy, in identifying excluded thinkers, and in critically assessing modern philosophy, and modern philosophers, from this perspective. Because of his importance, but also because he provides such an egregious example, it is not surprising that much of this new scholarship has focused on Kant (Allais 2016; Bernasconi 2001, 2002, 2003; Eze 1997; Hay 2013; Herman 1993; Hill and Boxill 2001; Langton 1992; Lu-Adler 2022a, 2022b; Mills 1997, 2005a, 2005b, 2017; Spivak 1999; Varden 2020).[38]

---

[38] I have been helped by thinking through these issues with Moya Mapps.

Some of this work provides detailed analysis of Kant's racism and sexism. And Kant provides much grist for the mill of racial and gender critique. As Huseyinzadegan notes, "Kant's problematic claims … range from the unnaturalness of a female philosopher, 'who might as well have a beard,' the stupid things that a black carpenter said 'because he was black from head to foot,' the poor women 'living in the greatest slavery in the Orient,' to the 'sheep-like existence of the inhabitants of Tahiti'" (Huseyinzadegan 2018: 1). Nor are these throw-away remarks. Kant had a theory of race that gave contemporary racism a philosophical pedigree (Kant 2013b). Moreover, Kant's racism and sexism directly influenced his moral and political philosophy, at least in applying it to actual circumstances. Thus, he held in *The Doctrine of Right* that women were justifiably denied voting rights and could at best be "passive citizens" owing to their dependency on their husbands (Kant 1996c: 6:314).[39]

Of course, this does not necessarily impugn Kant's fundamental moral and political ideas; perhaps he just misapplied them because of his various privileged biases. Some Kant scholars argue, indeed, that Kant's moral and political philosophy can be put to use to resist racist and sexist oppression. This is most obvious in the case of doctrines of equal dignity and rights that fueled so much of the civil rights and liberation movements of the 1960s and beyond. But it is also arguably the case in a more fine-grained way, as Helga Varden argues is true of some of Kant's moral and political doctrines in the *Doctrine of Right* (Varden 2020).

Perhaps the most interesting perspective that close study of Kant, and other modern moral philosophers, along these lines can reveal is its capacity to help us gain critical purchase on the role of bias in our own moral theory and practice. This is a point made by both Allais and Huseyinzadegan (Allais 2016; Huseyinzadegan 2018). Though we are the beneficiaries of an improved moral understanding that is partly the result centuries of resistance by oppressed theorists and activists, readers of this book, as well as its author, are likely subject to distortions by virtue of our own privileged sociopolitical positions. Taking account of these may help us to pursue moral theory and practice from a more critically informed perspective, as, indeed, Kant's critical philosophy itself encourages us to do.

But sociopolitical distortions run deeper. Perhaps it is the case, as Evgeny Pashukanis argued, following Marx, that the very concepts of modern moral philosophy – those of the moral subject, deontic morality, accountability, and so on – are the superstructural ideology of an underlying capitalist mode of production (Pashukanis 2003). Nietzsche, of course, makes a structurally similar argument in *The Genealogy of Morality* (Nietzsche 2007).

---

[39] He also says the same of wage laborers because of their dependency on their bosses.

But here again, perhaps these and similar genealogies, including evolutionary ones, that seek to debunk morality can be resisted on the grounds that modern moral philosophy and its history enable us to appreciate. Even if a given genealogy is correct, it does not follow that the ideas it explains are mistaken. Indeed, it may be possible to combine modern moral philosophy, sociopolitical history, and evolutionary theory to come to an overall understanding both of why core modern moral philosophical conceptions are valid philosophically and of how we have evolved, both biologically and socioculturally, to think they are (Tomasello, 2018; Buchanan and Powell 2018).

WORKS CITED

Abizadeh, Arash (2018). *Hobbes and the Two Faces of Ethics*. Cambridge: Cambridge University Press.
Abramson, Kate (2002). "Two Portraits of the Humean Moral Agent," *Pacific Philosophical Quarterly* 83: 301–334.
Abramson, Kate (2007). "Hume's Distinction between Philosophical Anatomy and Painting," *Philosophy Compass* 2: 680–698.
Albee, Ernest (1957). *A History of English Utilitarianism*. London: Allen & Unwin.
Alexander, Larry and Michael Moore (2016). "Deontological Ethics," *Stanford Encyclopedia*. https://plato.stanford.edu/entries/ethics-deontological/
Allais, Lucy (2016). "Kant's Racism," *Philosophical Papers* 45: 1–36.
Allison, Henry (1990). *Kant's Theory of Freedom*. Cambridge: Cambridge University Press.
Allison, Henry (1991). "On a Presumed Gap in Kant's Derivation of the Categorical Imperative," *Philosophical Topics* 19: 1–15.
Anderson, Elizabeth (1999). "What Is the Point of Equality?" *Ethics* 109: 187–237.
Anderson, Elizabeth (2010). *The Imperative of Integration*. Princeton: Princeton University Press.
Anderson, Elizabeth (2012). "The Fundamental Disagreement between Luck Egalitarians and Relational Egalitarians," *Canadian Journal of Philosophy* 36 (Supp.): 1–23.
Anderson, Elizabeth (2014). "Social Movements, Experiments in Living, and Moral Progress: Case Studies from Britain's Abolition of Slavery." The Lindley Lecture, The University of Kansas.
Anderson, Elizabeth (forthcoming). *The Great Reversal: How Neoliberalism Turned the Work Ethic against Workers*. Cambridge: Cambridge University Press.
Annas, Julia (1993). *The Morality of Happiness*. Oxford: Oxford University Press.
Anscombe, G. E. M. (1957). *Intention*. Oxford: Basil Blackwell.
Anscombe, G. E. M. (1958). "Modern Moral Philosophy," *Philosophy* 33: 1–19.
Aquinas, Thomas (1997). "*Summa Theologica*," in *Basic Writings of Thomas Aquinas*, v. II, ed. Anton C. Pegis. Indianapolis, IN: Hackett Publishing Company. Originally published in 1265–1273.
Aristotle (1999). *Nicomachean Ethics*, ed. and trans. Terence Irwin. Indianapolis, IN: Hackett Publishing Company.

Aristotle (2000). *Nicomachean Ethics*, ed. and trans. Roger Crisp. Cambridge: Cambridge University Press.
Arpaly, Nomy (2004). *Unprincipled Virtue: An Inquiry into Moral Agency.* Oxford: Oxford University Press.
Atherton, Margaret (1994). *Women Philosophers of the Early Modern Period.* Indianapolis, IN: Hackett Publishing Company.
Augustine (1990). *Homilies on the First Epistle of John*, in *The Works of Saint Augustine: A Translation for the 21st Century*, intro., trans., and notes Boniface Ramsay. New Hyde Park, NY: New City Press.
Aune, Bruce (1979). *Kant's Theory of Morals.* Princeton: Princeton University Press.
Austin, J. L. (1957). "A Plea for Excuses," *Proceedings of the Aristotelian Society* 57: 1–30.
Baier, Annette (1985). *Postures of the Mind: Essays on Mind and Morals.* Minneapolis: University of Minnesota Press.
Baier, Annette (1993). "Moralism and Cruelty: Reflections on Hume and Kant," *Ethics* 103: 436–457.
Balguy, John (1976). *The Foundation of Moral Goodness*, 2 vol. in one. New York: Garland Publishing Co., Inc. Originally published in 1728, 1729.
Barbeyrac, Jean (1718). Jugement d'un anonyme … avec dex reflexions du traducteur … in Pufendorf (1718).
Barbeyrac, Jean (1749). "An Historical and Critical Account of the Science of Morality," in *The Law of Nature and Nations*, eds. Samuel Pufendorf, trans. Basil Kennett, ed. Jean Barbeyrac, 5th ed. London, pp. 1–73.
Batson, C. Daniel and Laura L. Shaw (1991). "Evidence for Altruism: Toward a Pluralism of Prosocial Motives," *Psychological Inquiry* 2: 107–122.
Bentham, Jeremy (1838). *The Works of Jeremy Bentham*, ed. John Bowring. Edinburgh: William Tait.
Bernasconi, Robert. (2001). "Who Invented the Concept of Race? Kant's Role in the Enlightenment Construction of Race," in *Race: Readings in Continental Philosophy*, ed. Robert Bernasconi. Oxford: Blackwell, pp. 11–36.
Bernasconi, Robert (2002). "Kant as an Unfamiliar Source of Racism," in *Philosophers on Race: Critical Essays*, eds. Julia K. Ward and Tommy L. Lott. Oxford: Blackwell.
Bernasconi, Robert (2003). "Will the Real Kant Please Stand Up: The Challenge of Enlightenment Racism to the Study of the History of Philosophy," *Radical Philosophy* 117: 13–22.
Blackburn, Simon (1984). *Spreading the Word: Groundings in the Philosophy of Language.* Oxford: Oxford University Press.
Bodin, Jean (2004). *On Sovereignty*, ed. and trans. John H. Franklin. Cambridge: Cambridge University Press.
Boxill, Bernard (1984). *Blacks and Social Justice.* Lanham, MD: Rowman & Littlefield.

Boxill, Bernard (2003). "A Lockean Argument for Black Reparations," *The Journal of Ethics* 7: 63–91.
Brandt, Richard (1979). *A Theory of the Good and the Right*. Oxford: Oxford University Press.
Bratman, Michael (1981). "Intention and Means-End Reasoning," *The Philosophical Review* 90: 252–265.
Bratman, Michael (1987). *Intentions, Plans, and Practical Reason*. Cambridge, MA: Harvard University Press.
Brett, Annabel S. (1997). *Liberty, Right and Nature: Individual Rights in Later Scholastic Thought*. Cambridge: Cambridge University Press.
Broad, C. D. (1962). *Five Types of Ethical Theory*. London: Routledge & Kegan Paul.
Broad, Jacqueline (2006). "A Woman's Influence? John Locke and Damaris Masham on Moral Accountability," *Journal of the History of Ideas* 67: 489–510.
Broome, John (2013). *Rationality through Reasoning*. Oxford: Wiley/Blackwell.
Brown, Charlotte (1988). "Is Hume an Internalist," *Journal of the History of Philosophy* 26: 69–87.
Brown, Lesley (2007). "Glaucon's Challenge, Rational Egoism, and Ordinary Morality," in *Pursuing the Good: Ethics and Metaphysics in Plato's Republic*, eds. Douglas Cairns and Fritz-Gregor Herrmann. Edinburgh: University of Edinburgh Press.
Brunero, John and Niko Kolodny (2018). "Instrumental Rationality," Stanford Encyclopedia of Philosophy.
Buchanan, Allen and Russell Powell (2018). *The Evolution of Moral Progress: A Biocultural Theory*. New York: Oxford University Press.
Bukoski, Michael (2018). "Korsgaard's Argument for the Value of Humanity," *The Philosophical Review* 127: 197–224.
Burge, Tyler (1993). "Content Preservation," *Philosophical Review* 102: 457–488.
Butler, Joseph (2017). *Fifteen Sermons and Other Writings on Ethics*, ed. David McNaughton. Oxford: Oxford University Press. Originally published in 1726. Reference to sermon and paragraph numbers.
Cambridge Platonists Project, www.cambridge-platonism.divinity.cam.ac.uk/view/texts/normalised/index
Carter, Benjamin (2010). "The Standing of Ralph Cudworth as a Philosophy," in *Insiders and Outsiders in Seventeenth-Century Philosophy*, eds. G. A. J. Rogers, Tom Sorrell, and Jill Kraye. New York: Routledge.
Cassirer, Ernst (1951). *The Philosophy of the Enlightenment*, trans. Fritz C. A. Koelln and James P. Pettegrove. Princeton: Princeton University Press.
Cassirer, Ernst (1953). *The Platonic Renaissance in England*, trans. James Pettegrove. Austin: University of Texas Press.
Chappell, Richard Yetter (2012). "Fittingness: The Sole Normative Primitive," *Philosophical Quarterly* 62: 684–704.
Clarke, Samuel (1978a). *A Discourse Concerning the Being and Attributes of God*, in *Works*, v. ii. New York: Garland Publishing, Inc. Originally published in 1704.

Clarke, Samuel (1978b). *A Discourse Concerning the Unchangeable Obligations and the Truth and Certainty of the Christian Revelation*, in *Works*, v. ii. New York: Garland Publishing, Inc. Originally published in 1705.

Coady, C. A. J. (1992). *Testimony: A Philosophical Study*. Oxford: Oxford University Press.

Cohon, Rachel (2000). "The Roots of Reasons," *The Philosophical Review* 109: 63–85.

Colman, John (1983). *John Locke's Moral Philosophy*. Edinburgh: Edinburgh University Press.

Constant, Benjamin (2003). *Principles of Politics Applicable to All Governments*. Indianapolis, IN: Liberty Fund. Originally published in 1810.

Cooper, John M. (1996). "Justice and Rights in Aristotle's *Politics*," *Review of Metaphysics* 49: 859–872.

Crisp, Roger, *Sacrifice Regained*. Oxford: Oxford University Press.

Cudworth, Ralph (1969). "A Sermon Preached before the House of Commons," in *The Cambridge Platonists*, ed. C. A. Patrides. Cambridge: Cambridge University Press, pp. 90–127.

Cudworth, Ralph (~1670). Manuscripts on freedom of the will. British Library, Additional Manuscripts, nos. 4978–4982.

Cudworth, Ralph (1678). *The True Intellectual System of the Universe*. London: Richard Royston.

Cudworth, Ralph (1996a). *A Treatise Concerning Eternal and Immutable Morality*, ed. Sarah Hutton. Cambridge: Cambridge University Press.

Cudworth, Ralph (1996b). "A Treatise of Freewill," in Cudworth 1996.

Cumberland, Richard (1683). *De legibus naturae disquisitio philosophica*, 2nd ed. Lubeck and Frankfurt: S. Otto & J. Wiedemeyer. (First edition published in 1672.)

Cumberland, Richard (2005). *A Treatise of the Laws of Nature*, trans., with an intro. and appendix, John Maxwell, ed., with a foreword, John Parkin. Indianapolis, IN: Liberty Fund. (Based on 1727 edition.)

Daniel, Dafydd Mills (2020). *Ethical Rationalism and Secularisation in the British Enlightenment: Conscience and the Age of Reason*. Oxford: Palgrave Macmillan.

D'Arms, Justin and Daniel Jacobson (2000a). "The Moralistic Fallacy: On the 'Appropriateness' of Emotions," *Philosophy and Phenomenological Research* 61: 65–90.

D'Arms, Justin and Daniel Jacobson (2000b). "Sentiment and Value," *Ethics* 110: 722–748.

Darwall, Stephen (1977). "Two Kinds of Respect," *Ethics* 88: 36–49.

Darwall, Stephen (1980). "Is There a Kantian Foundation for Rawlsian Justice?" in *John Rawls' Theory of Social Justice*, ed. H. G. Blocker and E. Smith. Athens: Ohio University Press.

Darwall, Stephen (1983). *Impartial Reason*. Ithaca, NY: Cornell University Press.

Darwall, Stephen (1994). "Hume and the Invention of Utilitarianism," in *Hume and Hume's Connexions*, eds. M. A. Stewart and J. Wright. Edinburgh: Edinburgh University Press.

Darwall, Stephen (1995). *The British Moralists and the Internal "Ought": 1640–1740*. Cambridge: Cambridge University Press.
Darwall, Stephen (1997). "Reasons, Motives, and the Demands of Morality: An Introduction," in *Moral Discourse and Practice*, eds. S. Darwall, A. Gibbard, and P. Railton. New York: Oxford University Press.
Darwall, Stephen (1998). *Philosophical Ethics*. Boulder, CO: Westview Press.
Darwall, Stephen (1999a). "The Inventions of Autonomy," *European Journal of Philosophy* 7: 339–350.
Darwall, Stephen (1999b). "Sympathetic Liberalism: Recent Work on Adam Smith," *Philosophy & Public Affairs* 28: 139–164.
Darwall, Stephen (2000). "Normativity and Projection in Hobbes's Leviathan," *The Philosophical Review* 109: 313–347.
Darwall, Stephen (2002). *Welfare and Rational Care*. Princeton: Princeton University Press.
Darwall, Stephen (2003). "Autonomy in Modern Natural Law," in *New Essays on the History of Autonomy*, eds. Larry Krasnoff and Natalie Brender. Cambridge: Cambridge University Press.
Darwall, Stephen (2004). "Equal Dignity in Adam Smith," *Adam Smith Review* 1: xxx.
Darwall, Stephen (2006). *The Second-Person Standpoint: Morality, Respect, and Accountability*. Cambridge, MA: Harvard University Press.
Darwall, Stephen (2008). "Kant on Respect, Dignity, and the Duty of Respect," in *Kant's Virtue*, ed. Monika Betzler. Berlin: Walter de Gruyter, pp. 175–200. Reprinted in Darwall 2013c.
Darwall, Stephen (2012a). "Grotius at the Creation of Modern Moral Philosophy," *Archiv für Geschichte der Philosophie* 94: 296–325. Reprinted in Darwall 2013c.
Darwall, Stephen (2012b). "Pufendorf on Morality, Sociability, and Moral Powers," *The Journal of the History of Philosophy* 50: 213–238. Reprinted in Darwall 2013c.
Darwall, Stephen (2013a). "Bipolar Obligation," in *Morality, Authority, and Law: Essays in Second-Personal Ethics I*, ed. Stephen Darwall. Oxford: Oxford University Press, pp. 20–39.
Darwall, Stephen (2013b). *Morality, Authority, and Law: Essays in Second-Personal Ethics I*. Oxford: Oxford University Press.
Darwall, Stephen (2013c). *Honor, History, and Relationship: Essays in Second-Personal Ethics II*. Oxford: Oxford University Press.
Darwall, Stephen (2013d). "Respect as Honor and as Accountability," in Darwall 2013c.
Darwall, Stephen (2013e). "Kant on Respect, Dignity, and the Duty of Respect," in Darwall 2013c.
Darwall, Stephen (2013f). "Authority and Second-Personal Reasons for Acting," in Darwall 2013b.
Darwall, Stephen (2013g). "The Value of Autonomy and Autonomy of the Will," in Darwall 2013a.

Darwall, Stephen (2013h). "Forcing Freedom" (critical review of Arthur Ripstein's *Force and Freedom*), *Legal Theory* 19: 89–99.
Darwall, Stephen (2013i). "Demystifying Promises," in Darwall 2013c.
Darwall, Stephen (2014a). "Agreement Matters" (critical Notice of Derek Parfit's *On What Matters*), *The Philosophical Review* 123: 79–105.
Darwall, Stephen (2014b). "Review of Richard Sorabji's *Moral Conscience, Its History through the Ages: 5th Century BCE to the Present*." *Notre Dame Philosophical Reviews*. https://ndpr.nd.edu/news/56313-moral-conscience-through-the-ages-fifth-century-bce-to-the-present/
Darwall, Stephen (2014c). "The Social and the Sociable," *Philosophical Topics*, special issue, eds. James Conant and Sebastian Rödl 42: 201–217.
Darwall, Stephen (2016). "Making the Hard Problem of Moral Normativity Easier," in *Weighing Reasons*, eds. Errol Lord and Barry Maguire. Oxford: Oxford University Press.
Darwall, Stephen (2018). "Contempt as an Other-Characterizing, 'Hierarchizing' Attitude," in *The Moral Psychology of Contempt*, ed. Michelle Mason. Lanham, MD: Rowman & Littlefield.
Darwall, Stephen (2022). "Hutcheson in the History of Rights," *Journal of Scottish Philosophy* 20: 85–101.
Darwall, Stephen, Allan Gibbard, and Peter Railton (1997). "Toward Fin de Siècle Ethics: Some Trends," in *Moral Discourse and Practice*, eds. S. Darwall, A. Gibbard, and P. Railton. New York: Oxford University Press.
Dean, Richard (2006). *The Value of Humanity in Kant's Moral Theory*. Oxford: Oxford University Press.
Debes, Remy (2012). "Adam Smith on Dignity and Equality," *British Journal for the History of Philosophy* 20: 109–140.
De Grouchy, Sophie (2019). *Sophie de Grochie's Letters on Sympathy*, trans Sandrine Bergès, introduction, glossary, and commentary, Eric Schliesser and Sandrine Bergès. Oxford: Oxford University Press.
De Kenessey, Brendan (2017). *Joint Practical Deliberation*. Diss., Massachusetts Institute of Technology.
Della Rocca, Michael (2008). *Spinoza*. London and New York: Routledge.
Descartes, René (2017). *Meditations on First Philosophy: With Selections from the Objections and Replies*. Cambridge: Cambridge University Press.
Dorsey, Dale (2010). "Hutcheson's Deceptive Hedonism," *The Journal of the History of Philosophy* 48: 445–467.
Dreier, James (1990). "Internalism and Speaker Relativism," *Ethics* 101: 6–26.
Elster, Jon (1986). *An Introduction to Karl Marx*. Cambridge: Cambridge University Press.
Engelmann, Jan and Michael Tomasello (2019). "Children's Sense of Fairness as Equal Respect," *Trends in Cognitive Science* 23: 454–463.
Engels, Friedrich (1975). "Socialism: Utopian and Scientific," in *Collected Works of Karl Marx and Friedrich Engels*, v. 24. New York: International Publishers.
Ewing, A. C. (2012a). *The Definition of Good*. London: Routledge & Kegan Paul.

Ewing, A. C. (2012b). *Second Thoughts in Moral Philosophy*. Abingdon, Oxford: Routledge. Reprints. Originally published in 1959.
Eze, Emanuel Chukwudi 1997. "The Color of Reason: The Idea of 'Race' in Kant's Anthropology," in *Postcolonial African Philosophy: A Critical Reader*, ed. Emanuel Chukwudi Eze. Oxford: Blackwell.
Falk, W. D. (1948). "'Ought' and Motivation," *Proceedings of the Aristotelian Society* 48: 113–138.
Feinberg, Joel (1980). "The Nature and Value of Rights," in *Rights, Justice, and the Bounds of Liberty*. Princeton: Princeton University Press.
Fichte, Johann Gottlieb (2000). *Foundations of Natural Right*, ed. Frederick Neuhouser, trans. Michael Bauer. Cambridge: Cambridge University Press.
Fleischacker, Samuel (1991). "Philosophy in Moral Practice: Kant and Adam Smith," *Kant-Studien* 82: 249–269.
Fleischacker, Samuel (2004). *A Short History of Distributive Justice*. Cambridge, MA: Harvard University Press.
Fleischacker, Samuel (2005). *A Short History of Distributive Justice*. Cambridge, MA: Harvard University Press.
Fleischacker, Samuel (2013). "Adam Smith," *Stanford Encyclopedia of Philosophy*, https://plato.stanford.edu/entries/smith-moral-political
Foot, Philippa (1958). "Moral Arguments," *Mind* 67: 502–513.
Foot, Philippa (1959). "Moral Beliefs," *Proceedings of the Aristotelian Society* 59: 83–104.
Foot, Philippa (1972). "Morality as a System of Hypothetical Imperatives," *The Philosophical Review* 81: 305–316.
Foot, Philippa (1978). *Virtues and Vices, and Other Essays in Moral Philosophy*. Oxford: Basil Blackwell.
Foot, Philippa (2002). "Nietzsche's Immoralism," in *Moral Dilemmas, and Other Topics in Moral Philosophy*. Oxford: Oxford University Press.
Fordyce, David (2003). *The Elements of Moral Philosophy, in Three Books with a Brief Account of the Nature, Progress, and Origin of Philosophy*, ed. with an intro. by Thomas Kennedy. Indianapolis, IN: Liberty Fund. Originally published in 1754.
Forsyth, Murray (1982). "The Place of Richard Cumberland in the History of Natural Law Doctrine," *Journal of the History of Philosophy* 20: 23–42.
Frankena, William (1942). "Obligation and Value in the Ethics of G. E. Moore," in *The Philosophy of G. E. Moore*, ed. Paul A. Schilpp. La Salle, IL: Open Court.
Frankena, William (1955). "Hutcheson's Moral Sense Theory," *Journal of the History of Philosophy* 16: 356–375.
Frankena, William (1963). *Ethics*. Englewood Cliffs, NJ: Prentice Hall, Inc.
Frankena, William (1992). "Sidgwick and the History of Ethical Dualism," in *Essays on Henry Sidgwick*, ed. Bart Schultz. Cambridge: Cambridge University Press.
Fricker, Miranda (2007). *Epistemic Injustice*. Oxford: Oxford University Press.
Garrett, Aaron (2004). "Hume's 'Original Difference': Race, National Character and the Human Sciences," *Eighteenth-Century Thought* 2: 127–152.

Gauthier, David P. (1967). "Morality and Advantage," *The Philosophical Review* 76: 460–474.
Gauthier, David P. (1969). *The Logic of Leviathan: The Moral and Political Theory of Thomas Hobbes*. Oxford: Clarendon Press.
Gauthier, David P. (1979). "Thomas Hobbes: Moral Theorist," *Journal of Philosophy* 76: 547–559.
Gibbard, Allan (1990). *Wise Choices, Apt Feelings*. Cambridge, MA: Harvard University Press.
Gill, Michael (2006). *The British Moralists on Human Nature and the Birth of Secular Ethics*. Cambridge: Cambridge University Press.
Goldman, Alvin I. (1992). "In Defense of the Simulation Theory," *Mind and Language* 7: 104–119.
Gordon, Robert M. (1992). "The Simulation Theory: Objections and Misconceptions," *Mind and Language* 7: 11–34.
Grean, Stanley (1967). *Shaftesbury's Philosophy of Religion and Ethics: A Study in Enthusiasm*. Athens: Ohio University Press.
Green, Leslie (2003). "Legal Positivism," *Stanford Encyclopedia of Philosophy*. https://plato.stanford.edu/entries/legal-positivism/
Griswold, Charles (1999). *Adam Smith and the Virtues of Enlightenment*. Cambridge: Cambridge University Press.
Grotius, Hugo (1724). *Le Droit de La Guerre et de la Paix*, trans. Jean Barbeyrac. Amsterdam: Pierre de Coup.
Grotius, Hugo (1925). *On the Law of War and Peace*, trans. Francis W. Kelsey, intro James Brown Scott. Oxford: Clarendon Press.
Grotius, Hugo (1950). *De Iure Praedae Commentarius; Commentary on the Law of Prize and Booty*, trans. Gwladys L. Williams with the collaboration of Walter H. Zeydel. Oxford: Clarendon Press. Original manuscript of 1604.
Grotius, Hugo (2005). *The Rights of War and Peace*, 3 vols., ed. Richard Tuck. From the 1738 English translation by John Morrice of Jean Barbeyrac's French translation, with Barbeyrac's notes. Indianapolis, IN: Liberty Fund. Originally published in 1625.
Guyer, Paul (2006). *Kant*. New York: Routledge.
Haakonssen, Knud (1996). *Natural Law and Moral Philosophy: From Grotius to the Scottish Enlightenment*. Cambridge: Cambridge University Press.
Haakonssen, Knud (1998). "Divine/Natural Law Theories of Ethics," in *Cambridge History of Seventeenth-Century Philosophy*, vol. 2, 2 vols., eds. Daniel Garber and Michael Ayers. Cambridge: Cambridge University Press, pp. 1317–1357.
Haakonssen, Knud (2001). "The Character and Obligation of Natural Law According to Richard Cumberland," in *English Philosophy in the Age of Locke*, ed. M. A. Stewart. Oxford: Oxford University Press, pp. 29–47.
Habermas, Jürgen (1990a). *Moral Consciousness and Communicative Action*, trans. Christian Lenhardt and Shierry Weber Nicholsen. Cambridge, MA: MIT Press.
Hampton, Jean (1986). *Hobbes and the Social Contract Tradition*. Cambridge: Cambridge University Press.

Hannay, Alastair (2021). "Kierkegaard against the Herd," *iai News*. https://iai.tv/articles/kierkegaard-against-the-herd-auid-1826?_auid=2020
Hare, R. M. (1982). *Moral Thinking: Its Levels, Methods, and Point*. Oxford: Oxford University Press.
Hart, H. L. A. (1955). "Are There Any Natural Rights?" *The Philosophical Review* 64: 175–191.
Hart, H. L. A. (1961). *The Concept of Law*. Oxford: Clarendon Press.
Hart, H. L. A. (2012). *The Concept of Law*. 3rd ed., ed. Leslie Green. Oxford: Oxford University Press.
Hay, Carol (2013). *Kantianism, Liberalism, and Feminism: Resisting Oppression*. New York: Palgrave-McMillan.
Hegel, Georg Wilhelm Friedrich (1991). *Elements of the Philosophy of Right*, eds. Allen W. Wood and Hugh B. Nisbett, eds. Cambridge: Cambridge University Press. Originally published in 1821.
Herman, Barbara (1993). "Could It Be Worth Thinking about Kant on Sex and Marriage?" In *A Mind of One's Own: Feminist Essays on Reason and Objectivity*, eds. Louise M. Anthony and Charlotte Witt. Boulder, CO: Westview Press.
Heydt, Colin (2014). "Utilitarianism before Bentham," in *The Cambridge Companion to Utilitarianism*, eds. Ben Eggleston and Dale Miller. Cambridge: Cambridge University Press, pp. 16–37.
Hieronymi, Pamela (2005). "The Wrong Kind of Reason," *The Journal of Philosophy* 102: 437–457.
Hieronymi, Pamela (2013). "The Use of Reasons in Thought (and the Use of Earmarks in Argument)," *Ethics* 124: 114–127.
Hill, Thomas E., Jr. (1973). "The Hypothetical Imperative," *The Philosophical Review* 82: 429–450.
Hill, Thomas E. and Bernard Boxill. (2001). "Kant on Race," in *Race and Racism*, ed. Bernard Boxill. New York: Oxford University Press.
Hobbes, Thomas (1839). *The English Works of Thomas Hobbes*, 11 vols., ed. Sir William Molesworth. London: J. Bohn.
Hobbes, Thomas (1983). *De Cive, the English Version, Entitled in the First Edition, Philosophical Rudiments Concerning Government and Society*, ed. and trans. Howard Warrender. Oxford: Clarendon Press. References are to chapter and paragraph number.
Hobbes, Thomas (1994a). *Leviathan*, ed. Edwin Curley. Indianapolis, IN: Hackett Publishing Co., Inc. Originally published in 1651. References are to chapter and paragraph number.
Hobbes, Thomas (1994b). *The Elements of Law, Natural and Politic*, ed. J. C. A. Gaskin. Oxford: Oxford University Press.
Hobbes, Thomas (2014). *Behemoth, v. x of Clarendon Edition of the Works of Thomas Hobbes*. Oxford: Oxford University Press.
Hochschild, Adam (2005). *Bury the Chains: Prophets and Rebels in the Fight to Free an Empire's Slaves*. Boston: Houghton Mifflin Company.

Hockett, Robert and Aaron James (2020). *Money from Nothing: Or, Why We Should Stop Worrying about Debt and Learn to Love the Federal Reserve.* Brooklyn, NY: Melville House Publishing.

Hoekstra, Kinch (1997). "Hobbes and the Foole," *Political Theory* 25: 620–654.

Hohfeld, Wesley Newcomb (1923). *Fundamental Legal Conceptions as Applied in Judicial Reasoning and Other Legal Essays.* New Haven, CT: Yale University Press.

Hostler, John (1975). *Leibniz's Moral Philosophy.* London: Duckworth.

Howard, Christopher (2019). "The Fundamentality of Fit," *Oxford Studies in Metaethics* 14: 216–236.

Hruschka, Joachim (1991). "The Greatest Happiness Principle and Other Early German Anticipations of Utilitarian Theory," *Utilitas* 3: 165–177.

Hudson, W. D. (1970). *Modern Moral Philosophy.* Garden City, NY: Doubleday.

Hume, David (1932). *The Letters of David Hume,* ed. J. Y. T. Grieg. Oxford: Clarendon Press.

Hume, David (1978). *A Treatise of Human Nature,* ed. L. A. Selby-Bigge, 2nd ed., with rev. P. H. Nidditch. Oxford: Oxford University Press. Originally published in 1739, 1740.

Hume, David (1975a). *An Enquiry Concerning Human Understanding, in Enquiries Concerning Human Understanding and Concerning the Principles of Morals,* ed. L. A. Selby-Bigge, 3rd. ed., rev. P. H. Nidditch. Oxford: Clarendon Press. Originally published in 1748.

Hume, David (1975b). "An Enquiry Concerning the Principles of Morals," in *Enquiries Concerning Human Understanding and Concerning the Principles of Morals,* ed. L. A. Selby-Bigge, 3rd. ed., rev. P. H. Nidditch. Oxford: Clarendon Press. Originally published in 1751.

Hurka, Thomas (2014). *British Ethical Theorists from Sidgwick to Ewing.* Oxford: Oxford University Press.

Hursthouse, Rosalind (1999). *On Virtue Ethics.* Oxford: Oxford University Press.

Huseyinzadegan, Dilek (2018). "For What Can the Kantian Feminist Hope? Constructive Complicity in Appropriations of the Canon," *Feminist Philosophy Quarterly* 4.1: 1–25.

Hutcheson, Francis (1755). *A System of Moral Philosophy,* 2 vols. Glasgow: R. A. Foulis. Facsimile edition in *Collected Works,* vols. 5 and 6. Hildesheim: Olms, 1969–1971.

Hutcheson, Francis (2002). *An Essay on the Nature and Conduct of the Passions and Affections, with Illustrations on the Moral Sense,* ed. with an intro., Aaron Garrett. Indianapolis, IN: Liberty Fund. Originally published in 1728, 2nd ed., 1730, 3rd ed., 1742. This edition is based on the first edition but also includes passages from later editions.

Hutcheson, Francis (2004). *An Inquiry into the Original of Our Ideas of Beauty and Virtue in Two Treatises,* ed. with an intro., Wolfgang Leidhold. Indianapolis, IN: Liberty Fund. (Based on the 2nd edition, 1726; 1st edition published in 1725.) This edition also includes passages from the revised 5th edition 1753.

Hutcheson, Francis (2007). *A Short Introduction to Moral Philosophy*, ed. with an intro., Luigi Turco. Indianapolis, IN: Liberty Fund. Originally published in 1747.

Hutton, Sarah (1993). "Damaris Cudworth, Lady Masham: Between Platonism and Enlightenment," *British Journal for the History of Philosophy* 1: 29–54.

Immerwahr, John (1991). "The Anatomist and the Painter: The Continuity of Hume's Treatise and Essays," *Hume Studies* 1: 1–17.

Irwin, T. H. (2003). "Stoic Naturalism and Its Critics," in *The Cambridge Companion to the Stoics*, ed. Brad Inwood. Cambridge: Cambridge University Press, pp. 345–364.

Irwin, Terence (2007). *The Development of Ethics: A Historical and Critical Study, Volume I: From Socrates to the Reformation*. Oxford: Oxford University Press.

Irwin, Terence (2008). *The Development of Ethics: A Historical and Critical Study, Volume II: From Suarez to Rousseau*. Oxford: Oxford University Press.

Irwin, Terence (2009). *The Development of Ethics: A Historical and Critical Study, Volume III: From Kant to Rawls*. Oxford: Oxford University Press.

Israel, Jonathan (2001). *Radical Enlightenment: Philosophy and the Making of Modernity*. Oxford: Oxford University Press.

Jackson, Frank (1998). *From Metaphysics to Ethics: A Defence of Conceptual Analysis*. Oxford: Oxford University Press.

Johns, Christopher (2013). *The Science of Right in Leibniz's Moral and Political Philosophy*. London: Bloomsbury.

Johnson, Robert (2016). "Kant's Moral Philosophy," *Stanford Encyclopedia of Philosophy*. https://plato.stanford.edu/entries/kant-moral/

Kahneman, Daniel, and Amos Tversky (1982). "The Simulation Heuristic," in *Judgment Under Uncertainty*, eds. D. Kahneman, P. Slovic, and A. Tversky. Cambridge: Cambridge University Press.

Kail, P. J. E. (2001). "Hutcheson's Moral Sense: Skepticism, Realism, and Secondary Qualities," *History of Philosophy Quarterly* 18: 57–77.

Kames, Lord (Henry Home) (2005). *Essays on Morality and Principles of Natural Religion*, 3rd ed. Indianapolis, IN: Liberty Fund. Originally published in 1776.

Kant, Immanuel (1904). *Educational Theory of Immanuel Kant*, trans. and ed. Edward Franklin Buchner. Philadelphia: J. B. Lippincott Company.

Kant, Immanuel (1996a). "Groundwork of the Metaphysics of Morals," in *Practical Philosophy*, trans. and ed. Mary J. Gregor. Cambridge: Cambridge University Press. References are to page numbers of the Preussische Akademie edition. Originally published in 1785.

Kant, Immanuel (1996b). "Critique of Practical Reason," in *Practical Philosophy*, trans. and ed. Mary J. Gregor. Cambridge: Cambridge University Press. Page references are to page numbers of the Preussische Akademie edition.

Kant, Immanuel (1996c). "Metaphysics of Morals," in *Practical Philosophy*, trans. and ed. Mary J. Gregor. Cambridge: Cambridge University Press. Page references are to page numbers of the Preussische Akademie edition.

Kant, Immanuel (1998). *Critique of Pure Reason*, trans. and ed. Paul Guyer and Allen Wood. Cambridge: Cambridge University Press. Originally published in 1781. Page references are to page numbers of the Preussische Akademie edition.

Kant, Immanuel (2007). *Anthropology, History, and Education*, ed. Robert Louden and Günther Zöller. Cambridge: Cambridge University Press. Page references are to page numbers of the Preussische Akademie edition.

Kant, Immanuel (2009). *Idea for a University History with a Cosmopolitan Aim (1784)*, trans. Allen Wood, eds. Amelie O. Rorty and James Schmidt. Cambridge: Cambridge University Press.

Kant, Immanuel (2013a). "Of the Different Human Races," in *Kant and the Concept of Race: Eighteenth-Century Writings*, trans. and ed. Jon M. Mikkelsen. Albany: State University of New York Press.

Kant, Immanuel (2013b). "Determination of the Concept of Human Race," in *Kant and the Concept of Race: Eighteenth-Century Writings*, trans. and ed. Jon M. Mikkelsen. Albany: State University of New York Press.

Kant, Immanuel (2018). *Religion within the Boundaries of Mere Reason*, eds. Allen W. Wood and George Di Giovanni, foreword Robert Merrihew Adams. Cambridge: Cambridge University Press.

Kavka, Gregory (1986). *Hobbesian Moral and Political Theory*. Princeton: Princeton University Press.

Kavka, Gregory (1995). "The Rationality of Rule-Following: Hobbes's Dispute with the Foole," *Law and Philosophy* 4: 5–34.

King, Peter (1830). *The Life of John Locke, with Extracts from His Correspondence, Journals, and Common-Place Books*, 2 vols. London: Henry Colburn & Richard Bentley.

Kirk, Linda (1987). *Richard Cumberland and Natural Law: Secularisation of Thought in Seventeenth-Century England*. Cambridge: James Clarke.

Köhler, Wolfgang (1938). *The Place of Value in a World of Facts*. New York: Liverlight Publishing Corp.

Korsgaard, Christine (1996a). *The Sources of Normativity*. Cambridge: Cambridge University Press.

Korsgaard, Christine (1996b). *Creating the Kingdom of Ends*. Cambridge: Cambridge University Press.

Korsgaard, Christine (1996c). "Morality as Freedom," in Korsgaard 1996b.

Kosch, Michelle (2006). *Freedom and Reason in Kant, Schelling, and Kierkegaard*. Oxford: Clarendon Press.

Kosch, Michelle (2018). *Fichte's Ethics*. Oxford: Oxford University Press.

Kripke, Saul (1981). *Naming and Necessity*. Malden, MA: Blackwell Publishing.

Langton, Rae (1992). "Duty and Desolation," *Philosophy* 67: 481–505.

Law, Edmund (1824). "A Defence of Mr. Locke's Opinion Concerning Personal Identity," in Locke (1824), III, 179–198.

LeBuffe, Michael (2003). "Hobbes on the Origin of Obligation," *British Journal of the History of Philosophy* 11: 15–39.

Leibniz, Gottfied Wilhelm (1969). *Gottfried Wilhelm Leibniz: Philosophical Papers and Letters*, 2nd ed., ed. and trans. L. E. Loemker. Dordrecht: Reidel.

Leibniz, Gottfried Wilhelm (1985a). *Textes inédits*, ed. Gaston Grua. New York: Garland.

Leibniz, Gottfried Wilhelm (1985b). *Theodicy*, trans. E. M. Huggard. La Salle, IL: Open Court.

Leibniz, Gottfried Wilhelm (1988). *Political Writings*, ed. Patrick Riley. Cambridge: Cambridge University Press.

Leisinger, Matthew A. (2019). "The Inner Work of Liberty: Cudworth on Desire and Attention," *International Journal of Philosophical Studies* 27: 649–667.

Leisinger, Matthew A. (2021). "Cudworth on Freewill," *Philosophers' Imprint*, https://quod.lib.umich.edu/p/phimp/3521354.0021.001/1/--cudworth-on-freewill?rgn=full+text;view=image

Leiter, Brian (2015). *Nietzsche on Morality*, 2nd ed. New York: Routledge.

Lerner, Adam (unpublished). "Empathy as Evidence."

Lipscomb, Benjamin J. B. (2021). *The Women Are Up to Something*. Oxford: Oxford University Press.

Lloyd, S. A. (2009). *Morality in the Philosophy of Thomas Hobbes: Cases in the Law of Nature*. Cambridge: Cambridge University Press.

Locke, John (1824). *The Works of John Locke*, 12th ed., 9 vols. London: C. and J. Rivington.

Locke, John (1975). *An Essay Concerning Human Understanding*, ed. Peter H. Nidditch. Oxford: Oxford University Press. First edition, 1690; final, fourth edition, 1700,

Locke, John (1988). *Two Treatises of Government*, ed. Peter Laslett. Cambridge: Cambridge University Press. Originally published in 1689.

Locke, John (1990). *Drafts for the Essay Concerning Human Understanding and Other Philosophical Writings*, eds. Peter H. Nidditch and G. A. J. Rogers. Oxford: Oxford University Press.

Locke, John (1997). *Political Essays*, ed. Mark Goldie. Cambridge: Cambridge University Press.

Locke, John (2002). *Essays on the Law of Nature: The Latin Text with a Translation, Introduction and Notes, Together with Transcripts of Locke's Shorthand in His Journal for 1676*, ed. W. von Leyden. Oxford: Oxford University Press.

Løgstrup, K. E. (2007). *Beyond the Ethical Demand*, trans. Susan Dew and Heidi Flegal, intro. Kees van Kooten Niekerk. Notre Dame, IN: University of Notre Dame Press.

Løgstrup, K. E. (2020). *The Ethical Demand*, trans., intro., notes Bjørn Rabjerg and Robert Stern. Oxford: Oxford University Press.

Long, A. A. (1986). *Hellenistic Philosophy: Stoics, Epicureans, Sceptics*. 2nd ed. Berkeley and Los Angeles: University of California Press.

Lovejoy, Arthur O. (1908). "Kant and the English Platonists," in *Essays Philosophical and Psychological in Honor of Williams James*, ed. members of the Columbia University Philosophy Department. New York: Longmans, Green.

Lu-Adler, Huaping (2022a). "Kant and Slavery: Or Why He Never Became a Radical Egalitarian," *Critical Philosophy of Race* 10.2: 263–294.
Lu-Adler, Huaping (2022b). "Kant on Lazy Savagery: Racialized," *Journal of the History of Philosophy* 60: 253–275.
MacIntyre, Alasdair (1981). *After Virtue: A Study in Moral Theory*. Notre Dame, IN: University of Notre Dame Press.
Mackie, J. L. (1977). *Ethics: Inventing Right and Wrong*. New York: Penguin Books.
Mandeville, Bernard (1988). *The Fable of the Bees or Private Vices, Publick Benefits*, 2 vols. with a commentary critical, historical, and explanatory by F. B. Kaye. Indianapolis, IN: Liberty Fund, (1988). Originally published in 1714.
Martineau, James (1901). *Types of Ethical Theory*, 2 vols. Oxford: Oxford University Press.
Mautner, Thomas (1999). "Pufendorf and the Correlativity Theory of Rights," in *Grotius, Pufendorf and Modern Natural Law*, ed. Knud Haakonssen. Ashgate Dartmouth: Aldershot, pp. 159–181.
McIntyre, Jane (1994). "Hume: Second Newton of the Moral Sciences," *Hume Studies* 20: 3–18.
Mill, John Stuart (1924). *Autobiography*. London: Oxford University Press.
Mill, John Stuart (2002). *Utilitarianism*, ed. George Sher. Indianapolis, IN: Hackett Publishing Co., Inc. References to chapter and paragraph numbers.
Miller, Fred D., Jr. (1995). *Nature, Justice, and Rights in Aristotle's Politics*. Oxford: Clarendon Press.
Mills, Charles W. (1997). *The Racial Contract*. Ithaca, NY: Cornell University Press.
Mills, Charles W. (2005a). "Ideal Theory as Ideology," *Hypatia* 20: 165–184.
Mills, Charles W. (2005b). "Kant's Üntermenschen," in *Race and Racism in Modern Philosophy*, ed. Andrew Walls. Ithaca, NY: Cornell University Press.
Mills, Charles W. (2017). "Black Radical Kantianism," *Res Philosophia* 95.1: 1–33.
Moore, G. E. (1993). *Principia Ethica*, rev. ed. with the preface to the (projected) 2nd ed. and other papers, ed. with an intro. Thomas Baldwin. Cambridge: Cambridge University Press.
Moran, R. (2005). "Getting Told and Being Believed," *Philosophers' Imprint* 5: 1–29.
Muller, Jerry Z. (1995). *Adam Smith in His Time and Ours: Designing the Decent Society*. Princeton: Princeton University Press.
Murdoch, Iris (2001). *The Sovereignty of the Good*. London and New York: Routledge.
Nadler, Steven (2006). *Spinoza's Ethics: An Introduction*. Cambridge: Cambridge University Press.
Nadler, Steven (2018). *Spinoza: A Life*, 2nd ed. Cambridge: Cambridge University Press.
Nagel, Thomas (2022). "What Is Rude?" *London Review of Books*. www.lrb.co.uk/the-paper/v44/n03/thomas-nagel/what-is-rude
Neuhouser, Frederick (2008). *Rousseau's Theodicy of Self-Love: Evil, Rationality, and the Drive for Recognition*. Oxford: Oxford University Press.

Nietzsche, Friedrich (2007). *On the Genealogy of Morality*, rev. student ed., ed. Keith Ansell-Pearson, trans. Carol Diethe. Cambridge: Cambridge University Press.
Nisbett, Richard (2018). *Culture of Honor*. New York: Routlege.
Norton, David Fate (1982). *David Hume: Common-Sense Moralist, Sceptical Metaphysician*. Princeton: Princeton University Press.
Nozick, Robert (1974). *Anarchy, State, and Utopia*. New York: Basic Books.
Oakley, Francis (2005). *Natural Law, Laws of Nature, Natural Rights: Continuity and Discontinuity in the History of Ideas*. New York: Bloomsbury Academic.
OED (2021). *Oxford English Dictionary*. Oxford: Oxford University Press. www-oed-com
Olson, Mancur (1971). *The Logic of Collective Action*. Cambridge, MA: Harvard University Press.
Parfit, Derek (1986). *Reasons and Persons*. Oxford: Oxford University Press.
Parfit, Derek (2011). *On What Matters*, 2 vol. Oxford: Oxford University Press.
Pashukanis, Evgeny (2003). *The General Theory of Law and Marxism*, intro. by Dragan Milovanovic. New Brunswick and London: Transaction Publishers.
Passmore, John (1951). *Ralph Cudworth: An Interpretation*. Cambridge: Cambridge University Press.
Passmore, John (1968). *Hume's Intentions*, 2nd rev. ed. New York: Basic Books.
Paul, Joanne (2020). *Counsel and Command in Early Modern English Thought*. Cambridge: Cambridge University Press.
Pettit, Philip (1993). *The Common Mind: An Essay on Society, Psychology, and Politics*. Oxford: Oxford University Press.
Pettit, Philip (2009). *Made with Words: Hobbes on Language, Mind, and Politics*. Princeton: Princeton University Press.
Pettit, Philip and Michael Smith (1990). "Backgrounding Desire," *The Philosophical Review* 99: 565–592.
Pettit, Philip and Michael Smith (1996). "Freedom in Belief and Desire," *Journal of Philosophy* 93: 429–449.
Pink, Thomas (2007). "Normativity and Reason," *Journal of Moral Philosophy* 4: 406–431.
Plato (2001). *The Republic*, ed. G. R. F. Ferrari, trans. Tom Griffin. Cambridge: Cambridge University Press.
Platts, Mark (1979). *Ways of Meaning*. London: Routledge & Kegan Paul.
Price, Richard (1974). *A Review of the Principal Questions in Morals (1758)*, et. D. D. Raphael. Oxford: Clarendon Press.
Prichard, H. A. (2002). "Does Moral Philosophy Rest on a Mistake?," in *Moral Writings*, ed. Jim MacAdam. Oxford: Oxford University Press.
Pufendorf, Samuel (1672). *De Jure Naturae et Gentium*. Lund: Adam Junghans.
Pufendorf, Samuel (1710). *On the Law of Nature and Nations* (*De Jure Naturae et Gentium*), trans. Basil Kennett. Oxford: A. and J. Churchill.
Pufendorf, Samuel (1718). *Les devoirs du citoien*, trans. Jean Barbeyrac, 4th ed. Amsterdam: Chez P. de Coup.

Pufendorf, Samuel (1934). *On the Law of Nature and Nations*, trans. C. H. Oldfather and W. A. Oldfather. Oxford: Clarendon Press. Originally published in 1672.

Pufendorf, Samuel (1991). *On the Duty of Man and Citizen According to Natural Law.* trans. Michael Silverthorne, ed. James Tulley. Cambridge: Cambridge University Press.

Pufendorf, Samuel (2009). *Two Books of the Elements of Universal Jurisprudence*, ed. Thomas Behne and trans. W. A. Oldfather, with revisions by Thomas Behne. Indianapolis, IN: Liberty Fund. Originally published in 1660.

Railton, Peter (1986). "Moral Realism," *The Philosophical Review* 95: 163–207.

Raphael, D. D. (1969). *British Moralists: 1650–1800*. Oxford: Clarendon Press.

Rawls, John (1955). "Two Concepts of Rules," *The Philosophical Review* 64: 3–32.

Rawls, John (1971). *A Theory of Justice*. Cambridge, MA: Harvard University Press.

Rawls, John (1980). "Kantian Constructivism in Moral Theory," *The Journal of Philosophy* 77: 515–572.

Rawls, John (1993). *Political Liberalism*. New York: Columbia University Press.

Rawls, John (2000). *Lectures on the History of Moral Philosophy*, ed. Barbara Herman. Cambridge, MA: Harvard University Press.

Rawls, John (2007). *Lectures on the History of Political Philosophy*, ed. Samuel Freeman. Cambridge, MA: Harvard University Press.

Raz, Joseph (1972). "Voluntary Obligations and Normative Powers," *Proceedings of the Aristotelian Society* 46: 79-101.

Raz, Joseph (1977). "Promises and Obligations," in *Law, Morality, and Society: Essays in Honor of H. L. A. Hart*, eds. P. M. S. Hacker and Joseph Raz. Oxford: Oxford University Press, pp. 210–228.

Raz, Joseph (1986). *The Morality of Freedom*. Oxford: Clarendon Press.

Raz, Joseph (2002a). *Practical Reason and Norms*. Oxford: Oxford University Press.

Raz, Joseph (2002b). *The Authority of Law: Essays on Law and Morality*. Oxford: Oxford University Press.

Reid, Thomas (1969). *Essays on the Active Powers of the Human Mind*. Cambridge, MA; MIT Press. Originally published in 1788.

Reid, Thomas (2007). *Thomas Reid on Practical Ethics: Lectures and Papers on Natural Religion, Self-Government, Natural Jurisprudence, and the Law of Nations*, ed. Knud Haakonssen. Edinburgh: Edinburgh University Press.

Ripstein, Arthur (2009). *Force and Freedom: Kant's Legal and Political Philosophy*. Cambridge, MA: Harvard University Press.

Roberts, John R. (unpublished). "Virtue Has No Master: Cudworth's Metaphysics of Free Will."

Roberts, Robert (2003). *Emotions: An Essay in Aid of Moral Psychology*. Cambridge: Cambridge University Press.

Rosenkoetter, Timothy (2003). "A Semantic Approach to Kant's Practical Philosophy," presented at the APA Central Division 2003 meetings in Cleveland, Ohio.

Ross, W. D. (2003). *The Right and the Good*, 2nd ed., ed. Philip Stratton-Lake. Oxford: Clarendon Press.

Rousseau, Jean Jacques (2003). *The Social Contract and Other Later Political Writings*, ed. Victor Gourevitch. Cambridge: Cambridge University Press.

Rousseau, Jean Jacques (2019). *The Discourses and Other Early Political Writings*, ed. and trans. Victor Gourevitch. Cambridge: Cambridge University Press.

Sartre, Jean-Paul (1992). *Being and Nothingness*, trans. Hazel Barnes. New York: Washington Square Press.

Scanlon, T. M. (1998). *What We Owe to Each Other*. Cambridge, MA: Harvard University Press.

Scanlon, T. M. (2014). *Being Realistic about Reasons*. Oxford: Oxford University Press.

Schapiro, Tamar (2021). *Feeling Like It: A Theory of Inclination and Will*. Oxford: Oxford University Press.

Schiffman, Kelley (2015). Rethinking Reason and Right: Moral Rationalism in Eighteenth-Century Britain. Ph.D. Diss., Yale University.

Schliesser, Eric (2019). "Sophie de Grouchy, Adam Smith, and the Politics of Sympathy," in *Feminist History of Philosophy: The Recovery and Evaluation of Women's Philosophical Thought*, eds. Eileen O'Neill and Marcy P. Lascano. Springer: Springer Nature, Switzerland.

Schneewind, J. B. (1977). *Sidgwick's Ethics and Victorian Moral Philosophy*. Oxford: Oxford University Press, 1977.

Schneewind, J. B. (1990). *Moral Philosophy from Montaigne to Kant*, v. i. Cambridge: Cambridge University Press.

Schneewind, J. B. (1998). *The Invention of Autonomy*. Cambridge: Cambridge University Press.

Schroeder, Mark (2005a). "Cudworth and Normative Explanations," *Journal of Ethics & Social Philosophy* 1.3: 1–27.

Schroeder, Mark (2005b). "The Hypothetical Imperative?" *Australasian Journal of Philosophy* 83: 357–372.

Selby-Bigge, L. A. (1964). *British Moralists, Being Selections from Writers Principally of the Eighteenth Century*, 2 vols. Reprinted in one volume with a new introduction by Bernard H. Baumrin. Indianapolis, IN: Bobbs-Merrill.

Sellars, Wilfrid (1956). "Empiricism and the Philosophy of Mind," in *Minnesota Studies in the Philosophy of Science* 1: 253–329.

Sensen, Oliver (2011). *Kant on Human Dignity*. Berlin: DeGruyter.

Shafer-Landau, Russ (2003). *Moral Realism: A Defense*. New York: Oxford University Press.

Shaftesbury, Anthony Ashley Cooper, 3rd Earl of (1698). "Preface," in *Select Sermons of Dr. Whichcot*, ed. Anthony Ashley Cooper, 3rd Earl of Shaftesbury. London: A. & J. Churchill.

Shaftesbury, Anthony Ashley Cooper, 3rd Earl of (1900). *The Life, Unpublished Letters, and Philosophical Regimen of Anthony, Earl of Shaftesbury*, ed. Benjamin Rand. London: Swan Sonnenschein.

Shaftesbury, Anthony Ashley Cooper, 3rd Earl of (2001). *Characteristics of Men, Manners, Opinions, Times*, 3 vols., ed. Douglas J. Den Uyl. Indianapolis, IN:

Liberty Fund. (Based on 1732 edition; first edition, 1711.) References are to volume and page number from the 1732 edition.

Sharp, Franc Chapman (1912). "The Ethical System of Richard Cumberland and Its Place in the History of British Ethics," *Mind* 21: 371–398.

Shelby, Tommie (2005). *We Who Are Dark: The Philosophical Foundations of Black Solidarity*. Cambridge, MA: Harvard University Press.

Shelby, Tommie (2016). *Dark Ghettos: Injustice, Dissent, and Reform*. Cambridge, MA: Harvard University Press.

Sheridan, Patricia (2007). "Pirates, Kings, and Reasons to Act: Moral Motivation and the Role of Sanctions in Locke's Moral Theory," *Canadian Journal of Philosophy* 37: 35–48.

Sidgwick, Henry (1964). *Outlines of the History of Ethics for English Readers*, 6th ed. Boston: Beacon Press.

Sidgwick, Henry (1967). *The Methods of Ethics*, 7th ed. London: Macmillan.

Silk, Alex (2015). "Nietzschean Constructivism: Ethics and Metaethics for All and None," *Inquiry* 58: 244–280.

Skorupski, John (1999). *Ethical Explorations*. Oxford: Oxford University Press.

Slote, Michael (1992). *From Morality to Virtue*. Oxford: Oxford University Press.

Smith, Adam (1976). *An Inquiry into the Nature and Causes of the Wealth of Nations*, eds. R. H. Campbell and A. S. Skinner. Oxford: Clarendon Press. Originally published in 1776.

Smith, Adam (1982). *The Theory of Moral Sentiments*, eds. D. D. Raphael and A. L. MacFie. Indianapolis: LibertyClassics. Originally published in 1759.

Smith, Michael (1989). "Dispositional Theories of Value," *Proceedings of the Aristotelian Society* 63: 89–112.

Smith, Michael (1994). *The Moral Problem*. Oxford: Blackwell.

Sorabji, Richard (2014). *Moral Conscience through the Ages: Fifth Century BCE to the Present*. Chicago: University of Chicago Press.

Spinoza, Benedict (1985a). *Short Treatise on God, Man, and His Well-Being*, in *Collected Works*, v. i, ed. Edwin Curley. Princeton: Princeton University Press.

Spinoza, Benedict (1985b). "Ethics," in *Collected Works*, v. i, ed. Edwin Curley. Princeton: Princeton University Press.

Spinoza, Benedict (2016). "Theological-Political Treatise," in *Collected Works*, v. ii, ed. Edwin Curley. Princeton: Princeton University Press.

Spinoza, Benedict (2007). *Theological-Political Treatise*, ed. with intro. Jonathan Israel. Cambridge: Cambridge University Press.

Spivak, Gayatri Chakravorty (1999). *A Critique of Postcolonial Reason: Toward A History of the Vanishing Present*. Cambridge, MA: Harvard University Press.

Stevenson, Charles (1937). "The Emotive Meaning of Ethical Terms," *Mind* 46: 14–31.

Strawson, P. F. (1968). "Freedom and Resentment," in *Studies in the Philosophy of Thought and Action*. London: Oxford University Press.

Street, Sharon (2008). "Constructivism about Reasons," *Oxford Studies in Metaethics* 3: 207–245.

Suarez, Francisco (1944). *A Treatise on Laws and God the Lawgiver*, in *Selections from Three Works of Francisco Suarez, S.J.*, v. 2, trans. Gwladys L. Williams, Ammi Brown, and John Waldron, rev. Henry Davis, S.J., intro. James Brown Scott. Oxford: Clarendon Press, 1944. Originally published in 1612.
Thompson, Michael (2004). "What Is It to Wrong Someone? A Puzzle about Justice," in *Reason and Value: Themes from the Philosophy of Joseph Raz*, eds. R. Jay Wallace, Philip Pettit, Samuel Scheffler, and Michael Smith. Oxford: Oxford University Press.
Tierney, Brian (1997). *The Idea of Natural Rights*. Grand Rapids, MI: Wm. B. Eerdmans Publishing Co.
Tomasello, Michael (2018). *A Natural History of Human Morality*. Cambridge, MA: Harvard University Press.
Trianosky, Gregory (1978). "On the Obligation to Be Virtuous: Shaftesbury and the Question, Why Be Moral?" *Journal of the History of Philosophy* 16: 289–300.
Tschentscher, Axel (2012). *The Basic Law (Grundgesetz) 2012: The Constitution of the Federal Republic of Germany*. http://papers.ssrn.com/sol3/papers.cfm?abstract_id=1501131
Tuck, Richard (1981). *Natural Rights Theories: Their Origin and Development*. Cambridge: Cambridge University Press.
Tuck, Richard (1993). *Philosophy and Government: 1572–1651*. Cambridge: Cambridge University Press.
Tuck, Richard (2001). *The Rights of War and Peace: Political Thought and the International Order from Grotius to Kant*. Oxford: Oxford University Press.
Tucker, Robert C. (1969). *The Marxian Revolutionary Idea*. New York: W. W. Norton & Company.
Varden, Helga (2020). *Sex, Love, and Gender: A Kantian Theory*. Oxford: Oxford University Press.
Villey, Michel (1982). *Philosophie du Droit: 1. Definitions et fins du droit*, 3rd ed. Paris: Galloz.
Villey, Michel (1984). *Philosophie du Droit: 2. Les moyens du droit*, 2nd ed. Paris: Galloz.
Voitle, Robert (1984). *The Third Earl of Shaftesbury*. Baton Rouge: Louisiana State University Press.
Wahrman, Dror (2006). *The Making of the Modern Self: Identity and Culture in Eighteenth-Century England*. New Haven, CT: Yale University Press.
Watson, Gary (1975). "Free Agency," *Journal of Philosophy* 72: 205–220.
Watson, Gary (1996). "Two Faces of Responsibility," *Philosophical Topics* 24: 227–248.
Watson, Gary (2009). "Promises, Reasons, and Normative Powers," in *Reasons for Action*, eds. David Sobel and Steven Wall. Cambridge: Cambridge University Press, pp. 155–178.
Williams, Bernard (1981a). *Moral Luck*. Cambridge: Cambridge University Press.
Williams, Bernard (1981b). "Internal and External Reasons," in *Moral Luck*. Cambridge: Cambridge University Press.

Williams, Bernard (1985). *Ethics and the Limits of Philosophy*. Cambridge, MA: Harvard University Press.

Williams, Bernard (1995). "Internal Reasons and the Obscurity of Blame," in *Making Sense of Humanity*. Cambridge: Cambridge University Press.

Winkler, Kenneth P. (1985). "Hutcheson's Alleged Moral Realism," *Journal of the History of Philosophy* 23: 179–194.

Wisdom, John (1948). "Things and Persons," *Proceedings of the Aristotelian Society* 22: 202–215.

Wolf, Susan (1987). "Sanity and Moral Responsibility," in *Responsibility, Character, and the Emotions: New Essays in Moral Psychology*, ed. F. D. Schoeman. Cambridge: Cambridge University Press.

Wolff, Robert Paul (1970). *In Defense of Anarchism*. New York: Harper & Row.

Wollaston, William (1978). *The Religion of Nature Delineated*. New York: Garland Publishing Co., Inc. Originally published in 1722.

Wood, Allen W. (1990). *Hegel's Ethical Thought*. Cambridge: Cambridge University Press.

Wood, Allen W. (1999). *Kant's Ethical Thought*. Cambridge: Cambridge University Press.

Wood, Allen W. (2016). *Fichte's Ethical Thought*. Oxford: Oxford University Press.

Woolhouse, Richard (2007). *Locke: A Biography*. Cambridge: Cambridge University Press.

Worsnip, Alex (2015). "Hobbes and Normative Egoism," *Archiv für Geschichte der Philosophie* 97: 481–512.

Yaffe, Gideon (2000). *Liberty Worth the Name: Locke on Free Agency*. Princeton: Princeton University Press.

Young, Julian (2010). *Friedrich Nietzsche: A Philosophical Biography*. Cambridge: Cambridge University Press.

Yovel, Yirmiyahu (1992). *Spinoza and Other Heretics, Volume 1: The Marrano of Reason*. Princeton: Princeton University Press.

INDEX

Albee, Ernest, 100
Allais, Lucy, 12, 341
Allison, Henry, 280
Anderson, Elizabeth, 14
Anscombe, Elizabeth
  challenge, xi, 1–13, 16–20, 24, 35, 38, 101
  consequentialism, critique of, 1
  law conception, 1, 17–20, 25, 29
  legislation, divine, 2
Aquinas, Thomas, 11, 16, 17, 26, 64, 102
  Bonum honestum, 20
  eudaimonism, 26
  law
    eternal, 26–27, 92
    natural, 16–20, 26–27, 155
  Naturalism, Aristotelian, 17, 26
  perfectionism, 114
Aristotle, 4, 5, 11, 15, 23, 36, 167, 204
  justice, distributive, 29
  naturalism, 7, 11, 12, 16, 17, 19, 25, 26, 28, 30, 40, 92, 97, 101, 102, 122, 147, 151, 152, 163, 168, 189
  perfectionism, 114–115
  wisdom, practical, 108

Baier, Annette, 9
Balguy, John
  accountability, 248, 287
  agency, 248–249
  akrasia, 249
  approbation, 249
  benevolence as insufficient and unnecessary for moral goodness, 248
  fitness, 249–250
  in relation to

Butler, Joseph, 248–249
Clarke, Samuel, 237–239, 247–250, 287
Hobbes, Thomas, 287
Hutcheson, Francis, 248–249, 287
Price, Richard, 237–239, 287
Suárez, Francisco, 250
moral sense theory, rejection of, 252
morality, deontic conception of, 238–239, 256
motivation, 249–250
necessity, 249
obligation
  as normative relation, 242
  internal, 249–250
practical and theoretical reasoning, parallel between, 249–250
rationalism, 113, 229, 237–238, 248–250
reason as source of moral motivation, 238, 248–250
"the reason of the thing and the rectitude of the action," 283, 287
virtue as rational determination of the mind, 248
Barbeyrac, Jean, 27, 34, 87
  on Grotius, Hugo, 15, 22–24, 32, 35
  on Leibniz, Gottfried Wilhelm, 163–164
  on Pufendorf, Samuel von, 87
Bentham, Jeremy, 162, 205
  in relation to
    Hume, David, 205
    Hutcheson, Francis, 177
Bratman, Michael, 260

Butler, Joseph
  accountability, 169–172, 194–197, 200, 239, 246, 256
  action in circumstances as object of reflective judgment, 190
  agency, 168–172, 185–198, 200, 222, 241, 253, 256
    self-reflective, 165
  Anglicanism, 184
  approbation, reflex, 142, 170
  authority and mere power, distinction between, 185, 195, 209
  autonomy, 169–170, 187–188, 206, 221–222
  benevolence, 185, 186
  conscience, 147, 165–166, 168–172, 183–199, 200, 241, 248, 249, 255, 257, 259, 270
    and self-love, dualism between, 168–169
    authority of, 142, 151, 168–172, 184, 186–188, 192–197, 205, 222, 238, 240, 246, 253, 259, 261–263
      teleological argument for, 192–194
      theological argument for, 192–194
      transcendental argument for, 193–197
    in relation to self-love. *See* Butler, Joseph:Self-love:In relation to conscience
  "cool hour" passage, 56, 189
  egoism, rejection of, 185, 199–200
  eudaimonism, rejection of, 172, 189–190, 192
  "everything is what it is...," 172, 185
  God as designer, 193–194
  good and right, 197–199
  happiness, 186, 189
  hierarchy, normative, 186–188, 255
  in relation to
    Aristotle, 189
    Clarke, Samuel, 196
    Cudworth, Ralph, 169–170
    Cumberland, Richard, 170–171
    Hutcheson, Francis, 165–166, 169–171, 185–192, 195, 197–199, 205–206, 221–222, 238

  Leibniz, Gottfried Wilhelm, 166
  Locke, John, 100, 169–170
  Pufendorf, Samuel von, 194
  Shaftesbury (Anthony Ashley Cooper, Third Earl of), 142, 147, 151, 165–166, 169–170, 185, 189, 192, 195, 199, 222, 238
  judgment
    deontic moral, 188, 191–192
    normative practical, 171–172, 186–197
  morality, deontic conception of, 168–172
  nature, 168, 187–189, 192–193
  obligation, 172
  passions, private and public, distinction between, 185–186
  proto-utilitarianism, rejection of, 166, 199, 206
  psyche
    constitution of, 169, 185–188, 194–195
    economy, 169, 185–188, 191–193
  psychology, moral, 165–166, 185–188, 200
  reason, 127
  reflection, principle of, 165, 171–172, 186–197, 222, 249, 255, 263, 270
  Rolls Chapel, 184
  self-deception, 188
  self-love, 168–169, 184–193, 199–200, 261–262
    in relation to conscience, 186–188, 197
  self-reflection, 190–192
  sermons, overview, 183–184
  utilitarianism, indirect, 198, 200
  vice as misery, 169
  virtue
    as conscientious self-guidance, 165, 166, 206, 241
    reduction to benevolence, rejection of, 166, 170–171, 205, 257
  watch analogy, 194

Cassirer, Ernst, 140
Cicero, Marcus Tullius, 11, 156–157

Clarke, Samuel
　accountability, 246–247, 273
　agency, 10, 243, 245–247, 256, 273
　benevolence, universal, 246
　Boyle Lectures, 196, 243
　circumstances, 243–246
　conscience, 196
　　authority of, 246–247
　differences of things, 244–246
　equity, 243, 246
　fitness, 208, 241, 243–246
　　as founded in the nature of things, 243, 244
　　as synonymous with "right" and "reasonable," 243
　golden rule, 243, 287
　good, universal, 243
　in relation to
　　Balguy, John, 237–239, 247–250, 287
　　Butler, Joseph, 196, 243, 246–247
　　Cudworth, Ralph, 243, 248
　　Fordyce, David, 240–246
　　Hobbes, Thomas, 287
　　Hutcheson, Francis, 245–246
　　Leibniz, Gottfried Wilhelm, 157, 248
　　Price, Richard, 237–239, 273, 287
　　Reid, Thomas, 273
　　Shaftesbury (Anthony Ashley Cooper, Third Earl of), 142
　　Suárez, Francisco, 250
　internalism, motivational, 247, 255
　judgment, 244–247
　love, 243, 246
　mathematics and morality, analogy between, 244
　morality, deontic conception of, 238–239, 246–247, 256
　obligation, 196, 241, 244–246, 250
　　as "eternal reason of things," 246
　　as normative relation, 242, 246
　rationalism, 113, 229, 237–238, 241, 243–248
　　founder of British tradition, 243
　reason as the source of moral motivation, 238
　reasoning, practical and theoretical, parallel between, 247, 249
　relations, natural, 244–245
　supervenience, 245
　voluntarism, rejection of, 243, 248
　will, 247, 249
Cudworth, Ralph, 10
　accountability, 112, 128–129, 135–139, 145–146, 148, 169–170
　agency, 112, 148, 158, 169–170
　anti-positivism, 111, See also Voluntarism, rejection of
　atheism, rejection of, 128
　autexousy, 136–139, 261
　autonomy, 169–170
　believing and judging, distinction between, 136–137
　benevolence, 134–135
　blame, 128, 135–136
　charity, 112, See Cudworth, Ralph:Love
　conscience, 139
　determination, practical, 132–139
　eudaimonism, 169–170
　fault and sin, 137
　God, 117
　　as ideal of moral agency, 133–135, 139
　goodness, natural and positive, distinction between, 131
　government, divine, 128
　guilt, 128, 135–136
　honesty, 138, 139
　idealism
　　ethical, 131–134
　　metaphysical, 130–131
　in relation to
　　Hobbes, Thomas, 129, 130, 132–133, 136, 138, 152
　　Leibniz, Gottfried Wilhelm, 111
　　Locke, John, 112, 128–129, 131, 169–170
　　Plato, 130, 134
　　Plotinus, 130
　　Pufendorf, Samuel von, 128–129, 131, 138
　　Shaftesbury (Anthony Ashley Cooper, Third Earl of), 111, 151, 169–170
　　Spinoza, Baruch, 111, 128
　internalism, autonomist, 133

Cudworth, Ralph (cont.)
    judgment, practical, 112, 135–137
    justice, 134–135
    knowledge, 130–131
    life, "stories of," "animal" and "divine," 137, 139
    "light" in which agents view options, 137
    love, 112, 133–135, 138, 139, 141, 146, 243
    metaphysics, 128, 135
    mind, 130–135
        modifications of, 131–134
        of God, 131, 133–134
    morality, eternal and immutable character of, 111, 129–134, 208, 237, 252
    motivation. *See* determination, practical
    nature, necessary, 137
    obligation, 112, 131–133, 135–139
    rationalism, 270
    Sui-Potestas. *See* Cudworth, Ralph:autexousy
    virtue, ethics of, 113
    voluntarism, rejection of, 42, 70, 111–112, 128–134, 152, 248
    will, 260
        as "last practical judgment," 136–137
        free, 112, 128, 135–139
            animal and moral, 112, 136–139, 169
Culverwell, Nathaniel, 92
Cumberland, Richard
    agency, 88, 89, 101–108
    authority, divine, 103–104
        as epiphenomenal, 109
    benevolence, 88, 101, 102–105, 171
    best end as the greatest good of all, 103, 106–110, 171
    effects, 102–103, 105–108
    egoism, rejection of, 101
    empiricism, 87–89, 101, 102, 104–105
    envy and hatred, 105
    eudaimonism, rejection of, 101
    good
        as single normative standard, 109–110
        common, 88, 89, 103–108, 134, 177

    goods, natural, 106
    happiness, 102–104, 107–108
    in relation to
        Aquinas, Thomas, 102
        Aristotle, 101, 102, 104
        Grotius, Hugo, 87–90
        Hobbes, Thomas, 88–90, 101–102, 104–105, 107, 108
        Hume, David, 90
        Hutcheson, Francis, 90
        Leibniz, Gottfried Wilhelm, 90
        Locke, John, 88–90, 103–106, 109
        Pufendorf, Samuel von, 87–90, 103–104, 109
        Shaftesbury (Anthony Ashley Cooper, Third Earl of), 90
        Suárez, Francisco, 146
    instrumentalism, 105–108
    internalism, 90
    law, natural, 88–89, 102–105, 108–111, 141, 146
    love, 104, 105, 134
    morality as science, 87, 88
    naturalism, 87–90, 101–110
    nonaggression, mutual, 105
    obligation, 89, 103–104
        as epiphenomenal, 108–110
    peace, 105, 106
    propositions, practical, 102–103
    punishments and rewards, 103–104
    reason, practical, 107–109, 171
        standard of, 107–108
    reductionism, 87–89, 106, 108–110, 171
    right, the, 106
        as epiphenomenal, 108–110
    sanctions. *See* punishments and rewards
    utilitarianism, 88–89, 100, 106, 109
    voluntarism, theological, 90, 101, 108–109
    will, consequence-directed rational, 105–107

Descartes, René, 120
    dualism, 114

Fichte, Johann Gottlieb, 334
    in relation to Reid, Thomas, 265
    summons, xii

Florentinus, 21, 22
Fordyce, David
  accountability, 242, 246, 258
  affections, 240
  agency, 239–242, 258
  conscience
    authority of, 240–242
  conscientiousness and moral
      goodness, connection
      between, 241, 258
  empiricism, 239–241
  in relation to
    Butler, Joseph, 240–242
    Clarke, Samuel, 240–246, 251
    Hume, David, 240–241
    Hutcheson, Francis, 239–241,
      258
    Locke, John, 239, 258
    Price, Richard, 239, 258
    Shaftesbury (Anthony Ashley
      Cooper, Third Earl of), 240
  morality, deontic conception of,
    239–242, 246, 258
  motivation, 239–242
  obligation, 239–243, 245, 246, 258
    as indefinable, 239–241, 251
    as normative relation, 242
  reason, 239–241
  sense, moral, 239–242, 245, 258
  senses as source of ideas, 239–241
  sentimentalism, 239–246
  "state of moral obligation," 242
  "state of the case," 241, 244
  supervenience, 245
Fricker, Miranda, 14

Galileo, 45, 120
Grotius, Hugo
  accountability, 23, 31, 34–38, 91, 155
  autonomy, 35
  Carneades, challenge of, 16, 25–31,
    36, 156–157, 163–164, 197, 279
  collective action problem, 27–28, 37
  consentium gentium, 36, 40
  dignity, 33
  Dutch trading companies, 31
  equality, right of, 21, 38, 64
  eudaimonism, 25
  golden rule, 36
  in relation to
    Aquinas, Thomas, 19, 20, 24
    Aristotle, 23
    Florentinus, 21, 22
    Seneca, 21
    Suárez, Francisco, 17–21, 23–25,
      292
  individualism, 40
  ius, 20–25
  law, moral, 34
  law, natural, 11, 16, 19, 24, 29–30,
    36–38, 63–64, 111
  liberty, 32
  minimalism, 35, 36, 40
  morality as science, 34–36
  "morality," use of word, 87
  Naturalism, Aristotelian, 11, 16, 25
  necessity, moral, 155
  obligation, 24–25, 29, 32–38
    perfect and imperfect, 62–63
  principles, general, 37, 38
  punishment, 31, 33–34
  recognition, mutual, 64, 91
  reparation, 32
  restitution, 32
  right, fountain of. *See* Grotius,
      Hugo:Sociability
  rights
    claim, 31–33
    natural, 24–26, 31–33, 35
    perfect and imperfect, 16, 22–23,
      38, 62–63
  sociability, 19, 21–22, 24, 29, 34,
    36–38, 40, 63–64, 73, 91, 265,
    268, 269, 274, 277, 278
  sovereign, 31
  speech, 37
  superiority, right of, 21, 38, 64
  voluntarism, rejection of, 19, 24
  war and peace, 42–43
  Will, 31
Guyer, Paul, 288, 301, 306, 334

Haakonssen, Knud, 15
Hare, R.M., 162, 245
Hart, H.L.A., 31, 33, 50
  point of view, internal, 216
  rules, external and internal aspects
    of, distinction between, 219

368 INDEX

Hegel, Georg Wilhelm Friedrich, 10, 12, 265, 334
Hobbes, Thomas
   absurdity and injury, 51
   accountability, 36, 55, 56
   attitudes, reactive (Strawsonian), 59–61
   color analogy, 45–48, 89, 120
   conscience, 58
   consequence, 39, 43–44
   contract and covenant, 41–44, 48–54, 61, 125, 215, 216, 219
      violation of, 51–59
   creatures lacking conception of right and wrong, 59
   deliberation, 47–51, 60–61
   desire and the good, 41, 43–49, 219
      and the right, 48
      metaethics of, 48, 59–61
   egoism, 30
   empiricism, 39–40, 44, 59, 61
   Epicureanism, 89, 104
   evil, 45, 46
   expressivism, 45–48, 210
   fool, 25, 30, 56, 52–59, 279
   God, power of, 50
   Golden Rule, 36, 54, 59, 73, 87, 287
   in relation to
      Grotius, Hugo, 30, 40–43
      Suárez, Francisco, 18, 146, 292
   individualism, 40
   instrumentalism, 49
   judgmentalism, 60
   justice, 43
   law, 54, 55
      natural, 41, 44, 48, 52–59, 146
   liberty, 41, 42, 49–51, 53
      blameless, 33, 49, 55, 59, 75, 83
   materialism, 39–40, 44, 51, 59, 61
   minimalism, 40
   morality as science, 39–40, 43–44, 47, 51
   "morality," use of word, 87
   nature
      right of, 41, 49, 53, 55, 75, 159
      state of, 41, 52, 53, 55, 57, 58, 105, 213
   nominalism, 39, 43, 130, 132
   obligation and the right, 40–44, 54, 48–61, 68, 219, 239
   and the good, 52–54
   metaethics, 49
   obligation, natural, 49–50
   passions, 44, 45
   power, normative, 41–42, 44, 61, 215
   projectivism, 60, 61, 119–120,
      See also Hobbes, Thomas:expressivism
   reasonable, the, 54–56
   reciprocity theorem, 49, 54
   reductionism, 44
   sanctions, divine, 141
   scarcity, natural, 105
   self-preservation, 41, 48, 49, 53, 55, 59
   sense, 39
   slaves and servants, 57–58
   sovereign, 49, 54–59, 125, 215, 216
   subjectivism, 44–45
   utility, expected, 52
   war and peace, 41–45
   War, English Civil, 40
   will, 47, 51, 60, 120, 136
Hohfeld, Wesley Newcomb, 65, 159
   rights, claim, 32
   rights, liberty, 32, 33, 159
Hume, David
   aesthetic and moral assessment, analogy between, 143, 221, 230
   approbation, 249, 264
   as anatomist, 203
   autonomy, 206
   beauty, moral, 230
   benevolence, 204–205, 212–215, 218
   bigot, seditious, 205, 214
   causation, 252
   collective action problems, 204
   color analogy, 69, 237
   consequentialism, 211
   constructionism, social, 212
   convention, 205, 213–221
   creatures, rational, 220–221, 232
   desires, 201, 207
   empiricism, 151, 241, 252, 259
   Enlightenment, Scottish, 201
   expressivism, 210
   fact, matters of, 209–210

free rider. *See* Hume, David:knave, sensible
ideas, association of, 175, 204–205, 209, 211–212
ideas, relations of, 207, 209, 244
in relation to
    Balguy, John, 237–238
    Butler, Joseph, 184, 190–191, 205–206, 214, 221–222, 229, 238
    Clarke, Samuel, 208, 237–238, 243–247
    Cudworth, Ralph, 208
    Cumberland, Richard, 89–90
    Grotius, Hugo, 30
    Hobbes, Thomas, 213–214, 216–217
    Horace, 211
    Hutcheson, Francis, 166–167, 175, 177–179, 181–182, 201, 203–206, 210–211, 213–214, 218, 220–224, 229–230, 232, 237–241, 251, 254, 282
    Price, Richard, 237–238
    Shaftesbury (Anthony Ashley Cooper, Third Earl of), 113, 124, 140–144, 151, 172, 213, 238
    Smith, Adam, 201–203, 220–224, 229–238
    Spinoza, Baruch, 115, 122, 124, 127
"is"/"ought," 201, 209–210, 244
judgments, ethical, 201–202, 208–213, 222, 229–231
justice, 203–205
    artificial, 167, 204–205, 213–221, 232–233, 265
    motive of, 218–220
    practices, rule-governed cooperative, 205, 213–221
knave, sensible, 25, 30, 205, 217–218, 279
mind, secret springs and principles of, 203
"moral problem," 201
moral virtues and natural abilities, distinction between as purely verbal, 167, 177, 203–204, 211, 236
morality, deontic, rejection of, 167
motivation, theory of, 60, 206–212, 220

motives as object of approbation, 214, 218, 222, 229
naturalism, empiricist, 201, 203–204
Newtonianism, 203–204, 211
obligation, 89, 166, 171, 266–267
    interested, 141, 181, *See* Hume, David:Obligation:Natural
    moral, 181, 205, 213, 217–220, 232, 240
    natural, 141, 181, 213, 217–220, 240
    rule, 219–220
passion and reason, opposition of, rejection of, 206–208
passions, calm and violent, 127
performance, external, as lacking merit, 167, 213, 214, 220
perspective, observer's, 190, 203, 218, 221–223, 230
philosophy as science, 139
promising, 214–218, 266–267
property, 214–219
rationalism, rejection of, 201, 206–211
reason as "slave of the passions," 127, 316
reason as motivationally inert, 166, 201, 206–210, 247, 255
reasoning
    demonstrative, 207
    probabilistic, 207, 209
resentment, 221
rowing example, 216
seditious bigot, 37
self-interest, 205, 213–214, 217–220
self-love, 214–216
sense, moral, 113, 210, 259
    rejection of, 203–204, 210–211, 264
sentimentalism, 113, 143, 167, 190, 201, 206–212, 214, 218–220, 222–223, 229, 230, 237–241, 243–246, 263–264, 274
subjectivism, 210
sympathy, 175, 204–205, 209, 211–212, 220–224, 229–232, 264
    as emotional contagion, 211, 224
utilitarianism, 205, 211
utility as foundation of justice, 203, 205

Hume, David (cont.)
  virtue
    "in rags," 212
    amiable and awful, distinction between, 234
    artificial and natural, distinction between, 213
    ethics of, 167, 177, 204–205, 213–215, 251, 254
    will, 206–210, 220
Hursthouse, Rosalind, 9
Huseyinzadegan, Dilek, 12, 341
Hutcheson, Francis, 9
  agency, 248
  appetitus rationalis. See Hutcheson, Francis:will
  apprehension, rational, 179–180
  approbation and condemnation, 167–168, 174–177, 182, 204, 210, 211, 249, 251, 258, 263, 264
    moral, and nonmoral esteem, distinction between, 167
  beauty, 175
  benevolence, 133, 147, 151, 175–178, 199, 204–206, 211, 213, 214, 248, 254, 258, 261, 282–283
    calm extensive. See Hutcheson, Francis:benevolence, universal
    particular, 180
    universal, 166, 176–181, 184, 204, 232, 246
    universal, and self-love, dualism between, 168, 170, 181, 186
  choiceworthiness, moral, 133, 167, 168, 174, 177–178, 204, 205, 213, 218
  color analogy, 69, 176
  condemnation. See Hutcheson, Francis:approbation and condemnation
  desires, calm, 121, 127, 179–181
  desires/affections and appetites/passions, distinction between, 178–181
  egoism, rejection of, 173, 229
  Enlightenment, Scottish, 201
  eudaimonism, rejection of, 168, 173, 178–181
  expressivism, 210
  God, 170
  goodness, 173–181
    moral, 167–168
    moral and natural, distinction between, 167–168, 173–176, 179–181
    natural, 166
    public, 122, 168, 178
  greatest happiness principle, 166, 177, 179–180, 204, 205, 213, 232
  in relation to
    Aristotle, 167–168, 177
    Balguy, John, 237–238
    Butler, Joseph, 165–166, 169–171, 180, 183–192, 195, 197–199, 205–206, 221–222, 229, 238
    Clarke, Samuel, 237–238, 243, 245–246
    Cumberland, Richard, 89–90, 101, 105, 151, 168, 173, 177
    Hobbes, Thomas, 173, 174
    Hume, David, 177–179, 213, 220–224, 229–230, 232, 237–241, 251, 254, 282
    Leibniz, Gottfried Wilhelm, 124, 153, 166
    Locke, John, 167, 173–174, 239, 251
    Mandeville, Bernard, 173
    Price, Richard, 237–238
    Shaftesbury (Anthony Ashley Cooper, Third Earl of), 113, 124, 140–144, 147, 151, 165–166, 172–173, 177, 180–182, 204, 213, 238
    Spinoza, Baruch, 122, 124, 127
  instinct, 179
  judgments, moral, 222
  justice, 168, 232
  love, 166–167, 175
  moral virtues and natural abilities, distinction between, 211
  morality, deontic, rejection of, 166–168, 177, 204
  motives, contemplation of, 174–177, 198, 213, 214, 218, 222, 229, 251, 258
  naturalism, empiricist, 151, 166, 173–176, 201, 240, 241, 251, 259

obligation, 89, 171, 173, 177–178, 181–183
  of moral sense, 181–182, 213
  of self-interest, 181–182, 240
"ought" as "unlucky," 181
passions, calm and violent, 127
perspective, observer's, 165, 176–177, 190, 192, 198, 222–223, 232, 251, 258
proto-utilitarianism, 177–178, 199
psychology, moral, 165–166
rationalism, rejection of, 201, 229
reason as motivationally inert, 168, 179
reason, practical, 178–181, 184
reflection, calm rational, 168
right, the, 232
rights
  alienable and inalienable, 178
  perfect and imperfect, 174, 178
self-reflection as interfering with moral virtue, 165, 180
sense, moral, 113, 165–168, 173–183, 190–191, 198, 203–204, 210, 213, 218, 222–223, 229–230, 239–240, 248, 251, 259, 263
sentimentalism, 113, 143, 167, 201, 203–204, 218, 230, 237–241, 243–246, 248, 263, 274
utilitarianism, 162, 204, 205
virtue
  as coinciding with self-interest, 181
  ethics of, 166–168, 173, 176–183, 204–206, 213, 251, 254
will, 179

Irwin, Terence, xiii, 10–12, 15, 16, 19, 20, 28, 30, 64, 92, 97, 147, 151, 162–164, 189
Israel, Jonathan, 115, 122

Johns, Christopher, 159

Kant, Immanuel, 10
  accountability, 273, 280, 283, 285–288, 292–294, 309, 314, 324–325, 331, 333, 336
  agency, 208, 269, 322, 278–340

finite rational, 10, 273–274, 278–281, 284–286, 290–292, 324–326, 329–333, 339–340
perfect rational, 10, 273, 284, 285, 289–290, 324, 329–331, 334, 340
autonomy, 10, 136, 153, 221, 313, 322
  and heteronomy, distinction between, 271–272
  freedom, positive, 271, 309–312
  of the will, 271–277, 280, 287, 300, 302, 308–315, 317–323, 325, 333–334, 336, 337, 339
benevolence, 282–283, 285, 309, 314, 322, 324, 328
"categories of freedom," 271–272
challenge, morality as chimerical, 25, 30, 279–280, 288, 301, 309, 318, 321–322
common humble person example, 326–329
conscience, 330–331, 333
constraint, 284
  external, 335–339
  self, 314, 335–340
deliberation, 10, 273–274, 280, 285, 294, 300, 309–316, 321, 322, 327, 339–340
desire, 208, 286, 289, 299, 306–307, 309, 312–314, 316–321, 323–324, 328, 331
dignity, 12, 203, 234, 321, 322, 327, 341
  as an end in oneself, 299–308
  disposition, morally good, 307
duty, 273–274, 278–288, 290, 293–295, 301–302, 307, 326, 329–338
  as the necessity of an action from respect for law, 283, 330
  ethical, 335–336
  good will, 281–288
  of right, 335–338
  perfect and imperfect, distinction between, 295
  strict and wide, distinction between. See Kant, Immanuel:Duty:Perfect and imperfect, distinction between

Kant, Immanuel (cont.)
    to oneself, 335
    to others, 295, 302, 335, 338
    empirical, the, 271, 278, 316–320,
        325–326, 332
    false testimony example, 323–325
    force. *See* constraint
    freedom, 10
        as *ratio essendi* of the moral law,
            314, 323
        autonomy. *See* Kant,
            Immanuel:autonomy
        external, 272–273, 336–339
        laws of, 66, 127, 153, 278, 288–289,
            311
        negative, 309–311
        of choice, 272–273, 284, 306, 334,
            336
        positive. *See* Kant,
            Immanuel:autonomy:
            freedom, positive
    goodness, 279–293, 307–308,
        311–313, 317, 319–322, 325,
        330–334, 336
    hindrance, 283, 337
    idealism, transcendental, 273, 300, 314
    ignorance, veil of, 304–306
    imperative, categorical, 36, 208, 273,
        279–281, 285, 287, 288, 291,
        298, 309, 315, 317, 320–322
        Formula of Autonomy (FA),
            302–303, 306, 308, 321, 334
        Formula of Humanity (FH), 295,
            299–303, 306, 308, 321, 334
        Formula of the Kingdom of Ends
            (FKE), 206, 306, 308, 321
        Formula of the Law of Nature
            (FLN), 294
        procedure, 294–299, 303–306, 320
        universal law formula (FUL),
            285–290, 293–299, 301–303,
            306, 308, 321, 334
    imperatives, categorical and
        hypothetical, distinction
        between, 271, 288–291
    imperatives, hypothetical, 208, 271,
        288–292
        assertoric, 292
        problematic, 292
    in relation to
        Balguy, John, 283, 287
        Butler, Joseph, 221
        Clarke, Samuel, 273–274, 287
        Cudworth, Ralph, 270
        Grotius, Hugo, 30, 277, 279, 338
        Hobbes, Thomas, 279, 287, 292
        Hume, David, 221, 279
        Hutcheson, Francis, 221, 282–283
        Leibniz, Gottfried Wilhelm, 125,
            153–154, 157, 160, 270
        Locke, John, 100
        Paul the Apostle, 282–283
        Price, Richard, 252, 270, 273–274,
            287
        Pufendorf, Samuel von, 300, 309
        Rousseau, Jean-Jacques, 269,
            274–278, 300, 304, 308, 336
        Shaftesbury (Anthony Ashley
            Cooper, Third Earl of), 142,
            151
        Smith, Adam, 203, 221, 300
        Suárez, Francisco, 18, 292–293
        Wolff, Christian, 153, 270
incentives, 325–328
inclinations, 271, 273, 284–286,
    289–290, 313, 314, 316–317,
    323–324, 329–330, 334,
    339–340
insincere debtor example, 295–299,
    301–302
kingdom of ends, 304–306
law
    moral, 271–275, 278–281, 284,
        286–291, 303–310, 323–335,
        337–340
        as *ratio cognoscendi* of freedom,
            314, 323
        awareness of being bound by,
            272, 280, 314–315, 323–324,
            333
    moral and practical, distinction
        between, 271, 273, 279,
        286, 290–291, 303–304,
        331, 339
    practical, 271–273, 279, 281,
        286–287, 289–290, 293–295,
        299, 303–304, 311, 314–320,
        322, 330–332, 334, 339

lawgiving, 306, 308–309
    external, 334–339
    internal, 334–340
logic, transcendental, 271
love, 277, 282–283, 285, 314, 322, 324, 335
    self, 319, 328
lust and gallows example, 323–324
matter, 271, 316–319
maxims, 271, 275, 280–282, 285–289, 293–299, 302–303, 306, 315–320, 334
morality
    deontic conception of, 269, 273–274, 278–288, 290, 293, 301, 307, 308–311, 314–315, 318, 320–340
    deontic, normative epiphenomenality of, 273, 280–281, 283–285, 309, 333
    foundations of, *a priori*, 279
    supreme principle of. *See* Kant, Immanuel:Imperative, categorical
nature, laws of, 66, 127, 272, 278, 288–289, 311
necessitation, 273–274, 280–281, 283–285, 289–290, 302–304, 307, 309, 314, 325, 329–331, 334–340
    necessity, inner, 289–290
    necessity, natural, 289, 292
obligation, 153, 273–274, 278, 281, 283–287, 290, 293, 314, 324–325, 330–333, 335–337
    authoring of, 302–303
    narrow and wide. *See* Kant, Immanuel:duty:perfect and imperfect, distinction between
ought
    narrow and wide scope readings, 291–292
principles, material, 314–320
principles, material and formal, distinction between, 271, 294
prudence, 281, 292–293, 320

prudent shopkeeper example, 281
racism, 12–13, 340–342
rational egoist example, 297–298
rationalism, 10, 269–272
    critique of earlier rationalists, 270, 272, 320
realm of ends. *See* kingdom of ends
reason, objective law of, 284–286, 290
reason, practical, critique of, 272, 270–274, 276, 279–280, 284, 288, 294, 307–309, 314–323, 333
reason, pure practical, 208, 271–274, 276, 278–281, 283–284, 287–290, 301, 309, 314–315, 317–318, 322, 325–326, 330–334
    fundamental law of, 273, 315, 317–318, 322, 332
    synthetic use of, 279, 288
reason, pure, antinomies and paralogisms of, 270
reciprocity thesis, 280, 288, 322
respect, 283–285, 290, 299–303, 314, 325–330
    and humiliation, 328–329
    appraisal, 307–308, 327–329
    as *a priori* feeling, 326
    as phenomenal feeling, 273–274
    in relation to dignity, 300, 306–308, 321
    observantia, 307
    recognition, 307–308, 326–328
    reverentia, 307
Revolution, Copernican, 270, 320
right, the, 273, 287, 300–302, 306–308, 325, 330–339
Right, Universal Principle of (UPR), 272, 301, 306, 337–338
sciences, 278
self-conceit, 203, 326, 328–329
sexism, 12, 13, 340–342
sociability, 276–277
status, social, 326–329
sympathy, 282
thinking, form of, 270–271, 312
thought, theoretical, 272, 310–314, 320

374 INDEX

Kant, Immanuel (cont.)
  truth, synthetic *a priori*, 318
  value, priceable and dignity,
      distinction between, 306–308
  volition, objects of, 153, 271, 272, 276,
      279, 308, 311, 317–319, 325
  will
    determining ground of the, 271,
        316–319, 326
    form of the, 271, 272, 312, 317,
        319–320, 322, 325
    goodness of the, 280–286, 288,
        290, 293, 307, 308, 320, 327,
        329, 332
      and duty. *See* Kant,
          Immanuel:duty:good will
    hindrance, 339
    holy, 153, 290
    world, phenomenal, 284
    worth, moral, 142, 151, 206, 278,
        280–284, 325, 329
Kennett, Basil, 67
Kierkegaard, Søren, 10
Korsgaard, Christine, 300
  agency, deliberative, 313
  autonomy, appeal to, 321
  contructivism, 320–321
  normativity, source of, 8, 172, 201
Kosch, Michelle, xiii

Leibniz, Gottfried Wilhelm
  agency, free, 157–158
  anti-positivism, 112–113
  beneficence, 163
  benevolence, 124, 152–157, 163, 166
  charity, 124, 152, 155
  compatibilism, 158
  complaint, reasons of, 161
  demands, 153, 160–162
  eudaimonism, 124, 156, 163
  God, 117, 152
    as creator, 157
    as exemplar, perfectly virtuous, 152
    wise and benevolent nature of,
        154–159
  Golden Rule, 160–161
  good, the, 152–159
    dependence of moral goodness on
        motives, 154
  Greatest Happiness Principle, 153,
      156, 166
  harmonizer, as, 152
  in relation to
    Aquinas, Thomas, 155
    Cicero, Marcus Tullius, 156–157
    Clarke, Samuel, 157
    Cudworth, Ralph, 111–113, 152,
        158
    Grotius, Hugo, 155–157, 163–164
    Locke, John, 158
    Pufendorf, Samuel von, 112–113,
        152, 154–155, 163
    Shaftesbury (Anthony Ashley
        Cooper, Third Earl of),
        111–113, 152–155
    Spinoza, Baruch, 111, 122, 124, 156
  judge, sentencing criminal, 162
  justice, 152–157, 159–164
    as "the charity of the wise," 125,
        152, 155, 156, 159, 161
    as balanced relationship between
        self-love and love of others,
        159
    as universal benevolence, 152–154
  "Kingdom of Grace," 157
  love, 152, 156, 163
  metaphysics, 152, 155, 157–158
    teleology, 158
  moral quality, twofold, 159
  Naturalism, Aristotelian, 163
  necessity
    moral and metaphysical,
        distinction between, 157–158
    moral and natural, 124, 152, 153,
        155, 159
  obligation and the right, 152–155,
      158–164, 171
    "science of right," 153, 155, 158–159
    claim rights, 160
    modes of right, 155
    obligations, bipolar, 160
    precepts, deontic, 160–161
      equity, 163, 164
      piety, 160
  perfectionism, 153, 155–157
  pleasure as knowledge of perfection,
      156
  possibility, moral, 155

rationalism, 270
reciprocity, principle of. See
    Leibniz, Gottfried
    Wilhelm:obligation
    and the right:precepts,
    deontic:equity
reductionism, 124
respect, 153, 162, 163, 166
sanctions, eternal, 157
theodicy, 152
"Universal Republic of Spirits," 157
utilitarianism, 153, 156, 162–163
virtue, ethics of, 154–158, 163
voluntarism, rejection of, 111–112,
    152, 154–155, 248
wisdom, 155–157
Lloyd, Sharon, 54
Locke, John, 10
    accountability, 90, 95, 98–100, 145,
        148, 169–170, 239
    agency, 2, 98–100, 148, 158, 169–170,
        261
    archetypal and ectypal concepts,
        distinction between, 91, 97
    authority, divine, 91, 90–94, 98, 103,
        129
    autonomy, 98–100, 112, 169–170
    believing and judging, distinction
        between, 137
    bonum honestum. See Good,
        common
    collective action problem, 93–95, 103
    debitum naturale, 98
    egoism, 150
    empiricism, 167, 174
    Epicureanism, 104
    eudaimonism, 169–170
    externalism, 90, 96–98, 100
    Golden Rule, 87
    good, common, 95
    good, the, and the right, 92–100
    hedonism, rational egoistic, 91,
        93–97, 100, 170
    imputation, 99
    in relation to
        Aristotle, 97
        Confucius, 97
        Cudworth, Ralph, 100, 111, 112, 136,
            169–170
        Cumberland, Richard, 88–90
        Grotius, Hugo, 34, 88–91
        Hobbes, Thomas, 90, 98
        Hume, David, 90
        Hutcheson, Francis, 90
        Leibniz, Gottfried Wilhelm, 90
        Pufendorf, Samuel von, 88–92,
            95–100
        Shaftesbury (Anthony Ashley
            Cooper, Third Earl of), 90,
            111, 139–140, 169–170
        Suárez, Francisco, 93, 95, 97, 98
    internalism, 90, 96
    knowledge, three-fold division of
        logic and semantics, 97
        natural philosophy (theoretical
            knowledge), 97
        practical knowledge, 97
            ethics, 97–98
    law
        distinction between divine, civil,
            and law of "Opinion or
            Reputation," 96
        natural, 88–89, 91–95, 97–100
    morality as science, 88, 91
    "morality," use of word, 87
    motivation, moral, 95–98, 100
    naturalism, 89
    nominal and real essences,
        distinction between, 91
    obligation, 90, 95–96
    person, 2, 35, 87, 99
    property, 94
    punishment, 90, 93, 95, 96, 99
    sanctions, 91
        divine, 98, 91–100, 103, 141, 170
    scarcity, natural, 94
    self-determination. See Locke,
        John:autonomy
    souls, immortality of, 93–94
    utility, 92
    voluntarism, theological, 111, 117
    will, 96, 260
        divine, 103
        freedom of, 90, 98–100

MacIntyre, Alasdair, 9
Mandeville, Bernard, 173
Marx, Karl, 341

Masham, Damaris, 13, 111
Mill, John Stuart, 8, 162, 177, 183, 197, 205, 229, 257
Mills, Charles, 14
Moore, G.E., 6–9
    egoism, refutation of, 107
    fallacy, naturalistic, 209
    in relation to
        Butler, Joseph, 185
        Cumberland, Richard, 107
    supervenience, 245
    value, intrinsic, 122, 319

Nadler, Steven, 121, 125
Nietzsche, Friedrich, 3, 6–10
    in relation to
        Rousseau, Jean-Jacques, 274
        Spinoza, Baruch, 114, 115, 118–119, 121, 127
    morality, deontic, as illness, 115
    ressentiment, 118
    unconscious, "dark workshop" of, 118
    will to power, 121

Oldenburg, Henry, 117

Parfit, Derek, 6, 223
Pashukanis, Evgeny, 341
Paul the Apostle, 282–283
Pettit, Philip, 267
Plato, 4, 5, 127, 130, 134
    Socrates on justice, 4, 11, 16, 28, 217
Platonists, Cambridge, 113, 139, 144, 173
Plotinus, 130
Price, Richard
    accountability, 250–251, 253–254, 256, 273
    agency, 251, 253–256, 273
    benevolence, instinctive and rational, distinction between, 254
    capacity, moral, 253–254, 256
    fitness, 250–251, 253–257
    golden rule, 287
    ideas, normative, as indefinable, 239
    ideas, simple, 209, 250
    in relation to
        Balguy, John, 250–252, 255–256, 274, 287
        Butler, Joseph, 253–257
        Clarke, Samuel, 237–239, 243, 247, 250, 255–256, 273, 274, 287
        Cudworth, Ralph, 113, 252, 256
        Fordyce, David, 251
        Hobbes, Thomas, 287
        Hume, David, 251, 254, 255, 274
        Hutcheson, Francis, 251–252, 254, 257, 274
        Plato, 252
        Reid, Thomas, 237, 273
        Shaftesbury (Anthony Ashley Cooper, Third Earl of), 142
        Suárez, Francisco, 250
    internalism, motivational, 253–256
    intuitionism, 113, 252–253, 257, 263
    liberty, 253–254
    moral sense theory, rejection of, 251–252, 254, 258, 259
    morality
        as objective, necessary, and universally binding, 252–253
        deontic conception of, 113, 238–239, 251, 253–256, 258
    obligation, 242, 250–253, 256–258
        as indefinable, 250–253
    rationalism, 113, 229, 237–239, 250–258, 270
    reason, 250–258
        as the source of moral ideas, 251, 257, 258
        as the source of moral motivation, 238, 255–256
    Rectitude, 253–256
    self-determination through conscience, moral goodness as, 253–257
    understanding, the, 251–253, 258
    virtue
        abstract and practical, distinction between, 256–257
        heads of, 257–258
Prichard, H.A., 4–8, 219, 257
Pufendorf, Samuel von
    accountability, 61–62, 67, 66–69, 71, 73, 80, 86, 91, 96, 164, 194, 202, 219, 239, 256, 309
    agency, 79, 82–86, 239, 256

authority, divine, 62, 63, 65, 70, 76–82, 129
  imposition of, 41, 42, 61, 62, 64, 66–72
authority, mutual human, 76
causes, moral, 68
color analogy, 69
compensation, 77, 78
compulsion and obligation, distinction between, 69, 75, 82–86, 91, 96
conscience, 83
  and shame, distinction between, 83–84
consent, 81–82
creation, divine, 66–67, 70, 72
demands, authoritative, 62, 66
dignity, equal human, 42, 62, 64, 68, 69, 74–76, 78, 79, 86, 234, 300
effects, moral, 66–68, 75
empiricism, 41
entities, moral and physical, 65–67, 69, 72, 90
esteem, 73–74, 76, 78–79
goodness, natural, 69
imputation, 62, 68–69
in relation to
  Grotius, Hugo, 38, 42–43, 62–65, 73, 78
  Hobbes, Thomas, 41–43, 61, 65, 69, 83
  Locke, John, 96
  Suárez, Francisco, 62, 63
injury, 74
intercourse, 73–74, 83
law, natural, 42, 62–65, 70–71, 73, 76–77
"morality," use of word, 87
motivation, moral, 79–81, 84–86, 96
nature, state of, 83
necessity, moral, 155
obligations and rights, 62, 68–70, 75–86, 239
  bipolar, 64–66, 69, 70
  mutual, 42, 74, 76, 86
  natural, 160
  perfect and imperfect, 62–64, 67, 71–73, 76–79, 81
  to god, 42, 64, 67, 71, 76
  violation of, 78

pacts, 65, 66, 68, 79–81
powers
  natural, 68, 75, 83, 86
  normative, 41–43, 62–75, 78–83, 86, 90
  divine, 62, 83, 86
promising, 65–66
punishment, 77–78
recognition, 61, 62
  mutual, 62, 64, 67, 68, 72–73, 91
sanctions, 66, 67, 69, 75, 77, 80, 83–86, 96
self-defense, 76
sociability, 22, 62–65, 71–75, 78–79, 83, 86, 91, 265, 268, 269, 274
space, moral, 62, 66–67
voluntarism, theological, 41, 62, 111, 117, 164
war and peace, 42–43, 72, 74
will, 67, 79, 80, 84–85

Rawls, John, 9, 60, 116, 257
  categorical Imperative Procedure, 294–299, 305, 320
  constructivism, 320–321, 334
  ignorance, veil of, 304–306
  justice as fairness, 306, 331
  justice, conditions of, 215
  needs, true human, 305
  nullishing and telishment example, 296–297
  practice and summary conception of rules, 217
  rational, the, 54
  right, priority of, 331, 332
  "self-originating source of valid claims," 42, 300
Raz, Joseph, 65
  authority, theory of, 339–340
Reid, Thomas
  accountability, 260–262, 266–268, 273
  agency, 259–262, 273
  approbation, 263–265
  attention, 261
  benevolence, 261, 262
  children, 266–268
  cognitivism and noncognitivism, contrast between, 263–265

Reid, Thomas (cont.)
  common sense, moral, 259
  conscience, 261–263
  conscience and self-regard,
      relationship between,
      261–263
  deliberation, 261, 263
  empiricism, critique of, 259
  faculty, moral, 259, 262
  favor and injury, 265–266
  Golden Rule, 263
  gratitude, 265
  in relation to
      Balguy, John, 237
      Butler, Joseph, 259, 261–263
      Clarke, Samuel, 237, 273
      Cudworth, Ralph, 260, 261
      Fordyce, David, 258
      Grotius, Hugo, 265, 268
      Hume, David, 259, 263–267
      Hutcheson, Francis, 259, 261, 263–265
      Kant, Immanuel, 260
      Locke, John, 260, 261
      Price, Richard, 237, 258–260, 263, 273
      Pufendorf, Samuel von, 265, 268
      Smith, Adam, 265, 268
  incitements to the will and volition, distinction between, 260
  indignation, 265
  judgment, 259, 261–265
  justice, 260, 262, 265–268
  mind, power of, moral, 258–259, 262
  obligation, 259–263, 265–268
  power, active, 259–263
  promising, 266–268
  prudence, 260, 262–263
  purpose, fixed. see resolution
  rationalist/sentimentalist debate, reluctance to enter into, 237, 259
  resolution, 260–261
  self-condemnation, 261–262
  self-determination. see reid, thomas:self-government, capacity of
  self-government, capacity of, 259–263
  self-love. see conscience and self-regard, relationship between
  sense, moral, 258–259
  sentimentalism, empiricist, rejection of, 263–265
  sociality, 265–269
  subjectivism, rejection of, 259, 264–265
  testimony, 267
  the animal, the mechanical, and the rational, distinction between, 260
  trust and trustworthiness, 268
  virtue
      and the right, 259–262
      as conscientious conduct, 259–262
  will, 260–262
Ripstein, Arthur, 336
Ross, W.D., 185, 208, 247, 257, 258
Rousseau, Jean-Jacques
  Amour de soi, 277
  Amour propre, 277–278
  association, political society as, 269, 274–275, 304
  contract, social, 274–277
  dignity, equal human, 269, 274, 277–278, 300, 308
  freedom, 274–278
      common, 275–276
      moral, 275–276, 278
  in relation to
      Grotius, Hugo, 269, 274, 277, 278
      Locke, John, 100
      Pufendorf, Samuel von, 269, 274
      Reid, Thomas, 269
      Smith, Adam, 269
  law, 274–278
  slavery, 275–276
  sociability, 269, 274, 276–277
  will, general, 274–277
      as compared with the "will of all," 275

Saint Augustine, 124
Scanlon, T.M., 38
  reasonable, the, 54

Schapiro, Tamar, 313
Schneewind, J.B., 16, 152, 154, 163–164
Seneca, 21
Shaftesbury (Anthony Ashley Cooper, Third Earl of)
   accountability, 146
   "advice to authors," 147, 149
   aestheticism, 142–145
   affections, 141–147
      degrees of, 142
   agency, 151, 169–170
   anti-positivism, 112–113
   autonomy, 169–170, see Shaftesbury, Anthony Ashley Cooper, Third Earl of:self-determination, self-critical
   beauty. see Shaftesbury, Anthony Ashley Cooper:third earl of):goodness:as beauty
   benevolence, 142, 151, 180
   deontic conception of morality, absence of, 140–141
   desires, "sly" and "insinuating," 148–150
   education, liberal, 143
   egoism, rational, 147, 150
   enthusiasm, noble, 144
   eudaimonism, 141, 147, 151, 173, 181, 180
   God as unifying creative mind, 144
   goodness, 113, 141–145
      as beauty, 142–145
         first order of, 145
      as natural, 141–143, 151
   hedonism, rejection of, 150
   honesty, 149
   ignorance, motivated, 148–149
   in relation to
      Butler, Joseph, 238
      Cudworth, Ralph, 111–113, 139–140, 144–148, 150, 151, 169–170
      Cumberland, Richard, 89
      Descartes, René, 146, 147
      Epictetus, 146, 147
      Hobbes, Thomas, 139
      Leibniz, Gottfried Wilhelm, 111
      Locke, John, 100, 112–113, 138–140, 145–148, 150–151, 169–170
      Locke, John, 152
      Mandeville, Bernard, 173
      Platonists, Cambridge, 173
      Spinoza, Baruch, 111, 115, 122, 124
      Suárez, Francisco, 141, 146
      Whichcote, Benjamin, 113
   inspiration, 144–145
   inspiring disease, 149
   interest, public, 141, 143, 145
   love, 112, 142, 151
   mind, 142, 144–146
   natural order, teleology of, 141–145, 151
   Naturalism, Aristotelian. See Shaftesbury (Anthony Ashley Cooper, Third Earl of):*eudaimonism*
   obligation to virtue, 89, 140–141, 146–147, 171, 173, 180, 181, 213, 228, 240
   powers, creative and practical, 113
   psyche as system, 147
   rationalism, 144
   reductionism, 181, 182
   self, the, 140
   self-converse. see Shaftesbury, (Anthony Ashley Cooper, Third Earl of):soliloquy
   self-determination, self-critical, 142, 145–151, 165, 180, 238
   self-government, 150–151
   self-love, 142
   sense, moral, 113, 140, 142–145, 151, 173, 181
   sentimentalism, 124
   soliloquy, 147–151
   systems, scorn of, 140
   taste, cultivated, 143
   theism, 144
   therapy, self-analytic reality, 148
   virtue, 140–148
      as intrinsic good, 151
      ethics of, 113, 140–142, 151, 173, 177
   voluntarism, rejection of, 111, 112, 139, 151, 152
   will, 151
Shelby, Tommie, 14
Sidgwick, Henry, 161, 185, 197, 257
   ancient and modern ethics, contrast between, 4–7, 11–12, 19–20, 24–25, 28, 30, 62, 101, 151, 170, 200, 204, 217, 330–332

Sidgwick, Henry (cont.)
  benevolence, rational, principle of, 107
  "good from the point of view of the universe," 122
  in relation to
    Butler, Joseph, 168, 184, 186, 189, 200
    Cumberland, Richard, 101, 107, 168, 184
    Hutcheson, Francis, 168, 184, 204
    Shaftesbury(Anthony Ashley Cooper, Third Earl of), 140
  "ought," irreducibility of, 209
  reason, practical, dualism of, 168, 182, 184, 186
  utilitarianism, 162
Slote, Michael, 9
Smith, Adam
  accountability, 202–203, 221, 233–234, 236, 268
  Adam Smith Problem, 202
  adoption and approval of mental states, 225–226
  autonomy, 221–222, 229
  benevolence, 229
  condolence, 227
  dignity, equal human, 202–203, 233–236, 300
  economics, 202, 234
  empiricism, 201, 231
  Enlightenment, Scottish, 201
  expressivism, 231
  fellow-feeling, 202, 225, 226, 231
  fittingness. see smith, adam:propriety
  gratitude, 231, 265
  hand, invisible, 202
  in relation to
    Balguy, John, 229, 237–238
    Butler, Joseph, 184, 221–222, 229, 234, 238
    Clarke, Samuel, 229, 237–238, 243–244
    Grotius, Hugo, 233
    Hume, David, 201–203, 220–224, 227–238
    Hutcheson, Francis, 201, 221–24, 227–230, 232, 234, 237
    Price, Richard, 229, 237–238
    Rousseau, Jean-Jacques, 235
  Shaftesbury (Anthony Ashley Cooper, Third Earl of), 147, 222, 228, 234, 238
  inductivism, 229
  judgment, aesthetic, 230–231
  justice, 221, 231–234, 265, 268
  magnanimity, 235
  merit and demerit, judgments of, 231–232
  person outside society example, 230
  projection, imaginative, 202, 221–233
    epistemic function, 225–226
    normative function, 222–223, 225–229
  projectivism, 231
  propriety, 202, 221–236, 243
  prudence, 229
  punishment and reward, 231–234
  pyschology, moral, 202
  rationalism, rejection of, 201
  resentment, 221, 231–234, 265
  respect, 202–203, 234–236
  self-command, 222, 234–236, 238
    excellent exercise as perfect virtue, 222
  self-government. see smith, adam:self-command
  self-love, 234, 235
  sentimentalism, 201, 202, 230, 237–239, 244–246
  simulation, 224
  situation, 202, 223–230, 244
  slavery, 235
  sociability, 269
  spectator, impartial, 202, 227–228, 232–233, 235
  sympathy, 202, 224–225, 227–231
  virtue, 222
    amiable and respectable, distinction between, 234–236
    ethics of, 228–231
Smith, Michael, 201, 206, 209, 267
Spinoza, Baruch
  accountability, 117–118
  action, 117–118
  activity, 121, 125
  Amsterdam, Portuguese Jewish, 116, 126
  atheism, 116

badness as privation, 118, 119, 121
bearing calmly, 123, 125–127
blame, 118–119
blessedness. *see* spinoza, baruch:bearing calmly
conatus, 115, 118–121
consciousness, 114
consequence, causal, 118
demands, 123
doctrine of free will, rejection of, 115
duty. *see* spinoza, baruch:right, the
Enlightenment, Radical, 116, 122
eudaimonism, perfectionist, 114, 119–128
extension, 114
fatalism, 117
fear, motivation by, 118
freedom, 114, 121, 125, 127
God
   as substance, 116–119
   personal, rejection of, 115
good, the, 118–126
   apparent good and objective good, distinction between, 120–121
   common, 114, 122, 124, 125
happiness. *see* Spinoza, Baruch:bearing calmly
hate, 118–119, 126–127
ignorance, 118
in relation to
   Aquinas, Thomas, 114
   Aristotle, 114–115, 122
   Cudworth, Ralph, 111, 117, 118
   Descarte, René, 114
   Hobbes, Thomas, 114, 119–120, 125, 126
   Leibniz, Gottfried Wilhelm, 111, 117, 122, 124
   Locke, John, 117
   Pufendorf, Samuel von, 117, 118
   Shaftesbury (Anthony Ashley Cooper, Third Earl of), 111, 122, 124
indignation, 118, 126–127
inquisition, the, 116
intellect, 120, 126–127
jealousy, 119
joy, 126–127
knowledge, 114, 120, 121, 125

lens grinder, occupation as, 126
liberalism, 116
love, 118, 119, 126–127
metaphysics, 116–118, 123
   ethics as, 114–115
   monism, 114, 122, 125
morality, deontic, rejection of, 115–119
nature, 113–126
   human, model of, 121–122
necessity, natural, 117–119, 123–124
passions, 117–119
   emotions, taxonomy of, 126–127
perfection, 114–115, 119–126
politics, democratic, 115–116, 125
power, 118, 121, 122, 125, 126
projectivism, 119–121
reality, perfection as, 118
reductionism, 121, 124–125
remorse, 118
repentance, 118
right, the, 114, 122–125
sadness, 119, 126–127
sanctions, 117
striving. *see* conatus
virtue, 113–115, 121, 125
voluntarism, rejection of, 111
well-being, 114
will, 120–121
   appetites/desires and will/action, distinction between, 120
   doctrine of free will, rejection of, 117–118, 127
Stoics, 5, 11, 16, 28, 37
Strawson, P.F.
   attitudes, reactive, 30, 59, 196, 231, 239, 287
Suárez, Francisco, 26
   accountability, xii, 17–18, 164, 270
   agency, xii
   Bonum honestum, 20, 92
   eudaimonism, 26, 30
   externalism, 29
   in relation to aquinas, thomas, 17, 19–20, 92
   right, the, 68
   law and counsel, xii, 8, 11, 17–19, 23, 29, 54, 141, 146, 155, 159, 164, 171, 181, 238, 250, 292–293

Suárez, Francisco (cont.)
   law, natural, 16–20, 26, 62, 63, 92
   Naturalism, Aristotelian, 19, 26
   voluntarism, 18–19, 24
   voluntarism, theological, 164
   will, 18

Thompson, Michael, 159
Tuck, Richard, 19, 31, 33, 63
Tyrell, James, 87

Vázquez, Fernando, 32

Whichcote, Benjamin, 112, 113
Williams, Bernard, 3, 9, 165
   morality system, critique of, 269
Wolff, Christian, 153, 270
Wollaston, William, 113, 237, 243
Wood, Allen, xiii, 300, 302

Yovel, Yirmiyahu, 116

For EU product safety concerns, contact us at Calle de José Abascal, 56–1º,
28003 Madrid, Spain or eugpsr@cambridge.org.

www.ingramcontent.com/pod-product-compliance
Ingram Content Group UK Ltd.
Pitfield, Milton Keynes, MK11 3LW, UK
UKHW022025170226
468134UK00021B/586